1 MONTH OF
FREE
READING

at

www.ForgottenBooks.com

By purchasing this book you are eligible for one month membership to ForgottenBooks.com, giving you unlimited access to our entire collection of over 1,000,000 titles via our web site and mobile apps.

To claim your free month visit:

www.forgottenbooks.com/free752305

ISBN 978-0-364-63244-4
PIBN 10752305

REPORTS

FROM

COMMITTEES:

NINE VOLUMES.

— *(2.)* —

BUSINESS OF THE HOUSE (ABRIDGED PROCEDURE
ON PARTLY CONSIDERED BILLS);
CALEDONIAN RAILWAY (CONVERSION OF STOCK), &c. ;
CHILDREN'S LIFE INSURANCE [H.L.].

Session
11 *February* 1890 —— 18 *August* 1890.

VOL. XI. //

REPORTS FROM COMMITTEES:

1890.

NINE VOLUMES:—CONTENTS OF THE

SECOND VOLUME.

N.B.—*THE* Figures *at the* beginning of the line, *correspond with the* N° *at the foot of each* Report; *and the* Figures *at the* end of the line, *refer to the* MS. Paging *of the Volumes arranged for The House of Commons.*

REPORT

FROM THE

SELECT COMMITTEE

ON

BUSINESS OF THE HOUSE (ABRIDGED PROCEDURE ON PARTLY CONSIDERED BILLS);

TOGETHER WITH THE

PROCEEDINGS OF THE COMMITTEE,

AND APPENDIX.

Ordered, by The House of Commons, *to be Printed,*
14 *July* 1899.

LONDON:
PRINTED BY HENRY HANSARD AND SON;
AND
Published by EYRE and SPOTTISWOODE, East Harding-street, London, E.C.
and 32, Abingdon-street, Westminster, S.W.,
ADAM and CHARLES BLACK, North Bridge, Edinburgh;
and HODGES, FIGGIS, and Co., 104, Grafton-street, Dublin.

BUSINESS OF THE HOUSE
(ABRIDGED PROCEDURE ON PARTLY CONSIDERED BILLS).

Ordered, - [*Monday 23rd June* 1890]:—THAT a Select Committee be appointed to inquire whether by means of an abridged form of Procedure, or otherwise, the consideration of Bills, which have been partly considered in this House, could be facilitated in the next ensuing Session of the same Parliament.

Ordered,—[*Friday, 27th June* 1890]:—THAT the Committee do consist of Twenty-one Members.

Committee nominated of,—

Mr. Arthur Balfour.
Sir Algernon Borthwick.
Sir Edward Clarke.
Mr. Chamberlain.
Mr. Dillon.
Mr. Dillwyn.
Mr. Penrose Fitzgerald.
Mr. Goschen.
Mr. Gladstone.
Sir William Harcourt.
Dr. Hunter.

Lord Hartington.
Mr. Jennings.
Mr. Labouchere.
Colonel Malcolm.
Mr. John Morley.
Sir Stafford Northcote.
Mr. T. W. Russell.
Mr. Sexton.
Mr. John Talbot.
Mr. Whitbread.

THAT Seven be the Quorum of the Committee.

THAT the Reports of the Select Committees of the House on Public Business of the Sessions 1861, 1869, and 1878, and the Return "Parliamentary Proceedings," of the present Session, be referred to the Select Committee.

R E P O R T.

THE SELECT COMMITTEE appointed to inquire whether by means of an abridged form of PROCEDURE, or otherwise, the consideration of BILLS, which have been partly considered in this House, could be facilitated in the next ensuing Session of the same Parliament;——HAVE agreed to the following REPORT :—

FOUR times since 1880 the House of Commons has been obliged to revise its rules for the purpose of expediting public business. Four times in the same period exceptional methods of restricting discussion, not based upon the Standing Order or practice of the House, have been adopted, when, in the opinion of the majority, it became absolutely necessary to pass into law measures required to meet a pending crisis. The causes, legitimate and illegitimate, which stimulate discussion, have, however, counterbalanced, and more than counterbalanced, the effect of the rules designed to restrain it; the difficulty of legislation has not diminished; the exhausting labours imposed upon Members of Parliament, excessive at the beginning of this decade, have, if anything, increased; and experience shows that while closure, in the form in which it is recognised in the Standing Orders, may be, and, in the opinion of your Committee, is adequate to deal with single resolutions and short Bills, it is not adequate to enable the House to consider, within the compass of a Session of convenient length, measures which are both long, complicated, and controversial. Unless, therefore, the House is prepared to acquiesce in its increasing impotence to grapple with such measures, some further modification of its procedure seems to be necessary.

Such a modification can only take one of two forms. It must either, by some very stringent form of closure, enable Bills which would, if debate were free, be killed by a prorogation, to pass through all the stages in the course of one Session, or else it must revive them in the succeeding Session under such conditions that it would not be necessary, or indeed permissible, to repeat the discussion which had taken place upon the stages to which the House had already agreed.

As your Committee are of opinion that the first course might in certain contingencies seriously endanger that right of free criticism, which is one of the fundamental and most useful privileges of Parliament, they are driven to the consideration whether the second course might not safely be adopted, without introducing a more serious innovation into the practice of the House. Your Committee therefore agreed to the following Resolution :—

"That, in the judgment of your Committee, it is expedient that a Standing Order be passed for the purpose of abridging procedure in the case of Bills originating in the House of Commons which have been partly considered, and your Committee advise that such Standing Order should be adopted by the House in the following terms:—

"In respect of any Public Bill which is in progress in Committee of the whole House, or in a Standing Committee, or which has been reported therefrom, or which has reached any further stage, a Motion may be made (after notice given) by a Member in charge of Bill, 'That further Proceedings on such Bill be suspended until the next Session,' and no amendment shall be moved to such Motion.

"If such Motion be carried, then, in the ensuing Session (being a Session of the same Parliament), any Member whose name was on the suspended Bill may claim "That the Resolution of the previous Session be read." Thereupon the Speaker shall direct the Clerk to read the Resolution, and shall proceed to call on the Member to present the Bill in the form in which it stood when the Proceedings thereon were suspended; and the Questions on the First and Second Readings thereof shall be successively put forthwith.

"If both these Questions be carried, the Bill shall be ordered to be printed ; and, if it had been partly considered in Committee in the previous Session, it shall stand committed to a similar Committee, and it shall be an Instruction to such Committee to begin their consideration of the Bill at the Clause on which Progress was reported in the previous Session ; but if it had been reported from Committee in the previous Session, the consideration of the Bill, as reported, shall be appointed for that day week.

"Provided always, That, if the First or Second Reading be negatived, such Vote shall not be held to preclude the House from entertaining a Bill, on the same subject-matter under the ordinary Rules of Procedure."

This Standing Order, it will be observed, differs fundamentally both in its character and in its object from the various schemes with which it has a superficial similarity, and which have been more than once considered by the House of Commons during the last 40 years. Committees have sat upon three such schemes in the years 1848, 1861, and 1869, but in every one of these cases the object of the proposal was not to enable the House of Commons to deal effectually with measures submitted to it by the Government, or by private Members, but to enable the House of Lords to deal effectually with measures sent up to it from the House of Commons. This last object may be desirable or undesirable, and the means suggested for carrying it out may have been effectual or ineffectual, but your Committee desire to point out that neither the object nor the machinery for obtaining it were the same as those of the proposed Standing Order.

In spite of these essential differences, fears have been expressed lest the adoption of this Standing Order should supply a justification to the House of Lords for reviving and putting in force the rejected schemes of 1848, 1861, or 1869. But it must be observed, *in the first place*, that a plan by which one House is enabled more effectually to deal with business which has originated in it, and which has never left it, can hardly form a precedent for a totally different scheme by which one House may be able to postpone without rejecting Bills initiated in the other. And, *in the second place*, it is obvious that no endeavour on the part of the House of Lords to carry out the second of these objects can be effectual without the concurrence of the House of Commons. For the change of procedure must either be effected by Bill or by Standing Order. If by Bill, then the assent of both Houses is required. If by Standing Order, then only by Standing Orders adopted by both Houses, and to which both Houses, therefore, must be parties. "It has been alleged that the Standing Order now proposed would invite and countenance the adoption by the House of Lords of a similar Standing Order, and thus enable that House to postpone the consideration of all Bills passed and sent up from the House of Commons." In reply to this allegation, your Committee deem it right and necessary to record their opinion that any claim or attempt by either House of Parliament of its own authority, by Standing Order or otherwise, to postpone to a future Session of Parliament any Bill sent to it from the other House of Parliament, would be a breach of the constitutional usage of Parliament.

It has been suggested that, by suspending a Bill, the valuable power of amending it during the recess and reintroducing it in a better form, would necessarily be lost. Your Committee are not prepared to dispute the fact that changes which may also now and then be improvements, are often made in Bills which have failed to become law in the Session when they were first introduced ; but those who are of opinion that such amendments are necessary or expedient in the interests of good legislation, should be prepared to carry out their theory to its logical issue, and to propose a Standing Order under which no Bill should be passed in the same Session in which it was first read a second time. By this means the advantages, inseparable in their opinion from every abortive attempt at legislation, would not be arbitrarily confined to a few measures chosen at random. It may be noted in this connection, that those who are impressed with the advantages of not passing measures till they have been twice introduced into the House of Commons, are hardly in a position to regret that the proposed Standing Order may in certain cases extend legislation over two years instead of one.

The only other argument which it is necessary to consider is that based upon the fact that the House of Commons has already adequate powers, without a Standing Order, to repeat in an abridged form the stages of any Bill which have been already passed in a previous Session. In the words of Sir James Graham—"Whenever it may be thought "desirable promptly to pass and send to the other House for concurrence, a Bill passed "in a former Session, but set aside in the Lords, the Commons may pass the Bill rapidly "through

" through all its stages if they be so minded, and this course is not open to the objection
" of providing fresh opportunities for the postponement of legislation." No doubt the
House has such a power, as it has the power of deciding, if it so pleases, that the
First, Second, and Third Readings of a new Bill shall be put without amendment
or debate. But your Committee are of opinion that it is of the utmost importance
that Parliamentary practice should be guided as far as possible by settled rules,
deliberately adopted, and generally applicable. And it appears to them that every
argument which can be urged against the proposed Standing Order is equally effective
against the policy suggested by Sir James Graham's Report; while the latter is open to
the most serious objections, based not only upon the waste of time which any attempt to
carry it out must necessarily produce, but still more upon its sudden, occasional, and
arbitrary character, so little in harmony with the general spirit of House of Commons
procedure.

The preceding considerations may be briefly summarised as follows :—

The length of discussion to which it is thought necessary to subject measures
which are the object of party controversy has increased, is increasing, and does not
seem likely to diminish. As a result, the difficulty of passing such measures through
all their stages in the course of one Session has increased likewise. This difficulty
is especially felt in the case of long and complicated Bills, and it is precisely in the
case of these Bills that the closure of debate is most ineffective as an instrument
for facilitating the rapid progress of business. It is, therefore, desirable to increase
the power of the House of Commons to deal with such measures; it is also
desirable to shorten the length of Sessions, whose present duration overtakes
the endurance of Members and embarrasses the machinery of administration;
but it is *not* desirable, so long as any other alternative remains, to increase the
stringency of the existing machinery for closing debate. Your Committee believe
that if these three principles be accepted every possible alternative is excluded,
except one which shall relieve Parliament in certain cases from the necessity of
repeating in two successive Sessions the same debate upon the same questions.
They attach no weight, for reasons above given, to any objections that have
suggested themselves to this plan, based upon the relations now existing between
the two Houses of Parliament. They think the change, though undoubtedly an
important one, is much less violent in character and much less at variance with
the spirit of Parliamentary tradition than some alterations which have been made
of late years in Parliamentary procedure; and they point out that if, as they
recommend, it be effected, by Standing Order instead of by Bill, the experiment may
be purely tentative, and could be abandoned, should that course be subsequently
thought desirable, by the sole action of the House of Commons, without requiring
the consent of the other branch of the Legislature.

14 *July* 1890.

PROCEEDINGS OF THE COMMITTEE.

Monday, 30th June 1890.

MEMBERS PRESENT:

Sir Algernon Borthwick.
Mr. T. W. Russell.
Mr. Whitbread.
Sir Stafford Northcote.
Mr. Dillon.
Mr. Dillwyn.
Mr. Chamberlain.
Mr. Arthur Balfour.
Mr. Penrose Fitzgerald.
Mr. Goschen.
Mr. Gladstone.

Sir William Harcourt.
Lord Hartington.
Dr. Hunter.
Mr. Jennings.
Mr. Labouchere.
Colonel Malcolm.
Mr. John Morley.
Mr. Sexton.
Mr. Solicitor General.
Mr. John Talbot.

Mr. GOSCHEN was called to the Chair.

The Committee deliberated.

[Adjourned till Thursday next, at Twelve o'clock.

Thursday, 3rd July 1890.

MEMBERS PRESENT:

Mr. GOSCHEN in the Chair.

Mr. Arthur Balfour.
Sir Algernon Borthwick.
Mr. Chamberlain.
Mr. Dillon.
Mr. Dillwyn.
Mr. Penrose Fitzgerald.
Mr. Gladstone.
Sir William Harcourt.
Lord Hartington.
Dr. Hunter.

Mr. Jennings.
Mr. Labouchere.
Colonel Malcolm.
Mr. John Morley.
Sir Stafford Northcote.
Mr. T. W. Russell.
Mr. Sexton.
Mr. Solicitor General.
Mr. John Talbot.
Mr. Whitbread.

RESOLUTION, proposed by the *Chairman*, read, as follows :—" That, in the judgment of your Committee, it is expedient that a Standing Order be passed for the purpose of abridging procedure in the case of Bills originating in the House of Commons which have been partly considered, and your Committee advise that such Standing Order should be adopted by the House in the following terms :—

" In respect of any Public Bill which is in Progress in Committee of the whole House, or in a Standing Committee, or which has been reported therefrom, a Motion may be made (after Notice given) by a Member in charge of Bill, ' That further Proceedings on such Bill be suspended until the next Session.'

" If such Motion be carried, then, in the ensuing Session (being a Session of the same Parliament), any Member whose name was on the suspended Bill may claim ' That the Resolution of the previous Session be read.' Thereupon the Speaker shall direct the Clerk to read the Resolution, and shall proceed to call on the Member to present the Bill in the form in which it stood when the Proceedings thereon were suspended ; and the Questions on the First and Second Readings thereof shall be successively put forthwith.

" If

" If both these Questions be carried, the Bill shall be ordered to be printed ; and, if it had been partly considered in Committee in the previous Session, it shall stand committed to a similar Committee, and it shall be an Instruction to such Committee to begin their consideration of the Bill at the Clause on which Progress was reported in the previous Session ; but, if it had been reported from Committee in the previous Session, the consideration of the Bill as reported shall be appointed for that day week.

" Provided always, That, if the First or Second Reading be negatived, such Vote shall not be held to preclude the House from entertaining a Bill on the same subject-matter under the ordinary Rules of Procedure."

DRAFT REPORT, proposed by Mr. *Gladstone*, read the first time, as follows : —

" Your Committee have inquired into the matters referred to them, and have agreed to the following Report :—

" A Resolution has been submitted to your Committee by the Chancellor of the Exchequer in the following terms :

" 1. That, in the judgment of your Committee, it is expedient that a Standing Order be passed for the purpose of abridging procedure in the case of Bills originating in the House of Commons which have been partly considered, and your Committee advise that such Standing Order should be adopted by the House in the following terms :

" In respect of any Public Bill which is in Progress in Committee of the whole House, or in a Standing Committee, or which has been reported therefrom, a Motion may be made (after Notice given) by a Member in charge of Bill, ' That further Proceedings on such Bill be suspended until the next Session.'

" If such Motion be carried, then, in the ensuing Session (being a Session of the same Parliament), any Member whose name was on the suspended Bill may claim ' That the Resolution of the previous Session be read.' Thereupon the Speaker shall direct the Clerk to read the Resolution, and shall proceed to call on the Member to present the Bill in the form in which it stood when the Proceedings thereon were suspended ; and the Questions on the First and Second Readings thereof shall be successively put forthwith.

" If both these Questions be carried, the Bill shall be ordered to be printed ; and, if it had been partly considered in Committee in the previous Session, it shall stand committed to a similar Committee, and it shall be an Instruction to such Committee to begin their consideration of the Bill at the Clause on which Progress was reported in the previous Session ; but if it had been reported from Committee in the previous Session, the consideration of the Bill as reported shall be appointed for that day week.

" Provided always, that, if the First or Second Reading be negatived, such Vote shall not be held to preclude the House from entertaining a Bill on the same subject-matter under the ordinary Rules of Procedure.

" 2. Schemes similar, though not identical with the proposed Standing Order, have in various forms been repeatedly under the consideration of the House of Commons during a space of more than 40 years. They have been examined and reported upon both in principle and detail by Committees of the highest authority and experience, including the names of—

Sir R. Peel.	Mr. Walpole.	Lord Palmerston.
Sir G. Grey.	Mr. Hardy.	Sir F. Baring.
Mr. Hume.	Colonel Wilson Patten.	Mr. Bright.
Mr. Disraeli.	Mr. Bernal.	Sir G. C. Lewis.
Mr. Goulburn.	Mr. Cobden.	Mr. E. Bouverie.
Sir R. Inglis.	Mr. Henley.	Mr. Massey.
Lord Stanley.	Mr. Evelyn Denison.	Mr. Dodson.

" 3. In every instance, and in every shape, they have been universally condemned. These schemes had their origin in a Bill proposed by the late Lord Derby in the year 1848. The professed object of that Bill was to enable either House of Parliament by Resolution to suspend till a future Session the consideration of Bills sent up from the other House. The alleged necessity for such a measure was based on the excessive and protracted discussion of Bills in the House of Commons, and was admitted to be intended mainly to allow the House of Lords to postpone for a year Bills sent up from the House of Commons at a late period of the Session. This Bill was rejected in the House of Commons on the recommendation of a Select Committee of high authority and Parliamentary experience. In the year 1861 the subject was revived by proposals from a Committee of the House of Lords for the adoption by both Houses of Resolutions which would enable Bills passed by one House of Parliament to be carried over to a future Session in the other House of Parliament. These proposals were likewise rejected by a Committee of great weight, presided over by Sir James Graham, to whose Report further reference will presently be made. In 1869 a Bill, introduced by Lord Salisbury into the House of Lords, entitled ' An Act to ' facilitate the Proceedings on Bills in Parliament,' and also certain Standing Orders proposed by Lord Eversley and Lord Redesdale, were considered and rejected in a Joint Committee of the House of Lords and House of Commons, by the Commons' Members of that Committee. The

subject

subject was again brought forward in the year 1882, on a motion of the present Solicitor General, and rejected by a large majority of the House.

" 4. So conclusive do the successive Parliamentary judgments on this question appear to have been, that in 1886, when measures for expediting the public business of the House were considered by the Committee over which Lord Hartington presided, no one thought fit to revive any similar proposal. No evidence has been produced or reasons alleged in support of the proposed Standing Order which should induce your Committee to reject or reverse the conclusions sanctioned by so remarkable a concurrence of Parliamentary authority.

" 5. The objections which apply to all these proposals are set forth with great force in the Report of the Committee of 1861, drawn up by Sir James Graham, supported by the evidence of Mr. Speaker, and unanimously adopted. It is there shown that ' the power sought would only be exercised with respect to important measures, and the power of suspension would give increased facilities for retarding legislation . . . There is also much greater facility for altering in a new Session the frame and scope of a measure when it has been extinguished by Prorogation. The opportunities for re-considering, improving, and amply discussing important measures would thus be inconveniently abridged.' Your Committee attach the greatest weight to the views thus expressed. Your Committee concur also in the conclusion of this Report that ' in order to effect this object, if desired, the Resolutions, so far as the Commons are concerned, are not necessary. Whenever it may be thought desirable promptly to pass, and send to the other House for concurrence, a Bill passed in a former Session, but set aside in the Lords, the Commons may pass the Bill rapidly through all its stages if they be so minded, and this course is not open to the objection of providing fresh opportunities for the postponement of legislation.' These observations apply equally to the case of the carrying over to another Session in the House of Commons a Bill partly considered, and they derive greater force from the fact that, since the date of the above Report, the House of Commons has acquired much greater and more effective means of expediting the passage of Bills when it is so minded.

" 6. It is most material to observe that the Standing Order now proposed, though in form applicable only to the House of Commons, by the carrying over to a future Session of Bills which have been partly considered in this House, will, in its consequences, invite and countenance the adoption by the House of Lords of a similar Standing Order, and thus enable that House to postpone the consideration of all Bills passed and sent up from the House of Commons. The present proposal, therefore, implicitly involves all the consequences which would have followed from the adoption of the previous schemes above referred to, and all the objections which prevailed against those schemes apply with equal force to the present proposals.

" 7. Your Committee, therefore, have come to the conclusion that the proposed scheme is both objectionable in its nature and unnecessary for the purposes it professes to attain. The objections to it may be briefly summed up :—

" (I.)—The great advantage would be lost (as pointed out by the Committee of 1861) of altering in a new Session ' the frame and scope ' of a measure.

There are few Bills of the first importance which, after full discussion, and with a more complete knowledge of the sentiments of the House and the country, would not with advantage be re-cast ; and time would probably be saved, rather than lost, by reconsidering them as a whole in a new and reformed shape, rather than by seeking to remould them by amendments in their incomplete state.

" Of this, the Tithe Bill of last Session affords an apt illustration. It was found impossible to introduce into the Tithe Bill the desired amendments in Committee, and it was necessary to introduce a new Bill to accomplish the objects of its authors.

" (II.)—This further objection arises on the proposed Standing Order, by which it is provided that any Member in charge of any Bill which has arrived at the stage of Committee may move that ' further proceedings on such Bill be suspended until the next Session.' It is difficult to conceive how such a provision is calculated to economise the time of the House. Every Member who does not see a clear prospect of passing his Bill through the House, will make such a motion, upon which will arise what will become in effect a Second Reading debate. The Order Book of the House will, at the meeting of Parliament, be found clogged with the accumulated arrears of unfinished remnants from previous Sessions.

" This power of carrying over Bills might have a most prejudicial effect in inducing an apathy and laxity on the part of the Government and of the House in the prosecution of important measures, and afford a pretext for propounding plausible and specious schemes which it was never intended to pass, but which might be indefinitely hung up without the discredit of abandoning them. It might, on the other hand, have the result of giving to trivial Bills a vitality which they did not merit.

" A still graver objection arises in this case, that the power of a majority to select Bills to be carried over might be most oppressively exercised.

" (III.)—The scheme is unnecessary, because in a future Session of Parliament upon a new Bill the powers of Closure already possessed by the House are sufficient to expedite its passage where previous discussion seem to justify its employment.

" I V.—Then

"(IV.)—The ancient rule of this House that 'no Bill of the same substance be brought in the same Session,' is abrogated by the proposed Standing Order, and no method is provided for making a fair start for a new Bill except through the cumbrous process of rejecting the first or second readings of the suspended Bill by Vote of the House.

"(V.) It will invite and induce the House of Lords, through a similar Standing Order, to assume and to exercise an unlimited power of postponing Bills passed and sent up by the House of Commons. It is obvious that this power may be extensively used by the House of Lords for the indefinite putting off of measures sent up from the House of Commons, which the other House may regard with disfavour, and that without accepting the responsibility of rejecting them. So far from expediting legislation, such a scheme would greatly retard it. It would seem probable that the normal period for passing a great legislative measure might become under the operation of such joint Standing Orders two Sessions in either House of Parliament, or a period of three years. A further difficulty would arise in the case of Bills which had passed the House of Commons, and been sent to the House of Lords, that the House of Lords might pass in a future Session, without amendment, Bills which on further consideration the House of Commons, after the lapse of a year, might be anxious to alter or reject, but upon which it would have no opportunity to pronounce. Provision was made for this case in former schemes, but no such provision is to be found in the proposed Standing Order.

"8. Upon the question whether so grave a change in the constitutional practice of Parliament could be made otherwise than by Statute, your Committee find it unnecessary to express an opinion. It has certainly been assumed on every occasion when the subject has come under discussion during the last 40 years, that such a proceeding could not properly be taken independently by either House of Parliament through the operation of a Standing Order as now proposed. Whether by Statute or by joint Resolution, the consent of both branches of the Legislature has always been held to be indispensable, even apart from the question of the Prerogative of the Crown in respect to Prorogation.

"9. It is not necessary, however, to come to a decision as to the manner in which the thing should be done, because your Committee have arrived at the same conclusion as that reached by all previous Committees of this House, viz., that the scheme itself is one not to be recommended. If the object is simply to expedite in this House, in a future Session, a Bill which has been partially considered in a previous Session, the House of Commons possesses already, without any new Standing Order, ample power to accelerate, as occasion arises, and so far as it may think fit, any stages of the Bill when re-introduced.

"10. Your Committee have therefore come to the conclusion that the Standing Order proposed cannot be recommended for adoption by the House."

The Record of the Proceedings of previous Committees are annexed to this Report, as follows:

"PARLIAMENTARY PROCEEDINGS ADJOURNMENT BILL, SESSION 1848.

"A BILL, intituled, An Act to enable either HOUSE of PARLIAMENT to adjourn PROCEEDINGS during the PROROGATION of PARLIAMENT upon certain BILLS passed by the other HOUSE, and to resume the PROCEEDINGS thereupon after such Prorogation.

"WHEREAS by reason of the great increase of the public business it is expedient that additional facilities should be afforded for the transaction of the same, and especially for securing sufficient time for the due consideration by both Houses of Parliament of Bills to them submitted. Be it therefore enacted, by the Queen's Most Excellent Majesty, by and with the advice and consent of the Lords Spiritual and Temporal, and Commons, in this present Parliament assembled, and by the authority of the same, That from and after the passing of this Act it shall and may be lawful for either House of Parliament, if it shall so think fit, at any stage of its proceedings upon any Bill which shall have been passed by the other House of Parliament, to adjourn by Resolution the further proceedings upon such Bill, the consent of the Crown having been first duly signified to such adjournment to the then next Session of Parliament.

"And be it enacted, That when such Resolution as aforesaid shall have been passed, it shall and may be lawful for the House of Parliament which shall have passed the same, to proceed to the consideration of such Bill in the Session of Parliament next after the introduction of such Bill; and the previous proceedings had and taken upon such Bill in the two Houses of Parliament shall not in such case abate or be deemed to have abated by reason of the Prorogation of Parliament, but all such proceedings shall be and be deemed to all intents and purposes good and valid, as if no such Prorogation had taken place, and as if all such proceedings had been had and taken during the then Session of Parliament.

"Provided always, and be it enacted, That if any Bill so adjourned as aforesaid shall pass without amendment, it shall nevertheless be returned to the House of Parliament in which it shall have been introduced for the concurrence of such House; and it shall not be lawful to submit such Bill for the signification of Her Majesty's pleasure thereupon unless and until such House shall, by Resolution, have concurred therein, and shall have signified such concurrence, by message, to the other House.

298.   B   "And

" And be it enacted, That nothing in this Act contained shall be deemed to authorise either House of Parliament to proceed to the consideration of any Bill so adjourned as aforesaid if at any period subsequent to such adjournment Her Majesty, Her Heirs or Successors, shall have been pleased to dissolve Parliament, but that all proceedings in respect of any such Bill shall be deemed to have abated, by reason of such Dissolution, as if this Act had not passed.

" And be it enacted, That nothing in this Act contained shall be deemed to extend to any Bill passed by the House of Commons, the main object whereof shall be the imposing of any Tax upon the subjects of this Realm, or the repeal of any such Tax, or the levying any Revenue in aid of the Public Service, or the appropriation of any Supplies granted to Her Majesty, Her Heirs or Successors.

" And be it enacted, That this Act may be amended or repealed by any Act to be passed in this Session of Parliament."

" PARLIAMENTARY PROCEEDINGS [H.L.] BILL.

" A Bill, intituled, An Act to facilitate Proceedings on Bills in Parliament.

" WHEREAS by the usage of Parliament proceedings on Bills have not continuance after a Prorogation, and it is expedient that better provision be made in that behalf:

" Be it therefore enacted by the Queen's most Excellent Majesty, by and with the advice and consent of the Lords Spiritual and Temporal, and Commons, in this present Parliament assembled, and by the authority of the same, as follows:

" 1. Where a Bill passed in one House of Parliament is sent to the other House (not having been already under consideration of that House), and that House at any stage of the proceedings on the Bill passes a resolution to the effect that there is not sufficient time for the due consideration of the Bill in the then Session, and accordingly does not further proceed with it in that Session, then and in every such case, notwithstanding the Prorogation of Parliament, and as if there had only been an adjournment of the House in which the Bill was at the suspension of the proceedings thereon, the proceedings on the Bill may be resumed and carried on in the next subsequent Session, on the following steps being taken in that Session:

" (1.) On the consent of the Crown to the resumption of the proceedings being duly signified:

" (2.) On the House in which proceedings on the Bill were suspended passing a resolution to the effect that it is expedient that proceedings on the Bill be resumed.

" 2. Where proceedings on a Bill have been suspended and resumed in accordance with this Act, the Bill shall not be submitted for the Royal Assent unless and until the House in which the Bill originated has consented by resolution communicated to the other House to the same being so submitted.

" 3. Nothing in this Act shall authorise the resumption of proceedings on a Bill after a dissolution of Parliament.

" 4. This Act may be cited as The Parliamentary Proceedings Act, 1869."

" Extracts from the Reports of Select Committees on the Dispatch of Public Business.

SESSION 1848.—Report from the Select Committee on Public Business.

Lord John Russell.	Mr. Bernal.
Sir Robert Peel.	Sir William Heathcote.
Sir George Grey.	Mr. Cobden.
Sir James Graham.	Mr. Morgan.
Mr. Hume.	Mr. John O'Connell.
Mr. Disraeli.	Mr. Brotherton.
The Lord Advocate.	Mr. Henley.
Mr. Goulburn.	Sir George A. Hamilton.
Sir Robert Harry Inglis.	Mr. Evelyn Denison.

" Your Committee, having considered the provisions of the Parliamentary Proceedings Adjournment Bill, do not think it advisable to recommend it for adoption by the House.

" SESSION 1861.—Report from the Select Committee on the Business of the House.

Viscount Palmerston.	Mr. Disraeli.
Sir James Graham.	Lord Stanley.
Sir Francis Baring.	Sir John Pakington.
Sir George Grey.	Mr. Walpole.
Mr. Bright.	Mr. Sotheron Estcourt.
Sir George Lewis.	Mr. Hardy.
Mr. Edward Pleydell Bouverie.	Colonel Wilson Patten.
Mr. Gregory.	Mr. Maguire.
Mr. Dunlop.	Mr. Ker Seymer.
Mr. Massey.	Mr. Deedes.
Mr. William Ewart.	

" Your

"Your Committee have not overlooked a proposal made in the other House of Parliament, that a power should be given by statute to either House of Parliament of suspending (at any stage of proceeding) Bills which shall have been passed by the other House of Parliament, and of resuming such Bills in the succeeding Session at the precise stage where they had been dropped.

"The objections to this proposal are grave and numerous. The power sought would only be exercised with respect to important measures; and this power of suspension would give increased facilities for retarding legislation. There is also much greater facility in altering in a new Session the frame and scope of a measure when it has been extinguished by Prorogation. A Bill sent from one House and suspended in the other could not be amended in the Recess. It must be resumed as it was left; and all amendments, which might then be introduced, could be fully debated in one House only; for the House to which the amended Bill is returned cannot re-commit it, but must accept or reject the amendments proposed. The opportunities for reconsidering, improving, and amply discussing important measures would thus be inconveniently abridged.

"Moreover, this suspending power in either House of Parliament, if exercised at its own discretion, would be at variance with the Prerogative of the Crown. The deliberations of Parliament may be cut short at any moment by the exercise of the Royal power of Prorogation which quashes all proceedings pending at the time, except Impeachments by the Commons, Writs of Error and Appeals before the House of Lords, and trials in progress before Election Committees. Every Bill must be renewed after a Prorogation, as if it had never been introduced, though the Prorogation be for no more than a single day. In 1689, Parliament was prorogued from the 21st of October to the 23rd, for the purpose of re-introducing the Bill of Rights, concerning which a difference, fatal to its progress, had risen between the two Houses.

"In June 1610, the Commons established a rule 'that no Bill of the same substance be brought in the same Session,' and so imperative has this rule been regarded, that in 1707 Parliament was prorogued for a week, in order to admit the revival of a Bill which had been rejected by the Lords.

"If this power of suspending had then existed, in neither of these two cases could the prerogative of Prorogation have been exercised with its salutary effects; and the tendency of this new power would be to give to the House exerting it an equivalent to the Royal Veto in its mild form, when the Sovereign declares 'Le Roi s'avisera.'

"But in the Bill introduced in the House of Lords in 1848, there was a provision that the consent of the Crown should be first duly signified to such suspension. This consent of the Crown to the mode of dealing with Bills not perfected by the concurrence of the other Branches of the Legislature, would be a novelty at variance with constitutional practice, not to be defended by any necessity. The prerogative of the Crown, in all cases where the rights, interests, and property of the Crown are not specially affected, is limited to assenting to or rejecting Bills which have passed both Houses. It is barred from all interference during the discussion of them in either House of Parliament.

"On the whole, therefore, Your Committee adhere to the opinion expressed by the Select Committee in 1848, and which came to the Resolution, 'that, having considered the Provisions of the Parliamentary Proceedings Adjournment Bill, they do not think it advisable to recommend it for adoption by the House.'

"Your Committee cannot leave unnoticed an intimation, which they have received from the Select Committee of the House of Lords on Public Business, that they would suggest for adoption by both Houses the three following Resolutions:

"1st. That it is expedient, in certain cases, to adopt an abridged form of proceeding with reference to Bills which shall be again brought before this House after having been passed by it, in the immediately preceeding Session of the same Parliament.

"2nd. That the Bills in respect to which such abridged form of proceeding may be adopted, shall be *mutatis mutandis* the same Bills which this House may have passed and sent to the other House, and as to which that House may have resolved that there did not remain time for their due consideration in the Session in which they were received.

"3rd. That on a Resolution being moved, that it is expedient again to pass, and to send to the other House for its concurrence, any such Bill, the question shall be put whether the House will agree to the same, and on such Resolution being agreed to, the Bill to which it relates shall be forthwith sent to the other House for its concurrence, without any further question being put or any debate allowed.

"These Resolutions are not, indeed, open to the objection of interference with the Prerogative of the Crown, as they do not contemplate the actual suspension of Bills from one Session to another, notwithstanding a Prorogation; nor are they open to the objection of sanctioning a novel practice as to the concurrence of the Crown in the mode of dealing with Bills in progress through Parliament.

"But their avowed object is to provide, in certain cases, for the resumption, in a new Session of the same Parliament, of Bills passed by one House and not considered by the other, by means of new and summary forms of proceeding, which they declare it expedient to adopt.

"The objections already stated against a Statute for the purpose above-mentioned apply in a great degree to these Resolutions. They, in common with the Statute, would apply only to measures of importance, involving considerable detail ; and it is extremely improbable that, after an interval of several months, either House would desire to send up to the other House measures of this nature without any Amendment.

" In order, however, to effect this object, if desired, the Resolutions, so far as the Commons are concerned, are not necessary. Whenever it may be thought desirable promptly to pass, and to send to the other House for its concurrence, a Bill passed in a former Session, but set aside in the Lords, the Commons may pass the Bill rapidly through all its stages, if they be so minded ; and this course is not open to the objection of providing fresh opportunities for the postponement of legislation.

" With regret, therefore, Your Committee have come to the conclusion that the three Resolutions, suggested by the Committee of the House of Lords, cannot be recommended to the Commons for their adoption.

SESSION 1869.—Report from the Joint Committee of the House of Lords and the House of Commons on the Despatch of Business in Parliament.

Sir George Grey.	Mr. Walpole.
Mr. Disraeli.	Mr. Dodson.
Mr. Bouverie.	Colonel Wilson Patten.

" The Committee have considered the provisions of a Bill introduced into the House of Lords at the beginning of this Session by the Marquess of Salisbury, entitled ' An Act to facilitate Proceedings on Bills in Parliament,' the principle object of which was to enable either House of Parliament to resume, in a subsequent Session, Proceedings on Bills for which there had not been sufficient time for due consideration in the previous Session, thereby providing for a due supply of Bills to be submitted to the consideration of the House of Lords, early in the Session, avoiding the crowds of Bills at a later period, and spreading the legislative business more equally over the Session in both Houses. It was proposed by Viscount Eversley and Lord Redesdale to attain the same objects by Standing Orders. (*See* Appendix.)

" The Committtee admit, with some qualification, the existence of the evil which it is proposed to correct, but are of opinion that it can only be remedied by general consent, and believe that there are objections to all the proposed modes of obviating it which make it unlikely that the House of Commons would take a different view now from that which they took in 1848, when a Bill moved by the Earl of Derby, and passed through the House of Lords, was referred to a Select Committee of the House of Commons, who declined to recommend it for adoption.

" APPENDIX A.

" STANDING ORDER proposed by the VISCOUNT EVERSLEY.

" *Resolved,*—That whenever this House shall resolve that a Bill, not being a Bill relating to Revenue and Taxation, has been sent up from the Commons at a period when it cannot receive due consideration, a Message shall be sent to the Commons acquainting them with such Resolution ; and if the same Bill shall be presented in the next Session, it shall be passed *pro formâ* through all its stages prior to that at which it was laid aside ; and, when passed, shall be sent to the Commons with a Message stating it to be the same Bill (with or without amendments) as that sent up to the House of Lords in the last Session.

" APPENDIX B.

" THE LORD REDESDALE to move, That the following new Standing Order be added to the Roll of Standing Orders :

" Not later than ten days after the meeting of Parliament in any Session, notice may be given that on a day named, of which not less than one, nor more than two, weeks' notice shall be allowed, a Motion will be made to suspend the Standing Orders in relation to any Public Bill which shall have been introduced into and passed through this House in the preceding Session, after having been for eight weeks. at least, under the consideration of the House from the time of its first introduction, and shall not have been rejected by the Commons, the said Bill being laid on the Table at the time when the notice is given, and if the House when the Motion is made shall agree [*by a majority of   of those present*] that the Orders shall be suspended, the question that such Bill do pass shall be put and declared to be carried without further debate being allowed ; and the Bill so passed shall be sent to the Commons with a request that they will return it, if they agree to the same, for the further consideration of this House, whether amended by them or not, in order that the Lords may reconsider it in all its provisions in like manner as if every part thereof had been amended by the Commons, and the said Bill shall thenceforth be treated in this House as if it was a Bill amended in the ordinary way.

" In the event of a Bill passed by the Commons and sent up to this House in the preceding Session, and not rejected by this House, being sent by them to this House in the same manner and with a similar request, the Lords will return such Bill, if they shall pass it, to the Commons to be treated by them in respect to every part thereof, whether amended in this House or not, as if every provision therein contained had been introduced in this House."

The Committee deliberated.

[Adjourned till To-morrow, at One o'clock.

Friday, 4th July 1890.

MEMBERS PRESENT:

Mr. GOSCHEN in the Chair.

Mr. Arthur Balfour.	Mr. Jennings.
Sir Algernon Borthwick.	Mr. Labouchere.
Mr. Chamberlain.	Colonel Malcolm.
Mr. Dillon.	Mr. John Morley.
Mr. Dillwyn.	Sir Stafford Northcote.
Mr. Penrose Fitzgerald.	Mr. T. W. Russell.
Mr. Gladstone.	Mr. Sexton.
Sir William Harcourt.	Mr. Solicitor General.
Lord Hartington.	Mr. John Talbot.
Dr. Hunter.	Mr. Whitbread.

Motion made, and Question proposed, " That the Resolution proposed by the Chairman be now considered "—(The *Chairman*).—Amendment proposed to leave out from the words ' That the' to the end of the Question, in order to add the words, ' Draft Report proposed by Mr. Gladstone, be read a second time, paragraph by paragraph '—(Mr. *Gladstone*).— Question put, That the words proposed to be left out stand part of the Question.—The Commitee divided:

Ayes, 11.	Noes, 9.
Mr Arthur Balfour.	Mr. Dillon.
Sir Algernon Borthwick.	Mr. Dillwyn.
Mr. Chamberlain.	Mr. Gladstone.
Mr. Penrose Fitzgerald.	Sir William Harcourt.
Lord Hartington.	Dr. Hunter.
Mr. Jennings.	Mr. Labouchere.
Colonel Malcolm.	Mr. John Morley.
Sir Stafford Northcote.	Mr. Sexton.
Mr. T. W. Russell.	Mr. Whitbread.
Mr. Solicitor General.	
Mr. John Talbot.	

[Adjourned till Tuesday next, at Twelve o'clock.

Tuesday, 8th July 1890.

MEMBERS PRESENT:

Mr. GOSCHEN in the Chair.

Mr. Arthur Balfour.	Mr. Jennings.
Sir Algernon Borthwick.	Mr. Labouchere.
Mr. Chamberlain.	Colonel Malcolm.
Mr. Dillon.	Mr. John Morley.
Mr. Dillwyn.	Sir Stafford Northcote.
Mr. Penrose Fitzgerald.	Mr. T. W. Russell.
Mr. Gladstone.	Mr. Sexton.
Sir William Harcourt.	The Solicitor General.
Lord Hartington.	Mr. John Talbot.
Dr. Hunter.	Mr. Whitbread.

Main Question put, and *agreed to*.

Motion made, and Question proposed, " That, in the judgment of your Committee, it is expedient that a Standing Order be passed for the purpose of abridging procedure in the case of Bills originating in the House of Commons which have been partly considered, and your Committee advise that such Standing Order should be adopted by the House in the following terms:—

" In respect of any Public Bill which is in Progress in Committee of the whole House, or in a Standing Committee, or which has been reported therefrom, a Motion may be made (after notice given) by a Member in charge of Bill, ' That further Proceedings on such Bill be suspended until the next Session.'

" If such Motion be carried, then, in the ensuing Session (being a Session of the same Parliament), any Member whose name was on the suspended Bill may claim ' That the Resolution of the previous Session be read.' Thereupon the Speaker shall direct the Clerk to read the Resolution, and shall proceed to call on the Member to present the Bill in the form in which it stood when the Proceedings thereon were suspended ; and the Questions on the First and Second Readings thereof shall be successively put forthwith.

" If both these Questions be carried, the Bill shall be ordered to be printed ; and, if it had been partly considered in Committee in the previous Session, it shall stand committed to a similar Committee, and it shall be an Instruction to such Committee to begin their consideration of the Bill at the Clause on which Progress was reported in the previous Session; but, if it had been reported from Committee in the previous Session, the consideration of the Bill as reported shall be appointed for that day week.

" Provided always, that, if the First or Second Reading be negatived, such Vote shall not be held to preclude the House from entertaining a Bill on the same subject-matter under the ordinary Rules of Procedure."—(The *Chairman*).

Amendment proposed, in line 6, after the word " therefrom," to insert the words, " or which has reached any further stage."—Question, That those words be there inserted—(Mr. *Russell*),— put, and *agreed to.*

Another Amendment proposed, in line 8, after the word " Session," to insert the words, " This Question shall be put forthwith, without Amendment or Debate "—(Mr. *Chamberlain*).—Question put, That those words be there inserted.   The Committee divided :

Ayes, 5.	Noes, 6.
Mr. Chamberlain.	Mr. Arthur Balfour.
Mr. Jennings.	Sir Algernon Borthwick.
Colonel Malcolm.	Mr. Penrose Fitzgerald.
Sir Stafford Northcote.	Lord Hartington.
Mr. T. W. Russell.	The Solicitor General.
	Mr. John Talbot.

Another Amendment proposed, in line 8, after the word " Session," to insert the words, " and no Amendment shall be moved to such Motion "—(Lord *Hartington*).—Question, That those words be there inserted,—put, and *agreed to.*

Main Question, as amended, put, and *agreed to.*

Resolved,—" That, in the judgment of your Committee, it is expedient that a Standing Order be passed for the purpose of abridging procedure in the case of Bills originating in the House of Commons which have been partly considered, and your Committee advise that such Standing Order should be adopted by the House in the following terms:—

" In respect of any public Bill which is in progress in Committee of the whole House, or in a Standing Committee, or which has been reported therefrom, or which has reached any further stage, a Motion may be made (after notice given) by a Member in charge of Bill, ' That further Proceedings on such Bill be suspended until the next Session,' and no amendment shall be moved to such Motion.

" If such motion be carried, then, in the ensuing Session (being a Session of the same Parliament), any Member whose name was on the suspended Bill may claim ' That the Resolution of the previous Session be read.' Thereupon the Speaker shall direct the Clerk to read the Resolution, and shall proceed to call on the Member to present the Bill in the form in which it stood when the proceedings thereon were suspended ; and the Questions on the First and Second Readings thereof shall be successively put forthwith.

" If both these Questions be carried, the Bill shall be ordered to be printed ; and, if it had been partly considered in Committee in the previous Session, it shall stand committed to a similar Committee, and it shall be an Instruction to such Committee to begin their consideration of the Bill at the Clause on which Progress was reported in the previous Session: but if it had been reported from Committee in the previous Session, the consideration of the Bill, as reported, shall be appointed for that day week.

" Provided always, That, if the First or Second Reading be negatived, such Vote shall not be held to preclude the House from entertaining a Bill on the same subject-matter under the ordinary Rules of Procedure."

[Adjourned till Thursday next, at Twelve o'clock.

Thursday, 10th July 1890.

MEMBERS PRESENT:

Mr. GOSCHEN in the Chair.

Mr. Arthur Balfour.	Mr. Jennings.
Sir Algernon Borthwick.	Mr. Labouchere.
Mr. Chamberlain.	Colonel Malcolm.
Mr. Dillon.	Mr. John Morley.
Mr. Dillwyn.	Sir Stafford Northcote.
Mr. Penrose Fitzgerald.	Mr. T. W. Russell.
Mr. Gladstone.	Mr. Sexton.
Sir William Harcourt.	The Solicitor General.
Lord Hartington.	Mr. John Talbot.
Dr. Hunter.	Mr. Whitbread.

DRAFT REPORT, proposed by Mr. *Balfour*, read the first time, as follows :

" 1. Four times since 1880 the House of Commons has been obliged to revise its rules for the purpose of expediting public business. Four times in the same period exceptional methods of restricting discussion, not based upon the Standing Order or practice of the House, have been adopted, when, in the opinion of the majority, it became absolutely necessary to pass into law measures required to meet a pending crisis. The causes, legitimate and illegitimate, which stimulate discussion, have, however, counterbalanced, and more than counterbalanced, the effect of the rules designed to restrain it ; the difficulty of legislation has not diminished ; the exhausting labours imposed upon Members of Parliament, excessive at the beginning of this decade, have, if anything, increased ; and experience shows that while closure, in the form in which it is recognised in the Standing Orders, may be, and in the opinion of your Committee, *is* adequate to deal with single Resolutions and short Bills, it is not adequate to enable the House to consider, within the compass of a Session of convenient length, measures which are both long, complicated, and controversial. Unless, therefore, the House is prepared to acquiesce in its increasing impotence to grapple with such measures, some further modification of its procedure seems to be necessary.

" 2. Such a modification can only take one of two forms. It must either, by some very stringent form of closure, enable Bills which would, if debate were free, be killed by a prorogation, to pass through all the stages in the course of one Session, or else it must revive them in the succeeding Session under such conditions that it would not be necessary, or indeed permissible, to repeat again the discussion which had taken place upon the stages to which the House had already agreed.

"3. As your Committee are of opinion that the first course might in certain contingencies seriously endanger that right of free criticism, which is one of the most fundamental and useful privileges of Parliament, they are driven to the consideration whether the second course might not safely be adopted, without introducing any dangerous innovation into the practice of the House. Your Committee therefore propose that a Standing Order should be adopted by the House in the following terms :—

" ' That, in the judgment of your Committee, it is expedient that a Standing Order be passed for the purpose of abridging procedure in the case of Bills originating in the House of Commons which have been partly considered, and your Committee advise that such Standing Order should be adopted by the house in the following terms :—

" ' In respect of any Public Bill which is in progress in Committee of the whole House, or in a Standing Committee, or which has been reported therefrom, or which has reached any further stage, a Motion may be made (after notice given) by a Member in charge of Bill, " That further Proceedings on such Bill be suspended until the next Session," and no amendment shall be moved to such Motion.

" ' If such Motion be carried, then, in the ensuing Session (being a Session of the same Parliament), any Member whose name was on the suspended Bill may claim " That the Resolution of the previous Session be read." Thereupon the Speaker shall direct the Clerk to read the Resolution, and shall proceed to call on the Member to present the Bill in the form in which it stood when the Proceedings thereon were suspended ; and the Questions on the First and Second Readings thereof shall be successively put forthwith.

" ' If both these Questions be carried, the Bill shall be ordered to be printed ; and, if it had been partly considered in Committee in the previous Session, it shall stand committed to a similar Committee, and it shall be an Instruction to such Committee to begin their consideration

B 4   of

of the Bill at the Clause on which Progress was reported in the previous Session; but if it had been reported from Committee in the previous Session, the consideration of the Bill, as reported shall be appointed for that day week.

"'Provided always, That, if the First or Second Reading be negatived, such Vote shall, not be held to preclude the House from entertaining a Bill, on the same subject-matter under the ordinary Rules of Procedure.'

"4. This Standing Order, it will be observed, differs fundamentally, both in its character and in its object, from the various schemes with which it has a superficial similarity, and which have been more than once considered by the House of Commons during the last 40 years. Committees have sat upon three such schemes in the years 1848, 1861, and 1869, but in every one of these cases the object of the proposal was not to enable the House of Commons to deal effectually with measures submitted to it by the Government, or by private Members, but to enable the House of Lords to deal effectually with measures sent up to it from the House of Commons. This last object may be desirable or undesirable, and the means suggested for carrying it out may have been effectual or ineffectual, but your Committee desire to point out that neither the object nor the machinery for obtaining it were the same as those of the proposed Standing Order.

"5. In spite of these essential differences, fears have been expressed lest the adoption of this Standing Order should supply a justification to the House of Lords for reviving and putting in force the rejected schemes of 1848, 1861, or 1869. But it must be observed, *in the first place*, that a plan by which one House is enabled more effectually to deal with business which has originated in it, and which has never left it, can hardly form a precedent for a totally different scheme by which one House may be able to postpone or reject Bills initiated in the other. And, *in the second place*, it is obvious that no endeavour on the part of the House of Lords to carry out the second of objects can be effectual without the concurrence of the House of Commons. For the change of procedure must either be effected by Bill or by Standing Order. If by Bill, then the assent of both Houses is required. If by Standing Order, then only by Standing Orders adopted by both Houses, and to which both Houses, therefore, must be parties. It seems to be supposed that a mere alteration of the Standing Orders of the House of Lords, unaccompanied by any alteration in those of the House of Commons, would enable the former to suspend Bills sent up to them at the end of one Session, and to proceed to their consideration in the course of the next. This, however, is an error. It would be competent, no doubt, for the House of Lords, if they chose to suspend Bills which had not originated in their House. But since no Bill can receive the Royal Assent unless it has passed both Houses *in the same Session of Parliament*, this operation would be totally nugatory, unless the House of Commons, on its part, was prepared to pass the suspended Bill rapidly through the necessary stages in the *same* Session as that in which the House of Lords finally took it into consideration. The 'suspended' Bill would, on its re-introduction in the House of Lords, be to all intents and purposes a *new* Bill, and it would be for the House of Commons, and not for the House of Lords, to determine whether, when it came down to them from the Upper House, it should be passed either by the ordinary procedure, or an abridged procedure, or not passed at all. It seems clear, therefore, that no action undertaken by the House of Lords *alone* would enable them to attain the object which the late Lord Derby and others endeavoured to accomplish by Bill.

"6. It has been suggested that, by suspending a Bill, the valuable power of amending it during the recess, and reintroducing it in a better form, would necessarily be lost. Your Committee are not prepared to dispute the fact that changes which may also now and then be improvements, are often made in Bills which have failed to become law in the Session when they were first introduced; but those who are of opinion that such amendments are necessary or expedient in the interests of good legislation, should be prepared to carry out their theory to its logical issue, and to propose a Standing Order under which no Bill should be passed in the same Session in which it was first read a second time. By this means the advantages, inseparable in their opinion from every abortive attempt at legislation, would not be arbitrarily confined to a few measures chosen at random. It may be noted in this connection, that those who are impressed with the advantages of not passing measures till they have been twice introduced into the House of Commons, are hardly in a position to regret that the proposed Standing Order may in certain cases extend legislation over two years instead of one.

"7. The only other argument which it is necessary to consider is that based upon the fact that the House of Commons has already adequate powers, without a Standing Order, to repeat in an abridged form the stages of any Bill which have been already passed in a previous Session. In the words of Sir James Graham, 'Whenever it may be thought desirable promptly to pass and send ' to the other House for concurrence, a Bill passed in a former Session, but set aside in the Lords, ' the Commons may pass the Bill rapidly through all its stages if they be so minded, and this ' course is not open to the objection of providing fresh opportunities for the postponement of legisla- tion.' No doubt the House has such a power, as it has the power of deciding, if it so pleases, that the First, Second, and Third Readings of a new Bill shall be put without amendment or debate. But your Committee are of opinion that it is of the utmost importance that Parliamentary practice should be guided as far as possible by settled rules, deliberately adopted, and generally applicable. And it appears to them that every argument which can be urged against the proposed Standing Order is equally effective against the policy suggested by Sir James Graham's Report; while the latter is open to the most serious objections, based not only upon the waste of time which any attempt to carry it out must necessarily produce, but still more upon its sudden, occasional, and arbitrary character, so little in harmony with the general spirit of House of Commons procedure.

" 8. The

" 8. The preceding considerations may be briefly summarised as follows :—

" The length of discussion to which it is thought necessary to subject measures which are the object of party controversy has increased, is increasing, and does not seem likely to diminish.   As a result, the difficulty of passing such measures through all their stages in the course of one Session has increased likewise.   This difficulty is especially felt in the case of long and complicated Bills, and it is precisely in the case of these Bills that the closure of debate is most ineffective as an instrument for facilitating the rapid progress of business.   It is, therefore, desirable to increase the power of the House of Commons to deal with such measures; it is also desirable to shorten the length of Sessions, whose present duration overtaxes the endurance of Members and embarrasses the machinery of administration; but it is *not* desirable, so long as any other alternative remains, to increase the stringency of the existing machinery for closing debate.   Your Committee believe that if these three principles be accepted every possible alternative is excluded, except one which shall relieve Parliament in certain cases from the necessity of repeating in two successive Sessions the same debate upon the same questions.   They attach no weight, for reasons above given, to any objections that have suggested themselves to this plan, based upon the relations now existing between the two Houses of Parliament.   They think the change, though undoubtedly an important one, is much less violent in character and much less at variance with the spirit of Parliamentary tradition than some alterations which have been made of late years in Parliamentary procedure; and they point out that if, as they recommend, it be effected, by Standing Order instead of by Bill, the experiment may be purely tentative, and could be abandoned, should that course be subsequently thought desirable, by the sole action of the House of Commons, without requiring the consent of the other branch of the Legislature."

Motion made, and Question put, That the Draft Report proposed by Mr. *Balfour*, be read a second time, paragraph by paragraph.—The Committee divided:

Ayes, 11.	Noes, 9.
Mr. Arthur Balfour.	Mr. Dillon.
Sir Algernon Borthwick.	Mr. Dillwyn.
Mr. Chamberlain.	Mr. Gladstone.
Mr. Penrose Fitzgerald.	Sir William Harcourt.
Lord Hartington.	Dr. Hunter.
Mr. Jennings.	Mr. Labouchere.
Colonel Malcolm.	Mr. John Morley.
Sir Stafford Northcote.	Mr. Sexton.
Mr. T. W. Russell.	Mr. Whitbread.
The Solicitor General.	
Mr. John Talbot.	

[Adjourned till Twelve o'clock, on Monday next.

Monday, 14th July 1890.

MEMBERS PRESENT:

Mr. GOSCHEN in the Chair.

Mr. Arthur Balfour.	Mr. Labouchere.
Sir Algernon Borthwick.	Colonel Malcolm.
Mr. Chamberlain.	Mr. John Morley.
Mr. Dillon.	Sir Stafford Northcote.
Mr. Dillwyn.	Mr. T. W. Russell.
Mr. Penrose Fitzgerald.	Mr. Sexton.
Sir William Harcourt.	The Solicitor General.
Lord Hartington.	Mr. John Talbot.
Dr. Hunter.	Mr. Whitbread.
Mr. Jennings.	

Draft Report proposed by Mr. *Balfour* considered.

Paragraph 1.—Question put, That the paragraph stand part of the Report.—The Committee divided:

Ayes, 8.	Noes, 7.
Mr. Arthur Balfour.	Mr. Dillon.
Mr. Penrose Fitzgerald.	Mr. Dillwyn.
Mr. Jennings.	Sir William Harcourt.
Colonel Malcolm.	Mr. Labouchere.
Sir Stafford Northcote.	Mr John Morley.
Mr. T. W. Russell.	Mr. Sexton.
The Solicitor General.	Mr. Whitbread.
Mr. John Talbot.	

Paragraph 2.—An Amendment made.—Question put, That the paragraph, as amended, stand part of the Report.—The Committee divided:

Ayes, 10	Noes, 7.
Mr. Arthur Balfour.	Mr. Dillon.
Sir Algernon Borthwick.	Mr. Dillwyn.
Mr. Penrose Fitzgerald.	Sir William Harcourt.
Lord Hartington.	Mr. Labouchere.
Mr. Jennings.	Mr. John Morley.
Colonel Malcolm.	Mr. Sexton.
Sir Stafford Northcote.	Mr. Whitbread.
Mr. T. W. Russell.	
The Solicitor General.	
Mr. John Talbot.	

Paragraph 3.—Amendments made.—Question put, That the paragraph, as amended, stand part of the Report.—The Committee divided:

Ayes, 10.	Noes, 7.
Mr. Arthur Balfour.	Mr. Dillon.
Sir Algernon Borthwick.	Mr. Dillwyn.
Mr. Penrose Fitzgerald.	Sir William Harcourt.
Lord Hartington.	Mr. Labouchere.
Mr. Jennings.	Mr. John Morley.
Colonel Malcolm.	Mr. Sexton.
Sir Stafford Northcote.	Mr. Whitbread.
Mr. T. W. Russell.	
The Solicitor General.	
Mr. John Talbot.	

Paragraph 4.—Question put, That the paragraph stand part of the Report.—The Committee divided:

Ayes, 10.	Noes, 7.
Mr. Arthur Balfour.	Mr. Dillon.
Sir Algernon Borthwick.	Mr. Dillwyn.
Mr. Penrose Fitzgerald.	Sir William Harcourt.
Lord Hartington.	Mr. Labouchere.
Mr. Jennings.	Mr. John Morley.
Colonel Malcolm.	Mr. Sexton.
Sir Stafford Northcote.	Mr. Whitbread.
Mr. T. W. Russell.	
The Solicitor General.	
Mr. John Talbot.	

Paragraph 5.—Amendment proposed, in lines 11—20, to leave out from the words " It seems " to the word "consideration" (inclusive), and insert the words, " It has been alleged that the Standing Order now proposed would invite and countenance the adoption by the House of Lords of a similar Standing Order, and thus enable that House to postpone the consideration of all Bills passed and sent up from the House of Commons. Such a proceeding would, however, not only be contrary to constitutional usage, but, as no Bill can receive the Royal Assent unless it has passed both Houses in the same Session of Parliament, it would be useless, unless the House of Commons, on its part, was prepared to pass the suspended Bill rapidly through the necessary stages in the same Session as that in which the House of Lords finally took it into consideration "—(Mr. *Balfour*). Question, That the words proposed to be left out stand part of the paragraph,—put, and *negatived*.

Question proposed, That the proposed words be there inserted.—Amendment proposed to the proposed Amendment, to leave out the words " Such a proceeding would however not only be contrary to constitutional usage," and insert the words, "In reply to this allegation your Committee deem it right and necessary to record their opinion that any claim or attempt by either House of Parliament of its own authority, by Standing Order or otherwise, to postpone to a future Session of Parliament any Bill sent to it from the other House of Parliament would be a breach of the constitutional usage of Parliament "—(Sir *William Harcourt*).—Question, That the words proposed to be left out stand part of the proposed Amendment,—put, and *negatived*.

Question, That the proposed words be there inserted in the proposed Amendment,—put, and *agreed to*.

Another Amendment made to the proposed Amendment, to leave out from the words " but as no Bill " to the word " consideration," at the end of the proposed Amendment—(Sir *William Harcourt*).—Question, That the words proposed to be left out stand part of the proposed Amendment, —put, and *negatived* .

Amendment, as amended, *agreed to*, and *inserted*.

Another

Another Amendment proposed in paragraph 5, line 20, to leave out from the words " The suspended " to the end of the paragraph—(Sir *William Harcourt*).—Question, That the words proposed to be left out stand part of the paragraph,—put, and *negatived*.

Paragraph, as amended, *agreed to*.

Paragraph 6.—Question put, That the paragraph stand part of the Report.—The Committee divided :

Ayes, 9.	Noes, 7.
Sir Algernon Borthwick.	Mr. Dillon.
Mr. Penrose Fitzgerald.	Mr. Dillwyn.
Lord Hartington.	Sir William Harcourt.
Mr. Jennings.	Dr. Hunter.
Colonel Malcolm.	Mr. Labouchere.
Sir Stafford Northcote.	Mr. Sexton.
Mr. T. W. Russell.	Mr. Whitbread.
The Solicitor General.	
Mr. John Talbot.	

Paragraph 7.—Question put, That the paragraph stand part of the Report.—The Committee divided :

Ayes, 10.	Noes, 7.
Mr. Arthur Balfour.	Mr. Dillon.
Sir Algernon Borthwick.	Mr. Dillwyn.
Mr. Penrose Fitzgerald.	Sir William Harcourt.
Lord Hartington.	Dr. Hunter.
Mr. Jennings.	Mr. Labouchere.
Colonel Malcolm.	Mr. Sexton.
Sir Stafford Northcote.	Mr. Whitbread
Mr. T. W. Russell.	
The Solicitor General.	
Mr. John Talbot.	

Paragraph 8.—Question put, That the paragraph stand part of the Report.—The Committee divided :

Ayes, 11.	Noes, 8.
Mr. Arthur Balfour.	Mr. Dillon.
Sir Algernon Borthwick.	Mr. Dillwyn.
Mr. Chamberlain.	Sir William Harcourt.
Mr. Penrose Fitzgerald.	Dr. Hunter.
Lord Hartington.	Mr. Labouchere.
Mr. Jennings.	Mr. John Morley.
Colonel Malcolm.	Mr. Sexton.
Sir Stafford Northcote.	Mr. Whitbread.
Mr. T. W. Russell.	
The Solicitor General.	
Mr. John Talbot.	

Amendment proposed, That the following new paragraph be inserted in the Report :—" You Committee, however, adopt the view expressed by the Joint Committee of Lords and Commons in 1869, with respect to the plan then before them, that changes of such gravity in the constitutional practice of Parliament ought not to be carried into effect without such general concurrence as would secure their cordial adoption and harmonious operation "—(Mr. *John Morley*).—Question put, That this paragraph be inserted in the Report.—The Committee divided :

Ayes, 8.	Noes, 11.
Mr. Dillon.	Mr. Arthur Balfour.
Mr. Dillwyn.	Sir Algernon Borthwick.
Sir William Harcourt	Mr. Chamberlain.
Dr. Hunter.	Mr. Penrose Fitzgerald.
Mr. Labouchere.	Lord Hartington.
Mr. John Morley.	Mr. Jennings.
Mr. Sexton.	Colonel Malcolm.
Mr. Whitbread.	Sir Stafford Northcote.
	Mr. T. W. Russell.
	The Solicitor General.
	Mr. John Talbot.

Question put, That this Report, as amended, be the Report of the Committee to the House.—
The Committee divided:

Ayes, 11.	Noes, 8.
Mr. Arthur Balfour.	Mr. Dillon.
Sir Algernon Borthwick.	Mr. Dillwyn.
Mr. Chamberlain.	Sir William Harcourt.
Mr. Penrose Fitzgerald.	Dr. Hunter.
Lord Hartington.	Mr. Labouchere.
Mr. Jennings.	Mr. John Morley.
Colonel Malcolm.	Mr. Sexton.
Sir Stafford Northcote.	Mr. Whitbread.
Mr. T. W. Russell.	
The Solicitor General.	
Mr. John Talbot.	

Ordered, To Report, together with an Appendix.

A·P·P·E·N·D·I·X.

LIST OF APPENDIX.

APPENDIX.

APPENDIX, No. 1.

PAPER handed in by the *Chairman.*

TELEGRAM addressed by the Marquis of *Salisbury* to Her Majesty's Ambassadors at Vienna, Paris, Berlin, Rome, and Washington.

(Telegraphic.) P. Foreign Office, 17 June 1890.

PLEASE report by telegraph whether Parliamentary Bills lapse, as they do in this country, with each Session, or whether they are again taken up at the same stage which they had reached.

ANSWERS to preceding TELEGRAM.

AUSTRIA-HUNGARY

— No. 1. —

Sir *A. Paget* to the Marquis of *Salisbury.*—(Received 23 June.)

My Lord, Vienna, 20 June 1890.

I THINK it right to explain, with reference to my telegram of this morning, that, according to the information I have obtained, it was the habit, for the first 10 or 15 years after the establishment of the Parliamentary system in Austria, for the Parliament to be prorogued annually, as it is in England, by a Speech or Message from the Throne, which put an end to the Session, and on Parliament reassembling, a fresh Session was opened in like manner by another Message, or Speech from the Throne.

It was found, however, that so much time was consumed at the opening of each new Session by debates upon the Address in answer to the Imperial Speech or Message, that it was determined to adopt the system of adjournments instead of formal prorogations ; and since Count Taaffe has been Prime Minister, a period of upwards of 10 years, this has, with perhaps an occasional exception, been the invariable practice followed.

A Session therefore may, and generally does, last during the whole period of six years, the duration of the Parliament, for which the Members of the Lower House or Chamber of Deputies ("Abgeordneten Haus") are elected, so that Bills which have been presented, and are in an incomplete state when Parliament adjourns for the holidays, are taken up again at the stage which they had reached when the adjournment took place ; though, should there be a formal prorogation, with a Message from the Throne putting an end to the Session, which it is within the faculty of the Emperor, acting on the advice of his Government, to adopt at any moment, every Bill then before Parliament lapses, and cannot be taken up again at the stage it had reached in the last Session, but must be presented afresh in the new Session. The same thing happens of course when a dissolution takes place.

The same system of adjournment instead of prorogation prevails also in the Hungarian Parliament, and I may add that another reason for its adoption, besides that already given above, is to avoid the multiplicity in every year of Imperial Messages or Speeches, for as the Delegations are always opened and closed by an Imperial Speech, there would have to be made four more, namely, one on opening and one on closing the Austrian Parliament, and one on opening and one on closing the Hungarian Parliament, if the system of prorogation was the practice.

The Emperor, however, as already reported, fixes the period for the reassembling of the different Parliaments by letters addressed to his Austrian and Hungarian Prime Ministers respectively.

When I received your Lordship's first telegram, I turned to the printed Regulations for the conduct of business in the Lower House ("Geschäftsordnung für das Abgeordneten Haus des Reichsraths"), naturally expecting to find the information there, but they are entirely silent on the subject, and I was therefore compelled to have recourse to other competent sources, which at this moment, when almost every one has left the capital either to attend the Delegations at Pesth, or for the country, were not easy to find, but your Lordship may rely upon the correctness of the information which in my telegrams and in this Despatch I have had the honour to convey, as it has been given to me by the highest authority.

I have, &c.
(signed) *A. Paget.*

— No. 2. —

Sir *A. Paget* to the Marquis of *Salisbury*.—(Received 27 June.)

My Lord,   Vienna, 25 June 1890.

ON referring to my Despatch of the 20th instant, respecting the system of Parliamentary procedure in Austria and Hungary, I find that I inadvertently stated that the Delegations were always opened and closed by an Imperial Speech. I should have omitted the word "closed," for, as a matter of fact, the Emperor only delivers a Speech on the opening of the Session in reply to the Addresses which are made to him by the Presidents of the two Delegations when the members are received in solemn audience at the commencement of their annual sittings. The custom is for the Delegations to be closed by a few words from the Minister for Foreign Affairs, in which he expresses the thanks of the Emperor for the attention the Delegations have devoted to the various matters brought before them, but no political questions are entered into.

As Count Kálnoky will be unable to attend on the present occasion, it is probable that the valedictory words usually spoken by him will be delivered by M. de Szögyény, the Chief Under Secretary of the Ministry for Foreign Affairs.

I have, &c.
(signed)   *A. Paget.*

FRANCE.

— No. 3. —

The Earl of *Lytton* to the Marquis of *Salisbury*.—(Received 17 June.)

(Telegraphic.) P.   Paris, 17 June 1890, 5.45 P.M.

IN reply to your Lordship's telegram of this day, I have the honour to state that, in France, Parliamentary Bills do not lapse with the Session, but are taken up at the same stage in the ensuing Session. In some cases they can even be carried over to a new Parliament.

GERMANY.

— No. 4. —

Sir *E. Malet* to the Marquis of *Salisbury*.—(Received 17 June.)

(Telegraphic.) P.   Berlin, 17 June 1890.

WITH reference to your Lordship's telegram of to-day, in both Prussian and German Parliaments, Bills lapse with the Session, but a recess does not affect them.

— No. 5. —

Sir *E. Malet* to the Marquis of *Salisbury*.—(Received 20 June.)

(Telegraphic.) P.   Berlin, 20 June 1890.

IN reply to your Lordship's telegram of to-day, the word "recess" in my preceding telegram was intended to mean "adjournment."

A Session of the Reichstag has no limit of time, and is opened and closed by Imperial Decree; it generally lasts about one year, but may be more or less.

Five years is fixed as the duration of a Reichstag.

ITALY.

— No. 6. —

The Marquis of *Dufferin* to the Marquis of *Salisbury*.—(Received 18 June.)

(Telegraphic.) P.   Rome, 18 June 1890, 4.30 P.M.

WITH reference to the inquiries contained in your Lordship's telegram of yesterday, I am informed that the procedure followed in respect to Bills brought before the Italian Legislature is precisely similar to that at present in force in England. Unless a Bill passes three readings, and receives the Royal Assent in the same Session, it is lost.

UNITED STATES.

— No. 7. —

Sir *J. Pauncefote* to the Marquis of *Salisbury*.—(Received 18 June, 8 A.M.)

(Telegraphic.) P.   Washington, 17 June 1890, 11.23 P.M.

WITH reference to your Lordship's telegram of to-day, each Congress has two Sessions. Bills not passed in the first Session do not lapse, but may be again taken up in the second at the stage previously reached. If not passed in either Session, Bills lapse with the closing of Congress.

APPENDIX, No. 2.

PAPER, handed in by the Chairman.

MEMORANDUM showing the PARLIAMENTS in which the Consideration of BILLS partly considered in one Session is resumed in the next ensuing Session.

UNITED STATES OF AMERICA.

The House of Representatives is elected biennially. The 27th Rule runs as follows :—

" All Business before Committees of the House at the end of one Session shall be resumed at the commencement of the next Session of the same Congress in the same manner as if no adjournment had taken place."—(V. Digest and Manual of the Rules and Practice of the House of Representatives. 12th Edition ; by Henry H. Smith.)

*Foreign Parliaments (R. Dickinson) 2nd ed., p. 497.

FRANCE.

Under the present constitution Bills partly considered are carried on from Session to Session of the same Parliament. The Chamber of Deputies continues in existence for four years, unless previously dissolved by the President, and the Bills, if not otherwise disposed of, continue before it the whole of the time without being reintroduced. Indeed, they may remain under consideration even longer, for if a dissolution occurs after a Bill has been sent up to the Senate, which is never dissolved (one-third of its Members retiring every three years), that body may agree to such Bill, and, if not amended, it becomes law on receiving the President's assent ; but if amendments are made, the Senate sends it back to the new Chamber of Deputies, and that Chamber may either agree to it as a whole summarily, or treat it as a new Bill.

Foreign Parliaments, 2nd ed., p. 308.

The Senate, however, cannot proceed in the new Parliament with a Bill sent up by the old Chamber of Deputies unless before the dissolution the " Committee of Initiative," to which all Bills are referred by the Senate on their introduction, has reported the Bill ; but it must be remembered that this reference to the Committee of Initiative takes place immediately after what in England would be described as the Order of Leave, or introduction of the Bill, and not after the Second Reading.

AUSTRIA-HUNGARY.

The Austrian or Cisleithan Parliament, unless dissolved by the Crown, lasts six years. The duration of the Hungarian or Transleithan Parliament has been recently extended from three to five years,

In both Parliaments, up to some ten years ago, the English system prevailed, and all business came to an end at the conclusion of each Session. But this practice has been found to be so inconvenient that adjournment from Session to Session has been adopted in lieu of prorogation, and all business is taken up in the ensuing Session of the same Parliament as if there had been nothing more than an adjournment from one day to another. This change was introduced by Count Taaffe ; and besides allowing Bills in progress to proceed in a continuous Session of six years or five years, respectively, it did away with the Debate on the Address in answer to the Imperial Speech, which had become as obstructive of legislation in Austria-Hungary as it still is in England. Should, however, the Emperor exert his prerogative of prorogation, or of dissolution, all business lapses, as with us. The annual Speech from the Throne is now only addressed to the Delegations chosen from the two Parliaments.

The Austrian and Hungarian Parliaments, when they adjourn at the close of the Session, do not adjourn till a day fixed at their own pleasure. But at the proper time the Emperor fixes the day for the reassembling of each Parliament in a letter addressed to his Austrian and Hungarian Prime Minister respectively.

BELGIUM.

The Members elected to the Belgian Chamber of Representatives are elected for four years ; half the Chamber relieving every two years.

The Senators are chosen for eight years ; half retiring every four years, but in case of a dissolution the whose number has to be renewed.

Bills which have been partially considered in one Session may be taken up in the following Session at the same stage, except after a dissolution. It was proposed in 1874 by a Committee on the Rules of Procedure to do away with this distinction and carry on Bills partly considered in the old to the new Parliament, but the proposed change was not accepted.

Foreign Parliaments, 3rd ed., p. 209.

NETHERLANDS.

All the business of the Second, or popular, Chamber that has been left unfinished at the close of a Session (including that of the Committees elected by the Chamber itself, and those nominated by the President, or by the Sections, and also the proceedings in consequence of a Message from the Crown, on which proceeding Government Bills originate), is resumed in the next Session of the same Parliament, as of course, unless the Chamber decides otherwise.

Foreign Parliaments, 2nd ed., p. 235.

The same practice is observed in the First Chamber, although it is not prescribed by rule. But it must be remembered that in the Netherlands the First Chamber is not allowed to originate Bills.

---

* " Summary of the Constitution and Procedure of Foreign Parliaments," compiled by R. Dickinson. Second edition, 1890.

DENMARK, NORWAY, AND SWEDEN.

Foreign Parliaments, 2nd ed., pp. 303, 334, 335.

Bills which have been partly considered in one Session may be taken up in the ensuing Session of the same Parliament at the point at which they had attained in the previous Session, and in Norway, even a Motion stands over to the next Session, unless a reservation has been made by the mover.

SPAIN.

Foreign Parliaments, 2nd ed., p. 331.

In the Spanish Parliament, on the motion of the Member in charge, a Bill can be taken up at the stage to which it had attained in the previous Session. But a dissolution terminates all proceedings on Bills which have not passed both Houses.

PORTUGAL.

Foreign Parliaments, 2nd ed., p. 329.

In the Portuguese Parliament Bills which have passed one Chamber and been sent to the other, but have not been discussed in the other Chamber in consequence of a prorogation, may be taken up at the same stage in the following Session of the same Parliament. Before a dissolution Bills which have passed one Chamber only are returned to the originating Chamber, with a message that time has been wanting for their full consideration.

GREECE.

Foreign Parliaments, 2nd ed., p. 312.

Bills interrupted by a prorogation can be taken up again in the ensuing Session of the same Parliament.

The practice of carrying over business is therefore recognised in twelve national Parliaments, counting Austria and Hungary as two Parliaments, and it is understood that the change introduced into both these Parliaments ten years ago by Count Taaffe, of substituting adjournment for prorogation, has worked satisfactorily.

A. M.

R E P O R T

FROM THE

SELECT COMMITTEE.

ON

BUSINESS OF THE HOUSE
(ABRIDGED PROCEDURE ON PARTLY
CONSIDERED BILLS);

WITH

PROCEEDINGS OF THE COMMITTEE.

AND APPENDIX.

Ordered, by The House of Commons, to be Printed,
14 July 1890.

[Price 3 d.]

Under 3 oz.

298.

11.—18.7.90.

REPORTS

AND

SPECIAL REPORT

FROM THE

SELECT COMMITTEE

ON THE

CALEDONIAN RAILWAY (CONVERSION OF STOCK) BILL,

THE

GREAT NORTHERN RAILWAY (CAPITAL) BILL,

THE

LONDON AND SOUTH WESTERN RAILWAY (CONVERSION OF STOCK) BILL,

AND THE

ISLE OF WIGHT RAILWAY BILL;

TOGETHER WITH THE

PROCEEDINGS OF THE COMMITTEE

AND

MINUTES OF EVIDENCE.

Ordered, by The House of Commons, *to be Printed,*
13 *June* 1890.

LONDON:
PRINTED BY HENRY HANSARD AND SON;
AND
Published by EYRE and SPOTTISWOODE, East Harding-street, London E.C.
and 32, Abingdon-street, Westminster, S.W.;
ADAM and CHARLES BLACK, North Bridge, Edinburgh;
and HODGES, FIGGIS, and Co., 104 Grafton-street, Dublin.

225.

CALEDONIAN RAILWAY (CONVERSION OF STOCK) BILL, THE GREAT NORTHERN RAILWAY (CAPITAL) BILL, and THE LONDON AND SOUTH WESTERN RAILWAY (CONVERSION OF STOCK) BILL.

Ordered,—[*Thursday, 20th March* 1890]:—THAT the Caledonian Railway (Conversion of Stock) Bill, the Great Northern Railway (Capital) Bill, and the London and South Western Railway (Conversion of Stock) Bill, be referred to a Select Committee consisting of Nine Members, Five to be nominated by the House and Four by the Committee of Selection.

THAT, subject to the Rules, Orders, and Proceedings of this House, all Petitions against the said Bills be referred to the Committee, and that such of the Petitioners as pray to be heard by themselves, their Counsel, Agents, or Witnesses, be heard upon their Petitions, if they think fit. and Counsel heard in favour of the said Bills.

THAT the Committee have power to send for Persons, Papers, and Records.

THAT Five be the Quorum of the Committee.

Ordered,—[*Monday, 31st March* 1890]:—THAT the Isle of Wight Railway Bill be read a second time, and committed to the Select Committee on the Caledonian Railway (Conversion of Stock) Bill, the Great Northern Railway (Capital) Bill, and the London and South Western Railway (Conversion of Stock) Bill.

Committee nominated—[*Thursday, 24th April* 1890]—of—

Mr. Campbell-Bannerman.

Mr. W. Beckett.

Mr. Bristowe.   Nominated by the House.
                                    [*Thursday, 24th April* 1890.]
Mr. Buxton.

Mr. R. Mowbray.

Mr. Biddulph.

Mr. Chance.

Mr. Charles Hall.   Added by the Committee of Selection.
                                    [*Friday, 25th April* 1890.]
Mr. J. E. Ellis (Notts.)

Ordered,—[*Friday, 2nd May* 1890]:—THAT Mr. Chance be discharged, and that Mr. Dickson be added to the Committee.

R E P O R T S.

LONDON AND SOUTH WESTERN RAILWAY (CONVERSION OF STOCK) BILL.

THE SELECT COMMITTEE on the LONDON AND SOUTH WESTERN RAILWAY (CONVERSION OF STOCK) BILL have agreed to the following REPORT :—

THAT the Bill does not authorise the construction of any new works.

That they had examined the allegations contained in the Preamble of the Bill, and had amended the same so as to make it consistent with the provisions of the Bill as passed by the Committee, and found the same as amended to be true, and had gone through the Bill and made Amendments thereunto.

CALEDONIAN RAILWAY (CONVERSION OF STOCK) BILL.

THE SELECT COMMITTEE on the CALEDONIAN RAILWAY (CONVERSION OF STOCK) BILL have agreed to the following REPORT :—

THAT the Bill does not authorise the construction of any new Railway or work.

That they had examined the allegations contained in the Preamble of the Bill, and had amended the same so as to make it consistent with the provisions of the Bill as passed by the Committee, and had found the same as amended to be true, and had gone through the Bill and made Amendments thereunto.

GREAT NORTHERN RAILWAY (CAPITAL) BILL.

THE SELECT COMMITTEE on the GREAT NORTHERN RAILWAY (CAPITAL) BILL have agreed to the following REPORT :—

THAT the Bill does not authorise the construction of any new works.

That they had examined the allegations contained in the Preamble of the Bill, and amended the same so as to make it consistent with the provisions of the Bill as passed by the Committee, and found the same as amended to be true, and had gone through the Bill and made Amendments thereunto.

ISLE OF WIGHT RAILWAY BILL.

THE SELECT COMMITTEE on the ISLE OF WIGHT RAILWAY BILL have agreed to the following REPORT :—

THAT the Bill does not authorise the construction of any new Railway.

That they had examined the allegations contained in the Preamble of the Bill, and had amended the same so as to make it consistent with the provisions of the Bill as passed by the Committee; and found the same as amended to be true, and had gone through the Bill and made Amendments thereunto.

SPECIAL REPORT.

THE SELECT COMMITTEE to whom the CALEDONIAN RAILWAY (CONVERSION OF STOCK) BILL, the GREAT NORTHERN RAILWAY (CAPITAL) BILL, the LONDON AND SOUTH WESTERN RAILWAY (CONVERSION OF STOCK) BILL, and the ISLE of WIGHT RAILWAY BILL was referred;——HAVE agreed to the following SPECIAL REPORT :—

1. YOUR Committee, in considering the Bills referred to them, have been assisted by statements made before them by counsel for the promoters; and besides the evidence submitted on behalf of the Railway Companies, your Committee have invited, and have obtained, an expression of opinion from witnesses representing the Board of Trade, the Bank of England, the Committee of the Stock Exchange, and two important Joint Stock Banking Companies.

2. Although the proposals in the Bills referred to your Committee differ in points of detail, they all have for their principal object the division of ordinary stock into two portions, one of which shall have assigned to it a fixed rate of dividend, while the other shall be entitled to such an amount of income as, after the payment of this fixed dividend on the first portion, may remain available for distribution out of the earnings of the company. The railway companies are impelled to apply for power to make this alteration in their stock by the belief that the stock in its new form will be more convenient and attractive to investors, and therefore advantageous to the proprietors.

3. It appears to your Committee that two distinct questions present themselves for decision, viz. :—

   (1.) Whether the proposed change in the form of railway ordinary stock ought to receive the sanction of Parliament.

   (2.) How far it is necessary, or expedient, that Parliament should interfere with the method by which the change is carried out; and if Parliament does so interfere, whether the terms and conditions under which stock may be converted, should be prescribed in a General Enabling Bill.

4. With regard to the first question, your Committee see nothing unreasonable, or objectionable from a public point of view, in the conversion of ordinary stock into a preferred and a deferred class, and, therefore, recommend that the necessary power for that purpose should not be refused when a Railway Company desires it.

5. In order to come to a satisfactory conclusion on the second question it is necessary to bear in mind what has hitherto been the attitude of Parliament with regard to such matters.

6. Your Committee find the principle applicable to such questions very clearly laid down by the Royal Commission on Railways, presided over by the Duke of Devonshire, in its Report dated 7th May 1867. The Commissioners say (paragraph 90) : " In fact, these Parliamentary restrictions tend to give the investing public the idea that they possess some peculiar advantage, and to lull them into a false security as to the value of the debentures and of the share capital. But now that Parliament has adopted the policy of placing any lawful enterprise, conducted by means of a joint-stock capital within the reach of all associations of persons more than six in number, and has conferred upon them the privilege of limited liability, it would appear to be a more judicious course *that Parliament should relieve itself from all interference with the incorporation and the financial affairs of Railway Companies, leaving such matters to be dealt with under the Joint Stock Companies Act, and should limit its own action to regulating the construction*

of

of the line, and the relations between the public and Joint Stock Companies so incorporated; requiring such guarantees as may be necessary for the purpose of securing the due performance of the conditions upon the faith of which the Parliamentary powers of the Company have been granted."

7. The principle thus stated has been adopted by the Board of Trade, which is the public department concerned in the matter; it has been asserted and appealed to by successive Ministers, and accepted by eminent Parliamentary authorities. Its soundness, also, has stood the test of time. The only important departure from it occurred in the Regulation of Railways Act, 1868, into which a clause was introduced (Section 13) permitting the division of stocks, and laying down with great elaboration the precise conditions which should govern that operation. The result has, however, been that, except in a few cases which occurred shortly after the passing of the Act, no advantage has been taken of that section.

8. Your Committee recommend, therefore, that Parliament should continue to act upon the principle of . non-intervention in the financial affairs of Railway Companies, believing that while the public are naturally concerned in the solidity and stability of corporations, to which Parliament has given large exclusive powers, these objects are, in most cases, best secured by trusting to the self-interest of the shareholders.

9. There may be, however, in proposals such as those now under consideration, points directly affecting the public interest, and your Committee have carefully scrutinised these Bills with this possibility in view. In order to avoid any confusion as to the actual amount of the paid-up capital of a company, your Committee think it right to insist (1) that the dividend shall in all cases continue to be declared on the original stock, and (2) that the original stock or paid-up capital shall be recorded and shown in the accounts, as though no alteration had been made in the form of the stock.

10. It also appears to your Committee that all railway stocks converted into preferred and deferred stocks should bear a uniform nomenclature.

11. Subject to these provisions, your Committee, on the grounds above stated, submit that there is no reason why these Bills should not, with some amendments they have made in them, be passed into law.

13 *June* 1890.

PROCEEDINGS OF THE COMMITTEE.

Tuesday, 8th May 1890.

MEMBERS PRESENT:

Mr. Bristowe.
Mr. Biddulph.
Mr. Charles Hall.
Mr. W. Beckett.

Mr. J. E. Ellis.
Mr. Campbell-Bannerman.
Mr. Buxton.
Mr. R. Mowbray.

Mr. CAMPBELL-BANNERMAN was called to the Chair.

The Committee deliberated.

[Adjourned till Tuesday next, at Twelve o'clock.

Tuesday, 13th May 1890.

MEMBERS PRESENT:

Mr. CAMPBELL-BANNERMAN in the Chair.

Mr. Bristowe.
Mr. Biddulph.
Mr. W. Beckett.
Mr. Buxton.

Mr. Charles Hall.
Mr. T. A. Dickson.
Mr. J. E. Ellis.
Mr. R. Mowbray.

1. LONDON AND SOUTH WESTERN RAILWAY (CONVERSION OF STOCK) BILL.

Preamble read the first time.

Counsel:—Mr. *Pember*, Q.C., and Mr. *Worsley Taylor*.

Agents:—Messrs. *Rees & Frere*.

2. CALEDONIAN RAILWAY (CONVERSION OF STOCK) BILL.

Preamble read the first time.

Counsel:—Mr. *Littler*, Q.C., Mr. *Pember*, Q.C., Mr. *Saunders*, Q.C., and Mr. *Worsley Taylor*.

Agents:—Messrs. *Grahames, Curry, & Spens*.

3. GREAT NORTHERN RAILWAY (CAPITAL) BILL.

Preamble read the first time.

Counsel:—Mr. *Pope*, Q.C., Mr. *Balfour Brown*, Q.C., and Mr. *T. D. FitzGerald*.

Agents:—Messrs. *Dyson*.

1. Petition against the Bill, Nottingham and Grantham Railway Company.

Counsel:—Mr. *H. Saunders*, Q.C., and Mr. *Batten*.

Agents:—Messrs. *Sherwood*.

4. ISLE OF WIGHT RAILWAY BILL.

Preamble read the first time.

Counsel:—Mr. *Pope*, Q.C., and Mr. *W. H. Bolton*.

Agents:—Messrs. *Sherwood & Co.*

The

THE LONDON AND SOUTH WESTERN RAILWAY (CONVERSION OF STOCK) BILL.

Mr. *Pember*, q.c., addressed the Committee in support of the Bill, and called evidence.

Mr. *Scotter* and Mr. *Scott* were sworn, and examined.

This closed the case for the Promoters.

Further consideration *postponed*

[Adjourned till To-morrow, at Twelve o'clock.

Wednesday, 14th May 1890.

MEMBERS PRESENT:

Mr. CAMPBELL-BANNERMAN in the Chair.

Mr. Bristowe.	Mr. J. E. Ellis.
Mr. Biddulph.	Mr. R. Mowbray.
Mr. W. Beckett.	Mr. T. A. Dickson.
Mr. Buxton.	

THE CALEDONIAN RAILWAY (CONVERSION OF STOCK) BILL.

Mr. *Pember*, q.c., addressed the Committee in support of the Bill, and called evidence.

Sir *James King* sworn, and examined.

Further consideration *postponed*.

THE GREAT NORTHERN RAILWAY (CAPITAL) BILL.

Mr. *Pope*, q.c., addressed the Committee in support of the Bill, and called evidence.

Mr. *William Grinling* and Mr. *Richard Green* were sworn, and examined.

Further consideration *postponed*.

[Adjourned till To-morrow, at Two o'clock.

Thursday, 15th May 1890.

MEMBERS PRESENT:

Mr. CAMPBELL-BANNERMAN in the Chair.

Mr. Bristowe.	Mr. J. E. Ellis.
Mr. Buxton.	Mr. R. Mowbray.
Mr. Biddulph.	Mr. Charles Hall.
Mr. W. Beckett.	Mr. T. A. Dickson.

THE ISLE OF WIGHT RAILWAY BILL.

Mr. *Pope*, q.c., was heard in support of the Bill, and called evidence.

Mr. *Tahourdin* sworn, and examined.

Room cleared. Committee deliberated.

[Adjourned till Tuesday next, at Twelve o'clock.

Tuesday, 20th May 1890.

MEMBERS PRESENT:

Mr. CAMPBELL-BANNERMAN in the Chair.

Mr. Bristowe.	Mr. T. A. Dickson.
Mr. W. Beckett.	Mr. J. E. Ellis.
Mr. Biddulph.	Mr. Charles Hall.
Mr. Buxton.	Mr. R. Mowbray.

Mr. *Horace Tahourdin* re-called, and further examined.

Mr. *R. Giffen*, an Officer of the Board of Trade; Mr. *Frank May*, Chief Cashier of the Bank of England; Mr. *Rokeby Price*, Chairman of the Stock Exchange; Mr. *William Astle*, the Chief Manager of the London and Westminster Bank, and Mr. *C. Gairdner*, Chairman of the Union Bank of Scotland, were examined by the Committee.

Room cleared. Committee deliberated.

[Adjourned till Tuesday, 10th June next.

Tuesday, 10th June 1890.

MEMBERS PRESENT:

Mr. CAMPBELL-BANNERMAN in the Chair.

Mr. Bristowe.	Mr. T. A. Dickson
Mr. Buxton.	Mr. J. E. Ellis.
Mr. Biddulph.	Mr. R. Mowbray.
Mr. W. Beckett.	Mr. Charles Hall.

LONDON AND SOUTH WESTERN RAILWAY BILL.

Clauses considered, and *agreed to.*

Preamble read a second time.—Question, " That the Preamble is proved,"—put, and *agreed to.*

CALEDONIAN RAILWAY BILL.

Clauses considered.

Clause 3.—Amendment proposed to leave out Sub-section 5—(Mr. *Buxton*).—Question put, That Sub-section 5 stand part of the Clause.—The Committee divided :

Ayes, 4.	Noes, 3.
Mr. Beckett.	Mr. Biddulph.
Mr. J. E. Ellis.	Mr. Bristowe.
Mr. Charles Hall.	Mr. Buxton.
Mr. R. Mowbray.	

Clause 6.—Question put, " That the Clause stand part of the Bill."—The Committee divided :

Ayes, 2.	Noes, 6.
Mr. Buxton.	Mr. Beckett.
Mr. Charles Hall.	Mr. Biddulph.
	Mr. Bristowe.
	Mr. T. A. Dickson.
	Mr. R. Mowbray.
	Mr. J. E. Ellis.

Clauses *agreed to.*

Preamble read a second time.

Question, That the Preamble is proved,—put, and *agreed to.*

GREAT NORTHERN RAILWAY BILL.

Clauses considered, and *agreed to.*

Preamble read a second time.

Question, " That the Preamble is proved,"—put, and *agreed to.*

ISLE OF WIGHT RAILWAY BILL.

Clauses considered.

On Clause 8, Mr. *Tshourdin*, re-called, and further examined.

Clause 15, *disagreed to.*

Clauses, *agreed to.*

Preamble read a second time, and verbally amended.

Question, That the Preamble, as amended, is proved,—put, and *agreed to.*

[Adjourned till Friday next, at Two o'clock.

Friday, 13*th June* 1890.

MEMBERS PRESENT:

Mr. CAMPBELL-BANNERMAN in the Chair.

Mr. Bristowe.	Mr. J. E. Ellis.
Mr. Buxton.	Mr. R. Mowbray.
Mr. T. A. Dickson.	

DRAFT SPECIAL REPORT, proposed by the *Chairman,* read the first time, as follows :—

" 1. YOUR Committee, in considering the Bills referred to them, have been assisted by statements made before them by counsel for the promoters ; and besides the evidence submitted on behalf of the Railway Companies, your Committee have invited, and have obtained, an expression of opinion from witnesses representing the Board of Trade, the Bank of England, the Committee of the Stock Exchange, and two important Joint Stock Banking Companies.

" 2. Although the proposals in the Bills referred to your Committee differ in points of detail, they all have for their principal object the division of ordinary stock into two portions, one of which shall have assigned to it a fixed rate of dividend, while the other shall be entitled to such an amount of income as, after the payment of this fixed dividend on the first portion, may remain available for distribution out of the earnings of the company. The railway companies are impelled to apply for power to make this alteration in their stock by the belief that the stock in its new form will be more convenient and attractive to investors, and therefore advantageous to the proprietors.

" 3. It appears to your Committee that two distinct questions present themselves for decision, viz. :—

" (1.) Whether the proposed change in the form of railway ordinary stock ought to receive the sanction of Parliament.

" (2.) How far it is necessary or expedient that Parliament should interfere with the method by which the change is carried out ; and if Parliament does so interfere, whether the terms and conditions under which stock may be converted, shall be prescribed in a General Enabling Bill.

" 4. With regard to the first question, your Committee see nothing unreasonable, or objectionable, from a public point of view, in the conversion of ordinary stock into a preferred and a deferred class, and, therefore, recommend that the necessary power for that purpose should not be refused when a Railway Company desires it.

" 5. In order to come to a satisfactory conclusion on the second question it is necessary to bear in mind what has hitherto been the attitude of Parliament with regard to such matters.

225.   b   " 6. Your

" 6. Your Committee find the principle applicable to such questions very clearly laid down by the Royal Commission on Railways, presided over by the Duke of Devonshire, in its Report dated 7th May 1867. The Commissioners say (paragraph 90): ' In fact, these Parliamentary restrictions tend to give the investing public the idea that they possess some peculiar advantage, and to lull them into a false security as to the value of the debentures and of the share capital. But now that Parliament has adopted the policy of placing any lawful enterprise, conducted by means of a joint-stock capital within the reach of all associations of persons more than six in number, and has conferred upon them the privilege of limited liability, it would appear to be a more judicious course *that Parliament should relieve itself from all interference with the incorporation and the financial affairs of Railway Companies, leaving such matters to be dealt with under the Joint Stock Companies Act, and should limit its own action to regulating the construction of the line, and the relations between the public and Joint Stock Companies so incorporated; requiring such guarantees as may be necessary for the purpose of securing the due performance of the conditions upon the faith of which the Parliamentary powers of the Company have been granted.*'

" 7. The principle thus stated has been adopted by the Board of Trade, which is the public department concerned in the matter; it has been asserted and appealed to by successive Ministers, and accepted by eminent Parliamentary authorities. Its soundness, also, has stood the test of time; the only important departure from it occurred in the Regulation of Railways Act, 1868, into which a clause was introduced (Section 13) permitting the division of stocks, and laying down with great elaboration the precise conditions which should govern that operation. The result has, however, been that, except in a few cases, which occurred shortly after the passing of the Act, no advantage has been taken of that section.

" 8. Your Committee recommend, therefore, that Parliament should continue to act upon the principle of non-intervention in the financial affairs of Railway Companies, believing that while the public are naturally concerned in the solidity and stability of corporations, to which Parliament has given large exclusive powers, these objects are, in most cases, best secured by trusting to the self-interest of the shareholders.

" 9. There may be, however, in proposals such as those now under consideration, points directly affecting the public interest, and your Committee have carefully scrutinised these Bills with this possibility in view. In order to avoid any confusion as to the actual amount of the paid-up capital of a company, your Committee think it right to insist (1) that the dividend shall in all cases continue to be declared on the original stock, and (2) that the original stock or paid-up capital shall be recorded and shown in the accounts, as though no alteration had been made in the form of the stock.

" 10. It also appears to your Committee that all railway stocks converted into preferred and deferred stocks should bear a uniform nomenclature.

" 11. Subject to these provisions, your Committee, on the grounds above stated, submit that there is no reason why these Bills should not, with some amendments they have made in them, be passed into law."

Draft Report read a second time, and *agreed to.*

Question, That this Report, as amended, be the Special Report of the Committee of the House,—put, and *agreed to.*

Ordered, To Report, together with Minutes of Evidence.

MINUTES OF EVIDENCE.

LIST OF WITNESSES.

MINUTES OF EVIDENCE.

Tuesday, *13th May* 1890.

MEMBERS PRESENT:

Mr. W. Beckett.
Mr. Biddulph.
Mr. Bristowe.
Mr. Buxton.
Mr. Campbell-Bannerman.

Mr. Dickson.
Mr. Ellis.
Mr. Charles Hall.
Mr. R. Mowbray.

THE RIGHT HON. H. CAMPBELL-BANNERMAN, IN THE CHAIR.

LONDON AND SOUTH WESTERN RAILWAY (CONVERSION OF STOCK) BILL.

The Petition for the Bill was read.

Mr. *Pember*, Q.C., and Mr. *Worsley Taylor*, appeared as Counsel on behalf of the Promoters of the Bill.

Messrs. *Rees* and *Frere* appeared as Agents.

There were no Petitions against the Bill.

Mr. *Pember* was heard to open the case on behalf of the Promoters of the Bill.

Mr. CHARLES SCOTTER, sworn; and Examined.

Mr. *Worsley Taylor.*

1. YOU are the General Manager of the London and South Western Railway?—Yes.

2. What is the capital of the company?—The capital of the company is about 31,000,000 *l.*

3. How is that divided?—There are about 8,000,000 *l.* debenture capital, 11,500,000 *l.* preference capital, and 11,500,000 *l.* ordinary capital.

4. I think last year several influential shareholders of your company have brought under the notice of your board the desirability of some such power as you are now asking for?—Yes; the origin of the Bill really commenced with certain large shareholders in the London and South Western Company who brought the subject under the notice of the directors. The directors considered the question at various meetings, and it was pointed out to the directors that unless some steps were taken by the company to promote a Bill to duplicate or divide their ordinary stock, it would be done by outsiders for the

0.101.

Mr. *Worsley Taylor*—continued.

company; the directors preferred to do it themselves.

5. That really is the short history of this Bill?—That is the short history of this Bill.

6. Then I believe that the matter was very carefully considered in the ordinary way by the board?—Yes.

7. And this Bill is the result of that consideration?—Yes; the matter was not only considered at one meeting, but at several.

8. Without taking you into the whole detail of the Bill, it is as my learned friend Mr. Pember said, a Bill for dividing the stock by means of duplication?—That is the object of the Bill.

9. Has every possible means been taken to safeguard the interests of the shareholders and everybody in the matter?—Every possible means have been taken to safeguard everybody as we think; but if we have omitted anybody we are

A

quite

13 *May* 1890.]   **Mr. Scotter.**   [*Continued.*

Mr. *Worsley Taylor*—continued.

quite prepared that such additional safeguard should be inserted in the Bill.

10. First, on Clause 2 of the Bill, nothing is to be done until there has been a resolution of the ordinary shareholders of the company?—That is the first thing; that it has to be approved by the ordinary shareholders.

11. Sub-section 1 of Clause 2 provides that the preferred and deferred ordinary stocks are to be issued only in substitution of and for a corresponding amount of paid-up original stock?—Yes; of course the whole scope of the Bill is of an optional character.

12. That is provided for by the next section, which says that such issue and substitution may be made on the request in writing of the holder of paid-up original stock; but not otherwise?—Not otherwise; it is to be purely optional, and if any shareholder prefers to keep his stock as it is he can do so; a division can only take place upon an application in writing.

13. So that first of all you have the whole body of shareholders consulted, and secondly, the conversion can only take place upon the application of each individual shareholder?—That is so.

14. Sub-section 3 provides for the issue of certificates, and the next material one is Sub-section 5, defining what those two parts are to be entitled to; that the preferred is to be entitled to 4 per cent., if it is earned, and the deferred to the remainder in each year, which would have been payable to the holders of that particular amount of 100 *l.* of original stock?—That is the object of the Bill.

15. As to the ranking of these stocks, they will rank after all debentures, debenture stock, guaranteed, and preference?—Yes, the holders of preferred ordinary and deferred ordinary stand in precisely the same position as ordinary shareholders do, there is no priority over existing shareholders, whether preferred or deferred.

16. So that as regards priority, the two duplicate parts, preferred and deferred, will simply rank in the same way as the original stock?—That is plainly expressed in the Bill.

17. Then Sub-section 8 provides for the voting power, that may shortly be described in the same way; that the two parts together stand in precisely the same position as the original 100 *l.*?—That is the intention of the Bill; if it is not expressed, we desire to make it clear that the two shall have the same voting power as the one.

18. The next I will direct your attention to is Sub-section 13?——

Chairman.] May I draw your attention to Sub-section 9? I think Mr. Pember said that he would have something to say about that later on, but he has omitted it.

Mr. *Worsley Taylor.*

19. Sub-section 9 of the Bill is, "In respect of the qualification of a director, the holding of preferred ordinary stock shall be equivalent to a corresponding holding of original stock and deferred ordinary stock, shall be considered as equivalent to one-half the nominal value of original stock, as respects the respective hold-

Mr. *Worsley Taylor*—continued.

ings thereof of any proprietor in his own right. (To the *Witness.*) Now dealing with a suggestion that has been made on that point, that the qualification of the directors is really altered by that sub-section, what do you say upon that?—I say distinctly, that I scarcely know how the words have got into the clause. The intention was that the qualification of a director holding preferred and deferred stock should be precisely the same as the qualification of a holder of ordinary stock, and if it is not in the Bill, we are quite prepared that it should be so arranged. The intention being that the qualification of director shall remain precisely as it is at the present time. I think the qualification is 3,000 *l.* of ordinary stock, and I do not think any shareholder should be qualified as a director unless he held 3,000 *l.* of preferred, and 3,000 *l.* of deferred, that is equivalent to 3,000 *l.* ordinary stock.

Chairman.

20. Or 6,000 *l.* of either one or the other; 6,000 *l.* of the one, and none of the other?—The object of my answer is this. We intended, I do not know how it has got into the Bill differently, that the qualification of a director of the South Western Railway should not be altered in any way; therefore, as you suggest, 3,000 *l.* of each, or 6,000 *l.* of one would be equal to 3,000 *l.* of ordinary.

Chairman.

21. You would regard it as immaterial to you so long as the director had what was equivalent to 3,000 *l.* ordinary?—Yes, so long as he had what was equivalent to 3,000 *l.* ordinary, we do not care in what form it it.

Mr. *Bristowe.*] But it should be 3,000 *l.* of each, because the preferred might become of little value.

Mr. *Biddulph.*

22. As the object is to preserve the qualification of the director, as it is at present the director's qualification should consist of ordinary stock as at present, should it not? Why should a director have anything to do with the new stock? A director might buy other stock if he liked it, but I think he should keep his qualification as it is now?—I think a director should have the same option as an ordinary shareholder.

Mr. *Bristowe.*] Besides it might be that everything might be converted so that he could not get a qualification if it were limited to ordinary stock.

Mr. *Dickson.*

23. The qualification now is 3,000 *l.* ordinary stock?—Yes, it is 3,000 *l.* ordinary stock, and I think with all respect, you must have a proviso that a director should be qualified by this new stock, because taking an extreme view of the case, supposing that all the ordinary stock were converted!

Mr. *Ellis.*

24. You in no way wish to alter the qualification?—In no shape or form; that is the wish of no director.

25. Then

Mr. Buxton.

25. Then in that case it will not be the same qualification if he had 6,000 l. deferred?—The qualification of a director is merely to ensure that he shall have a certain money interest in the concern, and I think 6,000 l. preferred would be equivalent to 3,000 l. ordinary.

26. Except that he would have a greater interest in endeavouring to increase the dividend?——

Mr. Biddulph.

27. But surely the object of the director would be to represent the ordinary stockholders?—If that clause of the Bill is altered in any way you think proper we are quite prepared to accept it, but I think that a difficulty might arise if the Bill passed and the whole of the stock were converted, and the only qualification for a director were ordinary stock; you would then be landed in a difficulty; if you can meet that difficulty I do not see any reason why any reasonable alteration should not be adopted; there is not a single director upon the South Western board who seeks to lessen the qualification which now entitles him to sit at the board.

Chairman.

28. The director, as now entitled, is a person whose holding is 3,000 l. of ordinary stock?—It is 3,000 l. ordinary.

29. The ordinary stock, with its possible fluctuations would be more completely represented by the deferred stock than by the preferred stock, would it not?—No doubt; that is to say, the deferred people will be people having a contingent interest in the concern.

Mr. Worsley Taylor.

30. But as I understand you, you want to preserve the same relative qualifications?—Yes; we are quite willing to agree to any clause that would preserve that.

31. The mere method of carrying that object out in any possible way you are quite willing to discuss?—Yes.

32. The view of the matter I was going to call attention to is that dealt with by sub-section 13. Would there be in your view, with that, any doubt in the minds of the public, or any possibility of doubt, as to what the capital at any time was?—Not the slightest.

33. You have a form here in which you suggest it might be made out?—That has been circulated amongst the Committee. The whole of the figures in that part of the statement or form now submitted to the shareholders are in accordance with the model form issued by the Board of Trade many years ago, and there would not be the slightest alteration in that form. The capital account will stand just as it does to-day; the only alteration will be that there will be an explanatory clause showing how much of ordinary capital has been converted under the Bill; that will be plainly set forth upon the form circulated amongst the Committee. We suggest that as the manner of doing it; the figures upon that particular statement, with the exception of the amounts converted, being the exact figures appearing upon the last half-yearly report of the company.

OJ101

Mr. Worsley Taylor—continued.

34. The accounts are to be made up "so as to show the amount of the original stock authorised, created, and received as if such substitution had not taken place"?—That is my idea of the statement showing the amount of the capital preferred and deferred stock; but if any other suggestion is made, to show it in a better form, or in a form which would commend itself better to the mind of the Committee, upon that point we are prepared to adopt any suggestion that may be made. I am not tied to that particular form of showing preferred and deferred stock.

35. But except for these purposes of account, will there be anything like a doubling of your capital?—There is no doubling the capital at all.

Mr. Bristowe.

36. How would it appear upon the official list of the Stock Exchange; supposing you convert all your capital into 11,000,000 l. preferred, and 11,000,000 l. deferred, would it stand upon the list as 11,000,000 l. of each?—Yes.

37. Then according to the official list it would be doubling the capital; would there be any means of providing against that which might lead to misconceptions?—We have tried to meet that by insuring that on the certificates with the 100 l. of deferred stock there shall appear in plain letters the word "duplicate," that it shall be called not deferred stock, but duplicate deferred stock, and I think it would be very easy in the accounts of the company (and the Stock Exchange lists are made up from the capital account of the company) to insert the word "duplicate" so that there will not be any doubt.

38. But it would appear as two amounts of 11,000,000 l. if it were all converted?—If it were all converted without any explanation it would appear upon the Stock Exchange list, and such documents that the capital was double what it actually is.

Chairman.

39. Would the word "duplicate" be a very luminous word in that sense. I am afraid that the uninstructed mind would be apt to think it meant exactly the reverse, that instead of being half the original stock it would be twice the original stock?——

Mr. Dickson.

40. Is it not practically doubling the capital? —No, there is no doubling the capital; the capital is not increased a shilling.

41. But nominally?—Nominally the figures are doubled of course, but the capital account of the company is shown upon certain Tables 1, 2, 3, 4, and 5 of the accounts; in all those tables the capital of the South Western Company, assuming this Bill is passed through both Houses and becomes an Act, will remain the same as it is to-day.

42. But your accounts will show 11,000,000 l. preferred, and 11,000,000 l. deferred, stock?— Assuming it is all converted, that would be so.

Mr. Bristowe.

43. The Brighton Railway Company and the South Eastern Company I understood divided their

A 2

Mr. *Bristowe*—continued.

their stock, that is to say they gave 50 *l.* each, and I am inclined to think that there are other Companies that have duplicated their stock up to now?—There is only one case of duplication now; that is the case of the North British Company; the North British Company obtained power in 1888 to duplicate their ordinary stock.

44. In the same way as you are doing?—In a similar manner to that which we suggest, only in that case the preferred stock bore 3 per cent.

Mr. *Beckett.*

45. Why should you not have halved your stock instead of duplicating it?—I think Mr. Pember has very clearly pointed out the general objection made to splitting: if we had wanted to split we need not have been before this Committee, because there is an Act of Parliament already enabling it.

46. But that fixes 6 per cent.?—Yes; but if you reduce the preferred interest from 6 per cent. to any lower figure you only more largely increase the interest upon the deferred stock; the South Western Company paid 6 per cent. last year, and it may pay 7 per cent. this year, and I hope it will. If it does, the operation of that would be this; and my directors consider that it would be a most objectionable thing. Assuming that they paid 6½ per cent. under the Act of 1868, the preferred would get 6 and the other 10. I am taking the two half years, and am taking the actual figures, taking the 6 per cent. that we did actually pay in 1889; in the June half-year we paid 4½ per cent; and supposing the stock had been split under the 1868 Act, and the 6 per cent. preferred.

Mr. *Worsely Taylor.*

47. Take it for the whole year?—One would get 6 per cent. and the other 7; but under the duplication Bill we practically give the shareholders the option of obtaining a security almost as good as preference capital for two-thirds of their holding in ordinary stock; two-thirds of the holding in the ordinary stock is practically secure, assuming the Bill passes in its present form of 4 per cent. preferred and 2 per cent. for the deferred.

Chairman.

48. But the question that is asked is as between duplication and splitting; what are the advantages of duplication, and what are the dangers of duplication as compared with the advantages or dangers of splitting?—I do not think I can add anything to what Mr. Pember has said, because of course Mr. Pember has taken it from his instructions which have been prepared by the Company; I thoroughly agree with everything he has said in connection with it, that taking all things into consideration, duplication is infinitely better than splitting; and the reason I say that is this, that here is the splitting Act which has been in operation since 1868, and there is only one Company which has adopted it outside of the three Companies represented by Sir Edward Watkin.

Mr. *Beckett.*

49. But may not that be because they do not want to create a new 6 per cent. stock?—There is no doubt that that is so, the Act is not adapted to the present time. The next answer to that is that all the Stock Conversion Companies that have been formed, have adopted the duplicating principle.

50. Not quite so I think; I think we will have a Company before us which has not done so?—They have adopted the duplicate principle of issuing 100 *l.* of preferred stock, and 100 *l.* deferred stock, making in the total 1,200 *l.* in the case of the 600,000 *l.* which they hold in the Caledonian Railway.

Mr. *Worsley Taylor.*] Take this one case, the Stock Conversion Company have duplicated and issued against the 600,000 *l.*, 600,000 *l.* preferred at 85½ and 600,000 *l.* deferred stock, taking the remainder of the dividend; but of course the advantage of a Railway Company doing that is this: that the Stock Conversion Company must get a profit over the transaction, and they must be paid for the services they render; and under the prospectus which they issue to the public, when they issue these preferred and deferred stocks, they stipulate that one eighth per cent. shall be deducted from the dividend on every 100 *l.* of deferred stock.

Mr. *Hall.*] That was a very exceptional stipulation, was it not?

Witness.] I do not see any way in which they are to get a profit upon the transaction unless they deduct it from the dividend; the consequence is, that assuming our deferred were 2 *l.*, and the preferred 4 *l.*, the deferred stock holder would get 1 *l.* 17 *s.* 6 *d.*, whereas if the Railway Company did it themselves the deferred stock holder would get 2 *l.*

Mr. *Buxton.*

51. Your argument is that it would make the deferred stock very much less speculative than if it were split?—I do not place much reliance upon the speculative aspect of the question. I do not think railway companies should take that into their consideration.

Chairman.

52. But what the Right honourable Member asks you is whether this is a point of the first importance; whether, if this thing should be done it should be done by splitting or by duplicating, and Mr. Pember argued before us very strongly that if you duplicate, you avoid that excessive tendency to speculation: the excessive sensitiveness on the part of the deferred stock. You were asked if you agreed with that?—I do entirely agree with that, and for the reason, as Mr. Pember explained, that in the operation of splitting, the half per cent. in the ordinary dividend would make a difference of 1 per cent. in the deferred stock, and that 1 per cent. would make a difference of 20 *l.* in its market value.

Mr. *Bristowe.*

53. Are you prepared to say that you think that

Mr. *Bristowe*—continued.

that if the stock is doubled in quantity it reduces the speculative character of it; that is to say, if it is duplicated instead of split?—Of course I can only give my opinion upon the subject. I really think there would be less speculation with the deferred stock, as we suggest in our Bill, carrying 2 per cent. interest. Assuming on the last year's basis 4 per cent. preferred, and 2 per cent. deferred, I consider that there would be less speculation, and that it would be infinitely preferable to the shareholder compared to what it would be if it were split, and the deferred stock were likely to fluctuate in one year from 20 *l.* to 40 *l.*

54. But then you would have double the quantity of stock, which would fluctuate from 10 *l.* to 20 *l.*; do you really consider that it would reduce the speculative character. I am not saying that it would increase it, but I want your answer?—My clear opinion is that there will be less speculation in the duplicate deferred stock than in a split stock under the Act of 1868.

Mr. *Buxton.*

55. Take the case you give us in this paper of a 7 per cent dividend; as I understand, assuming the stock were split with a 4 per cent. dividend upon the preferred, there would be a 10 per cent. dividend upon the deferred; whereas if it were duplicated the dividend upon the deferred stock would be only 3 per cent.; so that it stands to reason that there would be much less chance of fluctuation upon the chance of a 3 per cent. dividend than in the other case?—Certainly.

56. What other reason have you for duplicating instead of splitting?—I do not assign any other reason, because I understood I was not to repeat what Mr. Pember said; I think I could not use any further argument than to say that railway companies ought to be allowed to do that which outside companies can do to the serious prejudice of the railway companies.

Chairman.

57. But upon the point of duplication as compared to splitting, is there any other argument beyond the fact that one class of operation would check extreme speculative action which makes you prefer duplication to splitting?—No, I do not think there is.

Mr. Ellis.

58. Suppose the figure in the Act of 1868 were four instead of six would that incline you in favour of splitting?—No; that would strengthen my opinion in favour of duplication, because then I say your deferred stock would rise to such an enormous rate of interest, 10 per cent. for instance, as you see, and 11 per cent., as it would in the second half year; the interest upon the deferred stock might rise to that in the case of the South Western, so that it would become an unwieldly and unmarketable stock; a stock rising by tens and fifteens of pounds I do not think would be desirable.

Chairman.

59. You would perhaps be obliged to come to 0.101.

Chairman – continued.

Parliament for another division?—We have tested it all round, and we think on the whole these clever financial men in the city have hit upon the right mode of doing the business by adopting the principle of deferred and preferred by duplication, and Parliament sanctioned it in 1868.

Mr. Ellis.

60. Now about the possible evil of trust companies; do you agree with what Mr. Pember said?—Yes.

61. That is all by way of assumption; of course you have had no experience yet?—There has been no experience of it as regards ourselves; but I have the speech of the chairman at the last meeting of the Trust Company this year, in which he stated that they had now under consideration the conversion of very large blocks of other railway company's stocks; but by implication he stated that they would not touch those companies which had Bills in Parliament to deal with it themselves. I can quite understand that it would be no use for the Trust company to attempt to attack the South Western Company if the South Western Company has power under the Act of Parliament to do what they wanted to do themselves.

62. But I want to get it upon the notes; the evil is that in the future; you have no experience of it?—None yet.

Mr. *Worsley Taylor.*

63. Just a word about these trust companies; although you have not had any very great experience of them, because they have not been in existence long, do you know whether, that one-eighth per cent. that you have heard of as being charged upon the deferred stock is the only profit they have made in the past?—I know it is not their only profit; I do not know how they make their profit, but in the last year they paid 20 per cent.

64. That must have been from this process of duplication?—I cannot explain that; I only know the fact that they paid 20 per cent. during the first year of their existence.

65. I do not know whether the speech of the chairman at their last meeting has been brought under your notice. I will call your attention to this: "During the past year," says the chairman, "they had converted in all 2,100,000 *l.* of railway stock, representing a capital value of some 3,400,000 *l.* From their participation in this conversion both in respect of stock which they themselves had purchased for conversion and from the charge which they had made to others, they had chiefly derived the sum at the credit of profit and loss account," so that the one-eighth charge is by no means their whole source of profit, they must get something out of the process of conversion?—It is easily explained. I have not the exact figures; they issued preferred Caledonian ordinary stock——

Chairman.

66. Who did?—The Stock Conversion Trust Company; they issued Caledonian ordinary stock at 87½, and they issued the deferred at 39; now

Chairman—continued.

now taking the two together, that is 126¼, and the market price of the Caledonian stock at that time, the ordinary stock was 119½, so you will see that they got a profit of 5 l. or 6 l. upon every 100 l. of ordinary stock by that conversion.

Mr. Worsley Taylor.

67. That conversion, as I understand, being by duplication?—Yes.

68. If that is done outside now without the assent of the companies, without their being consulted, and without Parliament being consulted, does it apparently to your mind indicate one of two things, firstly, a demand by the public for that principle in lieu of the principle of the Act of 1868, and secondly, that it can be done without any control of Parliament?—Yes; and that is distinctly stated in the report which I had from the Stock Conversion, that they can do this without an Act of Parliament, and do it upon their own terms, and take the best time for doing it.

69. As I understand, certain influential shareholders in your company said to your board, if this can be done without your consent why should you not be empowered to do it now?—We had already made a representation to Parliament, saying that we did not ask to water the capital in any shape or form, or to increase the capital, except nominally; we think that we are entitled to ask Parliament to give us power to duplicate the ordinary stock.

70. And secondly, though you have not had yet practical experience of the mischief such as Mr. Pember pointed out, do you regard it, especially looking to the fact that these operations may be largely used as a very real and possible danger?—We do.

71. Now you were asked with reference to speculation. I take it you cannot set up any endeavour to stop speculation, but is the element of fluctuation, as against stability in this stock, a legitimate interest in your view of the holders of that stock?—Yes. I have explained, in answer to an honourable Member, that in the case of splitting, the fluctuation is just double what it is in the case of duplication; therefore the element of speculation is not so rife naturally as it is in the case of splitting.

72. The fluctuation is halved by the duplication?—Yes.

73. By the splitting it is doubled?—Yes.

74. What do you say to the point of marketability; you have the Act of 1868 under which you may split your stocks, giving 6 per cent. to the preferred; what do you say as to the marketability of a 6 per cent. preference, the only one you may create?—That is a very unwieldy kind of stock. Experience shows that a 4 per cent. stock will fetch more money in the market relatively than a 6 per cent. stock.

75. Therefore, on the one hand, under the splitting, you get one unwieldy and unmarketable stock?—Yes.

Mr. Worsley Taylor—continued.

76. And one subject to greater fluctuations?—Yes.

77. Would the result be the usual one; would the deferred take the rest?—No, the deferred share would get half under the duplication to that which it would under the splitting with a 4 per cent. preferred.

78. But assuming your initial figure for your preferred to be rightly fixed, how about the reasonable certainty, as well as the reasonable stability of the deferred stock?—We proposed 4 per cent. for the preferred, and with 6 per cent. there is a reasonable certainty of 2 per cent., or a little more for the deferred stock.

79. Therefore you get what you may call a reasonable certainty of that amount of dividend upon that deferred stock?—Yes.

80. Therefore you get a certain greater stability upon that stock?—We get a certain greater stability upon that stock by duplication than we do by splitting.

81. I have only one other suggestion to make to you. Take instead of the 6 per cent. under the splitting, 4 per cent; was that matter well considered before you came for the Bill?—It was considered; and as I explained, we think that would increase the evil rather than lessen it.

82. Had your board in view any other object except this, which you have described; that is to say, an operation for the benefit of the shareholders, impressed upon you by the wish that it should be carried out for the reasons you have given with respect to this company?—There is no other reason why we are here for this Bill than the reasons that have been given by Mr. Pember and by myself; there is no other object whatever.

Chairman (to Mr. *Worsley Taylor*).] With reference to Sub-section 9 of Clause 2, perhaps you will be good enough on the part of the company to bring up to the Committee what you propose with the view to carrying out what has been stated as to your intention regarding the qualification of directors?

[The Witness withdrew.

Mr. *Worsley Taylor*.] That shall be taken into consideration.

Chairman.] If you would draft a clause to carry out what has been stated in evidence?

Mr. *Worsley Taylor*.] That shall be done. We have one other witness to call.

Chairman.] It had occurred to the Committee that possibly the accountant or financial officer of the company was here prepared to give evidence?

Mr. *Worsley Taylor*.] No, it was one who was formerly one of the directors, and a member of the finance committee of the directors.

Mr. ARCHIBALD SCOTT, sworn; and Examined.

Mr. *Worsley Taylor.*

83. FOR a good many years up to 1885 you were manager of the London and South Western Railway?—I was.

84. And you are well acquainted with all the history, and now you are a director you take an active part in all matters connected with it, and you have particularly to deal with the financial business?—Yes; and I have paid great attention to the present Bill.

85. I think I may ask you a comprehensive question shortly: do you agree with what my learned friend Mr. Pember has said, and with what Mr. Scotter has told us as to the desirability of the Bill in the interests of the shareholders of the company?—I do; but I should like to give to the honourable Committee a little more in detail the operations of the two companies, which I have endeavoured to put in a short form, but still in such a way as to be readily comprehended; I would like to say that in mentioning the operations of these two companies I do not presume for a moment to criticise the action of the Stock Conversion Company, for example, I merely wish to describe their action without questioning or criticising it. I would just mention, taking the two that the Railway Investment Company that was alluded to as being established in 1881, carried out their operations upon the ordinary stock of the London and North Western Railway Company, the North Eastern, the Midland, and the Glasgow and South Western Railway Companies in the way they invited from the public tenders for these separate railway stocks in exchange for shares of the Investment Company; for 375,000 *l.* of London and North Western Company's ordinary stock they offered in exchange the Investment Company's stock for 139 per 100 *l.* preferred and 139 per 100 *l.* of their deferred stocks, the two together amounting to 278 preferred and deferred. In the case of the North Eastern they offered to the holders of North Eastern stock for 139 per 100 *l.* of the preferred and 139 per 100 *l.* of their deferred stock. In the case of the Midland they offered for 400,000 *l.* Midland ordinary stock in exchange for 112½ per 100 *l.* preferred and 112½ per 100 *l.* of deferred stock; and in the case of the stock of the Glasgow and South Western Company in exchange for 186,000 *l.* they offered 95½ths each of their preferred and deferred. Now, as a matter of fact, those shareholders in those companies who accepted this Investment Company's preferred stocks have practically got 4 per cent., although in two years there was some delay in paying that 4 per cent., but on the deferred shares of this Investment Company, those who made the exchange have in some years got nothing, and in other years got about 1 per cent. Now, in the case of the Stock Conversion Company, the operation there is different. That Company has a nominal capital of 2,500,000 *l.*, of which only 200,000 *l.* has been paid up. Their first operation was to deal in 1,000,000 *l.* of London and North Western ordinary stock, and against that 1,000,000 *l.* of London and North

0.101.

Mr. *Worsley Taylor*—continued.

ordinary stock they issued first 1,000,000 *l.* of 3½ per cent. first charge preference stock, which is styled and called by them London and North Western ordinary stock, just as the railway company would call it. They offered that at par, entitled to 3½ per cent. per year, out of the income derived in each year from 1,000,000 *l.* of London and North Western ordinary stock. Then against that same 1,000,000 *l.* they issued another 500,000 *l.* of what was called 4 per cent. first charge preference stock London and North Western. That was offered at 104 per 100 *l.*, entitled to 4 per cent. per year out of the North Western dividend in excess of 3½ per cent., but they again issued another 1000,000 *l.* of what was called deferred charge stock, which was offered at 39 per 100 *l.*

86. Still, against this original 1,000,000 *l.*?—Yes, still against the 1,000,000 *l.* of the North Western Stock, 2,500,000 *l.* of the Stock Conversion Company's stock was issued to the public assuming the whole has been issued. I cannot, of course, say to what extent, but that was the operation. They exchanged against that 1,000,000 *l.* of the London and North Western Company 2,500,000 *l.* of the Stock Conversion Company's stock.

Mr. *Buxton.*

87. Could you give the Committee the market value of the 1,000,000 *l.*, and also what the Conversion Company received for their issues?—I can give you those: the first charge preference which was 3½ per cent. upon 1,000,000 *l.* was offered to the public at par; the price of that is now quoted in the market at par. The next 4 per cent. first charge was offered at 104 per 100 *l.* and that is now quoted in the market at 101 7-8ths; the next 1,000,000 *l.* deferred charge stock was issued at 39 *l.* per 100 *l.*, that is now quoted in the market at 36 *l.* The meaning of the operation practically was this, that the Stock Conversion Company estimated in their own minds that the dividend upon the North Western Stock would be 8 per cent., so they divided the first 1,000,000 *l.* into 3½ per cent., the second, which was 500,000 *l.*, issued at 4 per cent., which was equal to 2 per cent. upon a 1,000,000 *l.*; and the third issue of 1,000,000 *l.* was to get the balance 2 3-8ths, which, upon the whole, was 7 7-8ths, leaving 1-8th for the Stock Conversion Company's expenses. Then the next operation was that against 500,000 *l.* North Eastern Ordinary stock, they issued first 750,000 *l.*, 3 per cent. first charge preference stock, styled North Eastern Railway Company's Consols, which is just the title the Railway Company give it themselves; that was offered at 85½ per 100 *l.*, entitled to 3 per cent. per year out of the dividends in each year from 500,000 *l.* North Eastern Ordinary Stock; that was issued at 85½, the price of the stock is now quoted at 82 per 100 *l.* Then they issued another 500,000 *l.* deferred charge stock styled North Eastern Railway Consols offered at 56½ per 100 *l.*, entitled to the income derived in excess of 4½ per cent.

A 4

Mr. *Buxton*—continued.

cent. from an equal amount to 500,000 *l.* of North Eastern ordinary stock. The price of this deferred stock is now quoted at 54¾ per 100 *l.* In that case the estimated dividend on the North Eastern ordinary stock seems to have been 7 per cent. Then the next operation was that against 600,000 *l.* of Caledonian ordinary stock there were created and offered to the public 600,000 *l.* of 3½ per cent. first charge preference stock, styled Caledonian Railway Ordinary Stock, offered at 87½ per 100 *l.*, entitled to 3½ per cent. per year out of the dividends on the 600,000 *l.* of Caledonian ordinary stock. The price of this 3½ per cent. stock is now quoted at about 89¾ per 100 *l.* Then they issued against another 600,000 *l.* deferred charge stock, styled Caledonian Railway ordinary stock, offered at 39 per 100 *l.*, entitled to the income on the 600,000 *l.* ordinary stock in excess of 3½ per cent.; I cannot find any quotation for that last stock at the present time. Of course it is difficult to follow the precise operation of this Stock Conversion Company. I do not myself imagine that they at once purchase the whole block of the stocks that they offer in, because I observe that they always take care to say, not that they have stock, but that they have arranged for a transfer of stock, and I think they only purchase the stock in block to the extent to which they are able to issue beforehand their own ordinary stock, and I think that by the first deed which has been referred to, that is made clear that they undertake on the holder of the Conversion Company's stock, giving up to that company their own stock, he is entitled to have in exchange for it a corresponding amount of the railway stock. I do not think it is bought all at once as it were, but bought gradually, for the reason that the capital paid up is so small. I do not see how they could do it if it is not done according as the Conversion Company's own stock is taken up.

Mr. *Worsley Taylor.*

88. As I understand, you have given illustrations of very large operations by these conversion companies of the stocks of the railway companies?—Yes; and I may remind you that the Stock Conversion Company was only established last year.

89. And you can go into further details if the Committee desire?—Yes.

Chairman.

90. Do you draw any conclusion in your own mind from these transactions from the figures you have quoted?—From a railway director's point of view they seem to be likely, in the first place, to mislead the public, and rather to be dangerous in the public interest.

91. To mislead the public, owing to the duplication of these stocks, or what?—Owing to these stocks which are issued by the Conversion Company itself, by the same name as the railway stock properly so called.

Mr. *Worsley Taylor.*

92. Taking this Stock Conversion deed, it says on the back of it, "Caledonian Railway Company—Trust Deed"?—Yes, and as I have

Mr. *Worsley Taylor*—continued.

pointed out, the stock which they create and issue in the case of the North Eastern Railway Company, for example, is called North Eastern Consols, which is the very name the North Eastern Company give their own stock.

Mr. *W. Beckett.*

93. How are their certificates worded?—The certificates granted are the certificates of the Conversion Company not of the railway company.

94. They do not mention the name of the railway company on them, do they?—They do.

Chairman.

95. What we may call the short title of the stock is the same as the name and title used by the railway company?—Precisely.

96. You say they issue them; are those on the market quotable?—Yes.

97. Side by side with the railway stock?—No, they are quoted upon the market under the name of the Stock Conversion Company, but giving those stocks separately.

98. Then you think in the first place that it complicates matters and confuses the public mind with reference to those different kinds of stock?—I do. I also believe that it is not without danger to the railway companies if it were carried to a greater extent, which possibly it might in the future be, unless the railway companies themselves take means to afford the proper conversion under direct Parliamentary provisions and under the direct control of the railway companies themselves.

99. Further, I presume, you think that if profit is legitimately to be made out of this transaction that profit ought to go to the railway company themselves?—To the railway proprietors.

100. Do you also attach importance to the point that we have heard so much of, the power which it gives to a syndicate or a small body of men to control up to a certain extent the railway companies?—I think it is dangerous for this reason, that at railway meetings generally comparatively few proprietors attend, and even if the board send out proxies, very few proprietors take the trouble to return the proxies, and by their being in combination it would not be difficult to cause embarrassment and injury to the company.

101. Especially at those stated meetings where a certain fixed majority is required?—Precisely; and, of course, upon railway bills where a Wharncliffe meeting is held, generally a question of policy is involved, and outside people perhaps not legitimately interested in the company might take advantage of that.

102. Have you anything to add to the evidence you have given?—I would like to say a word upon what has been stated about the nominal increase of capital; there is no difficulty whatever upon the form of account as published by the railway company, and as given to the Board of Trade, in avoiding any appearance of the duplication of capital. So far as the accounts are concerned, that can be made quite clear, but I would like to say this in addition, that a nominal increase of capital is also usual in the ordinary operation

Chairman—continued.

operation of consolidating railway stocks; for many years past it has been the practice, and it has been found very convenient, to consolidate a large number of preference stocks, some at 5, and some at 4½ per cent. into a general consolidated 4 per cent. stock, it gets rid of priorities, and is found very convenient. Now in carrying out that operation it follows that the capital must be nominally increased. In the case of the London and North Western Railway Company through that consolidation the nominal increase has been 9,370,000 *l.*, and by the consolidation in the case of the Midland Company who got only last Session power to consolidate their 4 per cent. debenture stock into a 3 per cent., that means a nominal increase of 5,862,000 *l.*; so that whatever objection may be taken to a nominal increase under a conversion equally applies to a nominal increase under consolidation, and there has never been the slightest inconvenience felt by the public, or any one by consolidation schemes; they have found them advantageous. If the Committee would wish, I have some figures here which would very briefly show the extent of the fluctuations which have gone on for some years back upon the deferred stocks if the Committee would like any information upon that hand.

Mr. *Bristowe*.

103. May I ask whether you think duplicating a stock, instead of spliting it, will reduce the speculative element?—I have not the slightest doubt of it.

Mr. *Biddulph*.

104. I presume that you intend to duplicate the whole of the ordinary stock?—My own impression is that not more than one-half will be actually converted. In the case of the Brighton Company and the South Eastern Company, each of those have allowed the conversion to go on now, one for 20 years, and the other for 14 years. About one-third of the ordinary stock still remains unconverted; two-thirds have been divided. In the case of the South Western I think it would be less than that, about half.

105. Would it not be more equitable to make it compulsory, because a shareholder could have the benefit of his portion that was converted into a deferred stock, and he could then if he chose go back to his original holding?—I think compulsory conversion would never answer. I think it must be optional.

106. But take the case of a director's qualification, surely either the directors must hold ordinary stock as they do at present, or else they must hold *pari passu* proportions of the new stock?—Quite so. I am clearly of opinion that the qualification as it stands in the Bill, is now what it ought to be; the object is not to reduce the interests in the director's own connection; he must now hold 3,000 *l.* ordinary stock; he can now as the Bill stands hold 3,000 *l.* of undivided stock, he can hold 1,000 *l.* of the preferred, which is said to be equal to the ordinary, then to make up his other 1,000 *l.* he must hold 2,000 *l.* of the deferred; in that way he has his qualification,
    0.101.

Mr. *Biddulph*—continued.

and I think that is right. I do not think it would be right for a director only to hold 3,000 *l.* deferred; that would not be equal to 3,000 *l.* of ordinary capital, but 1,000 *l.* of ordinary undivided is reckoned as 1,000 *l.*; 1,000 *l.* preferred is reckoned as 1,000 *l.*, and 2,000 *l.* deferred is reckoned as 1,000 *l.*, and that carries him to his original sum. I think the Bill is right as it stands.

107. But if you do not compulsorily convert the whole of the original stock, will it not be better that the director's qualification should be ordinary stock only because that comes last after everything else, and it is the interest of the directors of the company to look after that form of stock, which comes last; that is to say, the ordinary stock of the company?—But the ordinary stock of the company does not come last in this case; the preferred does not have any preference over the ordinary stock; the deferred comes last; the preferred stands upon the same level as the ordinary, with a fixed dividend, namely, 4 per cent., but the ordinary stock does not lose its position in any way.

108. It might happen that the preferred would clash with the ordinary in some way?—I do not think there would be any clashing, but I am certain that compulsory conversion would never be approved of by any body of proprietors.

109. Then it is impossible for you to state how much would be converted if it were optional?—It is only a guess; but, as I say in the case of the South Eastern Company for example, which have had a conversion under this splitting system for 20 years, there is still one-third not converted; and the South Western Company being rather a conservative body of proprietors, I do not think would convert more than half; that is my opinion.

Mr. *Buxton*.

110. I suppose it would go on from time to time?—I am reckoning for a period of years.

Mr. *W. Beckett*.

111. As you say, you think this compulsory conversion would not be approved of by your shareholders?—I am sure not.

Chairman.

112. You have considerable acquaintance with other railways besides your own?—Yes, I have.

113. As regards these Bills before us, without considering those companies which already have those powers, there will still be large companies which will not have these powers, the London and North Western and the Great Western Companies, for example?—As far as I can judge there are some companies anxiously waiting to hear the result of the present Bill.

114. You are not aware of any reason why they have stood out?—I can at once say that taking the London and North Western there is a strong feeling upon the board of the London and North Western against any change whatever, and I believe the same is the case with the Great Western, but some of the directors, at all events

B   of

Chairman—continued.

of one of those companies, are strongly impressed with what is happening with these outside companies; it is making a great impression upon them.

115. If you shut your door against these outside companies the whole of their energies will be directed against the railway companies which are open to them, I presume?—I do not think it would take long.

[The Witness withdrew.

Chairman.] Have you any further evidence to call?

Mr. *Worsley Taylor.*] I think not, Sir.

Chairman.] We will not begin new matter to-day. We do not, I believe, give a decision, we shall report.

Wednesday, 14th May 1890.

MEMBERS PRESENT:

Mr. W. Beckett.	Mr. Campbell-Bannerman.
Mr. Biddulph.	Mr. Dickson.
Mr. Bristowe.	Mr. Ellis.
Mr. Buxton.	Mr. R. Mowbray.

THE RIGHT HON. H. CAMPBELL-BANNERMAN, IN THE CHAIR.

CALEDONIAN RAILWAY (CONVERSION OF STOCK) BILL.

The Petition for the Bill was read.

Mr. *Littler*, Q.C., Mr. *Pember*, Q.C., Mr. *Saunders*, Q.C., and Mr. *Worsley Taylor*, appeared as Counsel on behalf of the Promoters of the Bill.

Messrs. *Grahames, Currey*, and *Spens*, appeared as Agents.

There were no Petitioners against the Bill.

Mr. *Pember* was heard to open the case on behalf of the Promoters of the Bill.

Sir JAMES KING, sworn ; and Examined.

Mr. Saunders.

116. I BELIEVE you are Deputy Chairman of the Caledonian Railway Company ?—Yes, I am.

117. And you have been a member of the Board for some 15 years ?—For about 15 years.

118. You were Lord Provost of Glasgow up to November last ?—Yes, I was.

119. Besides that you are Chairman of the Clydesdale Bank ?—Yes, I am.

120. And you have been on the Board of that bank for 20 years ?—Yes, rather more.

121. I believe you are the Chairman of the Finance Committee of the Caledonian Railway Company ?—Yes, I am.

122. Will you just give me shortly what the capital of the Caledonian Company is ?—Shall I give it exactly ?

123. I do not know that the Committee want a great deal of detail ?—The capital of the Company consists of about 8,000,000 l. of debenture stock and loans, about 18,000,000 l. of guaranteed preference stocks——

124. Let us say 19,000,000 l. ?—19,000,000 l.; and close upon 11,000,000 l. of ordinary stock.

125. That makes in round figures about 37,000,000 l. of capital ?—It does.

Mr. *Saunders.*] We will give the figures exactly, if you want them, Sir.

Chairman.] That is near enough.

0.101.

Mr. Saunders.

126. (To the *Witness.*) You have to add to that the two peculiar stocks referred to in Clause 7 ? — We have the deferred ordinary stock, No. 1, amounting to exactly 2,508,026 l.

127. And 13 s. 4 d. ?—And 13 s. 4 d.

128. And the deferred No. 2 ? — And the deferred ordinary stock, No. 2, amounting to 276,666 l. 13 s. 4 d.

129. The first participate in dividend above 7 per cent.; the other participate in dividend above 9 per cent. ?—Yes.

130. If we take those two last figures accurately, they make 2,784,693 l. ?—That is so.

131. You may say altogether that your capitals represent about forty millions ? — Yes, rather over forty millions.

132. There is capital authorised by Acts of Parliament, not issued, which you can give, if the Committee wish it; but I do not know that it is important for this purpose?—Yes, we have (about) rather more than 3,000,000 l. authorised, but not yet issued.

133. And among your preference stock you have, I believe, about a million and a quarter, 4 per cent. preferred, convertible at any time into ordinary stock, at par, at the option of the holders ?—Yes, at the end of any half year, in perpetuity.

134. So that you may possibly have an increase

B 2

Mr. Saunders—continued.

crease of your ordinary stock by a million and a-quarter?—And a diminution of the preference.

135. I believe in the course of last summer you became aware that the Stock Conversion and Investment Company, Limited, had bought up 600,000 *l.* of your ordinary stock, and created a Trust, for the purpose of dividing it into preferred and deferred?—Yes, that is so.

136. When I say "preferred and deferred" stock, I mean stock of the Trust, not of the Company?—Yes.

137. I believe, speaking generally, that that stock conversions operation was successful, was it not?—It was successful, and it was undertaken after they had already succeeded with two larger issues; one of London and North-Western stock, and the other of North-Eastern stock. We had reason to apprehend that before long another operation in our own stock was likely to take place.

138. Was it that which expedited or promoted the action of the Board with a view to this Bill?—Yes; the Board were not anxious to have their stock divided; they thought there was an inconvenience, and that there might be a danger arising to the company if these large blocks of stock were made into successive Trusts, and that it was better that the company should ask for powers to enable their own shareholders, without going outside of the company, to divide their stock if so inclined, leaving it perfectly optional; and that is the reason of our being here with our Bill to-day.

139. If there was a profit, you mean, to be obtained it should be obtained by your own shareholders, through the operations of their own company, to begin with?—Yes, of course they might have got a profit to some extent through the Conversion Company, but it would be done more economically, I believe, through the Caledonian itself, and without any annual charge for the management of the divided stock, as in the case of the Stock Conversion Company.

140. Now, let me turn your attention to another aspect of the question: would the holding of large stocks in the hands of the new Trust, or any outside corporation, have any possible material effect upon the action of the Caledonian Company in its voting power?—No doubt it might, not only if it happened to be in unfriendly hands, but if by inadvertence on the part of those who held the several portions of the divided stock, the voting were exercised in such a way as to operate against the policy of the company, especially in a Wharncliffe meeting.

141. At a Wharncliffe meeting, I believe, the railway company is prevented from issuing proxies, is it not?—Yes; you cannot ask for proxies in favour of the directors. You must send out blank proxies to be filled up by the shareholders; the consequence is that on special occasions the number of proxies appearing at these Wharncliffe meetings is smaller than in the case of ordinary half-yearly meetings, and therefore the danger would be intensified.

142. Therefore if a large amount of the stock were held by one or two or any other number of

Mr. Saunders—continued.

companies, that might very prejudicially affect the policy of the Company in its action with regard to Bills in Parliament?—Yes, I have noticed the number of proxies, and indeed the number of votes, and the amount of stock voted upon at each of the last ten Wharncliffe meetings of the Company expending over the last 10 years; and I see that in the case of four of those the voting of this 600,000 *l.* would have entirely defeated the policy of the directors; that is to say, it would have turned the meeting.

143. It is very much better then that the people who really are shareholders in the Company should vote upon their own part than by the united action of a body who are their trustees for a particular purpose?—I think so.

144. The policy of bringing in this Bill has been before your own shareholders at two meetings; first, your half-yearly meeting in September, then the Wharncliffe meeting this year, is that so?—Yes.

145. How has it been met by your shareholders?—It has been unanimously approved of; and at the Wharncliffe meeting the number of proxies lodged was larger than on any former occasion within the last 10 years, showing that it is a very popular scheme among our shareholders.

146. I believe it really represented 5,143,000 *l.* of your stocks which have power to vote?—Yes, that is so.

147. Making 25 per cent., or a quarter of your whole voting capital?—That is so.

Chairman.

148. May I just interpolate one question. This was not the only subject brought up at that meeting, was it?—No; at that meeting the various Bills before Parliament were submitted.

149. There must have been other Bills which contributed to the interest of the shareholders?—Yes; but among the large number of proxies so lodged, as well as the large attendance at the meeting present in person, there was perfect unanimity with regard to these Bills.

Mr. Buxton.

150. May I ask did the trust company oppose this proposal?—No, they did not.

Mr. Saunders.

151. From what you know of the opinion of your shareholders generally do you believe that it does meet the views of your proprietors?—I believe it does.

152. Now let us see how you propose to carry out your object. You propose to issue ordinary stock certificates of two classes, I believe; one to be called Caledonian preferred converted ordinary stock?—Yes.

153. The other deferred converted ordinary stock?—Yes; subject to any alteration of name which the Committee may approve.

154. Each of them to be of equal nominal amount, and each of them to be equal in amount
to

Mr. *Saunders*—continued.

to the present value of the capital which may be converted ?—Yes.

155. In other words it is a duplication system and not a splitting?—Not a splitting.

156. Well, I will not go into the small details about multiples of 10 *l.*, which were explained by Mr. Pember.

Chairman.] I was going to say that, of course, counsel will know that it is not necessary to substantiate out of the mouth of a witness what we have already received from Mr. Pember.

Mr. *Saunders.*] No, Sir ; I assumed you would take that in a Bill of this kind as being admitted, if not disproved.

Chairman.] Quite so.

Mr. *Saunders.*

157. (To the *Witness.*) I will just take this from you, that the dividend on the ordinary stock will continue to be ascertained, and declared exactly after this Bill passes as it is at the present moment?—There is a special provision in the Bill to the effect that it is to be declared as on the ordinary stock.

158. The fifth section of the Bill ?—Yes.

159. That, of course, has a bearing especially upon the gentlemen who issued the statement which has been referred to ?—Yes.

160. You have selected here three per cent. as the maximum dividend for preferred stock; would you explain, in your own way, the reason for doing that?—I think Mr. Pember has pretty fully explained that. We found that the average dividend for the last 10 years was 4¾ per cent., but we felt that ¾ per cent. was too narrow a margin for security. Even as regards 3½, there were two cases within the last 10 years, in which scarcely 3¼ was reached, 3*l.* 7*s.* 6*d.* in one case, and 3*l.* 5*s.* in another. There again we felt that to name 3¼ might be to discredit tne stock which we hope to be a favouriite investment stock in the market ; accordingly we felt that we were obliged to come down to 3 per cent. before we were on thoroughly safe and sound ground.

161. That was after very careful consideration by the Board?—It was.

162. Taking into consideration the special peculiarities of your own stock and your own dividend?—That is so.

163. Have you had prepared a statement which would, if this Bill passed, be the kind of statement issued to the shareholders, showing as at present the actual capital authorised, and in a marginal note the amount converted, taking an imaginary sum ?—Yes.

164. We will hand copies round to the members of the Committee showing how that is done ? —It is shown on the third page. You will observe that the ordinary stock here is still shewn by 10,860,000 *l.*, and assuming for the moment that above one-third of the stock is converted, the marginal note represents the form in which this would be shown to the public so as to prevent any one from imagining that in consequence of the duplication of the converted stock our capital is larger than it really is.

165. Do you believe that a note of that kind 0.101.

Mr. *Saunders*—continued.

would remove any possible source of error in the public mind as to the capital being watered by the operation of an imaginary duplication?—It seems to me to be beyond a doubt that it would do so.

166. There is one provision peculiar in your Bill which I will just ask your attention to. To begin with, the stock can only be converted at the instance of the individual holder of the stock; it is not compulsory against any individual? —No, it is not.

167. Then you provide that in the case of a man having converted, or the holder of any stock which has been converted, wishing it to be re-converted back again into ordinary stock, he will be able to do. that ?—Yes ; we have so provided. We thought it advisable to make the provision, for this reason : that being, as I explained at first, only wishful to provide a facility, and not being in the position of desiring that it should take universal effect, or indeed wanting that our shareholders should use it to the largest possible extent, we thought it desirable to make provision that if any found that they did not receive the same advantages that they expected from conversion, there should be an opportunity afforded to them of coming back. In fact in order to save confusion in the public mind (if there was any existing) we thought we were in that way providing for the smallest amount of capital being put in the form of this marginal note.

168. Of course that re-conversion is not an essential part of your scheme ?—It is not.

169. But you think it would be an advantage to give every holder the opportunity of either holding converted or unconverted stock as he likes?—We thought so, and, of course, these Bills were prepared without consultation between the companies; and this provision is very much a suggestion which, of course, we do not stand upon. We think it an improvement ; but it is by no means essential to our scheme.

170. The principle of division of stock into preferred and deferred we all know has been accepted by Parliament in the year 1868, only that was by splitting and not by duplicating stock?—That is so.

171. Has your board carefully considered whether it would suit the circumstances of your case to adopt the position under that Act of 1868 ?—We think it exceedingly undesirable in our circumstances that the change should take place by means of splitting. In the event of 6 per cent. being adopted, then taking the basis of last year's dividend, which was 5 1-8th per cent., it would give a preference dividend of 6 per cent. to 50 *l.* of each 100 *l.*, and a dividend of 4¼ to the remaining 50 *l.* Now we think in the first place that 6 per cent. is too large a secured dividend for the ordinary purposes of investment. Trustees and others naturally prefer to buy into a stock which either is about par or does not much exceed par in price. We thiuk, therefore, that it would be an unwieldy and by no means a favourite stock. Then again, 4¼ might be large enough to attract the attention of the Stock Conversion Company or another stock conversion company, and our deferred stock might be split again ; and. indeed, the 6 per cent. preference

B 3

stock

Mr. *Saunders*—continued.

stock might also be split. Of course this, as regards the ordinary stock, would be intensified if the rate of dividend were reduced from 6 per cent. on the preferred to 4 per cent. In that case the dividend on the deferred stock if split on the basis of last year's dividend would be 7½, manifestly large enough to attract the attention of a stock conversion company. Therefore we think that it is altogether inapplicable for the special purpose we have in view in applying for this Bill, that is to say, splitting is not applicable.

172. That that has not been generally approved by railway companies is shown by the fact that I think only two or three companies have adopted it in the last 22 years?—Three companies.

173. And the Brighton or South Eastern 6 per cent. stock only stands at 158 to 161?—That is so.

174. Do you find that these high priced stocks do not stand at their full value in the market that they might be expected to?—What are called heavy stocks are not preferred by investors.

175. The only other subject remaining for me to ask a question about is, these two deferred stocks: the deferred stock No. 1 and the deferred stock No. 2. You have seen the statement, of course, that has been made?—Yes, I have.

Mr. *Saunders.*

176. I will not prove, Sir, the facts stated by Mr. Pember, and which, no doubt, will not be in dispute, as to how that stock came to be created. (To the *Witness.*) Do you see how they will in any way be prejudiced by the alteration *inter se* of the other stocks?—I do not think we touch them in the slightest degree.

177. Your accounts will always enable you to ascertain to a farthing what the amount of percentage of dividend on the ordinary stock would be if it had not been all converted?—That is so.

178. Therefore it would be quite as apparent on the face of the accounts, to any investor, what his rights are, as it is at the present time? —The procedure will be the same as before. Our dividends would be declared on the ordinary stock, and it would be a matter as between the company and those persons who had converted, that it should be paid to certain shareholders in two parts instead of being paid in one sum.

179. I need scarcely say that you would not be inclined to accept the proposal made in paragraph 15 of the statement of these gentlemen that they should give you some of their existing stock in lieu of the deferred stock?—It would be manifestly unjust to these shareholders (especially if we do not convert) that in order to afford an opportunity to those who wish to convert, we should deduct from the money which ought to go into the pockets of our ordinary shareholders an annual sum in order to pay the claims of those holders of deferred stock who have really nothing to say and no claim to make as long as we are not dividing a larger dividend than 7 per cent. in the one case and 9 per cent. in the other. These stocks would have been better described when they were formed as " contingent right stocks, No. 2 and No. 1."

Chairman.

180. Would it be within your right to change the title now?—I am afraid that would be re. garded as unjust to them.

Mr. *Saunders.*

181. I suppose you are not so very particular about the nomenclature of these stocks, that if any injustice were done you would wish to adhere to it?—Certainly.

182. But if several railway companies are adopting this system of having preferred and de. ferred ordinary stock, would it not be better if possible that your company should have the same? —It certainly would be better, but we would not stand upon that.

183. You would leave yourselves entirely in the hands of the Committee?—Entirely in the hands of the Committee.

Mr. *Ellis.*

184. You would admit probably that some confusion might arise, because even in this state. ment, which has been handed to us, the term " deferred ordinary " is used twice over, you see? —But we are willing to change the nomenclature. We thought that, perhaps, "converted ordinary stock, No. 1, and converted ordinary stock, No. 2," might suffice.

Mr. *Saunders.*

185. Of course, if they consented to it, there could be no difficulty in converting their name into something which would avoid the mistake between the two if they did not like to be called by the same name that your ordinary shareholders would be?—Certainly not; but I am afraid that would be interfering with their rights.

186. You think that is chimerical, do you?— Yes.

187. It seems to me the proper solution of it?——

Chairman.

188. You do not think that the duplication of of the stock, as it is proposed, will lead to over. speculation in the deferred stock?—I do not think it will. There are two classes of holders. There is a certain class of persons who wish to be moderately safe, and yet to get a little more annual return than they can have from first-class debenture stocks; first-class guaranteed stocks. These would, we think, be, on the whole, safe in investing in our preferred stock. And then, again, there is another large class who are willing to run the ordinary risks of the trade of the country, and we think that they might have an opportunity of making their investment, and buying and selling, changing them as often as they liked, without leading to undue specula. tion.

189. You expect that it will have the effect of improving the value of the stock in the market? —On the ground that you have two classes of buyers; two sets of buyers where you have at present only one.

190. And you think that your shareholders should get the benefit of that profit rather than any trust company, or outside body of specu. lators?—Yes, we think so.

191. That

Chairman—continued.

191. That is one of your objections?—That is one of our objections.

192. In the case of the North British Railway, who obtained powers to do this, that has been already effected, I believe?—To a very marked extent.

193. Then your other principal object is to avoid the danger or inconvenience that arises from your possibly being over-borne by the action of a combined trust company of the kind that has been described—That is so. A trust which is formed for a different purpose than to further the interests of the Caledonian Railway.

194. You are not altogether interested, only in your capacity of railway director, but I think it has been already stated that you are chairman of one of the largest Scotch banks, and are well acquainted wite the general feeling of the community?—Yes.

195. How do you think this scheme is regarded by bankers and all those interested in the community generally, and in its commercial standing?—I think that bankers and large merchants regard the necessity for such a step as this arising; but they almost all recognise the importance of securing the object in this way instead of allowing it to be done by any chance combinations which may be formed; that is to say, they would have preferred that no operations in the way of splitting stock had taken place, but having begun, they look upon the obtaining powers by the companies themselves as very much preferable indeed to its being done in an indirect way and through foreign hands.

196. You are, of course, aware that there are large railway companies subject to the same dangers or inconveniences that you think you may suffer from, who have not yet taken this step?—That is so. Some of them are so large that even the operations of several trusts would not affect them to the same extent as we would be liable to be affected.

197. Such as the London and North Western?—Such as the London and North Western, and the Great Western and the Midland.

198. But your general impression is that in the community of Glasgow and the West of Scotland, at all events (and no one knows it better than you do), and you conveyed to the Committee the impression on your mind that this is not looked upon as a dangerous proposal, likely to lead to what is called, in ordinary language, gambling or over-speculation?—I can unhesitatingly say that it is looked upon with favour by the great majority of the community.

Mr. *Buxton.*

199. Do you think that a large number of the holders will take advantage of this power?—It is not easy to form an opinion in regard to that. I have no doubt that a large number will. I would not be surprised to see between a third and a half converted, and probably after the lapse of time it may gradually increase and come to be the larger half.

200. Will the company do anything at the beginning to promote this duplication or other-

0.101.

Mr. *Buxton*—continued.

wise; the difficulty will be, will not it, that there will be no quotation for a small amount of stock if only a small amount of stock is converted?—I think that the applications even from the first will be quite large enough to secure a market; not only a quotation but a regular market.

201. And if a regular market is obtained, do you think the ground will be altogether cut away from the feet of these trust companies?—I think it will, I have no doubt it will.

202. You think, in fact, that the trust companies will not further extend their operations?—Not as regards our company.

Mr. *Beckett.*

203. As regards the reconversion, you do not seem to put much value upon that yourself?—No, we do not.

204. Would not it introduce confusion into the company's accounts and puzzle people very much as to what the present position is from half year to half year?—No; each half year of course the amount will vary, or may vary, and it will not introduce any more confusion if it were to become a little smaller than if it were to become a little larger.

205. You seem to have introduced, I suppose you have introduced it in order to make the whole measure as acceptable as possible to as many as possible?—Yes, and with the view rather of favouring stock being left as it is than of favouring conversion.

206. Favouring the stock being left as it is?—That is to say, favouring the largest amount of stock being left in its present form.

207. Then you are not anxious to see the conversion yourself?—I have not been anxious to see the conversion, but I look upon it as very important to obtain the opportunity for all shareholders who wish to have it to enjoy it.

208. Did your Board ever think of making it compulsory?—No, my board thought that that would be unjust and undesirable.

209. Your objection to splitting seemed to be on account of the 6 per cent. required by the Act of 1868, but you might have split of course the 4 per cent. stock?—I think I endeavoured to explain that if it were made 4 per cent. the danger would be intensified. Taking our dividend of last year, if it were 4 per cent. then it would be a dividend to the preferred shareholders on each 50 *l.* of 4 per cent. and 6¼ to the deferred; large enough to attract the operations of the Conversion company.

Mr. *Mowbray.*

210. Do you think it is necessary to alter the qualification of your directors?—The object we had in view in putting the alteration in was, as it were, to secure that where directors were proposed; directors holding the two kinds of stock; that they should hold in the combined form as much as would correspond to the full ordinary stock which they at present must buy (by the Act of Parliament) to hold.

211. But as you have the power of reconversion in your Bill it would always be open to them to reconvert their separate holdings into

B 4   the

Mr. *Mowbray*—continued.

the old ordinary stock?—Yes; in that case they would come in as holders of 2,000 *l.* ordinary stock; and they would be quite as acceptable in that shape.

212. I was going to suggest to you that as you seem not anxious to have more of this stock converted than necessary, whether that would not be an additional inducement to people to hold the ordinary stock if you made the directors' qualification as it is at present in ordinary stock only?—The amount of ordinary stock involved in the holdings of 14 directors would be only 28,000 *l.*, and that is very little out of 10,000,000 *l.* or 11,000,000 *l.*

Mr. *Ellis.*

213. As I understand, it is not essential for a director to have any ordinary stock?—It is not. We do not propose that directors should be disqualified by the want of ordinary stock now. It is only if they happen to take their qualification from the converted stock that we think they ought to hold the full amount of that converted stock in both forms sufficient to make an ordinary qualification.

214. You might have the Board consist of gentlemen who had no interest whatever in that 10,000,000 *l.*, I understand?—We might; but, in point of fact, every director has more than 2,000 *l.* of ordinary stock.

215. One other question: Have you had any instance of those connected with the Trust Companies appearing at your meetings, and manifesting any hostility?—We have not.

Chairman.

216. Has there been time enough for that?—There has scarcely been time. It is only a year old; and no burning question has come up in the meantime.

Mr. *Biddulph.*

217. Have you any means of knowing how much of your stock is held by Trust Companies?—Of course, the register would show that.

218. Quite so?—I cannot say offhand.

219. You have no means of telling the Committee?—I could get the information.

Mr. *Bristowe.*

·220· I understood you, on being asked under what circumstances, or for what reason, you would allow reconversion, to say: If the shareholders did not receive the advantages they expected of the conversion, would you tell me under what circumstances shareholders having converted into preferred and deferred could not reap the advantages that they had under the old system?—The chief object a shareholder would have in dividing or converting would, I presume, be to make his stock more valuable in the market. If that state of matters ceased to exist, and the price of the two combined was somewhat similar to the price of the ordinary stock, then he might say, I would rather have my stock as before in the shape of ordinary stock and come for the reconversion.

221. Might it not be very awkward in the

Mr. *Bristowe*—continued.

manipulations of stock which you know take place for people to have the opportunity of reconverting, thus "cornering" the market from time to time?—Well, that is a matter rather for the Stock Exchange.

222. I wanted to see under what circumstances the combined stocks could be less valuable than the other (I do not see how it could be so); but it seems to me that there ought to be some important reason for the re-conversion. The conversion I quite understand, but the re-conversion is a little awkward. Another question I want to ask you is with regard to the voting powers of the preferred and deferred stocks. I believe according to this Bill the preferred have three-fourths of the voting power and the deferred one-fourth?—It is not a point we are very strong upon. Indeed, I do not know that we thought quite alike with regard to that; but the reason that weighed with us was this: We looked upon the ordinary stock as bearing the risks of the trade and as being, whether in the shape of preferred or deferred converted stock, deeply interested and directly interested in the prosperity of the company to a larger extent than guaranteed and preference stockholders and still more than debenture holders, who under any circumstances are perfectly safe. We thought that it was desirable that the larger portion of the voting power should be given to the holders, to that portion of the convertible stock which was likely to be held continuously; and we thought that the preferred 3 per cent. stock would be held more by continuous holders, that it would be less likely to be changed and could be better trusted with the direction of the policy of the company than those who held the deferred stock, who might be holders this month and cease to be holders next month.

223. But is it not a fact that the bulk of the prosperity or adversity of the company would, if all the stock were converted, fall upon the holders of the deferred stock?—Well, the margin of security is comparatively narrow, and even those who hold the deferred stock would have a direct interest in the prosperity of the company, and in seeing that unprofitable undertakings were not proceeded with.

224. You are still of opinion that the preferred stock should have a greater voting power than the deferred stock?—I would prefer that; but we are quite willing to fall in with the wishes of the Committee, if it is thought desirable that one uniform scale of voting power should be found in all the Bills.

[The Witness withdrew.

Mr. *Saunders* was heard to address the Committtee in support of the preamble of the Bill.

Chairman.] I think the desire of the Committee would be to do neither any harm nor any good to these old deferred ordinary stocks. We do not wish either to improve them or to spoil them in any way.

Mr. *Saunders.*] Quite so.

Chairman.]

Chairman.] But seeing that they are recognised under the title of " Deferred Ordinary Stock, No. 1," and " Deferred Ordinary Stock, No. 2," I think it will be desirable that there should be some word, at all events, inserted in the new stock, in order to prevent confusion.

Mr. *Saunders.*] I think that word " converted " really does make the distinction.

Chairman.] Yes. Then that concludes the Caledonian case?

Mr. *Saunders.*] That concludes the Caledonian case, Sir.

Chairman.] Now we proceed to the Great Northern.

Mr. *Pope.*] If you please, Sir.

Wednesday, 14th May 1890—*continued.*

MEMBERS PRESENT:

Mr. W. Beckett.
Mr. Biddulph.
Mr. Bristowe.
Mr. Buxton.

Mr. Campbell-Bannerman.
Mr. Dickson.
Mr. Ellis.
Mr. R. Mowbray.

THE RIGHT HON. H. CAMPBELL-BANNERMAN, IN THE CHAIR.

GREAT NORTHERN RAILWAY (CAPITAL) BILL.

Mr. *Pope* was heard to open the case on behalf of the Promoters of the Bill.

Mr. WILLIAM GRINLING, sworn; and Examined.

Mr. *Balfour Browne.*

225. YOU are the accountant of the Great Northern Railway Company ?—I am.

226. And you have held that office for upwards of 20 years ?—Yes.

227. You are well acquainted of course with the financial history of the company and the terms and conditions on which the capital was created ?—I am.

228. The particulars of the capital stock are set out in the first schedule referred to by my learned friend, Mr. Pope. The first original stock there is 10,884,517 *l.*; A stock, 1,159,275 *l.*, and B stock, the same sum, making 13,203,067 *l.*? —Yes.

229. Certain of your original stock has been issued at a premium ?—It has.

230. And instead of the premium going, as some companies allow it to go, into the pocket of the shareholders, it has gone into the pocket of the company ?—Yes.

231. And appears on the capital account, but no interest is paid upon it ?—That is so.

232. How much is that ?—269,260 *l.*

233. That makes a total capital, although not a total interest bearing capital of 13,472,327 *l.*, is not that so ?—That is correct.

234. Now with regard to the preference, that is 15,789,010 *l.* ?—Yes.

235. And the debenture stock, 9,089,301 *l.*?— Yes.

236. That brings out the total figures mentioned by my learned friend, Mr. Pope. Now special powers were granted to the Great Northern under their Act of 1848, which enabled the shareholders to divide the original stock into equal moieties denominated A and B, B being entitled to a preference dividend of 6 per cent., is not that so ?—That is correct.

237. So that the principle of division of ordinary stock into preferred and deferred was re-

Mr. *Balfour Browne*—continued.

cognised by Parliament in our case as long ago as 1848 ?—It was.

238. In that case of course it was optional ?— Yes.

239. The A are only to have the balance of the dividend declared from time to time on the ordinary stock ?—Yes.

240. Therefore whatever dividend is divided on the ordinary stock, the B first get their 6 per cent. and the A get the remainder ?—That is so.

241. Now I need not go into the question of the litigation, but litigation did take place, and it came before that great judge, Vice-Chancellor Wood, and he decided that the B shares were cumulative ?—If you will allow me, I should like to say a word of explanation upon that first division, because it has a very important bearing upon what we now propose. The division in 1848, as you stated, was upon a 6 per cent. basis, and it was an optional division with the shareholders to convert or not. The result of that conversion has already been explained; but I may say that the Great Northern were the first company to introduce this method of dealing with stocks, and we have been more fortunate as respects the results than any other company who have divided stocks, that is, our divided stocks have stood at a higher price than the divided stocks of other companies, as compared with the original stock; and for two reasons; the first, as has been stated, that it was decided by Vice-Chancellor Wood that the B shareholders were entitled to a cumulative dividend, and then in 1851 the directors decided that they would not allow any more stock to be divided. The division was allowed for a specific purpose; that purpose had been answered, and the Board therefore would not allow it to be continued. But I think the Committee will at once see the effect of that, which was not only to limit the stock, but to increase the value; and therefore our A and B stocks have stood as a rule, as

Mr. *Balfour Browne*—continued.

as compared with the original stock, at about 12 per cent. higher value. The A and B would produce about 12 per cent. more than the price of the original stock for the time being.

242. Under the Act of 1848 it was optional on the directorate to allow that conversion to go on to any extent?—It was.

243. But they did not do so, they stopped it at a certain point, when 1,159,275 *l.* had been divided. So much for it, and so much for B?—They did.

Chairman.] I do not wish to interrupt you, but the witness said that it was stopped because the object had been attained. Have you asked what the object was?

Mr. *Balfour Browne.*

244. No, I do not know what it was, but I will ask Mr. Grinling. (To the *Witness.*) What was the object?—The object was this: during the payment of the calls on the original stock some of the shareholders experienced a difficulty in meeting them so quickly as was found necessary for the purpose of carrying on the construction of the line; it was pointed out to the directors and urged upon them that if they allowed this division they would enable the shareholders to tide over a difficulty; the arrangement was that any shareholder who had paid 17 *l.* out of 25 *l.* was allowed to divide or convert, and 12 *l.* 10 *s.* of that 17 *l.* was assigned to the "A" or deferred stock; that, therefore, was paid up; there was no further liability upon it. The balance of the call between the 12 *l.* 10 s. and the 17 *l.* was assigned to the "B" stock; but as that "B" stock carried 6 per cent. (true it was in the future) there was no difficulty whatever in the shareholders either disposing of their stock or carrying on their engagement for their calls. That was, I believe, the special reason, and I may add that the directors were never very favourably disposed towards a speculative class of shareholders; and it is not with the idea of introducing speculative shareholders into the company that we bring this scheme before you. When I come further to explain the scheme, perhaps you will allow me to explain that point.

245. I will give you an opportunity of amplifying that; but in the meantime I want to get this fact; a certain amount of conversion was allowed for the object you have explained?—Yes.

246. It is still in the power of the directors to allow conversion to go on at present if they choose?—It is.

247. That is provided for by the Act of 1848?—Yes.

Mr. *Bristowe.*] May I interpose and ask when Vice-Chancellor Wood's conclusion about this being a cumulative dividend took place?

Mr. *Balfour Browne.*] I would give it you, but I do not find it here. Mr. Grinling, I dare say, will tell you the date. I find I have the Report here and that will give it.

Mr. *Bristowe.*] The point is only to know 0.101.

whether it affected the decision of the directors in stopping the further division.

Witness.] Oh, no, not that I am aware of.

Mr. *Balfour Browne.*] This was discussed, and the decision given on the 28th and 29th January 1859.

Mr. *Bristowe.*] And when did they stop dividing the stock?

Witness.] In 1851.

Mr. *Balfour Browne.*

248. So it had not anything to do with that. (To the *Witness.*) Then, under the Great Northern Acts of 1872, 1875, and 1887, special powers were granted to them for the consolidation of several preferential stocks at varying rates of dividend?—That is so; and I should like to mention here that the addition to the preference capital by the consolidation of those stocks amounted to 1,803,000 *l.*

249. Just let us follow that process, because it seems important. You had various preference stocks at varying rates of interest?—We had; and I may say ——

250. Wait just a minute. I want to get question and answer, if you please, for a minute or two; then you shall go on and explain. Is it a disadvantage to a company to have a large number of different stocks at different rates?—Certainly not.

251. "Certainly not," do you say?—Yes.

252. I do not understand that?—I can best illustrate it in this way: I may say we had two consolidations of these preference stocks; I think the first one was in 1876, when we brought our five per cent. (that is when we could convert) into a four and a half, that being at that time about the current market rate at which the stock could be placed. When we came down to 1887, then we found that it was profitable to the shareholder to bring those stocks down to a four per cent., and that was done; the total increment or addition to the stock being the amount that I have stated. I should like just to dwell upon these two points for a moment to show that in the scheme we are now proposing we are following out the lines of past legislation. In the first place, we have been allowed (and as has been stated we still possess the power) to divide stock; or, what is sometimes called to split stock; I call it dividing the dividend, apportioning the dividend; that is, the dividend was apportioned. The stock was not affected beyond that; it stood in two amounts to correspond with the assigned amounts of dividend. We have, as has been stated again, that power still, but the directors consider that 6 per cent. is not a rate at which they would now place any guaranteed stock. And I should like to impress upon the Committee the position of railways in reference to those rates of interest in the past. Now, take for instance, our 5 per cent. stock, which was placed, I think, in 1849 at par. The result of the two conversions is that that stock stands at, or is worth now, 150 *l.* That falls

Mr. *Balfour Browne*—continued.

upon the back of the railway. We are not proposing (and never have proposed) in any way to alter the burden; but looking at the future I think the Committee will see how important it is, when you are placing capital, that you should place it on the lowest rate of interest for the time being that you can. If we could see our way, we would bring our 4 per cent. down below that, and ultimately I believe it will have to come below that; that is that all preference or preferred stocks will have to be placed at something like the current rate of the day.

253. Just let me put in a question there. As I understand, the right of conversion was conferred by the Act of 1848?—It was so.

254. But if that right was exercised it would still have to be exercised on a 6 per cent. basis? —And with cumulative rights?

255. And with cumulative rights, both of which you think wrong in principle?—Yes. Parliament have decided the question of cumulative rights.

256. Further than that, on the consolidation of your preference stock Parliament recognised the principle of the increase of the nominal value of the stock?—Yes.

257. So long as the dividend was not increased? —Yes.

258 And when that was done you reduced certain preference stocks in the amount of dividend to increase the nominal value?—Yes.

259. Leaving the holders of those preference stocks in precisely the same position as they were before?—With an improved market.

260. And when you answered that it was "not a disadvantage," I think you missed my word; it is a clear advantage to a railway company to have as few stocks of varying descriptions as possible, is it not?—Yes.

261. Now a general explanation of the grounds on which that took place you have already given. The share capital has been issued either as original or preference, as considered most advantageous by the company at the period of raising the capital, as you have explained?— Yes; and I should like to follow that out. There has been no rule for placing railway capital, and it certainly has occurred to me, sitting in this room the last two days, that the Bills which are before the Committee do not propose any rule now. They propose to add to the methods of creating stocks, in fact, to increase the number, which is manifestly undesirable, not only from the company's point of view, but from the shareholders' point of view; because a small stock does not produce so good a market as a large stock would.

262. May I just interpose there. One of the disadvantages to your A and B and Ordinary, is that the A and B are small stocks?—That is so.

263. And, as I understand, one of your main grounds for compulsory conversion is, that there shall not be those outstanding people who would make a separate stock?—Yes; and I should like to tell the Committee the result of our experience of having three sets of original shareholders; that is, an original shareholder, pure and simple; an original shareholder who gets a preferred dividend, and an original shareholder who gets a deferred dividend. Their interests can-

Mr. *Balfour Browne*—continued.

not be the same, and the company, although not placed in any difficulty at all by the arrangement, have at times found this conflict of interest a serious drawback very often in the management of their affairs. I may give one illustration with reference to the declaration of dividend. We were advised for years that in order to fulfil the engagement between the A and the B shareholders, that the A would guarantee the 6 per cent. to the B; that after A had fulfilled that guarantee, he was entitled to have the balance closely divided. That was done, and the consequence was, as compared with some of the large companies, our balance was an infinitesimal one, 2,000 *l.* or 3,000 *l.* Looking at the contingencies of working a railway, it is a very great inconvenience to have that state of things; but that was one of the conditions of having these separate classes of shareholders. I should like, if the Committee will allow me, just to finish, by saying, that if the scheme fulfils its object, instead of having, as in the case of the other Bills, or in the case of our own Bill, supposing our Bill was not compulsory, but optional, we should aggravate our difficulty, as we should have an original A and a B, and a preferred and a deferred stock. Therefore, one object of the scheme is to endeavour, as far as possible, to bring those stocks into one.

Chairman.

264. What you point out as affecting the holders of deferred stock is, that it is to their interest to use up the uttermost farthing of the earnings of the company so far as they are available. That will equally apply to your new *régime* with the two classes of shareholders?—I am very glad you have given me the opportunity, Sir, of answering that, because I think you will see that the position is altered. We shall no longer divide stocks partly into A and B, or preferred and deferred, that only operates as regards the past; when we come to deal with the future we shall have the preferred stock, which will practically be the preference, and the deferred will become an open stock. I may quote the North British as an illustration of how it has been carried out.

265. You think when the margin has been given to the 4 per cent. stock that the interest of the deferred shareholders will be practically equivalent to the interest of the preferred shareholder in an ordinary railway?—I think so.

Mr. *Balfour Browne.*

266. That is so. On the other hand, while it was a small stock, like 1,159,000 *l.*, or whatever it was, that did not operate; it was too small to bear that general interest?—At one time 3,000 *l.* or 4,000 *l.* made a difference of a quarter per cent.

267. You have already pointed out now, that the result of the operation, that is, of the conversion of your preference stock into one uniform stock, did increase the value of the stock to the proprietors?—Certainly.

268. It clearly could do no harm to any other body, the mere increase of the nominal value?— That is my view; I have not heard any complaints

Mr. *Balfour Browne*—continued.

plaints ; I think the shareholders are very well satisfied.

269. The original stock having been improved by division into A and B, and the preference by the consolidation into one stock at the reduced rate?—Just so.

270. Of course the disadvantage of trying to operate under the Act of 1848 would be with the six per cent. ; and that is an absolute amount of interest ?—Yes, it would not produce so good a return of dividend.

271. Now, let me ask you this, it is a matter outside of your proof, but it will save me perhaps calling another witness : Was this matter of conversion brought to the notice of the directors by the shareholders themselves ?—It was, on several occasions.

272. The initiative came from the shareholders ?—Certainly ; and I noticed in turning up the report of 1849, that that was the case with the first division of A. and B. ; that came from the shareholders.

Chairman.

273. That we quite appreciate, because you have explained to us the motive of it ?—Yes.

274. When the shareholders more recently moved in this direction, what was their motive ?—First, you see, Sir, they see, or perhaps they themselves are participators in the improved value of the 12 per cent. ; they, therefore, of course, wish to increase the stock with the view of getting a profit.

Mr. *Balfour Browne.*

275. Just let me ask you first of all with regard to that 12 per cent., to put it quite clearly ; you did mention 12 per cent., but you did not work it out ; just work it out in figures ; as you have it here 100 *l.* A. in market value was 102 *l.* ?—Yes.

276. £. 100 B. market value 165 *l.*, making for the two 200 *l.*, which was, split, 267 *l.* ; is not that so ?—That is it.

277. Now the average value of each 100 *l.* under that system, that is, when you have split, is 133½ *l.* ?—Yes.

278. The present market value of the original stock where no split has taken place is 121 *l.* ?—Yes, if you will allow me to say so ; it was so where I put that figure down.

279. Is that it ?—It is so for this reason, and it has a bearing upon the question ; that so soon as the Company had deposited their Bill for the Act for this further conver-ion, the original stock increased in value ; and it has a converse action ; sometimes it has effect on the original stock, and sometimes on the divided stocks ; the anticipatory value is, of course, to the original stock ; but when you get the stocks divided, of course it depends then again upon the position of the dividend. The 6 per cent. stock, if it is assured, as our B or preferred stock has been assured, by the large amount left payable for the A, quite apart from the cumulative rights which have never been exercised, except on one occasion, and that was during a period of misfortune ; I think the Committee will see that there are reasons why these stocks should go up in price. As I have put it, the position is just this : that an

0.101.

Mr. *Balfour Browne*—continued.

original shareholder, instead of being in possession of one security which he can take in the market, is in possession of two securities ; because I do not think it need necessarily be taken. It is all very well for a Trust Investment Company and stock-jobbing concerns to look upon these preferred and deferred stocks as separate ; but that has not been the domestic idea, and the variety of reasons that there are for these stocks improving in value gives the figure that has already been stated, that is the 12½ per cent.

Mr. *Bristowe.*

280. If you will allow me to put it to you : unless I am mistaken, this A stock has been a very violent speculative article in consequence of the very small amount in hand ?—Yes, mainly so.

281. It must not be taken as the normal value, the difference between the original of these two stocks, because it has been the subject of very violent speculations I suppose ever since the year it was created ?—Yes.

282. It is a fact, is it not, that you can easily control a small amount of stock ?--Just so.

Mr. *Balfour Browne.*

283. Very likely that calculation of the difference of 12 per cent. would not hold if you had large stocks ; I quite admit that. (To the *Witness.*) But still has the same operation ?—I should like, please, to answer that. That is not the general opinion. The larger the stock ——

Mr. *Bristowe.*] I am not giving an opinion about it ; I only ask the question.

Witness.] The larger the market the better the value ; that is what I am informed.

Mr. *Balfour Browne.*

284. That is true, no doubt ; but when you get the small stock, do not you send to introduce speculative operations ?—Certainly.

285. So that it may be run up or run down ?—Yes. The fluctuation in the rate of dividend has been considerable. At one time our dividend was 7½ per cent. The A shareholders were getting 8 or 9 per cent., whereas now they have to be content with a modest 3 7-8ths.

286. However, I understand one of the reasons for this compulsory conversion is to get the whole of the stock into two categories ?—Yes.

287. One the preferred and the other the deferred ?—It is so.

288. You think the amounts will be so great that they cannot be controlled by gentleman speculators, and that they will be sufficient to keep the affair steady ?—Yes, I think so.

289. To take another illustration of the effect of the consolidation of your preference stocks into a 4 per cent. consolidated stock, the price of 4½ per cent. preference prior to consolidation was 138 *l.* for the 100 *l.* ?—Yes, 4½ that is.

290. Equal to a 4 per cent. stock at 123 *l.* ?—Yes.

291. Now what is the price of a 4 per cent.

C 3 after

Mr. *Balfour Browne*—continued.

after consolidation ?—It has varied little because of the condition of the money market; but it did reach at one time 130 *l.*, and it has been very recently as high as 129 *l.*

292. There again, you believe that to a large extent that increase is due to the effect of consolidation ?—Yes, I know of no other cause.

293. You confuse a possible purchaser if you present him with a great number of different stocks at different prices with different dividends ?—Not only that, but you see the man has to wait a long time for a market.

294. No doubt?—We have had small stocks under 100,000 *l.* If a man wants to sell he may have to wait months before a purchaser comes.

295. That is a serious disability to certain persons ?—Yes, it depresses the value. Then there is a further reason : Of late years (I believe it has been due to the action of the Government with reference to consols) there has been a great demand for 4 per cent. preference stocks, which has assisted the upward movement.

296. Would the new 4 per cent. preferred stock which you are now seeking to create, attain a better price than the B. 6 per cent. ?—Relatively it would.

297. Relatively, of course I meant to say that ?—Yes.

298. That is to say, 150 *l.* of the 4 per cent. would get more than 100 *l.* of the 6 per cent. ?—Yes.

299. There is a demand; a good deal in the market too, is there not, for preferred and deferred ?—Yes.

300. Now assuming the market value of the new preferred or deferred stock to be 120 *l.*, what would be the result of the conversion of the B. into a 4 per cent. stock ?—I have taken it in this way : that 100 *l.* original, if we gave 75 *l.* preferred; that is 75 *l.* for the 50 *l.* which you will see is turning the 50 *l.* 6 per cent. into a 75 *l.* 4 per cent.; I have taken that at 120 *l.*; that would give 90 *l.* for the 75 *l.* of preferred stock.

301. Or is it not easier to do it in " hundred pounds "?—If you please

302. It would be 180 *l.* for the 100 *l.* ?—No, 120 *l.*

303. For the 150 *l.* ?—Yes ; well I would rather take it as I have got it here, if you would allow me (I have had figures enough lately), because it illustrates the mode in which the exchange takes place. After they converted 50 *l.* 6 per cent. the proprietor would get 75 *l.* 4 per cent. ; the 120 *l.* preferred would give 90 *l.* for the 75 *l.* ; the 50 *l.* A would remain the same ; and that is another feature in this scheme which the directors have considered an advantage, that we are not increasing the deferred stock. And I think when I point out to the Committee that the same result is obtained by this increase of the preferred stock ; that is, making the preferred stock in the ratio of 3-5ths and 2-5ths deferred, it produces about the same effect as if you were to defer both those stocks, and that it is more to the advantage of the shareholder to have a stock with a fixed value than to have a speculative stock ; and as I have already said the board do not view with very much favour the

Mr. *Balfour Browne*—continued.

increase of speculative stocks. The increase in the value by this arrangement would be 20 *l.* That is the estimate ; but I should rather put it at something like 15 *l.*

304. Now will you just go on with your calculation ; 50 *l.* at 6 per cent. equals 75 *l.* at 4 ; the market value would be 90 *l.* ?—Yes.

305. 50 *l.* A would be 50 *l.* deferred ?—That is it.

306. Market value probably 51 *l.* ?—Yes ; it would be in all respects in the same position as the present A. That would be equal to 141 *l.* for the 125 *l.* of preferred and deferred stocks.

307. Now what is the present value of the original ?—I put it at 121 *l.* at this time.

308. So that the increased value would be ?—20 *l.*, as I have already said ; the price would vary.

309. This system is to be applied to the new stock of the company ?—That is proposed in the clause that has been referred to.

310. Just let me see the effect of that. If it is applied to the new stock of the company and the increased market value yields anything like 20 *l.*, that premium would go into the pocket of the company and enure to the benefit of the public without paying any interest ? — It would.

Mr. *Bristowe.*

311. It would go into the pocket of the shareholder, would it not ?—No, if you will allow me just to put it to you. So far as regards existing or past stocks it would go to the shareholder; any new would come to the Company. We have 1,000,000 *l.* 6 per cent. to do now. The effect of it shortly is this : I think I can better illustrate it in rate per cent. ; suppose we had a 5 per cent. dividend and we were going to divide it in the ratio of the existing or proposed conversion, the conversion of existing stocks, we should take 3 *l.* out of it to represent the 75 *l.* preferred stock. If I was going to issue it first hand I should have this 25 *l.* (the addition) for the Company. I should only have to pay 2 *l.*, that is I have reduced the dividend to the rate of 4 per cent. The effect of the arrangement, I submit, is very important as affecting the issue of future capital, because it will enable the Company to place the capital upon a very low rate of fixed dividend.

Mr. *Balfour Browne.*

312. To some extent this in the case of railways anticipates the legislation which is in vogue as to gas companies, that they are bound to sell their shares by auction, and the premium goes to the benefit of the Company, not to the benefit of the shareholders, and does not receive any interest ?—Certainly it works in that direction.

313. It works in that way, that is compulsory in the case of gas companies, but it has not been applied to the case of railways at all ?—Yes; and I should just like to take up the point again as to the raising of future capital upon the accounts of the companies. Many companies (I would rather not mention names) if they had issued all their stock on the principle that you say the gas and water companies are now to be compelled to do, would have received a considerable

Mr. *Balfour Browne*—continued.

able amount of additional capital for the same annual charge, in fact some of the companies seem quite happy in falling back upon their misfortunes. When they approach paying a very low dividend, they say, Oh, well, if you spread it over the whole, it would give a very satisfactory result. But then unfortunately it has gone to other people. It does not come to the company, and our burdens are quite heavy enough, it goes on the market. Stock issued at par gradually rising to 10 or 20 per cent. gets dissipated, or if not dissipated it does not fall to the Company, yet the Company have for all time to carry that burden; and as far as I understand the proposals that have come forward, I do not know exactly how to submit it, but I think it is well worthy of consideration.——

314. I am getting now upon somewhat dangerous ground. Trust Companies have sought to attain similar objects to those you are seeking here by simply duplicating the stock?—Yes.

315. You have got some statistics to lay before the Committee as to that. I understand some of the other railway companies propose simply to duplicate the stock as against the proposal in your Bill?—Yes.

316. We will not go upon that; but will you give the figures you have got as to the result of the stock companies, operations?—This is worked out on the accounts of the Stock Investment Company. The London and North Western Stock (the figures have already been quoted) on a security of 1,000,000 *l.*; the Trust Company have issued 1,000,000 *l.* of their own stock, 3½ per cent.——

Chairman.

317. We have had this before?—Yes, you have had it before. You have had all these figures.

318. Unless you have some new or more forcible deduction to make we need not have it again?—It shows this, that they make a profit upon the present price of something like 7 *l.* That is the aggregate.

Mr. *Balfour Browne.*

319. I will not press it?—The product of those stocks take the London and North Western at 184 *l.*, and the present price of the London and North Western stock at 177 *l.* gives an improvement of only 7 *l.*; but then the Trust Investment Company do not make their money in that way.

320. What do you mean by that?—I mean that they buy and sell stock as I understand; they are a stock-jobbing company. I do not know the distinction.

321. We have that to some extent from the witnesses who have gone before. As I understand, the result of those figures that shows what you have already been illustrating; that there is a gain, at all events?—Yes, I should like to point out to gentlemen who talk about doing this through the Investment Company that they have to pay the 8 per cent. expenses, equivalent to something like 3 *l.*; they get a second-hand security (because the stock is really pledged to the Trust Investment Company), and those

0.101.

Mr. *Balfour Browne*—continued.

stocks are issued against it. Of course the integrity of the trustees is the guarantee, but still it cannot be considered as a first class security: and taking the operation as it is, it is not the best way. If you decide that it is advisable to water stocks, that is not the way to do.

322. Now we will go to the scheme we have propounded here. Just very shortly tell us what that is; the amount of existing stocks is shown upon the schedule?—Yes, which has been referred to.

323. Preferred and deferred to be issued in lieu thereof; that is, set out in Schedule 3, as Mr. Pope pointed out?—Yes.

324. The mode of carrying out the provisions of the scheme is contained in Sections 3 to 6 of the Bill?—Yes.

325. The scheme adopts the principle of the original division of A· into A. and B., modified only by substituting 4 per cent. interest in lieu of the 6 per cent.?—That is so.

326. And increasing the capital in accordance with the arrangement already recognised for the consolidation of the ordinary and preference stocks?—Yes.

327. There is nothing you do to-day that you cannot find a precedent for in the past history of the Great Northern Railway Company?—That is so.

328. There is one modification, and that is that this scheme does not go beyond the cumulative rights of the B. stock, and those rights would be met, to some extent, by the improved security of the preferred stock?—It does not go beyond; and as I have pointed out these cumulative rights have only come into operation once in something like 30 years. The value of the preferred stock after all does not depend on whether you call it 4 per cent. or 6 per cent.; it depends upon what is behind it; if therefore you were to give preferred stock behind your deferred stock, you secure it to all intents and purposes.

329. As I understand the scheme to-day, with reference to the future stock, it is always that there should be an amount of deferred stock issued comparable to and bearing a proportion to the preferred stock?—Yes, that is the three-fifths and the two-fifths.

330. So that the preferred stock always has the backing of an equivalent amount of deferred stock?—Yes.

Chairman.

331. What do you mean by "equivalent amount?"—I hesitated at that; not an equal amount, certainly; a proportionate amount.

332. How do you determine the equivalency of it?—It is two-fifths; that is 50 *l.* as against 75 *l.*

333. Quite so; I rather wish to know, and I think the Committee would like to know this: there are two particular points as to this individual scheme?——

Mr. *Balfour Browne.*] Yes.

Chairman.] The first, I think, Mr. Grinling has said a good deal about; that is why the 4 per cent. was fixed upon.

C 4   Mr.

Chairman—continued.

Mr. *Balfour Browne.*] Yes.

Chairman.] Or Mr. Pope explained it, one or the other ; I really forget which. The other point is, as to the 75 *l.* and the 50 *l.* You propose that 100 *l.* stock shall be represented by 75 *l.* preferred and 50 *l.* deferred.

Mr. *Balfour Browne.*] That is only changing the 6 per cent. into a 4 per cent. ; that is the whole, Sir. If you turn it into 100 *l.*, taking 100 *l.* 6 per cent. changed into 4 per cent., it becomes 150 *l.* ; divide that by half it becomes 75 *l.*

Witness.] But if you will allow me to put it in another way, and, perhaps, I shall at the same time answer both questions; it is really governed by the dividend.

334. Certainly ?—As to whether you split or whether you duplicate, I do not know whether any gentleman would think it worth while to duplicate London, Chatham, and Dover Original Stock, and there are some stocks where the margin is so slight that there is no room for duplication. As I have already said, if I could secure the value by the increase of the proportion of the deferred stock, I submit that that is a better method than watering or duplicating both preferred and deferred. Now, taking our dividend, I had better take 5 per cent., the dividend was 4 *l.* 17 *s.* 6 *d.* on the last year——

Chairman.

335. Would you state what the dividends of the Great Northern Railway have been, or can you state it for a number of years back. We have it for other railways ?—Yes, I have it here. I have the average, the average for the past 10 years.

336. The average is not much good ?—Here is the list. I have given the average for 20 years and the average for 10 (*handing in the same*).

337. I am speaking of the original stock only, and not of the A and B ?—The " original " is stated there. I think the average of the original for 10 years to 1889 is 4 *l.* 14 *s.* 3 *d.*

338. To get it on the notes will you read the particular dividends ?—Shall I read the figures for each year ?

339. Yes, for each year ?—For the original stock only: 1870 (that is the year when this Table commences), 6 *l.* 12 *s.* 6 *d.* ; 1871, 7 *l.* 2 *s.* 6 *d.* ; 1872, 7 *l.* 2 *s.* 6 *d.* ; 1873, 7 *l.* 5 *s.* ; 1874, 6 *l.* 17 *s.* 6 *d.* ; 1875, 6 *l.* 10 *s.* ; 1876, 5 *l.* 10 *s.* ; 1877, 5 *l.* 5 *s.* ; 1878, 5 *l.* 5 *s.* ; 1879, 5 *l.* 2 *s.* 6 *d.* ; 1880, 5 *l.* 2 *s.* 6 *d.* ; 1881, 5 *l.* 5 *s.* ; 1882, 5 *l.* ; 1883, 4 *l.* 12 *s.* 6 *d.* ; 1884, 4 *l.* 12 *s.* 6 *d* ; 1885, 4 *l.* 10 *s.* ; 1886, 4 *l.* 7 *s.* 6 *d.* ; 1887, 4 *l.* 7 *s.* 6 *d.* ; 1888, 4 *l.* 7 *s.* 6 *d.* ; and last year, 1889, it was 4 *l.* 17 *s.* 6 *d.* The highest dividend I can get that the A's have received in that period has been 8¼ per cent., and the lowest dividend has been 2¾ : so that will, of course, very well answer the question as to the fluctuation.

Mr. *Balfour Browne.*

340. Now, to make one point clear, we used the word equivalent, I see upon the 3rd Schedule

Mr. *Balfour Browne*—continued.

of the Bill the " A " stock is 100 *l.*, the " B " stock is 100 *l.* ; but the " B " stock is to be converted into 150 *l.* ?—Yes.

341. Because of the dividend being 4 per cent. instead of 6 ?—That is so ; and that ——

342. Now, wait a minute, please. Now, go back to the original stock. There the form of conversion is precisely the same. There is to be 75 *l.* preferred, which is exactly the same as 150 *l.* preferred 4 per cent., and 50 *l.*, which is the same as 100 *l.* deferred ?—Yes.

343. Now, is the relation between the preferred and deferred in future always to be the same ? —That is the proposal.

344. Therefore, for every 75 *l.* of preferred stock there will be a backing of 50 *l.* deferred stock ?—Yes.

Chairman.

345. Then am I to understand that the reason why you substitute for 100 *l.* ordinary stock 75 *l.* preferred and 50 *l.* deferred, is that that particular division falls in with the arrangement with regard to the " A " and " B " stocks ?— Not altogether, Sir, because I could have effected the same if I had made the " B " into a 3 per cent., and have increased the stock by 100 *l.*

346. What I wish to get at is this ?—The reason why we stopped at 4 per cent. was that we considered that that was a fair marketable stock, that we did not wish to place an additional stock on the market that would stand or might stand below par.

Mr. *Balfour Browne.*

347. The basis of the whole is a 4 per cent. dividend ?—It is so.

348 But it is a recommendation, is it not, that that does fall in with the arrangements of " A " and " B " ?—It is so, and that is very important. It meets we hope the case of the " B," although some of the " B " shareholders stand out very earnestly for their cumulative rights. But I think if we can show them that they can make 10 *l.* out of them they will be willing possibly to consider the 10 *l.* better than the probability.

Chairman.

349. The point is this, we have had other schemes before us where the companies propose to proceed by what we know as a duplication of stock ?—Yes.

350. Duplication being, giving 200 *l.* of stock of one sort or another for 100 *l.* Here we have your Company proposing that instead of giving 200 *l.* stock for the 100 *l.*, you should give 125 *l.* on certain conditions, that is the point ?—I have here a written memorandum. I would rather put it as I have it in writing, although I do not think it carries all the points. Remember, if you please, that the object of the conversion that we have in view, is to reset the original stock, and to avoid further increase of the number of stocks. If it were optional the stocks would remain as under : Original ; " A " ; " B " ; preferred ; deferred ; and on the compulsory scheme these stocks would ultimately be merged into preferred and deferred. Unless the scheme is compulsory there would not be the
same

Chairman—continued.

same inducement to the A and B shareholders to convert. By allowing the stocks to remain separate it would reduce the market value as the improvement to some extent is dependent upon the amount of the aggregate stock in the market.

Mr. *Beckett.*] The Chairman's question bears much more on splitting than upon duplication.

Chairman.] It has been called splitting to describe duplication.

Witness.] I should be very glad if I could duplicate.

Mr. *Balfour Browne.*

351. I think Mr. Grinling's answer to that (if I may take him back to it) was that it depended upon the amount of the dividend? —Quite so.

352. If you have dividend sufficient you can duplicate?—If I had 6 per cent. constant dividend, as my friend Mr. Scott said he had yesterday, I have no doubt that that is a case for duplication.

Chairman.

353. May I ask, would a smaller dividend suit your purpose equally, because the Caledonian Railway have a smaller dividend, and yet they duplicate?—I do not see the advantage.

354. You say you do not wish to do it?—I do, but I do not see the advantage. It would of course improve the larger amount of "A" and "B" stock; but taking the question of guaranteed (suppose the amount to be Caledonian preferred stock), and you found the stock quoted behind it was only getting say 1 per cent. dividend, I think that that of itself would very much affect the value of the preferred stock; you might say there is a larger amount; but still it would appear on the market that there was only a 1 per cent. dividend behind the preferred stock; and I think there must come a point where you cannot duplicate.

355. But you do not leave a very large margin even in the Great Northern?—We give 3¾; and if we paid 5 per cent. it would be four.

356. You have been paying 4 *l.* 12 *s.* 6 *d.*, 4 *l.* 10 *s.*, 4 *l.* 7 *s.* 6 *d.*, three years, and so forth of late years?—We hope to improve.

357. I say you propose, I am not arguing against it. I am only wishing to bring out the point?—If you will allow me to call your attention to this point which has been mentioned I think more than once, the argument is, not that I want us to lower, but that a low dividend is desirable for a deferred stock.

Mr. *Balfour Browne.*

358. You are dividing it, if I may say so, over the 100 *l.* instead of over the 75 *l.*?—Yes.

Chairman.] Yes, your margin is greater.

Mr. *Balfour Browne.*] It is greater than at first sight it seems if you divide it over the 100 *l.*

Chairman.] Of course.

Mr. *Balfour Browne.*

359. (To the *Witness.*) With regard to the 0.101.

Chairman—continued.

duplication, if you duplicate when the dividend is not large enough you have to reduce the dividend upon the preference stocks as in the case of the Caledonian?—That is right.

360. The Caledonian only offer 3 per cent. preference, do not they?—Yes.

361. Is it your view that a 4 per cent. preference is a more marketable stock than the 3 per cent.?—Yes; only we were told that in the north; I was surprised to hear it; they like low dividends, or were content with them.

Chairman.

362. I think you said in your own evidence that you thought 4 per cent. was a fair dividend to propose for that sort of stock just now?—Yes.

363. But that it would probably have to be lowered afterwards; I think you said something to that effect; that there would be a demand, I mean, for a lower dividend?—Suppose we had a 6 per cent. dividend, I think I could prove this to you, that we should be entitled then to issue 100 *l.* 4 per cent. stock, and I should do it upon this ground, that I was giving to the original shareholder the ordinary market rate of interest for his investment. It seems to me that we very much lose sight of the position of railways with reference to their dividends. We talk of 6 or 7 per cent. when it includes the interest on the ordinary use of money, and that the dividend on the preferred stock should represent that charge. Then I would let the other go to the deferred stock, and if it is a growing dividend I think the deferred holder having made the sacrifice by guaranteeing the preferred holder, is certainly entitled, as we have always considered in the case of our "A" and "B," to all the improvement.

Mr. *Bristowe.*

364. And all loss; all the improvement or the other way?—He has to bear the other.

Mr. *Balfour Browne.*

365. Of course he has to take his chance of both. (To the *Witness.*) Let me ask you this; is the 4 per cent. more likely to keep the preference stock at a par value?—I consider so.

366. Ought the preference stock, in your view, to be at a par value?—Looking at the character of the Company I think it should.

367. If it is not, if it is under par, is it likely to become a more speculative stock?—Yes.

368. Although we do not want to decry our neighbour's plan, you think the one you submit is the preferable one?—Well, it is adapted to the circumstances of my company.

369. I quite understand your view, but if you had a safe 6 per cent. dividend, duplication might absolutely be the better plan?—It might.

370. Or as good a plan?—Quite so.

371. But under the circumstances you think the one you have suggested to the Committee is the better?—Well, for the Great Northern Company, I do.

372. Now, I think upon the main features of the scheme we have already sufficiently enlarged. I want to ask you about a minor matter, that is, the

D

Mr. Balfour Browne—continued.

the consolidation of the debenture stock. The debenture stocks set out in the first Schedule are Great Northern, 4 per cent., 8,764,444 *l.*, and the West Yorkshire, 5 per cent. 53,000 *l.*, making altogether 8,817,444 *l.?*—Yes.

373. And by Section 13 that my learned friend, Mr. Pope read, it is proposed to consolidate these stocks into one class, at a uniform rate of 3 per cent. ?—Yes. It is very undesirable to have stocks placed from time to time bearing so high a premium. Of course we are subject to the fluctuation of the market; and it is to the Company's interest therefore to send debenture stock out at rates as near par value as we can arrive at at the time.

374. The security will remain to all intents and purposes the same, and the mode of carrying out the consolidation is prescribed by the Act? —It is. There is a slight improvement in the value.

375. In your opinion, is there any improvement in the market value of the stock?—Yes, compared with the present price; if it was at par, that is, it would be worth 133 *l.* 6 *s.* 8 *d.* of of 100 *l.* 4 per cent.; and the present value is 130 *l.* It is only a slight improvement.

376. What would be the improved value do you say ?—£. 3. 6 *s.* 8 *d.* per cent.

377. I do not think there is anything else I need ask you——

Chairman.] It is essential for your purposes, from your point of view, that this operation should be compu'sory on the shareholders.

—It is. Well, I am afraid I have not explained that quite so fully as I should have liked to have done; but, in the first place, we could not carry out our scheme; the "A." and "B." would not come in for one. Then we should have these five sets of shareholders, and it would be hopeless to suppose that the shareholders would come in if it were optional.

378. That is what I said; you regard it as essential to the scheme that it should be compulsory?—We do, and if you will allow me to follow it up we think this: Supposing the issue of capital upon some intelligible basis, instead of leaving the companies sometimes to issue original and sometimes preference, Parliament has not hitherto, as far as I am aware, at all interfered with the liberties of the companies in placing their capital; we could not go very well back on original. Of course it would be for the directors to say whether the future capital should be preferred and deferred, but I understand that they would wish to have the power of doing so.

379. Have you any provision in this Bill as there has been in the others for showing in the accounts the original stock as well as the new? —Oh yes; we publish a capital account as distinct from the stocks and shares.

Mr. Balfour Browne.

380. That is Clauses 9 and 10?—The capital account would not be interfered with in any way by this operation. That represents cash.

Chairman.

381. It will show the original capital as now shown?—Oh yes; any one could see that from

Chairman—continued.

the accounts. Here is the way in which it is carried out as regards the preference. This is a copy of our last half-year's accounts; that is the capital account. Perhaps you will let me quote the figure showing a total of 36,686,000 *l.* of share capital; but the nominal addition is shown there (*handing in the document*).

382. And if this Bill was passed you would show in some such way the effect of it?—We should. We must. We could not produce accurate accounts without.

Mr. Balfour Browne.] Might I just read Clause 10 to you if you please, Sir?

Chairman.] Of course.

Mr. Balfour Browne.] "Notwithstanding the conversion under the powers of this Act of any ordinary capital the statements to be made up in accordance with the provisions of the 'Regulation of Railways Act, 1868'" (you have had a form in your hand just now under that Act) "shall continue to show the amount of ordinary capital authorised created, and received as if no such conversion had taken place, but the statement of capital account shall set forth in addition to the particulars required by the First Schedule to the said Act the amounts of the preferred ordinary stock and deferred ordinary stock."

Witness.] I may say, that when we carried through the operation that was the statement we published with the accounts showing the increase of each stock, and you see what a multiplicity of Stocks there were dealt with at that time. (*Handing in a document.*)

Chairman.

383. I think you have said that this change has been asked for by shareholders?—Yes; very urgently. It was impressed upon the directors more than two years ago and then repeated. Then, I may say, not intensified, but of course it was brought, I was going to say, to an issue by the action of the Trust Investment Company. In fact, our Chairman stated to the shareholders his view that if this was a *bonâ fide* operation, and the shareholders could have their market value improved he thought it would be better done by the Company than by outside machinery, that is by the Trust Investment.

384. And the directors are not aware of any opposition or reluctance on the part of any considerable section of shareholders?—Well, we had a meeting of shareholders for the purpose of considering this scheme, and there was a large majority in favour of it. There were some who were not; but I am sorry to say I do not think they quite understood what was proposed.

Mr. Beckett.

385. What amount of capital did the dissentients minority represent, do you remember? —It was done by show of hands. There were no numbers taken.

Mr. Balfour Browne.] It was not a Wharncliffe meeting, it was merely a test meeting we held, not under the Standing Order. We

We have to have a meeting before this Bill passes into the other house.

Chairman.] That has not been held

Mr. *Balfour Browne.*] That has not been held. The formal meeting has not been held, not on the amended Bill.

Mr. *Dickson.*

386. Do I understand by your scheme in the First Schedule, original A stock and B stock, that you intend to have only two classes of stock, preferred and deferred? — Ultimately.

387. That you should have no stock known by the name of original stock, at all? — That is so. We propose to save the first operation of the issue of original stock. As I understand, according to the arrangements for the issue of capital hitherto, it has been the practice first to issue original; then the provision is for dividing the stock. We wish to do that in the first instance.

388. All I want to know is, do you drop the name " original stock " entirely? — It would be preferred ordinary and deferred ordinary.

389. Do you intend having that or not; because it is not in any of your clauses? — No, it would drop out, as I have said. There would be no original stock.

390. Do I understand that you would not have any original stock; but that you will have preferred ordinary and deferred ordinary? — That is so.

391. But you would have the word " ordinary " attached to both stocks? — Yes.

392. Because that word " ordinary " does not appear in any of your schemes, as far as I can see? — I think it is in the Schedule, if you will look at that.

Chairman.] It is on page 15.

Mr. *Dickson.*] No, it is only " ordinary."

Witness.] I thought it was in the body of the Bill. I think it is in the designation of the stock.

Mr. *Pope.*] I think if you refer to Section 3, sir, you will find that the stock is named preferred ordinary stock and deferred ordinary stock.

Mr. *Dickson.*] Yes, that is the point I wanted.

Mr. *Biddulph.*

393. Were you in the room yesterday, and did you hear Mr. Scott's evidence? — I did.

394. Did you hear what he said with regard to the question of compulsory conversion? — Yes.

395. Do you agree with him upon that point? — I must recall it; I am not quite sure what the point is.

396. I will give you the question that was put; read that to yourself, and you will see what was said. It is Question No. 105 (*handing document to the Witness*)? — He gave that answer as I 0.101.

Mr. *Biddulph*—continued.
understand upon the view that the shareholders would not adopt it.

397. He said it was impracticable? — It was done by the North British.

398. I believe the other Bills here do not propose to make it compulsory? — They do not. I am not sure about the Isle of Wight Bill.

Chairman.] Yes, it is compulsory there.

Mr. *Pope.*] Yes, in the Isle of Wight case it is compulsory.

Mr. *Biddulph.*

399. (*To the Witness.*) But you do not take any powers for re-conversion? — No, we do not, we do not want to go back.

Mr. *Bristowe.*

400. It is put before this Committee that there are several ways of converting these stocks; one was duplicating, and you had 25 per cent. to it; do you think that those varied changes or varied plans will lead to any misconception on the part of the investing public, or do you attach any importance to it? — I think if you multiply stocks, especially the arrangement that was talked of this morning as regards the Caledonian, it seems to involve the necessity of a knowledge of the accounts of the Company, whether that is desirable or not when you are buying; but on the arrangement as I have put it, it is sufficient of itself.

401. Except that the one duplicates it, and yours adds 25 per cent.; one adds 100, and you add 25 per cent.; and unless there is something to show this various splitting up of capital in the ordinary quotations of the official list, the public do not know exactly what they are buying; I do not mean to say that it is injurious, but I want to know what your view of it is? — Allow me to refer to the class of preference stocks; the difficulty has not arisen, the 5 per cent. has been converted to 4½ and 4. I have never heard of any such question arising.

402. Was there an increase of capital simultaneous with that? — Yes.

403. That was allowed in your Company? — Yes.

404. You do not consider really yourself then that the capital is of so much importance as the dividend? — The dividend.

405. You base your idea upon the dividend? — Certainly.

406. I rather gathered that you did say so before? — Certainly, I think that governs it.

Mr. *Mowbray.*

407. You do not take compulsory powers on the A and B? — No, we are not in a position to do so, because we cannot give them the stock with cumulative rights.

408. Then unless you can induce them to take the option of your new stock you will not carry out one of your main objects, which is the consolidation of your ordinary stock? — Not in its entirety, but when they have 10 *l.* offered, then I do not know why they should hold on.

409. But you are not prepared to leave to the ordinary stockholder that option with out-

Mr. *Mowbray*—continued.

out inducement?—The ordinary stockholder? Well I would not give it to the B if I could help it; but I am obliged to give it to him.

410. I only wish to know why you think that the inducement of 10 *l*. will be sufficient to induce the A and B holders to convert at their own option, but that in the case of the other stock holders you consider it necessary to take compulsory powers?—I do not know that I quite follow your way of putting it, Sir. I am afraid the only answer I can give to it is that I cannot help it.

Mr. *Beckett.*

411. Is it not this, that you cannot compel either A or B to convert, because he cannot convert without the cumulative right?—That is so.

Mr. *Buxton.*

412. Then I do not quite understand why you want compulsory powers. I understood you in reply to the chairman to say, you intend to unify your stocks, therefore you want compulsory powers; but under the Bill, as Mr. Mowbray has pointed out, you have no compulsory powers with regard to A and B stock; therefore unification gets you no further than at present?—So the case of the A and B stock, as I have said, if we could bring about the conversion by compulsory powers; if we had the right of doing it, I think it would follow there. As regards the original, we have to consider what is for the interest of the whole body of shareholders, and whether an individual or any number of individuals should be allowed to stand out upon an arrangement which is really for the benefit to the whole body, is a question which I must leave to the Committee.

413. I understand the question of compulsion has not yet been put before the shareholders, they have not had an opportunity of voting whether the scheme shall be compulsory or voluntary as in the other case, is that so?—Perhaps you will allow me to answer it in this way: Unless we can get compulsory powers the scheme cannot be carried out; we should have greater confusion with the multiplicity of stocks and interests than we have now.

414. That is so; but as a matter of fact the shareholders have not yet had an opportunity of voting as to whether they desired compulsory powers or not?—They will; it will be subject to the vote at the Wharncliffe meeting.

Mr. *Balfour Browne.*] As a fact at this informal meeting, although it was not held

under any statute, that matter was before the shareholders and they did not disapprove of it.

Mr. *Buxton.*] I understood from the witness that they did not understand what they were voting about.

Mr. *Pope.*] That is a minor part of the Bill.

Mr. *Buxton.*

415. One other point, that is as to the 4 per cent· proposed by you as against the 3 per cent. proposed by the Caledonian Company. We have understood that the advantage of duplicating the stock was that it would make both preferred and deferred stock less speculative. The Caledonian, in much the same position as yourselves, with a small dividend, propose to make their preferred stock a 3 per cent. stock in order to make that a steady stock, and in order to make the deferred stock steady. Would it not be better for your purposes, and for your shareholders' purposes, if you made the preferred stock a 3 per cent. stock and duplicated it, instead of this very complicated arrangement that you propose?—First, a 3 per cent. stock would not command par. As I have said, the Company would not desire to place a stock in the market below par. Your suggestion would add to their dividend, and I gather that the view of the deferred shareholder is that he profits by a low dividend.

416. Then, as far as you are concerned, you do not think that your deferred stock will be a very speculative stock?—Well, it depends upon a variety of matters. I think it will be speculative to a certain extent, but not so speculative as it would be if it were watered or duplicated.

[The Witness withdrew.

Chairman.] Do you propose to offer any other witnesses.

Mr. *Balfour Browne.*] I propose to call a shareholder before you. It is only one question, Sir, that I wish to ask him, and I daresay you can deal with him to night.

Chairman.] If there is only one more witness we had better proceed.

Mr. *Balfour Browne.*] I propose to call only one witness, and also to offer you the general manager if you want to ask him any questions; but I do not propose to ask Mr. Oakley anything unless you do.

Chairman.] No, we do not wish to ask him anything.

MR. RICHARD GREEN, sworn; and Examined.

Mr. *Balfour Browne.*

417. You live in Herefordshire, and were High Sheriff of the county last year?—That is so.

418. You are a considerable holder of the ordinary stock, and you have frequently I believe

Mr. *Balfour Browne*—continued.

pressed upon the board of the Great Northern the necessity of dividing?—I have.

419. I believe you have taken a considerable interest in the affairs of the company, and you generally attend their meetings?—I do.

420. Have

Mr. Balfour Browne—continued.

420. Have you been consulted yourself by other holders, with the view of adopting some trust for the conversion of stock in the Great Northern Railway Company?—I have.

421. And have you set your face against any trust, hoping that the company itself would take the action they are now taking?—I have.

422. And, I believe, it was partly upon representations made by you and by other shareholders, that the Board were induced to take this action and produce this Bill?—I think it was.

423. And, as I understood, you entirely approve of the scheme that is now submitted to Parliament?—I do, most entirely.

Chairman.

424. Is the object that you have, as a shareholder, and is the object of those who sympathise with you, to secure this profit, which it is supposed will be made by splitting the stock?—That is one chief object, without a doubt.

425. You do not wish to run the chances of that falling into outside hands?—I should be very sorry indeed to see it, and the reason I have pressed it is, because I felt sure it would be brought forward by outside companies, if our own company did not do it.

426. Do you attach importance to the other point we have heard a good deal of, the power of an outside body such as that to interfere with the policy of the company?—I do attach very much importance to it.

427. The particular scheme which is adopted

in this Bill evidently has reference to the necessities created by the A and B stock?--Quite so; I may just observe——

428. Is that the principal object with you also, to get rid of the A stock?—I should not like to say it is *a* principal object with me; it is not *the* principal object; but I think it is quite likely that in course of time the Company will get rid of both the A and the B stock if this proposal is carried out.

429. At present the A stock is a very speculative stock, is it not?—It is a very speculative stock: and one reason is that I think it would be much less so if this proposal was carried out; because it is well known that the A being a speculative stock is in consequence of its small amount; therefore, it is easily manipulated by a few capitalists where they take it in hand, and if it is augmented by several millions that manipulation, of course, would become much more difficult. I may just observe that (it has been frequently stated) I have from time to time mentioned this, and pressed this division upon the Board on the principle of the present A and B stock if they could do no other. I have always been met by the fact that they very much object to the 6 per cent. cumulative stock, and as I understand this proposal it is simply instead of a 6 per cent. cumulative stock a 4 per cent. non-cumulative stock; and therefore I very much prefer the proposal of the Company to adopting a division on the lines upon which the Act of 1848 gives them the power to proceed.

Thursday, 15th May 1890.

MEMBERS PRESENT:

Mr W. Beckett.
Mr. Biddulph.
Mr. Bristowe.
Mr. Buxton.
Mr. Campbell-Bannerman.

Mr. Dickson.
Mr. Ellis.
Mr. Charles Hall.
Mr. R. Mowbray.

THE RIGHT HON. H. CAMPBELL-BANNERMAN, IN THE CHAIR.

ISLE OF WIGHT RAILWAY BILL.

The Petition for the Bill was read.

Mr. *Pope*, Q.C., and Mr. *Bolton* appeared as Counsel for the Promoters of the Bill.

Messrs. *Beal* and *Co.* appeared as Agents.

Mr. *Pope* was heard to open the case for the Promoters of the Bill.

Mr. HORACE F. TAHOURDIN, sworn ; and Examined.

Mr. *Bolton.*

430. I BELIEVE you are Chairman of the Isle of Wight Railway Company ?—Yes.

431. That is a small line of about 11 miles in length, is it not ?—It is 12 miles in length ; it is the red line shown on this map (*producing a map*).

432. That line runs from Ryde to Ventnor, does it not ?—Yes.

433. Would you give me the capital of the company ; first of all of the debenture stock ?—The debenture stock consists of A, B, and C debentures ; the A comes before the B, and the B comes before the C. The A debenture stock is 68,536 *l.*; the B is 67,548 *l.* ; and the C, 11,916 *l.*; making a total debenture stock of 148,000 *l.*

Mr. *Bolton*—continued.

434. Each of those stocks bears a dividend of 5 per cent., I believe ?—That is so.

435. Now will you give me the amount of the preference stock ?—£. 67,210.

436. That also bears 5 per cent ?—Yes.

437. What is the amount of your ordinary stock ?—The ordinary stock issued is 149,572 *l.*

438. At one time this company paid no dividend, I believe ; but of recent years the dividend has been rapidly increasing, has it not ?—The dividend has got up very steadily for some years past.

439. Will you put in the statement which you have before you of the dividends, and also the statement as to the conversion of capital ?--Yes. (*The following statements were handed in.*)

STATEMENT A.

ISLE OF WIGHT RAILWAY.

DIVIDENDS since Opening in 1864.

	On Preference.	On Ordinary.		On Preference.	On Ordinary.
1865 - - -	5 per cent. - -	- nil.	1878 - - -	5 per cent. - -	4½ per cent.
1866 - - -	- nil - - -	- nil.	1879 - - -	5 „ - -	4½ „
1867 - - -	- nil - - -	- nil.	1880 - - -	5 „ - -	4 „
1868 - - -	- nil - - -	- nil.	1881 - - -	5 „ - -	4 „
1869 - - -	- nil - - -	- nil.	1882 - - -	5 „ - -	4¾ „
1870 - - -	- nil - - -	- nil.	1883 - - -	5 „ - -	3½ „
1871 - - -	- nil - - -	- nil.	1884 - - -	5 „ - -	4¾ „
1872 - - -	- nil - - -	- nil.	1885 - - -	5 „ - -	5¼ „
1873 - - -	- nil - - -	- nil.	1886 - - -	5 „ - -	5½ „
1874 - - -	5 per cent. - -	- nil.	1887 - - -	5 „ - -	5½ „
1875 - - -	5 „ - -	3½ per cent.	1888 - - -	5 „ - -	5½ „
1876 - - -	5 „ - -	3½ „	1889 - - -	5 „ - -	6¼ „
1877 - - -	5 „ - -	3½ „			

Average for last 3 years - - - - - - - - 5¾ on Ordinary.
Average since opening *nearly* - - - - - - - 2¾ on Ordinary.

STATEMENT B.

ISLE OF WIGHT RAILWAY.

STATEMENT as to Conversion of CAPITAL.—Session 1890.

CAPITAL ISSUED:		Required for Interest or Dividend.	PROPOSED TO SUBSTITUTE:		Required for Interest or Dividend.
	£.	£. s. d.	£. s. d.		£. s. d.
5 °/ₒ A Debenture Stock - -	68,536	3,426 16 -			
„ B „ „ - -	67,548	3,377 8 -			
„ C „ „ - -	11,916	595 16 -			
	£. 148,000	7,400 - -	185,000 - -	4 °/ₒ Debenture Stock -	7,400 - -
5 °/ₒ Preference - - -	£. 67,210	3,361 - -	84,012 10 -	4 °/ₒ Preference - -	3,361 - -
Ordinary Stock - - - -	149,572	—	149,572 - -	4 °/ₒ Preferred - - -	5,983 - -
Dividend for 1889 - - -	6¼ °/ₒ	9,348 - -	149,572 - -	Deferred 2¼ °/ₒ - -	3,365 - -
	£.	20,109 - -		£.	20,109 - -

The 68,536 *l.* A Debenture Stock has at present a margin of income behind it of - - - - - - - - 16,182 *l.* a year.
„ 67,548 *l.* B Debenture Stock - ditto - ditto - - - - 13,304 *l.* „
„ 11,916 *l.* C Debenture Stock - ditto - ditto - - - - 12,708 *l.* „

The substituted Stock will consist of one First-Charge 4 °/ₒ Debenture Stock of 185,000 *l.*, instead of three small Stocks, and it will have an ample margin of income behind it (about 12,700 *l.* a year).

Mr. *Bolton*—continued.

440. Can you tell me the average dividend for the last three years?—Five and three-quarters per cent.

441. Last year it was 6¼ per cent., I believe? —Yes.

442. Now one of the objects of this Bill is to consolidate your three classes of debenture stock? —Yes.

443. You propose to consolidate them into a 4 per cent. debenture stock?—Into one 4 per cent. debenture stock.

444. What is the object of that?—The object is this : At present we have three classes of debenture, A, B, and C stock. The A comes before the B and the B before the C, but investors do not exactly realise that, and they have to make inquiries about it, and the result is that we do not get as good a price for the debenture stock as we should get, and there is this curious thing that happens: that although the A is in front of the B, and the B is in front of the C, a seller often gets more for his C debenture stock which comes at the bottom, than for the A debenture stock which comes at the top, simply because he is perhaps, more clever in finding a purchaser for it.

445. Do you find that any difficulty arises from the smallness of each class of debenture stock?— We are continually bothered as to not getting a Stock Exchange quotation for the debenture stock, and the reason why we cannot get a Stock Exchange quotation for the debenture stock is that it is not a large enough amount. If it was 100,000 *l.* or over a 100,000 *l.*, we could easily get a quotation, as in the case of the larger railway companies. If we get this power to convert it into this 4 per cent. debenture stock we shall have, as is shown on the right hand side of this return which I have handed in, 185,000 *l.* at 4 per cent., and it will be a readily negotiable trustees' stock.

446. You propose to give each holder of 5 per cent. debenture stock, 125 *l.* for his existing 100 *l.* of debenture stock?—Yes, which will yield him exactly the same dividend as he gets at present. I may say in connection with that, that the total amount required to pay the interest at 4 per cent. on the whole debenture stocks when thus converted, will be 7,400 *l.*; whereas we have a net revenue of over 20,000 *l.*; so that there is ample security. I may add that we have got the consent in writing of more than three-quarters of our debenture-holders to this scheme.

Chairman.

447. Is this debenture stock held in large amounts or small amounts?—It varies. We have something like 120 holders for this stock.

Mr. Bolton.

448. Do you find that 4 per cent. debenture stock is more marketable than 5 per cent.?—Yes, 4 per cent. debenture stock we find is the most desirable form of security.

449. I think you have already said that this proposal has been submitted to your debenture-holders?—Yes.

450. And three-fourths of them have consented?—Yes.

Mr. Buxton.

451. Three-fourths of each class?—Yes, three-fourths of each class. We have more than three-fourths altogether.

Chairman.

452. Have you any reason to believe that the others object?—We have no others strenuously objecting. There are two or three people who do not understand the proposal, and also we have several people who are abroad, and whose consent consequently we cannot get. The amount of income behind it being so large in comparison (of course it is all on a small scale, it is a small thing altogether), there is really no objection.

Mr. Buxton.

453. No one class as against another is objecting?—No. We have had objections, but we have satisfied them.

Mr. Bolton.

454. You have satisfied the people that there is ample margin for all?—Yes.

455. Now let me take you to the second important proposal in the Bill. You propose to convert your ordinary stock by duplicating it, do you not?—Yes.

456. Will you kindly explain to the Committee what your object in making that proposal is?— We propose to exchange each 100 *l.* of ordinary stock into 100 *l.* of 4 per cent. preferred stock and 100 *l.* of deferred stock. According to this Paper which the Committee have before them, on the left hand you will see that the result of that, under the present dividend of 6¼ per cent., would be that the preferred stock would get 4 per cent., and the deferred stock would get 2¼ per cent, but of course also getting any further increase there might be. But by that means we should make a sort of preference stock there, not quite, perhaps, as good as the ordinary preference which we are in the habit of dealing with, but still a preference stock that trustees will take, and which will have a large value. I may also say that we have several large shareholders who have been in this concern for a very long time, who have put it in this way (indeed I may say that this Bill is altogether put upon us by our shareholders) : " We have held this stock for a long time ; we want to make provision for our families, and we prefer to give our daughters a stock that will bear a fixed dividend, and to give our sons stock with a fluctuating dividend which they may keep or sell for what it may be worth."

457. You have fixed the rate of dividend upon the preferred stock at 4 per cent., have you not? —Yes.

458. You consider that the dividend which you have been paying for the last two or three years quite justifies you in fixing that rate?— Yes. Our dividend has gone up very steadily for the last 15 years ; it has risen from 3¼ per cent., as it was in 1875, when we commenced to pay a dividend up to 6¼ per cent., as it is now, and I have reason to believe that our dividend will increase rather than decrease.

459. Are you able to speak to the opinion of your shareholders upon this matter?—Our shareholders were very unanimous about this at the special

Mr. *Bolton*—continued.

special meeting. The Bill was carried by the whole meeting with the exception of one shareholder, and he was a little bit doubtful as to his preference stock (he was not as to his ordinary stock), and he was afterwards convinced. Besides that we have, as it happens, written consents from a large number of shareholders who did not attend the meeting.

460. Was there a large amount of stock represented at the meeting?—More than two-thirds of the whole capital of the company.

461. I think you propose to make this conversion compulsory?—Yes.

462. In your opinion is that an essential part of a conversion scheme?—With a company so small as ours unless it was carried out completely we should never know where we were with our stock.

463. Of course, as you say you have no reason to believe that any of your shareholders object; but still, I suppose, you might have had one or two holding out, or you might have one or two who were ignorant of the conversion scheme?—Except two or three shareholders abroad, who have not really considered this scheme, I do not think there are any who are not very much pleased with it.

464. You also propose, I think, to convert your 5 per cent. preference shares into 4 per cent., giving each of the shareholders 125 *l.* for every 100 *l.* nominal capital?—That is so.

465. I do not think there is any clause in the original Bill carrying that out?—That is dealt with in a clause we have put in to satisfy some of our shareholders.

466. Would your object for that be the same as for the reduction of interest in the case of the debenture shareholders, namely, that you find a 4 per cent. security more marketable than a 5 per cent.?—Yes; the desire is now to make this entirely into a 4 per cent. stock; 4 per cent. debenture stock, 4 per cent. preference stock, and 4 per cent. preferred stock.

467. I think there is only one other clause to which I need call attention, and that is Clause 15, in which there is an option proposed to be given of converting their preference stock into preferred ordinary stock?—Yes; some of our shareholders think that it would be a great advantage to the company if, instead of having the preference stock and preferred ordinary stock and deferred ordinary stock, we could get rid of the preference stock or preferred stock, so that we should only have one preference stock, and it has been agreed with those shareholders that we should endeavour to get the option inserted in the Bill; at least there is the option there; but I do not think it is fully carried out in the printed Bill. Each individual shareholder is to have the option of exchanging his 100 *l.* of 5 per cent. preference stock into 125 *l.* of 4 per cent. preferred, with a bonus of some 10 per cent. of deferred stock for doing it.

468. That clause was submitted with the rest of the Bill to your shareholders, was it not?—No; that is a matter of arrangement since.

469. But it was submitted to your shareholders, was it not?—Yes, it was submitted.

0.101.

Mr. *Bolton*—continued.

470. And your shareholders approve of the preference shareholders having that option?—Yes.

Chairman.

471. The clause in the Bill does not express what you say, does it?—There is a written clause with regard to it, which I will hand in (*handing in the same*).

Mr. *Bolton.*] I have the limitation which is proposed to be inserted in the clause, in writing here; I will read it: " The company may from time to time issue to any holder of 4 per cent. preference stock; in the capital of the company, created under the authority of this Act, such amounts of preferred ordinary stock and deferred ordinary stock as may be agreed upon with such holder in exchange for the preference stock so held by him, but not exceeding 10 *l.* of such deferred ordinary stock for each 100 *l.* of ordinary stock." The limitation you will observe is 10 *l.*

Chairman.

472. In that case you would not have an equal quantity of preferred and deferred stock?—In that case as regards so much of this 67,000 *l.* preference as was converted into preferred, we should have so much more preferred than deferred.

473. Do you attach much importance to this clause?—I do not attach very much importance it. It is put in at the wish of a section of our shareholders. I do not myself think that so many of them will convert that it will really very much matter. Of course the main principle of the Bill is the consolidation of the debenture stock, and the division of ordinary stock into preferred and deferred, and making the 5 per cent. preference into 4 per cent.

474. That would have the effect of simplifying your stock?—Yes.

475. But this latter proposal would rather have the opposite effect, would it not?—Some of our shareholders are sanguine that everybody would, with the small bonus that we propose to give, take these preferred shares.

Mr. *Biddulph.*

476. Will you tell me where that 10 per cent. is to come from; is it to be created?—Yes; a further clause in the Bill says that.

Mr. *Bristowe.*

477. This is not in the Bill before us, I understand. We can hardly be asked to discuss a thing that is not in the Bill?—In all these Bills that you have before you, I think you will have to do something of the kind. For instance, in the case of the Great Northern, it is an entirely new Bill in some respects. We shall put in clauses to do this.

Mr. *Buxton.*

478. Do you see any objection, if this conversion were carried through, that it should be on the lines of giving to the preference stockholders

E   an

15 *May* 1890.]   MR. TAHOURDIN.   [*Continued.*

Mr. *Buxton*—continued.

an equal amount of preferred and deferred stock?
—There would be every objection to that,
because the preference shareholder is now fixed
at 5 per cent.

479. I mean to his taking the same proportionate amount of preferred and deferred instead
of giving him more deferred than preferred?—If
you mean an equality between each preference
shareholder, certainly.

480. I mean if a preference shareholder
desires to convert 100 *l.* of his preference stock
into ordinary preferred or deferred stock,
he should take the same amount of preferred
stock in exchange; I understand you propose to
give him a larger amount of deferred than of
preferred?—No. He is getting 5 per cent. just
now, and we propose to give him an option of
having, in exchange for that, 125 *l.* of preferred
stock, and giving not more than 10 per cent. of
deferred stock for his 100 *l.*

481. In fact, you create more preferred stock
than deferred?—In that case.

Mr. *Ellis.*

482. Do you propose to create something to
which you applied the word "bonus" outside
these figures in this statement which you have
put in?—Yes.

483. Then that alters these figures?—To a
trifling extent. There is a clause in the filled up
Bill which empowers us to raise the capital
necessary for the exercise of the option.

484. I wish to get this clearly on the Notes
that we may have it correctly before us. Is there
something in your proposition that is outside
these figures?—Yes.

Mr. *Beckett.*

485. That is to say if your proposition is
carried out at all, it will alter these figures
which you have given us?—To a very trifling
extent.

Mr. *Bolton.*

486. That is only to be done by arrangement with your shareholders?—Only by arrangement; but we want power to do that.

Mr. *Bristowe.*

487. Do you consider there is any importance
whatever in having exactly the same amount of
preferred and deferred stock?—No importance
whatever.

Mr. *Buxton.*

488. Under the proposal you make, if the
whole preference stock, which amounts to 67,000 *l.*
were converted, it would create a normal amount
of 84,000 *l.* preference?—Exactly; the figure
that is opposite to it, namely 84,012 *l.* 10 *s.*

Chairman.

489. There would also be what you call the
onus of the deferred stock?—There would be a
bonus of 10 per cent. on the 67,000 *l.*

Mr. *R. Mowbray.*

490. Do I understand the conversion from
5 to 4 per cent. to be compulsory under the Bill?
—Yes.

Mr. *R. Mowbray*—continued.

491. Do I understand that for every 100 *l.* of
this preference stock converted into the 4 per
cent., you are going to offer 125 *l.* of preferred
and 10 *l.* of deferred?—No; we only offer at the
rate of 125 *l.* for the old 5 per cent stock.

Mr. *Bristowe.*

492. After that, as I understand, this 84,012 *l.*
10 *s.* preference, if you carry out the conversion,
will create 84,000 *l.* preferred and 84,000 *l.* deferred stock, plus 10 per cent.?—No; it will
create 84,000 *l.* of preferred stock, and 6,720 *l.* of
deferred stock; that is the 10 per cent. bonus.
Then beyond that we shall have 149,572 *l.* of
preferred ordinary stock, and 149,572 *l.* of deferred ordinary stock in exchange for the original
149,572 *l.* of ordinary stock.

Chairman.

493. We have it from you that this has been
suggested by some of your shareholders, but the
company do not attach much importance to it?—
We do not attach very much importance to it;
it is rather done to suit a few people's views.
We thought putting it in as an option clause it
would not hurt anybody. The substance of the
Bill is not affected by it.

494. If any people were very anxious to be
holders of preferred stock and deferred stock
they might go out at one door and come in at the
other instead of passing through the wall; that
is, they may sell their preference stock and buy
preferred stock and deferred stock?—It is not
exactly that either; because a good many shareholders hold all classes, and it is these people
who do hold all classes who think we ought to
have only one preference; they think this will
be a very neat little scheme with 4 per cent.
debenture stock, 4 per cent. preferred and 4 per
cent. deferred only.

Chairman (to Mr. *Bolton*).] Have you
any other point to put to the witness?—

Mr. *Bolton.*] No, Sir.

Mr. *Charles Hall.*

495. As regards the third sub clause of the
twelfth clause, it is your intention that the
directors shall have the same qualification as they
had before?—Yes.

496. That is not expressed in that clause, is
it?—It is not in the Bill at all as printed. Our
agents have considered there was no necessity
to put anything in, as we did not propose to
change the qualification. The stock for which
the 250 *l.* qualification would be exchanged,
would be the qualification. But I may say that
we are quite willing to put that into the Bill or
to make any increase in the qualification, if the
Committee wish it.

Chairman.

497. I think that ought to be expressed in the
Bill?—It will be.

Mr. *Pope.*

498. It should be, Sir; otherwise it will remain that the preferred and deferred stocks will
be equal qualification, and therefore it should be
expressed

Mr. *Pope*—continued.

expressed in the Bill. (To the *Witness*.) There are one or two questions which I ought to ask you, just as a matter of form. You know Sections 4 and 8 of the Bill with regard to the acquisition of land for stations and the extension of time for selling surplus land?—Yes.

499. Those are, in your judgment, important for the company, and nobody opposes them?—Nobody opposes them; and we find that we shall make use of more and more of this land.

Chairman.

500. Turning to Sub-section 3 of Clause 12, it provides that the number of votes shall be practically doubled; does that affect the interests of the preference shareholders?—It does not affect anybody's interests. As this is placed at present it confers the same proportion of votes as before.

501. Not in comparison with the preference shareholders, does it?—But our preference shareholders have no vote, except a special vote at the Wharncliffe meeting.

502. But for that purpose according to this the holders of what is now ordinary stock will have their votes doubled?—Yes; the clause is drawn in that way; I think that is the true reading of the clause; but whether you make it double or half it makes no difference to the proportion. Supposing you have 100 *l.* stock just now for which you will get 100 *l.* preferred and 100 *l.* deferred, if the 100 *l.* carries the same voting in the new Bill as now, it simply means that it doubles the number of votes, but it is in respect of the same parent bit of stock.

503. In the other Bills before us it was otherwise arranged; it was halved really?—We have no objection to its being halved. The result is exactly the same whether you leave it as it is or make it one half.

Mr. *Buxton.*] Surely the result is not exactly the same when it comes to the question of the voting with the holders of preference stock.

Mr. *Bolton.*] At a Wharncliffe meeting they do not vote per head, but they weigh the amount of stock on each side.

Mr. *Mowbray.*

504. £. 100 of preferred stock or deferred stock is said to be equal to a like amount of ordinary capital?—It would only affect this Bill in the case of the option being granted and exercised as regards this 67,000 *l.* of preference stock. If it was converted into preferred stock it would then get the vote of preferred stock. It has no vote as it stands at present.

Mr. *Buxton.*

505. Would it not have a vote at the Wharncliffe meeting?—Yes, it has at the Wharncliffe meeting.

506. Why should the ordinary shareholders have their voting power doubled at Wharncliffe meetings as against preference shareholders?—I think I can put it right about the voting if you will allow me to explain.

Mr. *Pope.*] Mr. Beale will explain what is the process of voting at the Wharncliffe meeting. It is not by votes in the sense of putting the two classes of shareholders together; they vote separately, and their respective holdings dictate always the weight of votes.

Mr. *Beale.*] At the Wharncliffe meeting, the different classes of votes are reckoned separately; you have to have the statutory proportion in each class of stock if that class of stock is affected. In a case which does not affect the interests of all the classes, the examiner, as I understand the practice, would not take into account an adverse vote on the part of the preference shareholders, if their interests were not affected.

Mr. *Ellis.*] Therefore you might double the votes in one class without affecting the other class of shareholders?

Mr. *Beale.*] Quite so.

Mr. *Pope.*] That is all I have to submit with regard to the Isle of Wight Railway.

Witness.] I will hand in now, Sir, the amended Bill with the particulars in it (*handing in the same*).

Chairman.] I understand, Mr. Pope, you have nothing more to offer us.

Mr. *Pope.*] I have nothing more to say, Sir.

Chairman.] Then I think we have completed all the railway evidence upon these Bills.

Mr. *Pope.*] Yes, Sir.

The Counsel and Parties were directed to withdraw.

Tuesday, 20th May 1890.

Mr. W. Beckett.　　　　　　　　　　Mr. Dickson.
Mr. Biddulph.　　　　　　　　　　　Mr. Ellis.
Mr. Bristowe.　　　　　　　　　　　Mr. Charles Hall.
Mr. Buxton.　　　　　　　　　　　　Mr. R. Mowbray.
Mr. Campbell-Bannerman.

THE RIGHT HON. H. CAMPBELL-BANNERMAN, IN THE CHAIR.

Chairman.] I BELIEVE the Witness, who was examined on the Isle of Wight Bill, wishes to correct some part of his evidence, and it is thought desirable he should do so.

Mr. HORACE F. TAHOURDIN, re-called.

507. *Chairman.*] YOU were asked this question (494): "If any people were very anxious to be holders of preferred stock and deferred stock they might go out at one door and come in at the other, instead of passing through the wall; that is, they may sell their preference stock and buy preferred stock and deferred stock?" This was your answer: "It is not exactly that either; because a good many shareholders hold all classes, and it is those people who do hold all classes who think we ought to have only one preference ; they think this will be a very neat little scheme, with 4 per cent. debenture stock and 4 per cent. deferred only." I understand you wish to insert the words "4 per cent. preferred" before the "and 4 per cent. deferred"?—To make it read sense, that is necessary. It is evidently a slip.

The Witness withdrew.

Chairman.] I think it is understood that those witnesses, whom we propose to hear to-day, are not witnesses either on the part of any particular railway scheme or against it. They are general witnesses, and they will not be subject before a Committee of this sort to examination by counsel.

Mr. *Pember.*] Oh, no.

Chairman] At the same time, if any counsel is so interested in the subject that he wishes to be present, and any question occurs, as a desirable question to be put for elucidating or supplementing the information the Committee desire, then the Committee will be willing to receive any suggestion of that sort.

Mr. *Pope.*] The general practice in such cases has been, as you say, that the witness is examined by the Committee; but if any counsel behind the bar suggests a question, by leave of the Committee, he is generally allowed to put it in the shape of cross-examination.

Chairman.] Quite so.

Mr. *Biddulph.*] Are counsel allowed to address us afterwards?

Chairman.] No.

Mr. *Pember.*] Would you not allow us, Sir, in the event of its being thought necessary by us, just to sum up in a few words any point that occurs to our mind as worth elucidation, and worth statement. Perhaps you would kindly think of it, Sir.

Chairman.] I do not know whether that is usual. We wish to follow the usual practice. In my experience, and I have been several times on a hybrid Committee, I do not think that has been done.

Mr. *Pember.*] I will tell you what happened though last year or the year before, I forget which now, but I think probably last year : There was an inquiry which was known as the Hyderabad (Decan) Inquiry in which there was a Committee of this kind ; there was a great debate as to whether counsel should be heard at all there ; and finally they were to be allowed to be heard to
put

put questions in the same sort of way that you suggest, Sir ; and then we were allowed within certain limits to address ourselves to the evidence called, although all the evidence was called by the Committee.

Chairman.] Yes ; but I am not quite sure that that was a parallel case. That was a case of a semi-judicial inquiry by the House of Commons which was entrusted to a Committee. This is a case of certain Railway Bills, and learned counsel appear on behalf of those railways.

Mr. *Pember.*] Yes.

Chairman.] We have received all the evidence we wish to take on behalf of the railways, and we now proceed to take evidence on the general question from the more general point of view, as to the general policy which Parliament ought to pursue with regard to the whole question. That is the subject on which we are taking evidence to-day rather than any other.

Mr. *Pope.*] Perhaps, Sir, the better course would be to reserve any decision until the necessity arises.

Chairman.] Yes.

Mr. *Pope.*] It might be that something might occur in the evidence which the Committee might desire that the railway companies should have the opportunity of submitting further information upon either by way of evidence or argument.

Chairman.] Certainly.

Mr. *Pember.*] There is one point that occurs to me as an illustration ; perhaps you will allow me to mention it : for instance, that in the general evidence you should touch upon a by no means unimportant question ; as to whether this should be done by a Private Bill, as affecting the different cases, or whether it should be done by one Act affecting them all, so as to secure uniformity. I think certainly it would not be unimportant to us if you allowed us to emphasise (I speak for myself, when I say "us," by-the-bye) the difficulty there would be in providing uniform legislation for companies whose conditions vary so very much.

Mr. *Pope.*] I am afraid that would introduce discussion between the companies ; from my view it would be easy enough.

Chairman.] I think, perhaps, the Committee had better adopt Mr. Pope's suggestion ; because, if we were to consult over the matter, it would necessitate clearing the room, which would be an inconvenience to everybody.

Mr. *Pember.*] Quite so.

Chairman.] Therefore, perhaps, we had better reserve our decision upon that point.

Mr. *Pember.*] I think you kindly said you would think over it ; that is what I meant.

Chairman.] I was only anxious in what I said to maintain what I believe to be the precedents and the practical authority.

Mr. *Pember.*] Quite so.

Mr. ROBERT GIFFEN, called in ; and Examined:

Chairman.

508. WILL you state to the Committee the official position that you hold ?—I am one of the Assistant Secretaries of the Board of Trade, having charge of the Commercial Department of the Board of Trade, and in that capacity, although I have not charge of the railway matters of the Board of Trade, yet certain statistics under the Regulation of Railways Act come before my department ; so that I am, to some extent, acquainted with those matters.

509. Will you tell the Committee what has been the general policy of the Board of Trade in regard to the financial arrangements of railway companies ?—I may say that the general policy has rather been to favour the utmost liberty to public companies to arrange their capital in any way they please, as it is considered that, on the whole, the public interest will be best promoted by permitting this liberty.

Chairman—continued.

510. In 1868, the question of what is ordinarily called " splitting stocks " came up, did not it ?— That is so. In 1868 it came up, and at that time a clause was introduced into the Regulation of Railways Act of that year allowing the division into preferred and deferred ordinary. That clause was not in the original draft of the Bill ; but it was inserted in the course of the passage of the Bill through Parliament on a proposal by Mr. Cave, who was then Vice-President of the Board of Trade ; and the clause, according to the records in the Board of Trade, was taken from a similar clause in the South Coast Companies' Bills of that year, which had been prepared by Sir Francis Reilly.

511. He was then the Government draftsman, was he not ?—He was then one of the Government draftsmen, I think ; and although there was no debate on the clause in the Regulation of

Chairman—continued.

of Railways Bills itself, yet there was a debate in the House of Lords on the similar clause of the South Coast Companies' Bills on 21st July 1868, and you will find the debate in "Hansard," vol. 193, page 1545 that is one of the volumes for 1868.

512. That was the same year in which the Railways Regulation Act was passed?—The same year, and the clause in the Regulation of Railways Act was taken from the clause in these companies' bills, and is substantially the same clause. I could not say whether they are quite verbally the same or not, but they are substantially the same.

513. Can you say what view was taken in the course of that discussion in the House of Lords? —Yes; Lord Redesdale very warmly opposed the division into preferred and deferred as being in the interest of stockjobbing; but the Duke of Richmond, who was then President of the Board of Trade, supported the clause on the general grounds stated; and if the Committee would like I would propose to read what the Duke of Richmond said as representing the Board of Trade and the Government upon that occasion.

514. Yes, please do?— He said, "he had listened attentively to his noble friend, but the only reason he had heard advanced for objecting to the clauses was because, as he elegantly termed it, they were brought forward for stock-jobbing purposes. He could not agree with him in his view of the question. He thought the tendency of Parliament of late years had been not to interfere with the financial arrangements of these companies; providing, of course, that Parliament saw that no injustice was done to mortgagees, or other parties who might be injuriously affected by legislation. For that purpose the Joint-Stock Companies Act was amended last Session; and he also had the honour of conducting through that House the Railway Companies Act, by which certain restrictions were put upon the issue of shares at a discount and the limitation of the interest on debenture stock." I think that does not quite express the meaning. I think that it is a mis-report to some extent; because the point was that certain restrictions were removed in 1867. "Moreover, the course proposed by his noble friend was entirely opposed to the recommendations of the Railway Commission, which went very fully and carefully into the question, and gave it as their opinion that it was the more judicious course for Parliament to relieve itself from interference in the financial affairs of railway companies; that it should limit itself to the questions of the construction of the lines, the relations between the public and the companies, and the requiring from them of guarantees for the due performance of the conditions on the faith of which their powers were granted. The clause to which the noble Lord objected referred only to the shareholders themselves, who need not come into the proposed arrangement unless they pleased. Instead of proving injurious to the proper management of the company. he believed the proposed subdivision of the capital would tend to give all the parties concerned an additional interest in seeing that the directors did their duty, and in putting the undertaking into a better state. On these

Chairman—continued.

grounds, he hoped their Lordships would acquiesce in the Commons' Amendment." Lord Salisbury and Lord Chancellor Cairns took part in the debate, and supported the Duke of Richmond, and opposed Lord Redesdale on similar grounds.

515. Was there much public interest in the question at the time, do you know?—I am quite able to say that there was a good deal of public interest at the time. At that time I was connected with the "Economist," assisting Mr. Bagehot, whose name is well known, who took a good deal of interest in the subject himself, and I daresay was acquainted with what was going on at the Board of Trade. In the "Economist" of 22nd August 1868 there was an article warmly approving the division into preferred and deferred, which I happen to know expressed Mr. Bagehot's views.

516. Did this article and this general expression of opinion (the formation of opinion of which you speak) refer to stock splitting or to stock duplication?—Stock splitting.

517. Only?—There was no question of stock duplication with reference to that question of preferred and deferred at the time. I can state the effect of that article, if so desired; but I think the reference might almost be sufficient. The effect of it was, and the point to which it was addressed was, whether the public interest would not be affected by the creation of large classes of preferred stock, where the people would have the voting power, but would not have so much interest in the management of the company; but, on the whole, the opinion was expressed in favour of the division. That was the danger which was apprehended then.

518. Was there any movement at that time in the direction of the duplication of stocks?—There was no movement at that time in favour of the duplication of stocks; but you would notice in that passage which I quoted from the Duke of Richmond that he referred to certain measures which had been passed in 1867; and one of those measures to which he referred was a provision repealing a proviso in the Companies Clauses Act of 1863, which prohibited the issue of shares at a discount; and in the Act of 1867 (30 & 31 Vict. c. 127, s. 27) there is a clause directing that the clause in the Companies' Clauses Act of 1863 should be read as if that provision which prohibited the issue of shares at a discount had been omitted; and it is considered that by that amendment the issue of shares at a discount was allowed. Then this repeal of the proviso about issuing shares at a discount, which was applied by this Act of 1867 to railway companies, was applied generally to all the companies dealt with by the Companies' Clauses Act, by means of the Companies' Clauses Amendment Act of 1869, 32 & 33 Vict. c. 48, s. 6. Then I may say that I find no debate upon the issue of shares at a discount upon these public Bills. But the question as regards Railway Companies was debated in 1867 (July 12) in the House of Lords on a proposal in a Brighton Railway Bill to permit the issue of shares at a discount, to which Lord Redesdale, who was opposed, called the special attention of the House; but the general feeling was against him.

Chairman—continued.

him. One of the proposals at that time to get railways out of the mess in which they were, was to issue pre-preference stock which had been sanctioned; and it was considered preferable also to permit the issue of shares at a discount. That was thought to be the least injurious way in which the companies could take means to get themselves out of their difficulties. The reference to "Hansard" is volume 188, page 1422. I may say that in point of fact, there have been from time to time issues of railway shares at a discount, not upon a large scale, but still there have been some issues; and I may mention that in the accounts of the companies as at the 31st December 1889, and in previous accounts, it appears that the Great Eastern mentions discounts to the extent of 1,147,000 l.; the London, Brighton, and South Coast 127,000 l.; the London, Chatham, and Dover (I am afraid you will not find this in the accounts for 1889; but if you go back you will find it explicitly shown in the accounts for 1878) acknowledge discounts to the extent of 1,112,000 l.; the Manchester, Sheffield, and Lincolnshire 647,000 l.; the Metropolitan District 549,000 l. This is not a completed list, but these are cases which have come before us in dealing with the capital of those companies where railway shares have been issued at a discount.

519. What bearing do you regard that fact as having upon the question we are dealing with?—That to some extent the issue of shares at a discount is of the same nature as a duplication of stock.

Mr. *Ellis.*

520. Can you say how far that statement goes back. Have you looked right back?—These are discounts that appear in the accounts of the companies for the most part in 1889; but it may be taken to go back almost 20 years. It is not a large amount.

Chairman.

521. That is to say, that the issue of shares at a discount that is thus affected is not the actual amount; in other words, that the nominal capital does not represent actual capital employed?— Actual capital paid up; that is so. I may say, however, that although it was apparently the intention of the Legislature at that time by these general Acts to sanction the issue of shares at a discount, I am informed that it is not quite certain whether that really was effectually carried out, though no question has arisen upon it; but I am informed legally at the Board of Trade that there might be some question as to whether what was intended was effectually carried out. Then I think that, in the Companies' Clauses Act of 1863, a proviso of a similar nature is for the issue of shares at a premium; but the premiums to be received by the shareholders, and not to go into the accounts of the company. That is, 26 and 27 Victoria, chapter 118, section 17; and then another instance of the great liberty given to railway companies in arranging their capital is in the 32nd and 33rd Victoria, chapter 48, section 1, where all restrictions on the rate 0.101.

Chairman—continued.

of interest of debenture stock are removed, and the companies are allowed to give what rate of interest they please.

522. So that the whole tendency and policy of the Government, and of Parliament, so far as it has been continuous and consistent, has been towards freedom in arranging capital?—At that time; and reference was made by the Duke of Richmond, I think, to the Duke of Devonshire's Commission in 1867, the Royal Commission which reported in that year, as sanctioning that principle; and I would propose to read what the recommendation of that Commission was upon which a great deal of that action that I have referred to in 1867 and 1868 was taken. What they say is, "We recommend that Parliament should relieve itself from all interference with the incorporation and financial affairs of railway companies, leaving such matters to be dealt with under the Joint Stock Companies Act, and should limit its own action to regulating the construction of the line and the relations between the public and joint stock companies so incorporated, requiring such guarantees as may be necessary for the purpose of securing the due performance of the conditions upon the faith of which the Parliamentary powers of the company have been granted."

523. Is there not a Standing Order, however, which goes in the other direction, prohibiting an increase of capital when an amalgamation takes place?—That is so; that is Number 165 of the Standing Orders of the House of Commons; and I think there is a similar Standing Order of the House of Lords to the effect that, "In Bills for the amalgamation of railway companies, the amount of capital created by such amalgamation shall in no case exceed the sum of the capitals of the companies so amalgamated;" but the general policy has been what I have stated.

524. And has that Standing Order been enforced in all cases do you know?—I could not say whether it has been enforced in all cases; but what I have to draw attention to next is the case of the increase of the nominal amount of the stock of railway companies taking place at different times.

525. Has taken place?—Has taken place at different times in connection with, and to facilitate, amalgamations and consolidations of different stocks.

526. Of the same company?—Of the same company; I think the Clause in the Standing Orders refers to an amalgamation of two companies, a railway amalgamation; but what I have to draw attention to is the case of the increase of nominal stock to facilitate amalgamations and consolidations of different stocks of the same company. The first which I wish to mention is that of the London and North Western Company in 1878, when there was a nominal addition to the capital of 8,545,000 l.; the Lancashire and Yorkshire in 1879 in this way made a nominal addition to its capital of 1,703,000 l.; the Glasgow and South Western in 1881 made a nominal addition of 988,000 l.; the Caledonian also in 1881 made a nominal addition of 800,000 l.; the Metropolitan also in 1881 made a nominal

Chairman—continued.

addition of 400,000 *l.*; the London and South Western in 1881 made a nominal addition of 1,096,000 *l.*; the Furness in 1881 made a nominal addition of 478,000 *l.*; the Great North of Scotland made a nominal addition in 1882 of 704,000 *l*, having in 1879 made a similar addition of 336,000 *l.* The City of Glasgow Union in 1882 made a nominal addition of 300,000 *l.* Then in 1888 you have the case of the North British, which at that time made a nominal addition of 5,181,000 *l.*

527. That was a case of absolute duplication, was it not?—To that extent it was a case of duplication. There was an arrangement of preferred and deferred as well; but that was the extent of the duplication in that year.

Mr. *Bristowe.*

528. It was mixed up, was it not, with an amalgamation between it and another company; the Edinburgh and Glasgow, I think?—I think the amalgamation of the North British and the Edinburgh and Glasgow had taken place long before.

Mr. *Pember.*] That was 1865.

Mr. *Pope.*] The honourable Member is quite right. There was a financial question which arose in that Bill of the North British which did complicate that arrangement.

Witness.] I may say that in 1876 the North British had made a similar nominal addition to its capital of 2,386,000 *l.* In 1888 the Great Northern made a nominal addition to its capital of 1,803,000 *l.*; and last of all we have the Taff Vale, which made a nominal addition to its capital of 2,827,000 *l.* in 1889.

Chairman.

529. In most of the cases you have quoted, I gather that the addition was comparatively small; that is to say, it was small comparatively to the capital of the company?—That is so. The infusion of the new stock in proportion to the whole stock of the company was a comparatively small percentage.

530. Except in the case of the North British?—Except in the case of the North British; there the infusion was, at least, a very large infusion in proportion to the particular stocks dealt with; and in the Taff Vale case I think we may say it was very large in reference to the whole capital of the company; but these were the new departures that took place in 1888 and 1889.

531. Now coming to this Taff Vale, which is the most recent case; can you state what the view of the Board of Trade was in dealing with that Bill, and what was done with regard to it?—I may say that the matter was brought somewhat informally to the notice of the Board of Trade, because this question of dealing with capital in Railway Bills is not one of the subjects upon which it is the duty of the Board of Trade to examine the Bills, and make Reports to the Referees or whoever has charge of the matter; but still the matter was brought to the notice of

the Board of Trade in informal communications of different kinds; and the view which the Board of Trade took was, that while adhering generally to their opinion in favour of freedom in these matters, they thought the proposal of such extensive increase of nominal capital as was made by the Taff Vale Bill to be a new departure so important, that it ought not to be passed *sub silentio*; that is to say, while hitherto you had had nominal additions to capital under circumstances where probably the thing was done as incidental to other arrangements, and where it was not a large per-centage of the original paid-up capital, you would come to something quite different, in degree, at least, when you came to these nominal additions which were proposed in the Taff Vale Bill; therefore the Board of Trade thought that that was a matter so important that it should be dealt with rather in a public manner, and should not be allowed to pass as a matter of course, notwithstanding their general opinion that the greatest freedom should be permitted to companies to arrange their capital as they pleased. They thought that a sufficient case ought to be made out publicly for extending the liberty given by the provisions of the Act of 1868. In the communications which passed, the Taff Vale Company cited the North British Act of the previous year, which they seemed to have followed; but I may say that that North British Act of 1868 (which was the first on a large scale authorising something like duplication) had not been before the Board of Trade. We were not aware of it or of what was done under it, until long after that Act was passed. Eventually the matter in connection with the Taff Vale Bill was disposed of by the Chairman of Committees, who gave the Taff Vale large powers of duplication (more than had been given to the North British), subject to a provision that surplus profits above 15 per cent. on the old ordinary capital, or 6 per cent. on the new enlarged capital should be given to the public.

532. In the shape of reduced rates?—In the shape of reduced rates, or in any other way that Parliament might determine. It was further decided that the facts should also be shown in the published accounts of the company, that is to say, what the nature of the increase of nominal capital was, and that the old ordinary capital should also be shown.

533. That the ordinary capital should be put in front of the accounts of the company, so that every one should understand?—That was the general idea of the clause that was put in.

534. The Taff Vale Railway is a railway with some peculiarities about it, is it not; I mean 15 per cent. is a peculiarity to begin with?—The dividend is large, as you say, which is a peculiarity. Then in addition to what was done with the ordinary capital by that Bill, there was a clause in the Bill of the nature of an amalgamation and consolidation of other stocks as well as the ordinary stock (which made some excuse for something being done); but I may say that the nature of the powers asked for originally by the Taff Vale Bill was very extensive; and if the Committee have it before them, it might be convenient

Chairman—continued.

convenient to see how the matter was brought to our notice, and what was the thing that was really asked for.

535. I scarcely think it necessary to go into that. I understand from you that the course pursued with regard to the Taff Vale Bill was not suggested by the Board of Trade, but originated in the House of Commons?—It is difficult to say how it was suggested, because the whole communication between the Chairman of Committees and the Board of Trade was quite informal.

536. They were cognisant of it?—Yes, they were cognisant of it.

537. Then since that, what have you heard on this subject?—Since that the matter came informally before the Board of Trade (I believe in the recess of last year) in connection with proposals from the Caledonian Railway Company, proposals, I believe, of something of the same nature as those that you have before you now; and the Board of Trade, after the experience of the previous year, when it was found difficult to resist altogether these proposals of duplication, which were strictly within the principle of the general policy of freedom in such matters, took the view that if this freedom were to be at all generally conceded, it was most important that they should retain a record, for public purposes, of the actually paid up, as distinguished from nominal capital. They suggested that this should be done in the Bills, or by a general Bill as far as the accounts prescribed by the Regulation of Railways Act, 1868, are concerned, and the Board of Trade also propose under the General Powers conferred by the Railway Act of 1888, to obtain and record the same information in the annual returns under the Regulation of Railways Act of 1871; that is to say, the Act of 1888 gives the Board of Trade, by Clause 32, a general power of obtaining statistical information, and the Board of Trade, under that general power, propose in those returns, which are laid before Parliament, to have information of that kind, so as to show the public what the paid-up, as distinguished from the nominal capital is, if these duplications of stock should ultimately be sanctioned.

538. So that the effect of this would be, as you say, that the paid-up capital would always also be recorded, while the railway shareholders might have any units for their capital, for the purpose of buying and selling, that suited them best?—That is the idea; that it is important for public purposes that we should have a good record, whatever may be sanctioned for the companies themselves; and, I may say, that it is impossible to foresee all the occasions on which such a record might be useful; but we consider that it is within the clear right of the Government to have it. It might obviously prove important if such a question as the actual dividend paid arose upon the question of reducing fares and rates; or if schemes of purchase, which were once so common, should again come up. *Primâ facie*, it is important in the public interest, that a record of paid-up, as distinguished from nominal capital, should be maintained.

539. Yes, there are those two distinct objections, apart from others that might be thought

0.101.

Chairman—continued.

of; firstly, that there might be a question of reducing fares and rates; and, secondly, that Parliament, in its wisdom, might nibble at the idea of purchasing?—Some arrangement of that kind might arise; so that you really would like to have the information as to what the paid-up capital is as distinguished from these merely nominal figures.

540. Beyond this you tell us that the general policy and idea of the Board of Trade is that they should interfere as little as possible with the liberty of the companies, either to duplicate or to increase their nominal capital?—That is so; but subject to this: that we consider the present matter one of novel impression, a new case, and we think that it ought to be fully debated, and the public interest, or necessity for it, on the part of the railway shareholders shown, and that the whole matter should be discussed;· but we do not see any immediate necessity or urgent necessity for preventing that if a case can be shown for it.

541. As to the question of the alleged danger of stock-jobbing and other possible mischiefs to investors generally, or to shareholders in particular, you think that those matters are, if possible, best left to the shareholders themselves?—That is so; that we express no opinion upon that, as far as the public interest is concerned, that if there is no insuperable objection otherwise, they ought to be left to the shareholders.

542. The opinion of the Board of Trade, in fact, is rather a negative opinion?—Yes; it is one of suspense. We wish to see the matter debated and to have the whole thing brought out, subject, of course, to this, that we give you the information as to what the past history and the past view has been.

543. But you do not see any such objections likely to arise as would call for legislative restrictions of a strong kind upon the free action of shareholders, such as has been hitherto allowed?—Not at present, not so far as the thing has come before us; but this, of course, is subject to what you may find out in your own inquiry.

534. I think you have some point upon which you as *amicus curiæ* you would like to say something as to the special causes of fluctuation in deferred stock?—Yes. A good deal has been said in the public press and elsewhere about the importance of increasing the nominal capital so as to have stocks under par and things of that kind, rather than have them heavy stocks and so on; but the point I should wish to put with reference to the creation of deferred stocks is this, that the essential thing to keep in mind is always what the proportion of the net income given to the deferred stock bears to the total net income of the company. For instance, if a company has a million of net income, and out of that it pays half of it to the ordinary capital, then if you divide the ordinary capital equally into preferred and deferred, the deferred would receive 25 per cent. of the net income, and that of itself is a larger margin than some of the ordinary capitals of some of the railway companies now have. I do not like to mention names, but there is the case of a large company,

F   which

Chairman—continued.

which is before me at this moment where the amount of the net income paid to the ordinary shareholder is 50 per cent. of the whole amount that is paid in the shape of interest and preferance charges and profit to the ordinary shareholder ; that is to say, that the ordinary shareholder gets half. If you were to divide that income into equal parts, giving the first half to the preferred, and the other half to the deferred, the deferred would have 25 per cent. of the net income ; and there are other companies, I think (two or three of the leading railway companies) at this moment, where the ordinary shareholder get as little as 15 per cent.

545. The rest being all preferential of one kind or another ?—Yes, or preferential as far as that ordinary stock is concerned ; so that the deferred stock of the company that I have in my mind, if it should be created in the way I suppose, would be less subject to fluctuation than what you call the ordinary stock of another company which we might have in our mind. The important point with reference to fluctuation is the proportion of the total income which is given to the deferred shareholder.

546. To the deferred shareholder ?—Yes ; if that proportion is small the fluctuation on the deferred stock will be very great ; but if it is as large as something like 25 per cent. it may be no greater than the fluctuation upon the ordinary capital of other companies ; and that is the main point which causes fluctuation in deferred stocks. That is the main cause of fluctuation however you may arrange the nominal capital.

547. As I understand it, I take it to mean this, that in order to secure something like stability there ought to be beyond the new preferred stock a very substantial margin for the deferred stock ?—That is so.

548. And the more that margin is the more stability there will be in the stock, and the more security also there will be naturally for the preferred stock ?—That is so.

549. And you think that is a great object to secure, that the deferred stock should always bear a sufficiently substantial proportion to the dividend at present paid ?—Subject to the opinion that that is a matter rather for the shareholders themselves to regulate. If I was advising the shareholders as a private individual that is what I should say.

550. Quite so.　I began by asking you whether you did not express this opinion as *amicus curiæ*, which is the capacity in which you are here, and not as representing any official or authoritative dictum of the Board of Trade ?— That is so.

Mr. *Beckett.*

551. I would like to ask you one question. Have you got the Act of 1868 there ?—Yes, I have got the Act of 1868.

552. Could you refer to the 6 per cent. clause; sub-section 6, I think it is ?—Yes ; I have it.

553. Will you read that ?—" As between preferred ordinary stock and deferred ordinary stock preferred ordinary stock shall bear a fixed maximum dividend at the rate of 6 per centum per annum."

554. You do not know of your own knowlege, I suppose how that came to be put in, do you.

Mr. *Beckett*—continued.

What gave rise to Parliament fixing 6 per cent. to be the preferential dividend ? —Another part of the clause was that the privilege was only to be given to railway companies which should pay 3 per cent. per annum on the ordinary capital for a certain period, and then as the stock was split into half, which would give 6 per cent. to the preferred, the whole of that 3 per cent. I believe that that was the basis of the division. It was with reference to that clause only permitting it after companies had paid 3 per cent.

555. You see, I suppose, that the course of the dividend earning power of railways since then has so altered that that would be inapplicable now ?—That is to say, that the dividends of a great many companies have increased.

556. Have fallen so much ?—I am not quite quite sure that they have fallen.

557. Are you not ?—No.

558. Then you said just now that you thought it was desirable that the ratio between the preferred and deferred should be fixed so as to prevent speculation as much as possible ?—Will you repeat that question ?

559. I understood you to say that the relation of dividend between the deferred and preferred should be such that there should be as little ability to speculate as possible outside ?—I do not know that I went so far as that. I mentioned a certain case in which I would advise the ordinary shareholders, if I were advising them, to do certain things.

560. You may fix the ratio now applicable to it, but in 10 years' time things may so change that it would be quite inapplicable ?—That is always the case; that would be so.

561. So that there does not seem to be any general rule to be laid down, and that each company must be dealt with according to its own circumstances ?—I should not like to express an opinion upon that point as to whether general rules could be laid down.

Mr. *Dickson.*

562. Have you looked into the Bills now before the Committee ?—Not very minutely, and it was not considered desirable that I should go into the question of particular Bills. It was considered desirable that I should only deal with the general question of policy.

563. So that you cannot tell in what respect the proposals now before the Committee in these various Bills differ from what Parliament has already sanctioned in the case of the North British and the Taff Vale ?—I do not think I could go into detail to give any information to you that you have not got yourselves.

Mr. *Bristowe.*

564. I understood you to say that the Board of Trade were very particular that the real capital should be stated in all the accounts and publicity given to it, as separated from the nominal capital ?—If these extensive duplications and increases of nominal stock are carried on, we think it would be most important that that should be done. I may say that we share the common feeling rather against a watering of capital.　We think it is not a thing that we should advise; but looking at the question as a

_matter

Mr. *Bristowe*—continued.

matter of public interest, if the railway share-holders desire it, we incline to think, as far as we can judge at present, that it is rather covered by the general idea that they should be allowed to do what they please; but then we say, let us take care of the public interest so far as the record is concerned

565. That is a point I want to lead to. You, naturally are aware, with your knowledge of the thing generally, that when the stock is duplicated in the official list of the Stock Exchange it appears as a gross amount. Suppose there is 10,000,000 *l.* of the capital of a company and it is duplicated, it would appear then as 20,000,000 *l.*; do you anticipate that the public might be misled in any injurious manner by such an entry as that?—I should hope that to some extent the careful record of the actual paid-up capital might even tend to check the mischief to the public from the capital being described in that manner; but we propose to keep a record mainly in the interests of the Government and the public with reference to the powers with which the companies have been entrusted, and not for the purpose of benefiting or shielding the investing classes in any way.

Mr. *Mowbray.*

566. Is your view of this question at all affected by the coming into existence of these trust companies?—We think that that is a matter upon which the railway shareholders themselves must put forward their own case as to whether they think that they can show a case as far as they are to be affected by these companies, and that that is a matter upon which the Board of Trade will have better means of judging after the evidence which you are able to obtain. The Board of Trade have rather suggested that there ought to be an inquiry of this kind for the purpose of obtaining information.

567. But you have no opinion which you wish to express upon the subject now?—No, none which I wish to express.

568. Then I gather rather that when you said that these Bills are a cause of "novel impression," which, I think, was your word, you rather referred more to the amounts than to any principle of novelty?—But the amounts are of so unusual, and of so large a kind, that it makes a very great difference indeed, and it is quite likely that although some increase of nominal stock were permitted, without much remark as an incidental to an amalgamation or consolidation of stocks, it becomes a very different question when you have these very large additions proposed.

569. What was the proportional increase in the Taff Vale, can you tell me?—I think the ordinary capital was increased two and a-half times; and in the case of the North British, what was called the North British ordinary capital, I think, was exactly doubled.

Mr. *Buxton.*

570. Do I understand that, on the whole, you prefer each individual case to be dealt with on its merits, rather than by a fresh amending Act of the Act of 1868?—I do not think I went so far as that. In fact, I think the Board of Trade have made no suggestion on that point at all.

0.101.

Mr. *Burton*—continued.

571. You would rather not give an opinion?—I would rather not give an opinion at present.

572. I suppose, in your opinion, it would be well to have uniformity as far as possible in reference to this whole question; even if there was no special Act like that of 1868, a uniform clause ought to be inserted in all these Bills as far as possible?—I think that would be an advantage certainly.

573. Have you any strong opinion with reference to the question of duplication as against splitting?—It seems to me they are quite different; they are two things. You cannot set them off against each other. You may have stock splitting with duplication, but you may have duplication by itself.

574. You have no special objection to duplication then?—I think I have expressed already sufficiently the view the Board has upon that point, that we wish the thing discussed.

575. I gather that there would be no difficulty with regard to this question of the actual paid-up capital; all you want the record for, as far as I understand, is for the public purpose in case of a revision of rates or a purchase by the State of the railways. There would be no difficulty in having it accurately kept by all the companies, I suppose?—I think in future there ought to be no difficulty, and, I think, for a great many years past there will not be much difficulty; but I should not like to say there may not be some difficulty with reference to the earlier period of railway companies; but still we must get the best information we can, as far as it can be got.

Chairman.

576. There is one point we have heard a good deal about. I do not know whether you are prepared to give any opinion upon it; that is, whether, if a railway is to have this power of altering its stock, it should be a condition that all the stock should be so altered, or whether it should be allowed to be optional with the shareholders who hold the stock?—I think, giving a personal opinion, if I was advising the shareholders, I should recommend them to permit it to be changed backwards and forwards as people liked, as it is only a question of a unit for the purposes of buying and selling; but looking at it as a matter of public interest, I should rather be disposed to say, if you think it is a kind of liberty generally which ought to be permitted to the companies, that in a detail of that kind you should permit them to do as they please. It would be covered by the general principle of letting them do as they please.

577. You do not see from your point of view; from the point of view of the public interest, to which you have referred, as to your future relations with the companies, any great disadvantage in the comparative confusion which would arise from some shareholders having converted and some not having converted, and perhaps some having reconverted?—I think not; as we are always going to keep the record of the paid-up capital.

578. That is all you care for for your purpose?—For

F 2

Chairman—continued.

—For our purpose that is what we should look to.

579. For the purposes of the record, as to the "unit"; to use your own phrase ; they may have in dealing with their stock ; that you think is an affair for them rather than for you, as representing the public?—That would be an affair for them, if the Committee should eventually sanction these duplications.

580. Quite so. In which of your two capacities do you give that opinion?—I am speaking generally, of course, as to what has been the view of the Board of Trade, as far as the public interest is concerned, although on one or two points as *amicus curiæ* I have given a personal opinion.

Mr. *Buxton.*

581. Have you any opinion with reference to a point that was raised in the quotation you read from the Duke of Richmond's Report with reference to the voting power of the deferred stock ; do you think they ought to have equal voting power with the preferred stock ?— That raises also a question of very wide scope indeed, on which I think it is desirable that at this stage I should not give an opinion.

Chairman.] Is there any suggestion Mr. Pope, or Mr. Pember, that you would like to make on the evidence of this witness.

Mr. *Pember.*] There is one, Sir, which I venture to make. It is that the witness should emphasize a little more I think than he has, that the issue of shares at a discount, of which he spoke as being in the nature of duplication differs from duplication, inasmuch as it increases the capital amount which bears dividend, whereas duplication does not, I mean that if the share was not issued at a discount, or we will say, suppose it was issued at a discount of something like 20 per cent., 80,000 *l.* would have done duty for 100,000 *l.*, there would have been only 80,000 *l.* applicable to dividend ; whereas if the share is raised at a discount it brings it up to nearly 100,000 *l.* which is bearing dividend.

Witness.] I do not quite see the difference. If you have more duplication it is the same thing ; that is to say, you call a thing which is 100 *l.*, 200 *l.*; whereas when you issue shares at a discount of 50 *l.*, you call a thing which is 50 *l.*, 100 *l.* It seems to me exactly the same thing.

582. Surely is it not this : suppose that instead of raising 8,000,000 *l.* at par, I raise it at a great discount which makes my capital 10,000,000 *l.*, I have to declare dividends on 2,000,000 *l.* more ; but if I duplicate my capital under the scheme of the South Western of this year I do not have a shilling more of capital to pay dividend upon ;

Mr. *Buxton*—continued.

I declare a dividend on the old un-duplicated capital, and then divide it between preferred and deferred ?—Still I think for purposes of the public, unless the precaution had been taken by the Board of Trade to secure a record of the paid-up capital the thing would have appeared as the capital upon which a dividend was declared.

583. Quite so ; the operation would not be the same thing ; and if a record is kept, there would be that difference?—There would be that difference as regards these past issues of shares. I think it has not been to a very large extent.

584. Quite so ; that is what I mean. It is a different operation. May I venture to suggest this also, that the Taff Vale Act as it passed both Houses, if there had not been the limitation of dividend insisted upon by Parliament, would have allowed the Taff Vale Company to have declared, if their receipts would have permitted it, 15 per cent. upon the 250 *l.* instead of 15 per cent. upon the 100 *l.* ?—I doubt if that would have been so. I think it might have been a question. If ever the question had arisen as to the reduction of fares and rates, I think the point would have been raised whether you ought not have looked to the original paid-up capital. That would have been the question.

585. I think so too?—But I think that has been prevented by the course that has been taken.

586. Quite so ; that is precisely what I meant. There is only one other thing perhaps I might ask an expression of your opinion upon ; that is whether you would not think it advisable to put the preferred capital, if duplicated, in such a position that it would at least command the price of par ? —I should not like to express an opinion upon that point. I have spoken of the public interest.

Chairman.

587. You do not see the public interest involved in that?—Not so much. If you were to sanction these thing at all, it would certainly be important to leave a good deal to the shareholders themselves.

Mr. *Pember.*

588. Supposing you were advising the shareholders in the matter, you would suggest that they should give as much dividend to the deferred stock as would keep it at least at par? —Generally, perhaps ; but I should like always to know the particular circumstances under which the thing was to be done.

589. Therefore, uniformity as to the amount to be given to the preferred stock must depend upon the particular circumstances of each company ; uniformity is impossible ; and the amount to be given to the deferred stock must depend upon the circumstances of each individual case? —I do not like to go so far as to say it would not be possible to have general rules. I would not express an opinion upon that.

Mr. FRANK MAY, called in ; and Examined.

Chairman.

590. WILL you be good enough to say what your position is at the Bank of England?—I am Chief Cashier of the Bank of England.

Chairman- continued.

591. And you have come here in answer to the invitation of the Committee, in order to give the Committee any information in your power as

to

Chairman —continued.

to the effect of this general process of conversion of stock?—Yes, I have.

592. I need not ask you any question, I think, as to the necessity for the conversion of stock, or as to the effect of it upon the interests of the shareholders ; but do you see any disadvantage or inconvenience to the public from such conversion of stock as is contemplated in our days on such a scale?—No ; I think the division of stock would be a matter of, perhaps, convenience, and would not be attended with any disadvantages to the public interest.

593. It would afford to certain classes of investors a kind of investment which they at present desire?—I think so; I think it would add to the number of what we call first-class investments which sober investors like very much. They like investments at a fixed rate of interest. That is one reason why I think it would be in favour with the public. Another strong reason, as it seems to me is, that it would also place the management of the railway companies in the hands of those who are most interested in the management.

594. Would you explain how that would occur?—I mean, of course, with reference to these large stock conversions that have taken place under the trust companies. Under these companies, as I read it, a very small proportion of the large amounts of stock which have gone into the names of those trustees will enable the vote for the whole of that stock to be applied for or against the railway company for whom the trustees hold the stock.

595. You say "applied against the railway company"; but although, through the medium of a trust company, the holders of the shares in the trust company are still interested in the prosperity of the railway, are they not?—They are, certainly ; but they have no direct voice after they have parted with their stock. The stock has gone into the hands of certain persons who are the trustees ; they have lost the direct hold of their stock.

596. You think there is a danger of the power which a trust company gives being seized upon for sinister purposes by those who manage the trust company?—I think that is a danger.

597. At all events for purposes not identical with the desires and interests of the great mass of the shareholders?—No.

598. If it were not for that danger, do you think that the shareholders generally would have been anxious to embark in these schemes?—It is rather a large question to answer, but I think that a shareholder likes that which gives him an increased value in his property.

599. It does have the effect of actually increasing the value of his property, so far as our experience has gone ; is that your view?—I think so.

600. Have you any opinion to give as to the comparative advantages of what is known as "splitting," and is known as "duplication"?—I should say that "duplication" might be opposed on principle, although there are certain advantages in it; for instance, if you divide a stock, and give 100 *l.* of one stock and 100 *l.* of another, for the 100 *l.* original stock, it is very easy of calculation. The 200 *l.*

Chairman—continued.

of the joint stocks represented only 100 *l.* of the other after all. It is simply a measure of value ; it does not alter the intrinsic worth of the stock; still I think there are objections to it as a matter of principle.

601. You think it might deceive some people? —I do not know that. I think, as a rule, investors do not really trouble themselves much about the aggregate amount of stock in any company. That is my experience.

602. Do you think that one of those methods of dealing with the stocks would induce greater speculation of an improper kind than the other?—No, I do not. Of course as to interfering with speculation, I do not see how that is to be done. Of course people will speculate whether you have the stock 100 *l.* preferred, and 100 *l.* deferred, or half that amount.

603. Did you hear Mr. Giffen's opinion as to the expediency of having a substantial amount of net income available for the deferred stock so as to prevent undue elasticity in it?—Yes.

604. Do you agree in that opinion?—I did not follow Mr. Giffen in that, for I think that the deferred stock must always be liable to greater fluctuation, because on that stock would come the increased or the decreased cost of all the commodities, like iron and coal, and labour, and everything else, all that would fall on the deferred stock, and therefore it must fluctuate ; I do not see how the fluctuation could be avoided.

605. But the fluctuation would be greater or less according as the total amount of available dividend was small or great; that is to say, supposing a railway company at present pays 7 per cent. dividend, and you converted it into 5 per cent. preferred, and 2 per cent. deferred, and you compared that condition of things with a conversion into 4 per cent. preferred and 3 per cent. deferred in the one case, the fluctuation would be upon 2 per cent. in the one and in the other upon 3 per cent.?—Yes.

606. Therefore it would be more lively?—It might be so.

607. I think that was Mr. Giffen's view?—Yes.

608. You do not attach very much importance to that point?—I do not.

609. Do you attach much importance to one point that has been brought very much before us; that is, the question of making the preferred stock as near a par level as possible?—No, I do not ; I do not think that matters at all. I think from my experience of the necessities of investors they always choose those stocks that are below par ; good stocks.

610. If I may use the phrase, there is no sweet simplicity in a par figure which would recommend it?—No, I do not think so. I think a good investor would rather have a stock of 90 say than 100, because he has got ten points before it reaches par. That we find to be very much the case in the case of all first-class stocks.

611. Do you think that the position and interest of the Bank of England as a semi-State institution, would be at all affected by a large movement of this sort if it assumed general proportions?—I am afraid I am hardly authorised by the Corporation I have the honour of representing to answer a large question of that kind ; but

0.101.

F 3

but

Chairman—continued.

but for myself I do not see how it can be affected. We shall probably find that the effect will be to enhance the value of Consols, Bank stock.

612. It would enhance the value of Consols?—It would enhance the value gradually of all the highest class of stocks, I should think.

Mr. *Buxton.*

613. Why should the addition of a larger number of what you call first-class investments enhance the value of Consols and other first-class investments?—Because as those stocks were the more absorbed they would rise in value, and the others would by sympathy.

614. I do not gather, at least I could not understand, any actual objection that you had to duplication of stock. You did not state any definite objection?—No, I do not think I have any objection personally to the duplication of stock.

615. On the whole, do you prefer duplication or splitting of stocks?—I do not think there is much to choose between them. You may, of course, split your stocks in this way; for instance, take Caledonian Railway stock, which is, say, at 125; you may give 75——

616. I am not talking of splitting for a moment in equal proportions?—Then I do not see any advantage in that.

617. You do not think that, on the whole, the duplication would make the deferred stock less speculative?—I do not think so.

618. Its interest would vary less than by splitting, would it not; a less proportion of the dividend would go to that stock if duplicated than if split, would it not?—If split in equal amounts. I think, if you split 100 *l.* of stock into 50 *l.*, 6 *l.* per cent. stock, and the deferred into the balance, it is the same as if you divide 100 *l.* 3 *l.* per cent. stock, and the balance goes to the other hundred

619. Surely every additional 1 per cent. dividend would accumulate in a larger proportion on 100 *l.* than on the 200 *l.* stock; that is to say, on the 100 *l.* deferred rather than on the 50 *l.* deferred, would it not?—Yes, it would be less affected.

620. That is to say, there would be less variation of dividends on the deferred stock under the duplication scheme than under the splitting

Mr. *Buxton*—continued.

scheme, would there not?—Yes, probably there would.

621. I understand you have practically no objection to duplication, so long as it is a simple operation, namely, absolute duplication, instead of the percentage of stocks; I mean, for instance, that there should always be the 200 *l.*, the 100 *l.* preferred and the 100 *l.* deferred, for the 100 *l.* original?—Yes.

622. But you do have the objection to a scheme which would propose, for instance, to divide them into 125 *l.*, 75 *l.* preferred and 25 *l.* deferred?—Yes, I think so.

Mr. *Beckett.*

623. Why?—Because, although the stock may happen to be worth that in money, your 100 *l.* may be worth 125 *l.*; that is only the market estimate of it. There is no more money put into the company than there would be under a duplication scheme. There is no more money laid out on the railway. It is an arbitrary arrangement, after all, founded on simply the market price of the stock.

624. Both are?—Yes, both are.

Mr. *Dickson.*

625. Speaking generally, representing the Bank of England, you do not look with disfavour upon the proposals made to the Committee in these Bills?—No; we are rather inclined to believe that it is a matter of self-defence on the part of the companies. We do not see why the trust company should be able to do legally that for the shareholders of a railway company that the railway company cannot do for its own shareholders.

626. In other words, you are in favour of the shareholders being able to do by and through their own company what they are now forced to do, if at all, through the trust companies?—Yes.

Mr. *Buxton.*

627. Would it give greater facilities for lending and borrowing money if there were a larger amount of what you call these high-class or first-class investment stocks?—I do not think so.

628. You do not think it would?—I do not think it would.

Mr. ROKEBY PRICE, called in; and Examined.

Chairman.

629. WILL you state what your position is with regard to the Stock Exchange?—I am Chairman of the Stock Exchange.

630. You have been good enough to come here to give us any assistance you can; can you say generally how you regard this policy of conversion of stocks?—I think, speaking personally, I should prefer the companies keeping their stocks as originally created; but inasmuch as outside companies have been created for the purpose of creating stocks of their own to represent certain stocks bought of various companies, it appears to me that is a very left-handed way of providing investment for the

Chairman—continued.

public. I think that railway companies ought to have exactly the same power to deal with their stocks that those investment companies attempt to do through their own organisation. It would be done much more to the advantage of the shareholders, because the large salaries and commissions that are paid in these investment companies to their trustees must come out of the dividend apportioned to such stock of each company which that stock conversion company must hold; and I think the profit might much better go to the shareholders through their own directors than through an outside body.

631. Then

Chairman—continued.

631. Then if these trust companies had not been invented, you would not have seen any great object in this policy on the part of the railway companies themselves?—The first company to do this was the Great Northern under very peculiar circumstances; and a very admirable thing it was for them to have done it. The extreme opposition of the Midland, and the York and North Midland, and the London and North Western, and the old Eastern Counties, was so great that the 25 *l.* shares of the Great Northern Company went to a very low price. The result was that, if calls had been made to complete the line, the line would most probably have become bankrupt; and to the credit of the then chairman, Mr. Beckett Denison, and his colleagues, he advised the plan of dividing the 25 *l.* share into two shares; a 12 *l.* 10 *s.* share fully paid up, and a 12 *l.* 10 *s.* share with only 2 *l.* 10 *s.* paid up. A 12 *l.* 10 *s.* share was to be given to the shareholders who had borne a great deal of the burden of making the line and getting the Act, and that was to have 6 per cent., because it was thought that nothing less than 6 per cent. would make it worth the while of shareholders to take it. Then the other 12 *l.* 10 *s.* share, with only 2 *l.* 10 *s.* paid, because a speculative stock. But the Great Northern after a certain time were proh b ted by their own Act from making any further division of the stocks. I think that in that case, it was a great advantage to the shareholders and the public that that division was made. I do not think there was the same reason for making the division in the South Eastern and the Manchester, Sheffield, and Licolnshire and the Brighton. That was certainly done for the purpose, as I think, of giving a speculative element to a certain portion of that stock. At the same time it did provide a stock which has been very serviceable to investors and to some trustees, and that is a preferred stock with an ascertained annual interest, and that has been certainly of very great service. I think that the proposal, as I understand it, in these Bills to make the preferred stock a 4 per stock is a very great improvement upon the 6 per cent. stocks; and, practically, it does become, in a big company certainly it would become, equal to a preference stock; and that is a very great advantage to the public.

632. Will there be any confusion, do you think, in the minds of investors and the public at large between what we know as preference stock and this preferred stock?—The first company that came out was the Railway Investment Company, seven or eight years ago; and they improperly put in their prospectus that it was a preference stock; and we, in the committee, declined to quote it until it was altered. Then then they altered it to "preferred" to avoid any misconception. We thought it very wrong; in fact, we refused to put it in our list, I think, and they altered it to preferred.

633. And you think that is a sufficient distinction to keep the public straight?—I think so.

634. Can you give any opinion as the effect of this process in leading to undue speculation, or the reverse?—I think the duplication is merely a matter of self-defence. I would rather

Chairman—continued.

it was not duplicated. I would rather prefer deferred and preferred of equal amounts; but inasmuch as these other companies do duplicate a very large quantity of their stock (600,000 *l.* Caledonian, a great quantity North Eastern, and a great quantity Glasgow and South Western have already been duplicate), that throws that particular stock into the market, which is understood to be a duplication; and, therefore, I think, in defence the companies, if I may be allowed to say so, ought to be allowed to duplicate; and I think, too, that by duplication the speculation would be less, because, as we know from experience on the Stock Exchange, with the A. stocks, being comparatively small stocks——

635. The Great Northern?—No, the A. stocks, not the Great Northern so much, but the Brighton A. and the Chatham and Dover A. and the Sheffield A. being small stocks, they they are more easily manipulated by being small; whereas, if they were duplicated manipulation could not be so easy. On principle I do not like it; but I think the railway companies are bound to keep the management of the company in their own hands.

636. May I ask you why you do not like it? —Well it is a misrepresentation of capital. I mean to say that it does not represent the actual fact. There is not one nail, there is not one sleeper put fresh down on to the railway for this duplication.

637. Of course, you are aware that these companies all propose, and we have heard from Mr. Giffen, that the Board of Trade would be prepared so far as they are concerned, to insist that the original capital should always be placed on the face of the account, so that there should be no doubt as to what the real paid-up capital was?—That is very necessary.

638. Still the other you think is a little bit delusive, the fact that the other is being spoken of as actual capital?—I think if it was stated in the accounts so as to make quite clear what the capital of the company was before the duplication, and what the capital is after, that that will tend to keep before the public and before the shareholders their actual position, and by that means every person who buys or sells these shares will always have before him every six months what his position really is.

639. Have you any strong opinion as to the advantage or disadvantage of making this manipulation universal within the stock of one company as against allowing it to be optional?—I am against restriction. I think it ought to be left to the shareholders to determine. As a matter of account, and as a matter of convenience to suit stockbrokers, I think, perhaps, it would be better to make it compulsory; but I am not quite sure whether the interest of stockbrokers and the Stock Exchange is a paramount interest.

640. There is another point bearing on the same thing: In certain proposals power is sought to allow re-conversion back to the original stock? —Yes.

641. Do you approve of that?—That is what I meant; that the shareholders should have the power, if they thought fit, to do so.

642. To re-convert?—To re-convert.

643. You mean that they should work backwards

Chairman—continued.

wards and forwards as they like?—Work backwards and forwards as they like.

644. You do not think that would give rise to the possibility of " cornering," to use a common phrase?—It is a well-known word; I do not think it would. My own personal opinion of the matter as to keeping accounts and receiving orders from principals and executing them is that I would rather it was compulsory; and I am not at all sure that it would not be to the advantage of the company; but still I do not like to restrict shareholders if they do not wish to do so.

645. But you see nothing in the public interest to induce you to have a strong opinion on that subject?—No, I do not think so. I think that a great deal depends on the voting power. I do not know what the Committee may do with regard to voting power, but I think that ought to be regulated.

646. What are your views upon that subject?—I think they ought to have no more voting power than they have under the unchanged stock, that is to say, the old stock.

647. How would you distribute that voting power as between the preferred and the deferred?—I think the best way would be to consider it as a divided stock; each stock should have half just what it is; 100 *l*. stock is divided into two fifties, 50 *l*. preferred and 50 *l*. deferred; the 50 *l*. preferred should have half its voting power and the 50 *l*. deferred the other half. Then it would keep the voting power exactly as it was before the division took place.

648. And keep the relations between the two kinds of stock equal?—Equal.

649. Would you apply the same principle to the directors' qualification?—Certainly.

Mr. *Ellis*.

650. May we take it that you express the views of the association or committee of which you are chairman?—I think I do. I brought it before the committee meeting on Friday last, and I told them that I had been summoned to be here, and I gave them my views, which I have stated to you to-day. We had a very large committee (over 20 members being present out of the 30), and I found generally that they agreed with me; I do not think they quite agreed with me about the duplication. Some of the members of the committee were against duplication.

Chairman.

651. In favour of splitting?—In favour of the old plan; but I think it is a matter of some consequence to prevent what you have just called "cornering," Sir; I think the larger the stock is the less chance there is of cornering. I am not in favour of it in itself at all; it is merely a defensive operation against the action of outside bodies who might have no interest in the company; on the contrary, they might have a diverse interest. Speaking of what I know, as to one company, I can easily conceive that the Railway Investment Company (the shareholders) might direct their board to vote in a certain way in a company, with regard to a certain Bill, which might be in direct opposition to the inte-

Chairman—continued.

rests of that company; and that would be a very dangerous thing to do.

Mr. *Ellis*.

652. Speaking generally, then you are here in a representative capacity?—I am.

653. I gather that your view is based largely upon the desire to restore, or to keep, as you put it, the management of the railway company's affairs within their own hands?—Yes.

654. Would not you admit that the success (whatever it has been) of these trust companies has shown that they meet a public want?—Well, I am not so sure of that, because some of the stocks which they have created are at a lower price than they issued them at, the deferred stocks.

655. Then you would not admit that they had been an unqualified success at all?—No; they have been a qualified success; the preferred part of their bargain is an investment; but still the preferred part of the Stock Conversion Company is deceiving, because it is not a portion of the original company; it is a portion, it is quite true, of the Stock Conversion Company, but not of the original company.

656. Then you would not admit that they have forced the hands of the railway companies?—I do not know. I think they might do very easily.

657. You would not say that these railway companies come before this Committee, because, to a certain extent of the success of the Trust Company?—I do not say the success only; but I think it is a disadvantage to have an outside body, who may have diverse interests to those of a particular company, and to use that voting power.

658. That is not quite my point. My point is this: We had it opened by counsel here, that the railway companies, some of them, at all events, come before us, in consequence of certain action on the part of the trust companies. If it be so that action must have been successful, to a certain extent; would you say that it has been successful?—To a certain portion of their stocks, decidedly.

659. Would you say the trust companies have found a new vein, so to speak, on the part of the investing public?—I think they have, but not half so good a vein as it would have been if it been struck by the original company.

660. Quite so; then they have, to a certain extent, forced the hands of the railway company?—Certainly, to a certain extent.

661. But you would say distinctly that it would be much better that that should be done by the railway company themselves?—It should be done by the railway company for every reason I think.

Mr. *Beckett*.

662. In the interests of the investing public do you see any objection to each railway company putting forward its own scheme? You know we have four schemes here, and they are not identical at all?—Yes.

663. One is for duplication; another is for splitting; one is for 4 per cent. preferred; another for 3 per cent.?—Yes.

664. Do

Mr. *Beckett*—continued.

664. Do you see any objection to that?—No, I do not. One of the great advantages to the public has been that the 4 per cent. stock, or the 6 per cent. stock has become to be an assured 6 per cent., and an assured 4 per cent.; and, therefore, whatever interest the preferred stock bore it ought to be as nearly as possible an assured interest: therefore, if it is a company of a small revenue it might be very inadvisable and contrary to public interest to make the 4 per cent. stock what the 3 per cent. stock would be, assured. I would let each company do what it thinks best for its own purposes in that respect.

665. You personally seem to prefer duplication to splitting, do you?—On the whole I do.

666. Although you spoke approvingly of the Great Northern having been the first to introduce the splitting?—Under the particular circumstances of the Great Northern at that time.

667. Have you read their Bill?—I have just looked at it.

668. Do you see any objection to their scheme?—The Great Northern propose (I presume so at least) to take the present market value?

669. Yes?—And to capitalise as it were that market value; that is to say, to give 125 *l.* for each 100 *l.* of the stock.

670. Is there any objection to that in your view?—I would rather they were all done alike.

671. Why?—I am speaking as an investor now, or as an agent of investors.

672. Quite right?—It is much easier to us to explain to people. They see them all, and can compare the prices in our list, and they can say: this 4 per cent. stock gives us so much, this gives us so much, this gives us so much, and so on. If you have 3 or 3 per cent. it may make some difference, still you cannot avoid that.

673. Are not the public quite familiar with the present Great Northern system of splitting the A's and the B's?—Oh, yes.

Mr. *Dickson.*

674. Do you think the number of trust companies dealing with the railway stock is likely to increase?—I could not say that.

675. There is a tendency that way, is there not?—Yes; they pay very large salaries to their trustees and people of that sort, so I presume there is a tendency. Some people think they pay very well.

676. If there is a public want you would prefer seeing it met by the company directly instead of by the trust companies?—Certainly, at much less cost to the public.

Mr. *Biddulph.*

657. One question I should like to ask you with regard to what you said about reconversion of stocks, surely if a man converts his stock, and he changes his mind, all he has got to do is to sell that stock, and buy some of the other?—Then you have to pay broker's commission and stamps to the Government.

678. It is all the better for business, it is not?—I am not here to advocate broker's business.

0.101.

Mr. *Biddulph*—continued.

679. Surely, it would give rise to great confusion if a man were to change backwards and forwards, his stock, his first ordinary, then preferred, then deferred?—I do not see that it would be much acted upon.

680. If you will excuse my saying so I do not see the use of having that power to reconvert?—The only thing is that I would let shareholders in their own interest know what is best for themselves; it is not always they do know what is best, still——

681. Surely, if a may changes his mind he can sell his stock and buy some of the other. It comes to the same thing, does it not?—There may be a great loss in doing it. The market price of the two stocks may be at one particular time very different, he sells a stock at a price to buy something else.

682. If there is a difference in the price of the stocks, surely that everybody doing the same thing. If a man could convert his stocks and get something by it he would do so immediately, and there would be a perpetual shuffling backward and forwards?—In my experience very often people change their minds; they have got a speculative stock and do not like it; or they may wish to change deferred stock for preferred stock, or *vice versâ*; therefore I would not dictate to any shareholder whether he shall sell as you propose, Sir, and re-buy, or whether he should have the power to write to the secretary of his company and deliver up the certificates of his then holding and say, I want to reconvert. Of course the trouble to the company would be no more than the buying and selling would be, and the shareholder would be saved from the expense of stamps and brokers' commission, and besides the turn of the market.

683. Surely if there was to be a difference in value between the converted and the unconverted stocks, the moment the balance inclined one way you would find everybody coming in and reconverting. It would be an endless matter?—The South Eastern Company have not converted all their stock, and there is a certain amount of stock still unconverted, as also the Brighton; and the second half the year the South Eastern Company allow their shareholders to divide their ordinary stock into preferred and deferred; and at times it is quite as you say; at times it is a great advantage to them to do it. That falls to the jobber to do. He has a demand from brokers for a particular kind of stock. If he has got the old stock he then divides it at a profit to himself. I do not quite see your point, if I may be allowed to say so.

684. My point is, that it surely gives rise to great confusion to have stocks reconverted backwards and forwards?—With whom, Sir?

685. With the public; you do not know how much of the converted stocks there are in the market if a person can go into the office of the company any day and turn all his stock back again into ordinary stock?—That is his own private interest, and he is surely to be allowed to do what he likes with his own in that case.

686. Quite so; but it may have a great effect upon the market, and the outside public cannot know; there may be a large quantity of this particular stock in the market, or there may be

G   a great

Mr. Biddulph—continued.

a great scarcity of it; and one individual or a syndicate of individuals might, if they choose, for their own purposes go to the company and create on the spur of the moment a large amount of stock, or diminish the amount of stock, that there is on the market, according as they wished it?—There would be very few large holders who would do that. I should think the result of experience would be that it would be changed in very small amounts, and we (the committee) require our secretary of the share and loan department, Mr. Burdett, to see every half-year that he has every account of every company, and he is ordered by the committee to alter the capitals of the company according as they appear in that list. He also has to keep an account of all Acts of Parliament passed during the Session where either fresh capital has been created, or capital has been altered: those he has to take a note of, and when an Act has been passed, information is given to the committee, and the committee then order the capital in our list to be so altered; so that the time which would elapse between the conversion and any operation to speak of would be very small. I do not think you may consider that as really of any consequence.

687. To go back to my first point; if a shareholder wishes to reconvert his stock, he has only to go and sell his one stock in the market, and buy the other. There is no necessity for his going to the company to register fresh stocks, and to alter the amounts of the stocks?—Now he is obliged to do it in that way. The object of giving it to the company is to give the shareholder an easier, a quicker, and a cheaper way of doing that which he does at the present time.

688. I am sorry to say I cannot quite see it in that light myself. I think if a man does not know his own mind he must pay for it; if he converts his stock once he ought to be satisfied with that?—We have some companies now not exactly on all-fours, but there are many companies which have "registered stock" and "scrip stock." They give what are called scrip-warrants, and they allow their shareholders to convert either into "registered" or into "scrip," and vice versâ, and that is done now in several companies. It is a convenience. For instance, foreigners prefer a scrip stock; English people prefer a registered stock. The result has been in the case of the stocks of international companies that that power is given.

689. But it is rather different when you reconvert a stock?—I know it is different; only I am showing that it is a facility of a somewhat similar kind which is very much made use of.

Mr Bristowe.

690. On that point of reconversion; I do not wish to labour the subject any more; but you said you had a meeting of the committee at which the members were nearly all present; and as this is the first proposal made on the part of a railway, so far as I understand, and only on the part of one of them, to have the power to reconvert, I should like to know whether this matter was discussed between you and the committee?—No, it was not.

Mr. Bristowe—continued.

691. Then I want to ask you about the Stock Exchange official list. Mr. Giffen has stated that he anticipates that there is no objection to this scheme, because the accounts are all kept in such a manner as to show the real capital of the company, and not the duplicated or watered capital. Is it the fact that on the Stock Exchange official list if there is a capital of ten millions say, and it is duplicated, that will appear on your list as twenty millions? —Yes.

692. Is it not possible that that might deceive the public in some way?—We have had several companies, you know, where capital has been duplicated. The Great Western have made their 5 per cent. preference and debenture stocks into 4 per cent.; the income as been the same, but they have increased the capital by so much. The stock is actually in existence. There is no distinction between one portion of the Great Western 4 per cent. stock and any other portion of the Great Western 4 per cent. stock.

693. You do not anticipate that that list will deceive the public, or that there is any way by which you might insert in the list a statement that those stocks have been converted, bracket them in some way or other; perhaps you do not think that that is necessary?—No, I do not know how we could make a distinction of that sort; in fact, it would be more confusing to make the distinction because we should have to put two lines (I presume that is what you mean) we will say 100,000 l. of Great Northern debenture stock originally a 5 per cent., and 50,000 l or 100,000 l. debenture stock duplicated. It would make a great confusion.

694. You do not consider that a matter of any great importance?—No, I think not.

Mr. Mowbray.

695. I rather understood you preferred duplication, because you said that it would increase the size of the stocks, and it was more difficult to manipulate a large stock than a small stock?—Yes.

696. I also rather understand that in duplication what you double is the nominal value of the stock, the earning power is exactly the same?—Exactly the same.

697. Therefore would it be any more difficult to manipulate a large nominal stock which had the same earning power and the same real value as a smaller stock?—You have got more stock to buy.

698. But you do not want more money to buy it?—I do not know. It is the amount of stock that gives the extent of voting. The more stock you get the more voting power you get. You cannot get hold of a larger amount of stock so easily as you can a smaller amount of stock.

699. I was not looking at it from the point of view of voting, but rather from the point of view of the market. I thought that that was the point of view from which you were looking at it?—Yes; I think I am right. I think that would be so. I should not like to dogmatise upon it. You cannot prevent speculation.

700. You think that although the larger stock would be of no more real value than the smaller stock; the mere nominal size of it would

make

Mr. *Mowbray*—continued.

make it more difficult to manipulate?—I think so.

Mr. *Buxton.*

701. Just one question as to the point raised by Mr. Biddulph as to re-conversion; would there be any fear of a speculator buying up a large amount of either preferred or deferred and then converting it to and forcing the delivery of those who sold it?—I would not say that that could not be done.

702. But you do not anticipate that as a practical danger?—No, I do not.

703. I understand, in reference to duplication, you would much prefer if there is a system of duplication that it should be a simple one, namely, 200 *l.* for the 100 *l.* stock?—Yes.

704. And you rather object to such a proposal, for instance, as that of the Great Northern that it should be a nominal 125 *l.* for the 100 *l.*?—I am only speaking my own opinion. I do not want to limit the power of any of the shareholders to do what they like with their own capital. I think it would be much more to the advantage of the Great Northern if they followed the general practice rather than adopt one of their own. That is not of very much consequence, because after all the amount of the stock would be in our list as so much, whatever it was.

705. It is not A. and B. there simply, but a splitting of stock, was it not?—A splitting. By-the-bye, there was a peculiarity with the Great Northern B., which there is with no other B. stock. The Great Northern B. stock is a guaranteed stock. The Great Northern B. if it is not paid in one half year, the corresponding portion of the A. stock has to make it good in the succeeding half-years.

706. Do you think that cumulative system a good one or a bad one with reference to this preferred and deferred stock?—I would not have it for these, certainly.

707. Do you think it would be a good thing to have an Amending Act of the Act of 1868

Mr. *Buxton*—continued.

affecting railways generally, which they could come under or not as they liked, or to treat each individual case as it arises?—I think I should leave it to the companies to act as they think best. Six per cent is too high an interest for the preferred stock, and tends to make the A. stock much more speculative.

Chairman.] With regard to that last point of 6 per cent. named in the 1868 Act, we are to take it that it is distinctly the opinion of the learned counsel who are so acquainted with the matter, that that really means that the 6 per cent. is imposed as a necessary condition on all preferred stock.

Mr. *Pope.*] Certainly.

Mr. *Pember.*] Undoubtedly.

Chairman.] The words used are "fixed maximum rate."

Mr. *Pope.*] Quite so.

Mr. *Pember.*] Yes.

Chairman.] It cannot be taken to mean that it is a fixed rate, and that its maximum is to be six.

Mr. *Pope.*] No.

Mr. *Pember.*] No.

Mr. *Pope.*] In other words, you mean it would not be at the option of the company to fix a maximum within the margin of 6 per cent. It is an actual 6 per cent. We could not say 4 per cent., for instance.

Chairman.] Quite so.

Mr. *Pember.*] The word "six" means that. They shall not have more than 6 per cent., but 6 shall be the fixed rate.

Mr. WILLIAM ASTLE, called in; and Examined.

Chairman.

708. WILL you be good enough to state what position you occupy?—I am the Chief Manager of the London and Westminster Bank.

709. We have asked you to come here to give us your assistance in this matter. Can you say, whether with your large experience of the London and Westminster Bank, you have formed any opinion on the general policy of the Bills now before us?—I think that the principle of splitting the various stocks is one that should be left entirely to the disposition of the various companies; and probably a general Act passed that would enable the companies to deal with it as their shareholders pleased, would be the best way.

710. According to the circumstances of each company?—Exactly.

711. So far as this is done, do you think it will have the effect of increasing the number of 0.101.

Chairman—continued.

investments available for the public?—As regards the preferred stock it would give a very good security for timid people to invest in, who, perhaps, are not well able to judge for themselves. The preferred stock would be a very desirable thing, and I should think it would be as well that the dividend on that should be cumulative.

712. In order to prevent disappointment in any particular year?—Yes.

713. Do you think that this movement will have a tendency to increase speculation, by which I mean injurious speculation?—I should not like to go so far as to say "injurious"; but there is no doubt that the deferred stock is a stock in which a good deal of speculation does take place.

714. Do you attach importance to the point that a considerable margin of the average dividend

G 2

Chairman --continued.

dend of a company should be represented by the deferred stock?—A fair proportion should, after securing a decent rate for the preferred.

715. By "a decent rate," what do you mean? —Say 4 per cent.

716. You think there is an advantage in its remaining about that level?—I think so, in the present state of things. It is a very difficult thing to obtain a good and reliable security to pay you 4 per cent.

717. You are not afraid that the interests of bankers and others who are in the habit of advancing money upon the security of stocks would be affected by this process?—Not by the division of stocks. We are already hampered enough with other difficulties. We do not want to increase them; but they would not be increased by the division of the stocks.

718. You would still require a safe margin? —Undoubtedly, and require it to be kept up.

719. You could do that as easily under this new system as under the old?—Undoubtedly.

720. Do you see any objection to the great nominal increase of capital involved in a re-duplication system?—I must frankly say I cannot express an opinion upon that. I do not understand it sufficiently to tell you; therefore, I would rather not answer the question.

721. Your experience does not enable you to speak with authority upon the subject?—No, it does not.

722. Nor perhaps on the point whether the whole of the stocks of a company should be converted, if any are converted?—I should leave it entirely to the shareholders. I think they have the best right to deal with their own property.

723. From your point of view you do not see that there is anything to be said either *pro* or *con*?—No, I do not think so.

Mr. *Ellis.*

724. You mentioned 4 per cent. instead of 6; do you consider the case would be met by the insertion of 4 per cent. in a general Act instead of 6, as in the case of the Act of 1868?—If I understand the remarks that were made just now I should think that that was the best way of arriving at it, to fix the dividend with a maximum of, we will say, 6 per cent.

Chairman.

725. That is the law already?—It is, is it?

Mr. *Ellis.*

726. What you mean is that instead of having a statutory 6 per cent. you should allow a maximum 6 with power to go below 6. Is that your meaning?—Yes. The maximum of 6 might not be reached.

727. Then I quite apprehend that you mean that a general Act should be passed; only instead of the Act of 1868 which imposes an absolute 6 per cent., a fixed 6 per cent., you would allow a maximum 6 per cent. on anything below it?—Yes.

Chairman.

728. You do not mean do you that the deferred stock should have a movable dividend, the preferred stock would have a fixed dividend as I understand?—It would fixed at the time of the conversion.

729. It would be fixed at the time of the conversion, quite so?—But at the time of the conversion it should be open. It should be fixed, and at a cumulative dividend.

730. But at the time of the conversion it should be open to the railway company to fix their rate of dividend on the preferred stock at 6 or anything under?—Yes.

731. Once fixed, they could not change it of course?—No.

Mr. *Pope.*] Of course you are aware that the Act of 1868 only allows the splitting of stock; it does not allow a duplication.

Mr. *Ellis.*] I was only referring to the one point of the dividend in the Act of 1868.

Mr. *Pope.*] Quite so.

Mr. *Ellis.*

732. (To the *Witness*).] Can you give us any further light, from your banking experience; you have spoken of the shareholders' interests and the railway interest to a certain extent?—As bankers, I do not think we should be affected at all by the conversion.

733. You have no further opinion to offer as a banker?—No, none whatever.

Mr. *Beckett.*

734. You say you think it is desirable that there should be a cumulative dividend?—Yes; that would tend to keep the stock steady, and make it a safer investment.

735. Do you know that Parliament in 1868 passed a Bill forbidding that?—No, I do not; but what one Parliament does another can undo.

736. Yes; but I suppose there were good reasons for it at that time?—Yes.

Mr. *Biddulph.*

737. May I ask if you have any views with regard to the question of reconversion?—I am very doubtful whether that question of yours was understood before. Do I understand you to mean that when a man has converted his stock, where the railway company has divided their original stock into preferred and deferred, that they can go and turn that into original stock again?

738. That, I understand, is the proposal in the Caledonian Bill?—If that is the proposal, that I should not agree to.

Mr. *Bristowe.*

739. Generally speaking, do you say that there would be no risk, more than bankers usually run, if these Bills are acceded to?—I do not think it would add to the risk.

20 *May* 1890.

. Mr. CHARLES GAIRDNER, called in; and Examined:

Chairman.

740. YOU are the general manager of the Union Bank of Scotland?—I am.

741. And you have in that capacity an acquaintance with the feeling in that community on this subject?—Yes; pretty well.

742. You are acquainted with the nature of the Bills before us?—Yes.

743. In so far as you can judge, do you find that railway shareholders are in favour of this policy?—Yes; I think there is a pretty strong general feeling among the railway shareholders in favour of sub-division of the ordinary stocks.

744. What do you regard that as proceeding from?—I think it proceeds largely from the fact that preference stocks at present command an almost abnormally high price, a much higher price than they used to have, and shareholders like to get the benefit of that increased price. I think they expect that the conversion will lead to the increased market value of their security.

745. You think that there is a demand in the general community for that kind of investment? —I think so.

746. Then we are met by the fact that some railway companies propose to take this step, and others do not. Are the directors of railway companies anxious to do it?—I think the directors of railway companies generally, as far as I know their feelings, are very much opposed to it. I think the directors are not of the same mind, at least not all so strongly of that mind; I think they regard a sub-division with considerable doubt.

747. For what reason, do you suppose?— Well, I think the reason probably is that they know more about the risks that attach to railway property, and looking to the fact that a railway is intended to go on to a very remote future, I think that they consider it desirable that the ordinary stock, which must stand the brunt of adversity, if adversity should come, ought to be a large and substantial stock.

748. You mean if the ordinary stock is divided, that the deferred stock ought to have a large proportion?—Yes; if the ordinary stock is divided then, of course, the deferred stock will be of a much smaller amount than the ordinary stock at present is; and I think the question is that if sub-division is to take place the deferred ought to be maintained as a large and substantial stock, enjoying a substantial interest in the revenues of the railway company. I think there would be a very strong objection entertained by railway directors, in so far as I know, to making the deferred stock depend chiefly upon its speculative value as being a voting power more than as a revenue-producing investment; and I think there is an important difference in that way between the views of the directors and the shareholders in this matter.

749. The directors have perhaps more largely

0.101.

Chairman—continued.

in view the interest of the stability of the company?—I think so.

750. And of course the more substantial the deferred portion of the stock is the more safe (and therefore attractive) will be the preferred part? —The preferred also, of course, would have a higher value in the market presumably if the stock behind it is large and bearing a substantial dividend.

751. Then in these Bills, do you find this doctrine sufficiently observed?—Well, I have not studied the Bills with a view to apply it. I am speaking rather to the general principle and I do not know enough about the condition of any one of the railways I may say, although I do know about the Caledonian to some extent, but I have not studied them with a view to the application of the principle.

752. What would be your view on the question we have heard so much of, the question of duplication or splitting?—Well, I think it is the duty of the duplicators to prove their case; and I have not heard it proved to my satisfaction. I do not see what is to be gained by it. I understand some of the witnesses were of opinion that there would be less fluctuation if the stock were duplicated. I do not understand that. The thing which is to fluctuate is not the nominal amount of the stock; it is the value of the stock in the market; and I do not think the value of the stock in the market will be materially different, whether, after resolving on sub-division you split the stock or duplicate it. The thing is the same. It is a difference of nomenclature and nothing more. There may be a difference in value if you thereby meet a demand or even a sentiment, and you may make it a little more in the one case than the other; but I do not think it would amount to very much. As to its steadying fluctuation, I do not see why that should be at all, because it is not the increasing of the nominal amount of stock that is of importance; it is the market value of the thing which is going to fluctuate. The cause of fluctuations, of course, is mainly in the net revenue, and these fluctuations are applied in the one case to the present amount of ordinary stock split into two; in the other case to double the present amount of the ordinary stock standing in the books of the company. But it is not the application to these nominal amounts of stocks which is important; it is the market value of those two stocks. I do not see that the duplication will make you materially better or worse compared with splitting.

753. You say that any company proposing to duplicate its stock ought to prove its case; then you approve of splitting rather than duplication? —I think so; I think it is better; I think it is more intelligible, although I think there is really nothing in it, or rather there would be nothing in

G 3   it

Chairman—continued.

it if everybody was an expert in figures. I am afraid everybody is not an expert in figures, and that it may lead to misapprehension in the minds of investors.

754. Although, as we have heard so often, the original ordinary stock is shown on the face of the accounts in every case ?—Yes ; but very few people read those accounts.

755. With your experience and knowledge of public feeling, and of the public interest, what would you say ought to be the principle upon which this division of stock should take place ?— Well, you start with the Act of 1868, which has adopted a principle, and gives power to all railway companies, as I understand it, to divide their ordinary stock into two, provided they assign to the preferred portion not less than 6 per cent. dividend. That has not, I understand, been found to be of use, and very few railway companies have adopted it. Well, I think, in any legislation by way of amendment of that Act it is very important to have regard to the necessity of maintaining for the deferred portion a substantial interest in the company, so that it shall not become a mere plaything, possessing a value in the market, but yielding, perhaps, little or no dividend. I think the best line upon which to work this out, would be to proceed on the net revenue of the line ; and in future legislation, while I quite agree with the principle of giving as much freedom as possible to the shareholders, at the same time to enforce limitation. I think that before a railway company should be enabled to divide its ordinary stock it ought to have earned on the average of a certain period (say five years) a certain minimum dividend. I think if a railway was only paying one or two per cent. dividend, that it ought not to be authorised to subdivide its stock. The particular amount of dividend should be settled by Parliament, and I think there should be a limit, and that only railways that satisfied that condition should be in a position to subdivide their ordinary stock. Then, I think there should be a second condition : I think that in fixing the dividend to be appointed to the preferred stock, care must be taken that a substantial margin is left for the deferred, and that might be arrived at probably on the basis of the minimum dividend of a period like five years : Suppose the minimum dividend during five years had been 4 per cent. then that would give you datum on which to fix the limit of dividend to be assigned to the preferred stock ; but on one principle or another I think it is very important in the interests of the stability of the railway, as a great national institution, that the deferred portion shall possess solid value. I think it is not impossible to find a mode by which that could be settled, and yet sufficient freedom left to the railway companies to deal with their own particular circumstances.

756. You say, so far as you have just remarked in the interest of the railway as a State institution ?—As a national institution.

757. That is to say it has a certain status assigned to it, or given to it by Parliament in the

Chairman—continued.

public interest, and that the commercial interests of the community in which it exists are affected more or less by the fate of the railway company, so that it goes beyond the mere interests of the shareholders ?—Yes, I think the commercial interests would ultimately be affected if any railway company got into the hands of a merely speculative body.

758. The public might probably not be so well served, you mean ?—I think so.

759. And that there would be some sympathetic effect upon other commercial interests in the neighbourhood ?—I think so.

760. You are aware of all we have heard about the danger to railway companies by the creation of trust corporations ; would you give us your opinion upon that subject ?—Well, I have very little information upon that subject ; I have heard more of it since I came to London than before I came up. Of course it is a serious matter for any company to have a very large portion of its stock in the hands of any one person, I dare say it makes a very uncomfortable position for the directors, but I am not aware of any hostile intention on the part of any of those trust companies. I know nothing whatever about them ; but the railway directors seem to assume that there is a hostile purpose there, and if there be, it is a very serious matter. But in order to prevent hostile action on the part of those companies, it seems to me very doubtful if the dealing with the ordinary stock in the way proposed is either likely to be the best, or to be an effective mode of counteracting those companies. I do not see how it is to be effective at all. I do not see how duplicating the stock (which will duplicate the stock held by the trust company as well as by the shareholders) strengthens the hands of the directors. It may do so but I do not see it.

761. The whole of this transaction, if it is carried out, would prevent the further development of the action of those trust companies, would it not ?—It might do so ; but I do not know that it would. I am now assuming that the deferred stock would be left as a very substantial property. If it be so, then those gentlemen may operate upon that just as well as they operated upon the present stock. I do not see how you are to defeat them if they are determined to have it ; but I think they will defeat their own purpose if they go on. I do not think it is possible to go on buying 600,000 *l.* every year in a railway like the Caledonian Railway without raising the price to a point that would defeat their own purpose. At any rate, I think we do not know enough (I do not know enough) about the matter to form an opinion decidedly upon it ; but I should be very sorry to think it had become a necessity, so to treat the ordinary stock of the railway companies as to make it a much more speculative property than it is at present.

762. There are one or two points that we have become very familiar with now, on which you, perhaps, will give us your opinion ; first of all the question whether, if this operation is to be performed at all, it ought to be applied to the whole of the stock of the company, or whether it
should

Chairman—continued.

should be applied at the option of the shareholder?—The important feature in that question, I think, is the great importance of simplicity in the accounts. I do not suppose it would be done, or could be done, unless there was a very large proportion (probably a majority) of the shareholders approved of it; and if they approved of it, they intended to use it, to turn it to account. I think that to make it compulsory, would, in the interests of simplicity, be desirable; but there might be time allowed for it being done, and after a period it might become compulsory. I have no very strong opinion upon that point; but, I think, in the interest of the simplicity of the accounts, it is desirable, if possible, to supercede the old form by the new form.

763. That is a question rather affecting the company itself than the public?—I think so.

764. I mean the simplicity of their accounts is more an affair for them than for outside people? I do not think it is of importance to any one besides themselves.

765. Similarly, do you see any objection to the power of reconversion, or would you allow that freedom?—I do not like the idea of reconversion. I think a person should not be allowed to be always chopping and changing in a question of that kind. The last witness spoke of the preferred stock being made cumulative. That would make it quite impossible. You could not have it both cumulative and reconvertible, for you would get into hopeless confusion. I think it ought neither to be cumulative, nor should it be reconvertible; but that is a minor question also, I consider.

766. You see no particular way in which it will affect your interests as a banker?—None whatever: except that if they make the stock a very speculative thing, I think that would be contrary to the interests of bankers and of the public. We have plenty of speculative commodities in the country, and I do not think it is desirable that our great railways should become speculative institutions; and I assume that if a general Act were passed all the railways might end in having their stocks converted, more or less, into very speculative things. I think that would be a great public misfortune, and that the bankers would suffer with other people.

Mr. *Buxton.*

767. With reference to that point, while half the stock is made more speculative, the other half is made less speculative?—No doubt.

768. Would that affect you as a banker in the way of lending, and so on?—No, I do not think so.

769. I understand your objection to reconversion is simply that you think a person ought to make up his mind once for all, and have done with it?—I think so.

770. Suppose the stock gradually became converted, and yet somebody at some subsequent time preferred original stock, do not you think they ought to be entitled to get that just as much as before?—That is not a question on which my opinion is of any value, I think. I want to give as much liberty as possible; but I think that having the accounts of a railway in a clear and intelligible condition is important for the general investor.

0.101.

Mr. *Mowbray.*

771. Have you any definite propositions to make with regard to the voting power which you would give to the deferred stock?—I think voting power changes, or rather the railway company's mode of ascertaining the wishes of the shareholders undergoes very considerable change with the process of conversion. You must assume that the preferred may all get into the hands of an investing class, and the deferred may all get into the hands of a more active and adventurous class. The voting power, as I understand it, is to be divided between the two stocks, stocks held by two classes whose interests are antagonistic, and who may be positively hostile to one another. The preferred are only interested in getting their fixed dividend; the deferred may be interested in getting money to extend the line, to develop the line according to new conditions; yet they cannot get the money to do that without not only going to the preferred, but asking them to allow this new capital to take precedence of their stock in claiming upon the revenues of the line I could thus easily imagine that there might be hostility between the two classes of the ordinary stock. I think that is a very serious fact as affecting the whole question of sub-division.

772. That I rather gathered from your evidence before; but I wished to know whether you had any propositions to make to meet that difficulty?—Well, I have none. I think you cannot take away from the preferred their right of voting, and, of course, you mean to confer it upon the deferred, so it strikes at the whole principle of sub-division.

773. Would it be possible to meet it by allocating the voting power in different proportions? —I should be at a loss to know which was to have the larger proportion. You might argue the one way or the other, according to the condition of the particular railway.

774. Would you oblige your directors to hold equal qualifications in the two?—I have not thought of that.

775. Perhaps that is too small a point to be taken into consideration?—I think it is a very minor point. I do not even know what the present law in regard to qualifications is. I think directors may hold nothing but preference stock, if I remember rightly.

776. I think that is so in the Caledonian case? —That may be so.

Mr. *Biddulph.*

777. They may hold either?—They may hold either.

Mr. *Bristowe.*] They must hold 2,000 *l.* stock.

Mr. *Ellis.*

778. You speak, of course, as a banker, I apprehend?—No, I speak more as a man of business. I have no special interest that is to say in the matter as a banker, beyond what comes in the most ordinary way of business.

779. Then your evidence is not specially at all as a specialist; that is to say, as a banker?— No, not in the least.

Mr. *Dickson.*

780. Are you not largely interested in lending money upon these securities?—I am; but I do not think bankers have a very deep interest in this question further than I have tried to explain. It does affect us; but I am not influenced consciously in my opinions by that. I look at it more from the interest of the public in maintaining the railway companies in a strong position financially.

781. Then, as a banker you are in no way alarmed about the proposals put forward by the railway companies?—Well, I am not alarmed as a banker. I think there will be no great effect produced for a good many years. It will be some years before anything is done which will affect the position of bankers. It is not so much from the point of view of a banker that I have been speaking.

Mr. *Ellis.*

782. Do you attach great importance to what I may call the principle of uniformity and simplicity in any action that may be taken?—I do.

783. You would desire to see the result of any action such that, what I may call the ordinary investor, should not be led astray in any way?—Yes; I think that is desirable if it can be accomplished.

[The Witness withdrew.

Chairman] We have not asked any other witness to come to give us information, but I wish to say something more in the presence of counsel. The Caledonian Company is represented, I think?

Mr. *Saunders.*] Yes, Sir, I represent the Caledonian Company.

Chairman.] I wish to say this: I received a letter from Mr. Spens, the secretary of the Stock Conversion and Investment Trust, Limited, some time ago, asking to appear as a witness here in order to refute certain statements which had been made regarding that company, which he regarded as somewhat unfair; and I instructed a letter to be written to him to say that the Committee did not consider anything that had been said of his company as involving any imputation upon them.

Mr. *Pope.*] Not at all.

Chairman.] Therefore, we did not think it necessary that he should come to answer anything; but since then I have received a letter from him, and I think it is fairest to all parties, while still adhering to the opinion that it is quite unnecessary to enter upon any examination (because we have nothing to do with the operations really of the Trust Company), and I think it perhaps desirable, that I should read this letter, and read it in the presence of the learned gentlemen who represent the Caledonian.

Mr. *Saunders.*] I am much obliged to you, Sir.

Chairman.] " The Stock Conversion and Investment Trust, Limited, 218 and 219, Winchester House, Old Broad-street, E.C.,

London, 16th May 1890. F. Williams Wynn, Esq., Clerk to the Select Committee on the Caledonian, Great Northern, and London and South Western Stock Conversion Bills. House of Commons.—Sir, I am in receipt of your letter of yesterday, and note that the Committee do not desire to examine me as a witness in reference to those Bills. Lord Tweeddale, the chairman of this company, and my co-directors, request me to ask you to bring under the special notice of the Committee the fact that the trustees in whose names railway stock, against which converted stocks are issued by this company is placed, have under their trust deed, no power of voting at railway meetings in respect of such stocks unless they do so as instructed by a meeting of the holders of the stocks issued by this company, and of which meeting each holder of stock receives individual notice. This provision, we believe, secures any vote given being at least as representative of the wishes of the parties interested as that taken at any railway meeting. I also desire to bring under the Committee's notice the fact that, except at Wharncliffe meetings, the scale of voting is not regulated by the amount of stock held by individual shareholders, but that on all other occasions the vote of 600,000 *l.* stock held in one block is only equal to the vote of small shareholders holding an aggregate amount of, I think, some 60,000 *l.* stock. I may add, with reference to the remarks made in the opening statement of counsel with regard to Lord Tweeddale and Mr. Renton, that so far from those gentlemen or the company having any desire to do anything which might suggest personal conflict of interests that on more than one occasion opportunity was offered to the Caledonian Railway Company Board of Directors to appoint a trustee, for the conversion scheme applicable to their stock, who was agreeable to themselves. This company has all along expressed its desire that the railway companies, whose stocks are converted, should nominate trustees. In this state of matters I think the personal allusion of counsel should not have been made. Kindly lay this letter before the Committee. I am, Sir, yours faithfully (signed) *Nath. Spens.*" I think that by reading that letter I place his case in the best way possible; it goes on to the Notes and places his case not only before the Committee, but before all parties concerned.

Mr. *Saunders.*] Perhaps I may be allowed to say, and possibly it would be gratifying to the writer of that letter, that I should say it, and it is only right I should: I am quite sure that Mr. Pember, in making the statement he did, was only illustrating a possible evil, and was not pointing to any conceivable malpractice or any attempted control of the stocks of the Caledonian Company on the part of either Lord Tweeddale or of Mr. Renton, or of the Stock Conversion and Investment and Trust Company. I think Mr. Pember guarded himself against that, but he said that if such a thing were
done

done by people who were not as responsible as those gentlemen, it would be leaving a door open to attacks, either for stock jobbing purposes or for rival companies purposes to control stocks. Of course with regard to the argument as to the amount of stock represented at the meeting there might be an answer to that. It would not be proper that I should go into that; but I have to say, on behalf of the Caledonian Railway Company, that we are perfectly satisfied with everything that has been done by the Stock Conversion Company, and I am quite sure their action was not directed with the view in any way to control the stocks. Nothing they have ever done has been the cause of complaint. I am extremely sorry that any casual allusion by my learned friend, Mr. Pember, should have been interpreted as being a covert attack upon the company; and I am instructed to say so by the solicitor of the company.

Chairman.] I may say, for myself, it was quite in that sense that I understood Mr. Pember's allusion.

Mr. *Saunders.*] I am much obliged to you, Sir.

Chairman.] Now that the evidence is concluded, the Committee will have to deliberate to settle their Report; and that they will do after Whitsuntide, some time.

Tuesday, 10th June 1890.

MEMBERS PRESENT:

Mr. W. Beckett.   Mr. Biddulph.
Mr. Bristowe.   Mr. Dickson.
Mr. Buxton.   Mr. J. E. Ellis.
Mr. R. Mowbray.   Mr. Charles Hall.

THE RIGHT HON. H. CAMPBELL-BANNERMAN, IN THE CHAIR.

Chairman.] The Committee have passed the preambles of the several Bills, and will now go through the Bills to receive certain desired information from counsel as to particular clauses. The Committee will make a Special Report to the House on the subject. The Committee will require that in each Bill a provision is included, directing that dividends shall be declared on the original ordinary stock, and that the original ordinary stock shall be clearly set forth in the statement of capital account. This is already provided in certain of the Bills The Committee are also of opinion that the new stocks should have a uniform nomenclature, and should be known as " Preferred Converted Ordinary Stock," and " Deferred Converted Ordinary Stock." Now, with regard to the Clauses of the Bills we will take the South Western first. Clause 2, Sub-section 11, of the South Western Bill provides that " Preferred Ordinary Stock and Deferred Ordinary Stock shall respectively be held on the same trusts, and subject to the same charges and liabilities as those on and subject to which the original stock in substitution for which the same are issued was held immediately before the substitution, and so as to give effect to and not revoke any deed, will, or other instrument disposing of or affecting such original stock." I wish to ask the Counsel for the London and South Western Bill whether in his opinion that covers the whole ground covered by Clauses 8 and 21 of the Great Northern Bill, it obviously covers Clause 8, but it appears to us that a similar provision to Clause 21 should be inserted in the South Western Bill. In the Isle of Wight Bill there is a similar clause which is even perhaps better expressed.

Mr. Pember.] I see the point.

Chairman.] We hope you will be willing and ready to insert such a provision; the Committee find that in certain of the Bills and not in this Bill.

Mr. Pope.] Ordinarily railway companies do not recognise trusts at all, therefore the practical importance of it is but small.

Mr. Pember.] At present I am not sufficiently instructed to say whether there would be any objection on our part to the insertion of such a clause.

Chairman.] The Committee think it is a right clause unless some special reason is shown why it is not applicable to the particular company. It does not seem to us to affect the Company.

Mr. Pope.] No, it affects the trustees.

Mr. Pember.] Do not think that I am at all recalcitant about the matter, but that has not been brought to my attention before, and I confess that I would like a few minutes to think the point over.

Chairman.] The Committee has to meet again on Friday ; perhaps then you will be able to tell us whether you have any objection to the insertion of the clause.

Mr. Pember.] Yes.

Chairman.] I do not think there is any other point on the South Western Bill.

Mr. Pope.] Perhaps you will allow me to say this, that we inserted that clause in the Great Northern Bill and in the Isle of Wight Bill, not as affecting the Company at all because undoubtedly the stock itself is, by the ordinary provisions which have been introduced docketted, so to speak, with the character of a trust, but we thought it desirable that the trustees should be enabled to accept, in lieu of the corpus of their trust, converted stock, in order that it might not be said that they had committed a breach of trust by accepting converted stock.

Mr. Pember.] At the present moment, with all submission to the Committee, I am not quite clear whether it is right that trustees should be empowered to take converted stock.

Chairman.] Perhaps

Chairman.] Perhaps you will consider that before Friday. Then I wish to ask this question of the learned Counsel. Looking at Clause 2, Sub-section 13 of the South Western Bill, and the analogous sections in the other Bills, they meet the wishes of the Committee with regard to maintaining well in the front of the accounts the old original ordinary stock; but I wish to ask, for our information, whether that will carry with it the implied provision that the Board of Trade shall see that this is done.

Mr. Pember.] I may say at once we should have no objection to that being provided, for a moment: " If the company, under the powers and provisions of this section, create and issue any preferred ordinary stock and deferred ordinary stock, the forms of accounts and of returns prescribed by and referred to in the Regulation of Railways Act, 1868, and in the Railways Regulation Amendment Act, 1871, or in any Act amending the same, shall from time to time continue to be made up, so as to show the amount of original stock authorized, created, and received, as if such substitution had not taken place; but the statement of capital account shall set forth, in addition to the particulars required by the first Schedule to the Act first named, the amount of preferred ordinary stock and deferred ordinary stock respectively." I have very little doubt that that would give the Board of Trade power to see that it was done, but we should not have the slightest objection to make assurance doubly sure by saying that all the regulations of those Acts, so far as the Board of Trade is concerned, shall be applied to this Act.

Chairman.] Perhaps that is a point the learned Counsel would consider also.

Mr. *Pember.*] Yes.

Chairman.] It is not right in Bills, such as these, to put any new duties upon the Board of Trade; but we wish to bring it under the powers conferred upon the Board of Trade by other legislation.

Mr. *Pember.*] There is no doubt about it, because by Section 4 of the Regulation of Railways Act, 1868, first of all it says, that every statement of accounts and balance sheet are to be signed by the chairman and by the accountant; and then there is a distict injunction that every copy or statement of accounts shall be forwarded to the Board of Trade.

Mr. *Pope.*] We need not discuss it now.

CALEDONIAN RAILWAY (CONVERSION OF STOCK) BILL.

Chairman.] As to the Caledonian Bill, I have to say that the Committee have decided to strike out Clause 6, providing for the reconversion of stock. I think it was stated on the part of the Company that that was not insisted on in any degree by the Company, and for other reasons the Committee think it desirable to strike that clause out.

Mr. *Littler.*] We should have liked it, but, of course, we bow to the decision of the Committee.

Chairman.] I may mention that the title which we require, " Preferred Converted Ordinary Stock," was made particularly necessary by the circumstances of the Caledonian Company where there is already preferred ordinary stock. We desire that the Caledonian Company should insert the same clause with regard to the power of trustees as we desired should be inserted in the South Western Bill. That is the only point with regard to the Caledonian Bill, except the naming of the stock.

Mr. *Pope.*] That applies to all the four Bills.

Chairman.] Yes.

ISLE OF WIGHT RAILWAY BILL.

Chairman.] Now with regard to the Isle of Wight Bill, there are certain clauses in that Bill as to which, I think, we have heard nothing, namely, Clauses 4 to 8, " power to acquire lands," compulsory purchase of lands," and " restriction on displacement of persons of the labouring class."

Mr. *Pope.*] As far as I know those are unopposed powers. probably you would be content to take formal evidence here in support of the Preamble; they are unopposed clauses; they are not within the peculiar subject matter for which this Committee was constituted, and it would be convenient if you would simply take formal evidence, so as to report the Bill. I will put Mr. Tahourdin, the Chairman of the Company, in the box, and ask if that part of the Preamble is true.

Chairman.] We rather want an explanation of these clauses, especially Clause 7.

Mr. *Pope.*] That is a Standing Order Clause; that is a restriction on displacing persons of the labouring classes.

Chairman.] That is inserted formally in all Bills of the sort ?

0.101.   H 2   Mr.

Mr. *Pope.*] Yes.

Chairman.] Does that apply to Clause 8 also ?

Mr. *Pope.*] No ; as regards Clause 7, the Standing Order requires that where you take lands and buildings, you shall either make provision for the people you displace, or you shall not displace the people ; therefore that clause has to be inserted. Clause 8 extends the time of the General Act (The Lands Clauses Act) to ten years from the passing of the Act.

By the *Committee.*] What is the reason for that ?

Mr. *Pope.*] You will require some formal evidence of the reason for that ; it is not opposed. I will put Mr. Tahourdin into the box to explain the reason for putting that clause into the Bill.

Mr. HORACE F. TAHOURDIN, re-called.

Mr. *Pope.*

784. You are Chairman of the Isle of Wight Railway ?—Yes.

785. Will you explain the reason for putting in Clause 8 ?—We have several pieces of land up and down the railway, part of which are used at present and part of which will be used, and the time has expired and there might arise a question of their being surplus lands.

786. That is to say, you have acquired under previous powers certain lands ?—Yes.

787. The statutory period of 10 years is running out ?—It has nearly run out.

788. You still think that you may require these lands for the purposes of the railway, therefore you desire a removal of the powers for a further period of 10 years ?—That is it.

789. If you did not get this extension under the provisions of the Lands' Clauses Act you would have to sell the lands you hold now, at the expiration of 10 years from the passing of the original Act ?—Yes.

Mr. *Pope*--continued.

790. By the *Committee.*] Are these lands situate near any population ?—They are near stations.

Mr. *Pope.*] It is the ordinary clause.

Chairman.

791. If you had not been going to convert your stock, would you have come for this power ? —We should not have come to Parliament with a Bill simply for this purpose, but we have got a note for some time to put this in the first Bill we applied for.

792. By the *Committee.*] Do you require the whole of these lands for your own purposes ?—Yes.

793. You never would think of selling them for building purposes ?—Not outside of the works.

794. You put this clause in this Bill to avoid the expense of a separate Bill ?—Yes.

Chairman.] I think that is sufficient information on that point. I understand that Clause 15 is struck out of the Bill. I did not know that there was an absolute agreement that it should be struck out, but the Committee took some exception to it, and I think a willingness was expressed to omit it if the Committee desired.

Witness.] Clause 15, as amended, stands in the Bill. We said if 14a was adopted that Clause 15 might go out.

Chairman.] If the clause, as amended, was read to the Committee it would be an advantage ; it is not very easy to follow it as we have it here. It is a clause which provides for turning preference stock into ordinary stock, which is an unusual proceeding.

Mr. *Pope.*] The clause, as amended, reads in this way : the marginal notes is "conversion of 5 per cent. preference stock into 4 per cent. preference stock," and the body of the clause " is on the 1st of January 1891 the existing 5 per cent. preference stock in the capital of the Company shall be by virtue of this Act cancelled and extinguished, and on that day there shall be, by virtue of this Act without further or other authority, created a 4 per cent. preference stock of the Company to the amount of 84,012 *l*. 10 *s*. in lieu of and in substitution for the stock cancelled and extinguished as aforesaid." (To the *Witness.*) I suppose that that 84,012 *l*. is the proportion to which the stock would be increased by reason of the reduction to 4 per cent. ?—Yes.

Chairman.] That clause refers to a change from 5 per cent. preference stock to 4 per cent. preference stock. The clause I am referring to has, as its marginal note, "Conversion of 4 per cent. preference stock into ordinary stock."

Mr. *Pope.*] I confess I understood that Mr. Tahourdin said that would affect so small a number of shareholders that he would be quite willing that it should be struck out of the Bill ; I do not find it struck out of the Bill, but I am not dispose to go behind what Mr. Tahourdin said.

Chairman.] We do not wish to pin Mr. Tahourdin to what he said ; I do not think he implied that it would *ipso facto* be struck out, but he expressed a willingness to abandon it without much regret if the Committee desired that it should be struck out, and I think the Committee would rather that it was not in the Bill.

Mr. *Pope.*] Then we shall strike it out.

Chairman.] I think

10th June 1890.

Chairman.] I think Clause 14a is unobjectionable. We shall require clauses to be put into the Isle of Wight Bill to provide, as in the other cases, for the publication of the accounts in the way we desire, keeping the old original ordinary stock in the foreground, and also some limitation on the borrowing powers.

Mr. *Pope.*] It would be desirable possibly that some clause should be agreed on as a common clause to that effect, which would secure the object you have in view, which would be inserted in all the Bills.

Chairman.] There is such a clause in the South Western Bill which seems to us to be very well drawn.

Mr. *Pope.*] I do not see why that should not be adopted as a general clause.

Chairman.] There is another clause in the South Western Bill which you can adopt at the same time, Clause 2, Sub-section 14, a clause preventing any extension of the borrowing powers by this alteration of stock.

Mr. *Pope.*] Quite so, I do not think it will affect the Isle of Wight Company, for they have no borrowing powers to affect.

Chairman.] Possibly not, but we wish to make assurance doubly sure. It is to be understood that the general observations that I have made apply to the Isle of Wight Bill as well as to the others. Then any new clauses that may be necessary, can be submitted to the Committee on Friday.

Friday, 13*th June* 1890.

Mr. Bristowe.   Mr. Dickson.
Mr. Buxton.   Mr. John Ellis.
Mr. Campbell-Bannerman.   Mr. R. Mowbray.

THE RIGHT HON. H. CAMPBELL-BANNERMAN, IN THE CHAIR.

LONDON AND SOUTH WESTERN RAILWAY (CONVERSION OF STOCK) BILL.

THE Preamble having been amended in accordance with the decision of the Committee, the Preamble, as amended, was passed.

The clauses of the Bill were proceeded with.

Clauses having been incorporated in the Bill embodying the decision of the Committee, the clauses, as amended, were passed.

CALEDONIAN RAILWAY (CONVERSION OF STOCK) BILL.

THE Preamble having been amended in accordance with the decision of the Committee, the Preamble, as amended, was passed.

The clauses of the Bill were proceeded with.

Clauses having been incorporated in the Bill embodying the decision of the Committee, the clauses, as amended, were passed.

GREAT NORTHERN RAILWAY (CAPITAL) BILL.

THE Preamble having been amended in accordance with the decision of the Committee, the Preamble, as amended, was passed.

The clauses of the Bill were proceeded with.

Clauses having been incorporated in the Bill embodying the decision of the Committee, the clauses, as amended, were passed.

THE ISLE OF WIGHT RAILWAY BILL, 1890.

THE Preamble having been amended in accordance with the decision of the Committee, the Preamble, as amended, was passed.

The clauses of the Bill were proceeded with.

Clauses having been incorporated in the Bill embodying the decision of the Committee, the clauses, as amended, were passed.

The Committee deliberated upon a Special Report to the House.

R E P O R T S

AND

SPECIAL REPORT

FROM THE

SELECT COMMITTEE

ON THE

CALEDONIAN RAILWAY (CONVERSION OF STOCK) BILL,

THE

GREAT NORTHERN RAILWAY (CAPITAL) BILL,

THE

LONDON AND SOUTH WESTERN RAILWAY (CONVERSION OF STOCK) BILL,

AND THE

ISLE OF WIGHT RAILWAY BILL;

TOGETHER WITH THE

PROCEEDINGS OF THE COMMITTEE

AND

MINUTES OF EVIDENCE.

Ordered, *by* The House of Commons, *to be Printed*,
13 *June* 1890

[*Price 7½ d.*]

225.

H.—23. 6. 90.

Under 8 oz.

I N D E X.

[*N.B.*—In this Index the Figures following the Names of the Witnesses, and those in the Analysis of Evidence of each Witness, refer to the Questions in the Evidence; and the Numerals following *Special Rep.* to the Pages in the Special Report by the Committee.]

A.

ACCOUNTS. Advantage to railway companies in having as few descriptions of stocks at different rates as possible, *Grinling* 250-252. 261——Explanation in connection with the account of the Great Northern Company, as already showing the capital under the proposed conversion of stock into "preferred ordinary" and "deferred ordinary," *ib.* 379-382. 386-392. 400-406.

Stipulation on the part of the Board of Trade as to the accounts clearly showing the amount of paid-up capital as distinguished from the nominal, as a condition of further duplications being sanctioned; importance of explicit records on this point in the public interest, *Giffen* 537-539. 564, 565. 575, 582. 583——Approval, on the whole, of full latitude in the companies as to the amount of stock to be converted, and as to the reconversion, &c., so long as full records are kept of the paid-up capital, *ib.* 576-580. 587.

Importance of the accounts clearly showing the paid-up capital apart from duplication or splitting, *Price* 637, 638——Great importance attached to simplicity and uniformity in carrying out conversion so that the accounts may be clearly understood by the public, *Gairdner* 753, 754. 762-764. 770. 782, 783.

Satisfaction of the Committee with the provisions in the Bills for maintaining in the front of the accounts the old original ordinary stock, *p.* 59——Approval by the Committee of the clause in the South Western Bill on the subject of accounts, *p.* 61.

Recommendation by the Committee that, in order to prevent any confusion, the original stock or paid-up capital shall be recorded and shown in the accounts as though no alteration had been made in the form of the stock, *Special Rep. v.*

Astle, William. (Analysis of his Evidence.)—Witness is Chief Manager of the London and Westminster Bank, 708.

Opinion that railway companies should be empowered to split or duplicate their stocks according to the circumstances of each company, 709, 710. 722, 723——Advantage of the good investments created for the public by means of preferred stock; approval of the dividend being cumulative, 711, 712. 734-736.

Approval of the maximum dividend on preferred stock being fixed at 6 per cent., though 4 per cent. would be a fair proportion, 713-716. 724-731——Belief that the conversion of stocks would not affect bankers injuriously, 717-719. 732, 733. 739——Disapproval of any right to re-convert, 737, 738.

B.

Bank of England. Probable effect of extensive conversion of railway stocks in enhancing the value of Bank of England stock, *May* 611-613.

Opinion that the creation of large amounts of preferred stock would not facilitate loan transactions, *May* 627, 628—— Belief that the conversion of stocks would not affect bankers injuriously, *Astle* 717-719. 732, 733. 739; *Gairdner* 766-768. 778-781.

Board of Trade. General policy of the Board of Trade to favour the utmost liberty in railway companies as to the arrangement of their capital; instances to this effect, *Giffen* 509-543——Explanation that the Board of Trade express no opinion as to the expediency of duplication, but considers that the question should be carefully considered, as by the present Committee, *ib.* 540-543. 562, 563. 566-574.

Adoption by the Board of Trade of the principle of non-intervention in the financial affairs of railway companies, *Special Rep. v.*

Report, 1890—*continued.*

C.

Caledonian Railway Company. Particulars respecting the capital of the company; total of about 40,000,000 *l.*, of which about 11,000,000 *l.* is ordinary stock and 2,784,693 *l.* is deferred ordinary stock, *Sir F. King* 122-134——Great popularity of the present scheme with the shareholders of the company, *ib.* 144-151——Proposed issue of preferred converted ordinary stock and deferred converted ordinary stock, each equal in amount to the present ordinary stock, *ib.* 152-156——Provision as to the dividend being still declared on the ordinary stock, *ib.* 157-159. 176-178.

Reason for fixing 3 per cent. as the maximum dividend on the preferred ordinary, *Sir F. King* 162, 163. 209——Statement to be issued to the shareholders explaining that there would be no increase of capital, but only a duplication of stock, *ib.* 163-165 ——Question considered as to the names or titles to be given to the two stocks when duplicated ; willingness of the promoters to leave this matter entirely to the Committee, *ib.* 179-187.

Large number of shareholders expected to convert if the Bill be passed ; check thereby to further action of the Trust Company, *Sir F. King* 199-202——Preference on the part of the board for as little conversion as possible, the object being to give the option to the shareholders, and to exclude the operation of outside companies, *ib.* 205-208.

Approval on the part of the Committee of the adoption of the word "converted" in order to prevent confusion, *p.* 17.

Decision of the Committee to strike out the clause providing for the re-conversion of stock, *p.* 59.

Report by the Committee to the effect that the preamble of the Bill, as amended, is proved, and that amendments have been made to the Bill, *Rep.* iii. ix. ; *p.* 62.

See also Re-conversion.   Scotland.   Stock Conversion Trust.   Voting Power.

Capital. Facility of avoiding any appearance of duplication of capital under the Bill promoted by witness' company ; nominal increase, however, in carrying out conversion as in the case of the consolidation of the preference stocks of the North Western Company, *Scott* 102—— Statement as to the beneficial effect of the proposed conversion scheme of the Great Northern Company with regard to the future raising of capital, as an additional amount could be raised for the same annual charge, *Grinling* 310-313.

Restriction under one of the Standing Orders upon increase of capital when an amalgamation takes place, *Giffen* 523, 524——Repeated instances of increase of the nominal capital of companies, as on occasions of amalgamation, *ib.* 524. 530——Misrepresentation of capital where duplication takes place, *Price* 636.

Compulsory Conversion. Necessity of the proposed conversion scheme of the Great Northern Company being compulsory ; great confusion otherwise, *Grinling* 377, 378. 393-398. 407-414——Conclusion that compulsory conversion is very objectionable and would not be approved by the shareholders of the South Western Company, *Scott* 105-111.

Conversion or Division (Ordinary Stock). Expediency of the railway companies carrying out the conversion of their own stocks, under direct Parliamentary provision, rather than of the matter being taken up by outside companies, *Scott* 98, 99. 112-115—— Strong feeling at the boards of the North Western and Great Western Companies adverse to conversion, *ib.* 113-115.

Approval of full latitude in the companies as to conversion, *Giffen* 576-580. 587; *Price* 635. 639. 644. 662-673. 707——It is, in fact, a defensive operation against the action of outside bodies, *Price* 651. 674-676——Opinion that railway companies should be empowered to split or duplicate their stocks according to the circumstances of each company, *Astle* 709, 710. 722, 723.

Principal object of the several Bills to carry out the division of ordinary stock into two portions, one of which shall have assigned to it a fixed rate of dividend, while the other shall be entitled to such an amount of income as, after the payment of the fixed dividend on the first portion, may remain available for distribution out of the earnings of the company, *Special Rep.* iv.

Conclusion of the Committee that there is nothing unreasonable nor objectionable from a public point of view in the conversion of ordinary stock into a preferred and a
deferred

Conversion or Division (Ordinary Stock)—continued.

deferred class, and that the necessary power, when desired by any railway company, should not be refused, *Special Rep.* iv.

> *See also* *Caledonian Railway Company.*   *Duplication of Stock.*   *Great*
> *Northern Railway Company.*   *Isle of Wight Railway Company.*   *London*
> *and South Western Railway Company.*   *Splitting of Stock.*   *Trust Com-*
> *panies.*

Cumulative Dividends.   Objection to the cumulative system being applied to the preferred or deferred stock, *Price* 705, 706; *Gairdner* 765——Approval of the dividend on the preferred stock being cumulative, *Astle* 711, 712.

D.

Debenture Stock.   Reason for the proposed conversion of debenture stocks of the Great Northern Company into one 3 per cent. stock; improvement thereby in the aggregate value, *Grinling* 372-336.

Deferred Ordinary Stock.   Speculative character of the A. stock of the Great Northern Company, by reason of its small amount and fluctuating dividend; increase of value where there is an increased market, *Grinling* 261-263. 280-285. 293-295. 339——Less speculation and increased value where there is a large amount of deferred stock, *ib.* 261-263. 280-285. 293-295. 339.

Importance attached by witness (apart from his official position) to deferred stock receiving a substantial proportion of the net income; increased fluctuation and speculation accordingly as such proportion is small, *Giffen* 534-561. 588, 589.

Difficulty in preventing fluctuation and speculation in deferred stock; unimportance attached to a suggestion by Mr. Giffen on this point, *May* 602-608——Speculative character of the deferred stock, *Astle* 713——Views of witness as the importance of deferred stock being maintained at a larger amount, and participating substantially in the net profits; suggestions on this subject, *Gairdner* 747-751. 755-759.

Balance of earnings to be divided among the holders of deferred ordinary stock after the payment of a fixed dividend on the deferred stock, *Special Rep.* iv.

> *See also* *Accounts.*   *Caledonian Railway Company.*   *Conversion, &c.*   *Isle of*
> *Wight Railway Company.*   *London and South Western Railway Company.*

Dividends.   Recommendation of the Committee that, in order to avoid any confusion as to the actual amount of the paid-up capital of a company, the dividend shall in all cases continue to be declared on the original stock, *Special Rep.* v.

> *See also* *Preferred Stock.*   *Cumulative Dividends.*

Duplication of Stock.   Consideration of objections to the duplication of the stock of the South Western Company, instead of splitting it; grounds for the conclusion that duplication is far preferable in the interests of the shareholders, and that there will be less speculation than if the stock were split under the Act of 1868, *Scotter* 45-82—— Decided opinion that the speculative element is reduced where stock is duplicated instead of split, *Scott* 103——Opinion that duplication will not lead to speculation, whilst it will increase the value, *Sir J. King* 188-192. 198.

Grounds for preferring the scheme of the Great Northern Company to a duplication of the stock, though the latter might be the better plan if there were a safe dividend of 6 per cent., *Grinling* 334-371——Less speculative character of the deferred stock of the Great Northern Company than under a duplication scheme, *ib.* 416.

Explanation that there was no question of duplication of stock at the time of the Act of 1868, *Giffen* 516, 517——Doubt as to duplication being more open to objection than splitting, *May* 600, 601. 614-624.

Approval, on the whole, of power in the companies to duplicate; less speculation where there are large amounts of deferred stock than under the splitting system, *Price* 634, 635. 650, 651. 665. 673. 695-700. 703-706 ——Dissent from the opinion that there would be less fluctuation of stocks if duplicated; preference for splitting, *Gairdner* 752, 753. 761.

> *See also* *Accounts.*   *Conversion, &c.*

G.

Gairdner, Charles. (Analysis of his Evidence.)—Witness is General Manager of the Union Bank of Scotland, 740,741.

Belief that there is a strong feeling among railway shareholders in favour of conversion or subdivision of the ordinary stocks as increasing their market value, 743-745——Considerable doubt in the minds of directors as to the expediency of conversion and the creation of deferred stock, 746–749.

Views of witness as to the importance of deferred stock being maintained at a large amount and participating substantially in the net profits; suggestions on this subject, 747–751. 755–759——Dissent from the opinion that there would be less fluctuation of stocks if duplicated; preference for splitting, 752, 753. 761—— Great importance attached to simplicity and uniformity in carrying out conversion so that the accounts may be clearly understood by the public, 753, 754. 762-764. 770. 782, 783.

Question whether the schemes before the Committee would prevent trust companies from further operating in railway stocks, 760, 761——Disapproval of any re-conversion; increased confusion and speculation thereby, 765-770——Objection also to the dividends being cumulative, 765.

Opinion that bankers would not be affected by conversion, unless there were a great impetus to speculation, 766–768. 778–781—— Consideration of the effect of conversion as regards voting power; difficulty on this joint, 771–773.

Giffen, Robert. (Analysis of his Evidence.)—Witness is one of the Assistant Secretaries of the Board of Trade, certain statistics under the Regulation of Railways Act coming before his Department, 508

General policy of the Board of Trade as regards railways to favour the utmost liberty to the companies as to the arrangement of their capital; instances to this effect, 509-543—— Origin of the clause in the Regulation of Railways Act of 1868 as to the splitting of ordinary stock into preferred and deferred; views expressed in the House of Lords by the Duke of Richmond (then President of the Board of Trade) in favour of this clause, which was adopted, 510-518—— Explanation that there was no question of duplication of stock at the time of the Act of 1868; 516, 517.

Question in 1867 of the issue of shares at a discount, this having been done by several companies, without opposition on the part of the Board of Trade or of the Legislature, 518-521—— Recommendation in the Report of the Royal Commission on Railways in 1867 that Parliament should relieve itself from all interference in the financial affairs of railway companies, 522.

Restriction under one of the Standing Orders upon increase of capital when an amalgamation takes place, 523, 524 —- Repeated instances of increase of the nominal capital of companies, as on occasions of amalgamation, 524-530—— Large increase or duplication of capital of the North British Company in 1888; 526-528. 531. 569——Information respecting the large duplication in the case of the Taff Vale Company in 1889, and the conditions under which allowed, 530-536. 569. 584, 585.

Stipulation on the part of the Board of Trade as to the accounts clearly showing the amount of paid-up capital as distinguished from the nominal, as a condition of further duplications being sanctioned; importance of explicit records on this point in the public interest, 537-529. 564, 565. 575. 582, 583—— Explanation that the Board of Trade express no opinion as to the expediency of duplication but considers that the question should be carefully considered, as by the present Committee, 540-543. 562, 563. 566-574.

Importance attached by witness (apart from his official position) to deferred stock receiving a substantial proportion of the net increase; increased fluctuation and speculation accordingly as such proportion is small, 534-561. 588, 589—— Belief as to the origin of the 6 per cent. clause in the Act of 1868; increased dividends on ordinary stocks since that year, 551-557.

Approval, on the whole, of full latitude in the companies as to the amount of stock to be converted, and as to re-conversion, &c., so long as full records are kept of the paid-up capital, 576-580. 587——Effect of the issue of shares at a discount in increasing the capital bearing dividend, this not applying to the system of duplication, 582, 583.

Great Northern Railway Company. Total of 13,472,327 *l.* as the original stock or ordinary capital of the Great Northern Company, inclusive of 269,260 *l.* derived from premiums and not receiving dividends, *Grinling* 228-233——Total of 15,789,010 *l.* as the amount of preference stocks, the debenture stock being 9,089,301 *l.*, *ib.* 234, 235.

Special

Great Northern Railway Company—continued.

Special power obtained by the company, under their Act of 1848, to divide their original stock into equal moieties, the B. stock taking a preference cumulative dividend of 6 per cent.. and the A. stock receiving the balance, *Grinling* 236 -240. 252-255—— Explanation that it was optional in the directors under the Act of 1848 to allow conversion to go on, and that for special reasons a certain amount of preferred and deferred stock was issued, and the process of conversion was stopped, *ib.* 241-247——Consolidation of various preference stocks under the Acts of 1872, 1875, and 1887, the addition to the preference capital thereby being 1,803,000 *l.*, *ib.* 248-252. 256-260.

Initiation taken by the shareholders in pressing conversion on the board of directors; that is, in view of the large increase of market value thereby, this being about 12½ per cent., *Grinling* 271-279. 383-385——Statement as to the disadvantage of three separate stocks (ordinary, preferred, and deferred) in lieu of one ordinary stock in the case of the Great Northern Company; object of the present compulsory scheme to bring these stocks into preferred and deferred, *ib.* 286-288.——Higher relative value of the 4 per cent. consolidated preference stock than of the previous 4½ per cent. stock, *ib.* 289-295.

Recognition under the present scheme of the Great Northern Company of the original division into A. and B. stocks, with the modification that 4 per cent. interest is substituted for 6 per cent., *Grinling* 322-330——Arrangements as to the proportionate issue of deferred stock and preferred stock, there being 75 *l.* of the latter at 4 per cent., and 150 *l.* of the former for every 100 *l.* of ordinary stock, *ib.* 328-350——Statement of the annual dividend on the original stock of the company since 1870; average of 4 *l.* 14 *s.* 3 *d.* for the last ten years, *ib.* 335-339.

Reason for fixing the preferred dividend at 4 per cent. instead of 3 per cent., as in the case of the Caledonian Company, *Grinling* 340 368. 415, 416—— Prospect of the B. shareholders falling in with the scheme, though not retaining cumulative rights, *ib.* 348. 407-411.

Active part taken by witness, as a large holder of ordinary stock, in supporting the proposed conversion of the stock, instead of the matter being taken up by trust investment or other outside companies, *Green* 417-429——Prospect of both the A. and B. stocks being eventually got rid of under the present scheme; reference hereon to the very speculative character of the A. stock, *ib.* 427-429.

Special circumstances under which the Great Northern Company took the lead in converting ordinary stock into preferred and deferred; justification for their doing so, *Price* 631. 666——Questionable expediency of the arrangement proposed by the Great Northern Company in their Bill of this Session, *ib.* 667-673. 703-706.

Report of the Committee that the preamble of the Bill, as amended, has been proved, and that amendments have been made to the Bill, *Rep.* iii. ix. ; *p.* 62.

See also **Capital.**   **Debenture Stock.**   **Duplication of Stock.**

Green, Richard. Large interest of witness in Great Northern ordinary stock; active part taken by him in supporting the proposed conversion of the stock, instead of the matter being taken up by trust investment or other outside companies, 417-429 —— Prospect of both the A. and B. stocks being eventually got rid of under the present scheme ; reference hereon to the very speculative character of the A. stock, 427-429.

Grinling, William. (Analysis of his Evidence.)—Witness has been accountant of the Great Northern Railway Company for twenty years, 225-227.

Total of 13,472,327 *l.* as the original stock or ordinary capital of the Great Northern Company. inclusive of 269,260 *l.* derived from premiums and not receiving dividends, 228-233——Total of 15,789,010 *l.* as the amount of preference stocks, the debenture stock being 9,089,301 *l.*, 234, 235.

Special power obtained by the company under their Act of 1848 to divide their original stock into equal moieties, the B. stock taking a preference cumulative dividend of 6 per cent., and the A. stock receiving the balance, 236-240. 252-255   Explanation that it was optional in the directors, under the Act of 1848, to allow conversion to go on, and that for special reasons a certain amount of preferred and deferred stock was issued and the process of conversion was stopped, 241-247.

Consolidation of various preference stocks under the Acts of 1872, 1875, and 1887, the addition to the preference capital thereby being 1,803,000 *l*, 248-252. 256-260—— Advantage to a railway company to have as few descriptions of stocks at different rates as possible, 250-252. 261.

View of witness' directors that 6 per cent. is now much too high a rate at which to place any guaranteed or preferred stock ; opinion that in future all such stocks will have

160.   I 3   to

Grinling, William. (Analysis of his Evidence)—*continued.*

to be placed at something like the current rate of the day, 252 —— Statement as to the disadvantage of these separate stocks (ordinary, preferred, and deferred) in lieu of one ordinary stock, in the case of the Great Northern Company; object of the present compulsory scheme to bring these stocks into preferred and deferred, 261-270. 286-288 —— Speculative character of the A. stock by reason of its small amount and fluctuating dividend; increase of value where there is an increased market, 261-263. 280-285. 293-295. 339.

Initiation taken by the shareholders in pressing conversion on the board of directors; that is, in view of the large increase of market value thereby, this being about 12½ per cent., 271-279. 383-385 —— Higher relative value of the 4 per cent. consolidated preference stock than of the previous 4½ per cent. stock, 289-295 —— Calculations as to the much higher relative value of a 4 per cent. deferred ordinary stock than of the present 6 per cent. B. stock, 296-309.

Statement as to the beneficial effect of the proposed conversion scheme with regard to the future raising of capital, as an additional amount could be raised for the same annual charge, 310-313 —— Comment upon the operations of the Stock Investment Company, as in the case of the London and North Western Railway Company; considerable profit made by the former in their mode of dealing with the ordinary stock of the latter, 313-321.

Recognition under the present scheme of the Great Northern Company of the original division into A. and B. stocks, with the modification that 4 per cent. interest is substituted for 6 per cent., 322-330 —— Arrangement as to the proportionate issue of deferred stock and preferred stock, there being 75 *l.* of the latter, at 4 per cent., and 50 *l.* of the former for every 100 *l.* of the ordinary stock, 328-350 —— Grounds for preferring the proposed scheme to a duplication of the stock, though the latter might be the better plan if there were a safe dividend of 6 per cent., 334-371.

Statement of the annual dividend on the original stock of the company since 1870; average of 4 *l.* 14 *s.* 3 *d.* for the last ten years, 335-339 —— Reason for fixing the preferred dividend at 4 per cent. instead of 3 per cent., as in the case of the Caledonian Company, 340-368. 415. 416 —— Prospect of the B. shareholders falling in with the scheme, though not retaining cumulative rights, 348. 407-411 —— Reasons for the proposed conversion of debenture stocks into one 3 per cent. stock; improvement thereby in the aggregate value, 372-376.

Necessity of the proposed conversion scheme being compulsory; great confusion otherwise, 377, 378. 393-398. 407-414 —— Explanation in connection with the accounts as clearly showing the capital under the proposed conversion of stocks into "preferred ordinary" and "deferred ordinary," 379-382. 386-392. 400-403 —— Less speculative character of the deferred stock than under a duplication scheme, 416.

I.

Isle of Wight Railway Company. Total of twelve miles as the length of the railway; particulars as to the capital and dividends, *Tahourdin* 431-441 —— Ordinary stock of 914,572 *l.* dividends thereon not having been paid till 1875, and having gradually increased up to 6½ per cent. in 1889, *ib.* 437-441.

Statement explanatory of the proposed conversion of capital under the Bill before the Committee, as regards debenture and ordinary stocks, *Tahourdin* 439 —— Particulars respecting the proposed conversion of the three 5 per cent. debenture stocks into one 4 per cent. stock; consents obtained from more than three-fourths of the stock holders, *ib.* 442-454 —— Information as to the proposal for converting each 100 *l.* of ordinary stock into 100 *l.* of 4 per cent. preferred stock and 100 *l.* of deferred stock; unanimity of the ordinary shareholders in approving this scheme, *ib.* 455-463. 492.

Further creation of 4 per cent. stock by the conversion of each 100 *l.* of 5 per cent. preference into 125 *l.* of 4 per cent; contemplated bonus of 10 per cent. of deferred stock in connection with this conversion, the directors, however, not attaching much importance to the latter proposal, *Tahourdin* 464-494 —— Main principle of the Bill that all the stocks (except the deferred ordinary) shall receive 4 per cent., *ib.* 466. 473, 474.

Object of Clause 8 of the Bill to extend for another period of ten years the time for retaining certain lands for the purposes of the railway, *Tahourdin* 784-794.

Amended clause substituted for Clause 15, with reference to the conversion of 5 per cent. preference stock into 4 per cent. stock, *pp.* 60, 61.

Amendment of the preamble by the Committee; also, of certain provisions of the Bill, *Rep.* iii. ix.; *p.* 62.

See also *Voting Power.*

Issue

Report, 1890—continued.

Issue of Shares at a Discount. Question in 1867 of the issue of shares at a discount, this having been done by several companies, without opposition on the part of the Board of Trade or of the Legislature, *Giffen* 518-521——Effect of the issue of shares at a discount in increasing the capital bearing dividend, this not applying to the system of duplication, *ib.* 582, 583.

K.

King, Sir James. (Analysis of his Evidence.)—Long experience of witness in connection with the Caledonian Railway, of which he is now Deputy Chairman, 116-121.

Particulars respecting the capital of the company; total of about 40,000,000 *l.*, of which about 11,000,000 *l.* is ordinary stock and 2,784,693 *l.* is deferred ordinary stock, 122-134——Purchase of 600,000 *l.* ordinary stock by the Stock Conversion and Investment Company, for the purpose of dividing it into preferred and deferred; success of theoperation, 135-137.

View of the board that the shareholders should have the option of dividing their stock, instead of this being done through the Stock Conversion Company, 138, 139. 207——Prejudicial influence which might be exercised as regards the policy of the Caledonian Company, through the large voting power of the Stock Conversion Company, or other outside companies, 140-143. 193. 215-219——Great popularity of the present scheme with the shareholders of the Caledonian Company, 144-151.

Proposed issue of preferred converted ordinary stock and deferred converted ordinary stock, each equal in amount to the present ordinary stock, 152-156 —— Provision as to the dividend being still declared on the ordinary stock, 157-159. 176-178——Reason for fixing 3 per cent. as the maximum dividend on the preferred ordinary, 160-162. 209.

Statement to be issued to the shareholders explaining that there will be no increase of capital, but only a duplication of stock, 163-165——Explanation that not only will it be optional in every shareholder to convert, but that, if he should convert, he can reconvert into ordinary stock, 166-169. 203, 204. 220, 221 —— Decided objection to the stock being split instead of duplicated, 170-174.

Question considered as to the names or titles to be given to the two stocks when duplicated; willingness of the promoters to leave this matter entirely to the Committee, 179-187——Opinion that duplication will not lead to speculation, whilst it will increase the value, 188-192. 198——Favourable opinion of Scotch bankers and of the community generally as regards the proposed duplication, 194-198.

Large number of shareholders expected to convert if the Bill be passed; check thereby to further action of the trust companies, 199-202 —— Preference on the part of the board for as little conversion as possible, the object being to give the option to the shareholders and to exclude the operation of outside companies, 205-208.

Explanation on the subject of the qualification of directors, as affected by the Bill, 210-214—— Reason for proposing to give a much larger voting power to the preferred than the ordinary stock, though the board are quite willing to fall in with the wishes of the Committee on this point, 222-224.

L.

London and South Western Railway Company. Total of about 31,000,000 *l.* as the capital of the London and South Western Company, of which 11,500,000 *l.* is ordinary capital, *Scotter* 1-3——Object of the present Bill to duplicate the ordinary stock, the matter having been forced upon the directors by the shareholders, *ib.* 4-9. 82——Necessity of approval by the general body of ordinary shareholders, *ib.* 10.

Option to be exercised by every shareholder whether to keep his stock as it is or to have it divided into preferred and deferred, *Scotter* 11-13 —— Proposal in the Bill that the preferred stock shall have 4 per cent, and that any excess shall go to the deferred stock, *ib.* 14. 81—— Priority still to be possessed by the existing debenture and preference stocks, *ib.* 15, 16.

Willingness of the company to adopt suggestions as to the mode of showing in the accounts the amount of each class of stock after duplications; there is no doubling whatever of the capital, *Scotter* 32-44——Advocacy of duplication rather than splitting, *ib.* 45-82.

Grounds for the opinion that not more than one-half the ordinary stock of the South Western Company would be converted, *Scott* 104. 109, 110.

Report by the Committee to the effect that they have amended the preamble of the Bill, and have gone through the Bill and made amendments thereto, *Rep.* iii. viii.; *p.* 62.

See also *Capital.*

M.

May, Frank. (Analysis of his Evidence.)—Witness is Chief Cashier of the Bank of England, 950.

Opinion that the division of railway stock, as into preferred and deferred, is not attended with any public inconvenience, whilst it increases the range of safe investments, 581-593——Effect of the operation of trust companies in railway stocks in giving them a large voting power, 593-597——Increase in the market value of stock by conversion, 598, 599.

Doubt as to duplication being more open to objection than splitting the stock, 600, 601. 614-624——Difficulty in preventing fluctuation and speculation in deferred stock; unimportance attached to a suggestion by Mr. Giffen on this point, 603-608——Dissent from the view that it is expedient to keep the preferred stock up to par, 609, 610.

Probable effect of extensive conversion in enhancing the value of Bank of England stock, 611-613.

Approval of the railway companies being able to carry out conversion schemes, instead of this being left to trust companies, 625, 626——Opinion that the creation of large amounts of preferred stock would not facilitate loan transactions, 627, 628.

N.

North British Railway Company. Large increase or duplication of capital of the North British Company in 1888; *Giffen* 526-528. 531. 569.

P.

Parliamentary Restrictions. Conclusion of the Committee adverse to Parliamentary intervention in the financial affairs of railway companies; security to be obtained rather by trusting to the self-interest of the shareholders, *Special Rep.* iv, v——Adoption of this principle, as laid down by the Royal Commission in 1867, by the Board of Trade, and by eminent Parliamentary authorities, *ib.*

See also Conversion, &c.

Preferred Ordinary Stock. View of witness' directors that 6 per cent. is now much too high a rate at which to place any guaranteed as preferred stock; opinion that in the future all such stock will have to be placed at something like the current rate of the day, *Grinling* 252——Calculations as to the much higher relative value of a 4 per cent. preferred ordinary stock of the Great Northern Company than of the present 6 per cent. B. stock, *ib.* 296-309.

Belief as to the origin of the 6 per cent. clause in the Act of 1868; increased dividends on ordinary stocks since that year, *Giffen* 551-517——Dissent from the view that is expedient to keep the preferred stocks up to par, *May* 609, 610.

Great improvement by making the preferred stock 4 per cent. instead of 6 per cent., *Price* 631. 964. 707.

Advantage of the good investments created for the public by means of preferred stock, *Price* 631 ; *Astle* 711, 712. 734-736——Approval of the maximum dividend on preferred stock being fixed at 6 per cent., although 4 per cent. would be a fair proportion, *ib.* 713-716. 724-731.

Fixed rate of dividend to be assigned under the several Bills to the preferred ordinary stock, *Special Rep.* iv.

See also Accounts.   Caledonian Railway Company.   Conversion, &c.   Cumulative Dividends.   Public, The.

Price, Rokeby. (Analysis of his Evidence.)—Witness is Chairman of the Stock Exchange ; he represents generally the views of the Stock Exchange Committee, 629. 650-652.

Explanation that witness would prefer that there should be no conversion of railway stocks, but that, as trust companies are operating for this purpose, it is much better that the work should be carried out directly by the railway companies and their shareholders, 630, 631. 634-639. 651. 653-661. 674-676.

Special circumstances under which the Great Northern Company took the lead in converting ordinary stock into preferred and deferred ; justification for their doing so, 631. 669——Advantage of the creation of preferred stock as supplying a useful investment

Price, Rokeby. (Analysis of his Evidence)—*continued.*
investment for trustees and others, 631——Great improvement by making the
preferred stock 4 per cent. instead of 6 per cent., 631. 664. 707.

Adoption of the term "preference" by the Railway Investment Company; objection
on the part of the Stock Exchange, so that the term "preferred" was substituted, 632,
633——Approval, on the whole, of power in companies to duplicate; less speculation
where there are large amounts of deferred stock than under the splitting system, 650,
651. 665–673. 695–700. 763–766.

Expediency of full latitude in the companies to duplicate or split, as each company
may prefer, though witness would prefer one uniform system, 635. 639. 644. 662–673.
707——Importance of the accounts clearly showing the paid-up capital apart from
duplication or splitting, 637, 638——Approval of power in shareholders to re-convert;
consideration of objections thereto, 636–645. 657–690. 701, 702——Suggestion that
duplicated stock should have only half voting power, or the same power as before
duplication, 645–649.

Questionable expediency of the arrangement proposed by the Great Northern Company in their Bill of this Session, 667–673. 703–706—— Doubt as to any confusion of
the public through the quotations of capital in the Stock Exchange official list, after
duplication or conversion, 692–694——Objection to the cumulative system being applied
to the preferred or deferred stock, 705, 706.

Public, The. Opinion that the division of railway stock, as into preferred and deferred,
is not attended with any public inconvenience, whilst it increases the range of safe
investments, *May* 591–593——Advantage of the creation of preferred stock as supplying a useful investment for trustees and others, *Astle* 711, 712. 734–736;
Price 631.

View of the railway companies that the stock in its new form will be more
convenient and attractive to investors, and that the arrangement will be advantageous
to the proprietors, *Special Rep.* iv.

Q.

Qualification of Directors. Explanations upon the subject of the qualification of
directors of the South Western Company, as affected by duplication of the ordinary stock;
desire to preserve the same qualification as at present, without any diminution, *Scotter*
18–31——Approval of the qualification of directors, as under the Bill of the
London and South Western Company, *Scott* 106–108——Explanations on the subject of
the qualification of directors, as affected by the Bill of the Caledonian Company,
Sir J. King 210–214.

R.

Railway Investment Company. Summary of the operations of the Railway Investment
Company in the offer of deferred stock and preferred stock of the company in exchange
for ordinary stock held by shareholders in the North Western, North Eastern, and other
companies; unsatisfactory result as regards the return on the deferred stock,
Scott 85.

Adoption of the term "preference" by the Railway Investment Company; objection
on the part of the Stock Exchange, so that the term "preferred" was substituted,
Price 632, 633.

Re-conversion. Explanation that not only will it be optional under the Bill in every
shareholder of the Caledonian Company to convert, but that, if he should convert, he
can re-convert into ordinary stock, *Sir J. King* 166–169. 203, 204. 220, 221——
Approval of power in shareholders to re-convert; consideration of objections thereto,
Price 639–645. 657–690. 701, 702.

Disapproval of any right to re-convert, *Astle* 737, 738——Objection to re-conversion;
increased confusion thereby, *Gairdner* 795–770.

Rejection by the Committee of the re-conversion clause of the Caledonian Bill,
p. 59.

Regulation of Railways Act (1868). Clause introduced into this Act permitting the
division of stocks, and laying down the precise conditions which should govern the
operation, *Special Rep.* v——Very limited extent to which use has been made of the
foregoing section, *ib.*

Royal Commission on Railways. Recommendation in the Report of the Royal Commission
on Railways in 1867 that Parliament should relieve itself from all interference in the
financial affairs of railway companies, *Giffen* 522; *Special Rep.* iv, v.

S.

Scotland. Favourable opinion of Scotch bankers and of the community generally as regards the proposed duplication of Caledonian Stock, *Sir. J. King* 194–198——Belief that there is a strong feeling among railway shareholders in Scotland in favour of conversion or subdivision of the ordinary stocks as increasing their market value, *Gairdner* 743–745—— Considerable doubt in the minds of directors as to the expediency of conversion and the creation of deferred stock, *ib.* 746–749.

Scott, Archibald. (Analysis of his Evidence.)—Long experience of witness in connection with the London and South Western Railway, 83, 84.

Summary of the operations of the Railway Investment Company in the offer of deferred stock and preferred stock of the Company in exchange for ordinary stock held by shareholders in the North Western, North Eastern, and other companies ; unsatisfactory result as regards return on the deferred stock, 85——Particulars as to the operations of the Stock Conversion Company in the issue of different classes of stock in exchange for ordinary stock of the North Western, North Eastern, and Caledonian companies, 85–89.

Conclusion that the operations of these companies are very misleading to the public, and, if extended, may become very embarrassing to the railway companies, 90–101—— Expediency of the railway companies carrying out the conversion of their own stocks under direct Parliamentary provisions, instead of the matter being taken up by outside companies, 98, 99. 112–115.

Facility of avoiding any appearance of duplication of capital under the Bill promoted by witness' company ; nominal increase, however, in carrying out conversion, as in the case of the consolidation of the preferred stocks of the North Western Company, 102 ——Decided opinion that the speculation element is reduced where stock is duplicated instead of split, 103.

Grounds for the opinion that not more than one-half the ordinary stock of the South Western Company would be converted 104. 109, 110——Conclusion that compulsory conversion is very objectionable and would not be approved by the shareholders, 105–111 ——Approval of the qualification of directors as under the Bill, 106–108——Strong feeling at the boards of the North Western and Great Western Companies adverse to conversion, 113–115.

Scotter, Charles. (Analysis of his Evidence.)—Total of about 31,000,000 *l.* as the capital of the London and South Western Railway Company, of which 11,500,000 *l.* is ordinary capital, 1–3——Object of the present Bill to duplicate the ordinary stock, the matter having been forced upon the directors by the shareholders, 4–9. 82——Necessity of approval by the general body of ordinary shareholders, 10.

Option to be exercised by every shareholder, whether to keep his stock as it is or to have it divided into preferred and deferred, 11——Proposal in the Bill that the preferred stock shall have 4 per cent., and that any excess shall go to the deferred stock, 14. 81 —— Priority still to be possessed by the existing debenture and preference stock, 15, 16 —— Intended continuance of the same voting power as at present, 17.

Explanations upon the subject of the qualification of directors, as affected by duplication of the ordinary stock ; desire to preserve the same qualification as at present, 18–31——Willingness of the company to adopt suggestions as to the mode of showing in the accounts the amount of each class of stock after duplication ; there is no doubling whatever of the capital, 32–44.

Consideration of objections to the duplication of the stock, instead of splitting it ; Grounds for the conclusion that duplication is far preferable in the interests of the shareholders, and that there will be less speculation than if the stock were split under an Act of 1868 ; 45–82.

Speculation. See *Deferred Ordinary Stock.   Duplication of Stock.*

Splitting of Stock. Decided objection to the stock of the Caledonian Company being split instead of duplicated, *Sir J. King* 170–174—— Expediency of full latitude in the companies to split or to duplicate, as each company may prefer, though witness would prefer one uniform system, *Price* 636. 639. 644. 662–673. 707——Preference for splitting rather than duplication, *Gairdner* 752, 753. 760.

Origin of the clause in the Regulation of Railways Act of 1868 as to the splitting of ordinary stock into preferred and deferred ; views expressed in the House of Lords by the Duke of Richmond (then President of the Board of Trade) in favour of this clause, which was adopted, *Giffen* 510–518.

See also *Accounts.   Conversion, &c.   Duplication of Stock.*

Stock

Stock Conversion and Investment Trust (Limited). Particulars as to the operations of the Stock Conversion Company in the issue of different classes of stock in exchange for ordinary stock of the North Western, North Eastern, and Caledonian Companies, *Scott* 85-89——Purchase of 600,000 *l.* Caledonian ordinary stock by the Stock Conversion and Investment Company for the purpose of dividing it into preferred and deferred; success of the operation, *Sir J. King* 135-137——View of the board that the shareholders should have the option of dividing their stock, instead of this being done through the Stock Conversion Company, *ib.* 138, 139. 207.

Comment upon the operations of the Stock Investment Company, as in the case of the London and North Western Railway Company; considerable profit made by the former in their mode of dealing with the ordinary stock of the latter, *Grißling* 313-321.

Letter from the secretary (Mr. Spens), explanatory of the position and action of the company in the matter of voting power in respect of railway stocks held by them, as in the Caledonian Company, *p.* 56.

Statement on behalf of the Caledonian Company that they are quite satisfied with everything that has been done by the Stock Conversion Company, *pp.* 56, 57.

Stock Exchange. Doubt as to any confusion of the public through the quotations of capital in the Stock Exchange official list, after duplication or conversion, *Price* 692-694.

T.

Taff Vale Railway Company. Information respecting the application in the case of the Taff Vale Company in 1889 and the conditions under which allowed, *Giffen* 530-536. 569. 584, 585.

Tahourdin, Horace F. (Analysis of his Evidence.)—Witness is Chairman of the Isle of Wight Railway Company, 430.

Total of twelve miles as the length of the railway; particulars as to the capital and dividends, 431-441——Ordinary stock of 149,172 *l.*, dividends thereon not having been paid till 1875, and having gradually increased up to 6¼ per cent. in 1886; 437-441 —— Statement explanatory of the proposed conversion of capital under the Bill before the Committee, as regards debenture, preference, and ordinary stocks, 439.

Particulars respecting the proposed conversion of the three 5 per cent. debenture stocks into one 4 per cent. stock; consents obtained from more than three-fourths of the stockholders, 442-454—— Information as to the proposal for converting 100 *l.* of ordinary stock into 100 *l.* of 4 per cent. preferred stock and 100 *l.* of deferred stock; unanimity of the ordinary shareholders in approving this scheme, 455-463. 492 —— Further creation of 4 per cent. stock by the conversion of each 100 *l.* of 5 per cent. preference into 125 *l.* of 4 per cent.; contemplated bonus of 10 per cent. of deferred stock in connection with this conversion, the directors, however, not attaching much importance to the latter proposal, 464-494.

Main principles of the Bill that all the stocks (except the deferred ordinary) shall receive 4 per cent., 466. 473, 474——Explanation of the result as regards voting power of the proposed duplication of the ordinary stock; this would not prejudically affect the the voting power of the preference shareholders, 500-506.

[Second Examination.]—Object of Clause 8 of the Isle of Wight Railway Bill to extend for another period of ten years the time for retaining certain lands for the purposes of the railway, 784-794.

Trust Companies. Conclusion that the operations of the trust companies are very misleading to the public, and, if extended, may become very embarrassing to the railway companies, *Scott* 90-101——Approval of the railway companies being able to carry out conversion schemes instead of this being left to trust companies, *May* 625, 626.

Explanation that witness would prefer that there should be no conversion of railway stocks, but that, as trust companies are operating for this purpose, it is much better that the work should be carried out directly by the railway companies and their shareholders, *Price* 630, 631. 634-639. 651. 653-661. 674-676 — Question whether the schemes before the Committee would prevent trust companies from further operating in railway stocks, *Gairdner* 760, 761.

Trustees. Views of the Committee as to the insertion of clauses respecting the powers of trustees, *pp.* 58, 59.

U.

Uniformity of Nomenclature. View of the Committee that all railway stocks converted into preferred and deferred should bear a uniform nomenclature, *Special Rep.* v.

V.

Value of Stock. Increase of the market value of stock by conversion, *May* 598, 599.

    See also *Caledonian Railway Company.*   *Great Northern Railway Company.*

Voting Power. Intended continuance of the same voting power as at present, under the Bill of the London and South Western Company, *Scotter* 17 —— Prejudicial influence which might be exercised as regards the policy of the Caledonian Company through the large voting power of the Stock Conversion Company and other outside companies, *Sir J. King* 140-143. 193. 215-219 —— Reason for proposing on the part of the Caledonian Company to give a much larger voting power to the preferred than the ordinary stock, though the board are quite willing to fall in with the wishes of the Committee on this point, *ib.* 222-224.

    Explanation of the result as regards voting power of the proposed duplication of the ordinary stock of the Isle of Wight Railway; this would not prejudicially affect the voting power of the preference shareholders, *Tahourdin* 500-506 —— Effect of the operation of trust companies in railway stocks in giving them a large voting power, *May* 593-597.

    Suggestion that duplicated stock should have only half voting power, or the same power as before duplication, *Price* 645-649 —— Consideration of the effect of conversion as regards voting power; difficulty on this point, *Gairdner* 771-773.

W.

Works. Report by the Committee that no new works are authorised either by the London and South Western Bill, Caledonian Bill, Great Northern Bill, or Isle of Wight Bill, *Rep.* iii.

Brought from the Lords, 31 July 1890.

REPORT

FROM THE

SELECT COMMITTEE OF THE HOUSE OF LORDS

ON

CHILDREN'S LIFE INSURANCE BILL [H.L.];

TOGETHER WITH THE

PROCEEDINGS OF THE COMMITTEE,

MINUTES OF EVIDENCE,

AND APPENDIX.

Ordered, by The House of Commons, *to be Printed,*
2 *August* 1890.

LONDON:
PRINTED BY HENRY HANSARD AND SON;
AND
Published by EYRE and SPOTTISWOODE, East Harding-street, London, E C.,
and 32, Abingdon-street, Westminster, S.W.;
ADAM and CHARLES BLACK, North Bridge, Edinburgh:
and HODGES, FIGGIS, and Co., 104. Grafton-street, Dublin.

[ii]

R E P O R T.

BY THE SELECT COMMITTEE appointed to consider the CHILDREN'S LIFE INSURANCE BILL [H.L.], and to Report to the House.

ORDERED TO REPORT,

THAT the Committee have met, and considered the said Bill, and have examined several Witnesses.

The Committee have resolved that it is expedient that Clause 2, of which the marginal note is "Insurance Money to be paid to Undertakers," be withdrawn from the Bill; but owing to the approaching Prorogation of Parliament they have been unable to complete their consideration of the said Bill, and recommend, that in the event of the said Bill being re-introduced into the House next Session, the said Committee should be re-appointed.

And the Committee have directed the Minutes of Proceedings and Evidence, with Appendix, to be laid before your Lordships.

25th July 1890.

ORDER OF REFERENCE.

Die Lunæ, 16° *Junii,* 1890.

CHILDREN'S LIFE INSURANCE BILL [H.L.].

Order of the Day for the Second Reading, read: *Moved,* that the Bill be now read 2ª: After short debate, motion *agreed to:* Bill read 2ª accordingly, and *referred* to a Select Committee.

Petition against; of Executive Council of the Ancient Order of Foresters; read, and *referred* to the Select Committee.

Die Veneris, 20° *Junii,* 1890.

Select Committee on: The Lords following were named of the Committee:

Lord Chancellor.	Lord Clifford of Chudleigh.
Earl of Derby.	Lord Ker. (*M. Lothian.*)
Earl Spencer.	Lord Poltimore.
Earl of Harrowby.	Lord Brougham and Vaux.
Earl Beauchamp.	Lord Kinnaird.
Earl Selborne.	Lord Norton.
Lord Bishop of Peterborough.	Lord Herschell.
Lord Bishop of Ripon.	Lord Thring.

The Committee to meet on Tuesday next, at Three o'clock, and to appoint their own Chairman.

Die Martis, 24° *Junii,* 1890.

The evidence taken before the Select Committee from time to time to be printed for the use of the Members of this House; but no copies thereof to be delivered, except to Members of the Committee and to such other persons as the Committee shall think fit, until further order.

LORDS PRESENT, AND MINUTES OF THE PROCEEDINGS AT EACH SITTING OF THE COMMITTEE.

Die Martis, 24° *Junii,* 1890.

LORDS PRESENT:

Earl of Derby.
Earl Spencer.
Earl Beauchamp.
Lord Bishop of Peterborough.
Lord Bishop of Ripon.
Lord Clifford of Chudleigh.

Lord Poltimore.
Lord Brougham and Vaux.
Lord Kinnaird.
Lord Norton.
Lord Herschell.
Lord Thring.

The Order of Reference is read.

It is moved that the Lord Bishop of Peterborough do take the Chair.

The same is agreed to.

The course of proceeding is considered

It is moved by the Earl Beauchamp, "That it is expedient that no evidence shall be received, except on oath." Objected to.—On Question :

Content, 1.

Earl Beauchamp.

Not Contents, 10.

Earl of Derby.
Earl Spencer.
Lord Bishop of Peterborough.
Lord Bishop of Ripon.
Lord Clifford of Chudleigh.
Lord Poltimore.
Lord Brougham and Vaux.
Lord Kinnaird.
Lord Norton.
Lord Thring.

It is resolved in the negative.

It is moved that the Committee be an open one.

The same is agreed to.

Ordered, That the Committee be adjourned till Friday next, at Twelve o'clock.

Die Veneris, 27° *Junii,* 1890.

LORDS PRESENT:

Lord Chancellor.
Earl of Derby.
Earl Spencer.
Earl of Harrowby.
Earl Beauchamp.
Earl of Selborne.
Lord Bishop of Ripon.

Lord Clifford of Chudleigh.
Lord Poltimore.
Lord Brougham and Vaux.
Lord Kinnaird.
Lord Norton.
Lord Herschell.
Lord Thring.

The Lord Bishop of PETERBOROUGH in the Chair.

The Order of Adjournment is read.

The Proceedings of Tuesday last are read.

The following Witnesses are called in, and examined, viz. : *Sidney Barwise,* Esq.. ь.в., M.R.C.S., *John Branson,* Esq., M.R.C.P.

a 3

The

The Earl Beauchamp objecting to a question put to the last-named witness, moves, "That the question being as to a matter not within the witness's own knowledge, be not put." Objected to.—On Question, it is resolved in the negative.

The following Witnesses are called in, and examined, viz.: *J. Branson*, Esq., M.R.C.P. (further examination),·*W. J. Cleaver*, Esq., M.D., *H. B. Pullen Burry*, Esq., M.R.C.S.,·and *H. A. Hodson*, Esq., M.R.C.S.

Ordered, That the Committee be adjourned till Tuesday next, at Twelve o'clock.

Die Martis, 1° Julii, 1890.

LORDS PRESENT:

Earl of Derby.	Lord Poltimore.
Earl Spencer.	Lord Brougham and Vaux.
Earl of Harrowby.	Lord Kinnaird.
Earl Beauchamp.	Lord Norton.
Earl of Selborne.	Lord Herschell.
Lord Clifford of Chudleigh.	Lord Thring.

The Lord Bishop of PETERBOROUGH in the Chair.

The Order of Adjournment is read.

The Proceedings of Friday last are read.

The following Witnesses are called in, and examined, viz.: *George Thomson*, Esq., M.D. *M. F. Carter*, Esq., *John Troutbeck*, Esq., *Arthur Browne*, Esq., and *H. W. Hooper*, Esq.

Ordered, That the Committee be adjourned till Friday next, at Twelve o'clock.

Die Veneris, 4° Julii, 1890.

LORDS PRESENT:

Earl of Derby.	Earl of Selborne.
Earl Spencer.	Lord Bishop of Ripon.
Earl of Harrowby.	Lord Poltimore.
Earl Beauchamp.	Lord Thring.

The Lord Bishop of PETERBOROUGH in the Chair.

The Order of Adjournment is read.

The Proceedings of Tuesday last are read.

It is moved by the Chairman "That an Extract from the Report of the General Hospital and Dispensary for Sick Children, Pendlebury," be put in. Objected to—(The Earl Beauchamp). —On Question, it is resolved in the affirmative. (For Extract, *see* Minutes of Evidence.)

The following Witnesses are called in, and examined, viz.: Captain *Burnett* (Chief Constable, Rotherham), *J. J. Ritchie*, Esq., M.R.C.S., Mr. *James Tasker*, Mr. *William Hartopp*, Mr. *R. A. Leach*, and Mr. *James Kershaw*.

Ordered, That the Committee be adjourned till Tuesday next, at Twelve o'clock.

Die Martis, 8° Julii, 1890.

LORDS PRESENT:

Earl of Derby.	Lord Bishop of Ripon.
Earl Spencer.	Lord Clifford of Chudleigh.
Earl of Harrowby.	Lord Poltimore.
Earl Beauchamp.	Lord Brougham and Vaux.
Earl of Selborne.	Lord Norton.

The Lord Bishop of PETERBOROUGH in the Chair.

The Order of Adjournment is read.

The Proceedings of Friday last are read.

The following Witnesses are called in, and examined, viz.: The Honourable Mr. Justice *Wills*, and the Honourable Mr. Justice *Day.*

It is then proposed that the Reverend *Benjamin Waugh* be called in and examined.

It is moved by the Earl Beauchamp, "That it is expedient that the Reverend Benjamin Waugh be examined on oath." Objected to.

After discussion.—On Question:

Content, 1.	Not Contents, 9.
Earl Beauchamp	Earl of Derby.
	Earl Spencer.
	Earl of Selborne.
	Lord Bishop of Peterborough.
	Lord Bishop of Ripon.
	Lord Clifford of Chudleigh.
	Lord Poltimore.
	Lord Brougham and Vaux.
	Lord Norton.

It is resolved in the negative.

The following Witness is called in, and examined, viz.: The Reverend *Benjamin Waugh.*

Ordered, That the Committee be adjourned till Friday next, at Twelve o'clock.

Die Veneris, 11° Julii, 1890.

LORDS PRESENT:

Earl of Derby.	Lord Ker. (*M. Lothian.*)
Earl Spencer.	Lord Poltimore.
Earl Beauchamp.	Lord Brougham and Vaux.
Earl of Selborne.	Lord Kinnaird.
Lord Bishop of Ripon.	Lord Norton.
Lord Clifford of Chudleigh.	Lord Thring.

The Lord Bishop of PETERBOROUGH in the Chair.

The Order of Adjournment is read.

The Proceedings of Tuesday last were read.

The following Witnesses are called in, and examined, viz.: Mr. *W. Crooks*, and Mr. *A. Dobson.*

Ordered, That the Committee be adjourned till Wednesday next, at Twelve o'clock.

Die Mercurii, 16° *Julii*, 1890.

LORDS PRESENT:

Earl of Derby.	Lord Poltimore.
Earl of Harrowby.	Lord Brougham and Vaux.
Earl Beauchamp.	Lord Kinnaird.
Earl of Selborne.	Lord Norton.
Lord Clifford of Chudleigh.	Lord Thring.
Lord Ker. (*M. Lothian.*)	

The Lord Bishop of PETERBOROUGH in the Chair.

The Order of Adjournment is read.

The Proceedings of Friday last are read.

The Course of proceeding is considered.

After long discussion, it is moved by the Lord Bishop of Peterborough, "That it is expedient that Clause 2 be withdrawn."—On Question, resolved in the affirmative.

The following Witnesses are called in, and examined, viz.: Mr. *T. Dewey* and Mr. *Taunton.*

Ordered, That the Committee be adjourned till Friday next, at Twelve o'clock.

Die Veneris, 18° *Julii*, 1890.

LORDS PRESENT:

Earl of Derby.	Lord Poltimore.
Earl Spencer.	Lord Brougham and Vaux.
Earl of Harrowby.	Lord Kinnaird.
Earl Beauchamp.	Lord Norton.
Earl of Selborne.	Lord Herschell.
Lord Clifford of Chudleigh.	

The Lord Bishop of PETERBOROUGH in the Chair.

The Order of Adjournment is read.

The Proceedings of Wednesday last are read.

The following Witnesses are called in, and examined, viz.: Mr. *T. Dewey* (further examination), Mr. *David Fortune*, Mr. *W. H. Hambridge*, and Mr. *John Clensy.*

Ordered, That the Committee be adjourned till Tuesday next, at Twelve o'clock.

Die Martis, 22° *Julii,* 1890.

LORDS PRESENT:

Earl Spencer.
Earl of Harrowby.
Earl Beauchamp.
Earl of Selborne.

Lord Ker.　(*M. Lothian.*)
Lord Norton.
Lord Thring.

The Lord Bishop of PETERBOROUGH in the Chair.

The Order of Adjournment is read.

The Proceedings of Friday last are read.

The following Witnesses are called in, and examined, viz.: Mr. *Edwin Hooper,* Mr. *J. E. Cleveland,* Mr. *Wyatt Sargent,* and Mr. *M. J. Cunningham.*

A question arising as to the course of examination of the last-mentioned Witness:

After long discussion, it is moved by the Earl Beauchamp, That the questions and answers after Answer No. 4399, be struck out, and that the Witness be requested to point out the grounds upon which he supports the resolution he produces.

The said Motion is, after discussion, agreed to.

The following Witness is again called in, and further examined, viz.: Mr. *M. J. Cunningham.*

Ordered, That the Committee be adjourned till Friday next, at Twelve o'clock.

Die Veneris, 25° *Julii,* 1890,

LORDS PRESENT:

Earl Spencer.
Earl of Harrowby.
Earl Beauchamp.
Earl of Selborne.
Lord Ker.　(*M. Lothian.*)

Lord Boltimore.
Lord Kinnaird.
Lord Norton.
Lord Thring.

The Lord Bishop of PETERBOROUGH in the Chair.

The Order of Adjournment is read.

The Proceedings of Tuesday last are read.

The following Witnesses are called in, and examined, viz.: Mr. *J. E. Cleveland* (further examination), Mr. *T. B. Stead,* and Mr. *Walton.*

A Draft Report is laid before the Committee, and agreed to (*vide* the Report).

Ordered, That the Lord in the Chair do make the said Report to the House.

EXPENSES OF WITNESSES.

NAME OF WITNESS.	Profession or Condition.	From whence Summoned.	Number of Days Absent from Home, under Orders of Committee.	Allowance during Absence from Home.	Expenses of Journey to London and Back.	TOTAL Expenses allowed to Witness.
				£. s. d.	£. s. d.	£. s. d.
Pullen Burry - - -	Medical Doctor - -	Liphook, Hants - -	1	3 3 -	- 17 -	4 - -
Dr. Bransom - - -	Medical Doctor - -	Rotherham - -	2	6 6 -	2 7 8	8 13 8
Dr. Cleaver - - -	Medical Doctor - -	Sheffield - - -	2	6 6 -	2 6 10	8 12 10
Sidney Barwise - -	Surgeon - - -	Blackburn - -	2	6 6 -	3 1 6	9 7 6
H. A. Hodson - - -	Surgeon - - -	Brighton - -	1	3 3 -	- 17 -	4 - -
Dr. Thomson - - -	Medical Doctor - -	Oldham - - -	2	6 6 -	2 15 4	9 1 4
Arthur Browne - -	Solicitor and Deputy Coroner.	Nottingham - -	2	4 4 -	1 17 8	6 1 8
H. Hooper - - -	Coroner - -	Exeter - - -	2	4 4 -	3 - -	7 4 -
M. F. Carter - - -	Surgeon - - -	Newnham, Gloucester -	2	6 6 -	2 2 3	8 8 3
Captain Burnett - -	Chief Constable -	Rotherham - -	2	2 2 -	2 6 8	4 8 8
Dr. Ritchie - - -	Medical Doctor - -	Leek, Staffordshire -	2	6 6 -	2 6 6	8 12 6
James Kershaw - -	Union Officer -	Rochdale - - -	2	2 2 -	2 5 -	4 7 -
William Hartopp -	Union Officer -	Bradford - - -	2	2 2 -	2 6 -	4 8 -
James Tasker - -	Relieving Officer -	Sheffield - - -	2	2 2 -	1 18 10	4 - 10
R. A. Leach - - -	Clerk to Guardians -	Rochdale - - -	2	2 2 -	2 6 -	4 8 -
A. Dobson - - -	Insurance Agent -	Manchester - -	2	2 2 -	2 4 -	4 6 -
J. E. Cleveland - -	Secretary to Friendly Society.	Manchester - -	2	2 2 -	2 4 -	4 6 -
W. Crooks - - -	Mechanic - - -	Poplar - - -	1	- 10 -	—	- 10 -
F. H. Taunton - -	Secretary to Liver Friendly Society.	Liverpool - -	2	2 2 -	2 8 6	4 10 6
David Fortune - -	-	Glasgow - - -	3	3 3 -	4 10 -	7 13 -
Edwin Hooper - -	Coroner - - -	Birmingham - -	2	2 2 -	1 10 -	3 12 -
J. E. Cleveland - -	Secretary to Friendly Society.	Manchester - -	2	2 2 -	2 4 -	4 6 -
A. Peat - - -	Collector to Insurance Society.	Rotherham - -	2	2 2 -	1 19 6	4 1 6
J. E. Cleveland - -	Secretary to Friendly Society.	Manchester - -	2	2 2 -	2 4 -	4 6 -
J. B. Stead - - -	-	Hull - - -	2	2 2 -	2 1 9	4 3 9
T. Walton - - -	-	Southampton - -	1	1 1 -	1 - 6	2 1 6
					£.	139 10 6

MINUTES OF EVIDENCE.

A

LIST OF WITNESSES.

Die Veneris, 27° Junii 1890.

LORDS PRESENT:

LORD CHANCELLOR.
Earl of DERBY.
Earl SPENCER.
Earl of HARROWBY.
Earl BEAUCHAMP.
Earl of SELBORNE.
LORD BISHOP OF PETERBOROUGH.
LORD BISHOP OF RIPON.

Lord CLIFFORD of CHUDLEIGH.
Lord POLTIMORE.
Lord BROUGHAM and VAUX.
Lord KINNAIRD.
Lord NORTON.
Lord HERSCHELL.
Lord THRING.

THE RIGHT REV. THE LORD BISHOP OF PETERBOROUGH, IN THE CHAIR.

MR. SIDNEY BARWISE, M.B. Lond., M.R.C.S., is called in; and Examined, as follows:

Chairman.

1. YOU are an M.B., and a Member of the Royal College of Surgeons?—I am.

2. And you also hold a diploma of Public Health?—Yes, of the University of Cambridge.

3. You are now medical officer of health for Blackburn, in Lancashire?—I am.

4. The population of Blackburn is returned at 125,000?—Yes.

5. Previously you were parish doctor for Birmingham?—Yes.

6. There you had, upon the whole, or mainly, a large parish practice?—I had then between 15,000 and 16,000 parish patients in 3½ years.

7. You were in charge of the districts, Nos. 3 and 4 of the Birmingham Union for 3½ years?—I was.

8. Will you tell the Committee what was the class of population with which you came in contact mainly during that time?—It would be the very lowest class of population that there is.

9. Was your attention called to the practice of child-life insurance amongst the classes you mainly dealt with?—I dealt entirely with the pauper class; I had no private practice. I noticed that the children of the outdoor paupers were insured in large numbers.

10. Not only did you observe that the children of a very large class of persons were insured in large numbers, but did you observe any connection between the treatment of such children and the fact of their insurance?—I was convinced after a little while that the chief anxiety of the parents was to see the child dead from the moment of its birth; that was the case. I may say that during labour, I constantly heard the mother and the women in the room say, it would be a blessing if the child were born dead, and as soon as a child was born, whenever it was ill, I have often heard it said, "It will be a blessing if

(142.)

Chairman—continued.

the Lord takes it," or some other phrase equivalent to wishing it were dead.

11. Then this experience of yours led you finally to put the question generally, when visiting sick children, "Is this child insured"?—When I saw them being neglected.

12. In fact you frequently put that question?—I frequently put that question.

13. Did you take any steps to verify the answers which the parents gave you?—No, I did not.

14. Did they generally either deny the insurance or admit it?—They have denied it, and I have found out afterwards that the child has been insured; but that was not a general thing at all.

15. You had practically no means of knowing whether the child was or was not insured, except the statement of the parent?—None whatever.

16. In every case then in which the parents stated that the child was insured you could take that statement as a matter of fact?—Yes.

17. But you could not take the statement of the parent that it was not insured?—No, I could not.

18. Therefore it is upon the admitted cases of insurance that you formed your opinion?—Yes.

19. What was your opinion of the effect of insurance in such cases as those you did attend?—That a sum of 2 l. or 3 l is sufficient to upset the balance of the motives of the parents.

20. You thought that in such cases it led to the neglect of the children?—It was an additionl motive to neglect.

21. You thought that in addition to the obvious motive in some cases afforded by the expense of bringing up the child and the trouble of the child in sickness, this additional motive of a sum

A 2

of

Chairman—continued.

of money to be got when the child died acted as an incentive?—As an inducement.

22. What was the character of those cases which came at length to impress you with this opinion? — Generally, they were cases which were signed up when they died, as "marasmus," or "atrophy," or some other vague term which simply means wasting.

23. It would be difficult would it not for a doctor to distinguish between a case of wasting naturally, and a case of wasting due more or less to the withholding of food?—It would.

24. And in the case of withholding food, the doctor would be obliged in most cases to take the word of the parent that the child was being properly fed?—He would. I have often felt that I have not believed that the children were being properly fed, and have cross-examined the parent as to how and how often it had been fed; and have even gone so far as to examine the bottle in order to see any evidence of its being fed.

25. Do you remember any special cases of neglect of the kinds you speak of, which struck you most?—Yes; there were two forms which the neglect took, the one was that which I have mentioned in not feeding the child, and not attending to it; the other class of neglect was in not calling in a doctor at all, when the child was at death's door even. In many cases I have been called in when the child has been dead, and not until then.

26. Then, as a matter of fact, you were frequently called in very late?—Yes; very late.

27. In cases of bronchitis and pneumonia?—In cases of bronchitis and pneumonia I have been called in when the child was dead.

28. In cases of bronchitis and pneumonia it is clear that exposure, accidental exposure even, and still more, wilful exposure, would aggravate the symptoms?—It would produce the pneumonia.

29. And if the disease existed exposure would aggravate it?—It would.

30. If you had no knowledge of the history of the case, you would have no means of ascertaining whether this child was wilfully exposed or not?—None whatever.

31. A parent having a child suffering from bronchitis or pneumonia might bring it through the streets. and you would have no means of knowing whether the disease was aggravated in that way?—No; I remember a case of a child coming to me suffering from pneumonia, and I do not think it lived the day out.

32. Was that child insured?—I cannot say.

33. Were there other characteristics of the insured children amongst those classes which struck you; did you ever blame the parent for bringing a child out in that state?—Yes.

34. Were the parents in the habit of asking you carefully for your certificate in these kind of cases?—It is really that which attracted my attention to these cases first of all; when I have seen a woman, without showing any regard to the welfare of her child, asking me questions about whether the papers would come, or if she would get a certificate; or the way they would put it would be, "Would it be all right if any-

Chairman—continued.

thing happens," that is the common phrase, and a phrase I have heard a good many times; it was that I say which aroused my suspicions.

35. You thought that this eagerness for the certificate, and the question about "anything happening," and "it being all right," showed a guilty intent on the part of the parent?—It certainly showed what the parent was most thinking of; I should have expected the parent to have asked about what was to be done with the child.

36. Had you reason to believe that in any of the cases the children were insured when the parents said that they were not?—Yes, there was one case; I could not name it; but a case in which it came out at the inquest that the child was insured, and I had not filled it up in my form.

37. You say that it had become practically your habit in many cases to ask, "Is this child insured?" In what kind of cases did you generally ask that?—Generally in those cases of marasmus I should ask that.

38. Were you ever told that the parent was not quite sure whether the child was insured or not?—Yes, they used vague phrases; the phrase I have frequently heard is, "I think someone," a sister or a cousin, "has it in a bit of a club."

39. Would those people run any risk of losing their insurance policy if they deceived you on this matter?—I do not think so, but I do not know.

40. What is the exact nature of a doctor's certificate; it is simply a medical certificate as to the cause of death, is it not?—It is simply a certificate which goes to the registrar, and there is a penalty for using it for any other purpose.

41. The doctor is not called upon to say that the child died from natural causes; but he certifies to the nature of the disease?—Yes.

42. And whether the disease was superinduced by crime or neglect would not appear upon the certificate. he simply says the child died of such-and-such a disease?—That is so.

43. And that certificate goes to the registrar?—Yes, that certificate goes to the registrar, and a copy of it to the Registrar General.

44. Do you think that in those cases you speak of there was any temptation to the parent, arising from the balance between the insurance money and the expenses; that there was a money temptation to the parent?—I know that that was so; I know cases too where the money has not been spent upon the burial. I have found a case, it was only the day before yesterday; Mr. Waugh saw me and he asked me that question, and I found a case.

45. Will you state the case to the Committee?—It is not the case of a child, but it is to the point. A man named Powell who was insured for 3 *l.* 10 *s.* was buried by the parish.

46. This is a case of death insurance in which the person was buried by the parish?—Yes.

47. That goes to show that a person on whose life an insurance has been effected may, nevertheless, be buried by the parish?—Yes.

48. Could you answer the question whether the parish could in any case refuse to bury the child or person?—They can refuse if they know the

Chairman—continued.

the person is insured, but the burial would be effected by withholding the knowledge from the relieving officer.

49. You think that a very small money balance, speaking of the class of persons you are in the habit of attending, would be a temptation to them to neglect or do away with the child?—Yes.

50. Such a sum, for instance, as 30 s.?—Yes, indeed, a very few shillings; anything sufficient for drink.

51. To people in the lowest classes, you think the temptation of a few shillings would be an adequate temptation to induce them to neglect or improperly expose a child to get money?—Speaking of the people who systematically neglect their children, 2 s. or 3 s. extra to be spent in the case of death would be an additional inducement; that is to say, to persons of that class that I am speaking of, the very lowest class. One woman who neglected her child got her living by singing hymns in the street; she was drunk two or three days before, and she was drunk two or three days after, the child's death.

Earl Beauchamp.

52. Was that child insured?—I cannot answer that question.

Chairman.

53. In a communication you made to the editor of "The Birmingham Daily Post," in October 1888, you say that the medical man is compelled to grant a certificate even where he has the gravest misgivings of criminal neglect, "because he can prove nothing against the statement of the parents;" has that been your experience?—It has been my experience over and over again I have felt that the children have been neglected. In one case I was confident the child had been starved, and this case I reported to the coroner, but it went no further than having an inquest. The child was 2½ years of age, and weighed 7 lbs.

54. You think that in the case of a coroner's inquest the doctor in many cases can prove very little?—Very little; he can prove more if he has made a post-mortem examination.

55. Then I come now to the question of post-mortem examinations; is it not the case that a child may be killed by improper or over-feeding quite as easily as by starvation?—By improper feeding, certainly.

56. The parents may give the child a quantity of improper food?—Certainly, that would kill it.

57. I am told that one effect of improper feeding is convulsions?—Yes.

58. Is there anything, except the history of the case, which would enable a doctor to distinguish between convulsions brought on by improper feeding and convulsions arising from any other cause?—The commonest cause of convulsions is improper feeding. I would suspect improper feeding in every case until I found some other cause for it.

59. And the only thing that would detect that thoroughly would be a post-mortem examination?—Yes; unless the doctor obtained evidence of improper feeding.

(142.)

60. That is, in other words, unless he had the history of the case before him?—Yes.

61. Symptoms, as distinguished from the history of the case, would not be sufficient?—The convulsions produced by improper feeding he would not be able to distinguish from those produced by teething; and the only persons from whom he would be able to get the information would be the parents.

62. You also say that there are no certain signs by which starvation can be detected without a post-mortem examination?—And even with a post-mortem examination it is not always certain.

63. Have you sent many cases of this kind on to the coroner?—I have.

64. Do you send them to the coroner in the first instance, or to the police?—I send them to the coroner.

65. Then on what condition does the coroner hold the inquest?—He instructs one of his officers to make inquiries, and if it is a very bad case there is an inquest; in the majority of cases he does not have to hold an inquest.

66. Do the police generally report that an inquest is necessary or desirable?—The coroner's officer is a police officer, and he makes the inquiry; it is a separate department of the police.

67. When a case comes before the coroner and you are called as a witness, can you give any further evidence of the cause of death?—The history of the case, or such evidence as I have had given to me, is all I can say.

68. You can say, for instance, "This child died from bronchitis or pneumonia," but you cannot tell the coroner anything as to what aggravated or even caused that bronchitis or pneumonia, unless you know the history of the case?—No.

69. Then you might have given evidence that a child had suffered from this or that disease, but the jury would not be induced thereupon to say that the child had been done away with?—I know a case in which I gave the strongest evidence; in the case I have already mentioned the child weighed 7 lbs. at 2½ years of age, and the evidence there was very strong; I believe I had a post-mortem in that case, but the coroner, addressing the jury, said that it was a bad case; I think he advised them not to return a verdict of manslaughter, because those cases were so frequently thrown out at the assizes.

70. Did the coroner express the opinion that it was a bad case?—Yes; at the same time he advised the jury that it was a useless expenditure of the ratepayers' money to send such cases to the assizes, because they could not get quite legal proof.

71. You positively say that within your knowledge the coroner did say that; are you speaking of matters within your own knowledge?—Yes.

72. It occurred in a case in which you gave evidence?—Yes.

73. And you heard the coroner say that?—I have heard that said several times.

Earl Beauchamp.

74. Did you hear this said in that particular case?—In that particular case I cannot say that the coroner said it, but I have heard it said over

A 3   and

Earl *Beauchamp*—continued.

and over again. I have heard the coroner say over and over again that where we have these cases of neglect, and children dying from neglect, which are practically manslaughter, it is useless sending such cases to the assizes, as the accused have been so frequently acquitted.

Chairman.

75. Have there been many cases in which you have refused a certificate in which the case has reached the coroner's court?—Yes; I should think altogether there would be, perhaps, 20 cases a year.

76. Which have gone to the coroner's court? —Yes; those would not be all children, of course.

77. But of the children; how many cases would there be?—Only five or six cases would go to the court.

78. Cases in which you refused a certificate, and the cases went to the coroner?—Yes.

79. Not more than half-a-dozen cases in each year?—Not more.

80. Do you think that the conditions of evidence at courts of assize encourage doctors to give certificates and let the matter drop?—I cannot say that.

81. Would you say, then, that a reference to a number of cases tried at the assizes and the convictions obtained would give a true idea as to the extent of the criminal neglect of children? --I am sure it would not.

82. You are decidedly of opinion that there may be and have been many cases of neglect of children which, first of all, do not reach the coroner; secondly, which, having reached the coroner, never reach the court of assize; and thirdly, having reached the court of assize, no conviction was obtained in them?—Yes.

83. There are, in fact, those three safeguards to the criminal against the punishment of infanticide?—Yes.

84. Are there any special difficulties in getting evidence amongst the lower classes of crimes against children?—Yes.

85. What are they?—The way in which the cases break down, as to proof, before they get to the assizes. The evidence, as a rule, is fairly strong before the coroner, but the mother of the child is put on bail, as a rule, and has been visiting her neighbours in the meantime, and the evidence against her, as to her guilt, is certainly much weaker at the assizes than it is before the coroner. I believe the fact is, that the feeling of resentment which exists naturally in the minds of decent people, and which compels them to tell the whole truth before the coroner, has subsided in the two or three months which elapse before the assizes are held.

86. Do you think the people you speak of, whose children you knew were insured, all of them, lived on the parish?—I had no knowledge of anyone off the parish at all; I devoted the whole of my time to parish work; I had no private practice.

87. Did you find that those whom you attended, and whose children were insured, were also at the same time on the parish?—They were on the parish when I was attending them.

Chairman—continued.

88. You could not have been attending them unless they were on the parish?—I could not have been attending them unless they were on the parish.

89. And, although they received parish relief, they also insured their children?—Yes.

90. Did you ever know a case in which having to pay insurance money was the reason assigned for going on to the parish; that the parents said, " I shall have to go on the parish now because I am paying the insurance premiums, and it impoverishes me so that I must go on the parish "?— No; because all the cases I had were on the parish at the time of their coming to me.

91. What do you really think is the chief danger of child-life insurance?—That it certainly, with the lowest class, is an inducement, I believe, to neglect the children.

92 You think that in many cases the children who are made away with are made away with rather by letting the children die, than by any actual violence done to them?—Yes; it is passive.

93. What may be called constructive infanticide, letting the child die rather than save its life?—Yes.

94. Have you any idea of how the money may be spent when there is anything over from the funeral; have you ever known a case in which the insurance money has been paid, and you have seen that the parents have been spending it either in paying arrears of rent, or in drinking, or in any other way?—Not to my knowledge.

95. In all the cases you have spoken of you have been attending?—Yes, gratuitously, as parish doctor.

96. They have not paid for your attendance? —That is so.

97. Is it not the fact that gratuitous medical attendance can be obtained free in the large towns by people wishing for it?—In Birmingham, I believe, a third of the population, when ill, are treated gratuitously each year.

98. Are there a great many sick clubs, in which the people get allowances for themselves and children when they are ill?—There are two large general hospitals for medical attendance, and there is one large general dispensary in which they have tickets given them for relief, as well as medicine, gratis; there are altogether about 13 medical charities in the town.

99. Practically, any person who wanted medical attendance for his child could very easily get it? —Yes.

100. It would not be necessary to make a death insurance in order to get money to pay the doctor?--Most emphatically, that is not the case.

101. I presume, a doctor's fees, if you will pardon me for asking you, are not larger in the case of a child that dies than in the case of a child that lives, if he charge any fees?—I have no knowledge of their fees at all.

102. But, obviously, if a parent can get the child attended by the doctor for nothing or next to nothing, there is no occasion for insuring the child's death in order to pay the doctor?— Certainly not.

103. You

Chairman—continued.

103. You do not think that the payment of the doctor's fees is by any means a necessary part of the payment out of the sum for which the child is insured?—Certainly not.

Earl of *Derby.*

104. From what you say I infer that it would be absolutely impossible for the medical man, in the majority of cases, unless he had a previous knowledge of the family, to say decidedly that the child had been killed by neglect?—Yes; I mean that unless he knew how the mother had been attending to the child while he was away he would not know whether his instructions were carried out or not.

105. Practically, it is impossible to tell whether a child's death could have been averted by proper care or whether it has died in consequence of neglect; that is what you would put to the Committee?—That is what I mean.

106. Taking the case of parents who are willing to let their children die or to kill them for the sake of the few pounds or shillings of insurance, do not you think that the mere object of saving trouble and expense would operate in the same way?—I do.

107. Therefore, if you would entirely get rid of the temptation to infanticide which is said to be created by insurance the stronger temptation to infanticide would still remain, namely, that of getting rid of the cost of the child?—That is so.

108. Therefore, any check upon insurance would be nothing more than a partial check upon the evil you describe?—It could not be more than that.

Earl *Spencer.*

109. Is there much difficulty in a poor person receiving a medical order for getting a parish doctor in Birmingham?—There is no difficulty whatever; the medical order is always given in every case, and inquiries are made in the meanwhile. If it is found, as it sometimes is, that the parent of the child (if it is a child) can afford to pay he is made to pay for the order afterwards, but the order is always given in the first instance, and I should think there would be only half a dozen cases in a year in which they are made to pay.

110. When you are attending a case of that sort does the doctor allow medical extras for the proper treatment of the child out of the workhouse?—Yes.

111. In those cases where there is a balance from the insurance, have you ever known a case where the Poor Law authorities have claimed any part of the receipts?—No.

112. You spoke of the gratuitous medical treatment of the poor in Birmingham; are the two large dispensaries you mentioned gratuitous; are they not subscribed for?—There is one large dispensary with four branches: it is quite gratuitous.

113. They are not provident dispensaries?—No; there is a large provident dispensary in the town as well, but I do not call that gratuitous.

114. In some of those cases you speak of the neglect of the mother might have arisen from extreme poverty; is that the case or not?—They could always have obtained relief if they asked for it.

(142.)

Earl *Spencer*—continued.

115. In the case of convulsions is it not from ignorance and the result of the improper feeding that convulsions come on?—I do not think convulsions are (they were not in my practice) a case in which I should say there was much blame to be attached to the parent.

116. It was mere ignorance, was it, and improper feeding?—In the case of convulsions, I think it was.

117. Then you do not think they often improperly feed them in order to bring about death for the purpose of getting the insurance?—I do, but not by causing convulsions; the improper feeding I mean is that which does not introduce enough food into the stomach to cause convulsions.

118. It is generally by semi-starvation that the result is arrived at?—Yes, generally by semi-starvation.

Lord *Kinnaird.*

119. Was not your answer to a previous question that the commonest cause of convulsions was improper feeding?—Yes, but the commonest form of death is not convulsions.

Lord *Clifford of Chudleigh.*

120. Do the insurance officers require a doctor's certificate besides the certificate that you give to the registrar?—No; they require a certificate from the registrar, not from the doctor. I believe it is illegal for the doctor to fill up such a certificate; the registrars consider it taking a perquisite from them. I have frequently had a certificate brought me by a person whose child was insured to fill up, but I have always refused to do it and sent them to the registrar.

121. Do you know, in fact, what children amongst those you attend are insured, and what are not?—As a rule, I know.

122. You think that there are not many cases that would escape your knowledge?—I should only inquire into a case where the child had been neglected, but I could find out by asking; I have asked frequently.

123. By the insurance officer coming to the doctor who had been treating the child for the certificate, instead of his going to the registrar, you would be bound then to know every case in which the child had been insured?—Certainly.

124. But under the present system you have not an opportunity of doing more than asking?—It is not provided for, and I do not know unless I ask.

Lord *Kinnaird.*

125. I did not quite understand with reference to the certificate you gave; if you thought the child had been starved, would you not put that in your certificate?—When I had been attending the child for some time; it was always a point whether I had been attending the child for some time or not; I should make inquiries where I could and where I have not been satisfied in my mind, I have given certificates with the name of the deceased, and "marasmus." The registrars have received instruction from the Registrar-General to make inquiries into those

A 4

Lord *Kinnaird*—continued.

those doubtful certificates, and I have left it with the registrar.

126. Would not an insurance company take very good care that they would not pay in any such case?—I think the insurance companies pay, because it is to the agents' interest to make them pay; for instance [this is not the case of a child, but it bears upon your Lordship's question], I knew a man who was in an advanced stage of consumption who was taken into an insurance company, and when he died they came to me and asked me to put "bronchitis" upon my death certificate, because if I put "consumption" they would not get the money. I asked the woman where she got this information from; she said she got it from the agent. The agent certainly ought to have known, and would have known, that the man was ill, from his appearance; I think the agents try to get as many cases as they can.

Lord *Thring.*

127. Is marasmus, as you call it, or natural wasting, a common complaint amongst children?—It is rather common.

128. Is it a common complaint, or does it arise from the poverty of the parent?—I have to use the statistics; the death figures include a large number of those doubtful cases.

129. But I want to know whether, quite apart from doubtful cases or life insurance, taking the upper classes if you like, do children often die of marasmus, or wasting, in the upper classes?—Amongst the doctors who attend the upper classes marasmus is practically a symptom, and the doctor of the upper classes goes to the cause of a symptom.

130. The question I want to ask is whether we can draw any conclusion as to whether wasting is a natural complaint or what you may call an artificial complaint produced by neglect; do they die of marasmus when they are properly fed?—I do not think they do.

131. Then apart from quasi-artificial means, children do not die usually of marasmus?—Amongst the upper classes I do not think they do.

132. Then, if they do not die of marasmus amongst the upper classes, and they do die of marasmus amongst the lower classes, that shows that wasting is produced either by neglect or by what is the same thing, by the miserable poverty of the parents; that is the conclusion, is it not?—I have no experience of middle-class practice.

133. Then with reference to the grant of a certificate. When the doctor is called upon to give a certificate of death, he would have in most cases he had attended, personal knowledge before he gave the certificate?—The law says nothing about it.

134. Do I understand that you may be called in to see a dead human being and certify to his death, without having ever attended him before?—No; the certificate says that I "last saw him alive on a certain date," and as long as the doctor has seen the patient alive at all he can fill up the certificate.

135. That would be the legal construction?—That is the practice.

Lord *Thring*—continued.

136. Are you obliged to give a certificate; supposing you refuse to give one?—You are not obliged to give a certificate, but you are compelled to report the case to the coroner if you do not give a certificate. You have to give a certificate within a certain number of days; but in the meanwhile you have reported the case to the coroner, and he, in the meanwhile, makes up his mind whether he will hold an inquest or not.

137. Going back a little further, apart from parochial practice, supposing a person dies in London or Birmingham, what happens as regards the certificate?—I think this will answer the question. This I know to be the common practice. A doctor would have an unqualified assistant, who will have a doctor's door-plate put up, he will see the children regularly until they are just dying; then he will fetch the doctor, a regularly qualified man in practice, simply to see the child that he may sign the certificate; he will see the child alive upon the day of death, perhaps, and he will give a death certificate.

138. Without having the slightest knowledge of the cause of death except from the slight examination he can make of the child's body?—And what his assistant tells him.

139. You are a parish doctor?—I was; I am not now.

140. Supposing you went to see a child, and doubted the cause of death, do I understand you must either give a certificate, or must write to the coroner stating the reasons for not giving a certificate; I want to know what is the law?—You are compelled to give a certificate.

141. Supposing you had not seen the child at all, what happens?—Then you cannot give a certificate.

142. Supposing you had seen a child only alive once, what would you do?—I should refuse to give a certificate.

143. Must you assign reasons for that refusal to the coroner?—I should do so.

144. What reason would you assign?—That I could not fill up the certificate because I did not know what the child died from.

145. In those doubtful cases instead of stating that it was pneumonia, or something of that sort, might you not say you did not know; would not that be sufficient?—Those cases in which I had this doubt were cases which had been under my care for some time, and which I should certainly know more about than the coroner would by his inquiry officer.

146. Are you subject to any action for libel if you merely say, "I do not know the cause of death"?—No; but I believe you are liable to a penalty if you refuse a death certificate improperly.

147. Is there a fee given for a death certificate?—No.

148. It is gratuitous?—Yes; there is a penalty, I believe, for taking a fee for a death certificate.

149. The danger would be that you might be punished for refusing a death certificate improperly?—Yes.

150. That is the danger you run?—Yes.

151. "Improperly" would mean refusing it without sufficient reason?—Yes.

152. Now

Lord *Thring*—continued.

152. Now with reference to these insurance societies, do you know at all, within your own knowledge, how they collect their fees, or what they do to get this large business?—Not within my own knowledge. I have seen the collectors in the courts going from house to house.

153. You do not know whether there is a great deal of touting?—I do not.

154. Then you said something about the anxiety for the children dying before birth; of course the societies do not insure children before birth, do they?—No, but I brought that out because it is a thing that should be faced.

155. Do you mean that there is a natural tendency in the lower classes to wish their children not to come into the world at all?—Yes, not to come into the world at all.

Lord *Norton.*

156. You stated that you had known parents say, that it would be a blessing if the child were born dead; that must have been a case of insurance before birth?—Not necessarily, but on account of the trouble.

157. How could the parents say it will be a blessing if the child is born dead, if it were not insured?—I have no knowledge of children being insured before birth.

158. What is the greatest age of a child of which you have known a suspicious death of that sort?—I could not say.

159. What is the limit of the Act as to insurance, is it not the age of 10?—I do not know anything of the law on the matter.

160. Do you believe that in the case of an older child such a temptation would cease, the child's life being more profitable than the insurance?—Certainly.

161. Is it not often the case that parents of this class are out at work and have to leave their sick children to nurses?—That was not the case in Birmingham.

162. You said that sometimes parents do not know of the insurance of their children, but surely the payment from time to time must make them aware of it?—I said they professed not to know.

163. Do you suppose that many of the children in whom these suspicious cases of death occur are illegitimate children?—Most of them are, that would be in my practice.

164. What sort of undertaker is employed in the case of a funeral of a child of that sort?—I do not know exactly how to describe the undertaker; I know the shops they go to for the funerals, and I have seen the funerals in the streets.

165. There are actually professional undertakers employed in a case of that sort?—Yes.

Lord *Bishop of Ripon.*

166. May I ask whether the evidence you have been giving applies as much to Blackburn as to Birmingham?—I have not had time to go into the question yet in Blackburn, but the operatives are a much more respectable class in Blackburn than they are in Birmingham.

167. Do I understand (if I may go back to the question of the certificate given by the doctor) that, as a rule, the doctor would wish to give the

(142.)

Lord *Bishop of Ripon*—continued.

certificate, in fact, rather than withhold it?—Certainly.

168. So the weight of inducement is on the side of giving the certificate?—On the side of peace and quietness.

169. Otherwise he might be involved in great awkwardness by refusing?—Besides that, in private practice it would do a man damage to refuse a certificate; he would not be popular if he did. I was more independent because I had no private practice.

170. May I ask this; I did not quite understand your statement respecting the case you mentioned of the child two and a-half years of age, 7 lbs. in weight; you implied that the coroner recommended that that case should not go to the assizes, because of the difficulty of proving any neglect?—Yes, because those cases of manslaughter have gone from Her Majesty's coroner in Birmingham, time after time, and the accused have been acquitted.

171. In that particular case the coroner actually used such influence as he possessed to stop its going?—I do not remember whether he did, in this particular case, in fact, I think, that in this particular case it was not our proper coroner.

172. I only want to make it clear upon that particular case whether the fact was so or not?—I cannot remember; my opinion is that it was not our regular coroner.

Lord *Poltimore.*

173. I think you said that the large proportion of children who died from neglect were illegitimate children?—Yes.

174. Have you any idea what the proportion would be between legitimate children and illegitimate children amongst the deaths?—My opinion would give an exaggerated view of the facts, because I had more to do with illegitimate children than an ordinary practitioner would.

Earl of *Harrowby.*

175. How many years were you at Birmingham?—Three and a-half years.

176. What number of children roughly passed through your hands?—I had 15,600 cases in the three and a-half years, mostly children.

177. And in Blackburn you have only been a short time?—I am medical officer of health there; I have no practice.

178. How long have you been there?—Twelve months.

179. Would you go so far as to say that the greatest number of children you had to do with were insured?—I should not like to give the figures at all, but it was a very common practice.

180. Did you find very great ignorance as to the rearing of young children amongst that class?—The greatest ignorance.

181. Are many of them put out to nurse while the parent is at work or seeking for work?—That is not very common in Birmingham.

182. We understand you not to be speaking of artizans and operatives, but of the very lowest classes?—Of the very lowest classes.

B

183. You

Earl *Beauchamp.*

183. You told us of the Birmingham medical charities being so numerous that there was one-third of the whole population of Birmingham receiving gratuitous relief; does the same sort of thing exist in Blackburn ?—No.

184. Birmingham is exceptional in that respect ?—I should think Birmingham has more medical charities than any town in England.

185. Do I understand you to say that you refused certificates in five or six cases ?—There were inquests in five or six cases yearly.

186. Were those cases specially of children ? —Yes.

187. Do you know, taking the case of the last year you were in Birmingham, whether in the six cases in which you refused certificates, the children were insured or not ?—I cannot answer the question. I have tried to find out.

188. The object of the inquiry of this Committee is to understand how far insurance bears upon children's life ?—Quite so; but I have no record of whether those children were insured or not.

189. Possibly you might have a record referring to other years; have you no means of ascertaining or informing the Committee whether in the majority of cases in which you refused certificates, the children had been insured or not ? —I asked the question regularly and my impression is that the majority of them were insured.

190. Is it your experience that the majority of the children whom you attended were insured or not ?—I should think that at least 25 per cent. would be insured.

191. You have told the Committee that you blamed the parents for taking the children out, and that the parents in some cases have said to you, " Will it be all right if anything happens ; " in those cases had you any hesitation in giving a certificate ?—I certainly should hesitate ; I can remember children getting better and going under other doctors and dying afterwards.

192. They being no longer on the parish ?— Going away from me because I had talked to the parents severely.

193. I suppose they came to you as the parish doctor ?—Yes, because they could get me for nothing, as it were.

194. The doctors whom the poor employ would be men whom they would remunerate themselves ?—Yes.

195. You have told the Committee that in some cases you examined the bottle in order to detect improper feeding ?—Yes.

196. Would you tell us what happened after that examination of the bottle ?—I can remember examining the bottle. I could not say there was anything wrong with it.

Earl *Beauchamp*—continued.

197. Did you remonstrate in any way with the parents ?—No, I could not say there was anything wrong with it.

198. In answer to an early question you told the Committee that you were convinced that the chief anxiety of the parents was to see the child dead from the moment of its birth ?—In a large number of cases.

199. Would you wish to qualify that statement as a general proposition ? You stated that the chief anxiety of the parents was to see the child dead from the moment of its birth; do you propose to qualify that in any way ?—I should certainly say that that was not the majority of my patients' wish, but of a large number of them.

200. Have you found within your experience any instance of maternal affection among the patients you have attended ?—Very often.

201. Do you believe there is such an instinct as parental affection ?—Of course I do ; but it is certainly very slight amongst the very lowest classes, and does not exist in a large number of them at all.

202. Do you think that the parents who are so neglectful of their parental duties would be stimulated to take greater care of their children if they were restricted as to life insurance ?—I think they would not have such a direct motive the contrary direction.

203. Do you think that a parent who would lavish care and affection upon his child, if it were uninsured, would leave it to perish for the sake of a few shillings ?—No, I do not.

204. Then you do not consider that the few shillings would be a sufficient inducement to neglect ?—Not where there is any true parental feeling.

205. The mischief, if there be mischief, which follows from life insurance, would depend upon the amount of parental affection that exists ?— Certainly.

206. You have no statistics at all to lay before us with regard to the proportionate mortality between children insured and uninsured ?—I left Birmingham 12 months ago, and since then I have been out of practice, so that my attention has not been directed to this subject at all until last Tuesday ; otherwise I believe I could have got figures had I been asked while I was in Birmingham.

207. Did you collect any statistics when you were in Birmingham ?—I was commencing just when I left; I had made up my mind to take up the subject thoroughly.

The Witness is directed to withdraw.

Mr. JOHN BRANSON, M.R.C.P., Edin.; L.R.C.S., Edin.; L.S.A., Lond., is called in ; and Examined, as follows:

Chairman.

208. You are a Licentiate of the Royal College of Surgeons ?—Yes; and a member of the Royal College of Physicians.

209. And you are a licentiate of the Apothecaries' Society ?—I am.

210. Are you medical officer for the Rotherham district ?—I am.

Chairman—continued.

211. How long have you been so ?—Between three and four years.

212. Have you practised in Rotherham since 1875 ?—Yes.

213. For the last three or four years you have been medical officer ?—Yes, I have been for 33 years connected with medical practice.

214. What

Chairman—continued.

214. What is the main class of labour in Rotherham ?—Chiefly miners and ironworkers.

215. Are you medical officer of the Poor Law Board or of the Sanitary Board ?—Of the Poor Law Board of the Rotherham district.

216. Is child insurance practised largely by this class of persons you have spoken of ?—Very largely.

217. Mainly amongst the labouring class; the miners and ironworkers ?—Yes.

218. Can you say anything as to the character of the class amongst whom this practice has prevailed ?—Those who insure most are generally confined to the more improvident classes of the poor; in my experience the better-class poor do not insure the children as a rule, but it is very largely those who are improvident and very poor. Those are the baser class.

219. Those of bad character ?—Those of bad character. It is very common amongst them.

220. Then you would say that the majority of those insurances within your knowledge are not held by the thrifty and respectable, but by the lower class, the bad people ?—I meet occasionally with industrious and worthy amongst the lower class, but that is not the rule; they are, as a rule, the dissolute.

221. Have you observed any effect that this practice of insurance has had amongst this class ?—The general effect of infant insurance amongst this class I refer to has been to make them careless as to the treatment of their children, either with respect to giving them medicine, or food, or clothing; it has generally demoralised them; their natural care has been lessened by the inducement to neglect which insurance holds out to them.

222. You consider that insurance would offer a considerable added inducement to the natural dislike of the cost and trouble of bringing up the children ?—It is so; the people express themselves in a very indifferent way about the death of a child ; they look to death as though it were the natural sequence of insurance.

223. Have you any cases that you can give the Committee to illustrate that statement ?—I have had many cases which I could mention ; a little while ago I brought up two cases before the magistrates ; it is only the flagrant cases that we can lay hold of; nothing is more easy than to kill a child, but nothing is more difficult than to detect the crime; we can easily see what the result is, but we cannot tell how it is brought about. In April last two children were insured; the first child had been previously brought to me, and then the parents brought up a second child in a dying state from scarlet fever. My son, who is a qualified surgeon, helps me at home; he saw the child, and gave instructions respecting medicine and treatment, and the parents were to come for the medicine, but they never came near; the child died.

224. Were you aware of the case of a person of the name of Pritchard ?—That is the case I am now referring to.

225. You had two cases of the sort in question in one day, I think ?—There were three cases really in court that day, and we got convictions in two cases.

(142.)

226. What were they convicted of ?—Neglecting the child and of cruelty ; in the first child's case I sent for the father and mother, and told them I should give them the benefit of the doubt ; although I had not the slightest doubt in my own mind that they had neglected it, and had been very cruel, and I told them that they were not worthy of the name of father and mother; I gave them a certificate, but warned them that I should not do the same upon a similar occasion if it occurred again.

227. Have you known any cases of improper feeding ?—I might say that, in eleven days, this same woman came up with another dying child in exactly the same condition; it died in an hour-and-a-half after I saw it; it was patent to anyone when the child was brought to me that it was dying; it was full of dropsy and had inflammation of the lungs ; it had been ill above a week, but it had neither clothing nor the appearance of any kind of comfort, and it was upon that case, coming upon my warning which I had given only eleven days before, that I refused to give them a certificate, and referred them to the coroner. They were prosecuted and convicted, and the man has just come out of gaol.

228. How long a term of imprisonment did they get ?—Two months; but the wife escaped, by getting into the hospital ; she had been ill; the home was one of the most desolate I have ever been in.

229. Could you mention any other case ?—I am attending now three cases which bear upon this subject. I have one I was called to last week; it was scarlet fever again. I may say, that we never see the children, as a rule, until the case is hopeless; as a rule, in convulsions, it is generally from the uræmic poison of the scarlet fever; and death may occur at any moment ; ordinary starving is slower; they are better able to time it. When they wilfully mean to compass the death of the child, as I know they do in many cases, they can time it so as to kill it in a few days ; but in this kind of case they are often caught; the convulsions of scarlet fever often kill within an hour or two, and in this case, last week, the child died within a few hours. There are three other children now in the house whom I am attending ; they have no means of proper nursing; however, I insisted upon the bedrooms being changed and greater attention being paid to them, and those three are getting better. When one of the children died, I told the parents I should give a certificate that time, but I blamed them very much; they had had no regard whatever to preserving the life of the child. I may mention another case. A few days ago I was sent for to attend another child in convulsions, it was under two years of age, and the whole house are insured; the woman drinks, which is very common in connection with these cases. She had been feeding a child under two years of age with what is called "souse," often a miserable mixture of pig's skin and pig's ears, boiled, which had driven the child into inflammation of the bowels, and ultimately into convulsions; the little dress that it had on would almost have stood in dirt; it had inflammation of the throat as well ; there was no attempt at nursing; in the home the furniture would not

B 2   fetch

Chairman—continued.

fetch 3 *s.*; but all their concern was about these very certificates I hold in my hand; I have brought them with me (*producing the same*). They have just insured the child again. I am dealing with the system, not with individuals, so that the names will not appear; they had allowed the policies in the office to lapse, because the agent had failed to call; he had got into trouble himself, and so they allowed them to fall through after paying over two years. They immediately re-insured the children with the agent who had lost the first office, in this new office. On the day the child was in convulsions, the insurance agent, without having seen the child at all, gave them these policies, guaranteeing, as the outside stamp says, "Immediate full benefit." On the strength of a payment of 4 *d.*, in that case there is 3 *l.* payable; for 4 *d.* in another case, 3 *l.* 10 *s.*; and for another 4 *d.*, 10 *l.*; each policy stamped "Immediate full benefit." Inside the policy they follow the old lines, "a penny a week insuring quarter benefit for a quarter of a year; half benefit 26 weeks; full benefit, 52 weeks;" but from what is stamped outside and on the paying card, the people have the idea that they will get the money instantly they have made their first payment; so these had paid their 4 *d.*, and their policies were stamped to give "full benefit." The company are all right, because they have constant lapses, and in that way they are able to make these very sensational offers from the money that is everlastingly becoming lapsed. This woman, I may say, had no idea apparently beyond insurance; the one leading idea of her home-work is to keep these papers intact; she will sell the furniture, when she has it, and the first money from her husband's wages is taken to pay this agency, which has to be kept up. I believe, if she had not got ashamed, this child would have been dead already, but she is taking a little more care of it now, but I am very much afraid it will die.

230. How many of the family are insured?— The father and mother are both insured. There is a sister of 13, she has paid only 4 *d.*; here is a little child of 10 months, and this patient I am now attending of a year and 11 months.

231. The three children and the parents are all insured?—Yes.

232. You have not found, then, that the parental affection of mothers of that class makes them very careful of their children or very desirous of preserving their lives?—No, I find their natural affection seems to be so marred by their miserable surroundings and their loose habits, that they seem to have an unnatural wish to be rid of them; they do not make any trouble about them when they die; the tendency is towards death; the insurance is a powerful inducement in that direction.

233. You do not think, from your experience, that parental affection is in every case, or even in a great many cases, a sufficient protection for the children?—Certainly not; I have two cases side by side, which I am attending at present; one I may say fairly contrasts with the other. In one case the individual is a decent, honest, but very poor man, who had been paying for about 11 years, and nursing his children rightly; but

Chairman—continued.

he yesterday said to me, "These agents are never off the door-step; they are constantly pestering and plaguing us; but I shall not insure that baby." The baby was in danger. "I had insured the others, and after 10 years I got into poverty, and the policy lapsed, and all that money is lost," he said, "whereas if I had paid it into the Post Office Savings Bank I should have had something." That was a case in which the man really wished to do right by them. Next door to him I am attending an illegitimate child, and in the opinion of myself and the registrar, it is the intention of that woman to kill that child if she can. My son and I have been so frequently there, and watched her, that she does not neglect it to the same extent as she did; the child is living now and is three-quarters of a year old; I believe it will die; but we have made it a very difficult thing for her, because we knew that she had it insured directly it was born.

234. You have so carefully watched the mother of the child that you have prevented what you believed to be an intended murder?—Yes.

235. But in a great many cases that watchfulness would be impossible?—Quite impossible.

236. A busy medical man could not possibly give his attention to a case of that kind?—No. In scores and scores of instances I have written secondary causes in the certificate, when I have had plenty of moral evidence that the child had been destroyed, but, having no technical or legal evidence, I was powerless.

237. You had no such evidence in those cases as you thought would be in the least likely to get a verdict from a jury?—No; the past history of the case must be found, and to get that a detective would have to live in the house.

238. In most cases the doctor could not possibly know as much about the case as you know of the history of this woman?—No, he could not.

239. Therefore in most cases they feel themselves bound to give a certificate?—Yes, because it is so difficult to get legal evidence upon which to get a conviction. Besides that, there are so many other reasons; the doctor is not a prosecutor; he does not like to be in that position; that is rather the duty of the police; it is a great waste of his time; I have had many days wasted over the Pritchard case. It does not pay the doctor, in fact, and if he can give a certificate in any way without doing violence to his conscience, he will do it. The loss of time in attending before the coroner, and then before the magistrate, and then cooling his heels for two or three days at the assizes, is a very serious thing. And you have to bear in mind that if he fails to convict there is discredit to the doctor and damage to his practice, so that a doctor is very chary of refusing to give a certificate, even when he is morally convinced that it is a case of murder.

240. A doctor has every encouragement to give a certificate, and very little to refuse?— Very little, but I have refused many.

241. When certificates are refused the cases have to go to the coroner?—Yes.

242. Can you state whether, as a rule, those cases

27 *June* 1890.]   Mr. BRANSON, M.R.C.P.   [*Continued.*

cases end in conviction?—In most cases they fall through.

243. They fall through for want of sufficient evidence?—Yes; for want of sufficient evidence.

244. You could not give such evidence as would convict?—No.

245. Therefore it would have been a waste of time to have prosecuted such cases?—Yes.

246. Now with reference to prosecutions by the police; it is their duty, is it not, to take up those cases?—Yes.

247. Do they generally perform that duty?—They are more powerless even than the doctor.

248. Why?—The doctor has the best opportunity for getting information, such as it is; but going after the death the police have no means of knowing anything about the case, except through the doctor, or some other source; such information is very rarely to be obtained; the neighbours do not like to inform one against the other.

249. Then when a case does come before the coroner, I believe I am right in saying that in case of death the husband cannot bear witness against the wife, or the wife against the husband?—That is so.

250. Therefore, if only one of the parties was guilty even, and they did not both combine to bring about the death, the case would still fall through?—That is so.

251. Do you always, in case of suspicious death, refuse to give a certificate?—Whenever I am reasonably convinced that there has been neglect I refuse the certificate, and refer the parties either to the registrar or the coroner, but they are nearly always referred back again; they get a certificate from the coroner. He says, "I cannot get forward;" but still, whenever I am satisfied there has been criminal neglect I take a stand and refuse the certificate.

252. May I ask what is the precise nature of the doctor's certificate; he does not state the remoter causes of diseases; he simply says that death arose from a certain disease; is not that so?—We simply come in at the subsequent or secondary cause.

253. As to the cause of that cause you know nothing?—Nothing.

254. The case may be apparently one of natural disease; but it may be a natural disease produced, or greatly aggravated, by neglect or designed ill-treatment?—Yes.

255. It would be almost impossible, would it not, for a doctor to distinguish between the two cases?—The majority of the marasmus cases arise out of neglect and insufficient or improper food, and I believe I should be safe in saying that 90 per cent. of those cases are cases which might have been saved.

256. You give this as your opinion as a medical man; do you find that opinion is generally prevalent amongst the profession?—It is.

257. Do they hold the same views as you do?—The experience of every medical man I have spoken to has borne out the same thing, namely, the difficulty of giving certificates.

258. Practically then, as a matter of fact, for one reason or another, medical men do give many

certificates which they ought not to give?—Yes, we do.

259. Have you found out in what way the very bad class of people amongst whom the cases you speak of arise look upon insurance?—They look upon it very much as a lawful speculation; in the way in which a woman answered me the other day, when I was called in to see one of her children. It was a horribly neglected home, and several of the children were ill; this one was dangerously so from sheer neglect; it was patent to me, from the environments of the house, that there was no proper attention paid to the child. I inquired about the insurance. I thought there must be a motive for the neglect; and it was the case, that while there were so many children and such great poverty there was insurance. I said, "Why do you insure the children?" and the woman replied, "To put them away, sir." But I said, "God gave you these children to preserve and take care of;" the woman had never looked at it in that light; she was dumb; but the feeling was there, and came out, as it always does, when I speak to these people; that that is the tendency in their minds; the very fact demoralises them; the children will be put away, and they can afford to be careless. Careless people become criminal people; people drinking or beginning to drink soon come to think that this insurance and the doctor's certificate is all they need to think about; the clothing, the nursing, and the feeding, is less important.

260. People get dangerously familiarised with the possible prospect of the child's death?—They become perfectly wooden and indifferent to it.

261. The thought which is constantly before their minds is, "If the child dies I shall get so much money"?—Yes; it produces neglect, and in some cases positive criminality.

262. As regards the insurance of children, do you find that those bad classes of parents give much attention to your medical instructions when you tell them to treat the children in a certain way?—Never as we could wish; we find them almost invariably neglected; occasionally the medicine is poured down the sink and not given at all.

263. Though you have directed the medicine to be given you have no evidence that the medicine is given?—No.

264. And you believe that in many cases it has not been given?—Frequently, when I have ordered applications, I have turned down the clothing to see if my directions have been complied with, and I have found that my instructions had not been regarded at all; they have put out all sorts of excuses; that they had not got it, or had not the money to get it. The man I sent to gaol had 2 *l.* a week, and had always averaged 30 *s.*; so that it was not want of money, it was pure vicious neglect.

265. There would have been no difficulty in getting medicine?—No; they would get it, if necessary, for nothing from the union or hospital.

266. Are there any particular drugs that they may give to the children easily which will produce death?—It is a very common thing to give them soothing syrups and a little laudanum, now

Chairman— continued.

and then; it is a very common practice with the very worst characters, in nursing children, especially illegitimate children; but those who are clever and smart enough know that they do not need to give direct poison; simply sour milk will kill as surely as if they were poisoned with arsenic; the mere action of the acidulated milk destroys the digestive lining of the stomach and bowels, so that it is simply a question of time when the child is bound to die of starvation. The people who take charge of illegitimate children know this, and the parents of illegitimate children, too.

267. Do they put a little vinegar in the milk?—There is no need to do that; if they put it in the sun it will soon turn sour. There were two women I went sharply after to the Masborough side of Rotherham, a little while ago. I heard them singing and laughing away as lively as if they were at some merriment, as I was coming up, and when I got there they were at the wash-tub, those two strong young women, and the little child was in a cradle. I had previously ordered beef-tea and arrowroot to be given to the child. When I saw the child it was just alive; the eyes were glazed and blinded, it was so near death. I do not suppose it had had anything in its lips for some time; the lips were cracked and dry. I opened the child's mouth; the little tongue was like a bit of dried stick; it lay in a little wooden cradle, dirty and badly covered. I turned round and said to one of the women, "Where is the milk or the arrowroot which I ordered?" She said, "Oh, master, it could not take it." I said, "Then where is it; let me see it?" Then the mother went out of the house and rushed to the next house, and came back shortly with a dirty tin pot with some greasy water in it and said, "This is it." I felt very angry because the child looked so horribly neglected. I took a knife up from the table and, looking in the woman's face, I said, "If you would just draw that knife across the child's throat, that would be kinder than letting it die of starvation. This little child cannot speak to you and tell you what is the matter with it; if you let it die like this because you want it dead I will let you go to the coroner." They said, "Oh, master, we are ignorant and young." They had been singing like crickets before I got to the house.

268. You find, in many cases, a mother without a mother's feelings?—In innumerable cases; and it makes my practice very often painful to me, when I am powerless to protect the children as I would.

269. Do you think it is a reasonable accusation against those promoting this Bill to allege that they say that the working classes have no parental affection?—It is a great libel upon the working classes. These that I am speaking of are the dissolute classes, the offshoots, doing a little bit in the parish and a little bit in the house; they have no sense of moral and home obligations; there are not so many of the better class of working men who insure their children; they find they can invest their money to better advantage, and they are not short of burial money; it is those who waste their money who rely upon this suspicious basis for burying their children.

*Chairman—*continued.

270. I think you said something about lapses in the case of parents whose insurance had lapsed; as a matter of fact, do you know that there are a good many lapses?—They are very common. These two cases I am attending are both cases in point.

271. In those cases all the money that they have paid goes to the insurance company?—Eventually; there is a short period of grace allowed.

272. Is it not very probable that their getting all these lapses covers the cost arising from these cases of criminal neglect and murder, and makes the business pay pretty well in spite of them?—That is so. Take the case of Pritchard; they have no claim upon the company, but, although they were vicious people and deserved nothing, in each case half-a-sovereign was handed to them; that would be published in the company's statistics, showing that they were so generous, and that keeps up a fictitious idea.

273. Is it your opinion that the case of a donation or gratuity given on death in this way brings in fresh cases to the society, and makes it popular?—It is so.

274. Therefore the society can very well afford to write off these bad cases, as a shopkeeper writes off his bad debts?—And leave large balances.

275. It would not be a sound argument to say that murder in connection with insurance could not be committed, because the loss would be so heavy that the insurance society could not carry on its business?—That would be absurd, in my experience.

276. Do you think that there is great temptation in handling money, and that if the handling of the money were made impossible by law it would have a great effect in checking this bad practice?—As a practical man, moving in and out amongst this class of people, I do not think it would do that which is really needful; it would be a check, but not a sufficient check.

277. What do you think would be a sufficient check?—In my judgment, the best check would be registration; that every child insured should be registered, as in the case of vaccination or baptism registration; and that each child insured should be brought to the doctor when it was insured; but the greatest work is done by insuring dying children and weakly children, such as the one I am now attending. It is insured now, when it is practically in a dying state, and the agent has not seen the child.

278. Do you think that the agent either did not know that the child was dying, or that it was immaterial to him?—It is immaterial to him. I have heard many people complain that the insurance companies slide out of paying in all sorts of ways and that they, i.e., the people, are pinned down to certain conditions. Dr. Cobban, the police surgeon, told me only yesterday that he had a man come to him who had insured his child when it was born six months forward, in order to have it in immediate benefit. The company took the money, and it died in nine weeks. The man came back to say the agent would not pay, because the child was under three months.

279. Was

Chairman—continued.

279. Was this told you by Dr. Cobban ?—Yes, only yesterday.

Earl *Beauchamp.*

280. Where does Dr. Cobban live ? — In Rotherham ; he is the police surgeon there ; he said, " Go back and tell the agent you have paid the money."

The committee-room is cleared, and after a short time the public are re-admitted.

Chairman.

281. You were just now giving the Committee a statement you said you had heard from Dr. Cobban, the police surgeon, in your neighbourhood, as late as yesterday ; have you a very distinct recollection of what he did say ?—Yes, I have.

282. Perhaps you will proceed with your statement ?—He told me that in this case he had attended, and when the child was born it was insured and six months paid forward, which the agent received.

Earl *Beauchamp.*

283. It was insured after the child was born ? —Yes ; directly after the child was born ; the child died, if I remember rightly, when it was nine or ten weeks old ; it died within three months. On applying to the agent he declined to pay, saying that the child was not in any benefit. He came back and told Dr. Cobham that he had been refused, so he said " Go back again and tell him that as you have paid the money he must pay, or you will bring it into court, and that I will appear as a witness against them ; " the money was instantly paid.

Chairman.

284. I may ask you what facilities there are in Rotherham for obtaining medical attendance gratis; can a poor man easily get the attendance of a doctor for nothing ?— Very easily.

285. He may be a member of one of the friendly societies, which give a sick allowance ?— Yes.

286. Or he may be a member of a club which has a club doctor ?—And then there is the parish doctor and the hospital as well.

287. In point of fact, no member of the working classes need go without medical attendance for want of money to pay the doctor ?—Certainly not.

288. Then, if it be alleged that he must make a death assurance in order to get the money to pay a doctor to attend his child, the allegation is absurd ?— Yes.

289. The doctor's fee for attending a child which dies is not larger, is it, than if it recovers? —Certainly not.

290. And if he can pay for the attendance of a doctor when the child does not die, he can pay for the attendance of a doctor when the child does die ?—Yes.

291. When parents have insured the child, and you have attended a good many cases, have the parents paid you any money out of the insurance money after the child's death, or did you always attend as the parish doctor ?—In the case of Pritchard I attended as private doctor.

Chairman—continued.

292. Did the parents of the child pay you anything for attending ? — In the first case they came and paid 2 *s.*, but in this transaction upon. which I put them in prison they paid nothing.

Earl of *Derby.*

293. I suppose it is the interest of the insurance office to refuse payment in every case where any proof can be given that the child has come to its death by improper means ?—Decidedly.

294. Presumably, if the practice is so common as you have described it, the insurance offices must be very well aware that such cases frequently do occur ?—Yes.

295. If that is so, how is it that they make no attempt to detect these offences, and so save themselves from payments which they need not make ?—I have never known them attempt to prosecute in any case. They generally try to minimise the payment ; if there is anything shaky about the case as to age, or the child ailing at all when insured, they make their payment less.

296. I presume it is absolutely against the interests of the offices that such murders should take place ; they lose by every such case, do they not ?—I presume they do.

Chairman.

297. I omitted to ask you this : have you observed in the directions of one of those companies this direction to its agent : " You will be careful not to permit a claim to be allowed upon an infantile policy unless it has been in existence the requisite period, because it will bring discredit upon the company if they refuse to pay a claim after the necessary certificates have been procured ; " has your attention ever been drawn to that rule ?—No, it has not.

Earl of *Selborne.*

298. Are these all time policies ; policies for a limited time ?—All children's policies are, as I understand, under 10 years of age.

299. Is the insurance for a limited time ?—I believe it is in most cases.

Earl *Spencer.*

300. In the case of these prosecutions which you said you knew of (I think Pritchard was the name you mentioned) who was it instituted the prosecutions ?—I did.

301. You did, as medical officer of the parish? —I sent the particulars to the coroner, and gave the particulars to Captain Burnett, the chief of the police ; he took the case up upon the strength of my notes.

302. What were they prosecuted for ; what was the charge, neglect ?—Wilful neglect of the children in allowing them to die in an inhuman way.

303. They were not charged with manslaughter ?—No, the coroner refused to do it ; he did not have any inquest ; he referred the case straight to the magistrate without holding any inquest. He said, " I will send my certificate to bury, so you must send them on to the magistrate," and with my notes they were prosecuted.

304. The

Earl *Spencer*—continued.

304. The magistrate tried 'the case out?—The magistrate tried the case out, and they were convicted for neglect.

305. And upon conviction the insurance-money could not be paid, I suppose?—The society paid 10 *s.* in each case as a gratuity; the full benefit, if they had got the full amount, would have been 3 *l.*, but they were under three or six months.

306. Was it in consequence of the successful prosecution that the insurance was forfeited, or how was it?—It was forfeited because they were not in benefit according to the company's rules; it was a pure gratuity on their part to give this half-sovereign.

307. But in the case where the prosecution is successful, would the fact of conviction forfeit the insurance?—It would, in my judgment; but I do not know of a case.

Lord *Clifford of Chudleigh.*

308. Do policies often lapse from neglect of the agent to apply for the premiums?—Yes; and from the movements of the people and their carelessness they are very apt to get behind; they have a few weeks' grace; I forget whether it is eight or ten weeks.

309. Do I understand you to say the agents are careless?—In one case I have mentioned, the agent himself was to blame; he got into legal trouble over a case of arson he was charged with.

310. That, you think, is not a common thing?—It is common enough for the policies to lapse.

Lord *Thring.*

311. Are you personally acquainted with the manner in which these insurance companies conduct their business; how do they collect their subscriptions?—The agent goes round weekly. I know a case in point; they will have, perhaps, four or five or eight or nine, which they can very well get in one house, and it is worth the agent's time to go round every week.

312. Supposing the agent does not attend each week; if the people are careless they will allow the policy to lapse?—In that case, it is stated by the rules that if the agent does not call it is their duty to acquaint the office, or to take the money to the office. The agent not calling does not excuse them; but being careless people, they are very often caught.

313. Who gets the benefit of the lapsing, the shareholders or the directors?—That I do not know.

Lord *Norton.*

314. Should you say that the greater number of the cases of suspicious deaths have been of illegitimate children?—It is not uncommon; indeed it is very common amongst married people to have children die in this way; but it is a much more prevailing custom for illegitimate children to be treated so.

315. Have many cases come under your notice in which, the mother having died, the child has been in the care of a stepmother?—Not many cases; a few.

316. But you would say that, in all the sus-

Lord *Norton*—continued.

picious cases that have come under your notice, the parents are of the lowest class, and usually a drunken and ill-conducted lot?—Not all; a child, in one case I know, was left motherless, and is in charge of the grandmother. I found my instructions invariably neglected. The child was dying from this marasmus, and I got cross with her, and said, " I shall give the case up unless you carry out my instructions; the child is dying, and I will not be responsible." She nearly broke into tears, and said I was very severe upon her. I said, " I want you to see this; if you were struck with apoplexy now, and fell ill, I would look after your interests, and I want you to deal with the child in the same way as you would want to be dealt with if you were in the same position." She nursed the child. A little time afterwards I met the father, and said, " How is the child?" He said, " She is dead, sir. I called at your surgery, but you were not in; we called in another doctor."

317. What was the father?—The parents were in a very fair average position. They were in a good home; but I could see the child was in the way. The grandmother had a large laundry, and the child was a nuisance to her.

318. You said the better class of working men did not insure their children?—As a rule they do not.

319. But they provide for their children in better ways?—They have their own clubs, which allow so much for a child, and frequently they make provision by savings banks and Post Office savings banks. I do not find that they usually insure in these little offices such as I have named. It is not the custom amongst that class so much as it is amongst the dissolute.

320. Then the cases of insurance that you have been referring to are generally insurances in friendly societies or in burial clubs?—In the better class of working-men.

321. And not in clubs specifically for the burial money?—No; I apprehend rather in such as the Oddfellows and Masons.

322. In all cases there is not only the interest that my Lord Derby referred to of the officers of the society against imposition of this sort, but it is the interest of the neighbours to look after any suspicious case of maltreatment of a child, is it not?—It is never done; the neighbours will not often interfere even when a child has been neglected to death; they will not interfere or inform one against another; it is not their business, they think.

Lord *Bishop of Ripon.*

323. I think you said the society sometimes made the death of a child a kind of advertisement?—That is so.

324. So as to get fresh insurances?—Yes; they make it known that they have been especially generous in cases where they have had no claim upon them whatever; it is an inducement to the people to feel that they will always get something. In one case I am attending now the sister and sister-in-law have both got claims, they are both of them parish patients, and they are both very dissolute. The idea of insurance was regarded as a sort of legal speculation; they
lost

Lord Bishop of Ripon—continued.

lost sight of the individual in the money question absolutely.

325. But what I was thinking of was that the question whether the society would make a profit or not must depend upon the question of life or death. The death of a great number means loss to the society; but I gather from you that they speculate, so to speak, that although a death may mean a loss, yet a death, if it is well advertised, may mean a gain?—It is a gain to them, because they give a small grant, not a large grant; in this case it was 10 *s.* each.

Lord *Poltimore.*

326. You mentioned the bad case of Pritchard; was she a married woman?—Yes.

327. With one child?—Several.

Lord *Herschell.*

328. Are the societies you have been speaking of principally mutual societies?—I scarcely know what they are in themselves; I do not come in contact with them except through these children.

329. Are they societies constituted for the purpose of the shareholders gaining profits, or are they mutual societies?—I am not aware that any one gets a benefit, except the company itself; I am not aware that there is any benefit except the death-rate that is given when the insured dies; but the company is worked upon ordinary business lines for the benefit of the society.

330. They are not societies composed of members which pay into a certain fund for their own benefit?—I think not.

331. With reference to the inducement which the companies would have to pursue investigations in case they were suspicious of foul play, do you think it possible that the sum in a particular case which they would have to pay is so small that it might be disadvantageous to them, on the whole, even if there were suspicions, to take proceedings on account of the damage to their business generally?—That is so; they do not like to have any contention with reference to any of the insurances; they do the same thing with reference to adults. I have recently had two paupers, who both died in the union; they were insured all round to the extent of nearly 100 *l.* each; that is a very common practice; people all round making money out of their deaths because there is no limit.

Earl of *Harrowby.*

332. Had you had any experience of child insurance before you went to Rotherham?—Most of my experience has been in Rotherham; but I became aware of the very easy way in which children were disposed of, the easy transition from neglect to the grave, when I was a medical student in Liverpool; it was so very common there to get medical certificates; either a midwife, or a chemist, or any unqualified man of any sort, could get certificates from some medical man to any amount at a shilling each; he would sign them without demur and without question; this question of insurance, and of granting or refusing certificates, is a matter I have looked into a good deal; it has been a painful point with me all my medical life.

(142.)

Earl of *Harrowby*—continued.

333. Taking 3 *l.* as the amount payable on the death of a child, what proportion of that would be spent upon the burial expenses?—There is very little legitimate expense; 2 *l.* would cover all legitimate expenses. If it is an Irish death, the people generally spend a lot in drink, but it is very common generally to have what they call a spree.

334. But the legitimate funeral expenses, what would they come to?—The legitimate funeral expenses do not come up to the 3 *l.* 10 *s.* which they may receive; they generally have a little margin, and they make a little feast with it.

335. You have referred to the penalty upon a medical man for improperly refusing to give a death certificate; what is the position of a medical man with reference to giving a death certificate?—He is perfectly independent; he can refuse any time he chooses.

336. Can he refuse without assigning any reason?—No; he must give his reason to the coroner; he must say to the coroner why he refuses it, otherwise he is bound to give a certificate; but because of the difficulties I have just named the majority of general practitioners are conveniently deaf and blind to an evil they cannot cure; we cannot remedy the evil because of the want of technical evidence, so that a child has often passed away and a certificate been given, when we know morally that the child has not had a chance of life.

337. I understand you to say that it is not really the thrifty working classes who are affected by this question?—No; but the percentage of the others is so great that it becomes a burning question. I have nothing to say against the thrifty; and there are thrifty people in this line of life as in others.

Earl *Beauchamp.*

338. The workers in coal and iron are notoriously amongst the least cultivated of the working classes, are they not?—I think we may take it so, but it is not the better class even of those that I am referring to. We have some fine samples of homes and honest life amongst the workers of coal and iron in our neighbourhood; it is the offshoots of those people of a slavish type, who exist partly on parish, partly on a little work, and partly drunken; it is amongst those that this insurance evil is so mischievous.

339. Your duties as medical officer of the Poor Law Board brought you chiefly into contact with the worst part of the working classes?—Yes, in this particular I have come across all classes during my medical life, but the outcome of my experience is, that it is not the better working classes who lend themselves to this practice. I have, however, found that fairly decent people, when they have drunk, have degenerated into wilful neglect which borders upon criminal conduct; that is a very common thing.

340. I suppose the burials in Rotherham take place in the cemetery?—Yes.

341. Is there any bye-law restricting the time at which funerals are to be performed, as to the days?—No; occasionally they go by the doctor's advice; if it is a very infectious case, they would bury in a very short time.

C

342. Are

Earl *Beauchamp*—continued.

342. Are funerals allowed on Sundays?—Yes.

343. Is that day very much chosen by the working classes?—There is a large percentage buried on Sunday. I may say amongst the honest working classes they prefer the Sunday, because it does not take a day's work from them; it does

Earl *Beauchamp*—continued.

not matter so much to the poor and the more improvident; the Sabbath and week day are all alike to them, for they never trouble about losing a day.

344. Do you know at all what was the practice in Liverpool?—Not in reference to burial.

The Witness is directed to withdraw.

Mr. WILLIAM JACKSON CLEAVER, M.B., M.D., is called in; and Examined, as follows:

Chairman.

345. You are a Bachelor of Medicine?—Yes.

346. And a surgeon of Edinburgh?—Yes, M.D.

347. At present you reside at Broomhilll, Sheffield?—Yes.

348. You are surgeon to the Child's Hospital, Sheffield?—Yes.

349. For how long have you been so?—I have had 14 years' experience.

350. Is it long since your attention was called to the question of infant insurance?—It was four or five years ago.

351. May I ask what it was that first drew your attention to the subject?—What drew my attention first was what I read and saw in the newspapers, coupled with the cases brought to me at the hospital. In years gone by I used to have a great number of very weakly infants brought to me close upon their death, for whom I used to give a certificate, not thinking there was anything wrong about the case; it is only in the last four or five years that I have got to know that those children had many of them been insured.

352. Those children that were brought to you were brought towards the close of their lives?—They were.

353. You had no opportunity of attending them for any length of time?—Very often I only saw them once.

354. Probably once or twice would be about the most you would have seen any of them?—The majority of them I saw only once or twice.

355. A number of those were cases of emaciation presumably?—Yes, they were.

356. May I ask this; as regards emaciation it would appear upon your certificate as marasmus, would it not?—It would appear upon the certificate as marasmus, or congenital debility, as the case might be.

357. And as regards external features, are they pretty much the same whether the child is dying from inability to digest food, or from food not being given?—To a great extent.

358. You could not tell without a post-mortem examination which it was?—No.

359. The child being brought to you in a state of emaciation, the parents saying that "This child will not eat its food," or "would not take it," you would have no means of checking that statement?—None whatever.

360. Your certificate would be marasmus, or atrophy?—Yes.

Chairman—continued.

361. Your certificate is strictly as to the medical cause of death?—Yes, as to the medical cause of death.

362. When you were so much struck with those cases, which were brought to you, what action did you take?—I first began questioning the mother, more particularly where I did not like the statement as regarded the child; and if my suspicions were still further aroused by the answers, instead of giving a certificate I would write upon a slip of paper that the child had been brought to me in a state of extreme debility, that its death had ensued within a very short space of time afterwards, and that I could not give a certificate; that was taken to the registrar.

363. How many, upon the average, would there be of such cases?—There used to be, from six to ten years ago, a great number, but those cases have gradually dwindled away, and I cannot help thinking they have dwindled away because of the great care I have exercised in the last four or five years in questioning the mothers before granting death certificates.

364. You find that the parents rather avoid you?—They will not come to the hospital at all in cases of that kind.

365. Your suspicion arose, I may say, again from parents bringing them to you so late in the progress of the disease?—Yes, in the last two or three days.

366. Did the parents who brought those children so late to you show any particular parental affection or desire for their recovery?—Some of them did, I am sure; others just the reverse; but I often noticed that the children were brought not by their own mothers, but by some friend, and when I have asked where the mother was, I was told either that she was ill in bed or working, or was deaf, or that there was some reason why she did not come to the hospital with her child. I noticed that, in several cases; it seemed to me that to avoid questioning, somebody else brought the child.

367. In order to avoid the inconvenience of questioning?—Yes.

368. It would not be true to say that the people no longer brought their children to your hospital, because they could get better attendance elsewhere?—No.

369. The medical skill at your hospital was of a high class?—It is generally considered so.

370. You do not think then that the diminution in the number of cases you speak of is owing to the fact that the practice of insurance has

ceased

Chairman—continued.

ceased or diminished in Sheffield?—I am sure that is not the case.

371. The practice has greatly increased, has it not?—I believe it has, but I do not know of my own knowledge.

372. Do you think that all the persons who give medical certificates are as careful as you have described yourself to be?—I am sorry to say they are not.

373. Medical certificates are given carelessly, you think?—I am sure they are. I have given many carelessly myself from having no suspicion of their being anything wrong.

374. I suppose, as a matter of fact, a very busy medical practitioner has not time to look very closely in the cases brought to him for certificate?—They have no time, and, as it were, shift the responsibility on to the registrar of births and deaths.

375. And in the case of hospitals in the out-patient department, we all know that in large towns they are very crowded?—They are very crowded; you can only devote a very short space of time to each case.

376. A very great number of cases have to be dealt with in a very short time?—About a hundred cases have to be dealt with in about an hour and a-half.

377. It is impossible to give much attention in those cases to each?—It is.

378. Supposing a doctor orders medicine, has he much power of ascertaining whether that medicine is given or not?—None whatever; they have only the mother's word for it.

379. And similarly as regards that and medical comforts which doctor's order?—I can only rely upon what the mother tells me at the hospital, because I never see them at all elsewhere.

380. That observation would specially apply to what we call cases of out-patients?—Yes.

381. I think you stated that it would be difficult to distinguish in many instances between cases where the disease was natural, and cases where the natural disease was induced by evil intent?—It is absolutely impossible; you cannot tell.

382. You might have a very strong suspicion but you could not hold that a suspicion would warrant you in withholding the certificate?—Not unless I could gather suspicious circumstances from the neighbours or friends.

383. Not from the symptoms?—No.

384. If suspicious circumstances did not come to your knowledge you would have no reason for refusing a certificate?—I should have no reason for refusing a certificate.

385. Therefore, not only careless practitioners but a careful practitioner like yourself must frequently give certificates where they ought not?—Very often.

386. The medical certificate is, therefore, a very slight protection to the children?—It is hardly any protection.

387. When a medical certificate is refused and a case comes before the coroner, the doctor must naturally appear as a witness?—He must.

388. What more can he state except the circumstances which have come to his knowledge?—He can say nothing more than I am saying now, that

(142.)

Chairman—continued.

the case has not been treated properly, in his belief, but that he cannot verify it by actual facts.

389. That would not be evidence to warrant a conviction for wilful neglect, or manslaughter?—No.

390. Therefore, in your opinion, the majority of cases which come before the coroner get off scot free?—Yes.

391. From the inadequacy of the medical evidence?—Yes,

392. The only evidence the doctor could give would be the medical history of the case?—Yes, that is all.

393. And that he can only get from the parents of the child or those in charge of the child?—A doctor in my position can only get it from the parents.

394. Have you known of cases which have been brought before the coroner and which have failed?—I do not remember a single such case coming before the coroner; I can only think that the registrar of births and deaths on receiving my note, and not the certificate of death, has given the parent the certificate himself.

395. The registrar did?—Yes, because I have never yet been called before the coroner upon a single occasion for one of those cases.

396. Do you think the registrars are careless in giving their certificates?—I will not go so far as that, but they may err on the side of good nature and give the parent a certificate because they have no evidence and think they can get no evidence to inculpate him.

397. Is it generally the opinion of your profession, as far as you can gather, that there is a good deal of wilful neglect and child murder connected with insurance?—I believe it is a very common idea in the profession that there is a great deal of it going on. One cannot help thinking so, if one sees the cases that I see.

398. Do you ever attend those cases at the children's houses?—Never.

399. Always at the hospital?—Yes, always at the hospital; they come as out-patients.

400. Therefore if a child dies, you at the hospital have really hardly any chance of knowing the history of the case because you are not going backwards and forwards to the home?—I only get my knowledge from the parents the first time they bring a case, and that is often the only time. I had a case last week in which the mother brought a child to the hospital in the last stage of emaciation. I asked her whether the child was insured, and she told me it was not. Now we have in Sheffield an inspector from the society, and I wrote to him and asked him to inquire into the case before the mother came again. When I was at the hospital on the Saturday, I heard that a certificate was required for this child; I had only seen it once; the mother seemed a respectable woman; I questioned her very closely and gave her a certificate, but at the same time I wrote to the inspector, as I say, and he replied to me that he could find no evidence of wilful neglect or anything of the kind; but I cannot understand why it was the mother only brought this child to me within two days of its death.

401. Are you in the habit of asking the parents when they bring a child to you whether the

c 2   child

Chairman—continued.

child is insured?—I am now; I used not to do so.

402. Have you formed any opinion as to the number of insured children as compared with those who are not insured, who are brought to you?—I should think that somewhere about 25 per cent. of the children I have inquired into have been insured, but I have only the mother's statement to go upon, and the mother can easily say the child is not insured when it is.

403. Whenever the mother says it is insured, you know, of course, that it is insured?—Yes.

404. But it is by no means certain, when she says it is not insured, that it is not insured?—I cannot tell that.

405. Have you ever known any cases of this kind being brought before the assize court at Sheffield?—Not one.

406. And you know very few cases, I should presume, from what you have said, in which a coroner's jury has returned a verdict against the parents?—I have not had one.

407. Although you have had good reason for believing that in many cases you ought to have had them?—I know it.

408. You do not give that as a guess, but as a moral certainty?—A moral certainty as great as anything can be where I have not the actual facts to deal with.

Lord *Clifford of Chudleigh.*

409. Have you any reason to think that mothers do conceal the fact that a child is insured?—I am not aware of that from actual facts, but I have my suspicions very often that it is so.

410. You have never discovered a case, have you?—No; because it is only within the last year that we have had an inspector that I could apply to to tell me; in one case the mother told me that the child was not insured and it was insured, but in one case only, that I know of.

Chairman.

411. That was a recent case, I think?—It occurred about six months ago.

412. Since the inspector has been in Sheffield? Yes.

Lord *Norton.*

413. You seem to think that this class of cases has dwindled away since more care has been taken; does that mean that more inquiry has been made?—Yes; more inquiry has been made.

414. Have you any suggestion to make to the Committee as to improving the action of the certificate generally; one suggestion has been made that a certificate should be given on the first insurance only?—It is a very difficult matter to say; I have thought about it, but I have come to no definite conclusion as to what would be the best thing to do.

415. As the cases come to you at the hospital you can hardly tell much of the character of the people who come?—No, very little; because it is so very easy to keep a child in dirty clothes and unwashed at home, and yet to bring it up looking fairly respectable at the hospital.

Lord *Norton*—continued.

416. What is your idea of the character of parents generally in such suspicious cases?—I should say that it is about half-and-half. Some seem to have a great deal of motherly care and instinct about them, while others seem to be perfectly callous about it. There is no doubt that, so far as illegitimate children are concerned, there seems to be no motherly care whatsoever.

417. Have you any means of saying what proportion of the cases are illegitimate?—I cannot give the proportion; a large number of the cases in Sheffield are those of illegitimate children, but I could not give any percentage.

418. You do not know at all the proportion of the cases in which the child is in the care of a stepmother, the mother being dead?—No; I daresay there may be many such cases, but I do not know them; I take it for granted that the mother is the mother of the child and not a step-mother, unless there is something to arouse my suspicions.

419 When you say so generally that you cannot be sure whether the cases are truly stated to you, why, in those circumstances, do you suspect?—My suspicions are aroused in the first instance by the appearance of the child; if the child is very close to its death, as you can see by its appearance, my suspicions are still further aroused; and, unless the mother can very straight-forwardly answer all my questions, I am, of course, still further suspicious.

420. You say that the cases have been diminished by the employment of an inspector; who is the inspector and what is his business?—He is an inspector appointed by the Society for the Prevention of Cruelty to Children.

Lord *Poltimore.*

421. Are the children generally brought to you in the first stage of illness, or, as a rule, are they brought to you when they are very far gone?—A careful mother always brings the child at an early stage of illness, unless it is one of those numerous cases in which it has been seen by another doctor outside, and he says he believes he cannot get it better, and then they bring the child to me; there may be many cases in which the child has been treated quite properly out of doors, but the parent brings it up to me very near its death, hoping it may get better treatment, or different treatment, at the hospital.

422. Can you tell me at all the proportion of such cases?—No; but we get a very great number of cases. The out-patient visiting days are Mondays and Thursdays; and on Mondays I should say that, out of 100 children brought up, there would be three or four cases of emacia-tion, which be perfectly honest cases of emacia-tion due to marasmus, but I should feel perfectly sure, though I may be wrong in my opinion about it, that they are cases of neglect.

Lord *Thring.*

423. Why do they bring you up the neglected children?—For the certificate.

424. If the child is once seen by you at the hospital, and the mother comes to you another day and then says the child is dead, do you grant the certificate?—Very rarely of late. In some

cases

Lord *Thring*—continued.

cases I have written to the inspector to inquire into the case, but more frequently I have refused a certificate, giving only a slip of paper to take to the registrar.

425. How do you know that the child is dead? —I have only the mother's word for that; a mother brought up a child last Thursday week, and on the Saturday she applied for a certificate.

426. Do you grant a certificate without seeing that the child is dead?--Yes; the child is at home. I do not see the child.

427. Is that the practice of the hospital?—It is the practice of all hospitals in similar cases; we must take the word of the parent that the child is dead, because we are not an out-patient visiting hospital.

428. But it surprises me to learn that you grant a certificate at all?—In most cases I am not surprised to hear that the child is dead.

429. How many times would you have a child brought up before you granted a certificate?— I have done so when it has been brought up once, twice, or three times, quite according to the nature of the case; if it is a case which is to my mind free from suspicion, I should grant it.

430. The question suggests itself, of course; how do you know what the child dies of if you do not see the death; I suppose you presume that the disease continues?—If a child is brought up at three or four months of age only weighing 3 or 4 lbs., it would be a very great miracle that the child should recover, and I tell the mother, the first time she brings it up, that the child will most likely die, and that no medical aid will be of any avail. I lecture her, and ask her why she has not brought up the child before; she may give sometimes one reason and sometimes another, but I have not the slightest doubt that what the mother tells me afterwards is true, that the child died at a certain time, and I must give the certificate.

431. Supposing you did not give the certificate, what would happen to you?—If I did not give the certificate, and the registrar refused to give a certificate, the case would have to go before the coroner, and I should be called up to give evidence before the coroner, and also at the magistrate's court, I presume, and also at the assizes.

432. I do not mean that; but supposing you had not seen the child dead, and did not give the certificate, what would happen to you; is it not a sufficient justification for you to say that you have not seen the child dead?—If the child died between the two visiting days in the week, and I had no cause for suspicion, I should give the certificate, because I should know that the mother had not the chance of bringing the child up again to see me; but if the child was very ill, and very near death when brought to me, I should say to the mother, "This child is very ill; I cannot take the responsibility of giving you a certificate if it dies between Monday and Thursday. It is your duty to call in a medical man; if you cannot call in a medical man and pay him, there is the parish doctor you can call in."

433. I cannot understand why that parish doctor should give a certificate at all, and why you do not say, "I am not in a position to give a

(142.)

Lord *Thring*—continued.

certificate, I have only seen the child once previously, I do not know that the child is dead;" it is only an inference that the child died of the same disease as that for which it was seen?—It is only an inference that the child has died of that disease, but the inference is a fairly solid one.

434. I cannot understand why you do not refuse the certificate?—I think, in many instances, it would be a great unkindness to the parents to put them still further to the trouble if they are perfectly honest people and do not wish to call in other advice, or better advice than they have had.

435. How would you put the parents to trouble? —The trouble would be having the coroner's inquest upon the child; and again, the parents could not bury unless they got either my certificate or the registrar's certificate.

436. But if you are at all doubtful they ought not to bury under those circumstances?—I quite admit that. I freely admit that I must have given many certificates in my time which I ought not to have given.

Lord *Brougham and Vaux*.

437. In the event of one of these dissolute mothers telling you what was not true, and that you did not give a certificate, what would be the effect of your decision?—I could not imagine such a case; I never had such a case; it would defeat its own object, I should think; if I gave a certificate for a child which was not dead, I do not know what benefit the certificate would be to the people.

Lord *Herschell*.

438. The registrar does not register merely upon the medical certificate; he requires, does he not, the statement of some one who was present at the time of the death?—Yes.

439. So that the fact of the death does not rest upon the certificate, but rests upon the evidence of some one who was present at the time of the death?—Yes.

440. Then the medical certificate gives the probable cause of death (upon the assumption that the child is dead) which fact the registrar has learned from some other quarter, and, as I understand, if you had seen the child within a short period of its death, and learned that it was dead, and had seen from such-and-such conditions that it seemed to be due to that disease, it would be the ordinary course to give the certificate that it had died of that disease?—Yes.

441. I suppose, if the certificate were not granted under such circumstances, where there was no suspicion, the records of the cause of death would be nothing like as complete as they are; they are only obtained from the last medical practitioner who treated the patient?—That is so.

442. Supposing that you refused to give a certificate, under what circumstances ought the registrar to permit the funeral to proceed without the certificate of the coroner?—That I cannot say; of those cases that I have referred to not a single case has come before the coroner, I take it, because I have not been summoned.

443. Is there no cause of death registered at all in such a case?—I believe the registrar

c 3   simply

Lord *Herschell*—continued.

simply takes it from the mother's lips, ' She has wasted away."

444. But when a medical man has been attending the patient within a day or two of the patient's death, if the medical man states that he is unable to state the cause of death, do you mean to say that the registrar would insert simply what he has learnt from the mother ?—It must be so.

445. Or would he leave a blank ?—" Debility uncertified," I have seen in a certificate; " uncertified " is occasionally inserted.

446. The registrar, according to your idea, possibly communicates with the coroner, and the coroner thinks that the child may be buried without an inquest ?—I think it very possible that that may be so.

447. Could you communicate to the Committee some of those instances which would enable the Committee to know who is the registrar to apply to for an explanation as to what was done in the particular cases where you have refused to certify ?—Any of the registrars of births and deaths in Sheffield could do that.

448. Do you mean to say there could be cases in the districts of each of them, where you have refused to certify ?—No doubt there must have been cases in all of them in the last 10 years.

449. Would you have any means of referring, so as to enable you to know the particular cases in which you refused to certify ?—No; but I know a registrar's name in Sheffield at the present time who, I have no doubt, could give information upon the subject; he is one of the registrars of the Eccleshall district.

Earl *Beauchamp.*

450. The registrar's certificate is required for the ordinary burial ?—After the doctor has been, the doctor's certificate goes to the registrar.

451. No clergyman can bury except upon the production of the registrar's certificate ?—That is so.

452. The registrar's certificate is required for the purpose of burial ?—Yes.

453. But are you aware that under the Friendly Societies Act of 1875 a special certificate is required to enable the insurance companies to pay the insurance money ?—I do not know that.

454. Section 28 says, by sub-section 2, " No society shall pay any sum on the death of a child under 10 years of age except to the parent of such child, or to the personal representative of such parent, and upon the production by such parent or his personal representative of a certificate of death issued by the registrar of deaths, or other person having the charge of the register of deaths, containing the particulars after-mentioned." Then there are the particulars, and then another sub-section, sub-section 4, goes on to say, " No registrar of deaths shall give anyone or more certificates of death for the payment in the whole of any sum of money exceeding 6 *l.* on the death of a child under five years, or for the payment in the whole of a sum exceeding 10 *l.* on the death of a child under 10 years; and no such certificate shall be granted unless the cause of death has been previously entered in the

Earl *Beauchamp*—continued.

register of deaths on the certificate of a coroner or of a registered medical practitioner who attended such deceased child during its last illness, or except upon the production of a certificate of the probable cause of death under the hand of a registered medical practitioner, or of other satisfactory evidence of the same." You were not aware of those provisions ?—I was not.

455. Assuming these provisions to be the law, when you have signed that paper which you have described to us, the registrar might grant a certificate for burial, but he could not grant the certificate which would justify the insurance company in paying the insurance money ?—So I understand from what your Lordship has been good enough to read.

456. Will you describe to us more particularly the contents of the paper which you have signed in various cases in which you have refused the certificate ?—First there is the date, then " Child's Hospital, Sheffield. This child has been brought up to me in the last stage of emaciation," or " the last stage of congenital debility," or some similar term of that kind. " The mother now applies for a death certificate. I cannot give it." Then I sign my name.

457. You do not know the effect of the working of the law of insurance sufficiently to tell us any instance in which the insurance has been either paid or withheld after the signature of such a paper by you ?—No, I do not know that part of it at all.

458. Your withholding the certificate, and signing a paper of that description, would prevent the registrar giving such a certificate as would justify the payment of the money by the insurance company ?—So I believe.

459. By Act of Parliament ?—So I believe.

460. Would you describe to the Committee a little more in detail what the position of the Children's Hospital in Sheffield is ?—It is an out-patient and in-patient hospital; but it is a very much larger out-patient hospital, in proportion, than an in-patient hospital.

461. But your relations to anybody who comes in there are purely voluntary ?—They are purely voluntary.

462. Nobody is compelled to come to you ? —No.

463. You are not in a position of a parish officer ?—No; the only passport for admission is poverty and suitability, for both out and in-patients.

464. Then your experience is necessarily very different from that of a parochial medical officer? —It is very different because I never see a patient in his own home by any chance.

465. Whereas it is the duty of the parochial medical officer to see patients in their own homes? —Yes, it is, if they call him in, to do so.

466. It is no part of your business to visit them in their own homes ?—Not at all.

467. How long has your inspector been appointed ?—A little over a year.

468. I think you mentioned one case of a mother concealing the fact of a child being insured; has there been more than one case of that sort brought to your knowledge ?—And stating that it was not insured, only one case that I know

of;

Earl *Beauchamp*—continued.

of; but last Monday week I had what I thought was a very suspicious case, which I handed over to the inspector, but the inspector could not find out anything, because the neighbours will not deal hardly with one another unless there is something very gross, and a child can so easily be put away by slow degrees and by small opiates, as I have often found to be the case, that even the neighbours' suspicions are not aroused.

469. Have you found, generally, on the part of mothers, great intelligence with respect to the bringing up of their children?—There is a great deal of ignorance, but I think the majority are intelligent.

470. Where children are brought up by hand, do you find adequate intelligence shown on the part of the mother, as to the preparation of food, for instance?—There is very great ignorance in that respect. When I see an emaciated child I am in the habit of saying, "What are you feeding that child upon?" and if it is a child of 10 or 12 months, but not younger, and they say, "It feeds with us, sir," nothing can be worse than that.

471. And that on the part of parents who were supposed to be careful and affectionate?—Yes; I cannot help thinking that if it is not criminal it is very gross negligence, because they have other mothers older than themselves around and alongside of them, and they ought to be able to find out what to do, if they are ignorant themselves.

472. Do you think, speaking from your own knowledge, that it is fair to say that mothers of the working classes have an intelligent appreciation of the best way of bringing up children by hand?—I should say that 50 per cent. of them have an intelligent appreciation of how to bring up children by hand; they have been taught for many years now. We distribute leaflets from the Children's Hospital in any case where we think the mother is ignorant, giving directions for her to go by. For the last 14 years I have endeavoured, as far as I possibly could, by the aid of these leaflets, to inculcate that knowledge, and I think it must be only very young and reckless mothers who could feed their children in the way that some feed them.

473. What is the average rate of infant mortality in Sheffield?—I could not say, speaking from memory.

474. What is the average rate of general mortality in Sheffield?—The average rate would be about 22, I believe; that would be about the average death rate; it was 25 a little while ago.

475. Although you are surgeon to the Children's Hospital, you cannot give the Committee any information with respect to the rate of mortality amongst children in Sheffield?—Not from memory. I have known it and appreciated it, but at the present time I cannot bear in mind what it is.

Earl *Beauchamp*—continued.

476. Have you formed any comparison as to the proportion of children in Sheffield insured and uninsured?—I have not formed any such comparison; I have not studied the question in that light at all; it is only facts which have been brought before me at the hospital which I can at all deal with.

Lord Chancellor.

477. Have you any means of knowing how many children are insured?—Only those that I inquire into. I inquire into a good number. I might inquire into half-a-dozen cases a week.

478. What I mean is, have you any means of ascertaining how many are insured without reference to those that came before you?—I have no means of ascertaining that.

479. Will you tell the Committee what is the form of certificate you give in case of death?—Three is the name, age, and address of the child, with spaces for the primary and secondary cause of death, and also the length of time the disease has lasted; that is the certificate.

480. Then you certify, not the death but the cause of death, assuming the death to have taken place?—Yes; there is also a blank space in each certificate which has to be filled in or left vacant, according to what the medical man thinks that the child died of, as I am informed, if I have not seen the child dead. I ought to have mentioned that before.

481. What is about the average attendance of your out-patient children during the year?—The attendances are between 16,000 and 20,000, but the distinct or separate cases are between 4,000 and 5,000.

482. During the whole period you have been speaking of, how many times do you think you have refused to certify upon the ordinary certificate, and have given the paper you spoke of?—Not more than half-a-dozen times, perhaps, in a year, for the last three or four years; before that hardly any at all; because I had no suspicion then that the question of money was mixed up with the death of the child.

Chairman.

483. You stated that 50 per cent. of the parents were intelligent as regards the bringing up of children; therefore, 50 per cent. may be ignorant; that being the case, there being some ignorance and even considerable ignorance, a mother who wished to show a child foul play could always shield herself under the plea of ignorance?—I have no doubt they do so.

484. The amount of prevalent ignorance would become an easy and handy excuse for a person dealing out foul play?—I am quite sure it does.

The Witness is directed to withdraw.

Mr. HENRY BURRY PULLEN BURRY, L.R.C.P., M.R.C.S., is called in; and Examined, as follows:

Chairman.

485. You are a Licentiate of the Royal College of Physicians?—I am.

(142.)

Chairman—continued.

486. And a Member of the Royal College of Surgeons?—Yes.

487. You

Chairman-- continued.

487. You are also a general practitioner?—Yes.

488. How long have you been in practice?—12½ years.

489. You were first appointed as house physician, and afterwards as house surgeon at the London Hospital?—Yes.

490. Have you had any experience in rural districts?—Yes, ever since then; for a little over ten years.

491. Therefore, in fact, two years and a-half years in London, and 10 years in the country, cover your medical experience?—Yes, about.

492. Where has been your practice?—My practice has been in the north of Hertfordshire; I wish particularly to draw attention to this: at Baldock, in Hertfordshire; Stotfold, in Bedfordshire, and Arlesey, in Bedfordshire; those were three places at which child-life insurance was carried on to a varying extent, and, more or less, amongst differing classes of population; and now, for the last six years, I have been at Liphook, in Hampshire, and I observe a different state of affairs amongst the people there.

493. What was the occupation of the population at Baldock?—The population of Baldock was almost exclusively engaged in malting and brewing, and the women in straw-plaiting; but at Arlesey they were engaged in brick-making and clay-work, as well as straw-plaiting.

494. And at Liphook the occupation is chiefly agriculture?—Entirely.

495. In point of fact, you have had a very varied experience?—Yes.

496. Have you, during your experience in those respective places, had your attention called to infant insurance?—I have directed a great deal of attention to the subject.

497. In which of those places would you say infant insurance was carried on most?—I think it was about the same all round at each of the four places I have mentioned.

498. Have you formed any strong opinion upon the subject of infant insurance?—I have, a very strong one.

499. Against it?—Very strongly against it.

500. Will you give the Committee the grounds upon which you came to that strong opinion?—The great frequency with which I was called in to cases of moribund children. I had a branch surgery in Arlesey while living at Baldock, the two places being four or five miles apart, and was constantly called in to see moribund children: it was a matter of constant occurrence while I was there.

· 501. When did you see the children?—On the point of death, and they were dead within a few hours.

502. Those illnesses were not, I presume, what would be called sudden and rapid illnesses which would have prevented the parents calling in assistance?—Not at all; they were all cases in which a certain amount of medical attention and skill would probably have pulled the child through; they nearly all seemed to be suffering from lung troubles; they appeared to be children who had been allowed to catch a cold and had not been properly looked after for it, but had been allowed to get into that state.

503. Are you aware what number or proportion of those children were insured; did you

Chairman—continued.

take any means of inquiry?—Nearly all were insured.

504. You ascertained that?—Yes, or rather I did not ascertain it; the people do not make any secret about it; they openly admitted it; it had become a notorious thing in Arlesey.

505. You were just called in in time to enable them to get a certificate for registration?—Just that and nothing else.

506. Did you notice that that was very frequently the case?—Yes.

507. Especially and almost exclusively in the insurance cases?—My impression is that it was exclusively in insurance cases, but I would not be positive about it.

508. But you are positive that the large majority were insured cases?—Distinctly; the very large majority.

509. How did you know they were insured cases?—Either the people told me beforehand, or came to me afterwards to ask about the certificate.

510. And you would sometimes ask whether the child was insured?—Yes, occasionally.

511. The parents had no hesitation at all in telling you that the child was insured?—I never met with any.

512. There was no attempt at concealment at all?—I never met with any.

513. What would you say was the character of the people who thus insured their children?—The people who insured their children were of all sorts, good, bad, and indifferent; but the classes amongst which this neglect took place, the cases in which there were deaths brought about in this way, were the most profligate, adulterous, drunken, and dirty; everything is abominable and filthy in those people's places.

514. Were many of those children illegitimate?—About half the children in the place were illegitimate: at any rate, an enormous number.

515. It was not your experience apparently that the fact of a man receiving weekly wages made him always kindly and affectionate?—Not at all; many of those men were making good money, from 1 *l.* to 30 *s.* a week in the brick fields.

516. I suppose a great many of them were intemperate?—All of them, more or less.

517. What would you say of the mothers?—I did not know much about the mothers.

518. But the fathers?—The fathers were an awfully drunken lot.

519. You say, in your notes, that the children of the married people, as well as the unmarried, were neglected until it was too late to save life; you did not observe any difference?—I do not think I did; the people used to live together as man and wife and have children, any number of them; I came across cases in which people had lived together as man and wife and had several children, and then got married, so that you could not tell whether you were treating legitimate children or not; you might say that five out of six of the weddings that took place were necessary, or that there had been children before.

520. You are speaking specially of Arlesey?—Yes.

521. Was

Chairman—continued.

521. Was it your opinion that the insurance money was any temptation to people of this class?—I think so, and I have always thought so.

522. A drunken, intemperate, and debauched man would be tempted by money, which he could spend in debauchery and drink?—I have always thought so.

523 Parental affection for his child would not prevent that?— There is very little parental affection amongst the average of those people.

524. Because they were a hard-up, drunken, and worthless people?— They simply care for nothing but drink.

525. Were you called in as parish doctor or as an ordinary practitioner?—As an ordinary practitioner.

526. As an ordinary practitioner you were, of course, entitled to fees; did you generally find when a child was insured by the parent, and died, that you got your fees pa d pretty regularly?—I got almost no fees at all. i

527. You found the parents got the insurance money, but you, at all events, were not benefited by it?—I do not know anything about the insurance money; I know I got no fees. I used to reckon about 50 per cent. bad debts in the place.

528. You did not find that in the case of the insured children you were better paid than in the case of the uninsured children?—I cannot tell that.

529. You did not get the fees, at any rate?—No; I used to make 50 per cent. bad debts.

530. Had you any sick clubs in your neighbourhood?—Yes, there were sick clubs in the neighbourhood.

531. In those sick clubs the patients could get the doctor's attendance for nothing?—But that only related to the labourers themselves, not to the children.

532. It would apply, would it not, to cases where parents in various benefit clubs made their children members of the clubs. Children can be made members of those clubs, can they not?—Not in the ordinary sick clubs; but in that neighbourhood every doctor had a little club of his own for children.

533. And the parents paid so much a week or so much a year in those clubs?—Yes.

534. And then got doctor's attendance for nothing?—Yes.

535. Did you notice that those who provided for sickness through your club sent for you as late as those who had their children insured?—I do not remember a single case of those in my club having a sudden or suspicious death.

536. You drew a distinction between those who were insured in such sick clubs and those who were insured in other insurance societies?—I did not as a general principle, because I did not know; but as to that particular case, it was so, that none of the members of my little club died a suspicious death.

537. Did you often have occasion to refuse a certificate in an insurance case?—No; my practice, as a rule, was not to refuse a certificate unless there was something definite, absolutely certain.

(142.)

538. Was that on account of the difficulty of proving the facts before the coroner afterwards?—That is one reason; another is, that if you see a child or person before death, the certificate is expected of you.

539. It would be an injurious thing for a private practitioner, not a parish doctor or official, if he got the name of frequently refusing certificates?—That is so.

540. Parents would not like to call him in?—Not only parents, but other people also.

541. Do you think there are many cases of criminal neglect which in this way escape the law?—I do not believe the law knows anything about the cases, or gets hold of 5 per cent. of the cases.

542. Did you ever know a case brought up before the coroner?—Yes, I knew one, and in that case the coroner could do nothing but censure the woman. This was not at Arlesey, but in another part of Hertfordshire.

543. The coroner did not send the woman on to the assizes?—No, he could not do that.

544. It is your distinct opinion that in the cases you have mentioned, the insurance money was an inducement to the parent either to do away with the child or to criminally neglect it?—I am strongly of that opinion.

Lord *Clifford of Chudleigh.*

545. Upon the question of certificate you say you sometimes know that a child is insured by the parents coming to you for a certificate; has that to be handed to the insurance office?—That is what it is wanted for, but it is of no good.

546. The parents tell you it is wanted in order to insure their getting the money?—Yes.

Lord *Herschell.*

547. You alluded to those different places apparently for the purpose of drawing some distinction between them; I should like to know what that was?—At Arlesey the population was of the wretched and fearful description I have mentioned, and that is where the suspicious deaths took place in much the larger proportion. At Stotfold a place of the same size, but not so depraved, it was less; and much less also at Baldock; but at Liphook, where I live now, there is almost purity, I should think, in this matter; I have never seen a single case in six years that was suspicious.

548. So that although you think that infant insurance prevailed about equally at the several places, the evils of it depended upon the character of the population?—Yes, exactly.

Earl *Beauchamp.*

549. You told the Committee that at Baddock, and also at Stotfold, all the moribund children brought to you were insured; speaking generally; were all the children in the district insured?—I could not say that; a very larger number were.

550. It was the prevailing habit of the district?—Child insurance was very prevalent in the district.

551. In the case you have just given the Committee
D

Earl *Beauchamp*—continued.

mittee where the coroner censured the woman, was she the mother of the child ?—I am almost positive she was.

552. But you cannot say for certain ?—I cannot say absolutely for certain, but I am almost certain she was.

553. Might she have been a nurse or stepmother?—No; I am almost certain she was the mother.

Lord Chancellor.

554. Were you called before the coroner ?—I was.

555. What was the cause of death?—Bad feeding.

556. Not starvation ?—Physiologically it was starvation, but not in the other way ; the child had had food, but it had had food that it could not digest.

557. But it was established that the child had been fed by the mother ?—Yes ; it had been fed on biscuits and boiled bread ; it was a very little child of about six weeks or two months old. It simply could not digest the food.

558. The result of that was that the view ultimately entertained was that the child had not been wilfully put out of the world ?—I do not think it was.

Chairman.

559. It is quite easy, is it not, for a parent who knows how to do it, to kill a child by overfeeding or cramming it ?—I do not know about its being easy ; but it is not difficult if you have

Chairman—continued,

a child which is at all weakly, by giving it the wrong food, to kill it. There is one case which it would be as well to mention, because it perhaps shows another aspect of the case, and that is this : There was one case I knew of two years ago, in which there were four or five children ; I think it was five then in the family, one of whom was a delicate one, and that was the one that was insured ; none of the others were insured, until I pointed it out to the people, and I refused to admit it.

Earl *Beauchamp.*

560. With reference to those insurance societies which you speak of, were they local or branches of any great central body ?—One is certainly a branch of a large central body. I do not quite know what the other is ; we had two in our neighbourhood.

561. Could you tell the Committee how the payments are made ?—Weekly or fortnightly.

562. To whom are they made ?—They are made to a canvassing agent ; a man who goes round trying to get new business and collecting the pence at the same time.

563. Have you any objection to tell the Committee the name of the central society ?—I do not know that I have ; the Prudential Society is one. I do not know what the other is ; they call themselves by so many names ; it is some society with head-quarters at Croydon.

The Witness is directed to withdraw.

Mr. HENRY ALGERNON HODSON, L.R.C.P., M.R.C.S., is called in ; and Examined as follows.

Chairman.

564. YOU are a member of the Royal College of Surgeons and also a Licentiate of the Royal College of Physicians?—Yes.

565. You are at present a physician practising in Brighton ?—Yes.

566. Before you practised in Brighton you had a large practice in the county of Devon?—Yes ; before that I was house surgeon to a large London hospital.

567. Have you formed a strong opinion as to the connection between murder or the putting away of children and insurance ?—A very strong opinion.

568. Was that founded upon your experience in London and in the country, or only in the country?—Principally in the country.

569. In what part of the country ?—In Devonshire.

570. It was an entirely agricultural population, I presume ?—No, it was not an entirely agricultural population ; there were potteries and clay-works, brick-making.

571. In what part of Devonshire?—A place called Bovey Tracy.

572. Would you kindly say to the Committee upon what grounds you formed this unfavourable impression as regards child insurance?—My attention was drawn first to the subject by finding that the children did not get well, as they should. I found small babies who really ought to get well, did not get well, and then on careful

Chairman—continued.

inquiry, by being able to see the children at their homes, I found they were simply ill-fed ; they were fed with bad food, and certainly, to the best of my belief, no medicine was given them ; and I am sorry to say that in every such case I found out that the child was insured.

573. That caused your unfavourable opinion upon the subject?—Yes, it did.

574. Is it an easy matter to bring home this crime of wilful neglect and child murder to the parent?—It is impossible, under the present state of the law, for this simple reason ; that although one is perfectly satisfied, as I have been in many cases, that a child has been literally murdered, for I can call it nothing else, yet if you get them up before the coroner you are asked, Are you prepared to swear that that child would have lived if it had been properly fed ? Of course you cannot swear that, and then the case falls through at once.

575. Have you had a case of that sort before the coroner ?—Yes, it was a case where the child was, practically speaking, starved to death ; an inquest was held and the verdict was "Died from natural causes."

576. Did you give notice that in every such case in which you knew the child was insured, you would refuse the certificate ?—I did.

577. Do you think the company were cognisant of this announcement?—I do, because an agent came to see me about it.

578. As

Chairman—continued.

578. As regards the symptoms of foul play, would you say the mothers are becoming quite skilled and crafty in the way of putting away children?—I think they are.

579. They can put them away without starving them, can they not?—They can put them away by simply giving bad food and feeding them irregularly; they give them food; they do not directly starve them, but improper food is as bad as insufficient feeding.

580. When you ordered medicine for a child, had you any power of testing whether the medicine was given or not?—Simply by cross-examination; occasionally you could tell, but it was very difficult to ascertain. In the hospital you can tell exactly, because your own nurses give it, but in their own houses it is impossible to tell.

581. What kind of character did those people bear who you thought were doing away with their children?—I should call them decidedly dissolute.

582. Were there a considerable number of them?—Yes.

583. You did not find that their parental affection was very strong?—Not in those cases.

584. Of course the respectable poor——?—The respectable poor do not insure their children.

585. You think the majority of the respectable poor were not in the habit of insuring their children?—Yes.

586. It was only this very low and bad class, you think, who were in the habit of insuring?—That is so. The same thing is taking place now. I am connected with the General Hospital at Hove, Brighton, and there the same thing takes place; of course I do not see the poor at their homes there, but the house surgeon told me yesterday that it is very largely done there; he says that they have had a very large number of cases of marasmus, which is wasting disease, in which we are perfectly satisfied that the children are simply starved for the sake of the insurance money.

587. Is it the case that doctors do not care very much to bring those cases before the coroner because they know it is no use?—It is an utter waste of time.

588. The doctors no not care to do it knowing that it is no use?—It being of no use.

589. Your experience at Brighton goes to the same point as your experience in Devonshire?—That is so, only that I have not the same experience at Brighton, because I only see the children that are brought to the hospital; I do see cases of it, but not so many as I did in Devonshire, but every one I speak to makes the same remark as to insurance; it is simply a premium for murder.

Lord *Norton.*

590. When you say that the respectable poor do not insure, do you positively state it as your opinion that the great mass of the insurance of children is by dissolute parents?—I stated that that was simply my experience of people in a certain locality; my experience of people in this locality was that the dissolute people insured their children.

591. And that the others did not?—In that particular locality.

Lord *Norton—continued.*

592. D) you mean in Brighton or Devonshire?—I do not know enough about the people in Brighton; I see a very large number there, but they are brought to the hospital; I do not know about them at home.

593. Have you any idea whether a very large number of those children who are insured would be illegitimate children?—I do not think that makes any difference.

Earl of *Selborne.*

594. I suppose you would have no means of judging what sort of proportion those who live bear to those who die?—I cannot form an opinion upon that.

595. Or what amount they are insured for?—I know nothing about the amount they are insured for.

Lord *Norton.*

596. What age would they be insured at?—From six weeks up to two years.

Lord *Chancellor.*

597. From what time to what time were you in Bovey Tracy?—I was there from 1879 to 1883, I think it was; I was there about five years.

Lord *Poltimore.*

598. Did your practice extend there beyond the Potteries into the agricultural districts, or was it simply confined to the Potteries?—It was a general practice; it was a very small pottery, comparatively speaking.

599. Was there any distinction between the pottery people and the agricultural classes?—It was not the pottery people, they were of a very superior class; it was the brick-making class that this practice prevailed amongst.

Lord *Thring.*

600. Is marasmus a common disease amongst the better classes?—It is becoming very common amongst the lower classes.

601. You said that you believed that a great number of cases of marasmus were produced artificially?—Yes.

602. Therefore natural marasmus, not produced artificially, is a very rare disease; that is to say, children properly cared for do not die from marasmus?—Not usually.

Earl *Beauchamp.*

603. Will you give the Committee the area over which you had charge at Bovey Tracy?—I could not.

604. Could you give the population?—It is a small place. I suppose there are not above 3,000 inhabitants, between 2,000 and 3,000. Then, of course, there are outlying places; there is a place called Chudleigh Knighton, and the surrounding districts.

605. You were poor law medical officer?—Yes.

606. And you cannot tell the Committee what the population under your care was?—I cannot, it was seven years ago.

607. You cannot give the Committee any approximate estimate?—Not nearer than 2,000 or 3,000.

　　　　　608. Then

Earl *Beauchamp*—continued.

608. Then your deduction is based upon a population of 3,000?—I beg pardon, I stated that I had also seen it working at the London Hospitals. Then I have also seen it working at Brighton, and I saw quite enough in this one place alone to show me the undesirability of allowing this insurance.

609. At the hospital they were brought to you as out-patients?—Yes.

610. And you have no opportunity of visiting the children in their own homes there or of knowing anything about them, except what their parents tell you?—That is so.

611. A question was asked with regard to the intelligence which mothers show as to bringing up children by hand; do you find that mothers are apt to be successful in that sort of thing?—I think they are.

612. Do you find that they always carefully prepare the food for their children?—Not always; but I think they are very careful as a rule; a woman who cares for her child is very careful about the food, and you will see children among the lower classes brought up by hand quite as well nourished as amongst the upper classes.

The Witness is directed to withdraw.

Ordered, That this Committee be adjourned to Tuesday next, at Twelve o'clock.

Die Martis, 1° Julii, 1890.

LORDS PRESENT:

Earl of DERBY.

Earl SPENCER.

Earl of HARROWBY.

Earl BEAUCHAMP.

Earl of SELBORNE.

LORD BISHOP OF PETERBOROUGH.

Lord CLIFFORD OF CHUDLEIGH.

Lord POLTIMORE.

Lord BROUGHAM AND VAUX.

Lord KINNAIRD.

Lord NORTON.

Lord HERSCHELL.

Lord THRING.

THE RIGHT REV. THE LORD BISHOP OF PETERBOROUGH, IN THE CHAIR.

DR. GEORGE THOMSON, is called in ; and Examined, as follows :

Chairman.

613. YOU are Coroner of Oldham ?—I am.

614. You are also a medical man ?—I am.

615. Have you, in your capacity as coroner, and also as a medical man, formed any opinion as to the effect of child life insurance on child mortality and life ?—I have in both capacities formed the opinion that it has a decidedly prejudicial effect.

616. From what circumstances do you draw these conclusions ?—As a medical man I chiefly draw it from my earlier experience in practice. I came in contact with cases where I was not summoned until the child was beyond the possibility of hope of benefit by treatment, and I was also compelled to notice that parents under these circumstances were more anxious about the certificates for clubs than they appeared to be for the recovery of the child.

617. These were cases of insured children ?—Yes, cases of insured children.

618. And what led you to suspect foul play ; was it the greater neglect of these children by their parents ?—Undoubtedly.

619. In what class of people did you generally find these cases ?—Amongst chiefly the class that spend their money carelessly, intemperate people, betting people, the baser sort of workpeople generally.

620. Not thrifty and respectable people ?—As a rule not.

621. These were, in point of fact, not persons who, from a desire of thrift and care for their children, would be likely to have insured them ?—Certainly not.

622. Therefore they were not people whose motives for insuring their children would have been thrift, and saving to the rates ?—I should say not.

623. Have you had a large number of in-

Chairman—continued.

quests on insured children ?—Not a large number.

624. Do you mean a large number actually, or in proportion to the cases?—I say not a large number in proportion to the death rate of young children.

625. Can you tell us what have been the actual number of cases from August 1887 to June 1890 out of the 407 inquests you have held ?—I can give you the precise number out of these 407 inquests ; 71 were on children under a year ; about half of those were under three months, and either not in benefit, or uninsured.

626. When you say not in benefit you mean insured, but not yet entitled to benefit ?—Yes.

627. That is to say more than half were insured ?—A great deal more than one-half.

628. But a certain proportion of the insured had not reached the age of three months at which they would come into benefit ?—Exactly.

629. Perhaps you will go on ?—Forty-two inquests were held on children over one year of age and under five.

630. How many of these were insured ?—Of those nearly the whole.

631. From five years and under 10, how many were insured ?—Twenty-two inquests, and those nearly all insured.

632. Much the larger proportion then of inquests on children were held on children under one year ?—Certainly.

633. Has there been any diminution of late in such cases to your knowledge, that is in cases of insured children coming before you as a coroner? —No ; I do not consider there has been any diminution in numbers.

634. Were there any number of cases during the period we are referring to where the child was buried without investigation, and which were

Chairman—continued.

cases which you think ought to have been inquired into?—I am sure there have been cases, but I can only estimate the number.

635. Have you any rough idea as to the number of cases?—I have formed a rough idea that probably there would be about 150 of those during the three years referred to.

636. During the three years?—Which ought to have been investigated.

637. Which you think ought to have been inquired into?—Yes.

638. How do you account for that fact?—I account for that by the fact that medical men, as a rule, certify those cases.

639. When a doctor refuses to certify, do the persons having the custody of the child report the death to the police?—They go to the police.

640. What action do the police generally take in such cases?—The police make some inquiries as to the circumstances, and as a rule they are satisfied, or, at any rate, are unable to find circumstances which they consider evidence of negligence, or worse.

641. Then the police do not invariably report to the coroner under such circumstances?—Hardly ever.

642. How does this come about; are the police satisfied generally with the statements of the parents?—I assume they are satisfied, or at any rate they are satisfied that they cannot get evidence.

643. For one or other of those reasons they do not in very many cases report to the coroner?—They do not.

644. Is there any attempt ever made to induce the medical officer to give a certificate by the police?—Oh, yes; it is not uncommon for the police to send an officer to a medical man where he has refused to certify after they have made inquiries, and to assure him they have no ground for suspicion.

645. If he still refuses, what do the police do then?—Then they send the persons in charge of the child to the registrar.

646. And do they direct them to inform the registrar that the police are satisfied?—They do; they sometimes send an officer with these persons to the registrar in order to get the case registered.

647. They ask the registrar to register the death?—Yes.

648. Do you know what payment is made to the registrar for issuing a certificate of death; what does he get on each certificate, do you happen to know?—I am not able to answer from personal knowledge, but I believe it is about 1 *s.* 3 *d.*

649. If the registrar is not satisfied with the cause of death he communicates, I presume, with the coroner?—He does.

650. Is it his legal duty to do so?—He has instructions from the Registrar General as to certain circumstances under which he ought to communicate to the coroner, in cases for instance of sudden death where the cause is unknown; that is to say, where the cause alleged to the registrar is, in his opinion, insufficient.

651. It will depend entirely then upon the judgment and integrity of the registrar whether the case reaches the coroner, or not at all?—Certainly to some extent, only he would be liable,

Chairman—continued.

I believe, to be checked by the Registrar General if it did not.

652. I think you stated that there were about 60 cases of insured children where there was ground of suspicion of improper feeding or negligence or worse; how many of these were so reported by the registrars?—Thirty-five cases in all.

653. Had all these cases been previously reported to the police?—Nearly all; I cannot vouch for all.

654. Amongst these cases there were several from suffocation in bed with parents from what is called overlaying?—That is so.

655. That is not an uncommon case?—Not very uncommon.

656. In the case of overlaying, would it be almost physically impossible to produce evidence that this was either intentional or accidental. If a mother overlay her children, would it be at all likely that there would be proof of her having done so either designedly or undesignedly before you, the coroner?—Very unlikely; it is very unlikely that we should get evidence that a jury could depend upon.

657. In fact, then, the police really come between you and the doctor who refuses the certificate?—Certainly they do.

658. And they may be called practically the judges of the case as to its fitness for you or not?—Yes, to a great extent.

659. Do you think that is altogether a proper and safe position for the police?—I think not; I think that it perhaps goes a little beyond their strict duty.

660. Do you consider this practice of the police responsible for all cases passing without investigation?—Indirectly so; I should not say all, but I say that indirectly it is responsible to a considerable extent.

661. In the majority of cases the police are responsible for cases not coming before you?—Either directly or indirectly. By indirectly, I do not suggest that many of these cases were reported to the police, but that medical men, after experiencing the futility of withholding a certificate, as a rule grant certificates in such cases.

662. At all events it is clear that the police have very great power in the matter from their position?—Undoubtedly.

663. Is it your opinion that in those cases that do come before you infant insurance tends to the neglect and death of the insured?—Yes, I have formed that opinion.

664. Have you in any such proceedings before you in these cases taken any further proceedings such as sending cases for trial to the assizes?—I have not.

665. Will you say why?—The principal reason is that it is almost impossible to get evidence that people could be convicted upon.

666. Do you find that juries as a rule are reluctant to return verdicts of manslaughter or murder?—I should say that I am generally obliged to advise them that it would be useless; juries are certainly reluctant, unless they have very strong evidence before them.

667. You have to advise the jury?—I have to advise the jury that there is no evidence to convict.

668. Is it your experience that in such suspicious cases the agents of the insurance societies

Chairman—continued.

societies give you any help at all in getting at the truth?—Never.

669. You have never had an insurance agent come to you and say, " I think this is a suspicious case, and you ought to inquire"?—Never.

670. You have got no help from them?—Never.

671. Have you ever known an agent call personally on you and ask you to falsify a medical certificate as to the duration of disease?—Yes, that has happened to me personally.

672. Would you give any further explanation of the circumstances of that case?—Yes, that occurs under these circumstances: if a child or adult has died from a disease of considerable duration, and the medical man certifies the disease as lasting so many months, it sometimes happens that the case has been insured within that period, and then a certificate dating the disease further back than the date of the insurance prevents the insurance money from being got. Then the relatives come to ask to have the certificate altered. It has happened to me in certainly a few cases to have an insurance society's agent come upon a similar errand.

673. You are speaking now as a medical man, not as a coroner?—As a medical man.

674. They could not apply to you as coroner to do anything of the kind; you were asked to falsify your certificate as a medical man?—Exactly.

675. To what extent do you find children insured in cases that come before you?—Nearly all are insured under 10 years of age ; it is exceptional to find them not insured.

676. Do you find them insured in one or more societies; do you ever ask this question in the case of a child?—I always ask the question and press the inquiry as to unregistered societies as well, but I find that it is not common to have children insured in more than one society in Oldham.

677. Is it a common thing for a patient then to tell you that the child is not insured in more than one society?—That is so.

678. Have you any means of testing that statement?—I have taken every trouble to test it. For the last six months I have gone over the registrar's books with their permission, and compared them with the depositions in my possession, and I have found the statements made in court correct.

679. The Committee of the House of Commons in their Report make the following statement: " From the nature of the cases it is almost impossible to obtain direct and inculpating evidence of criminality of this character, which is chiefly committed by a single individual in the privacy of the home ; " does that correspond with your experience as a coroner?—Entirely so.

680 For that reason you have not in many cases sent down the cases for trial at the assizes?—I have not in any case.

Earl of *Derby.*

681. You said, I think, that it was very common for you not to be called in to a case of infantile illness until too late?—That is so.

682. Do you at all confine that to the case of
(142.)

Earl of *Derby*—continued.

insured children, or does your remark apply equally to all?—I should say that the remark applies chiefly to insured children. I should not like to say entirely so.

683. You have not the means, I presume, of distinguishing between the effect of unintended neglect or ignorance, and the effect of wilful neglect?—Only one's knowledge of the world. One forms an opinion from the character of the people in charge of the child.

684. You may know that a child has died mainly in consequence of neglect, but you cannot say whether that neglect has been intentional or not?—That, of course, would be very difficult to get at.

685. It is a common thing, is it not, among the class whom you are describing, to treat children with great neglect, whether they are insured or not?—Among the baser class of workpeople, yes.

686. We are speaking of that class?—Quite so.

687. You gave us some figures as to the number of inquests held on children, and you gave us the number of inquests on children who died under a year old; can you say whether the number of deaths under a year old was greater in that case than, according to statistical laws it ought to be?—I do not know that I quite catch your meaning.

688. A certain number of children everywhere, and all over England, die under a year old?—Quite so.

689. A certain per-centage of the whole mortality occurs in such cases. I want to know whether the infantile mortality upon which you have given evidence is greater than the average of England?—I can give you the figures ; I have got the figures from 1882 to 1889, if you wish to have them. The deaths in Oldham of children under a year to a thousand births which is the usual way of putting it, were as follows: in 1882 the figures were 180 ; in 1883, 159 ; in 1884, 183 ; in 1885, 167 ; in 1886, 174 ; in 1887, 187 ; in 1888, 157 ; and in 1889, 178. I believe the average of England is 147, if I remember rightly.

Lord *Clifford.*

690. Do people who are careful and thrifty insure their children equally with those who are careless and dissolute in Oldham?—I believe so ; that is my experience.

691. Do you find that in a family of careful and thoughtful and good parents they make a distinction between their children, and insure some and not others?—I cannot say so.

692. You have never noticed that?—No, I have not observed it.

693. Do you find any difference with those who are not so careful ; do you find generally that they insure some children and not others?—No, I cannot say I have observed that. My attention has not been particularly directed to that point, but I have not noticed that.

Lord *Norton.*

694. Can you state whether of the suspicious cases that come under your notice any large proportion of the children are illegitimate?—I think I can answer by referring to figures for 1888,
D 4   but

Lord *Norton*—continued.

but I cannot answer offhand. I can give you the number of illegitimate cases up to seven years of age for the year 1888, if that will assist you. In that year there were two male illegitimate children and five female illegitimate children on which I held inquests.

695. Out of what total number?—The total number under seven years is 36.

696. Then it is a small proportion of the children who are illegitimate?—A small proportion.

697. Are there many cases, do you know, where the mother having died the child has been under the care of a stepmother?—I cannot answer from recollection.

698. It has not come under your observation? —Not particularly so.

699. You say in every suspicious case the parents have been dissolute and heartless, and with very little natural affection for their children? —Yes.

Lord *Brougham and Vaux.*

700. In your experience as a medical man will you go so far as to say that an insured child is less carefully managed than an uninsured child? —Amongst a certain class.

701. Amongst the class we are now discussing? —I should certainly say so.

Lord *Thring.*

702. You said, as I understood you, that during the three years 150 children had been buried without investigation whose deaths ought to have been investigated; on what ground do you form that calculation?—I base that chiefly upon my own early experience as a medical man; it is simply an estimate.

703. You may tell us how you do form it; why do you say 150 more than 1,000, or any other number?—I am estimating the number of unsatisfactory cases that probably come before medical men in the town. As I say, I base it upon the numbers which I myself saw in my earlier experience in practice.

704. What experience are you talking of; at what time?—Fifteen years ago, perhaps.

705. Fifteen years ago you were a medical man in Oldham?—I was.

706. I understand that you calculate these 150 children were buried improperly; under what circumstances?—I calculate it roughly upon my estimate of the number of cases which medical men are likely to meet with in which they hesitate to certify death.

707. What number of cases is a medical man likely to meet with, according to your experience?—My experience in these cases was, I should say, that I met with an average of six or eight such cases during the year.

708. You met with six or eight cases in which you hesitated to grant a certificate?—Yes.

709. That would make, in your experience as a medical man, 18 cases in three years?—Yes.

710. How do you put 150?—I should say we have 40 odd medical men in the borough, and of these probably something like one-third or one-fourth are comparatively young men, and have chiefly to deal with that class of case.

711. As I understand you, you calculate it in this way, that each medical man in Oldham has

Lord *Thring*—continued.

four or five cases which he ought to report, and then you multiply that by the number of medical men in Oldham?—No; you have not caught my meaning.

712. With respect to the police, I want to know this; suppose a medical man refuses a certificate, under what law does the person apply to the police; the police have no power to grant an order for burial?—No; but the police are the people who make inquiries if there is anything supposed to be wrong.

713. Supposing you refused to grant me a certificate, why should I apply to the police; what good do I get in applying to the police?— It is simply the only machinery that exists as between the people and the registrar. They might, if they chose, go to the registrar.

714. The legal course would be to go to the registrar?—That is what I say.

715. Then they apply to the police with the view to get the police to help them?—I do not think that would be quite the way to put it.

716. What I want to get at is this; when they apply to the police, is not the inference that they wish to have the case investigated? — They generally apply to the police because they are directed to do so by the medical man when he refuses to give a certificate.

717. The medical man has no right to refer them to the police?—It is simply the custom.

Lord *Poltimore.*

718. I understood you to say that the better class of working men insure their children's lives as much as the more dissolute class?—I think so.

719. If that is so, upon what do you base your belief that a very large number of these children among the more dissolute classes die of neglect; why should not the result be that the dissolute condition of the parents causes the death of the children without their actually causing it?— Undoubtedly the death-rate would be likely to be larger among that class of people in any case; but my observation has led me to think that it has increased amongst the children who are insured.

720. The number of suspicious cases, in fact, among the children of these dissolute parents who die is a considerable one?—I do think so.

Earl of *Harrowby.*

721. What proportion of the working classes of Oldham do you group into this category of the thriftless and dissolute whose children suffer in this way?—It is rather a difficult question to answer.

722. Are we talking of a fourth?—No, not nearly that; I think the proportion is small in Oldham; we have an exceptionally good working class in Oldham.

723. It is a small proportion?—It is a small proportion.

724. But the whole of them, speaking roughly, insure their children?—I believe so; that is my belief.

725. Would you consider it any great temptation to the doctor to certify even in a dubious case?—No; the reason a doctor certifies, as a
rule

Earl of *Harrowby*—continued.

rule is, that he discovers by experience that it is no use not certifying.

726. But in a case in which he has a good deal of doubt, why should he not refuse to certify?— Because he finds if he does not nothing comes of it, and the odium of what the people call trouble falls upon his shoulders.

727. And he does suffer considerably, does he? Undoubtedly.

728. So that there is great temptation to adopt it?—Yes, in that way.

Earl *Beauchamp*.

729. May I ask what your experience was before you were a coroner; were you parish officer?—I am still parish medical officer; I have a district in Oldham.

730. How long have you been parish medical officer?—For 11 years.

731. Of the cases of which you told us, where you were invited to falsify the medical certificates, in how many cases did the agents of the insurance companies come to you?—I should say it has happened to me six or eight times, speaking from memory.

732. Could you discriminate at all between children and adults?—I think it has happened oftener in the case of adults than in the case of children, in my recollection.

733. In how many cases do you think it would have occurred to children?—Really it is difficult to answer the question; I cannot speak from memory.

734. Our inquiry is not dealing with the whole question of life insurance, but with the question of infantile insurance?—I should think probably, in the case of children, it may have occurred two or three times; I cannot answer precisely, because I am speaking of things that have happened, most of them, a good many years ago.

735. May I take it that this application on the part of agents of the insurance companies happened a good many years ago?—I have not had recent applications, but I had one last year in the case of an adult.

736. How long would it be since you were last asked to falsify a certificate in respect of a child?—Probably, at least, five or six years ago.

737. Would that have been by the insurance company, or by the parents of the child?—It has happened by the agent of the insurance company; it is more common from parents.

738. What would be the last occasion of an application of that nature made by the agent of any insurance company, of a child?—Do you mean the case of a child?

739. Yes?—I am afraid I could not give you dates.

740. Was it within the last five years?—I should say within five or six years.

Earl *Beauchamp*—continued.

741. Within six years?—I should say probably within six.

742. But you do not remember the circumstances of the case?—No; I cannot give you precise information about that. It is a matter of distinct recollection that the thing happened, but I have no date of it to refer to.

743. It appears to you to be a matter of such minor importance to be invited to falsify a certificate that you took no memoranda?—No memoranda.

744. You thought it was a matter of no consequence?—Of consequence, but one does not make memoranda of everything of that kind unless one thinks there is something to come of it. If I had thought of it, no doubt I should have made memoranda.

745. You told us one of your difficulties in dealing with these cases was the lack of evidence?—I was not coroner at that time.

746. But you were the medical officer of the parish?—Yes.

747. When a suggestion of that sort was made to you you contented yourself with simply refusing?—Exactly.

748. Then, with regard to an answer that fell from you at the very beginning of your examination, you were asked what effect the system of life insurance had, and you said a prejudicial effect; would you explain that a little more; prejudicial to whom?—Prejudicial to the lives of the children.

Lord *Norton*.

749. In the case in which you were pressed to falsify a certificate by an insurance agent it was the interest of the company not to falsify your certificate?—Most certainly.

750. Why should you be pressed by an insurance agent to do that which was against the interest of the company?—I presume it may have been in the interest of the agent; I am not in his confidence, but I presume that was his reason.

751. How could it be the interest of the agent?—I suppose to increase his popularity in the district.

Chairman.

752. There is only one question more I should like to ask you in respect of these cases, in which you were asked to falsify the certificate; you stated that you made no memoranda, nevertheless the case made such a deep impression on your mind that you remember it to this day?— Undoubtedly; these cases always strike me very forcibly.

The Witness is directed to withdraw.

MR. MAURICE FREDERIC CARTER is called in; and Examined, as follows:

Chairman.

753. YOU are Coroner for the Forest Division of the County of Gloucester?—I am.

754. And you are also Clerk to the Guardians of the District of Newnham-on-Severn?—Yes.

755. What is the population in your division (142).

Chairman—continued.

of the county?—There is a mixed population in my division of 60,000; about 20,000 in the mining division of the Forest of Dean, and fishing and manufacturing also.

756. And agricultural?—Yes.

757. In

E

Chairman—continued.

757. In fact it is a fairly representative population of the population of England?—Yes.

758. It contains agricultural, fishing, mining, and manufacturing inhabitants?—Yes.

759. What is the population of the division?—About 60,000.

760. How long have you held office as coroner in this division?—Upwards of 22 years.

761. How many inquests do you hold in a year?—An average of 52.

762. In all you have held something between 1,100 and 1,200 inquests during your tenure of office?—Yes.

763. In the course of holding these inquests has your attention been called to the practice of child-life insurance?—It has.

764. Have you formed any opinion upon it?—I have.

765. What is your opinion?—I think it is very prejudicial, it tends to crime; that is the opinion I have formed.

766. Your distinct impression and belief is that it tends to crime?—Certainly.

767. That is founded on an experience as coroner of 22 years?—Yes.

768. Could you give the Committee an idea of the reasons which have induced you to form the opinion that child-life insurance leads to crime?—The case I should like to speak to your Lordships about, and hand in if necessary a note of, is a case which is strongly impressed on my mind, that occurred in 1880. The reasons which induced me to come to this conclusion were these, that I found, in the first place, there was a neglect to send for a medical man in proper time.

769. In the case of insured children?—Yes. Then there was a disregard of his advice; but thirdly, and most important, was the giving food which was absolutely improper, and which generally caused death by convulsions.

770. The parents did not call in a doctor till too late, they gave improper food, and they paid no attention to the doctor's instructions?—Yes.

771. Those were the circumstances that induced you in the case of insured children to suspect foul play?—Yes.

772. Can you give any case to illustrate what you have been saying?—The case, I think, that first most strongly impressed itself on my memory was a case in the year 1880, a case of a child named Boyce Wilkes. The child was eight years of age, and for some reason which has never been known it strayed from its father's house, and at the end of three days it was found in the forest; it was taken home. The first result was a loss of three toes; the child became imbecile, and there was a terrible shock to the system. In a few months afterwards, when the life would not, under any circumstances, be insured by any cautious or proper agent, the agent who did not exercise any ordinary care or caution, or any care or caution, insured the child for a sum of 10 *l.*, a sum which would not be wholly payable until the child became 10 years of age. The child died; I held an inquest, and I have the notes of the case. The medical man, Dr. Carleton, stated that he examined the child, he found it in a very emaciated condition, and that in his opinion the life would have been prolonged if more careful treatment had been exercised and proper nourishment

Chairman—continued.

given. That case has more strongly impressed itself on my mind than any other case that I have had, and, in consequence, I strongly expressed myself upon it.

773. Do you know of any other case?—I have also brought a note of the last inquest I held in such a case; that was in February 1889.

774. Last year?—Last year. That was the case of the child of a drunken father who had lost his situation through impropriety of conduct. I should add that they had had 14 children, eight of whom had died. There was an inquest on one, and that child was insured at Cardiff. This child being seriously ill, always in delicate health, was taken to Dr. Halpin, and he recommended that they should apply for assistance to the union. No application was made, but in the month of November, the day before it died, on a cold and miserable day, it was taken down to Dr. Carter, of Sydney, and the next day it died. That child was insured when it was known to be in a serious state of health, and when they were told that it was in a bad state of health by Dr. Halpin; and when I examined the woman she said she insured it because she thought the money would be acceptable. I found in this as in many other cases that the jurors will not find culpable neglect; they always attribute it to the ignorance of the parents.

775. Reverting to the second case you have just mentioned to us, this was the second child that had been insured in the family?—There was another child also insured, and that child was ill also.

776. How many died?—I cannot tell; eight out of 14.

777. There were 14 children in the family?—Yes.

778. These three children were insured?—Yes.

779. These three children were sickly children?—The first died and an inquest was held in Cardiff. The second was insured; and the third died, and an inquest was held by me; and it was also insured, and insured at a time when it was an imbecile.

780. I suppose a reasonably intelligent agent could have seen from the appearance of the child that it was in a very bad state of health?—Yes.

781. There could have been no doubt whatever?—No; just as in the case of Boyce Wilkes.

782. Speaking of agents, do you happen to know, as a matter of fact within your own knowledge, that insurance agents are paid considerable premiums upon every fresh case?—I know it is to their interest to insure as many cases as possible.

783. You are not able to state of your own knowledge what percentage of cases there is?—No.

784. We have had it in evidence from medical men practising in various parts of the country that they give certificates in cases of doubt, and only in a glaring case do they refuse it; do you think that is the case with the medical men in your division of Gloucestershire?—Certainly not; I do not think there is a medical man in the whole of Gloucestershire who would venture to give a certificate in a doubtful case.

785. Do you ever ask the parents, when a suspicious

Chairman—continued.

suspicious case comes before you, whether the child is insured?—Always.

786. Do they very often say no?—No, I think not.

787. When they do say no, do you take any steps to verify the statement?—No.

788. Are there any steps you can take as coroner?—I can only do so by asking the police to inquire of all the agents in the district.

789. That is the only step you can take?—Yes.

790. Meanwhile the jury must give their verdict?—Yes.

791. In all suspicious cases do you find the parents show any reluctance to admit the fact of insurance?—No.

792. Even in all cases you have found that to be the case?—I should say I sometimes find from the notes of the police cases where a question is always put to the police, "Is the child insured?" and it sometimes happens that the answer of the police is "No," and I find upon inquiry that it has been.

793. At what age do you find children insured; very young?—Yes; I think two years.

794. Had you a case reported to you in which a woman who had just been confined was solicited to have her child insured?—I have been told of the case.

795. Did it come before you personally?—No.

796. Do you think then, from your experience of insurance and the profits of insurance, that the familiarity of the parent's mind with the death of the child being connected with money has a tendency to deprave the mind of the parent?—Yes, I think so.

797. The idea of profit in connection with the death of the child is constantly before the parent's mind?—It seems to me to be so.

798. And you find it to have that effect; have you known any case in which a child was not insured until it was ill; is that the case you have been giving us; what you call the Bream case?—The last case was the Bream case.

799. Do you think that the cases of fatal neglect of children which have come before you have been amongst the very poor?—No, I think not.

800. Are they as common among people with high wages as with low wages?—I think so.

801. How would you describe the class of people who, in your opinion, allow their children to die wilfully neglected?—People who are dissolute and of drunken habits.

802. Their homes are very miserable, wretched homes?—Unfortunately the homes of the poor are very unsatisfactory.

803. Is that generally on account of their poverty?—I think not.

804. Or on account of their vicious habits; does it come very often from the vicious habits of the parents?—Yes; but I do not think that is so in my district.

805. In these cases of strongly suspected neglect of insured children that have come before you, have you ever committed any for trial?—Never.

806. Can you give the Committee the reasons why you have not committed the cases for trial?—I have never been able to obtain a verdict

(142.)

Chairman—continued.

from the jury to enable me to do so. They always stop short of culpable neglect. They find neglect, but never culpable neglect.

807. They will not find criminal neglect?—No.

808. Why do you find juries do that?—Very often they are persons of the same station of life as the person who is incriminated.

809. They do not wish to be hard on their own neighbours, perhaps?—One would take the most charitable view.

810. You are obliged to tell them in certain circumstances that there is no legal evidence to justify them?—When there is none.

811. You think it is your experience that juries do acquit where, in your opinion, after having heard the case, there ought to have been a committal and trial?—Undoubtedly.

812. And that very often?—I cannot say very often. In certain cases, certainly, if I had been a juror I should have found a verdict.

813. And in many cases where you have not been able to recommend a jury to find a verdict on the facts you have morally no doubt that it was a guilty case?—None.

814. Have you formed any opinion from your experience as to the causes why insurance money is a temptation to the parents?—I know that in cases before me, for instance, of improper treatment or neglect to send for a medical man, those cases do not always apply to those who are insured, but also in cases where people are not insured. If people are wicked enough to want to get rid of the burden of the maintenance of their children, *a furtiori* they would, if in addition to getting rid of the burden they get money.

815. It is a double temptation?—It is a double temptation.

816. The person who is hardhearted enough to get rid of a child because he does not like to bring him up would be the very person who would feel the temptation of the money gained by the child's death?—Yes.

817. You are clerk to the Newnham guardians?—To the guardians of the Newnham-on-Severn Union; I have been for 40 years.

818. Many persons who insure their children send for the parish doctor, when they send for one at all?—Yes.

819. The parish doctor attends them for nothing?—Yes.

820. It would not be true then to say, in a great many of these cases, that the parents require the insurance money in order to pay the doctor?—Oh no, but I should say that in many of these cases they would not obtain an order from the relieving officer to get the attendance of the medical officer, because he would say this is a case where they are able to pay.

821. In cases of inability or difficulty to pay they have no difficulty in getting gratuitous attendance from the parish doctor?—None.

822. Are you aware if there is any law which compels the guardians to compel a parent to bury a child if he is insured?—No.

823. Have the guardians any power of compelling the parent to bury?—None whatever. The only thing they would do would be to issue a distress upon any furniture in the parents' possession.

824. Take a case where a parent has insured a

E 2   child's

Chairman—continued.

child's life, and the child dies, and the parent has got the insurance money, and that is known to the guardians, and the guardians demand payment for the funeral?—I am afraid, legally, the guardians would have no power. If the funeral expenses were paid by way of loan, possibly they might, but I know of no other mode in which they could get payment.

825. They have no power of enforcing payment of the burial expenses?—No.

826. The parent might take the whole of the insurance money, and might still leave the parish to bury the child?—Quite; but I do not think it would be possible in the union to which I belong. It may be so elsewhere, and I am told it is so.

827. But there is no power to compel him to do so?—No.

828. As you say that these bad cases that have come before you have directed your attention to crime in connection with insurance, have you thought of any way of stopping this, judging from your own experience?—Do you mean as to the verdict of jurors?

829. No; I mean as to the temptation to the parents to commit crime?—I have during the last 10 years over and over again said that, in my opinion, one of two things should happen, either that the insurance should be abolished, that it should not be permitted by law, or that no larger sum should get into the hands of the parents except sufficient to provide a decent and proper burial, so that no profit should be made out of it.

830. In other words, you think that the only practical legislation on the subject would be legislation of some kind or other that prevented the insuring parent making a profit on the death of the child?—Certainly.

831. Unless you can stop that you think we shall not be able to stop crime in connection with insurance?—I think not.

832. You think that would be effectual?—I think it would.

· · Earl of *Derby*.

833. Then I understand you propose to limit the sum total to the parents to what would be required to meet the expenses of the funeral?—Yes.

834. Would you fix the amount at the lowest rate for which a funeral can be conducted?—No.

835. In what manner would you secure the money obtained by insurance being applied to the purpose of the funeral?—I suppose it must be paid into the hands of the person who undertook the burial.

836. Paid direct to the undertaker?—Yes, or some person appointed by law.

Earl of *Selborne*.

837. Is there any legitimate object of insurance except burial; would not the expenses of medical attendance come under the same principle?—I do not know how that is at all. I thought it was only for burial, but I cannot speak of my own knowledge.

Earl of *Selborne*—continued.

838. In what proportion of the cases of neglect that have come before you do you consider there has been wilful neglect; can you give the proportion?—I have a great difficulty in saying, but during the last five years I should think there have been five or six cases, probably.

839. Out of about 50 a year?—That is the whole number; it would not be 50 children.

840. How many cases of inquests on children have you in a year?—I think about one-third of the number would be under 16 years of age, and I think that during the last five years I had about 15 cases which were suspicious and bad.

841. Cases where you think there has been moral proof, though perhaps not legal proof?—Yes.

842. Were there many of those cases where you think the jury might have found a verdict, and yet were unwilling to do so from private circumstances?—In my opinion the juries ought to have so found.

843. There was sufficient evidence?—I thought so in some few cases. Very often there is great difficulty as to the question of means. Unless means are proved, in some cases difficult, although the power is absolutely insufficient, it would be impossible to convict.

Lord *Clifford of Chudleigh*.

844. Do you know if the agents of the companies make any medical inquiry before insuring?—I believe it is not the practice to do so, except in cases above 50 *l.* I asked that question in the case of Boyce Wilkes, and I said, "Why was not that done, seeing the terrible condition in which the child was?" and they said, "It is not the practice in cases under 50 *l.*, certainly not under 10 *l.*"

845. They trust, in fact, to the medical certificate they get after death?—Yes. I should say I have never received any assistance from the agents of the companies to enable me to conduct any inquiry into any of these cases.

846. You are dependent entirely for information as to whether the child has been insured or not upon the answers of the parents, or people connected with them?—Yes. As to the last question, in every case of sudden or violent death, or where the cause of death is unknown, the police make inquiries, and at once report to me; but suppose it should not happen to come to their knowledge, and the medical man did not certify, then they go to the registrar, and the registrar at once fills up a form, sending it to me, asking me whether, in my opinion, it is a case in which an inquiry ought to take place. If I think the inquiry is unnecessary I say so. If I think it is I send it to the police and ask them to make full inquiry; but I have never found any difficulty, either with the registrar or with the police. The police report every case, except by accident, but I sometimes have both at the same time; that is, I have a notice from the registrar and a notice from the police.

Lord *Norton*.

847. Do you think that the limit of money insured for should not exceed the burial expenses?—Yes.

848. In

Lord *Norton*—continued.

848. In answer to Lord Selborne, it seems you did not include in that the medical expenses?—No.

849. Do you not think there should be included the expense of medical attendance?—I think they are proper, no doubt.

850. Do you think the limit which the law now imposes is too large a sum for that double object, burial and the medical expenses; would you make the limit narrower than it is now by law?—I think so.

851. By how much; what sort of a sum do you say, on an average, should be the limit for burial expenses and medical expenses?—It would be impossible for me to give an answer to that question. The sum reasonably and properly incurred should be paid. That is the limit I should give.

852. Have you any sum in your mind as to the average limit for the burial expenses in the case of a child in that class of life?—No.

853. Do you not know what the burial expenses are for a child in that rank of life?—I forget the sum. I know the sum for the coffins from the tenders to the guardians. The coffin would not be more than 6 *s.* or 8 *s.*, and not higher than 15 *s.* for any coffin.

854. Then in your mind, recommending as you have recommended to us, that the sum should be limited to the burial expenses, do you mean a sum of about 1 *l.* or 2 *l.*?—That would depend on age. I should think 1 *l.* would be sufficient.

855. £.1 ought to be the limit?—Yes.

Lord *Brougham.*

856. Are you a medical man yourself?—No.

Earl of *Selborne.*

857. If the same principle were adopted as in the case of fire insurance; that is, that it should be for the person insured to make out the actual loss, do you see any objection to that?—None whatever. I am inclined to think that is the better course.

Lord *Thring.*

858. The mortality of children is in inverse proportion to their age; that is to say, more children die during the first three months than during the next three months, and so on?—I believe so.

859. Do you know in suspicious cases whether the children were under two or three years of age or over two or three years of age?—I think in some cases they were certainly above one year.

860. You are not a medical man, but you know it is much easier to kill a child without being detected under two years than it is afterwards?—I should think so.

861. Do you think there would be any great harm in prohibiting the insurance of children under a certain age, for example prohibiting the insurance under one year altogether. Would that be any hardship upon the poor, or can you give any opinion upon it?—I know they say so, because the case put to me very often by the parents is this, that they feel it is an absolute necessity to do so. It is their duty to do so, and by insuring they assist the rates.

(142.)

Lord *Thring*—continued.

862. You think that the prohibition of the insurance of children under one year of age would be regarded certainly as a grievance by the poor?—I think so. I am inclined to think that any prohibition would be regarded as a hardship by the poor.

Lord *Poltimore.*

863. Have you any means of judging of the proportion of legitimate and illegitimate children among these suspicious cases?—In my opinion, there are more legitimate children; for this reason, the parents of illegitimate children have not the means. The sum which a woman having one of these children would get would be the minimum of 2 *s.* 6 *d.* and the maximum of 5 *s.*, and, therefore, she would not be in the same position to insure as the working man getting 30 *s.* or 40 *s.* a week. That is my opinion unquestionably, that the cases have been more legitimate than illegitimate.

864. I think you said in your evidence that there were cases in which the parents applied to the parish to bury although the child was insured?—No; on the contrary I said it certainly would not be so in my district.

Lord *Herschell.*

865. In those doubtful cases where the medical certificate is refused, what happens; is there always an inquest or how is the burial permitted?—Where the medical man refuses to give a certificate the case then, as I have said already, is left to the police. The police give me as full an account as they can, and if necessary I inquire of the doctor, and if after the investigation made by the police and myself and the questions I have asked the doctor, I think that an inquiry should be held, I always hold it, and in the case of an illegitimate child I hold it in every case of death, whether insured or not.

866. In some of these cases if you were satisfied that although there was suspicion, nothing more than suspicion could be proved, and there can be no advantage in holding an inquest, do you authorise burial without an inquest?—No, that is not my practice.

867. If you think after your investigation is concluded that the case is one of suspicion you would always hold it?—Yes, and I believe my district is now in a fairly satisfactory condition, because through the length and breadth of it I have stated the course I should take, and I have also told people in every part of my district that it would be useless to attempt to get out of the difficulty by attempting to tell me that the impropriety of food arose from ignorance, because they know after what I have said that cannot be held to be good, and that in every case I shall hold an inquiry.

868. Do you think that the practice, when it has become known, of holding an inquest in all cases where a certificate has been refused, and there are suspicious circumstances connected with the death has had a tendency to produce a more healthy condition of things, and diminish suspicious cases?—I can only say that since this case of which I spoke most strongly, the last case in November 1889, I have not had to make an observation of the same kind up to this date, nor to hold an inquiry of a similar kind.

E 3

869. I do

Lord *Herschell*—continued.

869. I do not think you told us the age of the child in the case you mentioned ; you said it was soon after he attained the age of ten; can you tell us how soon ?—I cannot tell you how soon. The agent said he was about 10, or just past 10.

870. Therefore he died too late to secure the surance money for the parent ?—He died just in time to enable them to get the money.

871. Then he was under 10 ?—No, he was over 10 ; I said the whole money was not payable until he attained the age of 10 years. It so happens that there was a coincidence that the child had attained the age of 10 years, and then died.

872. A question has been put to you with regard to preventing the evils which now exist by providing for the payment of the money required for the funeral only to the undertaker. Do you think such legislation would necessarily prevent the evil ? Might you not have an arrangement made between the undertaker and the parent that something should be paid by the undertaker to the parent ?—I am afraid there is hardly a law which cannot be evaded. That might be so. Speaking of my own district, I do not think it would be possible, because I know all the people, and I think they are people who would be incapable of acting in collusion with people insured, but I believe in some districts in England it might happen.

873. Supposing instead of the money being paid to the undertaker it were required before the payment was made that there should be a statutory declaration by the undertaker as to what his charges were ; do you think that might have the same effect ?—No doubt.

874. Still, if the undertaker were a dishonest man, after having received the money absolutely, he might give some back to the parent ?—That would be subject to the same difficulty as the payment to the undertaker.

875. What I meant was rather this : an exception has been taken to the payment being made to the undertaker as putting the whole of the funeral expenses out of the control of the parent ; do you think if the society were prohibited from paying in respect of the funeral expenses any sum beyond what the undertaker declared to be his charges, that that would be as effective as payment direct to the undertaker ?—I am afraid not. I should think the proper course would be to pay to the undertaker. Your Lordship assumes that it is to go into the hands of the parent after the declaration made ?

876. Yes ?—I am afraid that would be hardly satisfactory ; I mean with such a class of persons, who could be guilty of doing a wrong, for instance.

Earl *Beauchamp.*

877. I understood you to say that, in the case of Wilkes, the medical man who conducted the post-mortem examination gave his opinion that the death might possibly have been prevented ? —I will give the exact words he used. The child's life may, possibly, have been prolonged if careful treatment and nourishment had been given.

878. Do you think that an opinion expressed in those guarded terms threw any reflection on

Earl *Beauchamp*—continued.

the parents ?—No, not necessarily. In this case there is the extraordinary fact that they paid no attention whatever, although the child was known to be in that serious condition of health, and no medical man was called in from the time it was insured to the time it died, on no occasion.

879. There was no evidence of any ill-usage or actual neglect ?—No, except so far as you find that the doctor was of opinion that the nourishment appeared to be insufficient. That he drew, no doubt, from the emaciated state of the child.

880. Did the doctor express an opinion that the nourishment was insufficient ?—He said, if careful treatment and nourishment had been given, the child's life might have been prolonged. That, I think, is the sort of evidence one generally gets from medical men. They scarcely ever go further than that. They do not say " I am absolutely certain," but they say, " It is possible that life would have been saved, but I cannot say."

881. Amongst other illustrations of neglect, you mentioned that one was improper food ?—Yes.

882. Do you find that parents in the lower classes are familiar with the best and most improved methods of bringing up children by hand ? —I cannot say that, but I think they ought to know that milk or milk and water is a proper diet for children, and they are always told so, but they give all kinds of things. They give potatoes, biscuits, boiled bread, and all sorts of things.

883. Would that be true of children whose lives were uninsured as well as of children whose lives are insured ?—I have said so.

884. It is not characteristic of parents of children who are insured ?—I have said so.

885. Though they may possess this knowledge they do not always practise it ?—That is so.

886. Juries you say always attribute the death to the ignorance of the parents ?—That is so.

887. After all the juries are in a position to form a sound opinion as to the intelligence of the parents, are they not ?—In my experience they are not.

888. Will you explain that a little more from your experience ?—I said, taking the case of people whose education is very imperfect, of low position in society and in life, they are hardly people I should think to form an opinion like a doctor for instance or myself.

889. Not as to the cause of death undoubtedly, but as to the habits of the parents ?—Yes, I think it is very possible that they come to the conclusion that it is from ignorance, because the habits of these persons are exactly their own habits. No doubt that is so.

890. With regard to these insurance societies, are they mostly local, or do they belong to any large organisation ?—A large organisation. The society with which I am most familiar is the Prudential.

891. To come to another point, you have been clerk to the guardians I think ?—Yes, for 40 years.

892. Have you observed at all whether the tendency of medical relief is to bring persons on the list of paupers who before they received medical relief were not on that list ?—I think it has that tendency.

893. And

Earl *Beauchamp*—continued.

893. And that therefore it would be a matter contrary to public interest to encourage persons to receive medical relief and so become familiar with the habit of receiving assistance from the rates?—That has been my opinion for many years.

Chairman.

894. May I ask in point of law are coroners paid a fixed salary or paid according to the number of inquests they held?—A fixed salary.

895. That is at least your own experience?—Yes.

896. As regards these cases of neglect to which you were referring in your opinion on a bad case, one clear evidence of neglect was neglect in calling in the doctor?—Yes.

897. They did not call in the doctor although the child was so seriously ill?—They never called in the doctor.

898. That you would regard distinctly as neglect?—Yes.

899. And as approaching to criminal neglect, wilful neglect certainly?—No doubt if you prove they had the means of paying for the medical man.

900. Even if they had not the means they could have got the gratuitous attendance of the parish doctor?—That does not follow. The Guardians may say this is a case in which we are of opinion you can pay.

901. Either they had means or they had not means; if they had means they could have paid the doctor, and if they had not means they could have got him?—Yes.

Chairman—continued.

902. Therefore, in either case there was neglect?—Undoubtedly.

903. I wanted to put a question or two as regards the payments of doctors; let us take the case of a child who is taken ill, and the parents send for the doctor and the child recovers and does not die, in that case how would the doctor be paid?—He must be paid by the parents who were able to pay unless they had an order from the guardians.

904. There would be the necessity to pay the doctor whether the child recovered or died?—Yes.

905. And the same necessity in each case?—Yes.

906. A doctor would not charge more for medical attendance in the case of a child that died than in the case of a child that recovered?—I apprehend not.

907. Then there is no necessity apparently for effecting an insurance which will pay the doctor if the doctor can be paid or left without payment, which comes to the same thing, in case the child does not die?—Yes.

908. It is exactly the same thing?—Yes.

909. Therefore, there is clearly no necessity for an insurance in the case of death any more than for an insurance to pay the doctor when the child recovers; am I not right?—Yes.

910. In fact this claim for death insurance to pay the doctor will not hold water?—I never heard it suggested until to-day.

[The Witness is directed to withdraw.

MR. JOHN TROUTBECK is called in; and Examined, as follows:

Chairman.

911. You are Coroner for the City and Liberty of Westminster?—Yes.

912. And your area extends from Temple Bar to Knightsbridge, and from Oxford-street to the river?—Yes.

913. You are a solicitor?—Yes.

914. And Master of Arts and Bachelor of Civil Law?—Yes.

915. Have you any knowledge of what the population of this district of yours is?—I have not been able to find out. I was only asked to give evidence on Saturday, so that I have not been able to find out.

916. How long have you held your office?—For four years, two of which was as deputy.

917. Two as deputy, and two as coroner?—Yes.

918. How many inquests do you hold in the year on the average?—The average is about 350, or a little over.

919. Including inquests on persons of all ages?—Yes.

920. Has your attention been called to cases of insured children in your capacity as coroner?—Yes, it has.

921. Have you formed any opinion of the effect of child life insurance?—Yes.

922. What is your opinion?—My opinion is, that it is prejudicial to child life.

923. What were the features in cases of insured children which attracted your attention,

Chairman—continued.

and made you form this opinion?—They were badly fed, and insufficiently fed, and exposed to cold and rain, and they were found suffocated in bed with their parents. That struck me most. I also notice that there is a great deal of drinking. The parents are very often drunk when in charge of them; I have often noticed that.

924. You have found the parents come to your inquest drunk?—Yes, I have found them come to my inquest drunk; sometimes from the proceeds of the insurance.

925. All these facts apply to insured children?—Yes. They also apply, but not to such a great extent, to children not insured.

926. You found them in both cases, but in a greater number in the insured than in the uninsured cases?—Yes.

927. How do you ascertain that a child is insured?—My officers always make a report, and one of the questions they have to fill in is whether the child is insured.

928. Supposing the parent says the child is not insured, do you take any steps to verify the statement?—I ask when the parent gives evidence.

929. Do you find that that evidence is always correct and truthful?—It is not always the same as what is stated to the officer. I sometimes find that they have told the officer that the child is not insured, and when on oath they admit that the child is insured.

Chairman—continued.

930. In what class of people do you generally find that these neglected children are insured?—In the lowest classes, at Clare Market, and that part.

931. Leading improper and depraved lives?—Yes.

932. Have you formed any idea as to what proportion of this kind of people there are in your district; are there many of them?—Yes, there are a great many. Westminster is not so bad as it was, but the worst part now is in Clare Market, where there are the Covent Garden porters and people of that kind, and those who live by selling things in the street, a general hand-to-mouth existence.

933. Is it your opinion that these are a class of people to whom a few pounds on a child's death would be a temptation?—Certainly.

934. Supposing that the child were not insured, there might, notwithstanding, be neglect on the part of the parent?—Yes, there often is.

935. Is it your opinion that, supposing the parent is disposed to neglect his child from other causes, viciousness, or drunkenness, or cruelty, that the possibility of making money by the child's death would be an additional temptation?—Yes, I think so.

936. With people of this class?—With people of this class.

937. Can you give us any illustration of suspicious cases that may have come before you?—I have in my mind the case of a strong child of, I think, six months old, and the parents were in poor circumstances. I think the father was a Covent Garden porter. They had more than one child, and this child was insured. The child became ill, and on the point of death was taken to King's College Hospital, and it was found to be dead just as it was taken in. An inquest was held, and the post-mortem examination showed that the child had been suffering for at least 36 hours from inflammation of the lungs; it had had no attention; and, I think, the mother was a flower seller, or some kind of seller in Clare Market; she took it out with her up to the day of its death. It was cold weather at the time, but she denied that the child had had anything the matter with it. The medical evidence was to the effect that it was impossible not to have noticed that something was the matter with the child.

938. Inflammation of the lungs we all know is a very acute and painful disease?—Yes.

939. A mother could not be ignorant that her child was suffering from inflammation of the lungs?—That was the opinion of the doctor.

940. Nevertheless she took it out with her?—Yes.

941. Were there any dispensaries at hand?—Yes; there are many dispensaries, and the hospital is quite close.

942. Was the parish doctor about in the neighbourhood?—He would be quite available if wanted.

943. Neither to the dispensary, nor to the hospital, nor to the parish doctor did this mother make any application whatever?—No, she said the child did not need attendance.

944. Are you aware what money came to that parent; did you hear it was an insured child?—

Chairman—continued.

I undetstood it was about 2 *l.* 10 *s.*, but I do not know that exactly.

945. That is an instance of what you would call a suspicious case?—Yes. I may say that that is a common kind of case.

946. You have had many similar cases?—Yes.

947. And they all more or less have that suspicion attaching to them?—Yes.

948. You have not found that parental affection in these cases makes the mother very careful about the child?—No.

949. The mother did not show much parental affection?—She did not seem to me to show any.

950. In other like cases you have not seen much parental affection?—It is very difficult to say. Sometimes there is a great show of grief at the death, and sometimes, when I am certain there is a great grief, there is nothing shown at all; it is very difficult to say.

951. Is it your opinion from what you know of this class of people, these depraved and worthless people, and from their habits of life, and so on, that, generally speaking, they are people whom strong parental affection would keep from ill-using their children and neglecting them?—No, I do not think they have such parental affection as other parents.

952. You do not think we can safely rely on the instinct of parental affection in all cases of insured children?—Not in my experience in that class.

953. Do you commit for trial in all these suspicious cases?—No; it is very rare to get a verdict.

954. What would you say were your reasons for not committing for trial when you have the suspicious cases?—The first is the very great difficulty in getting evidence, except that of the parents, and then the chief witnesses are usually friends of the parents and of the same class, and they obviously make the best case out.

955. You can perceive that they are doing so? Yes, it is quite evident.

956. Screening the parents as far as they can?—Yes, they do.

957. Even when you get very strong evidence do cases of this kind generally break down, or not?—It is very common when they are sent to trial to break down.

958. In the case of a trial for homicide or manslaughter, am I right in saying that a husband cannot give evidence against a wife, or a wife against a husband?—I believe so.

959. In that case the only evidence forthcoming would be that of the children of the family, the other children, if there were such, or the neighbours?—Yes, and the police.

960. The evidence of the children would be worth very little, if anything, for the want of understanding the treatment of a child by a parent unless there was violence?—Sometimes children are very clever and very sharp.

961. A child would not have sufficient medical knowledge or experience to see that the parent was treating the child improperly, giving it improper food?—I should look with great suspicion upon whatever a small brother or sister of the child might say. There is no knowing what home influence might have been brought to bear on what they were saying.

962. The child would give evidence under considerable

*Chairman—*continued.

considerable terror of the treatment it would receive from the parents, afterwards if it gave evidence against the parents?—Oh, yes.

963. And the evidence of the neighbours you say for the reason you have given is generally worth very little?—Generally worth very little.

964. What is the locality you specially refer to as regards these cases?—Clare Market.

965. You have cases of insured children from Clare Market?—Yes.

966. A good many of them?—I cannot give you the exact numbers; I have not been able to get them.

967. Could you tell the Committee anything about what is known as the Strand case?—The Strand fire case?

968. Yes?—That was a case where two children of a man who took a house in the Strand were insured. I think they were respectively about 9 and 10 years old, and they were insured for sums of about 7 *l.* and 10 *l.* The house was insured as well, and the man was a hairdresser. The house was burnt down one night; there was evidence that it had been prepared for burning, and the two children were burned to death. There was an inquest, of course, on the bodies, and the man was committed for trial for murder; he was also tried at the same assizes for arson, and he was convicted of the arson, but acquitted of the murder. There was no direct evidence except the evidence of the wife, who gave evidence in my court, and the children. There was no other evidence except one other man and an assistant, who was also tried for the same offence and acquitted. The mother's evidence was not, of course, given at the trial.

969. The mother's evidence was against the father?—To some extent it certainly was.

970. But could not be admitted at the trial at the assizes?—No, I think it affected the jury at the inquest materially.

971. What was the verdict of the jury at the inquest?—They returned a verdict of murder.

972. The case then, of course, went before the assizes?—It went to the Central Criminal Court.

973. Was the parent convicted?—No.

974. Then you think that the inability to receive the mother's evidence conduced to the case breaking down?—Yes, I think it does.

975. Do you know any other case which broke down; do you know what is called the Serné case?—The Strand case is the Serné case. I remember another case of an illegitimate child; I am not quite sure whether that was insured. It was a second child; it was supposed to be killed by its mother. I had not much doubt about it. It was sent for trial, but it broke down on the medical evidence.

976. Do you find many cases of overlaying of children?—Many.

977. In those cases it is almost impossible to prove an evil intent?—Yes; I may say I held 51 inquests on children under 12 months old this last year, from June to June, and 18 of those were suffocated while in bed with their parents.

978. You have not sent all the strongly suspicious cases of neglect to the Central Criminal

(142.)

*Chairman—*continued.

Court?—No; the jury does not return a verdict against them, and nothing is done.

979. And a jury, as a rule, will not return these verdicts?—No.

980. Although in your opinion, having watched the case, they ought to have done so?—There is a very strong case made out, and I think they ought to.

981. Do you remember the case of a girl who was brought before you for neglect of her child; it was her second child, was it not?—I have tried to look it out, but I have not been able to find the case.

982. You have not got notes of the case?—I have notes.

983. You remember there was such a case?—There was such a case, but I cannot remember the details sufficiently.

984. The case of a girl who was brought before you for neglecting her child; it was her second child, both insured, and the jury let her off. This was the second child?—Yes, perhaps that is the case you referred to first. I do not think it was neglect; I think there was distinct evidence that the child was deliberately killed. I have had another case like that, but I do not know the details of it.

985. The reason that you do not get so many cases sent to the court, is that juries, in point of fact, let the woman off; they do not like to send it?—They do not like to send it; they very often ask, if it is an illegitimate child, where the father is. That seems to be a sufficient reason to them.

986. Is there any other reason why these kind of cases do not go to the Central Criminal Court, besides the reluctance of juries?—There is a great deal of difficulty in getting up the cases; I do not think very often the cases are worked up enough.

987. In the case of these insured children, have you ever known a case in which an insurance agent has come to you and offered to give you help in proving that it was a bad case?—No, never.

988. It would be to the interest of the insurance company of which he is the agent to prove that it was a bad case, because they would not have to pay the money?—It might not. They might lose all the insurance business in that neighbourhood.

989. They might lose the insurance business in the neighbourhood by being too strict?—I only know they never have helped me.

990. Do you know much, or do you know anything about the extent to which child insurance is carried on by agents in your district. Are there many agents going about?—I have been told so, that, generally speaking, a parent is always asked to insure a child, and very many of them insure.

991. In different societies?—Yes; most respectable families.

992. Is it your opinion, from what you have experience of, that there is a certain amount of competition among these societies through their agents for insurance?—I cannot say.

993. Do you think that this amount of crime in connection with assurance will ever be checked so long as there is a profit accruing from death?

F   —I think

Chairman—continued.

—I think it would make a certain difference if a parent knew that there could be no profit accruing from death.

994. It would tend to check the crime in connection with insurance?—Yes.

995. The class of persons of whom you have spoken are many of them in a very low state of life?—Oh, yes.

996. Do you know anything about their wages? —It depends entirely; sometimes a Covent Garden porter will earn a great deal of money, as, for instance, just now, and then he will earn very little in the winter.

997. Most of these men would be able to pay 1 *d.* a week for six months, say without feeling it very much if they were in work?—I should think so.

998. That would suffice as we know to bring the insurance money. No dread of being pauperised, or being humiliated would come upon these people's minds, so very low as they are?— They do dread being pauperised, however low they are.

999. Why do they dread being made paupers of?—I think the restraint is one thing, and the natural feeling of shame that they have.

Earl of *Derby*.

1000. Do you know whether, as a rule, the children are only insured in one office, or in several?—I only get reports of insurance in one office; I do not remember a case of two; there may be such cases, but they are not reported to me.

Lord *Norton*.

1001. Of course if there were no profit in the insurance money all your suspicions of foul play would cease?—Yes, often.

1002. What suspicion of foul play could there remain if there was no profit in the insurance money?—I think that very often children are neglected when there is no insurance.

1003. What is the inducement of a parent to neglect a child which is dying if he makes no profit by it?—They make a profit indirectly by no longer having to support the child.

1004. Do you think that accounts for a good many of the cases which you consider suspicious, the mere wish to remove the burden of the child's support. Do you think that accounts for many of the cases of suspicious death which have come under your notice?—I think very often they simply neglect the child without much thought at all of what the consequences are.

1005. Without any thought of the insurance money?—Yes.

Earl of *Harrowby*.

1006. Do you find that all the working classes in your district in Westminster insure as a rule? —I think they insure largely.

1007. All the honest working people?— Yes.

1008. Can you give us any idea of the proportion of those who come into the category of the vicious and degraded, who are likely to try and make a profit by their children's deaths?— Compared with the respectable?

Earl of *Harrowby*—continued.

1009. Yes?—No, I cannot.

1010. Then it is a great indictment to bring against a class of people?—I may say this, that amongst the cases of children that come under my knowledge, the large majority of them belong to the poorest and almost the dissolute classes, and it is a rare thing to get a case from a respectable working man's family.

1011. You say, therefore, it is rather the vicious and dissolute parents than even the very poor that resort to this expedient to raise money?— Yes.

1012. And only a small proportion of the working people of Westminster come into your category?—Yes, it is chiefly in places like Clare Market; Westminster is changing from day to day. Just about here they are putting up artizan's buildings, which will change the character of the poor very much.

1013. Have you had any opportunity of judging of the feeling of the honest working class as to this question of children's life insurance, whether they think any further restriction is needed?—I do not think they like any interference. Those with whom I have talked, certainly say that it is a great boon to them to be able to insure their children, and I think it would be resented if it were stopped.

1014. They would resent any interference?— Yes.

1015. Of course they are aware that we have our feelings about the horrors of the system, as far as it affects a small number?—Yes.

1016. Can you tell us what the legitimate cost of the burial of a child under 10 years of age in Westminster would be?—I think about 30 *s.*

1017. And what they can get from the life insurance is about 2 *l.* 10 *s.*?—£. 2 10 *s.* after the child is three months old.

1018. Then there is the payment of the doctor's bill over and above that?—Yes, if there is any doctor.

1019. Would you tell me what happens in London if the doctor refuses to certify the cause of death; what is the next step?—Either the doctor reports the case to me, or the registrar does.

1020. Is the doctor bound to report the case? —No, he is not bound, but he often does.

1021. Supposing he does not report, and simply refuses, what happens?—The child cannot be buried, and nothing can be done until the death is reported to the registrar, and the registrar always reports it to the coroner.

1022. Then it comes to you in that way?—It comes to me in that way.

1023. The registrar must report to you?—Yes, and in addition a report always comes through the police; I sometimes get three reports of one death, one from the doctor, another, from the registrar, and another from the police.

1024. You get three reports, you say?—I may in some cases.

1025. And those three parties are bound to report to you as coroner?—Two of them are; I consider the police and the registrar are bound to do so.

1026. What happens if you do not see cause to hold an inquest?—There is a form which has lately been issued by the Registrar General, which is filled up to the effect that "I have caused inquiry

Earl of Harrowby—continued.

inquiry to be made into the death, and I do not consider it a proper case in which an inquest should be held."

1027. And upon that the burial may take place?—The death is registered, and the registrar gives his permission to bury.

1028. After the doctor refuses a certificate you have an informal investigation, not an inquest, and upon that you allow the funeral?—That is so, if it is a case in which an inquest is not necessary.

Earl Beauchamp.

1029. You told us that 30 s. was the undertaker's charge; does that include the cost of transit to the place of burial?—Yes, that is the cost of the funeral. That is only what I have been told on inquiry. I have asked people how much has their funeral cost them.

1030. Is there any prejudice on the part of the poor, of whom you have been speaking, at being buried at the expense of the parish?—Yes, I think there is a strong prejudice.

1031. Do you speak of Westminster, or other parts of England, as to the prejudice of the poor to being buried by the parish?—I cannot speak as to other parts of England so well, but certainly as to Westminster.

1032. It is considered rather a loss of caste and a stigma to be buried at the cost of the parish?—Yes, they feel it a slight on the dead person.

1033. The respectable working classes try and avoid that as much as they possibly can?—Yes.

1034. I think you told us that the evidence given before you on oath varied from the information obtained informally by the police?—It does often.

1035. You attach great value to evidence given on oath, as contrasted with evidence given loosely, and not under the sanctity of that ob-

Earl Beauchamp—continued.

ligation?—Certainly, I think the formality makes a great difference as far as I have been able to judge. I think people in the lower classes have a belief that there will be very serious consequences if they do not tell the truth under oath.

1036. You told us some thing which I did not quite follow about a child which was deliberately killed?—Do you mean the case of a mother who had had a second illegitimate child.

1037. I think that was the case. That was the expression you used. There was no doubt the child had been deliberately killed?—Suffocated.

1038. Deliberately killed was your expression?—By suffocation.

1039. Deliberately?—Yes, that was my opinion.

1040. What was the verdict in that case?—By my jury it was murder, and it was sent for trial, and the mother was acquitted.

1041. Where was the trial?—It must have been at the Central Criminal Court.

1042. The trial there was by a jury?—Yes.

1043. They heard evidence on oath?—They heard evidence on oath in the same way.

1044. And there was a conflict of opinion between your jury and the jury at the Central Criminal Court?—Yes.

1045. What was the exact verdict of your jury in your court?—Wilful murder against the mother.

1046. That was not sustained in the Central Criminal Court?—No.

Chairman.

1047. Did you form any opinion why it was not sustained; did you give any attention to the trial?—Yes, I thought it broke down through the medical evidence.

The Witness is directed to withdraw.

MR. ARTHUR BROWNE is called in ; and Examined, as follows :

Chairman.

1048. YOU are Deputy Coroner for the town and county of Nottingham?—For the town and county of the town of Nottingham, but not for the county at large.

1049. You are also a solicitor?—I am.

1050. Do you know what is the present population of the town and county of the town of Nottingham?—I believe about 235,000.

1051. How long have you held this office of deputy coroner?—Nearly 14 years, and for the last six or eight years I have done nearly all the duty.

1052. Could you say about what number of inquests you have held annually in those 14 years?—I believe the average is about 240.

1053. Of inquests on persons of all ages?—Yes.

1054. Amongst these, were there many children's cases?—A great many.

1055. Have you any idea as to the proportion between the children and adult cases that came before you?—I cannot give the percentage ; the infant mortality in Nottingham is very high,

(142.)

Chairman—continued.

owing to the large number of women employed in our factories and warehouses.

1056 In these cases of children has your attention been called to insured children?—Very much.

1057. Have you formed any opinion of the effects of child insurance as regards child life?—I have.

1058. What do you think they are?—My opinion is this, that in cases of neglected children the insurance money is very often the climax, or, I may say, the last incentive to allow the child to die. What I mean by that is this, that the insurance money is not the only incentive. The child, to begin with, is a burden, especially if it is illegitimate and it is first neglected ; its health becomes degenerated, and then the insurance money, I think, comes in and operates as a bait to continue that neglect.

1059. In most of these cases, then, it is your opinion that there has not been violence used to the child, but it has been wilfully and criminally

F 2   neglected?

Chairman—continued.

neglected ?—In the case of suffocation of children I think that there is very frequently violence used, because I find distinct evidence of pressure upon the children's faces, the noses being pressed in, but it is impossible to say whether that is wilful or accidental.

1060. You have had a considerable number of those over-laying cases as they are called ?—A very large number. I think during the time that I have held office I must have had at least 100.

1061. Of children overlain by the mother ?—Yes, the mother or the father, or both. Sometimes there are three or four, and I have known even five people in one bed.

1062. What kind of parents, in your opinion, are they whose children are thus illtreated, being also insured ?—I should say that in almost all cases they are poor people, but in very many cases they are depraved people, of depraved habits, living in filthy houses frequently.

1063. There are a great many of those in Nottingham ?—Yes, my Lord.

1064. Do you consider it to be any libel upon the respectable and properly conducted working men of Nottingham to say that there is a considerable number of working men who are drunken and immoral ?—Whether it is a libel or not, I am afraid it is true. The greater the truth the greater the libel, one of our judges said.

1065. Then it is not always from extreme poverty that the child is neglected or ill-fed, but sometimes it comes from the parent being drunken or immoral ?—I am satisfied that is so; and if your Lordship likes I can give an instance which recently happened. The case was one that happened in the winter time towards the end of last November. The deceased child, on whom I held an inquest, was one of four, all of whom were insured.

1066. In the same family ?—In the same family. This child was allowed to sleep upon a mattress which the jury and myself saw, and which was in a disgusting state, completely rotten and saturated through with urine. The only clothing which the child had was one or two old jackets. In that case the father was in regular receipt of wages as a warehouseman, and he to some extent excused himself by stating that he was at work all day long and had not the care of the child. If your Lordship wishes I would give the verdict in that case, as it is instructive.

1067. If you please ?—The verdict was this: "That on the 24th of November the said Alice Verney Barrett died from inflammation of the right lung ; that there is evidence to show that the deceased has been systematically neglected, and that the parents of the child, George Barrett and Alice Barrett, are censurable for such neglect, but that the evidence fails to show positively that the neglect was the direct cause of death; and the jury recommend that criminal proceedings be taken against the parents for the said neglect."

1068. Were criminal proceedings taken ?—They were.

1069. What was the result ?—With this result, that the mother was sentenced to 15 months'

Chairman—continued.

imprisonment, the longest term of imprisonment I have known in such a case ; and the father to three months' imprisonment.

1070. How long ago did that occur ?—A few months ago.

1071. Was that since the law passed last year for the better protection of children ?—I think it was ; it was just after.

1072. It was one of the cases in which the Society for the Prevention of Cruelty to Children prosecuted ? — No ; in Nottingham the police take upon themselves the duty, and so long as they do their duty there is no necessity for anyone else to interfere, and they do their duty to the best of their ability.

Earl of Selborne.

1073. The case you have just mentioned was an insured child ?—It was. There were four insured, and they were all grossly neglected. I only had to do with one case, but all the others were in a very bad condition.

Chairman.

1074. What was the age of the child ?—It was a year and 11 months old.

1075. On the death of that child, do you know what sum the parents were to receive ? — The father of the child said that he was insured, but was not in benefit ; but I should like to state my Lord, that at Nottingham there is a practice that even where the child is not in benefit parents still apply for and obtain a portion of the insurance money. If a child is insured for 30s. they will get perhaps 15s. or 1l.

Earl of Selborne.

1076. What do you mean by being in benefit? —When they have not been insured for a sufficient time, say three months.

1077. The insurance is not ripe ?—The insurance company is not legally responsible, but as a gratuity they pay them 15s., or 1l. or so.

Chairman.

1078. You ask parents in suspicious cases whether the child is insured ?—I almost invariably do so ; if I do not it is through inadvertence.

1079. When the parents deny it, do you take any steps to see if they have told you the truth? —I have not done so.

1080. Could you do very much to find out whether the parent was telling you the truth or not ?—I could. I could ascertain it definitely, and that is through the registry offices. In fact I have been told by one registrar that of the children under 12 months that die about three-fourths are insured. In every case I believe in Nottingham the parents come to the registrar for a certificate, for this reason, that I refuse to give them. In many cases the parent, or the agent of the insurance company, presents to me a printed form of certificate which I invariably refuse to sign.

1081. In such cases ?—In such cases. The result is that they are bound to go to the registrar to get a copy of the certificate before they can get the insurance money. So that I believe in

Nottingham

Chairman—continued.

Nottingham in every case the registrar must know whether the children are insured or not.

1082. Have you found it to be the case that where you have refused a certificate the registrar has given one ?—Always. They always do that, I believe

1083. Your certificate does not go as to whether the death is by natural or unnatural causes, but simply as to the nature of the disease that existed, that the death was from pneumonia or from bronchitis ?—Yes, with the addition that if it is caused by neglect I should put that in a certificate, as in a case of this kind I have just quoted; I should certify in that case the death would have been caused by inflammation of the lungs aggravated by neglect probably.

1084. Thereupon the registrar is bound to give his certificate ?—I believe so.

1085. And thereupon the funeral takes place ? —Yes.

1086. There could not then be a case of a child remaining unburied because he had got no certificate from the registrar ?—No, because in that case if the parent refuses to bury the child, the parish would be bound to do so.

1087. You think in some cases the parents would deny the fact of insurance ?—I think it is possible, but I have not investigated that subject.

1088. Do you often find a case of a person, being a parent, giving you evidence which you are afterwards able to prove to be untruthful?—Yes, I had a case a very short time ago where I put two questions to a mother, and I got two very significant answers. The first question asked was as to how the child had been fed. She at once denied having fed it on bread and milk, she said, " I knew it was not proper food." I had said nothing to her about it being proper or improper. The second question I asked was, was the child insured. She said, " Yes, but I hope you do not think I have killed it." Then she stated that she had not given this child improper food. The child was examined by a medical man, a post-mortem examination was made, and it was found that the child's stomach was completely filled with bread, stuffed with it.

1089. You did not ask her whether the child had been fed on bread and milk ?—I asked her how it had been fed. I did not know at that time that the medical man had found the bread. I examined him afterwards, and then I re-called her.

1090. Your question then, in the first instance, was simply a general question?—Yes.

1091. This was a volunteered statement, " I had not fed it on bread and milk " ?—Yes, and she said, " Because I knew it was not proper food."

1092. Then it appeared after the post-mortem examination that the child's stomach was full of this bread and milk. which the mother said she knew was improper food and she had not given ? —Yes, and the verdict was that the child had been suffocated after having been improperly fed, or something to that effect.

1093. Did that child bring the mother any money at its death as an insured child ?—I think it brought 30 *s.*

1094. Do you make it a rule to put such

(142.)

Chairman—continued.

questions, especially in the cases of illegitimate children, as to whether they are insured?—I always do so where I suspect there is any neglect.

1095. Do you generally find that the illegitimate children are insured ?—Almost invariably, I think.

1096. Are there any kind of cases in which you ask this question about insurance. A child may be killed in other ways than by improper food, for instance ?—If it is a case of accident, I should not trouble about it.

1097. If you suspected that a child had been drugged with syrups and improper medicines ?— In cases of that kind I should ; and I have frequently known of laudanum poisoning, and poisoning by Godfrey's cordial infants' preservative, and in cases of that kind I should ask. Those are cases that occur frequently with the children of young women who are at work in the day-time, and I believe that there is a very common practice in Nottingham of leaving a child in the care of some other person during the day-time, and to make it sleep for several hours it will have a dose of laudanum given to it; sometimes too much is given, and then it comes under my hands. I have had many cases of poisoning in that way.

1098. You said to us that juries are very easily moved by the parents to let them off?—I should say this, that that remark applies to juries at the assizes more than to juries who come before me. My experience has been this, that if a jury of men had been encouraged in cases of this kind such as the one I have quoted, they would have returned a verdict of manslaughter, but I have discouraged such a verdict.

1099. Would you say why ?—The reason I have done it is this ; as I have stated over and over again to juries that if they send a case for trial the case will be stale when it is tried at the assizes, perhaps two or three months old, and the sympathies of the jury will be worked upon in favour of the prisoner ; and, if I may say so, the judges appear to be over protective of criminals ; they seem to throw a mantle round them which it is almost impossible to remove. If there is any technicality which can be taken advantage of the prisoner gets the benefit of it, and the public in cases of that kind do not appear to be considered. There was a case at Derby a few months ago which appeared to me from the report to be a gross case of neglect, but it broke down. There was another case at Liverpool which was sent for trial for manslaughter, and the jury refused to convict.

1100. In point of fact, then, it is your opinion the chances of escaping before a jury of assize are even greater than they would be before a coroner's jury ?—Very much so, and still greater than at the sessions. There is a case pending now which is coming on in a few days which came before me, a very gross case of neglect. My practice has been to recommend that my jury should not return a verdict of manslaughter, but that the mother should be censured, and that the prosecution should be undertaken by the guardians. That was the law before the recent Act was passed, that the guardians had to take it up. That has been done with success in

F 3   several

Chairman—continued.

several cases. The guardians have prosecuted, the parents have been brought before the magistrates almost immediately after the offence, and have been dealt with at once, before the offence was stale, and whilst the facts were in the memory of the witnesses, and in several cases of the kind that have been brought forward and dealt with by the magistrates there have been convictions.

1101. Those would not be convictions for manslaughter or murder, but convictions for cruelty and wilful neglect?—Wilful neglect. In a case I speak of now, which is pending, the matter has been tried once at the sessions. The magistrates thought it too serious a case to deal with themselves, and she was sent for trial at the sessions. The jury in that case did not agree, and she was remanded to the next sessions to be tried again. In that case the evidence showed that she had grossly neglected this child, and had obtained assistance from the union on a doctor's certificate. She had had two doctors who had both recommended her not to feed the child on bread and milk or bread, but she admitted to me that she had fed it down almost to the day of its death on bread. She had continued to feed it on bread. She had also got milk from the workhouse which she had drunk herself, and cod-liver oil which she got from the same source, she said she had thrown on the back of the fire, and allowed the child to die.

1102. And this was the child's own mother?—Yes.

1103. Have you ever known a case where evidence of character, and evidence that the child was well cared for affected the verdict of your jury, which evidence afterwards proved to be untrustworthy; do you remember the case of a clergyman who spoke of care being bestowed on a child?—I have found this, that clergymen are very apt to give certificates of respectability where they know little or nothing about the case. One case I had was where an illegitimate child had been farmed out to a village near Nottingham, and it was brought into Nottingham in a dying condition, and died immediately afterwards. I held an inquest upon it, and at the inquest a sort of testimonial of respectability or certificate of respectability was presented to me from the parish clergyman, who said that he believed the woman in whose charge the child had been was a very respectable and honest woman, and had done everything she could for the child. I found at the inquest that 5 *s.* a week had been paid for the child, and all the other income was about 2 *s.* a week made by the husband, so that the whole family had only about 7 *s.* a week to live upon, and the post-mortem examination made disclosed the fact that the child had literally been starved to death. If I had relied upon that clergyman's certificate I should not have held an inquest.

1104. The clergyman declared that he knew the child was well cared for, and he had only seen it when he christened it?—I believe that was the only occasion when he had seen it.

1105. That letter, of course, would influence both you and the jury, if the case were before a jury?—It did not influence me, but it might have influenced the jury.

Chairman—continued.

1106. There was one thing which has been said which you can perhaps tell us about. Is it the feeling with doctors, or is it your own feeling, that in cases which fail, we will say, at the assizes, and the doctor has given evidence as to how the child in his opinion has come to its death, that gives very dangerous teaching to other persons as to how they may get rid of their children?—I can only infer that is so. It is a matter one can hardly define or prove positively, but I do find this, that where medical men give very definite evidence of neglect and absence of disease, there is great difficulty in getting a conviction. In the case I mentioned as pending now three medical men had given evidence that the child had apparently been starved to death, and that there was no evidence of any other disease, any constitutional disease whatever, and still there is great difficulty in getting a conviction.

1107. Taking all these things into account and the comparative facility with which doctors' certificates are given, and the difficulty of proving cases before the coroner's jury, and the still greater difficulty of proving cases at a court of assize, do you think that it is a reasonable demand to make that those who promote this Bill should produce a great number of cases of conviction and punishment for infanticide; do you think that criminal courts are, after all, the proper test, and a sufficient test, of crime in connection with insurance?—No, my Lord, I think they would be very insufficient tests, for the simple reason that a very small percentage of cases go before the judges for trial.

1108. To demand, then, that we should produce cases of conviction for infanticide is, under all the circumstances you have described to us, an unreasonable demand?—Certainly; even in cases of charges of wilful murder a jury, as we have all seen, will almost invariably acquit of the higher charge, but convict in many cases of concealment of birth, if possible. That is very frequently done; in fact, the greater the punishment the greater the difficulty in obtaining a conviction.

Earl of Selborne.

1109. You said just now that there was a case in which three medical men gave consistent evidence that a child had not been properly used, but that there was no conviction?—I say the jury disagreed, and the case is now pending for a second trial.

1110. What sort of evidence was given against the evidence of those medical men?—Practically no evidence at all, except what was elicited from the medical men themselves, that in some cases children would die notwithstanding every care and attention, but I believe all three medical men qualified their statements by this answer, that in this particular case there was no disease.

1111. Your attention no doubt has been directed to the requirements of the law in this case with regard to the certificates to be given upon which the money is to be paid. Do you think the certificates are sufficient?—Does your Lordship mean the copy of certificates obtained from the registrar?

1112. Yes; I have the Act of Parliament under my eye, which provides that the registrar
is

Earl of *Selborne*—continued.

is to give a certificate which is to state certain particulars, one of these particulars is to be the cause of death, and that must be the cause of death, as entered in the register by the certificate of a medical practitioner, I asked you whether you thought that anything more might be usefully certified by the medical practitioner in such a case?—I think, my Lord, that if the medical practitioner knew all the circumstances that had preceded death for a considerable time he would, in many cases, refuse to certify.

1113. Of course if he refuses to certify, how is the cause of death entered upon the register? —Then the case, as a matter of course, is referred to me.

1114. It goes to the coroner?—It cannot be registered until reported to the coroner.

1115. Would it be possible to require the medical officer in a case in which he is of opinion that there has not been proper care to add that to his certificate of the immediate cause of death? —No my Lord, I do not think that would be desirable; I think the better course is not to certify at all.

1116. I am supposing the case that he does certify, and of course if the law required him to state anything that he knows about the ill-treatment of the child he would be subject to penalties, I suppose, if he does not to do so?—No, my Lord, he is only subject to a penalty if he refuses to certify without reasonable cause.

1117. Even if the law required that in those cases, he should not only certify the immediate cause of death, but what he has observed about ill-treatment of the child, of course he would be at liberty to do so, and bound to do so. I wanted to know whether such a requirement would be any protection against abuses of this kind?—I think not more protection than we have at present.

1118. We have had evidence that medical practitioners do certify very easily?—That, I believe, is not my experience. I believe that the medical practitioners in Nottingham refer suspicious cases to the coroner.

Lord *Kinnaird.*

1119. What proportion of your 240 inquests per annum, do you think, are children under two years of age?—I can scarcely answer that question at present, for I have not calculated the percentage.

1120. A considerable proportion?—Yes, a large proportion.

1121. Fifty or 100?—I could not say definitely what proportion.

1122. In the case you mentioned, where a man was getting good wages, would that mean 2 *l.* a-week?—Thirty shillings or 2 *l.*

1123. Would 15 *s.*, do you consider, be an inducement to a man in that class, to make away with a child?—I think that would act as an extra inducement. I stated previously that I do not think it would be sufficient inducement alone, but the child already being somewhat of a burden, I think that that would act as an additional incentive.

1124. Is that a common feeling among a certain class that all children are a burden?—

(142.)

Lord *Kinnaird*—continued.

I believe with the respectable poor it is not so. I believe that many are extremely fond of their children, and are sorry to lose them when they die.

1125. Do not the disreputable parents get regular work in factories?—Very frequently, either in the factories or doing work outside. What they do is to get work from the warehouses, and do it at home, lace work.

1126. Do you think that the want of funds has anything to do with not getting up a case before the assizes; you said that before your court the jury very often convict, and then afterwards they do not; do you think that is caused by want of funds to get up the case?—No; I believe that in all cases where there was a likelihood of conviction the police would take up the case. I do not believe want of funds would come into the question.

Lord *Norton.*

1127. You say you never knew of children of decent parents dying suspiciously?—Very seldom.

1128. And you say that of all the deaths coming before you three-fourths are insured?— That I have learnt from the registrar. I personally have not the means of knowledge, but that was the result of an inquiry that I made.

1129. In fact, all those cases must have been cases of parents leading a dissolute sort of life?— Generally so. I mean to say that a very large number of the suffocation cases occur between Saturday night and Sunday morning.

1130. When you use the expression making away with a child, I suppose you mean, generally speaking, rather neglecting the child in a case of illness rather than taking actual steps to hasten the death?—I do not think I made use of that expression. If I had said so it should be in that sense.

1131. It is a very rare thing that a parent should take an actual step to hasten the child's death in your opinion?—I should not say so. I think there are many cases so suspicious that one might naturally infer that the neglect had been intentional. I have in my mind suffocation cases.

1132. But, generally speaking, it would rather be a negative act of neglect than a positive act of hastening the child's death?—In cases I have had there has been very positive evidence of positive neglect, where children have been left in the house in a starving condition for hours together, without any food or anyone to take care of them.

1133. They seldom go a step beyond giving unwholesome food?—I have given a case of a mother feeding a child on bread and milk after being told by two medical men not to do so.

1134. Do you think the greater number of cases of death of children have been those of illegitimate children?—I can hardly answer that question definitely, but I have reason to believe that most of the illegitimate children, or nearly all, are insured.

1135. You do not make the opposite statement that the greater part of those die suspiciously?— No, not the greater part.

F 4   1136. You

Earl of *Selborne.*

1136. You said just now that of the suffocation cases, a great number occured between the Saturday night and Sunday morning; do you attribute that to the parents getting drunk after receiving their wages on the Saturday?—I should infer that; it is very difficult to obtain definite evidence of it; but when I find five or six cases in succession, as I have done, occurring in that way I naturally suspect it.

Lord *Thring.*

1137. Do you think that the better class of our poor look with a feeling of abhorrence at their neighbours who murder, or are supposed to murder, their children?—I think in many cases that would be so, but the respectable poor would scarcely live in the slums where such cases would occur.

1138. But you think a respectable poor person would view the ill-treatment of children with the same horror as he would the ill-treatment of an adult?—I think so.

1139. Do you know whether the better class of poor would object to any check being put upon insurance or any partial prohibition; for instance, if a prohibition were put that they should not be insured within the first year, or three months, or six months?—I think very likely that a proportion would object.

1140. They would look on it as a hardship?—It is very possible they may.

Lord *Poltimore.*

1141. I suppose it is almost impossible to prove a case of suffocation, or what they call overlaying?—On the contrary, it is proved in every case that I have by the medical evidence on a post-mortem examination being made.

1142. But that it is done purposely or accidentally?—I cannot say whether it is done purposely or accidently, but in every case of suspected overlaying I have a post-mortem examination made, and there I have definite evidence of the death being caused by suffocation.

Earl of *Harrowby.*

1143. What is the cost of the burial of a child of this tender age in Nottingham?—I have no personal knowledge of that, but I should say that 1 *l.* or 25 *s.* would be ample for a child under 12 months of age.

1144. And what they get is about 2 *l.* 10 *s.*?—30 *s.*, 2 *l.*, and 2 *l.* 10 *s.* for a young child.

1145. And is it the habit of the working classes to insure in Nottingham, as we have heard in certain cases?—A very large proportion.

1146. It is the habit of the class?—Yes.

1147. And these sad events occur principally in the families of the vicious; it is not merely the very poor?—That is so in cases that I have to deal with.

1148. It is more the degraded poor, it is not mere poverty that induces to this crime?—In cases that I have come across, I cannot speak to those the registrar has come across, where no inquest is held.

1149. Have you thought of any remedy for meeting this evil?—Yes; I have stated, a long time ago my opinion that it might be a good

Earl of *Harrowby*—continued.

thing to prohibit insurance of children under a certain age, say 12 months, and one reason that I have for that is that the expense of burial is so small that I do not think it would be any serious obstacle. I have found that there is generally no difficulty in raising a little money to bury a person with, among friends and neighbours.

1150. To bury a child of that tender age?—Yes.

1151. Under 12 months?—Yes; and over 12 months ago they have a better chance of living.

1152. That would be your remedy to forbid insurance for a child under 12 months?—I should forbid it unless for a very small amount; I should forbid it unless for an amount less than the burial money would be.

1153. Might I repeat the question of the noble Lord just now; do you think the respectable working class would be at all injured in their feelings by a provision of that kind?—I think to a very small degree, where the smaller number must give way to the larger.

Lord *Thring.*

1154. I think you rather reform the answer you made to my question, because it was with that very object I asked you; I asked you whether you do not think that putting any restriction on child insurance for the first year, or even for the first three months, which is the most dangerous time, or the first six months, the better poorer class would not complain as being unfair to themselves?—I answered it in the way I did, because I wished to give a simple answer to your Lordship's question without going any further, but when I am asked further, I give the further answer that I think the insurance on a child of such young age should be limited to an amount which would be under the expense of the burial.

1155. But you would not prohibit it altogether?—Either prohibit it altogether or restrict it in that way so that no profit should be made.

1156. If you prohibit it altogether, we will take the first period, I mean particularly the one when the children mostly die, within the first three months?—Or six months.

1157. I want to know, do you think that if we prohibit altogether the insurance of children within the first six months that would afford any ground for the poor to complain, and, consequently, if you think it would, whether it would be a reasonable ground?—To a very small extent, indeed.

Earl of *Derby.*

1158. Up to what age would you prohibit insurance; up to 12 months?—If prohibited at all, I should draw the line at 12 months, because I think that when a child begins to walk about at 12 months it can sometimes get food for itself, and it has a better chance of living.

1159. I suppose after a certain age it would be able to say what was the matter with it, and then to complain, and not be so easily put out of the way?—That is so.

1160. At what age do you think it would be comparatively safe?—The word "comparatively" is a large one.

1161. Safe as we have been hearing of?—
After

Earl of *Derby*—continued.

After twelve months I should say it would be much safer than before twelve months. After two years it would be much safer than at twelve months.

Earl of *Selborne*

1162. I should like to ask you this question : one must assume, I suppose, that in the great majority of cases in which children's lives are insured they do not die, otherwise it would be no profit to the insurance company ; is not that so ? —I do not know the proportion, my Lord, but I believe the insurance premiums are so high that the companies still make a profit notwithstanding the great amount of infant mortality.

1163. Even in the case of death when the insurance money has to be paid ?—Yes, my Lord, I believe that the amount of money that comes to be insured is not more than 30 or 40 per cent. of the premiums paid.

Lord *Norton.*

1164 Do they not make a great deal by forfeited premiums ?—A large amount.

1165. I suppose that is one of the largest sources of profit ?—I have little doubt it is.

Earl *Beauchamp.*

1166. Do you think the evils of infantile insurance are very much brought about by undue pressure on the part of agents of insurance companies ?—I have very great reason to think so, because I have had cases where the mother has said to me she has had no peace until she has insured her children. The agent has been hardly off the door step.

1167. Would the registration or licensing of agents of insurance companies tend to keep this class of persons more under control ?—It is very difficult to form an opinion upon that, because it is very easy to get registered.

1168. Then there is another point upon which I wish to ask you a question with regard to Nottingham ; do all the funerals take place in the cemeteries ?—Yes, mostly ; we have other burial grounds.

1169. Are there any restrictitions with regard to the days on which interments can be performed ?—There are no interments on Sundays, I believe, but on all other days.

1170. Interments on Sundays are prohibited? —I do not know that they are prohibited, but it is not the practice to inter on Sundays, unless in some very special cases.

1171. When you say it is not the practice, surely in the case of the working classes who would lose a day's work by attending a funeral on any other day, Sunday is the most natural day, unless there is some restriction or prohibition ?—Perhaps that would be so, but the officiating clergy or ministers make it a rule not to inter on Sundays.

1172. Then, practically, there is a prohibition to the use of Sundays ?—When I say there is no prohibition that I know of, there is no legal prohibition.

1173. But there may be bye-laws ?—I believe there is no bye-law to that effect ; I believe it is a practice.

1174. I did not quite understand what happened in cases when a certificate is refused by the medical man and it is then reported to you ; how

(142.)

Earl *Beauchamp*—continued.

is the money paid ?—The case is this, that before the child can be buried they have to get a certificate.

1175. I am not talking about the burial, but I am talking of claiming the insurance money ?— They have to get a certificate from the registrar, and in order to do that the case must be reported to him. If there is no doctor's certificate he reports the case to me for investigation, and then I either hold an inquest, if it is a suspicious case, or if I see no reasonable suspicion I send a notice to him that I do not consider an inquest necessary, thereupon he registers the death, and gives a copy of his certificate upon which the insurance money is obtained.

1176. Who certifies the cause of death ?— Practically it is uncertified.

1177. But the law provides that no certificate shall be granted unless the cause of death shall be previously entered on the register of deaths, on the certificate of the coroner or registered medical practitioner who attended such deceased child during its last illness ?—The provision is made for a death being registered without a medical certificate, or the registrar might register it on the coroner stating he does not think it a case requiring an inquest.

1178. The cause of death must be certified ?— The alleged cause. It is not what is called a certified cause of death ; it is the cause that one can best get at.

1179. Alleged by whom ?—The coroner makes his preliminary investigation, and if he is satisfied that it is a natural death he does not hold an inquest, and informs the registrar what he believes to be the cause of death. For instance a weakly delicate child that has suffered from convulsions since birth.

1180. Supposing he does not certify that and he is not satisfied ?—Then he will hold an inquest, then there is a certificate giving the verdict of the jury.

1181. If the verdict of the jury is unsatisfactory, say, wilful murder, is the insurance money claimed ?—Probably it would not be paid ; it would be very likely to be claimed, but in such a case as that I think the insurance company would scarcely dare to pay it.

1182. Do you think it would be possible by strengthening the provisions of the law in respect of the certificate to obviate the difficulties of which you have spoken ?—I doubt whether it would where the cause of death is fully stated.

1183. Where the cause of death is fully certified there is no difficulty, but in cases where the cause of death is not fully certified or improperly certified ?—I have in my mind cases of medical men giving certificates of death from marasmus, which is a very common cause of death, meaning consumption of the bowels ; but there is no evidence brought to the medical man's mind as to how that consumption of the bowels has been brought about. Still, if he does not actually see suspicious circumstances, he does not refer the case to the coroner.

1184. That I understand ; when he does see suspicious circumstances, and suppose he does not certify, I want to know how the money reaches the hand of the parent ?—It cannot then reach the hands of the parent until the case has

G   been

Earl *Beauchamp*—continued.

been returned to the coroner, and either an inquest held, or he has certified himself that one is unnecessary.

Chairman.

1185. I have only one question to ask you; have you ever in your coroner's experience, had any assistance volunteered by any of these

Chairman—continued.

insurance agents in suspicious cases, or in other cases?—Never. I have always found them ready to assist the people to get the insurance money.

1186. To what do you attribute that?—I think it is a desire to obtain popularity amongst the classes who are likely to insure.

The Witness is directed to withdraw.

MR. HENRY WILCOCKS HOOPER is called in; and Examined, as follows:

Chairman.

1187. YOU are a solicitor by profession?—I am.

1188. You are now coroner for the city of Exeter?—I am.

1189. I think you state that you have been coroner for 37 years?—I have been coroner of the city of Exeter for 37 years.

1190. During that time how many inquests do you say you have held?—The average number I should say was 60, save and except in the year 1887, when I held an inquest on the Exeter Theatre fire, I do not take that into account, but generally speaking, it is about 60 a-year.

1191. So that you have had upwards of 2,000 inquests?—Upwards of 2,000.

1192. Have many of these inquests been on children?—A very large number.

1193. You could not tell from your notes or recollection what proportion?—No, I cannot.

1194. Has the proportion of these inquests on child cases increased or diminished during that time?—It has increased undoubtedly.

1195. Do you think the number of child cases has increased together with the increase of the practice of child insurance in Exeter?—I do, undoubtedly.

1196. You have seen a relation between the two things?—I have.

1197. That as child insurance has increased the number of child cases brought before you have increased?—Yes.

1198. Have you formed an opinion on the effect of child-life insurance on children's lives? -I have.

1199. What is that opinion?—An unfavourable one.

1200. A very unfavourable one?—A very unfavourable one.

1201. Do you think that child-life insurance is an incentive to neglect?—I do, I think it is an incentive to cruel neglect, and what is, morally speaking, murder.

1202. What were the features of the cases that came before you that first made you of this opinion?—There were cases of inanition, atrophy, marasmus, and improper feeding.

1203. Were there any other features in these cases that struck you, not merely as regards the nature of the disease, but as regards the circumstances of the case?—Yes, my Lord, there were general carelessness and the neglect to send for a doctor until the child was *in extremis*, and in very many instances not carrying out his instructions.

1204. These were in the cases of insured children?—Many of them. I cannot say to what extent.

Chairman—continued.

1205. Would you say the majority of them? —I can hardly say that, but in a large number of cases.

1206. In a very large number?—I think so.

1207. Were you always in the habit of inquiring whether a child was insured or not?— No; I have not been until the last few years, when the subject came prominently before the public.

1208. In consequence of the unfavourable impression made on your mind by the cases of these neglected children, you did begin some years ago to inquire in each case whether a child was insured?—I did.

1209. Had you anything for that but the parents' word?—No, nothing.

1210. And you were obliged to take the parents' word?—The evidence of the parents is given on oath, and I thought that my duty ended there. Could it be proved that the parents were stating that which was false they were liable to be indicted for perjury.

1211. It would be nobody's business in particular in the case of an inquest to come forward and prove that the parents' evidence on this point was false?—No, not at all.

1212. There is no prosecutor, properly speaking, at an inquest?—No.

1213. There is no one specially concerned in proving that the parent has told you a lie?— No one that I can see.

1214. You took, then, the parents' word?—I did.

1215. What proportion of the children can you say in these child cases that came before you were cases in which the child was admittedly insured?—I can scarcely answer that. I have taken out a number from February 1888 down to May 1890, and they amount to about 44, and in about half those cases I should say that the children were insured. I always ask the question now in every case, whether the child's life is insured.

1216. You are speaking now of the last few years since February 1888?—I am.

1217. Then it appears that, roughly speaking, in about one half of these cases that came before you the parents admitted having insured the child?—Yes.

1218. But as regards the other half, you could not be quite certain that when they denied it they were saying the truth?—I could not say that; I assumed they were speaking the truth under oath.

1219. Do you think you get all the cases of insured

Chairman—continued.

insured children before you that have had any suspicious circumstances?—No, I do not think so.

1220. Could you give us anything that would tend to show that?—The difficulty is in bringing home criminal neglect to the parties.

1221. Do you know what the opinions of medical men in your city are on the practice; are you a medical man yourself?—I am a solicitor of 50 years' standing.

1222. Is it, generally speaking, their opinion?—I think I may say it is unanimously in the city of Exeter the opinion of the medical profession.

1223. To your knowledge and the best of your belief it is unanimous?—I have had a long experience and that is my opinion.

1224. Did you ever ascertain the opinion of other coroners besides yourself on this subject?—Yes, I have. I have solicited the opinion of the coroners of the county of Devon, the whole of whom from my long experienc in that office I am well and personally acquainted with, and I should be quite ready to hand in these notes to your Lordship if you think it is a proper course for me to do so. I would mention first the opinion of the coroner of the borough of Barnstaple. He says, "I consider policies on young children's lives are indirect incentives to murder." Then the opinion of Mr. Vaughan, the coroner for the borough of Devonport, is, "I believe, speaking generally, the system at present in use with the canvassers, &c., is a very bad one and much abused, and I have no doubt tends with other causes to the destruction of infant life." Then I have the opinion of Mr. Clark, the coroner for the county borough of Plymouth. I may say that the late coroner for the borough of Plymouth died about 12 months ago, and the present coroner says, "The short experience I have had convinces me that you are quite correct in stating that the practice of insuring the lives of very young children tends to the destruction of infant life." That is as regards the boroughs of Barnstaple, Devonport, and Plymouth. Then the opinion of the coroner for the Okehampton district of Devon, Mr. Burd, is, "I look upon the system as tempting and dangerous, and in many cases to be the moving cause to murder. In one portion of my district, and that a sparsely populated one, I think the practice prevails extensively, and in same proportion I find inquests are necessary on infant children." Then Mr. Burrow, the coroner for the Crediton district of the county of Devon says: "As to the practice of insuring the lives of very young children tending to the destruction of infant life, I quite agree with you." The opinion of Mr. Hacker, coroner for the Totnes district of Devon is. "My opinion, as coroner, from what I have seen of the working of the present law as to infant insurance is the same as, I believe, is the opinion of most coroners, that it constitutes a great evil." Then Mr. Cox, the deputy coroner for the Honiton district of Devon, whose father is in a state of illness, and he takes his business for him, expresses their entire agreement with these views. The like from Mr. Rodd, the coroner for the Stoke Dameral district of Devon.

1225. Do you commit all cases for trial where
(142.)

Chairman—continued.

you are morally certain that there have been cases of wilful neglect?—No, my Lord, I do not, not when only morally satisfied. I require to be legally satisfied, as far as I can, that there is a probability of obtaining a conviction, and I am sorry to say that is very difficult at times to obtain, looking at the general view taken by Hei Majesty's judges on infanticide. When there are cases which are very flagrant, of which I have had one or two before me of a serious nature, I have committed, and one was a question of ill-treatment of a child of a very brutal character which came before Mr. Justice Day, and where he sentenced the woman to 15 years' penal servitude; and the man, as an accessory before the fact, to five years' penal servitude. That was about five years ago.

1226. Was that a case of insurance?—I am not sure. Mr. Justice Day knows the case very well; it happened to be tried before him.

1227. I have no farther question to ask you except this: this matter pressed itself so much on your mind that you voluntarily wrote to me to say you would give evidence?—Yes.

1228. You were not solicited by anyone else?—No, I have taken a very strong view of the case for four or five years since the matter has more particularly engrossed the public attention, and it is from that time to the present that I have made it a point in all inquests I hold to inquire and take some particulars as far as I can as to whether the lives are insured or not.

Earl of *Derby.*

1229. Do you think the majority of the cases where deaths of childen occur under suspicious circumstances are cases where the child is not above 12 months old?—Yes; I think it is under 12 months; I have taken them out: 14 days 6 days, 11 months, 11 weeks, 6 months, 6 weeks, 4 months, and so on. There are 30 or 40 of them within the last few years, and out of 44 there are 38 under a year

Lord *Clifford.*

1230. Do you many applications from the registrars of births and deaths for your certificate in cases in which the medical men have refused to give a certificate?—I do not get any application from the registrars themselves. They only report to me cases which they are to do by order of the Registrar General. Others report cases to me which when they get the notice of death they do not think they are able to register, but I get no application for certificates from the registrar. I have never had an application.

1231. As I understand the registrar cannot register the death unless he has a certificate?—He must have a certificate from me of the result of the inquest.

1232. You give no certificates to the effect that you have examined the case and think it unnecessary to hold an inquest?—That is prior to an inquest. I have given such a certificate.

1233. Where a registrar writes without your actually holding an inquest or getting the verdict of a jury, you do not give certificates?—No, I do not.

Lord *Kinnaird.*

1234. Do the insurance company pay at any age, say a few days old?—I believe they insure them as soon as they are born, some of the offices,

G 2   and

Lord *Kinnaird*—continued.

and I am given to understand, although I do not know it of my own knowledge, that they insure in one, two, and three offices.

Lord *Norton.*

1235. Do you think if the insurable sum paid was smaller, the temptation would cease?—I do not know; I do not think it would.

1236. Do you think the limit now fixed by law is more than the burial expenses?—Unquestionably, I should say so.

1237. Very considerably more?— I should say so.

1238. Even including medical expenses?—I cannot answer that question.

1239. Have you in your mind any limit that you think would be a proper limit to prevent any temptation to neglect a child?—No, I cannot say that I have.

1240. What is your idea of the smallest possible expense of the child's funeral at the age of a few months, or one year?—I should think a pound ought to cover it.

1241. Do you think if the insurable sum was limited to 1 *l.* there would be no temptation to neglect the child?—I think there would be much less temptation than there is at present.

1242. You think there would still be some?—Yes.

Lord *Thring.*

1243. What remedy do you suggest?—I can hardly suggest any. I know the feeling of the coroners of the whole county is that no life ought to be insured under six or seven years. That is a very strong feeling in the West of England.

1244. Do you not think that would produce also a very strong feeling amongst the honest poor?— I do not quite understand your question.

1245. Do you not think that if insurances under six or seven years were prohibited, that prohibition would produce a very strong feeling of wrong amongst the honest poor?—I think it is possible it would irritate them.

1246. Would it not reasonably irritate them that they should be prevented from insuring their children?—Possibly it might. The insurance at present is indiscriminate: it is difficult to discriminate between the honest poor and the other side of the question.

1247. Is not that a difficulty in all legislation?—Yes, I have no doubt it is; I do not wish in any way to say anything to the prejudice of the honest poor. I am one of those who would support them by all means.

1248. I only want to know whether it is not your opinion that a prohibition of that sort would justly cause a great feeling of irritation amongst the honest poor?—I think, possibly, it is very likely to do so.

Lord *Poltimore.*

1249. Do the more respectable members of the working class insure their children as much as the very dissipated and dissolute class?—I think not. I think the more dissipated are a majority of insurers; that is my impression.

1250. Can you form any opinion as to whether most of the suspicious cases are those of legitimate or illegitimate children?—No, I cannot answer that question.

Earl of *Harrowby.*

1251. You do not think you can say generally of the Exeter working people that they all insure their children's lives?—Not all of them.

1252. It is not the habit of the class?—There is a very large number, your Lordship possibly knows that there are offices that have certain canvassers, and that is the root of the evil, in my opinion. They go from door to door solicit. ing insurances, and pointing out the advantages in cases of death. Then as soon as insured, I am sorry to say, I think there is great neglect used, and there is not that care and supervision over them which is possible and right, and which I think there should be.

1253. About these terrible cases, they occur principally I think in your opinion, amongst the most dissipated part, of the most poverty-stricken working people?—I think so, more especially amongst drunkards.

1254. You are not bringing it as a general accusation against the working people?—I wish that to be distinctly understood.

Earl *Beauchamp.*

1255. Have you any opinion in your own mind as to the proportion between the honest poor and the dissolute poor?—I think the dissolute poor are in a large minority.

1256. You think, in order to restrain a small minority of a small minority, it is worth while to adopt legislation which would irritate the whole of the honest poor?—That is not a question for me to say; that is a matter for Parliament.

Chairman.

1257. As you have been asked that question, which do you think is most important, not to irritate the working classes or to prevent child murder?—I think child murder should be put down with a very strong hand.

1258. Do you really think that if the working classes had it made perfectly clear to them how much of child murder goes on under this system they would not submit to a certain amount of restriction in order to prevent it?—I think they would.

1259. A reasonable and right-minded man would see there was some reason for restraining him, though he might not need it, because the same restriction might apply to others who did greatly need it?—Yes.

The Witness is directed to withdraw.

The *Chairman* reads the following letter to the Secretary of State for the Home Department: " Sir, I have the honour to inform you that at the conclusion of the inquest held before me on the 9th inst. on the bodies of Sidney Bolton, William Sutton, and Elizabeth Jane Frost, which had previously been exhumed at St. Paul's, Deptford, Kent, the jury added to their verdict the following rider: ' The jury are of opinion that the facilities given by the loose system of life insurance practice by some companies is an incentive to wilful murder for the sake of the insurance money,' and they desire me to forward this expression of opinion to you, in the hope that the Government may initiate some

1 *July* 1890.

some legislation to remedy this evil. I am, Sir, your obedient servant (signed) *Edward N. Wood*, Deputy Coroner for London, Greenwich Division.'

The *Chairman* also read a second case sent to him by the clerk to the borough justices of Leicester, containing the report of a trial of a woman before magistrates for ill-treating her child, aged five years, when the Bench gave the following decision : " The Bench have no hesitation at all in convicting you upon the evidence given of gross cruelty and neglect of this child. It appears to the Bench precisely one of those cases which the Act was intended to meet. The poor little child should have looked to you for protection, but instead of that it received nothing but brutal ill-usage. The fact of the child's life having been insured for 5 *l.* throws a very grave doubt on the matter as to whether you were not guilty in intent of a very serious crime. It is perfectly clear that a woman like you, brutally neglecting this child, would have no idea of insuring its life except for the purpose of obtaining a premium on its death. We hear that three of your children are already dead, and that a fourth is in Dr. Barnardo's Home, whilst now you are brought here for treating the fifth child in this brutal manner. It is really difficult to use moderate language in describing a case like this. You will go to prison for three months with hard labour."

Ordered,—That this Committee be adjourned to Friday next, at Twelve o'clock.

Die Veneris, 4° Julii 1890.

LORDS PRESENT:

Earl of DERBY.	LORD BISHOP OF PETERBOROUGH.
Earl SPENCER.	LORD BISHOP OF RIPON.
Earl of HARROWBY.	Lord POLTIMORE.
Earl BEAUCHAMP.	Lord THRING.
Earl of SELBORNE.	

THE RIGHT REV. THE LORD BISHOP OF PETERBOROUGH, IN THE CHAIR.

THE *Chairman* reads the following extract to the Committee, from " The Sixty-First Annual Report of the General Hospital and Dispensary for Sick Children, Pendlebury and Gartside-street, Manchester, 1890 ": " We again feel bound to record our experience of the old subject of infant insurance, believing that in so doing we may assist in calling attention to the subject. Out of the 251 children whose deaths took place, 184 had been insured, though at the time of death only 162 were 'in benefit.' The average amount received by the friends for each child was 3 *l.* 4 *s.* 7¾ *d.*, a total sum of 523 *l.* 13 *s.* One record is interesting. In one family there had been five children, four are dead, and one is now living. The first died at 11 months, the friends received 4 *l.* in money, and 3 *s.* in drink ; the second died at 11 months, 4 *l.* and 3 *s.* in drink were received ; the third died at 15 months, 4 *l.* and 3 *s.* in drink were received ; the fourth died at one year and nine months, and 5 *l.* and 3 *s.* in drink were received. During a considerable part of this period the husband was out of work. Now, while we have no warrant for putting the worst construction on these facts, we cannot but feel that the influence of the worst form of " death clubs " is wholly bad, and we trust that further restrictive legislation will be enacted. In making these observations we must make it clear that our remarks principally apply to those clubs which insure infants a few hours old, and which disgrace themselves by giving a portion of the benefit money in drink."

[The same is directed to be recorded *quantum valeat* on the Minutes.

CAPTAIN LINDSAY ROBERT BURNETT, is called in ; and Examined, as follows :

Chairman.

1260. YOU were lately Captain in the 95th Regiment ?—I was.

1261. And you are now chief constable of Rotherham ?—I am.

1262. How long have you held that position ? —For nearly three years.

1263. Previously you were chief constable of Wolverhampton ?—I was acting chief constable of Wolverhampton.

1264. What is the population now under your care ?—Approximately 50,000.

1265. In the discharge of your duties as chief constable has your attention been called to the subject of child life insurance ?—It has.

1266. For how long ?—More especially for the last 18 months or so.

1267. What opinion have you formed upon the effect of this practice of child insurance upon a child's life ?—I have formed a very strong opinion ; I formed the opinion that it is an incentive to gross neglect, and very often an

(142.)

Chairman—continued.

incentive to death being compassed ; I have formed the strongest possible opinion to that effect.

1268. What is the character of the population under your charge ?—By far the larger portion of them are miners ; there are a considerable number also of ironworkers, brassworkers, potters, glassblowers, and canal loafers ; it is a maritime population a good deal.

1269. Are those labourers generally in receipt of good wages ?—The wages are particularly good at present ; they have been very fair for some time past.

1270. Among what class have you noticed the bad effects of this practice of child insurance ?—Among the dregs of each of these classes, the residuum of the whole lot.

1271. Is there any considerable amount of them ?—Not numerically, I should think ; perhaps you might say, approximately, a thousand of them out of about 50,000. I only say 1,000

G 4

quite

Chairman—continued.

quite roughly; I could not be positive as to that.

1272. Is it your opinion that those cases occur largely among illegitimate children?—I have had only one case brought to my notice of the insurance of an illegitimate child; the others have all been children of married people, or people passing as married.

1273. You do not think the question of marriage or illegitimacy has much to do with those evil cases?—No, I do not think so.

1274. What do you think it is?—I think it is simply callousness and selfishness, and the desire for gain.

1275. Have you, in the discharge of your duties, brought any of those cases to justice?—I have, several

1276. Have you had any recent cases?—I had one yesterday.

1277. Would you give the Committee some particulars of that case?—If you will allow me to take them from my note book, they were as follows: A man and his wife, Samuel and Ann Price; the man was a miner, and had six children; the eldest girl, Mary Ann, was 12 years of age, Lydia was 10 years of age, Caroline was seven; John, six; David, three; and George, 15 months. From information received on 24th of last month, I instructed the police surgeon and a detective serjeant to visit the house occupied by those people, and, from their verbal report to me, I obtained the parents' arrest upon a warrant, and had the six children removed to the workhouse. The doctor's report and the police serjeant's report as to the nature of the house, and the surroundings of the children, were very strong indeed; it could not be stronger. I called the next morning, myself, at the workhouse, and saw the children; they were all in a state of utter misery, semi-starved; the youngest child, George, was 15 months' old, and he was supposed to be dying; he was in a moribund condition that day. Subsequently, my detective serjeant, on searching the house, found the insurance policies for all the six children, who were insured in the " Pearl " Insurance Office on the 7th August 1889; those policies were all current at the present time. We also found a fresh insurance upon the life of this infant, George, of 15 months; a second insurance. I should say that, under the six insurances effected in August last, the children were insured in their proper Christian names, but in the surname of Davis, not the parents' proper name; but under the second insurance, effected on the 17th of last June, the child was insured in its proper name of George Price; this insurance was effected in the London, Edinburgh, and Glasgow Office. The condition of the child was so bad that I had the child photographed and weighed.

1278. This youngest child was, in fact, insured in three societies, was it not?—I shall prove that he was insured in three societies; I have proved two already; the third came out in the subsequent evidence. Then, speaking of the state of the child, he was supposed by the doctor not likely to survive the night, and the mother

Chairman—continued.

volunteered the information that the child was dying from consumption; that the child took food, but could not thrive upon it; the child has since then been fed in the workhouse, and has gained, in the short space of eight days, 1¾ lbs. in weight; he was weighed again yesterday. I have brought with me the photograph of the child, taken a week before the insurance, in case your Lordships should like to see it, as a curiosity. I may say that the normal weight of a child of that age should be from 19 to 21 lbs. instead of from 10 to 11 lbs.; it weighed 11 lbs. and some odd ounces in its clothes, and with a poultice on its head; in a flannel, a jacket, a night-gown, and a poultice. The children were all in such a state of vermin that the workhouse authorities found it necessary to shave their heads, and poultice them and isolate them. The parents were remanded, at my request, until yesterday, and, having ascertained that the children were insured, I subpœnaed both the agents of those two insurance offices, the " Pearl " and the " London, Edinburgh, and Glasgow Office," as witnesses for the prosecution. During the course of the proceedings a medical certificate was handed to me. signed by a doctor in the town, that the agent for the Pearl Office was ill or well, to attend. He did not give any specific disease that he is suffering from; but the other man, whose name was William Ashmore, attended, and, in cross-examination, he admitted he had insured this child, George Price, on the 17th of last month. He was asked by me his reason for going there; to endeavour to ascertain whether he had been sent for by the parents, and, in reply, he said he was going down the yard collecting from other houses, and that he went into the house occupied by the Prices because this same child was in arrears upon a third insurance (which was then brought to light) effected in his office, to the amount of 1 s. 3 d., and that insurance would expire on the 24th of last June, or seven days after the time he visited; so that the time he visited, when the child was moribund, the child was insured in this third office, and the reason he went to the house was that he went to renew the insurance or to effect a fresh one. I asked him if he had a medical examination before insuring the life; he said, No; that it was only in cases where the amount insured for exceeded 10 l. that they made a medical examination; otherwise they never did. I then asked if he noticed the condition of the child at the time he made the entry, and he said, No, he did not notice whether the child was ill or well, he took the mother's word for it; he presumed the child he saw upon the mother's knee was the child he insured. I then pressed him whether he got any per-centage from effecting these insurances; he hesitated considerably; he said, " Must I answer the question? " I said, he must. He then admitted that in those houses where the payment of a penny a week had commenced, and the weekly premiums had been paid for 12 weeks, he received a shilling, and that, therefore, it was his interest to effect a third insurance upon the child to get another shilling; the result of the case was that the father and mother were committed to gaol for three months' hard labour.

1279. Upon

Lord *Thring.*

1279. Upon the charge of neglecting their children?—Yes, upon the charge of neglecting their children. The child is now so much improved that I thought it was no use keeping the parents for the sessions.

Chairman.

1280. What was the total amount payable upon the death of those children?—So far as I could calculate it, I made it out to be 28 *l.* 17 *s.*, and that I believe to be correct, within a shilling or two.

1281. How much a week did the parents pay to obtain that sum?—Sevenpence.

1282. In consideration of the payment of 7 *d.* a week they could receive a sum of 28 *l.* 17 *s.*?—Yes; the eldest child's life would be worth about 9 *l.* 7 *s.*, and so on down to the youngest life, about 2 *l.* 15 *s.*

1283. Sevenpence a week would be 2 *s.* 4 *d.* a month?—Yes.

1284. The child comes into benefit at the end of three months?—Yes, it comes into benefit partially at the end of three months.

1285. Therefore, for the sum of 7 *s.* expended by the parent, he might obtain, if the children died, 28 *l.* 17 *s.*?—That is so.

Earl of *Selborne.*

1286. With reference to the premium, what was the aggregate premium upon the lives of all the children?—Sevenpence a week.

Chairman.

1287. If all the children had died the parent would have received 28 *l.* 17 *s.*, and he need have paid only 7 *s.* for all that sum?—That might be the case possibly, but in this case it would have been more because the children were insured in August last. In this case it would have been from 12 *s.* to 14 *s.*

1288. What was the character of this man?—He was a worthless idle man; when he chose to work he could get from 20 *s.* to 25 *s.* a week; he would work for two or three days and then he would drink the proceeds.

1289. Were the children produced in court during this inquiry?—Two of them were produced in court. I was informed by a police inspector, when the case was resumed, that the mother had been seen threatening the two children; during adjournment she was in the dock and the children were in the court.

1290. Has your bench of magistrates ever expressed an opinion as to this system of child life insurance?—Yes, they have always expressed their opinion strongly when I brought the matter before them.

1291. Reverting to this particular case, if the insurance agent had exercised anything like proper care or made proper inquiries, he could no doubt have ascertained the condition of these children?—He must have seen it.

1292. Do the parents conceal from the police the fact that a child is insured?—I have never had any information from them of the fact.

1293. How do you get at the fact of insurance?—By chance purely; in this case we found the actual policies; sometimes we get information and trace them up, but we have no actual means of getting at it.

(142.)

Chairman—continued.

1294. It was by searching the house in this case that the fact of insurance was discovered?—Yes.

1295. If the police had not searched the house you would have known nothing about the fact of the insurance?—No.

1296. The parents would have given no information about it?—They would probably, or possibly at all events, have denied it.

1297. Do you think it is desirable that there should be some process of registration by which you could know the fact of insurance?—I think so.

1298. Would you have such registration enforced by law?—Certainly. I think the sanitary and parochial authorities should also have access to the same register as well as the police.

1299. You think every insurance society should be bound to place in some public register the name of every child insured?—I do.

1300. And that the register should be accessible to the public authorities?—Yes.

1301. Of course that would have to be enforced by a penalty?—Yes, it would have to be enforced by a penalty. My police surgeon, Dr. Cobban, has drawn up a suggestion for the certificate, of which I have a copy with me.

1302. Will you lay it before the Committee?—This is the idea of what should be the form of certificate: first of all, in the first column there would be the number on the register, then the child's Christian name, and then the date and place of birth, and then the parents' names, with an asterisk under that stating whether the child was illegitimate or not, in which case then stating the mother's name; then the office in which the child is insured, and the amount of insurance and premium; the provisions as to benefit, how much after each three months, then the signature and address of the agent issuing the policy. This should be countersigned by the registrar of births and deaths, or whoever might be the authority constituted to keep the register; it also should have in the body of it the medical certificate from a qualified medical practitioner stating that he had examined the child, and whether the child in question was well nourished and healthy and free from organic disease; or on the other hand, that it was an unhealthy child suffering from any hereditary or other disorder, in which case the insurance officer would be justified in taking the child's life only at an increased premium. With a memorandum to the effect that, "When the insurance has been effected, this form, duly filled up, must be returned by the person effecting the insurance to the registrar who has granted the same for entry, then to be returned to insurer. In case of death, the person registering the death must produce this certificate to the registrar, without which a duplicate certificate for insurance purposes will in no case be granted. Persons using the ordinary certificate of death, or insurance companies accepting the same as a guarantee for payment of insurance money, render themselves liable to a penalty not exceeding *l.*," as may be settled.

1303. You have spoken of insurance agents, do you find that there are many of those insu-

H   rance

Chairman—continued.

rance agents about?—A great many; there is great competition amongst them.

1304. The House of Commons in their Report state this, "That the business of these insurance societies is highly competitive;" do you agree with that?—They are immensely competitive.

1305. An agent who was very particularly careful about his cases would know that if he rejected a case it would be taken by some other agent?—The case would be snapped up at once. I have been informed that the competition is carried on to this extent, that the monthly nurses and midwives who attend women in this class of life are actually in the employment of these agents, to give them notice of the birth of children, and that a child is actually insured before it is many hours in the world, that is, from a doctor's statement to me; it is not within my own knowledge.

1306. At any rate, from your knowledge the business of these agents is highly competitive?—It is highly competitive.

1307. Have you ever received any assistance from any insurance agent in any cases of neglect?—Never.

1308. Although it would be presumably to the interest of insurance societies that death should not occur?—Upon the face of it it ought to be so, but I doubt whether it would be so.

1309. Notwithstanding that, the insurance agents never assist you to trace out those cases?—Never.

1310. You think, I presume, that it would not be to their interest to help you?—No, the effect of it would be to take the business out of their office and to take the grist to the other mill, as it were.

1311. Even supposing the societies were careful, the only result of that would be that doubtful cases would go to other societies who would be less careful?—Yes.

1312. A society would get a bad name and would have less business if it disputed its policies?—Undoubtedly it would.

1313. You stated that you had summoned one of those agents to the police office yourself?—Yes; that is the case I mentioned.

1314. One of them produced a medical certificate that he could not attend; the other gave, you considered, unsatisfactory and reluctant evidence?—He gave reluctant evidence, but I considered it satisfactory evidence because I got what I wanted out of him.

1315. But he gave reluctant evidence, you say?—Yes, he gave evidence very reluctantly; he came without his books, although he had been warned to bring them, and they had to be sent for.

1316. Do you consider that all cases of cruelty to insured children come under your knowledge?—No; a small percentage only, I should imagine.

1317. Have you any remedy to suggest for the evils of which you have spoken so strongly?—I suggest the remedy of registration; it would be very hard on the deserving struggling and thrifty poor to take away insurance from them altogether, I think.

1318. But I suppose you think that the danger

Chairman—continued.

arises from the parent having a certain margin to spend over and above what the legitimate funeral expenses would be?—Certainly, I do.

1319. Do not you think that as long as that profit by death exists, there will always be to the baser sort a temptation to criminal neglect in those cases?—Always, no doubt; and I think that, in many cases, if the child were insured, and the premium were paid on the death, the parents would not inform the parish authorities, they would get the whole money, and the child would be buried by the parish as like as not; it would be quite probable.

1320. There is no compulsion upon the parent to bury?—No; if the parent is a pauper and cannot bury, the parochial authorities are bound to bury the child.

1321. What remedy have the parochial authorities; can they proceed against the parents?—If the parent is a pauper they have no remedy whatever; I think it would be a very difficult thing to levy an execution upon them.

1322. And probably if they did, the execution would produce very little?—Very little or nothing, judging by the executions that we get in rate cases.

1323. The most certain way in which the evil could be dealt with would be by preventing the insurer by some mode or other from deriving any profit by the death of children?—Certainly.

1324. What is your opinion of the original law respecting insurance laid down in the Statute of George III., "That there should be no gambling on death"; is that a sound principle?—Certainly.

1325. Do you see any reason why a working man should have a privilege in that respect which others have not?—He has not the command of money that others have; most of those people live from hand to mouth. They get 1 *l.* a week or 25 *s.* and have to live upon it; they have to struggle very hard.

1326. Do you think this low class of people (for instance, the loafers and so on) would be very much afraid of coming on the rates and being pauperised?—Not the slightest; they come on and they go off again.

1327. They have no sense of shame or degradation?—Not a bit.

1328. The dread of their going on the rates would not operate on their minds at all?—They utterly neglect that altogether; it would not in any way affect them.

1329. Do you know, as a matter of fact, how the respectable poor are supplied with medical attendance; there are sick clubs, I suppose, in Rotherham?—There are many sick clubs; the men who belong to those sick clubs, and keep up their contributions, do not suffer much when they are on the sick list, because they get an allowance for some time.

1330. Do they get the medical attendance for themselves and their children?—Yes, for themselves and their children, in most cases.

1331. Respectable working men can secure medical attendance by belonging to one of those clubs for a small sum?—Yes.

1332. And that medical attendance would be

given

Chairman—continued.

given in every case of a child's sickness?—In every case of sickness in the family.

1333. A man could secure that attendance without having to resort to a death insurance to pay the doctor?—He could. I cannot tell you what amount the club subscription would be, but I can ascertain that. These are the policies, and these are the account books in the Price case to show that the premiums are paid (*handing in the same*).

Earl of *Derby*.

1334. In your experience are not the majority of cases where death is caused by neglect or cruelty, cases of children under the ages of 12 months?—I should be far more inclined to say under the age of two years; I have had many cases of children verging on two years. I should say certainly the majority of them would be under two years.

1335. Then if insurance were prohibited under the age of two years, that would considerably diminish the inducement you have stated to exist?—It would diminish it to some extent, no doubt, but then children vary so much, especially among the poor; some of the children of three or four years old are mere infants, they cannot speak or defend themselves.

1336. You do not think that would be a sufficient remedy?—I do not.

1337. You would have complete publicity by registering the names of all the children insured?—I would.

1338. Who would keep the register?—Some authority should be constituted for the purpose. I should suggest the parochial authority; not the police, certainly.

Earl *Spencer*.

1339. With reference to registration, would you have on the register the lapses that occur entered, as well as the fact of insurance?—Yes, I think it would be necessary to do so, because if the child died, then the premiums would have either to be shown to be paid or the office would not pay the policy.

1340. Are there a good many lapses?—The lapses are what pay the offices so much.

1341. It would complicate the register too much, would it not?—I do not think it would.

1342. You think it would be hard upon the deserving poor to do away with insurance?—I think it would, upon many.

1343. It is the practice of the deserving poor to insure largely?—It is the practice largely, I think.

1344. What do they insure for?—Mainly for the burial expenses; and then there is a large desire for mourning, besides the expenses of the illness, and so on.

1345. Have you known many cases of neglect in Rotherham by parents, when the children were not insured?—Frequently.

1346. I suppose there is considerable inducement for parents who do not care for their children to neglect them, in order to get relieved of the responsibility of keeping them?—I have had as many cases of uninsured children neglected as of insured. I had a case yesterday of

(142.)

the same nature as that which I just mentioned; but there the children were not insured.

1347. You say you have heard of midwives acting as agents for the insurance agent?—I have heard so from a parish doctor.

1348. You have not heard that direct?—No; it is only hearsay.

Earl of *Selborne*.

1349. Are there many of those insurance societies at Rotherham?—Yes, a considerable number; I cannot tell you how many; I know certainly of the existence of five or six of them.

1350. Do those offices insure any other class of lives except these young lives?—Some do. Some of the offices are of a very different character from others, and bear a different reputation.

1351. Do you say they get their chief profit from the lapse of policies?—They get a very large portion of their profit from lapsed policies; the parents pay for a few weeks, then they get into arrears and the policy drops, then they effect it again and perhaps drop it again.

Lord Bishop of *Ripon*.

1352. You mentioned the idea of registration, was that with a view of letting the parish authorities know that an insurance policy existed?—For the purpose of letting not only the parish authority, but every authority who could be interested in the matter, the parish, the sanitary authority, and the police.

Lord *Thring*.

1353. Why do you think that your system of registration would stop murder?—Because it would bring light to bear upon it; we should know what children were insured, and if the parents were in a poor and struggling position we should have power to deal with them.

1354. Why should you suspect them if you say the uninsured children are neglected quite as much as the insured?—I do not think they are starved so much as the insured children, the cruelty cases amongst the uninsured are more cases of beating and burning than of starvation.

1355. You think the police would have the opportunity of watching these insurance cases?—We know the character of the people. Police who are well looked after ought to know the character of most of the loafing fellows in the town; and if their children were insured we should be able to watch them to a certain extent.

1356. You think you would be able to detect the crime?—In a great many cases where we cannot at present.

1357. The Committee have been told that these young children under six months old can be killed by sour milk?—They can be killed in a great number of ways that we cannot trace, such for instance as overlaying, nobody can trace those cases.

1358. Do you approve of the form of certificate which your surgeon gave?—I do.

1359. You propose to have a medical certificate

H 2

Lord *Thring*—continued.

cate that the child is in good health?—Or otherwise.

1360. Who would pay for that?—The long-suffering ratepayer, I suppose; I do not know who else would.

1361. You propose that the expenses of registration, including the expense of the medical certificate, should be at the expense of the parish?—I do not know who else would pay for it; I was not thinking of the money at the time.

1362. But it is a material question, because if the registration expenses are not payable by the parish, that would be absolutely prohibitory upon it?—The insurance societies would not pay the doctor's fee; you could not make them pay.

1363. The insurers could not pay it?—The insurers could not pay it.

1364. Therefore your plan really and truly depends upon the question of whether or not the ratepayers, in other words the parish, could pay for the registration?—Yes, in the same way as vaccination is kept up.

1365. Entirely at the public expense?—Yes, entirely at the public expense; it would be a public duty.

Lord *Poltimore.*

1366. Supposing the insuring of lives of children under two years of age were prohibited, would not that press rather hardly upon the deserving and respectable poor?—I should think if the child died no doubt it would press upon them, but of course the expenses connected with the funeral of an infant would not be so great as the expenses connected with the death of an older child.

1367. You said just now that the more respectable poor wish to have money for mourning and various expenses besides the actual funeral; would not that equally be the case with the younger children?—Yes, that would be just the same whether the child was two years or six years old.

1368. Then, in fact, it would be impossible to devise a system of prohibition which would not press heavily upon those insuring?—That is a very difficult question to answer.

Earl of *Harrowby.*

1369. What is your ground for imagining that only a small proportion of the insurance cases come under your knowledge?—Because there are so very few of the cases of children that die that I can trace in any way; I know from hearsay many things which I cannot prove. I get a variety of information given me, which information is not good enough to act upon, and would not justify me in acting, but which greatly influences my mind in knowing that other cases go on.

1370. That would apply to a large number of the cases; you said only a small number of cases?—I imagine only a small number of cases come within my knowledge.

1371. Do doctors communicate with you confidentially upon the subject?—Some of them; not all of them.

1372. What class of persons are the insurance

Earl of *Harrowby* —continued.

agents in Rotherham?—One of them is a baker who failed in business; another is an ex-police officer, and some clerks; they are largely people who have other callings besides.

1373. Are they what you would call generally a respectable class of persons?—A struggling class; slightly educated people living by their wits many of them.

1374. With reference to the societies of Rotherham, are they principally local societies?—I do not know of any local society; they all have a head office elsewhere.

1375. Are they managed by local agents?—They are managed by local agents.

1376. What is the class of men who manage these branches?—They are much the same class as the agents who insure; some of them are men who have other callings; some of them sell various things on the weekly payment system.

1377. Are they men of considerable standing in Rotherham?—Certainly not; of no social standing whatever.

1378. Are not those who manage the local branches of considerable standing?—No, there is no one of any standing.

1379. Have you any other idea beyond this scheme of registration, which you would suggest to meet this evil?—I know of no other remedy except total prohibition of insurance.

1380. Up to what age?—Up to the age, I should say, of five or six years.

1381. You think the evil is so great that you would be justified in imposing this disability upon a thrifty parent?—I almost think so; it is a very serious evil. I admit that it would be a very serious thing for some of the people; but still the evil is very great.

Earl *Beauchamp.*

1382. Can you tell the Committee at all as to the proportion between insured and uninsured children in Rotherham?—No, I cannot.

1383. Would the majority of the children be insured?—I should think amongst that class of life they would be, but I could not state positively. I have no means of knowing; my general and strong impression is that the majority of children of this kind of people are insured.

1384. What I understood you to say was that you had as many cases of neglected children who were uninsured as were insured?—I have had as many cases. I have had 30 cases within the last 13 months, and I should say about half were insured.

1385. Have you brought several of those cases to justice?—I have.

1386. Have you had any difficulty in obtaining a conviction?—No, I have obtained a conviction in almost every case.

1387. What would be the nature of the penalty?—The penalties vary. Yesterday there were four parents brought up, and they each had three months' hard labour; sometimes the punishment has been as low as 14 days.

1388. Have you known of any cases of child murder beyond cases of neglect?—No, I have not.

1389. Have

Earl *Beauchamp*—continued.

1389. Have you not ordered a prosecution to be instituted in any case of child murder ?—No ; nor a case of manslaughter.

1390. Therefore there has been no failure of justice in any case of child murder ?—I have not had any case in which I could absolutely call it child murder.

1391. You hold a very strong impression that child insurance leads to evil practices ?—I have that decided impression.

1392. The information you receive you see through spectacles tinged with that pre-possession ?—Perhaps I do, but it is so very patent that I cannot help seeing it.

Chairman.

1393. I think you spoke of an equal number of cruelty cases of insured and uninsured ?—They are in about equal numbers.

1394. Those, as you have said, occurring amongst the uninsured, might be cases of cruelty in which there was no desire to destroy life ?—Yes ; cases of sudden ebullition of passion, excessive punishment, and so on.

1395. Were the cases of cruelty to insured children cases of angry passion of the moment, or were many of them cases of deliberate starvation ?—Many of them were deliberate slow cases.

1396. Then the character of the cases differs decidedly ?—Distinctly.

1397. The number of cases of cruelty in uninsured cases might be equal to the number in insured cases ; but in the latter, was it apparent to you that the neglect was caused by a desire to extinguish life ?—Yes, that was my impression.

1398. Many of the other cases were cases of brutality, beating, and so on ?—Yes.

1399. That is to say, you saw a marked difference between the character of the offence in the insured cases and the uninsured cases, though the number was equal ?—They were perfectly different characters.

Earl of *Selborne.*

1400. Do you mean that there were no cases of neglect of the same sort amongst the uninsured ?—I have had no cases of starvation, or approaching starvation, amongst uninsured children.

Chairman.

1401. I think you also stated that a good many, both of the agents and their local superiors, were people in a small way of business ?—Yes.

1402. Therefore, if they were very strict and

Chairman—continued.

particular in examining into suspicious cases, they run the risk, do they not, of injuring themselves in their business ?—They might do so, no doubt.

1403. They would not like to make themselves unpopular ?—Certainly, they would not.

1404. As regards those convictions for child murder, you say you have had no case of a person brought before you on a distinct charge of manslaughter ?—I have had none.

1405. But you have had cases of cruelty such as this which you have adduced here, which if it had gone on a little longer would have ended in manslaughter ?—I have had one case in which a woman was sent to prison for starving her illegitimate twins, and three or four days after she had been sent to prison, and had been punished for it, one of the twins actually did die.

1406. This was the case you put before the Committee in which, if you had not come in and stopped the cruelty, it would have ended in death ?—Yes.

1407. I am requested to ask you this : if it were required that every person acting as an insurance agent should have his name placed upon a public register, do you think that would increase their public responsibility, and tend to check the evils complained of ?—It would undoubtedly increase their responsibility, and I should imagine it would tend to check the evil.

1408. To any great degree ?—I have not had time to form any opinion upon that.

Earl of *Selborne.*

1409. I suppose they do not do their business secretly, do they ?—Quite the reverse ; they are always pushing their business.

1410. Then what difference could it make that their names should be put upon a register ?—(*No answer.*)

Earl of *Harrowby.*

1411. Have you, as a matter of fact, a register of all the agents ?—No ; I have not. I ought to say that I hardly even know all the agents yet.

1412. Would it be of assistance to the police to have a register open to public inspection ?—Certainly it would be ; it might be.

Lord *Poltimore.*

1413. I suppose you would have no difficulty in finding an agent if you wanted him ?—No, if I could once get the policy, I could get the agent, because it requires to have his initials upon it ; there would be no difficulty about that.

The Witness is directed to withdraw.

MR. JOHN JAMES RITCHIE, M.R.C.S., L.S.A., is called in ; and Examined, as follows :

Chairman.

1414. ARE you a member of the Royal College of Surgeons ?—Yes.

1415. And a licentiate of the Royal College of Physicians ?—No.

1416. You are medical officer of health for the urban sanitary district of Leek in Staffordshire ? —I am.

(142.)

Chairman—continued.

1417. How long have you been so ?—Since the year 1859.

1418. Has your attention been called to the practice of child-life insurance ?—Yes.

1419. What is your opinion of the practice as carried on ; is it unfavourable to child life ?—Generally, yes.

H 3

1420. Have

Chairman—continued.

1420. Have you any experience as medical officer of health which confirms that view?—Yes, I have.

1421. Decidedly so?—Yes.

1422. You produce the health report of the year 1884, by the local authority?—Yes, I do.

1423. In which you made the following statement, which I will read, and you will tell me whether it is correct: "In connection with this subject, the question of insuring the lives of infants is just now engaging a good deal of public attention, and the history of our experience at Leek may be interesting and useful. There has been a burial society here for upwards of 30 years, which has been well worked, and proved of great service to the inhabitants. For certain reasons the directors saw fit in the year 1876 to discontinue the insuring of lives of children under one year. At that time the infant mortality was 156 to 1,000 children born," which is admittedly over that of the general average of England?—Yes.

1424. "In the following year this mortality dropped to 109, the lowest point ever reached"; that was the year following that when the local society discontinued child insurance?—Yes.

1425. "As soon as the local society declined this class of business, the branches of several large insurance offices took it up, and vigorously canvassed for the same; and in the year 1878 the mortality rose to 170"?—That is true.

1426. "The average rate for the last seven years has been 170, and during the year just closed it reached 186"; that is correct, is it not? That was in the year 1884.

1427. "While that for the whole of England and Wales was 147?"—That is correct.

1428. It appears, then, from this evidence that in child mortality there was a fall or a rise according to the age of the children under one year of age were insured, or were not insured?—It looks very much like that; that was the result of the figures.

1429. You are also a medical practitioner?—Yes.

1430. Does your experience as a medical practitioner bear out your experience as a medical officer of health?—Yes.

1431. With reference to the bad effects of this insurance system, is that, in your opinion, mainly confined to what are known as collecting societies, as distinguished from benefit societies and friendly societies?—Yes; because there is so much more influence brought to bear by a local society, well worked, upon the lives insured, and upon the attention given to those lives. We find in the burial society of Leek, which is rather more of a friendly society than anything else, that there we get a very much smaller mortality of children at the age mentioned than we do in the town generally.

1432. You are of course aware of the distinction between friendly societies and collecting societies?—Yes.

1433. The main object of friendly societies is relief in sickness?—Yes; of course that is not done in a burial society.

1434. Of course it cannot be; but in ordinary friendly societies the main object is relief in sickness?—Yes.

Chairman—continued.

1435. The collecting societies do not give relief in sickness?—That is so.

1436. They simply go in for payment upon death?—Yes.

1437. In friendly societies the contributions are generally brought by the members to some local centre, and in that way they become acquainted with each other?—That is so.

1438. But in a collecting society the collector goes from door to door and gathers the money?—That is so.

1439. Friendly societies are conducted for the benefit of the members, and the collecting societies for the benefit of the managers?—Exactly.

1440. In your opinion those are important distinctions between those two kinds of societies?—They are.

1441. Your experience, both as a medical practitioner and a medical officer of health, is that the bad cases occur more largely, if not entirely, with the collecting societies than with the friendly societies?—Much more largely. I will not say entirely, but much more largely.

1442. The majority of the bad cases are connected with those collecting societies?—Yes.

1443. The other societies are much more respectable in every way? — They are; the persons conducting them are persons well known in the town and persons of some standing and influence.

1444. You say that the main object of the friendly societies is relief in sickness; does that relief in sickness include medical attendance and medical comforts?—It does.

1445. A man belonging to one of the friendly societies can get the attendance of a doctor and medical comforts without going to the parish for them?—Yes, if you mean by "medical comforts" medical attendance; we do not of course supply them with food; merely with medical attendance.

1446. Have you thought of any way in which the law could prevent the evils you appear to find?—I should think it would be injudicious to stop insurance altogether; I think that would be very hard indeed upon a great number of people; but if we could give a sort of premium upon life instead of upon death in any way, that would be a great object to be attained. I do not profess to know how to do it; that does not belong to my department.

1447. There has been a proposal by more than one witness to fix the age below which no insurance should be allowed; would that in your opinion press unduly upon respectable parents?—I think it would.

1448. You think they would resent that?—I think they would; that is my belief.

1449. If you fixed a minimum of cost, a respectable parent who wished to give his child something better than a pauper's funeral would resent that also?—Some might; that is a question of sentiment.

1450. I am speaking with reference to sentiment?—I think they would.

1451. You are aware that the legislation now proposed is very strongly opposed on the ground that

Chairman—continued.

that it is opposed to the sentiments of the respectable working class; I want to know whether certain alternatives which have been proposed to that Bill would not also offend the susceptibilities of respectable parents; if you said you shall not insure under two years, you would offend their susceptibilities; and if you said to a respectable parent, you shall have nothing but the very cheapest funeral, he would resent that; both of those things you think would be distasteful to the working man?—Yes, under the present feeling and sentiment of the people.

1452. Do you see any objection to saying, instead of paying this money into your hands, this club or society shall pay the undertaker; the money shall not pass into your hands?—Probably some persons might feel even that rather distasteful; but I think that generally a person thinking the question thoroughly out would agree, on account of the mischief done in bad cases, that they would give up that sentiment; but it may be a question of education to a certain extent.

1453. You do not think they would resent that?—Speaking for my own town, I do not think the mass of the people would like it at all; we have comparatively little evil in connection with this question, because of the good working of the local society.

1454. Do you think the other societies would resent that?—I think they would resent the giving them only the bare money.

1455. The preservation of the lives of children being the object of the legislation, you think these alternative proposals for effecting that object would be just as disagreeable to this class as the paying of the undertaker would be?—It is very difficult to say; I am not connected with any society. I am chiefly here to speak to the medical facts of the case. I do not wish to give an opinion upon that point, because I am not able to give an opinion upon that view of the question.

Earl of Derby.

1456. Are the majority of cases of cruelty and neglect which have come under your notice, cases in which the age of the child was under twelve months?—Chiefly; but there really are not very many cases which have come under my own absolute knowledge; I have nothing to do with parish practice or anything of that kind, so that, really and truly, I do not know very much of the thing actually, except so far as the returns coming to me as the medical officer of health, are tabulated and referred to in my report.

Earl Spencer.

1457. You said that the local society managed its affairs very well, and that notwithstanding that when they gave up paying insurances on children under one year, the mortality fell from 156 in 1,000 to 109?—Yes.

1458. And that when the competing societies came in, the mortality rose to 170 per 1,000?—Yes.

1459. There is a considerable difference between 156 and 170; do you attribute that to the laxer management of the new competing societies?—I do, to the taking in of any child;

(142.)

Earl Spencer—continued.

because they canvassed the town for anybody that they could pick up.

1460. When this fall took place from 156 to 109, could you say whether that was amongst children of a particular age?—They were all under the age.

1461. Under what age?—Under one year.

1462. What is the maximum age for children?—These figures you have before you all refer to children under one year.

1463. Entirely?—Entirely.

1464. Were there any circumstances which might have created this great increase from 1883 to 1884, from something like 107 to 180?—In 1882 there was a very large mortality from an epidemic of measles; that was the largest year, and no doubt that had something to do with the large mortality of children under that age.

Chairman.

1465. For that year?—For that year, but there was a general increase after the adoption of the system of collection by insurance officers, that is to say after the local society discontinued.

1466. And there were no other circumstances to account for the increase?—No; the general sanitary condition of the town was even better attended to than before, and it has been better looked to gradually.

1467. The general condition of the people was the same, they were not poorer?—No.

Earl of Selborne.

1468. What is the population of Leek?—Fourteen thousand

1469. How much have you had yourself to do with collecting the facts which appear upon that report which has been put in?—The sanitary inspector and myself solely do that, except so far as the registrar's returns go, which are sent to me monthly.

1470. This report comes down to 1884; could you tell me whether the experience of the subsequent years has been the same or different?—In the year 1885 the number was 145.

1471. That is about the normal average of England?—Yes. Then in 1888 it was 135, which is lower still; but I may say that nearly all the children now are insured in the local society, at all events to a great extent, and I made inquiry as to whether there were many children insured in both the local society and a collecting society, and I find that that is not the case; the local society is being so well managed that the people generally insure in that in preference to any other.

1472. I thought you told the Committee that the local society discontinued infant insurance?—That was in 1876.

1473. Then they resumed?—They were obliged, or at least they thought they were, to resume it in self-defence, because the collecting society's agent went into all the houses and took in children, and in taking in the children they took in everybody else they could canvass for; the consequence was that the local society was obliged to take that class of work as well, only under better management.

1474. Is this the result of your experience, that when the local society discontinued and the

H 4   other

Earl of *Selborne*—continued.

other society did not come in, there was a marked diminution; and that when the other society came in there was a marked increase to considerably more than the general average for England?—Yes.

1475. Then when the local society resumed the practice of insurance and recovered their influence, the average went down largely, and came to be equal to or less than the average for England?—Last year it was down to 113.

1476. I should like to ask you a question about your burial society; you have said that the burial society only pays for burials; at least, I understood you to say so?—That is so.

1477. Does it require evidence of the cost of burial or does it pay a fixed sum, without looking into that matter?—They pay a fixed sum, but they do not pay that without looking into the case.

1478. Is it a contract of indemnity or an absolute contract to pay that sum. When I say a " contract of indemnity," I mean like a fire insurance to insure the amount of loss?—They pay the sum, if there are no circumstances which interfere with that payment. There is a rule of the society which states, that the local committee have to investigate each case of death, and if they find circumstances of neglect in relation to that death they do not pay the money.

1479. That would be an objection to paying at all?—Yes, that would be an objection to paying at all.

1480. If they find no such objection to their paying at all they pay the full sum?—Exactly.

Earl *Spencer.*

1481. What was the year in which the local society resumed their rule as to infant insurance? —It was in 1880.

Lord Bishop of *Ripon.*

1482. Then it is the case that the local society adopted rather a different method from an ordinary collecting society?—Yes.

1483. In fact it is their interest to look into the cause of death?—Yes.

1484. Would that lead you to the idea that if rules of that kind obtained in other societies there would not be the same encouragement to neglect?—There would not; because the people would not get the money for which they had insured.

Lord *Poltimore.*

1485. What is the name of the local society which has worked so beneficially?—The Leek Benevolent Burial Society, I believe, is the name.

1486. It is only a burial society?—It is only a burial society; we have of course a number of friendly societies; but that special thing is only a burial society.

1487. Therefore, in your opinion, a burial society properly conducted is rather a safeguard than a danger?—Yes. These figures show that when the society in 1880 commenced the practice, in the same population the burial society of Leek containing perhaps between 8,000 and 9,000 persons out of the 14,000, the deaths of children under one year in the burial society

Lord *Poltimore*—continued.

were 88, but in the town generally they were 175. In the year 1881 they were 90 as compared to 137; in 1882 they were 148 as compared to 193; that was the time when there was a large epidemic of measles; in 1883 the numbers were 104 as compared with 118, and in 1884 they were 112 as compared to 186.

1488. Then the effect of your burial society has, in your opinion, been beneficial, not detrimental?—Yes.

1489. How is that burial society managed?— There are trustees in Leek and a general committee elected from the members annually.

1490. Who takes the profits?—The society generally takes the profit.

1491. Amongst the members?—Yes.

1492. You stated, as I understood, that in the collecting societies the benefits went to the managers, and in friendly societies to the members; what did you mean by that?—I mean in the collecting societies; it appears that the managers of the societies take all the money, and that a great deal of it goes in expenditure; some 40 or 50 per cent.

1493. You mean it enriches the managers?— I do not know whether that is so.

1494. But you have this local society which you contrast very highly, apparently, with the collecting society, and you say the difference is that in one case the money goes to the managers, and in the other, the burial society, amongst the members?—The remark that I made to the noble Chairman referred to friendly societies.

1495. This local society appears to be an extremely good society according to your account?—Yes, but it is purely a burial society.

1496. I simply want to know how does it manage its business; does it collect by its members only, or by paid agents; does it grant commissions, or not?—I know nothing in the world about it, except what I see from the report, and the report, which is before the Committee, of the Leek Burial Society will give the whole information.

1497. I wanted to know how that society collected its money?—I do not know anything about the management, except so far as I see in the report; they have their yearly meeting; they appoint a certain number of collectors from among themselves as a committee, and these men go round and obtain the money required for the carrying on of the business, whether it be little or much; sometimes they do not want very much to pay the regular amounts they require; they collect as much as they need as far as I understand from the report.

1498. I will not trouble you further except to ask you this question: do you consider that this particular burial society is successful because it is managed by peculiarly honest people, or because the system upon which they work is a good system, while the other is a bad one?—I think that is it.

1499. Then, with reference to the amount of insurance, is it within your knowledge that the poor insure not only for the purpose of paying the expenses of the funeral, but for the purpose of procuring mourning?—They generally like to have some sort of respectable dress at these

4 *July* 1890.]   Mr. RITCHIE, M.R.C.S., L.S.A.   [*Continued.*

Lord *Poltimore*—continued.

times, there is no doubt, but I think they only go in just for that sum, as a rule.

1500. Have you found that the honest poor man, as a rule, when he insures his child, or the funeral of his child, does it partly with the view that he may appear at the funeral of that child in respectable mourning?—Yes, I think so.

1501. Therefore he applies the money partly in mourning?—No doubt he does.

Earl *Beauchamp.*

1502. I did not quite understand whether the local society which investigates cases of death, exercises any choice in the admission of children who are insured; for instance, if a child were sickly would that child be refused?—It would if they knew that it was so; I have known cases where they have been refused.

1503. I think you told the Committee that there were not many cases of child neglect which came within your knowledge?—Not within my knowledge; some do now and then, but nothing very striking; I have heard of such cases, but I wish simply to speak of what I know.

1504. Respecting the cases which have come within your knowledge, be they few or be they many, have you any reason to think that those children were insured or not?—They have been insured in those cases.

1505. And there have been cases in which they have not been insured; may I take it in that way as well?—I have not had many cases of neglect where the children were not insured; not many within my knowledge.

1506. Have you had any experience as to any prosecutions of parents?—I have had none.

1507. Neither for neglect nor child murder?—None.

Chairman.

1508. You say this local society is very well managed, because the members know one another?—Yes, all of them.

1509. The population of Leek is 14,000?—Yes, 14,000.

1510. Would that apply to a very large town of 220,000, say?—Not to the same extent; it could not do so.

Chairman—continued.

1511. The power of a local society for finding out character and checking bad cases is in inverse ratio to the population?—It must be so.

1512. The power to do this in a very large town would be very much less than in a very small town or village?—Certainly, unless it were divided into districts; people then would be able to know each other.

Earl of *Harrowby.*

1513. What class of life do the managers of this local society belong to, could you give the Committee their position?—They are in a very fair position in life.

1514. Not working people; not people in receipt of weekly wages?—Yes, the Committee are.

1515. Who is there above the Committee?—There are three trustees; I really do not know at the moment who they are.

1516. Who are the people who actually manage this society?—The operatives themselves.

1517. Those are really the practical managers?—Yes.

Lord Bishop of Ripon.

1518. These societies are divided, as I understand, from what we have heard, into two classes, one which I may call the profit-making society, and the other the mutual?—Yes.

1519. Is it your opinion that when a society is arranged upon what we may call the mutual system, where there are no profits, then these evils do not exist to the same degree?—That is my view.

1520. But that in the case of profit-making societies there is that incentive?—That is my belief.

Chairman.

1521. You have given the Committee in your report the proportions between the death-rate of the burial society and that of the town from the year 1880 to 1884; could you furnish the Committee with a similar return from the years 1884 to 1890?—I can do so; I will supply that information.

The Witness is directed to withdraw.

Mr. JAMES TASKER, is called in; and Examined, as follows:

Chairman.

1522. YOU are now employed as Rate Collector and Vestry Officer at West Bar, Sheffield?—I am.

1523. And you have been Relieving Officer in Sheffield until recently?—I have for 11 years.

1524. What was the population of your district?—About 32,000.

1525. In the discharge of your duty as relieving officer you had to visit those people?—I had.

1526. Constantly?—Constantly, all through the district.

1527. Was your attention called to the practice of child insurance in the district?—Not officially, but it was called to cases of insurance frequently.

(142.)

Chairman—continued.

1528. From your experience and knowledge of the district?—Yes.

1529. What was it that called your atttention to the subject?—I frequently saw that people whose children were poor and neglected often had plenty of money to spend, particularly after the death of a child.

1530. You saw money coming in to this class of parents who were neglecting their children after the death of the children?—Yes, upon the death of any of their children.

1531. You think that the coming in of money constituted a temptation to neglect?—Yes, I believe so.

1532. Had you reason to think that they were

I   making

Chairman—continued.

making a profit by the death of their children?
—That was so.

1533. In what sort of people did you find
that?—In the lower grade of society.

1534. There were a good many of that lower
grade of people in the town of Sheffield. were
there not?—Particularly in the district I was
in; it was the lowest part of Sheffield.

1535. There were a large number of the lowest
class of people in that district?—There were.

1536. Did you observe amongst the people you
had to deal with that insurance was used to keep
off the parish for the child's funeral?—Quite the
contrary.

1537. They did not seem to care about going
on the parish?—No; the first thing they did
would be to come to us to ask for the burial of
the child although they would very likely have
the child insured at the same time; but the
difficulty was to know that.

1538. Although they had the child insured
they came to you to get it buried at the cost of
the parish?—Yes.

1539. The parents told you, I suppose, that the
child was not insured?—Very often; whenever
the question was asked it was most frequently
answered in the negative.

1540. You had not time to verify the statement; you had to bury at once?—Yes, they
simply represented themselves as paupers and the
child would be buried.

1541. Had you any reason to believe when
they told you the child was not insured that they
were deceiving you?—I had.

1542. Have you ever taken proceedings in
such cases?—I have not taken legal proceedings,
but I have recovered the money in several cases
by threatening proceedings. After they had got
the money to bury the child I have ascertained
that the child was insured, and then I have got
our costs back from them.

1543. Why did you not take proceedings in the
numerous cases you spoke of?—Perhaps no proceedings could have been taken, because there
was nothing in the house; if you had taken the
whole house from the top to the bottom there
would have been nothing in it when you had
sold it.

1544. When you had recovered the cost of the
parish funeral, do you think there was still a
profit left to the insurers?—Yes, to the party
insuring.

1545. A child insured at six months may be
insured for 6 *l.*, may it not?—It may be by law,
but mostly in Sheffield it runs from 2 *l.* to
2 *l.* 10 *s.*

1546. What would be the cost of a parish
funeral?—In my parish it would have been about
12 *s.*

1547. Including all expenses?—Yes.

1548. A child of six months old whose life is
insured for 2 *l.* 10 *s.* could be buried for 12 *s.*?—
Yes.

1549. If then the parish could get a child
buried for that sum of course the parent could
get it buried for that sum?—Yes, I presume so.

1550. That was the charge the undertaker
made?—Yes.

1551. Then the insurers, supposing them to be
badly disposed, would get 2 *l.* 10 *s.*, and all they

Chairman—continued.

would have to pay would be 12 *s.*, leaving them
consequently, a profit?—Yes, of 1 *l.* 18 *s.*

1552. If the child were insured in a second
society there would be still more profit, because,
although there were two insurances there would
be only one funeral of the child?—Yes.

1553. Therefore, the insurance money in the
second case would be net profit?—Yes.

1554. A parent insuring in two societies might
get 5 *l.* insurance money upon the child?—I dare
say that would be so, but I doubt whether we
had many cases of their being insured in two
societies; I do not think we had in our district.

1555. There might be cases in which the
parent had the child insured in two societies?—
Undoubtedly; but I do not think we had many
cases of that in my district.

1556. Do you think that the parish was very
often applied to, to bury insured children?—I
think we were very often; the difficulty was to
find out whether they were insured.

1557. Why did you suspect them to be insured?
—Because after a death I found them very flush
of money which I knew could not have been come
by in any other way than from an insurance
society.

1558. They seemed to be very poor people,
and after a child was dead you found them to be
spending money?—Yes; having good parties and
drinking.

1559. Now as to the proportion of child
insurance in your district; did you find this to
be larger among the lower or the better class?—
I think it was rather amongst the lower class
that the largest amount of insurance was effected
in my district.

1560. The lower you went down the more
child insurance you found?—Yes.

1561. You have many betting men in Sheffield,
have you not?—Yes.

1562. Betting men and betting women?—
Yes.

1563. They are very much given to betting in
Sheffield, are they not?—Yes.

1564. Did you find this class of people very
much given to insurance of children?—It is very
hard to say that, because nearly all the lower
classes in Sheffield go in for betting little or
much.

1565. Do you think that affects the extent of
the insurance of children; that they look upon it
as a kind of bet against the children's lives?—I
should not like to look at it in that light; they
might look at it as a sort of provision.

1566. At any rate, they do not insure to keep
themselves off the parish?—Certainly not.

1567. Do you think that if you prevented the
parent handling the money and making a profit
in this way, it would greatly tend to check these
bad practices?—It would.

1568. Have you ever considered how you
could prevent a parent making a profit on his
child's death?—I have not formed an opinion as
to how that could be done, but I think it ought
to be done, because while there is a profit attached
to it, the poor people will insure, and they do not
spend the money judiciously.

1569. As long as there is money to be obtained
on the death of children those things will go on?
—The

*Chairman—*continued.

—The children will tend to be neglected in my opinion.

1570. It tends to continue these evils?—It does.

1571. Supposing the parent insured in a society, and the society instead of paying the money to the parent paid it to the doctor and undertaker, do you think that would tend to check these evils?—I should think that would have a tendency to check these evils; considerably so.

1572. Do you know how the parents in sick clubs and benefit societies pay the doctor?—In the sick societies that we have in Sheffield, to my knowledge the doctors do not attend to the children; that is done through the friendly societies.

1573. In friendly societies do you know how the club doctor is paid?—He gets so much per head per male member; either 2 *s.* 6 *d.*, 3 *s.*, or 3 *s.* 6 *d.* a year for each member.

1574. Who pays that?—That is paid from the club.

1575. It does not pass through the patient's hands?—No; but that does not apply to the children.

1576. Can a child become a member of a friendly society?—He can after 16 years of age.

1577. The money is paid to the doctor, not by the insurer, but by the club?—That is so; no matter how many members of the society there are, the doctor is paid so much each per year.

1578. And he is bound to attend them without charge?—Yes.

1579. This money he gets comes to him from the club?—Yes, certainly.

1580. Do not you think it would be possible to make some arrangement by which the insurance club or society should do the same thing with the undertaker as the friendly societies do with the doctor, namely, pay him without the money passing through the parent's hands?—I am afraid the people would rather object to that; the poor would certainly, and the better class would feel offended almost.

1581. I was not so much speaking of the offence, but of the possibility of doing it; it would be as possible in the one case as in the other, would it not?—I do not see the way in which it could be done.

1582. Supposing these societies were to be their own undertakers; supposing the society were to say. We will select one or two undertakers, and if you want to have your child buried it must be done by one of those; that could be done, could it not?—I think it could be done.

1583. And the child could be buried by a respectable undertaker?—Yes.

1584. If the undertaker proved disreputable or dishonest, then he could be superseded by another?—Yes.

1585. The societies could be their own undertakers?—Yes.

1586. Just as some shipping companies are their own insurers?—Yes, certainly.

Earl of *Derby.*

1587. You said there was most insurance amongst the lowest class?—In my district.

(142.)

Earl of *Derby—*continued.

1588. Do you mean by the lowest class, only the poorest class, or the least reputable?—Both; if you take the poor you take the disreputable too, because most of them insure to the man who goes round, and they can insure for such a very small sum of money; a halfpenny or a penny a week will effect an insurance, so that even these very poor people do it.

1589. Supposing a law were passed prohibiting the insurance of children under 12 months of age, do you think that would have the effect of diminishing the abuse?—I think it would have the tendency of allowing the children to get over 12 months, and becoming older and stronger; they would be able to defend themselves a little even at that age.

1590. And if it were made two years the change would be still better?—Yes.

1591. Do you think that that restriction would be much objected to by the better part of the working classes?—I do not.

1592. Supposing the plan were adopted of the insurance money being paid direct to the undertaker, so that the parent had not the handling of it, do not you think that would tend very much to diminish the practice of insurance altogether?—I think it would.

1593. The people would not care to insure under those circumstances?—No, not that class we are speaking of particularly, because it is the balance that they want to get hold of.

Chairman.

1594. You mean by the class you were speaking of, the poorest class?—Yes.

1595. The reason they would not insure would be that they wanted the balance of the money after the funeral?—Yes.

Earl *Spencer.*

1596. How did the question of infant insurance come before you in your capacity of relieving officer?—I often had complaints made, " so-and-so came to you and got the funeral fees and buried the child, and now they have got the insurance money."

1597. That was when you were relieving officer?—Yes.

1598. Was it part of your duty to inquire into matters of that sort?—If they came and made application to me, and I afterwards ascertained that they got insurance money it was my duty to inquire, and I did inquire, and whenever I could, I got the money back.

1599. Were there many cases in which the poor law authorities attempted to get the money back when the children were insured?—Not many.

1600. Did you ever try?—I think we have had cases; but I could not recollect positively.

1601. Do you ever remember recovering any of this money when proceedings were taken?—No; I have never recovered any money under proceedings, but I have recovered in several cases without taking proceedings. I have gone to them and got the money under threat of legal proceedings. Their goods would not be worth taking in any case that I had to deal with.

1602. Did they pay it out of the insurance money?—I should think not. I should think

I 2　　　　　　　　　that

Earl *Spencer*—continued.

that the money would have been spent long before.

1603. Then you were not successful in your proceedings?—I got the money; but I daresay not out of the money the people got from the society; that would have been spent before I could make the investigation.

1604. How many cases of this sort do you think, in your experience as a relieving officer, you had to investigate?—I really could not say the number. Of course those cases were continually cropping up, and we did not recover, except in very infrequent cases.

1605. Do you suppose that you inquired into 100 cases when you were relieving officer?—No, I do not think I did.

1606. Did you find often cases of children dying of neglect when they were not insured?—We have had cases of that sort, but not often.

1607. You cannot compare the number that you found died from neglect when they were not insured, with the number of children who died when they were insured?—I had no means of doing so. I had no account of it.

Lord *Thring*.

1608. Do the poor attend the funerals of their children in their working dress, or in mourning?—Usually they have mourning, but only of a very poor kind.

1609. They are very anxious to have mourning, are they not?—Yes.

1610. I presume when an honest poor man insures his child, he does it also with a view to enable him to procure mourning?—There is no doubt that when honest people do it, they do it for that purpose.

1611. And there is, I will not call it a superstition, but a strong feeling amongst the honest people, that their children should have a decent burial not at the expense of the parish, and that they should be able attend the funeral in decent raiment?—That is so amongst the better class of poor.

1612. I understand that your experience has been, not with the better class of poor, but with the worse class of poor?—Yes.

1613. Therefore you cannot tell the Committee whether the better class of poor in Sheffield insure in those societies, or not?—I can speak from many cases that I know, that the better class do insure with those societies and with those societies which collect.

1614. You would say then that, supposing we prohibited insurance, that would prevent the better class of the poor from getting what they particularly wished, namely, decent burial for their children and raiment for themselves to attend it in?—But from my acquaintance with that better class, I do not think they insure their children so very young; but when they come to about five years old they begin to insure and with an honest intention, no doubt.

1615. You would agree that if under the age of two years insurance were not allowed, that would not, in your opinion, affect or disgust, or whatever term you like, the better class of poor?—I do not think it would do them much harm.

Lord *Thring*—continued.

1616. What would you say, under one year or under two years?—Under two years I should say.

Earl of *Harrowby*.

1617. Did you find, in going about amongst the class of people who were under your special charge, that there was a general opinion that this insurance system brought all sorts of evils with it?—I do not know whether there was such an opinion generally entertained, but it was my own opinion that it did.

1618. Was it a matter of notoriety in these poor neighbourhoods that a good number of children were illtreated in order to get the money?—They were very much neglected.

1619. That is your opinion, I know; but did you find that that was a prevalent opinion in the district during the nine years that you were there?—A good many cases of that kind have been reported to me which I have gone to see, and I have gained my knowledge from persons in the immediate neighbourhood who have seen it, and who have reported the facts to me. I have myself gone and seen it.

1620. Have you ever considered the effect of the compulsory registration of these insured children?—I have not thought about that at all.

1621. Are the societies principally local societies which deal with insurance in Sheffield?—I think the principal ones are the Royal Liver and the Prudential societies.

1622. What are the local managers of those branches; what class of persons?—Very respectable persons are the managers of them.

1623. Do they take any active part in the management of the whole concern in Sheffield?—I cannot tell you that exactly. I know there is one gentleman in each society who is appointed resident manager. He has under him so many collectors, and each one has a district, and he takes a book and goes out to collect from door to door. I do not know that he takes any active part, except collecting from those people.

1624. You do not thing he inquires into the circumstances?—Certainly not; he cannot do it.

1625. And there is no inquiry into the circumstances of the death?—The society would require some kind of a certificate; but I really do not know what these societies require.

1626. So far as the agents go, you believe there is no inquiry by the agents of these societies?—I do not.

1627. Have you thought of any remedy for the state of things you describe?—It has been said that if the children were not allowed to be insured until after the age of two years, that would tend a great deal to decrease the danger to their lives; it is when they are young that they are most neglected, I think.

1628. That is the only remedy which suggests itself to you?—That is so.

Earl *Beauchamp*.

1629. A child dying of neglect would not necessarily be neglected with criminal intent?—Perhaps not.

1630. You would not necessarily infer when a child

Earl *Beauchamp*—continued.

a child died of neglect that the parent had neglected it for his own gain?—Not necessarily.

1631. Do you find amongst the classes you are speaking of, that the mothers are well instructed as to the proper method of taking care of their children?—Yes, I suppose they will have the knowledge, but they appear to and they do, no doubt, wilfully neglect them when they ought to be carefully looking after them.

1632 You have said that you suppose they have the knowledge, but that they wilfully neglect them?—Yes.

1633. Apart from your suppositions, so far as your observation goes of the class of people you speak of, the mothers frequently do neglect their children, and show ignorance of the proper method of bringing them up; is that so?—Yes.

1634. When the children cease to be at their mothers' breast, their mothers very often give them food which is very unsuitable to them?—Yes, and leave them in the gutter or on the causeway, or anywhere else.

1635. But not necessarily with criminal intent, with the view of making away with them?—No, they simply leave them and neglect them.

1636. Have you had anything to do with any prosecutions for neglect of children?—I had one, but it is some years ago now. I prosecuted a man and his wife for neglecting their children at the Leeds Assizes, and they were sent up for two months each.

1637. Were the children in that case insured?—I am not sure. I do not think they were.

1638. You told the Committee that the cost of a pauper funeral might be taken at about 12 s.?—Yes.

1639. As a matter of contract?—The union makes it, or the guardians make it, into a contract.

1640. Then a parent would not have the advantage of that contract if he paid for the funeral himself?—There are numbers of undertakers in the town of Sheffield now who will furnish a funeral throughout for a very small sum. You can get a very decent coffin and coach for a matter of about 14 s. or 15 s.; a private person can do that.

1641. But you have told the Committee, I think, that the average amount they insure a child for was from 30 s. to 50 s.?—In my district it was not so much as that.

1642. If you deduct 15 s. as the cost of what the parent would have to pay, that leaves, say 35 s. for mourning and whatever he may have to pay the doctor?—Yes.

1643. Are there fees for the burial?—Yes; the 15 s. does not cover the burial fees.

1644. What would the fee be in Sheffield?—For a child I should think about 4 s. 9 d. to 5 s. 3 d.

1645. Do funerals take place on Sundays in Sheffield?—Yes.

1646. At the cemetery?—Yes.

1647. We have had it in evidence in another case that the clergy object to bury on Sundays, that is not the case in Sheffield, is it?—Sunday is a very popular day for funerals.

Chairman.

1648. With reference to these costs for burial fees and funerals and mourning and doctors' fees, those of course would be expenses in the case of

(142.)

Chairman—continued.

a decent and respectable parent who wishes to give his child a decent and respectable funeral; but in the case of a parent who wished to make money by the death of his child he would not go in for those expenses?—No, if an honest parent wished to bury his child decently, it would cost him pretty nearly all his insurance money.

1649. I suppose if a parent wants to make money out of his child's death he is not likely to engage a nurse or to send for the doctor until just before the child's death, so that he may get the certificate?—That is so.

1650. He will not go to more expense than he can help?—That is so.

1651. In calculating what a disreputable and dishonest parent would do, it is quite beside the mark, is it not, to talk about the expenses that an honest and respectable parent would go to?—That is so, it is not the same thing at all.

1652. When you are talking of death profits in such cases, you mean that a man will go to as little expense as he could?—That is so.

1653. Therefore, to say that a respectable person would have to go to a certain expense for his child's funeral, has nothing to do with what a disreputable person would do?—That is so; nothing whatever.

1654. You find the societies, like the Liver and the Prudential, compete with each other?—Yes, they do, very keenly.

1655. Do you think they make very careful inquiries as to the character of the persons they insure with?—I do not think they inquire at all; they go from door to door and get as many people to take out these insurances as they possibly can.

1656. The fact that the woman is a profligate, or the man a drunkard, does not matter to them?—Not in the least.

1657. Have you ever had an agent come to you and say, " I suspect that this is a bad case, and you had better look into it?"—Certainly not.

1658. Have you ever known them give any assistance to justice?—Not any.

1659. Although it is the interest of the society that there should be no bad cases, it is not the interest of the collector?—Not in the least.

1660. Therefore, he is not the least interested in preventing all these cases?—Certainly not; it is his interest to get as many insurances as he can by which he gets a certain commission.

1661. If he were very particular and got the society to dispute every policy, he would not be a very popular agent?—No, I do not think he would get any business.

1662. Therefore he has a direct interest in taking business without inquiry?—That is the case.

1663. The society is very largely in the hands of its agents?—That is so.

1664. They have no means of checking the statement of their agents?—I do not think they have.

1665. In point of fact, the interests of the society and the lives of the children are in the hands of a set of men who do not care a pin about either; that is what it comes to, is it not?—I do not think they have any care in the matter.

The Witness is directed to withdraw.

J 3

4 *July* 1890.

MR. WILLIAM HARTOP, is called in; and Examined, as follows.

Chairman.

1666. YOU are the relieving officer of No. 1 District, Bradford?—Yes, I am.

1667. And you have been so for the past nine years?—I was appointed in December 1881.

1668. What is the character of your district? what kind of people live in it?—I have some of the lowest people in my district; it is the lowest part of the town.

1669. You have bad dwellings and bad people?—Yes; we have bad dwellings and bad people.

1670. In the district of the bad dwellings and the bad people, is there a considerable practice of insuring children's lives?—There is.

1671. Have you given any attention to the subject of insuring children's lives?—I have thought a little of it sometimes.

1672. Have you come to any conclusion upon the subject of child insurance?—I think it has a very bad influence with the very low and debased people.

1673. You find that even the most improvident and base insure their children's lives?—Yes, they do.

1674. Then being improvident and being base, it is not for thrift and respectability's sake they insure their children's lives?—It is simply for the money.

1675. They even insure the very old people, their parents, do they not?—Yes, I have known as many as 12 policies on one man's life, a case of cancer in the mouth which is a very slow process. The agent insured the man without ever seeing him, but his friends knowing that it was cancer, knew it would be fatal in the end.

1676. And the agent never took the trouble to see him?—He could not have done else he would have seen it at once.

1677. Either then the agent did not know that the man had a cancer, or he did not care, because the insurance put money in his pocket?—He could not have taken the trouble to see the man.

1678. Have you found that the effect of insurance has been to make parents neglect their children?—Yes, the idle and the dissolute ones.

1679. As to those unnatural parents, who it is said would neglect their children in any case, do not you think that the inducement of a pound or two of money in their hand to spend would be an additional inducement?—I do.

1680. Supposing that a man was unnatural enough not to wish to bring up his child on account of the expense and trouble, if the agent assures that man that he will have a couple of pounds when the child dies, that increases his temptation to do away with the child, does not it?—Certainly.

1681. More especially if he is an improvident and base fellow and fond of drink?—Yes.

1682. Is the poverty you find in the district only such poverty as comes from want of work, or does it arise from idleness?—It varies; there

*Chairman—*continued.

are times of bad trade when distress comes upon the district, and they are the class of people whom we have the greatest difficulty in keeping off the rates; if they can have anything by false statement and misrepresentation they will have it. Bradford is a manufacturing town, and there are times when a depression comes on when we have really deserving poor upon our books.

1683. You have found that those people have tried to deceive you about their insurance?—Yes, I have.

1684. You have found it out after burial, I presume?—Yes.

1685. You could not leave a child lying unburied in a poor person's room while you were making investigations?—Not at all times; there are times when people come and state that they have nothing to bury the child with; the relieving officer must deal with it according to the statement made at the time. After they have got the coffin, and sometimes after the child is buried, they will go to the registrar and get a certificate and get the insurance money; but we do not get deceived so often as some relieving officers do, for this reason: Our clerk is a very old gentleman, over 80 years of age, and he has an assistant clerk who is registrar. We have telephone communication between the workhouse and the clerk's office, and if people say they have no insurance, I go at once to the telephone and ascertain whether they have obtained a copy of the certificate of the registrar, so that it is only when they deceive and get the child buried before they apply for a copy of the certificate that I am deceived, otherwise I should have a great deal more of such cases than I have.

1686. That is owing to the accidental circumstance of your assistant happening to be the registrar?—That is so.

1687. Other relieving officers have not that advantage?—They have not.

1688. Have you any idea of the proportion of those cases where there would be death-money where there was neglect?—I have thought the matter over, and I think I should be safe in saying that in one case in 50 there would be neglect.

1689. Have you ever given information to the police with a view to taking proceedings against those people?—I have not.

1690. Why not?—It is only circumstantial evidence; we have no direct proof; of course you can judge from seeing the condition of the children, and the way they are allowed to lie unattended to, and without care, the place being in such a miserable condition, but we cannot bring any legal proof against them; we should not get a conviction.

1691. In point of fact, you did not bring those cases before the justices at Bradford, because you could not get anything done; it would be practically useless?—Yes, at Bradford it would.

1692. What

Chairman—continued.

1692. What circumstances induced you to think that in these cases there was criminal neglect for the sake of money?—When I first became relieving officer, I was astounded to see children in such a condition; and sometimes when I have gone to a house the mother has been out and perhaps one child, a young child, being in the house alone, I have gone and asked the neighbours where the woman was, the neighbours would say they did not want to interfere, they would not have anything to do with it. Then I have found that the mother was at the public-house, and I would say: Why did not they report the case, and they would say, "It is all right, the child is insured;" that was what gave me the idea at first.

1693. You found that these people applied for medical relief very late in the case?—Yes, sometimes at the very last moment.

1694. That would be presumably not for the sake of getting the child better, otherwise they would have come sooner. Your presumption would be that they came for the sake of the doctor's certificate?—Yes, that is so.

1695. Do you think that all the cases of bad treatment of young children in your district come under your notice?—No, I do not.

1696. Do the parents resort to cheap dispensaries to get medical attendance?—Yes, we have several in Bradford; they can go to a cheap medical man and have his advice and medicine for sixpence; and, even if they only went once and the child died, they would be able to get his certificate.

1697. He gives it quite promiscuously for sixpence, does he?—I do not say that he would give the certificate for sixpence, they would have to pay perhaps 2 s. 6 d. for the certificate; but they would get the medicine and his advice for sixpence in the first instance.

1698. Do you find that the fact that the funeral is paid for, and that they will besides get drink out of it, has any effect with the people in inducing them to insure?—In some parts of the district.

1699. It is an inducement to people to insure?—Yes, when they see how their neighbours go and do it, and get nicely over it, it is a temptation to them to go and do it too.

1700. Have you had any case in which you knew exactly how the money was spent when the parish buried the child?—Not exactly; but I have known them to have a tea going to one of the coffee taverns, and paying 9 d. a head for about 40 or 50 people.

1701. Upon the day of the funeral?—Yes, upon the day of the funeral.

1702. Which they paid for out of the insurance money?—Yes, when the child was buried, and they had done with their expenditure in clothing.

1703. Have you ever known insurances effected up to 20 l.?—Not with a young child; I have with a grown-up person.

1704. Do you know the opinion of your fellow relieving officers upon this subject?—Yes, it is practically the same as my own.

1705. They all, or most of them, agree with you that there is a great deal that is very bad connected with child insurance?—There are two districts where they would not get quite so many

as I do; I have the largest district in the union, and also the worst part of the town.

Earl of *Derby.*

1706. What is the largest amount of insurance upon a child's life that you have known?—On a young child, I think about 3 l. is the most they would get; that is for one policy; sometimes they will have more than one policy upon the same child.

1707. Is it common to insure in more than one office?—Yes, with some of them, and also there are people in Bradford who will insure a neighbour's child, although they have no interest in it, only for the money.

1708. As a mere gambling speculation?—Yes.

1709. We have heard of cases of neglect and cruelty which have come under your knowledge; should you say that the majority of them take place when the child is under 12 months of age?—Not exactly under 12 months of age, because a woman who drinks will many a time have the child in her arms, and go gossiping about with the child getting the breast; I should think it is more when the child is being weaned; when it is put on to bread and other things, and is left to be fed by the other children, which affects its digestion and brings on convulsions.

1710. But you are not speaking of cases in which it is intended that the child should die?—I think they do wilfully neglect and leave them.

1711. You said something about going to cheap dispensaries; is that to obtain a certificate?—Yes.

1712. Or in order to be able to say that they have come for advice and medicine?—And to get a certificate also.

Earl *Spencer.*

1713. You gave an instance, I think, of several insurances being effected on an old man, or a man who had cancer; you gave that as an instance of the recklessness with which the agents take up insurances?—I think that if the agents had to be more careful there would not be so much of it.

1714. Do you think that they very often take up insurances when a child is ill, or seriously neglected?—I do not think they take the trouble to see which is the child they are insuring; in fact, I know it.

1715. Do not they have to produce a medical certificate as to the health of the child at the time of its insurance?—No; if they had to produce a medical certificate with a child the same as an adult joining a friendly society, that would do away with a lot of it.

1716. The insurance is simply effected upon the report of the agent, who is careless as to the state of the child when he is making his report?—With a number of agents it is a matter of business; the more insurances they get the more money they get.

Lord Bishop of Ripon.

1717. You used the expression just now, "the same as with the friendly societies;" do you mean by that that the friendly societies insist upon

Lord Bishop of Ripon — continued.

upon a certificate?—They insist upon a medical examination.

1718. Do they insist upon that if it happens to be a child's life?—A child could not join any friendly society that I know of; they are only for adults, but an adult member can, by paying 10 s. 6 d. a year, have medical attendance for his children. In Bradford we have what is called a medical aid association in connection with the Odd Fellows' Club, and every working man, by paying, I think it is 10 s. 6 d. can have medical attendance for his children as well, and for 10 s. 6 d. he can have his wife attended to in her confinements.

1719. Do they accept children's lives in the burial society?—No; it is only for adults

1720. Then all the cases you are speaking of, of agents collecting the insurance money, are cases in which they are agents of what we may call a profit-making society?—Yes.

1721. And not a friendly society?—No.

1722. And not a mutual society?—No.

Lord Thring.

1723. You say that a medical certificate of the health of a baby would be a safeguard: I do not see that, because, supposing the parent wanted to destroy the child, there would be nothing easier than to overlay the child, or feed it with sour milk, or all sorts of things to bring on convulsions?—In many cases they do not insure the child at all until it is sick.

1724. But if the parent wishes to destroy the child, it appears to be so easy to destroy it, I do not see how the fact of requiring a medical certificate would help you?—It would prevent a good many from ever attempting to join.

1725. In other words it would cost them so much that it would prevent them from joining?—Yes.

1726. Who would pay for the medical certificate?—I suppose the society would have a doctor of its own; if an up-grown person joins for an insurance of 100 l., he is examined by the doctor of the society, and the society could have one for the children.

1727. But the sum paid is so small; a penny a week, or something like that; how would you pay for the cost of the certificate?—If the doctor had all the cases——

1728. But if it is so easy to kill a baby, I cannot see how a certificate that the child to-day is well, prevents its being killed to-morrow or next week?—I do not say it is done so quickly as that; it is done by a very slow process.

1729. But there might be many opportunities of doing it after the parent had got the certificate?—Still, I think that if a medical certificate were required, it would prevent many of them insuring their children.

Lord Poltimore.

1730. Do you think that a limit of age would meet with opposition from the more respectable classes?—Not in the slightest.

1731. And it would not be unfair towards them?—Not at all. I think the idea that when they attained a certain age they should draw a certain amount, would be very good, and also that if it did not attain that age the funeral

Lord Poltimore—continued.

money should be paid, so as to insure its being buried properly. I think many of the working people would agree to that.

1732. What limit do you think there should be before it could be insured?—At that rate I would insure it at two years of age.

Earl of Harrowby.

1733. Will you tell the Committee what the lowest cost of a child's funeral at Bradford would be; that is to say, supposing the parent buries the child himself?—I should think a working-man's child might be buried for about 1 l.

1734. Would that include the burial fees?—It would include the coffin and the burial fees, and the conveying of the child to the cemetery.

1735. That would be the least sum?—Yes.

1736. Therefore a dissolute parent would have to pay at least 1 l.?—Yes; if they buried it themselves.

1737. Can you tell me who manages the insurance companies in Bradford?—I do not think any of the managers live in Bradford; there are several district superintendents, and each district superintendent has a number of collectors under his own supervision.

1738. Are they local societies, or are they branches of great societies like the Liver and the Prudential?—It is those societies; the Refuge, the Prudential, the Liver, and the Pearl are the societies that we have in Bradford.

1739. It is those societies; not burial societies?—No.

1740. But you have burial societies in Bradford, have you not?—Yes, connected mostly with the Sunday schools.

1741. But they are mostly on a small scale?—Yes.

1742. Is there any manager who takes any care as to the cause of death before the sums are paid?—I am not aware of any; the people have to produce a certificate and it is sent away to the head office; some of them pay them directly they are due, and some of them will not pay until the following day. I have known it two days before they have got the money, because I have known people come to us and say they were afraid they were not going to get any money, because they had got the funeral paid for; and then they have got the money afterwards; but as a general rule in those cases we have got the money from them.

1743. There is no careful inquiry, is there, as to what is the cause of death?—Nothing beyond the registrar's certificate.

1744. May we suppose generally that all the artizans in Bradford insure as a class?—It is a very common habit.

1745. Do you think a system of compulsory registration of children insured would be of any use in preventing these abuses?—I scarcely see how that could be worked.

Earl Beauchamp.

1746. I do not quite understand this: you have just said that all the artizans insure; if all the children that come before you are insured——?—I do not say that they all are insured.

1747. I understood you to say, speaking generally, that all the artizans in Bradford insured?

Earl Beauchamp—continued.

sured?—I understood your Lordship's question to mean the better section of the working classes; most of the working classes do insure in Bradford.

1748. Then if most of the working people in Bradford insure their children, and you have only one in 50 cases of neglect, why do you say that child insurance stimulates neglect?—It does in the lower districts; I say that when a low debased woman sees her neighbours get the insurance money, and get her child buried by the parish, having got the money, and get out of it without being punished, it is an incentive to her to do the same.

1749. You say that, judging from your general knowledge of human nature, but I do not understand that the figures you produced at all bear out that contention?—I do not think I have had more than one in 50 that I have really thought had been wilfully neglected. I do not want to exaggerate it.

1750. Then I did not quite understand how the case of insurance of the man with the cancer bore upon the question of child insurance?—It

Earl Beauchamp—continued.

was simply a question that was put to me as to whether I found that the people who insured were healthy people; as well as children; it was not a voluntary statement given by me; I simply answered the question.

1751. Do you think that immoral and dissolute parents come to attend their children's funerals?—Not at all times; some of them do, but I have known cases in which they have not been able even to go to the funeral on account of having been drinking.

1752. That is when the children have been buried by the parish?—Yes.

1753. I understand you to say in answer to a question that when children were weaned the parents frequently neglected them and left them to be fed by other children?—Yes.

1754. Should you say that was the case more where the children were insured, or where they were not insured, or that it was a general practice amongst that class?—It is a general practice amongst the low class of people.

The Witness is directed to withdraw.

Mr. ROBERT ALFRED LEACH is called in; and Examined.

Chairman.

1755. YOU are clerk to the guardians of Rochdale?—I am.

1756. You are also the superintendent registrar of births, deaths, and marriages?—I am, for the same district.

1757. How long have you held that office?—I have been clerk and superintendent registrar for four years, and I was assistant clerk and deputy superintendent for ten years preceding that time.

1758. Being both clerk to the guardians, and registrar of births, deaths, and marriages, you have special opportunities for knowing whether the children buried by the parish are insured?—I have more than most people.

1759. You know what the provisions of the Friendly Societies Act are with reference to medical certificates and registrars' certificates?—Yes.

1760. Do you think that those provisions are sufficient to prevent the parish from having to bury an insured child without knowing that it is insured?—They are not, for this reason, and I speak from my knowledge of my own district. There are many societies which pay money upon the death of infants without any certificate at all, that is to say, without the registrar's certificate.

1761. Are there societies which do actually pay the insurance money without the production of the registrar's certificate?—Yes.

1762. The registrar's certificate is supposed to be a very special protection both to the society and to the child, and you say that there are several societies which pay without requiring this registrar's certificate to be produced?—There are several societies, local societies certainly, but very large ones in my district which pay their death money without the production of the certificate. These societies, I ought to say, are not registered under the Friendly Societies

(142.)

Chairman—continued.

Act, 1875, nor are they industrial insurance societies; but they are incorporated under the Companies Acts, and have been so during the last two or three years. Formerly they were registered under the Friendly Societies Act, and up to that time, about three years ago, of course they could not pay money on the death of a child without the production of the registrar's certificate; but once they became incorporated under the Companies Act, the articles of association would differ very considerably from the requirements of the Friendly Societies Act, 1875.

1763. Is there any legal penalty on the society for doing that which you have described?—The Friendly Societies Act of 1875, Section 28, applies to all friendly societies and benevolent societies, whether registered or not, and by Subsection 7, the Act is made applicable to industrial assurance companies. By the 39 & 40 Vict. c. 22, trades unions, whether registered or not, which insure or pay money on the death of a child under 10 years, are also brought within the provisions of this section; but the societies I now refer to, which have become incorporated under the Companies' Acts from 1862 to 1886, do not require (I do not think they are brought within the provisions of this Section 28) to produce a certificate of death.

1764. Can you give us the name of any society which you say pays death money without getting the registrar's certificate?—Yes, there is the Newbold Friendly Society, which I can give as an instance.

1765. Can you produce the rules of that society?—I have the Newbold Society's rules here (*producing the same*).

1766. Is there any rule of that society which requires that the registrar's certificate should be produced before payment?—The rule is as follows: "In the event of the death of any

K　　　　　　　　member,

Chairman—continued.

member, immediate notice shall be given to the collector of the district, who shall receive the certificate of death from the parents or guardians of the deceased, and forward the same to the president, vice president, or secretary; or the committee may, at their discretion, dispense with any such certificate. The collector of the district shall view the corpse, and receive sixpence from the society for each such inspection." So long as that society was registered under the Friendly Societies Act, as it was up to two years ago, there was no such discretion to dispense with the production of the certificate, because they had to act upon the registrar's certificate only under the Act.

1767. What was the reason for the collector viewing the corpse; the person viewing the corpse could say nothing except that the child was dead; he could say nothing about the cause of death?—He would not be entitled to do so, as a layman.

1768. What is the number of the members of this society, as far as you know?—I cannot say positively, but I have an idea that they have about 25,000.

1769. Where are its meetings generally held? —Its meetings are generally held at a public-house in the district; several of these societies have their registered office at public-houses.

1770. Are there many of the same class of clubs in your town?—There are several; I cannot say how many there are.

1771. Then practically you have no means of knowing whether the child's life is insured or not; it may be insured in one of these societies, but no certificate comes before you?—No certificate comes before me. I could trace it in the case of an ordinary friendly society or an industrial assurance society, such as the Prudential, but in these societies we cannot trace the fact of insurance.

1772. Then as regards the amount that may be insured, we know a child may be legally insured for 6 *l.* up to five years in a friendly society, but not more; but it may also be insured in the Newbold Society for 5 *l.* more, may it not?—I have amongst these counterfoils (*producing*) papers to show that a child has been insured in four societies; it has died under the age of five years; the registrar has been asked to give certificate for this amount, and he has given certificates for a total amount not exceeding what is allowed by law. But I take it that if the parents had been able to draw from each society what the rules of the Act would allow, irrespective of any limit by the Friendly Societies Act, namely 6 *l.*, allowed in that case for each child under five years, that amount would be considerably exceeded.

1773. It might run up to 10 *l.* and 12 *l.*?—And more than that.

1774. The registrar has no power of ascertaining whether a child is assured in this Newbold Society or not, has he?—I do not know of any means that we have to get at the information.

1775. Then, in fact, a child might be insured in four societies without your knowing anything about it?—Yes.

1776. And then buried at the expense of the

Chairman—continued.

parish?—And then buried at the cost of the parish, at the end of it all.

1777. And you would have no power of tracing that fact?—We should have no power of tracing the fact.

1778. What do you pay for the funeral of a child under 12 months of age, in your town?— Speaking of pauper cases, a child's funeral costs about 12 *s.* or 13 *s.*; but that includes about 8 *s.* for the registrar's fee for the interment at the cemetery; the remainder goes for the coffin: it does not include anything for the grave, or anything for the hearse, except horse-hire, because my board keeps a very respectable hearse for the interment of paupers.

1779. A child of six months old might be insured for 11 *l.*, might it not?—Not in the Newbold Society.

1780. But counting up the different societies, the insurer might get this amount; he might get 3 *l.* from one society, 3 *l.* from another, and 5 *l.* from the Newbold?—He would not get 5 *l.* from the Newbold Society, for the reason that the rules in the table do not permit the membership of children younger than three months. Then I see by the rules that they must pay 12 fortnightly payments before they are entitled to any money at death; so that that would bring the child up to the age of nine months.

1781. However, in the case of a child of nine months old, this sum of 11 *l.* might be taken?— Yes, possibly.

1782. Without you or anybody else having the least power to detect the fact?—Yes, or having any power at all to deal with it.

1783. Do you suppose, if it were possible to enforce by legal penalty that no society should insure a child which was known to be insured in any other society, that would have any effect in checking these bad practices?—Yes; my opinion is that the Friendly Societies Act of 1875 attempted to do that; but these societies have become incorporated, I believe, under Acts which it was never intended that friendly societies, pure and simple, should become incorporated under.

1784. In point of fact, it is your opinion that the Friendly Societies Act does not really touch a great many societies; there are some within it, and others have contrived to get outside it, or are outside it?—I do not think it goes far enough.

1785. The provisions of the Friendly Societies Act in that respect are very deficient?—Yes, its provisions are very deficient.

Earl of *Derby*.

1786. You think it is a common case for a child to be insured in more societies than one?— From inquiries that I have made, and the counterfoils I have seen, I should think that near on to 30 per cent. are insured in more than one society.

Lord Bishop of *Ripon*.

1787. This Newbold Society is called a friendly society, is it?—Yes, it is called the Newbold Friendly Society.

1788. But

Lord *Bishop of Ripon*—continued.

1788. But it managed to contract itself out of the provisions of the Friendly Societies Act ?— The certificate of incorporation was given by the Assistant Registrar of Joint Stock Companies. Up to three years ago, it registered under the Friendly Societies Act ; the society did not take itself from out of the Friendly Societies Act on account of this matter, but I believe it was owing to the difficulty of making out the valuation which the friendly societies have to make out to the registrar of friendly societies every five years ; they found a great difficulty in doing it, and they found that under the Companies Act that that would not be needed.

Lord *Thring.*

1789. I do not understand how the fact of your knowing or not knowing of a child being insured would prevent child murder ; when you say you cannot find it out, and you lay such stress upon it, what would be the advantage in your knowing it?—I have not ventured an opinion that there is any child murder in my district.

1790. But you ventured the opinion that it is injurious to child life, did you not?—No ; I have not given that opinion ; but it does not appear to me to be decent that a child should be insured for death benefit in as many as four societies, as they can do, under four years of age.

1791. But what advantage would accrue from your finding out that they were insured ?—I say the Friendly Societies Act of 1875 set up a certain safeguard as regards the insurance of children for death money. The friendly societies safeguard is this, that any child under five should be insured for not more than a maximum of 6 *l.* ; that was to secure that not more than 6 *l.* should be paid on the death of a child under five years of age ; and the same Act required that the society should not pay without the production of the registrar's certificate, which is a certificate of death, and a certificate of the amount which the society was liable to pay. Supposing that a child were insured in two societies, for 5 *l.* death money in each, and died under five years of age, the parent would come and register the child's death. I am now speaking of societies under the Friendly Societies Act ; he would ask the registrar for a certificate for one society, and he would get out the full 5 *l.* ; but he would not get a certificate for the second society except for 1 *l.*, and the society under a penalty would not dare to pay more than 1 *l.* ; but in the case of societies which have gone under the Companies Act, I say there is no production of a certificate required ; their articles of association do not require it ; hence it is possible that a parent getting his child insured in four different societies where no such certificate is required, the safeguard of the Friendly Societies Act of 1875 being done away with, a child might be insured for 20 *l.*

Lord *Thring*—continued.

1792. You think these societies should all be registered under the Friendly Societies Act ?— Yes, certainly ; I do not go into the question whether the Friendly Societies Act is good or not, but assuming it was the intention of the Legislature to set up that safeguard, all similar societies should be brought under its provisions.

1793. Would you say that the certificate under the Friendly Societies Act is a safeguard which should be enforced against all these societies ?—Certainly.

Earl of *Harrowby.*

1794. From your knowledge of Rochdale would you say that the whole of the artizans, speaking roughly, insure their children's lives ? —The population of the Rochdale borough is about 70,000, and of the union over which I am superintendent, about 130,000 ; this society, the Newbold, has a membership of 20,000 ; they are not all resident in the district, but there is no doubt that numbers of the respectable artizan class insure in these societies ; there are, of course, sick societies as well as death societies.

1795. It is the habit of the class as a whole to insure their children's lives ?—Yes.

1796. Do you think there is a difference between the habits of the more and the less respectable class, that the more respectable only insure children of about two years of age, whereas the thriftless and the immoral insure as soon as the child is born ?—My opinion is that the worst class of people do not insure at all. I am speaking now of the class of people who come to the guardians at any time they want assistance. I have no doubt there are cases in which we inter at the cost of the union, where the insurance money has been obtained. There is a great traffic in adult deaths.

Earl *Beauchamp.*

1797. Did I understand you to say that you do not express any opinion as to the effect of children's insurance upon infant mortality ?—I have not expressed such opinion.

1798. You express no opinion, but have you formed any opinion ?—I think that the provisions of the Friendly Societies Act, 1875, are prudent provisions, and I do think that it is wrong for those societies, which are purely friendly societies, to get away from those provisions and safeguards, by being incorporated under another Act.

1799. You think that until those safeguards were evaded, the Act of 1875 afforded all proper safeguards for children's lives ?—I should couple with the provisions of the Friendly Societies Act of 1875 the provision of registration.

1800. Of what ?—Of the registration of the child insured.

The Witness is directed to withdraw.

4 *July* 1890.

MR. JAMES KIRSHAW, is called in; and Examined, as follows:

Chairman.

1801. You are Relieving Officer at the Union Office, Town Head, Rochdale?—Yes.

1802. What is the size of your district?—There are about 40,000 population there.

1803. How long have you been an officer in that district?—Twelve years.

1804. What character of people reside in your district generally?—In one district I have some of the low characters.

1805. Are there any of the better class?—A small proportion only.

1806. Your attention has been confined chiefly to the lower class, and the improvident people, naturally, as relieving officer?—Yes; in one particular district.

1807. Do those people insure their children; I mean these very low class of people?—I believe they do.

1808. Have you formed an opinion as to why they insure their children's lives?—I believe they do it to make money.

1809. Do you think that the prospect of handling a few pounds would induce a parent of this class to let his child die?—I am inclined to think so.

1810. Have you noticed whether in many cases the parents let their children die for the sake of the insurance money?—I have thought so, in some cases.

1811. Do you think the people of this class insure the lives of their children merely to keep themselves off the parish?—I do not think they care anything about it.

1812. You do not think that they care how the children are buried?—I do not think they care.

1813. Can you give any case of an insurance funeral, that is to say, the funeral of a child who has been insured, coming to the parish?—Yes.

1814. Have you had any very recent case?—Not recently.

1815. Do you know any case where a shilling a week has been paid to a collector?—Yes.

1816. And in that same case the parties coming to you for relief?—Yes.

1817. Do they deposit the policy with you?—Yes.

1818. As security for the money?—Yes.

1819. Have you any reason to think that the parish has had to bury insured children?—I believe so.

1820. In that case it could not be done without people deceiving you?—I found that out after the child was buried.

1821. Do you find that the agents of the insurance societies give you any help in detecting these matters?—I have found one agent who has given us information.

1822. But do the others generally?—I have found two other agents who have helped to cheat us in the matter.

1823. By getting the funeral on the parish?—Yes.

Chairman—continued.

1824. Are there so many of those agents that they compete with one another?—Yes.

1825. The fact of an agent helping to get a funeral on the parish would make him very popular with that class of people?—It would incline them in that direction.

1826. The agents never volunteer information, do they?—Only one agent ever did.

1827. What reason have you for thinking, as I understand you do, that in certain cases the parents have taken the insurance money for drink?—I have found that a day or two after the death, the child having been buried, they have been drinking, and their neighbours drinking with them.

1828. And giving up work?—Yes, and giving up work.

1829. They were flush of money; they gave up work and they drank immediately after the funeral?—Yes.

1830. Upon that you concluded that these, being very poor persons, spent the insurance money not on the funeral, but upon this drink and dissipation?—I thought so.

Earl of Harrowby.

1831. With regard to the class who insure, do you think the most immoral and the most thriftless in your district insure young children's lives?—I think both classes insure, both the better class and the worst class, as far as my knowledge goes.

1832. It is a habit throughout the whole class, from the most respectable to the most thriftless?—Yes; this large club which has been referred to is spread all up and down the town; I should think there is hardly a street but where there are some members in that local club.

1833. Can you give the Committee the cost of a non-pauper child's funeral?—I should think about 1 *l.* would be the cost for a non-pauper child.

1834. The absolutely necessary expenses?—Yes.

1835. That would cover everything?—Yes.

Earl Beauchamp.

1836. Do funerals take place in Rochdale on the Sunday?—No.

1837. They are prohibited on the Sunday?—I believe they are.

1838. So that in addition to the cost of the funeral there would be the loss of a day's work, or half a day's work incurred in their attending it?—There would.

1839. I do not quite understand the instance you gave us of 1 *s.* a week being paid by parents who, I think you said, came to you for an order for a funeral?—That was not the case of a child, it was the case of a very old woman.

1840. You are here to speak about child insurance?—That case did not refer to child insurance at all.

1841. You

Earl *Beauchamp*—continued.

1841. You told the Committee that on one occasion you went a few days after the burial of the child and you found there had been a great deal of drinking, was that a case where the funeral had been paid out of the insurance money ?—Yes, it was.

1842. And there was a surplus over which was spent in merry making ?—Yes.

1843. Was that the case in which a wake would be held ?—It was.

1844. Were they Irish?—Yes; it so happens that I have a large proportion of Irish in that particular district ; it is my worst district.

1845. What you have said with regard to this merry making would apply in the other cases, to those cases of persons who are accustomed to

Earl *Beauchamp*—continued.

celebrate their funeral rites with a wake ?—Yes.

Chairman.

1846. Do you think that the spending of the funeral money upon a wake tends to thrift ?—I do not think it does ; just the opposite.

1847. The great argument in favour of insurance is that it tends to thrift ; you do not think that parents who get a tolerably cheap funeral and spend the balance of the insurance money upon a wake, are thrifty people ?—I do not think so.

1848. It is not necessarily a proof of thrift upon their part ?—No.

The Witness is directed to withdraw.

[*Ordered,* That this Committee be adjourned to Tuesday next, at Twelve o'clock.

Die Martis, 8° Julii 1890.

LORDS PRESENT:

Earl of DERBY.
Earl SPENCER.
Earl of HARROWBY.
Earl BEAUCHAMP.
Earl of SELBORNE.
LORD BISHOP OF PETERBOROUGH.

LORD BISHOP OF RIPON.
Lord CLIFFORD OF CHUDLEIGH.
Lord POLTIMORE.
Lord BROUGHAM AND VAUX.
Lord NORTON.

THE RIGHT REV. THE LORD BISHOP OF PETERBOROUGH, IN THE CHAIR.

THE *Chairman* reads a report of proceedings before the magistrates at Newcastle subsequent to a coroner's verdict of manslaughter. " At the Newcastle police-court, yesterday, Sarah Ann Grieves and John Grieves on remand were charged with causing the death of their child, John Henry Grieves, aged two months, by starving it while in a house, 22, Napier-street, on the 22nd June. At the coroner's inquest last week a verdict of manslaughter, it may be remembered, was returned against both parents. Mr. Edward Clark defended the male prisoner. The evidence previously given having been repeated, the Chairman said, never during the whole course of his thirty years' experience had he heard a more unnatural and brutal case. He thought it ought to have been the duty of those other relations if they had any feeling of humanity to have tried to do something for the child. Both parents were committed to the assizes on a charge of manslaughter. Mr. Clark said he did not wish to put the police to any unnecessary labour. He had felt it his duty to ask the man if his children were insured, and he said they were all insured. They were insured in the Prudential, but he did not know for what amount. *Chairman.*] What is the usual amount?—Mr. *Clark.*] Thirty shillings and two pounds, and for that insurance they pay one penny, or perhaps more, per week. *Chairman.*] Then a child just born can be insured ; it dies, and the parents get this sum of money?—Mr. *Clark.*] Yes. *Chairman.*] And how much does it cost to bury a child?—Mr. *Clark.*] I do not know exactly, but I should say probably 8 *s.* *Chairman.*] And the parents net a sovereign?— The Clerk (Mr. *Roberts*). It is a premium on manslaughter and murder. *Chairman.*] It is scandalous. And have we any more companies like that?—The Clerk.] Oh, plenty."

The extract is ordered to be entered on the Minutes, *quantum valeat.*

THE HON. SIR ALFRED WILLS, is called in ; and Examined, as follows :

Chairman.

1849. YOU are one of Her Majesty's Judges? —I am.
1850. I think you have been so for about six years?—Six years, very nearly.
1851. In the discharge of your duties in criminal courts, has your attention been called to the connection of crimes against children with insurance on their lives?—It has more or less. I do not know whether it would be convenient to your Lordships that I should just state in my own fashion the views which I entertain on this

Chairman—continued.

subject. If quite convenient to your Lordships I think I would prefer so to do. My Lords, the conviction that there is a certain degree of connection between insurance and the death of children has been gradually, if I may use the expression, filtering into my mind ever since it became a part of my duty to pa careful attention to questions of this kind. My convictions have been formed partly upon cases which I have tried, partly upon the natural interchange of views between myself and my colleagues, not in any

K 4

formal

Chairman—continued.

formal way, but in the course of friendly discussion and conversation, and I may add that some very specific information, which I think has been very useful to me, has come to my mind in the course of two or three cases which I have tried of frauds practised by the insurance agents who are the canvassers for business of this kind. In the course of those trials the veil has been lifted off some portions of their doings and their ways in a manner that one could not have expected under any other circumstances. I think, as far as my own personal experience is concerned, this has been the most instructive part of it. I may add, that in conversation with my learned brother, Baron Pollock, yesterday on this very subject, he said to me spontaneously, that he thought he had learned more with reference to this matter from some cases of that nature of frauds by insurance agents, which he has tried, than from everything else in his judicial experience. Of course, my Lord, I may add that I found my views partly upon the result of that sort of critical, though I hope not uncharitable, study of human nature which is part of my daily duty, and without which one has little chance of doing justice either in civil or criminal cases. Now, my Lords, subject to some observations with which I should like to conclude I cannot doubt that there are a vast number of instances of child insurance which lead to no mischief to the child, and which, subject to some considerations that I hope to be allowed to mention presently, may be called legitimate; the business could not go on at all if there was any very large portion of insured children who were done to death for the sake of the insurance. We are, therefore, necessarily dealing with the residuum—I hope a small percentage of the aggregate—which represents the dealings with children of bad parents and bad people. But then there must be a certain percentage of people of that sort, and taken on the whole it certainly amounts to a very considerable number of persons. No one who has sat in a criminal court at the Assizes, especially in the great centres of population, Lancashire, Yorkshire, Warwickshire, and so on, can doubt that there is in the aggregate a very considerable and lamentable amount of abuse of children by the most arrant neglect and cruelty. I try a very great many more cases of this kind into which the element of insurance does not enter, than of those into which it does enter, but I think that observation of itself has a material bearing upon the question of insurance, because I am satisfied that after making the largest allowance for pure ignorance (which accounts for a good deal of what is sometimes set down as cruelty) there is a very considerable residuum left of downright sheer wanton cruelty. I should like to add that in my own opinion we make too much allowance for ignorance rather than too little. It is absolutely necessary, in dealing with criminal cases, to err on that side, if at all, and I think that accused persons, in cases of this sort, get a larger credit for mere ignorance and poverty, and those things which they cannot help, than they very often are really entitled to. After every allowance which justice and charity can make, there are I have no doubt, a very considerable num-

ber of children in this country who are starved to death by parents who could prevent it if they chose, but who prefer either not to earn, or, when they have earned, to spend their money in drink and dissipation. Now if that be so when you come to throw in the incentive of a pecuniary benefit, which to many of these people is enormous compared with their daily earnings or any sum which they can hope to have in hand by any other means; when you add that temptation to the mere temptation to avoid a burden, I cannot help thinking that it must have a very bad effect, and that, besides the actual percentage added to the proportion of children done to death in this way, it must have a bad moral effect generally. That independently of this motive, children are habitually starved to death, I have no more doubt than that I sit here. I have tried cases over and over again where no one could have the smallest doubt that the helpless children had been subjected to a long course of systematic starvation, sometimes to avoid a burden, sometimes that their wretched appearance might excite sympathy on the part of the public, and so further the selfish ends of the parents. If you add to the temptation to get rid of a very serious and unwelcome burden the temptation of what to the kind of people I am speaking of is an enormous sum of money in hand, I think it requires no great acquaintance with human nature to know what the results must be, and that it must be to considerably increase the sorrows and the destruction of children. I have no wish or right to speak for anybody but myself, but I think I cannot be wrong in saying that I have never talked on this subject with any of my colleagues who is not substantially of a like opinion, and, I have every reason to say that the views which I am expressing to your Lordships are not, taken generally, my own isolated views. The system, as it seems to me, of this insurance on its present basis works badly in many ways. One of the great evils of the system appears to me to be this, that it is necessary for the insurance societies which indulge in it to tout, and they do tout to an enormous extent, and the heaviest pressure of persuasion is put upon the poor people to insure their children's lives, as it is called. I am sure that that goes on to a very great extent; it is very difficult for anybody who does not sit habitually in a criminal court, or learn something about it in other ways, to appreciate the extent to which it does go on. Agents, who are touting for business of this kind, cannot possibly be nice as to what they say, or what inducements they hold out of profit from the death of children, and I cannot help thinking that it brings about necessarily an unwholesome preaching in a most practical way as to the benefit to be derived from the early death of children, which cannot fail to demoralise, and against which you may preach in vain from the pulpit or from the bench, or from anywhere else, whence you cannot offer the same pecuniary advantages. The people who tout for these societies must preach the gospel of profit to be derived from the death of children, and it seems to me difficult to conceive a more unwholesome teaching than that, enforced as it is in practice by an utter absence

8 *July* 1890.]   Hon. Sir A. WILLS.   [*Continued.*

Chairman—continued.

absence of inquiry, or of precaution in making payments which become due upon the death of a child, which is undoubtedly the rule, and without which they might ply their vocation in vain. It is a necessary part of this system, and I believe its universal concomitant, that when death takes place no inconvenient questions should be asked. That seems to me to be most demoralising in itself, because you have the spectacle of a person who is above many of these people to whom arguments of this kind are addressed, who winks, and must wink if he is to carry on his trade successfully, at anything that is suspicious or unwholesome in the story of death with which he has to deal. Let me add this, if I may, that the poor themselves, I think, are a great deal deluded by this system of insurance, because the premiums which they pay are and must be very high in comparision with the results which are obtained, because there is so much necessarily of the illegitimate element in the system, and so much that is on the borderland that it must be absolutely necessary to charge higher than you would if there was no element of this kind introduced. I believe that the poor are really paying a vast deal more than they are at all aware where they are effecting what they consider to be legitimate insurance. They also, I think, are subjected to pecuniary loss, which they themselves hardly appreciate, by reason of the great number of lapsed policies. They cannot keep up the payments, there are a great number of lapsed policies where the poor, of course, get nothing, and they lose all that they have paid up to the time; so that, I believe, the result is that if you were to take an average, the amount of premiums actually paid, spread over the number of cases in which payments are kept up, gives a much higher rate than most people have any idea of. I believe that lapsed policies of the kind we are dealing with form a serious source of profit to the insurance companies. Of course the lapsed policies represent so much dead loss to the poor. To a considerable extent it is a system of wagering on the double event of the power to keep up the payments and the death of the child, and I believe that the stakes which the poor really pay are, in the aggregate, much higher than they imagine. It is said sometimes that all this is disrespectful to the working classes, and that it does not credit them with the good feelings and the sense of right which they really have. My answer is two-fold. First, I say nothing of them which I would not say of any other large masses of mankind if you put equal temptations in their way; and, secondly, it matters not to whom it is disrespectful if it is true. The working classes are, at all events, numerous, and amongst them a very small percentage gives a large aggregate.

1852. I think I understood you to say that though the percentage of bad cases of cruel parents in the working classes might be a small percentage, yet that the actual amount of such cases might be very large?—Of that I am quite certain.

1853. You speak of the touting of these agents.

142.

Chairman—continued.

They compete, I presume, against one another, a good deal necessarily?—That is hardly within my department, but it must be so. I am satisfied, from cases that have been tried before me, that they put a great deal of pressure on the poor people.

1854. I think you said you had cases of actual fraud on the part of insurance agents, which have come before you. It would appear that these agents are capable of fraud?—Yes.

1855. Would your Lordship say whether the fraud was on the parents or on the company?—The cases which I have tried have all been cases of fraud on the companies.

1856. Then the companies are liable, it would appear, to be deceived by their own agents?—There is no doubt about that.

1857. Therefore we may assume that however well-intentioned the company may be, it is very much in the hands and at the mercy of these agents?—No doubt.

1858. These agents having a direct and considerable profit on commission and on each policy that they effect, are naturally exposed to a very strong temptation to deceive and keep their employers in the dark?—There is no doubt about that. I think I must add that the impression left on my mind by six years of attention to this subject, because it comparatively early attracted my attention after I became a judge, is that, as a rule, many of these insurances are effected perfectly recklessly, without any regard at all to the health or condition of the child, or to the probable duration of life.

1859. In point of fact all that the agent appears to care about, in most cases, is getting his percentage?—That is undoubtedly so.

1860. I think your Lordship spoke of it being your opinion that poor men's money was very largely wasted and thrown away in many of these insurance cases?—Of that I have no doubt at all. There are a very great number in which the poor people cannot keep up the policies, or in which they get tired of keeping them up, and those cases are all so much directly to the good of the society.

1861. So far as that consideration goes, you would be disposed to say that insurance rather tended to waste a poor man's money than to thrift or to saving?—I think insurance of the kind we are dealing with is wasteful. I think also that it leads to thrift in the wrong direction, if I may say so, because it cannot, I think, be right that the parent should have a large pecuniary interest in the death of his child. It seems to me to be against all our notions of the principles on which insurance ought to be effected.

1862. It is all distinctly against the principle on which the original statute of George III. was framed, that there should be no wagering or gambling in human life?—It is so.

1863. And that statute forbade any person to insure the life of another unless he could show in the life an insurable interest?—That is so.

1864. All these cases which have been occurring under the Friendly Societies Act are occurring under a statute which so far as persons concerned

L   cerned

Chairman—continued.

cerned under those Acts go was practically a repeal, in fact literally was a repeal of the statute of George III.?—That is so.

1865. Then, in point of fact, the permission to insure under certain conditions and safeguards given by the Friendly Societies Act is an exceptional privilege given to the class concerned?—It is.

1866. In order to give that exceptional privilege it was actually necessary to repeal, so far as they were concerned, the wholesome statute of George III. which forbade all wagering?—It is so.

1867. Of course, it would be your Lordship's opinion then that in any case in which an exceptional privilege is conferred on any class, or any person, the onus lies on that class and person to justify that exceptional privilege?—Certainly.

1868. The whole of this exceptional privilege is a pure creation of law?—That is so; that is to say, a statutory exception out of statutory law which was passed to prevent these evils.

1869. Even if no cases such as your Lordship and other witnesses have mentioned, could be adduced of abuse of these privileges, the onus would always lie on the person possessing the privilege to justify it?—I think so.

1870. The Friendly Societies Act, your Lordship is aware, imposed certain restrictions on insurance. Lives under a certain age were only to be insured for a certain sum?—Yes.

1871. Those restrictions, like all restrictions, imply an imputation on somebody. If nobody was inclined to do wrong, I presume nobody would be required to be restrained?—It is an imputation, if at all, upon the frailty of human nature.

1872. It is an imputation upon human nature, but not necessarily more upon the human nature of the working classes than any other class?—Might I answer your Lordship in two lines of Horace :

" Jura inventa metu injusti fateare necesse est,
Tempora si fastosque velis evolvere mundi."

1873. Your Lordship speaks of there being a kind of wagering as it were, on the part of the insurance company as to the double event between the parent's payments and the child's insurance. In point of fact, that is a kind of wagering on the life?—I think so.

1874. I think your Lordship will remember that wagering on human life was the very thing which the statute of George III. was intended to prevent?—That is so.

1875. Then to sum up your Lordship's evidence it would appear to be this, that although there may be a small per-centage of the working class really guilty of this matter, yet the actual amount may be great?—I think so.

1876. In the next place it would appear that your Lordship has not found the parental affection in every case, or even in many cases, a sufficient safeguard for infant life?—I think it would be the idlest affectation to doubt that there are not a few parents in this country who would starve their children for 5 *s.* a-piece. I

Chairman—continued.

do not mean to say that represents any large per-centage, but I do mean to say that, taking the enormous numbers of the working classes, and the classes below the working classes, there are a good many cases of cruelty and starvation in the whole. They consist largely, however, not of working people, but of people who do not work, and who will not work, and I think that there is no doubt that there are many children who are simply given over to death for the sake of the insurance.

1877. What you say of these persons, and this per-centage, is therefore no libel or insult to the majority of the working classes who are presumably affectionate?—Not at all.

1878. And the cry that I and others promoting this Bill are offering a foul insult to the working classes is simply so much claptrap?—To me it seems the absurdest attack upon an endeavour to get at a right principle that could possibly be. I cannot understand myself why a right-minded man should have any wish to make a profit out of the death of his child. To myself, it is forbidden by law, inasmuch as these small insurances would offer no temptation, and, in respect of large sums, I should come under the general law. Now there is no doubt whatever that the amount that is insured is in many of the cases under consideration a large profit, and I think that is one of the things that ought to be struck at.

1879. As regards the cases being tried in a criminal court, I should like to ask your Lordship, supposing the charge is one of manslaughter or murder, the evidence of the husband would not be admissible against the wife, nor the evidence of the wife against the husband, would it?—That is so.

1880. Then even in the case where the husband and wife do not conspire to do away with the child, and where only one of the parties is guilty the other party however much he or she might contest the proceedings could give no evidence against the other in a court of justice on a charge of manslaughter?—That is so.

1881. Therefore in point of fact the difficulty of getting a conviction for manslaughter or murder must be very great, on account of the want of evidence?—That is so undoubtedly. I have no doubt that some cases which I have tried of criminal neglect would have had different results if the one parent could have been heard against the other. Of course that opens a very wide question.

1882. In the cases which have been brought before you, are you of opinion that the result of that difficulty of conviction for manslaughter or murder has led in many cases to the parent being indicted on a minor charge with a view to getting a verdict?—Yes, I think that possible. I cannot say that I have had my attention very much drawn to that distinction, nor do I, perhaps, attach quite so much importance to it as some people would, because, in my judgment, it is far more important that punishment should be pretty certain than that it should be severe ; and, therefore, to my mind, it does not so much matter what these wrong-doers are convicted of, if they are convicted of something.

1883. My

Chairman—continued.

1883. My question really had reference to the argument brought against the promoters of this Bill, that we cannot produce many cases of murder or manslaughter, and my question went rather to this, that one of the reasons why we cannot do so, in addition to the difficulty of evidence, is the temptation to prosecutors, or the inducement to prosecutors, to prefer a minor charge with the view to getting a verdict, rather than prefer the graver charge?--That is so, no doubt. I cannot entertain any reasonable doubt that in cases which I have tried, where the conviction has been for some minor offence, it has really been a case of manslaughter, if not of murder.

1884. Then the demand that the promoters of this Bill should produce a great number of cases of proved and convicted and punished infanticide is an unreasonable one under the circumstances?—I think so; besides which there is an enormous amount of cruelty practised upon children, which is short of actually killing them. Some society steps in, some visitor finds it out, and the matter is stopped it may be a few weeks or days before it will ripen into a case of manslaughter. People who starve their children are very often very desirous, whether with or without insurance, to be able to get a certificate of death, and a constant incident in these cases is a visit to the doctor with a moribund child; and I have tried several cases in which I have had little doubt that such was the motive for the visit, and in which the visit and the consequent interference of the medical man has led to the separation of the child from the parent and so saved its life.

1885. Has it at all occurred to your Lordship what amendments in the law, or what provisions might be desirable in order to prevent all this evil?—I cannot help thinking that the greatest improvement that could be introduced by way of safeguard would be to prevent people from making a profit of it. I have no doubt at all that the sums which are paid by the insurance offices are largely in access of the actual loss. A child dies. It can be buried, I know from evidence in matters of this kind having come before me, we will say for between 15 s. and 20 s.; many of these insurance offices insure up to 6 l., and I am not at all sure that they do not go higher, but 6 l., I think, upon a child not five years old. That is really 6 l. very often upon an infant of a few weeks or months' age, and that to many of the persons concerned, it is no disrespect to them to say, is an enormous sum.

1886. It has been suggested that a desirable amendment in the law would be this, that the contract between the insurance company and the insurer, should take the form of a contract of indemnity, that is to say, as in the case of a fire insurance, that the company should not be bound to pay a sum of money to the parent at all, but there might be a contract that the company would pay to the amount of the policy, and bear all the death expenses, including the funeral; do you think that if that were possible, it would have an effect in checking these evils?—I think that would be much better than leaving things as they are. I think it would be wise also to establish some very moderate pecuniary limit, because

(142.)

Chairman—continued.

I think the moment you open the door to the uncertain, you open the door to fraud. The resources of fraud, and the resources of people who wish to do wrong, are simply endless, and I think that if the margin of possible profit was large, there might be collusion between the insuree and the undertaker.

Earl *of Derby.*

1887. I think your Lordship told us that you had no doubt there were many parents who would starve their children for 5 s.?--I am sure there are parents who would do it.

1888. In that case would there not be a stronger inducement to cause the death of the child, arising out of the mere desire to be free of the burden of its support?—I think that my be; my point is that when you come to add to that desire to get rid of a burden, the putting in the pocket of 3 l., 4 l., or 5 l., you greatly add to the temptation, in a particularly attractive way, and to no good end.

1889. I am only putting it in this way: you may remove part of the temptation by doing away with the practice of insurance, but will not a much larger part of the temptation remain, inasmuch as the relief caused by the death of the child is considerably more important in a pecuniary point of view than the sum gained by its death?--I think I should say about that that the class of persons to whom anything of this kind applies, are people to whom the immediate possession of a 5 l. note is something like what we read of sometimes as the wealth of Golconda, and it does really afford an enormous temptation. Your Lordships will remember also, that in a very great many cases where one has reason to fear criminal neglect and foul play, with regard to children, the period of life has not arrived when the expense is anything appreciable. I may tell your Lordships, *apropos* of this, that in certainly the worst case of this kind that I have tried, there really was to my mind the strongest possible reason for believing that a woman with a perfectly good supply of milk withheld it from the child, and got rid of it somehow for the purpose partly of exciting compassion by the aspect of the child, and partly, I have no doubt, of not being too long burdened with it. I have a very strong impression, though I cannot give chapter and verse for it, that that represents a very considerable class of cases.

1890. I suppose you have no means of knowing, among the children who die under suspicious circumstances, what is the proportion who have been insured?—No; that I have no means of ascertaining. But one brings one's ordinary knowledge of human nature to bear, and one is satisfied that with bad people who are not restrained by considerations of morality and right and wrong, the prospect of the immediate acquisition of a 5 l. note, which is a thing which they have heard of but, as a personal possession, have never seen, is a temptation of which it is very difficult for us to measure the extent.

1891. You spoke of the competition between these various insurance societies as being very keen?—There is no doubt about that.

L 2   1892. And

Earl of *Derby*—continued.

1892. And you also spoke of the premiums which the poor have to pay to them being very high?—I think they are.

1893. Do not those two statements to some extent at least neutralise one another. If there is a very keen competition between the various societies would not that tend to lower the premiums to the lowest amount at which business would be profitable?—I doubt that, because these premiums are paid in pence and halfpence, and collected from week to week, and so on, and I do not think that the people who pay them have any idea how much they are paying. Into scales of payment so made it is not easy to introduce fine shades of difference. I think that is one of the mischiefs of this system. Then it very often happens that after having paid up for a considerable time, they cannot pay any longer, and then all the money which they have paid is forfeited. I am sure that is a very large element of pecuniary success to those who undertake this business.

1894. That occurs, does it not, in cases of other insurance besides the insurance of children. Insurance offices, in general, profit by lapsed policies, or am I mistaken in that statement?—Yes; but it is amongst the very poor that there is likely to be such a large percentage of lapsed policies. I suppose in rather a better class of life, where poverty is not so habitual, the percentage of lapsed policies is likely to be very much smaller than it is with regard to business of this kind.

1895. Quite apart from the question which we are considering before this Committee, the question of infanticide caused by insurance, do you think that the poor are unfairly, or even fraudulently treated, first, in having to pay too much in their premiums, and next in having often to lose the benefit of what they have paid for by their policies lapsing?—I should not like to apply the word fraudulent to those embarking in this business. I think they have done great mischief, and that a system has grown up of which the consequences were not originally foreseen, and that it involves much recklessness in the way of carrying it out; but I should not like to say that the offices are fraudulent in their dealings. But the actual rate of charge is concealed under these small weekly or monthly payments, and I feel sure the poor pay very highly. They could not possibly insure such lives as these unless they did; and I am also very sure that a very great many policies lapse because people get into trouble and cannot keep up their payments, and that is a very large source of profit.

1896. You think that an alteration of the sum for which children might be insured might be effective in diminishing the evil of which I have spoken?—I cannot help thinking so. In so saying, I am rather applying well-known principles of human nature than doing anything else.

1897. I presume in that case it would be necessary to lower the amount payable at the death of child to the very smallest amount which would suffice for funeral expenses?— I do not see, if I may take the liberty of saying so, what else the parents want in the case of the death of a child. The tendency among the poor to be

Earl of *Derby*—continued.

extravagant in regard to funerals is, I should think, already sufficiently pronounced. I think it would be not a bad thing if they did not have a chance of a very expensive funeral in cases of this kind.

1898. You told us in your evidence that you could not understand a right-minded man wishing to make a profit out of the death of his child?—Yes.

1899. In that I should agree. Can you not understand a right-minded man in very poor circumstances wishing to provide for the exceptional misfortune of having to bury a child?—That I quite agree in, and if some means could be devised which should make it impossible that a profit should be made out of it I should see very much less objection to it.

1900. You have no objection to the funeral being paid for out of insurance, provided the parents make no profit?—Make no profit. I am told that 6 *l.*, and I believe larger sums even than that, are paid for a poor child's funeral. I am satisfied if that does not represent a profit it represents an amount of merry-making which is very unsuitable to the occasion.

1901. Do you think an alteration of the age at which children may be insured, so as to exclude those under 12 months, or, perhaps, under two years, would have any considerable effect in diminishing the cases of crime?—I do not, think, my Lord, that any opinion I could give on such a subject as that would be worth having. The matters which come under my notice in a criminal court hardly enable me to give a satisfactory answer to that question; but it seems to me that the objectionable elements of this kind of insurance are greater the lower the age of the insured.

Earl *Spencer.*

1902. I think you are aware that a good many perfectly honest poor do value this, and insure their children's lives?—I have not the least doubt of it.

1903. In those cases is it always a profit that they get. Is it not possible that there are other matters besides the funeral expenses that they pay out of the sum they receive, such as nursing, or doctors, or mourning?—It is possible; but my experience would not enable me to answer your Lordship's question on that point with any satisfaction.

1904. Have you any experience of different kinds of societies; you spoke of touting, and you might call them the touting, of the collecting societies. Have you any experience of other societies who do not employ touting for their purposes?—No; I should say that in all the cases which have come before me which have enabled me to form any judgment on this subject—I think in every case—the society has had its canvassers.

1905. You have not had any cases of this sort coming from friendly societies, who rely on local knowledge, and do not have actual collectors?—No; I do not think so; I cannot recall any.

1906. You

Lord *Norton*.

1906. You clearly think that if the profit could be removed there would be no harm in insuring against the absolute expenses of a child's funeral?—I cannot see the least reason why there should be any objection to that.

1907. You seem to think that the maximum expense of a small child's funeral in that case would be from 15 *s.* to 1 *l.*?—I have been told by those who know better than myself that that is about the sum often paid, but I do not say that is the maximum of legitimate expenditure.

1908. Do you not think that the matter of the doctor's attendance ought be added to that?—I think if you could secure that the doctor would get it there is no objection.

1909. Do you think, supposing the law restricted the amount of such assurances as these, we will say to 2 *l.*, that the objections to the system would be removed?—I think *pro tanto* they would be removed. There might remain a residuum who would be tempted even then.

1910. Do you think there are other ways in which a thrifty parent could provide against such casual expenses, such as laying by money in the savings' bank for the purpose?—That is a matter in respect of which my judicial experience would give my opinion no special authority, and I would rather confine myself to such matters as I really have thought of in connection with my every-day work.

1911. Supposing it may be an object to thrifty parents to provide against the expense of a child's funeral, and such parents being, by your own testimony, by far the majority of all, would it be right to sacrifice their expenses as a death, such as laying by money in a savings bank?—I think that if in any way it could be rendered impossible for the parent to make a profit out of the transaction, a great many objections would be removed. I know that sometimes it is said that to speak in this way is speaking disrespectfully of the working classes. I cannot quite myself see that anybody ought to be offended at legislation which would proceed upon the footing that no profit ought to be possible out of such an event.

1912. From your statement as to the very high payments which their interests for the sake of a small number of unnatural parents who would be capable of abusing such things?—It has never entered my head to sacrifice their interests in any way. The thing that does seem to me to be dangerous, and to be very dangerous to infant life, is the probability of the parents being able to make a profit out of the death.

1913. What I wanted to know is whether you think that the injustice of sacrificing the interests of a great majority of parents for the sake of the abuse by the small minority of unnatural parents, might be removed by another mode of insurance against which parents have to make for such insurances as this, would not an investment in the savings bank be a much more economical mode of providing for the same?—I should think if you take it over a large area, that would be undoubtedly true, but of course the object of a system of insurance is to meet the cases where the deposits in the savings bank have not gone on long enough to cover the money wanted.

(142.)

Lord *Norton*—continued.

1914. It is from the loose way in which these insurance companies are conducted that the payment is necessarily high. Is not the profit that they make chiefly by lapsed policies?—I should think that is very likely, but really that is an actuarial question that I am not prepared to give any opinion about.

1915. In the case of elder children, where a child is an absolute profit, or may be a profit by his work to his parents, there can be no such temptation in the way of a temptation to neglect the child's life?—Clearly.

1916. When the child is old enough to earn money the temptation ceases?—Clearly if the money earned is adequate.

1917. In your experience is there any defect in the law which impedes convictions in cases of this sort?—I do not myself see any alteration in the law short of the great question which underlies a great many of the questions of criminal jurisprudence, that is, whether the prisoner should be examined. I am myself a convert to the view that prisoners should be allowed to give evidence.

1918. You have no other remedy to suggest have you than that which you have suggested of reducing the amount of such insurance?—The question of remedy has hardly fallen within the scope of my particular studies, and I do not feel myself competent to do more than point out to your Lordships such things as have forced themselves upon my notice during my judicial life.

1919. You do not suggest altogether the prohibition of child insurance?—No. I do not see any reason at all for that. If I may take the liberty of saying so I think that would be a mistake.

Lord Bishop of *Ripon*.

1920. May I ask your Lordship whether the opinions you have expressed are based on the facts which have come out mostly in various trials?—I think entirely. I had no opinion on this subject before I came on to the judicial bench. I had no occasion to study it. I have given a good deal of attention to it since; it has occupied my thoughts very much and very often.

1921. Did the action of what we may call the touts in connection with collecting societies come out in the trials at all?—I have heard a good deal of that, but not in trying cases of cruelty. I have already said that in the cases of fraud by insurance agents, which I have tried, I have seen that there is a great deal of it. I have not the least doubt of that. They go into every back street in a large town to an extent that is really astonishing.

1922. And I gather you felt there was some objection to that because it tended to suggest, perhaps, that there was gain to be made at the death?—I do not think it works well myself in more ways than one. I think, in the first place, that it induces a good many people to begin insurance with no reasonable prospect of keeping it up, and to whom, therefore, it is an unmitigated loss. I think, also, that there are a great many people who have at one time a reasonable prospect of keeping it up, who are almost certain in the course of years to fail in it.

L 3

1923. I was

Lord *Bishop of Ripon*—continued.

1923. I was rather putting the question with a view to gather whether you thought that it incited to wrong doing; whether those who thought they could make a profit out of the child had the first suggestion made by some of these agents?—My own personal experience hardly entitles me to express an opinion upon that point. It is rather a question of what is likely to be the case in human nature than from anything that has actually come under my observation.

Lord *Brougham and Vaux.*

1924. From the various conversations which you had with your colleagues on the subject, would you say they generally share your opinions?—I think so. I have no right to commit anybody else to my opinions, but I really do not know anyone who does not hold, as I think, substantially the same views. Baron Pollock did give me leave to say, if the question arose, that this is his view as well as mine, and that in his opinion, and to use his words, the system is not only indefensible in theory but bad in practice.

Lord *Poltimore.*

1925. Would not the fact of limiting the amount payable at death to the bare expense of the funeral act prejudicially and unfairly upon the more respectable working class who would wish to insure sufficiently perhaps to pay for mourning, or perhaps the doctor's bill?—It might. Of course, in a life like mine, I am perfectly well aware that I see, as it were, one side, and I know there may be another side, and I am sure I do not desire to dogmatise at all. I only desire to place before your Lordships the things that I see, and that present themselves to my mind as very distressing elements of the present system. I do not say for one moment that it is general amongst the poor people to starve their children, and to be cruel to them for the sake of insurance money; such a thought never entered into my head; but that there is a certain per-centage to whom it is an enormous temptation, I really have no more doubt than that I sit here.

Earl *Beauchamp.*

1926. You have told us that you have tried a great many more cases in which the element of insurance did not enter than cases in which it did?—A great many more.
1927. Referring to the case you mentioned just now of a woman who withheld milk from her child, was that child insured?—No.
1928. That was not a case of insurance?—No.
1929. The mother was not prompted to withhold sustenance from her child by the desire of the petty gain she would receive?—No.
1930. What was the result of that trial?—That child died.
1931. What was the result of the trial?—The father and mother are now undergoing a sentence of penal servitude, the mother for 10 years and the father for five.
1932. Do you find any indisposition on the part of juries to convict in cases of this kind?—I think, my Lord, that juries exercise a prudent

Earl *Beauchamp*—continued.

and wise reserve in matters of this kind, and I think that both judges and juries, if they do their duty, are obliged to be very cautious how they sanction convictions. I try many cases which end in acquittal, and which, in my opinion, properly end in acquittal, and in which, if you ask me what my belief is in my heart of hearts, I have very little doubt that there has been criminal neglect, but then you must be absolutely certain of it before you allow a conviction to take place if you can help it.
1933. And criminal neglect stimulated by the desire of insurance money?—Where there is the disposition on the part of the parent which would lead to criminal neglect, I think it is impossible to doubt that if there is a possibility of getting insurance money it is perfectly certain to sharpen it.
1934. Do you think the adoption of any system which saps the independence and self-reliance of the working classes would act injuriously upon society?—I have no doubt about that.
1935. Do you think that undue restrictions upon child insurance might have the effect of driving parents upon the rates and familiarising them with the idea that they are not required to maintain themselves?—Undue restrictions upon the thrift of the poor and upon their own methods of exercising it are, in my opinion, eminently undesirable, and, of course, the practical question lies in the word undue. Everything depends on what view you take of that.
1936. Any restriction that went further than was absolutely required would, in your opinion, be mischievous?—I think so. I have not the slightest feeling myself that the poor are not to be trusted, because they are poor or anything of that kind; but I would apply to my own class, if a question arose, exactly the same principles that I apply to them, and I never can understand why it is an insult to any particular class to apply the general principles which actuate human nature to them, and that there is in human nature a deep-seated selfishness against which a great deal of our legislation is directed nobody can doubt. I think in this particular the poorer people are, broadly speaking, the more liable they are to be actuated by motives of that kind.
1937. Is it not a matter of public advantage to develop in the working class the desire of providing for themselves whatever they may require, rather than throw this expense on society at large?—I think there can be no doubt about that at all.
1938. In applying this principle, like applying all other general principles, it would be impossible to prevent some cases of difficulty emerging?—Undoubtedly; that is so as things are now, if I may venture to say so.

Earl of *Selborne.*

1939. With reference to what you were just now saying about a class, we do apply the principle which you contend to our own class in cases of fire insurance and marine insurance, do we not?—I have always understood nobody can recover more than he has lost. Why there should be this exceptional principle applied to people as to whom it is not disrespectful to say
that

Earl of *Selborne*—continued.

that *ex necessitate rei* they must be tempted by lower sums than would tempt myself or people in my own class of life I cannot understand.

1940. In respect to life insurance, we require proof of interest ?—Proof of interest. There has been very exceptional legislation in regard to this kind of insurance. I cannot help thinking myself that it has really led to a great many deaths which would not have occurred without it.

Earl *Spencer.*

1941. When you were asked that question before, I think you said that you were afraid that any application of what was called the contract of indemnity might create fraud. Is not that so ?—I do not think I said that.

1942. Is not that your opinion ?—Would your Lordship kindly put the question again.

1943. When the question was asked you before with regard to this contract of indemnity, which Lord Selborne has just been asking you

Earl *Spencer*—continued.

a question upon, you said something as to being afraid that anything of that sort might induce fraud. It was so easy to have fraud in matters of this sort, and it was not desirable to encourage it ?—Yes. I think that in regard to these insurances upon very small children there very rarely indeed, as a rule, is an insurable interest which is commensurate with the sum insured.

1944. You do not mean that the proof of the bill of the undertaker, or the doctor, or the nurse would create fraud ?—No, my Lord. I do not mean that. I think my experience in criminal courts would lead me to suppose that it is perfectly possible that occasionally there might be collusion between the undertaker and persons for whom they undertake, and I think that an undertaker who was known to share the proceeds with the family might very likely be a favourite one in a great many districts that I have seen something of in my judicial life.

The Witness is directed to withdraw.

THE HONOURABLE SIR JOHN CHARLES DAY, is called in ; and Examined, as follows:

Chairman.

1945. YOUR Lordship, of course, is one of Her Majesty's Judges. May I ask for how many years have you held that office ?—Eight years.

1946. In criminal cases brought before you have you noticed or had your attention called to the practice of child life insurance ?—Yes.

1947. In what ways has it been brought before you ?—In trials for manslaughter of children and criminal neglect of children, and my attention has been called to the subject many years before I was on the Bench.

1948. Have you formed a strong opinion on the connection of this practice with crimes against children ?—I have.

1949. An unfavourable impression ? — Very unfavourable.

1950. You think then that there is a connection of crime with child insurance, even where only a small profit accrues by the death ; it need not be a very large profit ?—Certainly not. The amounts insured are generally small.

1951. I think you had a case once before you at the Wells Assizes, where four children were insured ?—Yes. Fortunately I can speak more particularly as to that than as to any other of the many cases I have had before me, because the papers have been looked up in that case, and I have had the opportunity of perusing them.

1952. Your memory having been refreshed, would you kindly state to the Committee what is your recollection of that case ?—That was a case in which a man and woman who lived in the neighbourhood of Swindon, who were in exceedingly poor circumstances, carried on the trade of baby-farming. In the autumn of 1886, they were visited by the county court bailiff, who then observed seven of those children on their premises. I refer to the county court bailiff as some evidence of their position and circumstances. They had barely means to keep themselves, but received in respect of these children sums either in gross, or in periodical payments to a certain

(142.)

Chairman—continued.

extent, which made it, at any rate, worth their while to carry on this business. They moved from one house to another, and were observed at most of these places by their neighbours and by the police. The children were in a wretched pitiable condition, a disgusting condition in fact of filth and starvation and disease, so that the smell of the place was very noisome. It was a very shocking case of the kind. In 1888, in May or June of that year, the Society for the Protection of Children from Cruelty took up the case, and the prisoners were tried before me at the summer assizes of that year; they were tried at Wells, and they were convicted. It was shown that in the December previous four of the children were insured. Three of them had been insured, so the prisoners stated to the insurance agent, some time before that. It would follow from that, that all seven children were insured. Altogether the children were in a state of utter, I might say almost hopeless starvation ; they were reduced to a condition of body that is very sad to describe, and no attention of any sort or kind was given to them, and probably they would all have died in a very little while, if they had not, happily, been rescued, and taken off to the union, where I have since heard two of them have died notwithstanding the care that was given to them. But this woman was waited upon by one of the canvassers for an insurance company, and she was induced to insure them at, I think it was, a penny a week, or some very small sum, that was payable in respect of them, and they continued insured up to the time they went to the union workhouse. I say these people managed to find the means for insuring the children, although they did not provide them with the commonest necessaries of life to keep body and soul together. It was a very shocking case of the kind, and I may say I have tried a great number of cases of this description generally.

1953. You have tried a great many similar cases ?

L 4

Chairman—continued.

cases ?—I have tried a great many similar cases. I will not say that the parties have been insured in all the cases; that is not always made to appear; but I have tried a great many cases of manslaughter and cases of criminal neglect in the case of children. I may say I have had occasion to administer criminal justice in everyone of the great centres of population. I have been at the assizes at Liverpool 13 times, Manchester 13 times, Birmingham, Leeds, Newcastle, Bristol, and all our great centres, and I am sorry to say I have had a great many cases of cruelty to children to deal with.

1954. Have you had any experience at all or knowledge, in your courts, of trying cases of collecting agents of these societies which insure children?—I have tried some. I remember one, because it occurred at the last assizes but one that I have been. It was in June 1888, and I think I tried this man at Wells. He was a canvasser who was charged with forgery and fraud by the society. In the course of that trial the course of business had to be gone into for the purpose of showing the embezzlements, and it certainly gave one cause to believe that comparatively little care was taken in controlling the conduct of these men, who derive a large bonus or benefit from every insurance they effect, and that is without reference to its continuance. They get a certain number of premiums paid down to them in advance on effecting the insurance.

1955. Has your Lordship heard that amounts to the amount of eight payments were made, or have you not heard the exact amount?—I did hear the exact amount, but I hesitate to state it.

1956. It is a very considerable amount?—A very large amount.

1957. Not merely a commission on the premiums collected, but in the case of every fresh insurance effected?—Yes, and that is supposed to be repaid to the office in some way. They do get a certain sum of money at once in bringing in the insurance. It is a small amount because the sum insured is small, and the premium is small, but still the profit is paid at a very early period; they get it at once for a considerable time. Therefore, there is a direct object in bringing in the insurance; whether they are kept up or not is quite a different thing. In the case I referred to, the man had insured persons who were in a very sad condition of health, representing them as good lives, because they do not have medical examinations, but they take the examinations of their own agents, or, at least, the reports of their own agents, and this man reported the lives as excellent and good, although some could not be found, and one when found was found in a very desperate state of health. The business is carried on in an exceedingly careless manner, and that the premiums are out of proportion to the benefit conferred there can be no question. The poor, I do not hesitate to say, are not benefited by the system of insurance, because they pay pay a great deal too much for what they are to get, owing to the costliness of the system, and the exertions that are stimulated by considerable payments so as to induce the canvassers to get in business are so

Chairman—continued.

great that the poor do not get anything like what they ought to get in respect of the premiums which they have paid. It is an extravagant system of insurance.

1958. The whole system, then, apart from this tendency to crime, is a wasteful system to the poor themselves?—I think a most wasteful system. The most unhappy system of what is called thrift.

1959. Apparently, then, these agents, with this great inducement to effect insurance, do not take the trouble of investigating the health of the children, or the circumstances of the parents, before they make this insurance?—I should say most certainly not, when you consider that it is not to their interest to do so. The great interest is to find people who will entrust them with their first penny, or whatever the sum is, and thereupon the agent gets his commission.

1960. Have you ever known in your judicial experience one of these companies disputing a policy?—I do not think such cases would come before me. They are too small; I forget, really (I ought to be ashamed to say so) what the tribunal is in which they obtain payment under the Friendly Societies Act; whether it is before magistrates.

1961. At all events, it has not come before your Lordship?—No.

1962. Is it your opinion, then, that this insuring of children, and touting of agents, and bringing before the parents the idea of the death of their children as a means of profit, tends to familiarise the minds of the parents with the idea of profit, as connected with death?—I should think so, certainly.

1963. It is demoralising?—I should think so, certainly. Take the case of Hays, to which reference has already been made. Here are people in an exceedingly poor condition themselves, who were tempted by the prospect of receiving something when these dying children do die. It suggests to my mind, as knowing something of human nature, that that is an inducement to get the money as quickly as may be.

1964. Have you thought of any remedy for this evil state of things?—I can only think of one practical remedy, and that is restoring the law to the state in which it was before the Friendly Societies Act was passed. On this subject let the working people be in the same position as other people are. Let there be no gambling in human life. It is not a fit subject for speculation.

1965. It is contrary to public policy that the law should allow any profit on death?—Certainly.

1966. You see no reason why an exception should be made in favour of one class more than another?—None whatever.

1967. In point of fact, if I might put your Lordship's opinion, it would be something like this; that thrift is a very good thing, but that it may be too dearly purchased by infanticide?—Certainly; that is a very happy way of expressing it.

1968. In point of fact, that the law ought to regard human life as of a greater value than the consideration of thrift?—The two have no common measure.

1969. It is the first business of the law and the

Chairman—continued.

the Legislature to protect human life?—I should think so.

1970. If it could be shown, then, ever so clearly, that the remedies of this evil state of things would lessen the amount of thrift, that would not, in your opinion, be sufficient reason for not passing such measures if it could also be shown that such measure saved human life?—I was going to say, quite apart from the latter branch of your question, I consider that it is a form of thrift, if it be thrift at all, that, in the interest of those who practice it, should be stopped or checked. I think that thrift is badly exercised in the form of insurance under such circumstances as undoubtedly now do and necessarily must exist.

1971. In point of fact, then, I may sum up in two sentences, first, that human life is not to be set against thrift, or thrift against human life; and secondly, that the system is by no means so promotive of thrift as it is alleged?—Certainly not.

1972. That it is a wasteful system?—Most wasteful.

Lord *Clifford of Chudleigh*.

1973. The law in the case of adult life insurance requires an insurable interest in the life insured. Would it be true to say that the principle of the law in the case of adult life insurance is precisely the same as that of an ordinary insurance, but that the difficulty of proving the pecuniary loss occasioned by the death of a person insured renders it possible to effect an insurance above the pecuniary loss occasioned?—In the case of adults there must be an insurable interest in the person on whose behalf the insurance is effected.

1974. The difficulty in the ordinary case of ascertaining whether that insurance is above the actual loss or not is so great that it is practically impossible to prove it. The law does not admit it?—Although it is not ordinarily done, if there is any reason to suspect that there is no insurable interest, proof will be required.

1975. Therefore it would be only carrying out what really is the principle of the law if you restricted infant insurance to the exact amount of loss?—A parent has no insurable interest, ordinarily speaking, in the life of its child. There are cases in which a parent may have an insurable interest in a child's life. That is not the ordinary case. For instance, if a parent had an income of so much a year so long as the child lived, he would have an insurable interest in the child's life, but that is not the ordinary case.

1976. You think that infant insurance stands on a different footing from ordinary insurance?—Yes, certainly; because it tends to deaden the natural instinct which a parent is supposed to have to take care of and prolong the life of its child. The interest is put in the other scale; the parent will receive money when the child dies.

1977. That will go almost as far as establishing the principle that you ought to prohibit infant life insurance altogether?—I see no reason why infant life assurance should be allowed at all. That is the view I take.

(142.)

Earl of *Selborne*.

1978. In the common case of life insurance the law, though it requires an interest, does not make it a contract of indemnity, so as to make the value of the interest the exact measure of the recovery?—No.

1979. With regard to adult persons, the facilities for malpractice are not, ordinarily, great enough to amount to a serious drawback?—No.

1980. I suppose in those cases of infant insurance the facilities for malpractice are very much greater?—Very much greater. The child is dependent entirely on the good offices of its parent.

1981. Even amongst adults sometimes it has been known to lead to murder?—Oh, yes, not unfrequently.

1982. But still the risk is not so great in the ordinary case as to be a counterbalance to the loss?—Certainly not; the adult, ordinarily speaking, can take care of himself.

Lord *Norton*.

1883. Would not the repeal of the provisions of the Friendly Societies Act be an injury to a very great number of honest parents in the country?—I should think not. It is not a matter on which I can express any well-founded opinion, but I should think it would not be. I should think that the event of the death of a child is a matter that might be provided against in the way that other misfortunes of life are provided against.

1984. There are other means of providing for such casualties since the Friendly Societies Acts, such as the Post Office Savings Bank?—That is a perfectly legitimate means.

1885. Is that your idea that these honest persons who wish to secure against such a casualty might find in the Post Office Savings Bank, not only a better and safer, but a more economical mode of insurance?—Much more economical, much safer, and in every way much better.

1886. As soon as the child is old enough to be profitable to his parents, the parent has an interest in his life?—Yes; so long as he remains with the parent, and works.

1887. Therefore there will be no danger of insurance of children at such an age?—When a child is 10 or 12 years of age there would be practically no danger. The mischief is with young children under the age of two or three years.

Lord Bishop of *Ripon*.

1988. Supposing you abolished all insurance how could a thrifty poor person meet the sudden pressure of expense arising from the death of a child?—In the same way as he has to deal with the expense of sickness, which is often very much greater.

1989. In the case of a child, the expense of the sickness and death might have to be added together?—It might be, but it must be dealt with in the ordinary way in which other misfortunes are dealt with.

1990. Does it not occur to you that a Post Office Savings Bank could only, of course, give

M   the

Lord Bishop of *Ripon*—continued.

the amount of money out which the parents had put in ?—Certainly.

1991. Therefore there is no protection against a rainy day, as we say ?—If the parents have been thrifty and have invested their little savings from time to time, they have a fund available which ought to be sufficient, unless mortality is very great amongst their children, to bury them at any rate from time to time.

1992. The death of a child is not an event of frequent occurrence ?—Would you feel the sa e objection to the poor being members of benefit clubs and burial societies which are managed on mutual principles ?—Local benefit clubs are very beneficial no doubt if they are properly managed, and a local burial club would be free from a very great number of objections which I find in the large insurance companies, which live upon infant and small insurances.

1993. What I was wanting to get at was this : it seems to me there are two systems in which the poor may provide for the contingency of death, and one is by putting into one of these profit-making societies, and the other is putting into what is normally called a club?—That is a local institution.

1994. You would not have the same objection, I imagine, to the club; you would not abolish the club?—I should not interfere with the club. The club is a local institution, where people have the means of knowing one another, and seeing what is going on, and so acting as a check upon frauds in their own interest. The burial clubs, no doubt, do exist, and they exist for the benefit of burying the adults as well as the children. They are all mixed up together in one interest, and watchful of one another more or less. My attention has never been called to that class of insurance in criminal courts.

1995. I gather from your evidence generally that you felt there was a great deal of evil resulting from what I may call the touting system ? —No doubt in every way.

1996. The interest then turns in the wrong direction ?—Yes. I should tell you, as far as I can gather, the number of those who insure in these societies do not, ordinarily speaking, seek them out. They are sought out by the canvassers; they are urged to contribute their pennies, and, of course, when they have contributed their pennies, I will not say naturally, but they do acquire an interest in looking for some return. They have no other return but upon the death of the child.

Lord *Brougham and Vaux.*

1997. You yourself are against infant insurance, even if it can be proved that it never tempted parents to commit crime ?—Yes, very much against it.

Earl *Beauchamp.*

1998. The case you described to us at the beginning of your evidence was known as the Swindon baby farming case, was it not?—Yes, it was.

1999. What relation to the children were the man and woman who were sentenced for mis-

Earl *Beauchamp*—continued.

demeanour towards the children ?—No other than commercial relations to them.

2000. That was not a case of a parent ?—No; that was a case of baby farming.

2001. That was not a case of a parent insuring the life of the child with an object ?—No.

2002. Nor was it a case of a parent putting out of the way a child whose life was heavily insured ?—Originally the negligence began, as far as I know, before there was any insurance. There were three insurances, which were not traced.

2003. My point is that the cruelty was not cruelty on the part of a parent ?—Oh, no, the parents had placed the children with this baby farmer. The parents were in no case traced.

2004. And the baby farmer insured these lives ?—Yes.

2005. Was that a legal transaction?—Certainly not. I am wrong in saying that, because it was legal under the Friendly Societies Act.

2006. What insurable interest had the woman ? —No insurable interest. I am not sufficiently familiar perhaps with the terms of the Friendly Societies Act to answer that question very distinctly, but it certainly would have been an illegal insurance under the Statute of George III. They had no interest whatever in the children.

2007. Under the Friendly Societies Act?— That allows persons to insure for these sums ?—

2008. In what societies were these children insured ?—Four children were insured in the Liverpool Victoria Legal Friendly Society, but the chief office I see is in London.

2009. Surely the Friendly Societies Act applies ; " No society shall pay any sum on the death of a child under 10 years of age except to the parents of such child, or to the personal representative of such parent " ?—This woman was a personal representative of the parent I suppose.

2010. How would she be that ?—She was the person in charge of the children, and they take the insurance.

2011. A person in charge of a child does not become the personal representative as the phrase is known to the law ?—Certainly not. I have the evidence of the insurance in this card, so that the children were insured, and the baby farmers, no doubt, believed in the validity of the insurance, or they would not have subscribed this sum of 1 *s.* 8 *d.*

2012. You think that the insurance societies are anxious to observe the law, so far as it is brought to their knowledge ?—I must say I do not want to give any opinion upon that. I may say that I tried these people for cruelty to the children, and the instance of the insurance was merely brought before me with a view of showing motive.

2013. Did any of the children die before the trial ?—Not that I am aware of. I cannot remember that. I do not remember hearing of any death.

2014. I thought your Lordship told us you had refreshed your memory ?—I have been told (it does not appear on these papers) that since the trial two of the children have died.

2015. I am talking of the time of trial ?—No;

I have

Earl *Beauchamp*—continued.

I have no reason to suppose that any of the children were dead. They were not tried for manslaughter, they were tried simply for the criminal neglect.

2016. That case, so far as it goes, does not in any way touch the question of the parents insuring the lives of their children?—Not of parents. It does touch the question of the insurance of lives of infants.

2017. You have told us that many cases of cruelty to children have come before you. Have you taken any pains to ascertain in those cases whether the children have been insured or not?—I have in some cases inquired, but I cannot remember the answers I got to the inquiries. I know I have in one or two cases made inquiries.

2018. Do you find any indisposition on the part of juries to find either child murder or criminal neglect?—None whatever. Child murder I exclude from my answer, but with regard to criminal neglect I have found none whatever. The difficulty of a judge, if there be a difficulty, is rather to restrain juries. I know no class of cases that raise more feelings among juries hostile to the person charged than charges of criminal neglect to children.

2019. If you were told that persons whose business it was to prosecute refrain from prosecution, for fear of not getting a conviction, you would think they were rather slack in what they did?—I believe the difficulty arises sometimes in the quantum of proof of the means of the person who has charge of the child. Judges may differ as to the amount of proof that is requisite to support an indictment of that description, because it has been held by some judges that there ought to be evidence of the actual means of the parent. I believe I am right in saying that some have taken another view, and consider that where there is a workhouse within hail that a child is not to be allowed to starve, even though the parents themselves are poor, and upon that subject there have been some differences of opinion.

2020. My question had reference not so much to the case of judges as to the willingness of juries to convict on the evidence before them;

Earl *Beauchamp*—continued.

juries always require, as I say, restraining rather than influencing in favour of conviction; juries are always keen to convict in all such cases in my experience.

Chairman.

2021. Keen to convict of cruelty?—Yes.

2022. Not keen to convict of murder or manslaughter?—No. There is always naturally an unwillingness to convict anyone of murder in all cases. As to neglect, juries require restraining rather than urging.

Lord *Norton.*

2023. There is not much difference between permitting criminal neglect of a child and committing the child to a baby farmer where it is known to be criminally neglected?—Morally speaking, not.

Earl of *Selborne.*

2024. I should like to ask this one question: was the society which insured those lives, and which has a long name, of which the word friendly was part, a friendly society registered under the Friendly Societies Act?—I have no doubt it was; from a portion of this paper, "Members' forfeiture notice, in accordance with the Friendly Societies Act 1875, Section 30, Sub-section 2," I should infer that it was.

2025. Of the societies so registered there are some which are and some which are not local?—Yes. I should think very few are local in any strict sense. They are mostly established in our great cities, and they have canvassers in all the villages of England.

Lord *Norton.*

2026. Do you recollect what the sentence was in 1888 on the conviction of these baby farmers?—The woman I sentenced to two years, I think, and the man, I think it was, to three months, if I remember rightly.

The Witness is directed to withdraw.

The Rev. BENJAMIN WAUGH, is called in; and Examined, as follows:

Chairman.

2027. You are honorary director of the National Society for the Prevention of Cruelty to Children?—I am.

2028. Since its formation in the year 1884?—Yes.

2029. May I ask you if you receive any remuneration in your capacity as director?—None.

2030. What is your special function as director of this society?—I have to determine on the officers' reports whether warnings or proceedings at law shall be taken.

2031. In cases of alleged cruelty?—Yes.

2032. Therefore it would follow that no prosecution for cruelty or criminal neglect could take place without your direction?—No prosecution up to the end of last month took place,

(142.)

Chairman—continued.

without my direction, in any of the 50 branches of the society, as well as the central office.

2033. Why do you say up to last month; did any prosecution take place without your knowledge then?—I have had to give up that department to a barrister who has temporarily acted whilst I have been giving myself to this work. I still occupy the position, but as a matter of fact I have not performed its duty.

2034. Your office as director brings you into direct knowledge of every case of alleged cruelty and every case of prosecution for cruelty in connection with your society?—Quite so.

2035. Have you had many such cases of cruelty reported to you?—I have made some statistics out which the Committee will allow me to quote from. We have had reported to us until

M 2

Chairman—continued.

until March last 5,314 cases from London and the conntry.

2036. Since the year 1884 ?—Since the year 1884 ; that is for the whole country, as well as London.

2037. In how many of these cases did you prosecute ?—We have prosecuted in 752 of them.

2038. In how many of these cases did you obtain convictions ?—670.

2039. Have any of these cases been cruelty of parents as distinguished from cruelty of those having charge of the children ?—Yes ; the number of cases of cruelty of parents, prosecuted cases, is 335.

2040. Out of 752 ?—335 were own fathers and mothers, and we convicted of that number 299. I may add, if your Lordship will allow me, that we imposed 49 years of imprisonment on fathers and mothers. 24 years of imprisonment on step-fathers and stepmothers, and 63 years of imprisonment on others ; that is, on step-parents and on fathers and mothers, 73 years in London alone. Now, in the country, we have given 88 years to fathers and mothers, 28 years to step-fathers and step-mothers, making a total of 116 years imprisonment for cruelty to children by step-parents and own parents.

2041. Were the cases of cruelty like that of parents of the milder or severer class of cruelty ? —Some of the most horrible cases have been of parents. One case, I may mention, that last week we prosecuted where a child was burnt in three places by its own mother, who deliberately made the poker red hot in the fire, and then applied it to the bottom of the back and under both arm pits. Another case I may mention, it is a celebrated case, and it is in our report, of Teresa Smith, who burnt the child in five or six different places, filed the thin shoulder blades until the flesh was completely cut away, and also burnt her child in four places at the bottom of the back. She further (this is in the course of six weeks) perforated the bottom of the feet of the child with a toasting fork, and then turned that toasting fork into a sort of wire scourge, and beat the child on the back. It was scarcely a human thing when we got possession of it.

2042. This was a case in which you prosecuted ?—In which we prosecuted.

Earl of *Selborne.*

2043. For murder ?—No ; the child was alive.

Chairman.

2044. Did you obtain a conviction in that case ?—We obtained a conviction in the case. It was six months of hard labour. Another case I might mention of a mother in a better rank of life, where we prosecuted a woman for opening windows at night when her two children were dying of bronchitis. The case attracted a good deal of attention at the time, and I should like to be allowed to to say that I am not making these statements about parents in a humble condition of life alone. I have brought the photographs of a few of the respectable children we have had to defend from cruelties in cases of their own parents, and in three cases not of their

Chairman—continued.

own parents, simply to avoid disparaging the poor.

2045. Just confine yourself to answering my exact questions. Has your attention been called to the practice of insuring children ?—Yes, we cannot help its being so.

2046. In what way has it been called. Is it in connection with cases of cruelty ?—Yes ; here is a case in which the emaciated child was an insured child. This is a case we have in the shelter now.

2047. Your attention was first called to the connection between crime and insurance by the number of emaciated or wasted children who are insured ?—It was.

2048. That was greater from the fact you state, than the number of less wasted children who are not insured ?—I am prepared to submit to your Lordships statistics later on which will show that.

2049. Did any specific case of child insurance attract your attention ?—The special feature is the one I have mentioned of emaciation going with insurance.

2050. Were there many cases of overlaying in the case of insured children ?—Yes ; here is a return of overlaying cases in London for one year, which shows that 600 children were overlaid last year, and the coroners' returns show that 50 per cent. of the overlaid cases brought before them were insured.

2051. Fifty per cent. were known to be insured ?—Known to be insured. These are the returns of the Registrar of Deaths.

2052. Were there many cases of convulsions in insured children ?—A great many, but often associated with emaciation, which brought on the convulsions, improper feeding, and other things.

2053. Have you any very recent cases of this kind ; I wish you to observe that I now wish you to direct your evidence entirely to the cases of insured children ?—I am directing my evidence entirely to those cases.

2054. Have you any more recent cases of cruelty or the criminal neglect of insured children ?—I have here five cases of prosecution last week. The first case is of four children where the total insurance was 28 *l* 12 *s.* The father was sent for three months, and the mother for three months, with hard labour. I have another case last week where at Preston two children were insured for 5 *l.* 13 *s.* 9 *d.* the total. The bench considered it a scandalous case, and committed it to the assizes. That is not yet determined.

2055. They committed the parties accused ?— They committed the father in this case, the mother being dead. I have another case last week where a boy was insured for 20 *l.* His age was 12, and the evidence showed that the boy had been insured for 10 *l.* up to a given date. up to which time he had been well treated. Within a few weeks of the time that he had come into the 20 *l.* benefit, the starvation began, which finally brought the boy into our hands. I have his photograph here, if you wish to see it. On Thursday last the father and mother were sent to gaol for six months each for having starved this boy. In another case at Yarmouth we had a child 16 years of age, insured for 10 *l.* The

case

Chairman—continued.

case was acquitted last night. I have received the telegram since I compiled these returns, "Acquitted." It was at the Yarmouth quarter sessions. I believe that it was acquitted, as there was no proof of motive, because the child was insured by one brother and starved by another. I have another case at Leicester of four children, one ten years old insured for 10 *l.*, another child of eight insured for 5 *l.*, another of seven insured for 5 *l.*, another of three insured for 5 *l.* The father went to prison for three months. That was at Leicester last week. That is to say, there were 12 children on whose behalf we took proceedings last week who were insured for a total sum of 87 *l.* 5 *s.* 9 *d.*, and all but one of the offenders have been sent to gaol.

2056. That, I presume, includes the boy of 16?—That includes the boy of 16, where there was an acquittal. If the Committee would like to see the boy of 16, whose photograph I have here, I should be pleased to submit it.

2057. As there was an acquittal we need not trouble?—That is a very important point. Acquittal does not mean that there was no guilt; it might mean that there was no proof of means. I should like to say that in this case we have not the means of knowing why the jury said not guilty. I am speaking only of the general principle.

2058. Passing from this case, will you come to this question: do you always prosecute in these bad cases?—No, my Lord, we very seldom prosecute.

2059. What is the reason you do not always prosecute when you get reports of bad cases?—Because of the pitiable character of the people who have been tempted. We consider it would be adding another wrong to take a case into court, because of the neglect which most pitiable and weak characters have shown in consequence of their temptation. As a sample of the proportion we do not prosecute, I should like to submit this Cardiff list of cases, from which you will see that we warn about seven cases where we prosecute one, and I will also, if you will allow me, lay upon the table our instructions to officers as to prosecutions.

2060. Do you encourage your officers to prosecute?—We do not.

2061. Do you always prosecute in cases where neglect ends in death?—No, we do not. We do so less frequently in those cases than we do in cases alive.

2062. Why is it in a case where death results from ill-treatment that you prosecute less than in cases where life is simply in danger?—Because we lack the principal witness who can speak to conduct, namely, the child who was alone in the bedroom at the death, besides the culprit.

2063. You state in your notes to me that in case of manslaughter, or alleged manslaughter, you have to prove means. What are we to understand by the word "means"?—We have to prove income. At common law no person can be convicted of starving to death, unless it is proved that he had the means. Under statute law you can.

2064. Prove that they had the means of feeding the child?—Yes.

2065. And you have to prove in every case of manslaughter by starvation that the parent (142.)

Chairman—continued.

had sufficient means of feeding the child?—Yes, that is so at common law.

2066. What is the difference you refer to, between that and statute law?—By the statute law, say you proceed under the Prevention of Cruelty to Children Act of last year, or under the Guardians Act of 32 & 33 Vict., the parish is counted means.

2067. Why then do you not proceed under the statute law in which this would be proved?—You cannot proceed under statute law for manslaughter. It must be at common law.

2068. Do I understand you to mean that manslaughter is not a statutory offence?—It is not a statutory offence.

2069. But only an offence at common law?—Only an offence at common law, and so is murder.

2070. So that it would follow from this. That if the father and mother are earning nothing, you cannot convict for manslaughter at common law?—No.

2071. You cannot convict at all for manslaughter?—Where a person has no means we cannot.

2072. Suppose they use violence, you can then?—If they use a hammer or knife we can convict.

2073. If they use starvation, it appears that you cannot?—We cannot without proving means.

2074. Do you often have cases where parents are out of work coming before you?—A large number.

2075. Where the parents are permanently out of work?—A good many of them insure their children who have no means of getting their living.

2076. Parents who have no means of getting their living, do apparently insure their children?—A large number, but I do not know what proportion they would be of the whole.

2077. Is that frequently the fact in cases of suffocation or overlying?—A great many of them our officer looks upon with great suspicion on the ground that there is no income whatever and the child is overlaid.

2078. Obviously where the parent has no money, the parent can have no object in insuring for saving money for funeral expenses, because he is without any means at all?—Possibly they insure to pay their rent.

2079. You mentioned Derby just now. What was that case?—It is a case the particulars of which I have here. It was one that was before Mr. Justice Wills, and he had to dismiss this case on the ground that he could not find means. I have got the particulars of the case.

2080. Will you state the particulars?—The case was a case of two drunken people who never earned anything, and who were voluntarily, as the judge said, poor, but on that ground they were not the less without means. This case came before his Lordship at Derby, and the jury acting on the statement that he made on the law of the case, dismissed the case. There were two doctors' certificates that the child had died of starvation. The child had been insured three months; immediately after it came into benefit the child was left alone without food for five hours at a time, three or four times, and it was heard to moan and cry by the neighbours next

M 3   door,

Chairman—continued.

door, but the door was always locked and they did not enter the house. The particulars of the case are rather long, but the doctor's statement was clear, the child had died from starvation.

2081. You put in those particulars?—I put in the particulars and the photograph.

2082. Do I understand you to say that the cruelty, or at least the great aggravation of the cruelty, arose as soon as the child came into benefit?—That was the testimony of the neighbours.

2083. That as soon as the child came into benefit, the cruelty which existed before, greatly increased after?—It greatly increased after. I should like on that point just to put in another statement made, and I give the particulars of it. It is a case of a child who is called Ernest Bastan; the child was 11 years old. He was well treated, everybody says, until two years ago, or about 18 months ago, at which time he had come into benefit for 20 *l.* instead of what he had been before, 10 *l.* From that time he was kept in; he was never out of doors; the neighbours now and again gave him food, sometimes saw him at the door, and the like, but he was reduced below his normal weight to 39 lbs. 3 ozs. in the course of 18 months, during which time he had not been allowed to go out. When the father was put on his trial he pleaded in extenuation that he had got 50 *l.* in arrear of rent by being out of work.

2084. I presume the only meaning of that would be that he had wanted the insurance to pay the rent?—It would appear so.

2085. Otherwise he would not have pleaded it as an excuse?—I take it that it is an excuse.

2086. This is the second case in which you find that criminal cruelty to children either begins or is greatly increased after the death of the child becomes largely profitable?—It is the second I put in. I could give a great many more.

2087. You know of other cases?—Yes.

2088. These two cases were cases in which you prosecuted?—In both cases. In one we obtained a conviction, in the other we failed. This man had means. There was furniture.

2089. He was convicted?—The question of means did not arise; he was convicted.

2090. In cases under the Cruelty to Children Act, at what period in the trial would the fact of insurance be brought forward?—It would be put in after the hearing of the case, and after the verdict of the jury, as you put in previous convictions.

2091. You do not mean the verdict of the jury; you mean the sentence of the magistrate?—No, after the jury has said guilty.

2092. In cases of summary jurisdiction there is no committal?—In cases of summary jurisdiction it does not come in at all. It is only on an indictment that you can bring it in, when it has been committed to quarter sessions. Then it is, as provided in the Act, that it must be introduced into the case, as is the practice as to previous conviction.

2093. As regards poisoning cases, a very remarkable poisoning case occurred at Greenwich which is known as the Sidney Bolton case, to

Chairman—continued.

which a reference was made in the evidence before this Committee. Were you informed of the illtreatment of this boy, Sidney Bolton?—We were. I cannot say exactly how long before, but about five or six months before the boy's death.

2094. That he was being illtreated?—That something was wrong. It was an anonymous letter.

2095. You had no idea of poisoning until after the death?—We had no idea that illtreatment was taking place. The boy was well-fed, had no marks upon him, and looked kindly treated; our officer came back and said there was nothing in it; it was a mere hoax, he thought.

2096. Your informant could not give you any sufficient reason for prosecuting in that case?—There was no reason even for censuring.

2097. How many policies were there in that woman's house?—According to the Registrar of Friendly Societies Returns, there had been 22 issued by the Liverpool Victoria Legal Friendly Society, and 13 in the Prudential.

2098. Then the boy was insured in two societies?—There were two children, one a sister and a brother, and their policies were both increased in amount just about the time when the poison was administered.

2099. The increase in the amount of the policy coincided with the time of the administration of the poison?—It seems so. I give that on the authority of the Registrar of Friendly Societies.

2100. In that case, if I remember, there was not a conviction of murder, the evidence being insufficient, but there was a conviction of forgery?—There was not a conviction of murder, because the woman died of a broken heart, Mrs. Winter, because she was committed for trial.

2101. At the death of this poisoned child a doctor's certificate was given of the cause of death?—A doctor's certificate was given by the doctor. I believe the symptoms were those which were common both to a bad cold and to strychnine.

2102. There was no difficulty in that case about obtaining a certificate from the doctor?—No, the doctor gave his certificate.

2103. You have had another poisoning case recently; when was that?—That was the Birkdale baby farming case; it is known as the Pearson case.

2104. In that case you assisted the police?—We assisted the police in that case, and a conviction was obtained.

2105. I omitted to ask you whether it is not the case that the late Commissioners of Police, Mr. Monro and Colonel Fraser, have directed the police to co-operate with you as far as possible?—They have directed the police to report to us every case coming to their knowledge of an offence against a child. The whole of the police cases are to pass through our hands.

2106. Will you proceed with this case; this was a case of insurance?—It was a case of insurance where the children were in a baby farm. On the insurance money being received by Mr. Pearson, who had insured these two farmed children, he got so drunk that he threatened he would throw the coffin out of the window, and that

Chairman—continued.

that led to a neighbour fetching a policeman to prevent it, which led the police to suspect something was wrong, and in consequence of that mere act of indiscretion of his, the child was not buried; a certificate of the death had been obtained; it was the third child that had died in the same house; a certificate had been obtained for all, and I volunteered, if they would exhume the other children, to pay the expenses of an analysis of the stomach, and the result of this was the discovery that the other two children died of poisoning, and this child had also done the same, and yet three medical certificates were given of death from natural causes. The man was sent for seven years' penal servitude, and the woman for five.

2107. This was a case which resulted first in prosecution, and then in conviction?—Yes.

2108. Were the parents implicated in this case?—The mother was implicated in this case and acquitted.

2109. Was the father implicated?—There was no father; they were illegitimate children of a lady who had some position in the town of Southport.

2110. Who was it that insured the children's lives?—The man Pearson, who was a baby farmer.

2111. May I ask you this question with respect to the insurance of baby-farmed children generally; it would appear that the baby farmer, who received a certain sum per week, would not be disposed to extinguish the life of that child, because the baby farmer would lose the weekly payment; is it the case often that the baby farmer receives a lump sum down?—Very frequently, but there is a motive for extinguishing life even in weekly payments; there are plenty to come. If a child is paid for, we will say, at the rate of 5 *s.* per week, and there are four payments for, say, four children, that is 1 *l.* a week, and each child is kept on 1 *s.* a week, and it starves to death; it is almost impossible to convict anybody for doing that. Four children at 4 *s.* profit leaves 16 *s.* So that the woman's interest is to keep the child, within certain limits of the law, as low as possible, so that it will die from wasting, convulsions, or other things, which would naturally happen to ill-fed children. Thus 16 *s.* a week on four children can be made, and the four children die little above the normal rate of young children without attracting any attention.

2112. Has it ever come to your knowledge that in cases of this kind the insurance agent knew that the person was not the parent, and knowing that the person was not the parent, and had no interest in the child's life, refused to grant a policy?—No, my Lord, we have had seven baby farmers' cases, and in all of them the children were insured.

2113. Therefore, in none of them did the agent refuse to grant the policy?—The agent in one case was told that they were the children of the people keeping the baby farm, who were both about 60 years of age, and there were four under two years.

2114. In the case that you have just spoken

(142.)

of, the Birkdale cases, the doctor gave the death certificates?—He did.

2115. It was only on the post-mortem examination taking place, at your instance, that the poisoning was discovered?—Quite so.

2116. And you said that this poisoning came after a large amount of insurance was effected?—Yes.

2117. You have had a recent case at Leicester which was not proceeded with; why?—We did not proceed with it because the baby farmers had a kind of ring in which, when a child is dying, it is sent round. The child was insured, and it was passed on from one to a second, and to a third, and to a fourth person who took charge of it, and when it finally died it had been in the last care three weeks. We could not take any proceedings against the person in whose care it had been.

2118. Are you of opinion that such cases of poisoning are common?—I should not like to say. There are a great many suspicious cases we have had to look at that we have not examined into, but it is a very striking fact that all the cases of hanging that we know of, I think, except one, in this country for poisoning children, have been cases where the discovery has been made after death by some accidental circumstance. Mrs. Flanagan, for instance, had got rid of 13 children it was alleged in the course of the evidence. It was believed she had so got rid of them all, and insured them, before it was discovered by Dr. Lowndes, the medical officer for the police of Liverpool, that there was foul play in the matter.

2119. These were all insured children?—That it is impossible to prove, because the evidence did not show that the other children that were dead were insured, but there had been a practice of insuring, and it was supposed the others had been treated in the same way.

2120. You say these cases are generally discovered by accident?—Yes, from some quarrel. Take the Winter case at Deptford. The case had been completed. The child Bolton, the sister of Sydney, was being made ill with strychnine. The woman next door told the little girl she had better go to the hospital. Mrs. Winter told the little girl if she went to the hospital they would cut her leg off. She did not go to the hospital. The father came to Mrs. Winter, and they had a dispute over the insurance money; that led the next door neighbours to know of the circumstance, and they reported to the police, and that is the way in which it was discovered that this child had been poisoned. This led to the suspicion as to poisoning in other cases.

2121. Do you find in many cases parents deny having insured the children?—Often they deny, or admitting they have insured, but say they are not in benefit or that the policy has lapsed, or something of that sort. Our officers find it very difficult to get information, especially in London.

2122. Can you tell in how many cases you know that insurance has been admitted. Have you any return to that effect?—I have now a return from some branches; we have 50. With your Lordship's permission I will put that in.

M 4　　　　　　　　　　　2123. Have

Chairman—continued.

2123. Have you made any analysis of the return?—I have the analysis. They are of returns for an average period of eight months, some 12, and some three. We have only appointed officers say, in Bath, three months; in Yarmouth, two months; in Rotherham, three months; but taking the whole list it is nearly eight months for the following aid committees, namely, Barnsley, Bath. Birmingham, Bolton, Bristol, Burnley, Cardiff, Chester, Darlington, Dublin, Durham, Halifax, Ipswich, Leeds, Leicester, Middlesborough, Newcastle, Portsmouth, Preston, Rotherham, Sheffield, Southampton, Stockton-on-Tees, Yarmouth, York.

2124. Just give us the analysis?—The number of cases of insured children dealt with in the eight months in those places is 160. The average during which cases have been dealt with as I have stated, is eight months.

2125. One hundred and sixty cases in eight months?—Yes, the number of children insured in these cases was 375. Of these, ended in death, 30. The amount for which they were all insured, 1,637 *l.* 4 *s.*

2126. Are you able to tell the Committee what is the amount of the insurance in the case of the 30 children who died, taken separately?—That I cannot say; it would be possible to get it. The whole returns are here, and I will get it out. The offences charged were 124 neglect, 14 ill-treatment, 14 starvation (which is a more serious form of neglect which has got to the emaciation stage), assault 8. They were dealt with thus: prosecuted, 53; convicted, 37; discharged or remanded, 16. Those who are remanded are so because the list is completed up to last Saturday. Total penalties imposed, imprisonment, five years and five months; fines, 7 *l.* 10 *s.* Beside the prosecuted, we warned in 87 cases, and here are the warning notices we sent, which I should like the Committee to see. " This is to inform you that your conduct to your child, ——, has been the subject of inquiry by this Society, and you are now warned to prevent the necessity for further proceedings. The object of the Society is to prevent cruelty; where monition fails, by prosecution, which it always undertakes with great reluctance. Your attention is called to section 8 or 6, as the case may be, of the 52 & 53 Vict.," or something of that kind, according to the Act we might proceed under. Besides this, we give them a list of convictions, something like 300 convictions, and pretty nearly an average of a year's imprisonment in each. These are given in addition to the other in bad cases.

2127. That is evidence as to the mode of your proceeding, on which point we are not engaged at the present moment. Have you any statistics showing the number of insured children in London?—May I be pardoned, I have not quite finished the answer to your previous question. Transferred and dismissed, 18. The classification of offenders was, 93 fathers, 98 mothers, 4 step-fathers, and 12 step-mothers; others, 10.

2128. The great majority of the cases were either mothers and fathers, or step-fathers and mothers?--Yes.

Chairman—continued.

2129. Were those prosecutions or convictions? —These include warned, prosecuted, and convicted.

2130. All cases of cruelty that came to your knowledge?—All cases of cruelty to insured children.

2131. Everyone of them?—Everyone of them.

2132. Have you any statistics to show the number of children who have died without having had doctor's called in?—I have a return here of inquests that our inquest officer attended which comes nearly to this. There are 96 cases of children that have been brought before the coroner in about 18 months.

2133. In London? — In London alone, all insured, and most of them dying under circumstances which render conviction impossible; the only person who was a witness of the last act, whatever that might be, being the mother, who was called as the sole witness at the inquest.

2134. All these cases, if I understand rightly, were sufficiently suspicious to require a coroner's inquest? — They were all before these three coroners, Mr. Baxter, Mr. Wyatt, and Dr. Danford Thomas.

2135. Everyone of these cases you have mentioned were cases which were brought before the coroner?—Yes.

2136. And all of them were insured?—All were insured, and I should like to mention one or two remarkable facts. One mother, seeing her child had tumbled into the copper, went out to look for a neighbour to get the child out, and found it drowned before she came back. Another woman, seeing that her child had fallen into soapsuds that she herself had been washing in at that time, lifted the child out, took it to the hospital, and it died of congestion of the lungs. The doctor certified congestion of the lungs, aggravated by burning. This is an illustration of the very little care doctors may give at hospitals to these cases. The next case is a case where a woman hired her child out to a woman to beg with in the streets in the east of London; this child died at our Shelter. It was first taken out of the hands of a prostitute, who was hawking it, by a policeman, and taken to the workhouse. The next day the mother took it from the workhouse, and when we heard that, we sent an officer to her, and took it to Harpur-street.

2137. Harpur-street is the office of the society?—The Shelter of the society. The child died the same night. The next day there was an inquest, and at the inquest two doctors certified that the child had died of starvation. We applied to Mr. Partridge for a summons. Mr. Partridge said it was manslaughter or nothing; that he could not allow it to be proceeded with as a misdemeanour. We then applied to the Public Prosecutor. The Public Prosecutor looked through the evidence, and did not see that if it went to the Assizes there would be evidence enough to obtain a conviction, and it was dropped. These are illustrations of the sort of thing that goes on every day in every town all over England.

2138. Have you any other returns of inquests?

Chairman—continued.

inquests?—I have no returns of inquests outside London.

2139. Have you a table of inquests attended by the society's inquest officers for London?—I have some returns of Dr. Macdonald's clerk.

2140. Dr. Macdonald is the coroner?—Yes; this is a return from the coroner's clerk, showing the number of children that died insured, in the inquests held by Dr. Macdonald. Under one month 46 children.

2141. Insured?—No, my Lord, deaths. Number of deaths, 46; insured, five. Over one month and under three, 37 children died; insured, 22. Under six months and over three, 39 deaths; 24 of which were insured. Six months and under 12, 36 deaths; 26 insured. One year and under two, 20 deaths; 12 insured. Two years and under three, 18 deaths; 11 insured. Three years and under six, 27 deaths; 16 insured. Six years and under 10, 19 deaths; 10 insured. The total number of deaths, 262; the total number of insured cases, 126.

2142. Will you allow me to ask you, referring to the first of these periods, I think it is a period of very early child life, is it not?—The first period, 46 deaths under a month?

2143. At that time the child would not have come into benefit under the regulations of the society?—It would not, under the regulations of the society, but there are what are called gifts and grants.

2144. It would not?—It would not.

2145. And the proportion is less in the case of death than it is in subsequent months, when the child would have come into benefit?—It is 5 in 46.

2146. You will understand the point I want to bring out. The ratio of insured children in deaths of children under a month is below that of the deaths of children when they come to three months?—It is, my Lord; in one case it is 10 per cent, and in the other it is 48.

2147. I mean to say that the ratio of the deaths in insured children rises rapidly after the time they come into benefit?—That is so, and sustains that rise until 10 years of age. I have similar returns from Mr. Wyatt.

2148. On this point I have another question. I believe it is perfectly well known that the ratio of infant mortality is greater in the first month than in the subsequent months. The infant mortality decreases as the child gets older? —Very much.

2149. Therefore, we have this fact, that the proportion of deaths of insured children is less during that very time when it ought to be, according to the ordinary tables of mortality, greatest?—Quite so.

2150. And that is the case where the children have not come into benefit?—Yes.

2151. How do you come to be represented on these inquests, or any of them?—The three coroners to whom I have referred have been in the habit, when their clerk has thought there has been a suitable case, to send for our inquest officer.

2152. It has now become a common thing for the coroners to send for your officer?—Very

(142.)

Chairman—continued.

often. Indeed, in various parts of the country we have sent officers.

2153. Can you give us the particulars of a case which I think you called the Dorin case? —That is an illustration of the difficulty we have in prosecuting, even where cases are very bad. I will read to your Lordship, if I may do so, the medical report in the case. I have here also the report taken from our officer's report. This is the report given by a doctor on a child which had been insured for 2 *l.*, and being in the custody of the person who insured it six months, and it had just come into benefit. The child had been well, and a beautiful child, until it went into their custody. It was a child of a widower, a stockbroker, "Body thin and emaciated; not a particle of fat about it; weight 16 pounds (ought to be 40 pounds). Lacerated wound on little toe of right foot; wound on right knee; bruises on the shin; left leg bruised. In small of back a scar; on outer side of right wrist, an old wound; on left wrist, a fresh wound and a scar. Two front teeth knocked out. On both cheeks old bruises. Behind right ear, wound nearly healed. Right side of forehead, a wound an inch long, caused by a severe blow with blunt weapon. Skull bone, inflamed wound three inches long. The brain wholly inflamed. On the left side of head a similar wound. Symptoms on head, result of blows. The marks on the wrist, result of tight drawn cords." Because two persons had the custody of that child, nobody could make a charge against one as to who had done it. In this case we could not prosecute.

2154. The reason it was not prosecuted was that there was no evidence which of the two parties having custody of the child was the guilty person?—We could make no charge.

2155. You give that as a case of the difficulty of obtaining a conviction in a case of gross cruelty?—I do, in domestic cases.

2156. Who were the persons having the charge of this child?—As there was no conviction, would it be desirable to mention the names.

2157. I do not want the names, but what relation were they?—The person having the charge was the married sister of the mother, the maternal aunt.

2158. Who was the other person? — Her husband.

2159. They were the persons having the custody of this child?—Yes.

2160. One of them the nearest relation, except the mother?—Yes.

2161. Who effected the insurance in this case? —That I cannot say, but I believe it was effected after the child went to its relations. That I cannot be sure about.

2162. The case was that of an insured child? —It was an insured child; a child that went to that house well, and came out of it in that condition.

2163. These would be the legal representatives of the child?—The mother was still living.

2164. You mentioned another case, which you speak of as the Thompson case?—It is a similar case to the one I have just referred to, and perhaps, to save the time of the Committee, I had better not go into it.

N

2165. At

Chairman—continued.

2165. At all events you put it in?—I put it in as an illustration of the impossibility of dealing with those cases in which a crime is committed in a bedroom, where the only person present is the person who is the possible culprit, and the child is dead.

2166. The Committee of the House of Commons in that report say, that it is manifestly impossible in a great majority of cases to procure conviction for crimes committed in the privacy of a house or a bedroom. That exactly agrees with your experience?—Thoroughly so.

2167. Did the coroner commit in either of these cases that you speak of?—No. In both cases they censured.

2168. Why do you think they did so. Do you blame the coroner for that?—Certainly not. The coroner knows better than I do, a great deal, that it is useless to send such cases on.

2169. You think that the only reason of the coroner for not committing was the impossibility of getting a conviction at the Assizes?—Mr. Wyatt said, " I hope you will get a conviction, but my experience is that you will not," and he was quite right; we could not get a conviction.

2170. For the legal difficulties you mention? —Quite so.

2171. The evidence of horrible cruelty is patent?—Quite clear; but who committed it there is no evidence.

2172. It must have been one or other of these two persons?—So we think.

2173. It is not probable that anyone would break into a house to treat a child in this way? —Not likely.

2174. It must have been those who had the custody?—I should think so.

2175. What were the principal characteristics or circumstances of the inquest cases on insured children, where you had notice from the coroner. Can you mention the apparent causes of death? —The apparent causes were mainly convulsions, overlying, and emaciation.

2176. The coroner, I suppose, would not send to you unless in a case where he suspected cruelty or wilful neglect?—I doubt whether the coroner had it under his consideration. I think it is the clerk who receives this information first.

2177. The coroner's clerk would not do so obviously?—I should think not; but I have no means of knowing.

2178. There was no reason for sending for you as the person to protect children from cruelty in a case where the coroner's clerk suspected no cruelty?—No.

2179. You have had some experience of different forms of cases. The one you mention at Birkdale, and the one at Leicester, and there was one at Swindon?—There was one at Swindon where we found four children insured. There were seven children; four were insured. These were the four where there were no payments due on behalf of the children, and they were dying. The other three had money still to come in, and they were fairly well, and not insured.

2180. What do you mean by money coming in?—The baby farmer received money down, 10 *l.*, 20 *l.*, or 30 *l.* When the money was all

paid, the child was insured and was starved. In the other three cases the children were not insured, and there were liabilities still on the part of the persons sending them. In one case 15 *l.*, and in another I think it was 5 *l.* Mr. Justice Day tried this case.

2181. The children on whom the baby-farmer had got all the profit he could were being done to death?—That was so; and two afterwards died.

2182. The children on whom the baby-farmer had still some money to get were comparatively well?—Yes.

2183. And all the four were paid for?—All the four; but not the other three.

2184. Had you a case at Finsbury?—We had a very bad case there; but we never proved that the child was insured.

2185. Had you a case in Whitechapel where the child was insured?—We had. There we warned and did not prosecute, because we found the sort of people who were sensitive to fear of the eye of our officer being on them.

2186. You found in that case a warning was sufficient?—Quite sufficient.

2187. As regards Upper Broughton, had you a case of an insured child?—We have had a very dreadful case just completed. Since we entered upon the investigation, the woman emptied her drawers, and burned all her letters, and all the policies and books and everything that could give a clue. We were unable to discover anything. I understand she will be able to renew the policies after destroying the papers.

2188. This was a baby-farmer?—Yes, an advertising baby-farmer.

2189. These are very bad cases, the abuse of insurance by baby-farmers. Is it your experience that these bad cases are mostly by baby-farmers?—Oh, dear no.

2190. You find quite as bad cases which are not by baby-farmers?—Quite as bad.

2191. Both of personal cruelty and criminal neglect?—Quite so.

2192. What is the reason that you have so many cases of baby-farmers tried, and verdicts obtained?—I do not think we have so many cases tried, but more of them are reported. It seems as though the reporters at police courts like to get hold of a good baby-farming case. And so the public is led to believe that a large proportion of this sort of thing is by baby-farmers. Parents' cases are not so popular, and they are not reported. Then it is much easier to convict a baby-farmer, because the man and the woman are not the parents of the children, and their evidence against one another can be taken if they make any statements, whereas the evidence of fathers and mothers on behalf of a child is not evidence. No conviction can be obtained on it. A further fact which is important to remember is this, we find neighbours hate baby-farmers; while they are quite willing to swear up to the hilt about a baby-farmer, they are very unwilling to interfere with a known parent; thus the difficulties of getting evidence are very great in cases of parents.

2193. A good deal has been made of the statistics by insurance societies, as showing that the totals of the deaths of insured children are lower than those for all children; have you any opinion

Chairman— continued.

opinion as to the correctness or otherwise of those statistics ?—I am unable to give an exact statement, but I have a very clear idea as to the direction in which the explanation of these statements may be found. First, I take such an office as the Prudential, and I mention it because it is one of the most respectable. It declines to take illegitimate children. Secondly, the mortality is 50 per cent. greater before three months old than it is after. This 50 per cent. of the whole 12 months takes place before three months is passed, and according to their rules the children do not come into benefit, and there is no liability until the child is three months old. That is a second fact ; and the third fact is that lapses, of course, take place ; and in some cases it is said a third of the policies lapse. One of the agents of one of the best societies said that at this early age quite half lapsed of the children, though it might be a third of the whole. Assuming it is the fact that about one-third lapse, and 50 per cent. do not come to the society as claims, and the mortality, which is so much higher among illegitimate children, is avoided by not taking illegitimate children, the comparison is vitiated.

2194. In point of fact, your objection to the statistics is twofold ; first, that they do not come out of one area, and second, that the conditions are not the same, one society, for instance, rejecting all illegitimate cases ?— Quite so.

2195. And all those illegitimate cases would appear in the registrar's report ?—Every child would appear in the registrar's report.

2196. Has your attention been drawn to the opinion expressed by the Committee of the House of Commons as regards statistics in their Report ?—My attention has been drawn to this, that they say their opinion is that the statistics published by the society and those which have been published in reply are not reliable.

2197. Has that Committee expressed an opinion that no trustworthy conclusion can be drawn from statistics on either side ?—Yes.

2198. Were statistics of the Prudential and other societies before the Committee ; did they make any communication before them ?—I have not taken any note of that.

2199. The Committee say in their Report : "A large quantity of figures have been submitted to the Committee by various witnesses, purporting to show results favourable or unfavourable to infantile insurance, but your Committee are not disposed to base any recommendations upon them one way or another, owing to the difficulty of drawing therefrom a safe conclusion "?—That is so.

2200. This difficulty is further alluded to by Mr. Sutton ; can you tell the Committee who Mr. Sutton is ?—Mr. Sutton is, as I understand, the Official Actuary of the Registrar's Department on Friendly Societies ; I am not sure about that ; I am only speaking from memory.

2201. This is what Mr. Sutton says, and I suppose he is an authority, as the Committee quote him. " It is well known that during the first year of life the risk of dying rapidly decreases day by day, it might almost be said ; so that any comparison made between the death rates under one year of age, say, of societies and

(1 42.)

Chairman— continued.

companies which only begin to assure infants when one month, two months, or three months old, with the Registrar General's mortality rates for the year 0 to year 1 might easily mislead"?—That is so.

2202. " Further speaking, quite generally, a heavy purse means a light mortality, and particularly so among the very young and the very old ; so that as those assured with these societies and companies are almost universally not favoured with a superfluity of worldly riches, the mortality among them would naturally be found higher than the Registrar General's figures deduced from all classes." This is an argument on both sides, for and against ?—Quite so.

2203. And the Committee rejected both those, did they not ?—It did.

2204. You have, of course, paid great attention to this subject, and it is an open secret that it is you who have drafted this Bill which I am now bringing before Parliament ; what is your opinion as to the probable and only possible remedy for all these evils ?—I think in order to preserve the benefits which accrue to the poor by having provision for funerals, and at the same time to avoid the temptation to weak moral characters, and to persons who are vicious, the first thing to be done is to take away from the insurer the handling of the money. That, I think, is a sort of compromise. It abolishes, practically, ordinary life insurance, and makes a funeral insurance. Life money you do what you like with. That, I think, is the first remedy. The reduction of the sums would be a consequence of that, because the undertaker would not require as much as 6 *l.* to bury a baby, which can be insured on its life now.

2205. The money obtainable upon the death of a child under five years for funeral expenses is 6 *l.* ?—It is.

2206. And the sum obtainable on the death of the child for funeral expenses at the age of five years six months might be 10 *l.* ?—Yes.

2207. It is obvious, of course, that the funeral expenses, and the doctor's attendance, in the case of a child of five years and six months, cannot possibly be greater than in the case of five years ?—Quite so.

2208. Yet, in the one case, the parent gets 6 *l.*, and in the other he gets 10 *l.* ?—Yes.

2209. Therefore, if 6 *l.* is a sufficient provision for all the death expenses at five years, 10 *l.* is an absurdly large provision for all death provisions at five years and six months ; that is obvious ?—Yes.

2210. What is the law in England for all the societies in which the middle and upper classes insure ?—No life can be insured where the insurer has no insurable interest.

2211. Is that the rule of any of the working men's own benefit clubs ?—It is in principle applied in sickness, but not in funerals, in most of their mutual clubs. Boys at 11, when they come into half-time, can have half-time pay allowed out of these clubs for sickness. They will not allow a child to receive any sick-pay until it reaches an age at which it may earn a wage.

2212. That is to say until the parent has some

degree

Chairman—continued.

degree of insurable interest in the child's life?—
That is the case in their own sick clubs and
benefit clubs, throughout the country.

2213. Supposing the sum insurable for funeral
expenses was reduced to a minimum, say the
very smallest sum at which the funeral could be
performed, and the doctor paid, that would have
the effect you say not of preventing one of the
better class of artisans from giving his child
something better than a pauper's funeral?—The
better class of artisan, having other means, would
be able to make additions.

2214. The scale at which you propose in your
drafted Bill, or in mine as I have adopted it, is, if
I am not mistaken, the same scale as was proposed by the Committee of the House of Commons?—It is suggested by them with favour
because it comes from an admitted authority, Mr.
Ludlow.

2215. It is recommended by them?—I am not
sure that it is recommended, it is mentioned with
favour.

2216. In that respect this Bill would be no
stricter in its regulations than the proposal made
by, I think, Mr. Ludlow. Who is Mr. Ludlow?
—He is Chief Registrar of Friendly Societies.

2217. The Chief Registrar of Friendly Societies represented to the Committee those
figures?—He did.

2218. Those figures the Committee regarded
as figures drawn up in no hostility to the
societies in question?—Not at all.

2219. It has been proposed or suggested that
if this Bill were prepared, and the death claim
were reduced from a possible 6 *l.* at a year old to
10 *l.*, and an advance of 5 *s.* a year was afterwards to be made up to 16, or as long as the
child lived, that would save these societies a considerable sum?—An enormous sum; I am not
able to say what, but I think that question might
be put to some witness who will follow.

2220. If some such scheme as that were introduced, the tendency of it would be to make the
thrifty parent keep his child alive rather than
have any inducement to his being put to death?—
Yes; if you reduced the money payable, say 2 *l.*
on a child's death at one year into a payment of
25 *s.* at death, and then allow the money to accumulate, with all the saving which I think would
result from preventing the present fatal neglect,
if that sum accumulated until a boy was 14 and
a girl 16, there might be a double insurance, so
much for death and so much as an endowment.
This would encourage a higher form of thrift,
and would tempt people to keep children
alive.

2221. There would be no waste?—On the
other hand, there would be compound interest
arising; the gain would be the parents'.

2222. The insurance society would obviously
make no objection to that. It would not injure
their interest?—I should think not.

2223. Nor would it injure the interests of the
parents apparently?—Not at all.

2224. Has it ever occurred to you that an insurance society, might simply contract to pay all
funeral expenses on the production of vouchers,
and so be, as it were, their own undertakers, to
use the common expression. The insurance
societies may say, "We make a contract with

Chairman—continued.

you to clear you of all funeral expenses as far as
your policy goes, on your production to us of
sufficient vouchers." Would that be any
to the societies?—I should not like to give an
opinion upon that, I have not thought much
about it.

2225. You have not thought how that would
work?—No.

2226. So as to be what is commonly called a
contract of indemnity?—I have not thought at all
of that.

Earl of *Derby.*

2227. You represent the Society for the
Prevention of Cruelty to Children?—I do.

2228. And we hear from you, and of course
we take it from you that you have no personal,
that is, no pecuniary interest, in it?—No, my
Lord.

2229. I suppose your society collectively depends upon public support, does it not?—It does,
wholly.

2230. Upon the contributions of the public?—
Entirely.

2231. And I suppose the extent to which those
contributions come in depends a good deal upon
the success of the society in obtaining convictions?—No, I think convictions are rather unpopular. In localities we have aid committees,
and these aid committees take charge of the cases.
Say Nottingham has an aid committee; if prosecutions there were numerous we could not get
many subscriptions. Putting down cruelty without conviction is more popular than prosecutions.
We give publicity to these cases when they are
scandalous.

2232. Where a case is settled without prosecution and merely by warning the parents or
the other accused parties, that does not become
public, and therefore nothing is known of what
is done?—Nothing is known.

2233. Therefore, if the success of the society in
obtaining assistance from the public depends
upon publicity, that publicity can only be obtained
by means of prosecutions?—Quite so.

2234. You said that there are cases in which
you did not prosecute on account, as I understood
you to say, of the conduct of the people who were
accused?—Yes.

2235. Does that mean that you abstain from
prosecuting out of a compassionate feeling for
them?—No, partly that. We abstain, with
young people especially, out of compassion.
Callous people we have no compassion for, and
we would prosecute many more of these than we
do if the conditions of the law were favourable,
but we hold that to fail in a court encourages
the bad far more than not to prosecute.

2236. It comes to this, that you do not pro
secute in cases where you do not think you will
obtain a conviction?—There are probably two
causes where we should prosecute instead of
one if the law were more favourable, but in
many cases we should not prosecute. The putting
down of cruelty in these is accomplished by
their fear of us.

2237. What do you mean by the law being
more favourable to you?—Take one illustration:
if fathers and mothers could give evidence in the
case of the death of a child, as they can now, in
certain

Earl of *Derby*—continued.

certain other cases, against one another, we should prosecute more than we do now.

2238. It is an alteration of the law of evidence that you want?—In the common law, not the ordinary statute law. We got that altered last year in the 52nd and 53rd Vict.

Lord *Clifford of Chudleigh.*

2239. The Committee of the House of Commons in their Report say, under Section 28, Sub-section 3, of the Friendly Societies Act, " no money can be paid on a child's death by a society or company, except to the parent of such child, or the personal representative of such parent. Your Committee assume that the words ' personal representative' are used in the Act in th r strict legal meaning; but it must be doubtful whether they are taken in this sense by many of those who are called upon to comply with the Act." Have your society got any experience in the case of insurances of that mistake being made?—I think the law is practically worthless.

2240. I do not mean that. My point is this, that an insurance company or insurance agent consider that a person having charge of a child is the personal representative of the parent, and, therefore, effects the insurance, which is strictly not legal?—They do effect insurances with persons who are not the parents of a child, because they hold that baby-farms say, when the children have been adopted on a lump sum payment, are in the place of the parents, and so are legally entitled to insure, and I think they are right.

Chairman.

2241. They are *in loco parentis* ?—Yes.

Lord *Norton.*

2242. What proportion of cases come before you of criminal neglect of children not insured. Is it anything like half?—I can give you the exact figures. I will submit them to your Lordship next week. I have not the general returns from these towns, but I should think not more than about 18 or 20 per cent., judging from the cases I happen to know. That is to say admittedly insured cases.

2243. In those cases does it appear that criminal neglect arose from a wish of a parent to get rid of the expense of the child?—I should scarcely think so. I think that wish is scarcely felt. The child is as nothing to them; the wish is to get possession of the money.

2244. I am talking of non-insured cases. A motive was to wish to get rid of the expense of the child?—I think it is more, what an American would call, in a large number of cases, mere cussedness of nature. They are intolerable of anything which limits their liberty. That is my belief.

2245. It is simply to get rid of the child?—Partly, and partly to get rid of the trouble of having it in the room.

2246. Are there a considerable number of cases of neglect by step-parents ?—To a small extent. I should say that probably the number of step-parents being smaller than those of own

(142.)

Lord *Norton*—continued.

fathers and mothers, the proportion might be perhaps, about the same or a little more.

2247. Are there a great number of cases where they are illegitimate children ?—There are cases of illegitimate children ; but the parents of illegitimate children are like married parents, they vary very much. Natural love exists often in a mother of an illegitimate child, and is often absent with a married woman.

2248. What was the exact nature of the remedy you proposed in the way of providing for burials?—That the funeral should be carried out by some recognised agent in a locality, just as now the grave is provided by a public body : the funeral should be provided on the same principle, under supervision if possible.

2249. At whose expense ?—At the expense of the society that undertakes according to scale to supply a funeral on certain terms.

2250. The parents bearing no part of the expense?—The parent may add as much as he thinks fit. Say the allowance is 2 *l.*, and the parent wishes to bury at 4 *l.*, and he is a man in a good position having 2 *l.*, he might put 2 *l.* more to it.

2251. Would it be in the nature of a burial club?—Yes, but without what the burial club now gives, the handling of the money to spend on anything a man likes.

2252. Where you have a reduction of premium what is the sum in your mind. Would 1 *l.* be the sum ?—We have three undertakers who have agreed to bury the dead children in our shelter at Harper-street, at 15 *s.*, 17 *s.*, and 18 *s.*, and supply a coach on the condition that the coffin is on the front seat.

2253. Would all danger of child insurance cease if the sum was limited to 1 *l.* ?—No ; 1 *l.* would be a fortune to a gin-drinking woman who has already pawned her husband's tools and clothes, and the babies' cot and the babies' clothes.

2254. You do not propose to abolish child insurance altogether ?—I would abolish child insurance altogether, and insure for a funeral. Life insurance permits persons to do what they like with the money. I would not give this liberty with the money, but permission to secure a free funeral according to a scale which should be paid for by arrangement with the society.

Lord Bishop of *Ripon.*

2255. You say you would abolish insurances up to that point, so that there would be no handling of the money ?—Yes.

2256. May I ask, have you noticed that there is a difference between the class of society that do the insurance work ?—Yes ; very great.

2257. May they be divided into two classes, those who make profit, and mutual societies that have no profit?—That is so.

2258. Would the incentive, so to speak, to crime, if I may use a strong word, exist as strongly in the case of one society as another ?—I must appeal to facts. You may probably remember the evidence of Dr. Ritchie, of Leek, that infant mortality fell from 156 to 109 per thousand after the Leek Burial Society ceased to insure

N 3   young

Lord Bishop of *Ripon*—continued.

young children. I may not put the figures accurately. Remembering that the society was a mutual society, and in its own interests it declined to insure children, the incentive would seem to exist in both kind of societies. That society had a high mortality, and ceasing to insure, the mortality went down. It was not a collecting society to which that happened.

2259. Does not that fact also point in this direction, that where you have a mutual society, the public opinion, so to speak, of the members, is against the person who does away with the child?—Quite so.

2260. Whereas in the case of the collecting society, if I understand it, the death is a good advertisement?—Quite so.

2261. Is that your impression?—That is so.

2262. So that on the whole there is an advantage on the side of the side of the mutual society?—A great advantage on the side of the mutual society.

Lord *Poltimore.*

2263. You said just now that children do not get into benefit until they are three months of age?—That is the case in the printed rules of the society. I do not think it is always the case that they keep the rules. I should like you to ask some agents. This is the Prudential's book of insurance: three months, 30 *s.*; six months, 2 *l.* 10 *s.* That is the rule throughout the country.

2264. Is that never varied from. Do they never depart from that?—Their rule never varies, but the practice I know nothing of.

Lord *Poltimore*—continued.

2265. Does the practice depart very often from that?—Practically, very much indeed.

2266. There is one question I omitted to ask you. It is obviously the interest of these societies to detect very bad cases, because they would not be obliged to pay the policy. Detecting cases, apparently, is in the interest of any insurance. I am not speaking of what you know, but apparently. Presumably it is in the interest of the societies that every case of crime and murder, where they have insured a life, should be detected. May I ask-have you ever got any assistance at all made by these societies in cases of criminal neglect or wilful neglect. Did they ever come to you and say, "We suspect here is a case, we wish you would help us to find it out"?—Never.

2267. Did you ever get assistance from an insurance agent?—Certainly not.

2268. I do not say it actually is, but it is presumably the interest of every insurance company to detect crime, because every crime is a fraud on the company?—Quite so.

2269. You never had that assistance from insurance companies?—Not once in the whole of the seven years. I should like to put in a case of a child beggar in the street, insured for 20 *l.* 12 *s.*, in a filthy condition, taken from the beggar, and sent to an industrial school. It was subsequently discovered that the death of that child would have brought to its owner 20 *l.* 12 *s.*, insured in the Liverpool Legal Friendly Society.

The Witness is directed to withdraw.

Ordered, That this Committee be adjourned to Friday next, at Twelve o'clock.

Die Veneris, 11° Julii, 1890.

LORDS PRESENT:

Earl of DERBY.
Earl SPENCER.
Earl BEAUCHAMP.
Earl of SELBORNE.
LORD BISHOP OF RIPON.
Lord CLIFFORD of CHUDLEIGH.

Lord KER (*Marquess of Lothian*).
Lord POLTIMORE.
Lord BROUGHAM AND VAUX.
Lord KINNAIRD.
Lord NORTON.
Lord THRING.

THE RIGHT REV. THE LORD BISHOP OF PETERBOROUGH, IN THE CHAIR.

THE following letter, and enclosed statements, are read by the Chairman:—

Justices' Room,
Town Hall, Leicester,
My Lord,   10 July 1890.

I beg to enclose a copy of the evidence in a case heard by the borough magistrates this morning, and which I mentioned to your Lordship. It will be seen that the child in question was insured for 30 s.

Eleven of the woman's children died in infancy, and it has been ascertained that two of that number were also insured for the same sum each, neither being more than 12 months. Inquiries are still being made as to whether any of the other children were insured; should this prove to have been the case I will let your Lordship know.

I have, &c.
(signed)   R. R. *Blackwell.*

The Right Reverend
The Lord Bishop of Peterborough.

[*Endorsement.*] Walker v. Rodwell (James) and Scott (Elizabeth), charged with neglect of George Rodwell, an infant. Convicted, Rodwell, six weeks; Scott, three months, hard labour. Copy Minutes of Evidence.

Frederick William Lewitt, upon his oath, saith:

I am a physician and surgeon; on the 5th May last the female defendant came to my surgery with a child, named George Rodwell, aged two months. It was suffering from atrophy, or wasting. I saw the child on numerous occasions between that day and 5th July instant, when it died. The child from the first was not properly attended, both as regards food and clothing. On three or four occasions I found the child alone in the house. I prescribed milk and water. I spoke to the female defendant several times. I warned her as to her neglect, and told her that if anything happened to the child she would get into trouble. I particularly remember the 3rd July instant. I then found

(142.)

the child alone in the house. I found the feeding-bottle empty, fittings in a shocking condition, teat very foul. I made a post-mortem examination of the body of the child, by direction of the coroner. I found no organic disease which would account for the child's death. The wasting was due to neglect in feeding. In my opinion, had my instructions been carried out, the child might have been alive now. I never saw the male defendant. I did not give a certificate on the death of the child. I did not prescribe laudanum, and was not aware that it was being given. The normal weight of a child of the age of the deceased one would be 10½ lbs.

Richard Walker, on his oath, saith:—

I am an inspector of the Society for Prevention of Cruelty to Children. On Friday last, 4th July 1890, I visited the house of the defendants, 3, Bailey's-yard, Sandacre-street. I saw the female defendant, who gave her name as Elizabeth Rodwell, wife of James Rodwell. I told her that I had received a complaint about her infant child, George Rodwell. At my request she produced the child and the feeding-bottle. The child was exceedingly emaciated; the scalp was caked with dirt. I called the attention of the female defendant to it. She said all her children had been like that. She took off the child's napkin, which was cold and wet. The child's buttocks were red and raw. There was some milk in the feeding-bottle quite sour. The teat and tubes were clogged with milk. I gave her the money for new fittings for the bottle, which she procured whilst I remained. She gave me some fresh milk, and I fed the child, which had been making a low cry during the time I was there, but which ceased when I fed it. It took the milk ravenously, and soon went to sleep. I told her I should report her for neglect. She admitted having given the child laudanum; two drops at night and two drops in the morning. I asked her if the child was insured. She hesitated, and then produced a book, showing the child to be insured in the

N 4   Royal

11 *July* 1890.

Royal London Friendly Society for 30 *s.* She said she had had 13 children, 11 having died in infancy. I told her I should come again in the evening and see her husband. She had told me she was married to the male defendant. Before leaving I examined the child's bed; bolster and pillow black with dirt; piece of calico used as a sheet; offensive through vomit. I went again the same evening at 8.45; saw both defendants. I told him the female defendant had said in the afternoon that she had given the child laudanum. He said he did not know of it. That she had told me she had been feeding it on corn-flour, boiled bread, and biscuits; but not for the last three weeks, as the child would not take them. He said, "Yes, she has been giving it food." I told them both I should report them for neglect. Rodwell said, "You can't do anything at me." I went to the house next morning, 5th instant, at 11.45, and weighed the child; it weighed 6 lbs. 8 ozs. The female defendant stated to me that the vicar of the parish had sent a pint of milk a day since 21st June.

Examined by *Rodwell.*

You said: "I washed the bottle every night, it was my job"; there was milk boiling on the fire at the time, and Rodwell said, "Look here, we don't pine our children." The female defendant told me she was the wife of Thomas Scott, dyer, who is living, and that she had been living with Rodwell for the past 16 years.

Mary Bale, upon her oath, saith:—

I live next door to the defendants. They have lived together next door to me since just before Christmas. I knew the child now dead. She used to go away, locking it up in the bedroom, and leaving it alone. She was a glove-stitcher, working at home. The child was left for three or four hours at a time. I have several times taken the feeding-bottle away from the child, in consequence of its filthy condition. I have heard the child crying hour after hour. I have several times spoken to Scott about the child, telling her she ought to be ashamed of herself for leaving it; and that she would get into trouble. A few weeks ago she told me she had not given the child the doctor's medicine; and only had the doctor in case anything happened. Last Thursday, when she came home, she woke the child, who cried, and I heard her say, "You little b——, I wish I could tie your jaws up before this time to-morrow." I have seen a great deal of beer go into the house before breakfast. Last Friday night, after Inspector Walker had been down, Rodwell said, "It would be better if the b—— inspector came and stirred up the closet pans than stir up a half-dead kid."

A newspaper cutting, containing the following extract, is also read:—

Mr. Justice Charles, in charging the grand jury at Newcastle Assizes, yesterday, referred to a case in which the parents were indicted for causing the death of their child through culpable neglect, and said it was a question whether some legislation ought not to take place; not for preventing entirely the insurance of children's lives, but, at all events, for preventing the proceeds of the insurance from getting into the pockets of the parents of the children.

It is directed that the foregoing be inserted in the Minutes of Evidence.

Mr. WILLIAM CROOKS, is called in; and Examined, as follows:

Chairman.

2270. WHERE do you live?—At No. 28, Northumberland-street, Poplar, East.

2271. What is your occupation?—I am a journeyman cooper.

2272. Would you object to telling us what your weekly wage is?—Certainly not: 2 *l.*

2273. I think you have some objections to the Children's Life Insurance Bill; would you kindly state those objections to the Committee?—My objection to the Bill is the payment of the funeral insurance money to the undertaker; if that was all the expense that workmen were put to, undoubtedly the Committee would be justified in pushing forward a Bill of this description, but it is not so. Amongst the working men who have a great difficulty in making both ends meet from week to week, unless they prepare themselves for the emergency for meeting these and other expenses, if death should overtake one of their children, and the consequence would be that they are plunged into debt, not only for the funeral expenses, but for the various other expenses that would be necessarily attendant on the funeral, and incidental to it.

2274. Do you mean by the "incidental expenses" of the funeral, the doctor, for instance?—And the black to be obtained for the parents

Chairman—continued.

on account of the children, which you must know, amongst the very poor, is looked upon as necessary. For poor people not to show a little respect to those they have buried, is looked upon as a kind of disgrace by those amongst whom they live. I may say that I do not know another working man who is so well acquainted with his own class as I am. I know some thousands of families, and out of the whole of those families, I do not know one neglectful mother. I find always mothers willing and very ready to make every sacrifice to keep their children alive, and it seems to me to be the case that the most thrifty of the very poor alway insure. I do not find in my experience anyone who has not that maternal affection for their children which it seems to be the general opinion that we lack as poor people. There is also an argument brought forward in favour of the Bill with regard to neglect to call in a doctor. I may say that any chemist in a poor neighbourhood would be willing to tell you that there is an immense amount of suffering which is caused by want of knowledge, and more frequently by want of funds to pay the doctor. It happens very often, that a dock labourer for instance has only got one day on in the week, and on coming home, if he

finds

Chairman—continued.

finds one of his children sick, the first thing he says to his wife is, "What have you done?" She will say, "l have been to the chemist to get something for it." A neighbour would probably have recommended something, and out of his very small earnings he cannot get enough money to call in the doctor, or if he does, he has to borrow the necessary fee to pay him; it is not out of want of natural affection on the part of either father or mother, it is only the want of the necessary funds to pay the doctor that leads to his frequently not being called in.

2275. Is there anything else you wish to say to the Committee?—Yes, I might say that if this Bill becomes law we shall in all probability go back to the old times of "friendly leads," which were of frequent occurrence, held in public-houses; it was a common thing when a man had lost a child for a friend to go about remarking, "So-and-so has lost a child, and we are going to have a friendly lead to help him." The consequence was that many would go to the public-house where it was held, and put their sixpences in the plate, and spend, perhaps, a shilling for the good of the house, and as likely as not wind-up with a good round "drunk" all round. Now, when this insurance system came in people would very naturally say that they would not give their shillings to help people who could help themselves. I know instances of people who have got enormous sums through the assistance of their friends. I know one instance in which 18 *l.* had been gathered, whereas if it had been known that the parties had been insured the chances are that the parties who had put their money into the plate would not have put in anything at all, and if assurance is interfered with, the consequence may be that we may come back to that state of things; my neighbour would say to me, "If the money is to go to the undertaker, let the undertaker insure, I will not." Further, it appears to me that this Bill as it stands now would not prevent collusion between the person insuring and the undertaker; the undertaker might offer some clothes to be worn, and if there was a very bad father or mother there would be nothing to prevent them pawning those clothes to get drink. Under any circumstances a bad mother will be a bad mother, whether there is an insurance upon the child or not; it amounts to the same thing. If there is a father or mother who is likely to put an end to their child's life (I am not acquainted with any such people) they would be just as likely, or more likely, to put an end to it quickly, so that they should not be troubled with it; but, practically, the longer one has a child the more likely affection is to spring up in the parents. With regard to the remarks which have fallen in the sick-room, "It would be a blessing if this child were to die," I may say that that is a common remark in a sick-room with poor people when they see their child suffering, not knowing whether it will live or die, the poor people would say, "Rather would I see it dead," and not unnaturally; but not with the ulterior motive of seeing the money come in. I have a boy 11 months old, not an ordinary child, but an exceptionally fine lad. When he was a month old he was very ill, and I myself have prayed by the bed, "God grant that he
(142.)

Chairman—continued.

may not live a quarter of an hour." What would have been the cry if there had been an inquest upon that child, and it was said that I had made the remark that it would be a good job if it would be dead? Supposing it had been insured, the remark would have been declared to have been made on account of the insurance. I cannot see how this Bill will meet the case it is intended to meet; if there are bad fathers and mothers then the criminal law should be able to find them out. With reference to medical jurisprudence, there is a continual conflict of evidence amongst the doctors as to whether a parent has neglected her child, whilst those who have lived amongst them for years are better able to tell than the doctors. One doctor will argue that the child has been neglected, and another will argue that it is not starvation, but that it is suffering from some complaint by reason of which it cannot assimilate its food. There are many instances of lung complaints, which, as you know, carry the children off very rapidly, and the cause is ordinarily attributed to natural death. If this occurs in a very poor case, and one of the jury were to ask, "Is it insured?" and the answer should be, "Yes," then an immediate suspicion runs through the mind of the jury that the child has not been properly cared for. One might say that the doctors were inclined rather to court inquest for the sake of the fee, than to give a certificate of death. My reason for saying this is, that in very poor neighbourhoods, where this class of people live, the doctor would, perhaps, only charge sixpence for his visit, and he would have to sit and prescribe for 40 odd patients before he could make up the guinea fee which he would get at the inquest, earning it in a very few moments, because you know that the doctor generally only stops a few moments, and says that he was called in at a very late period of the case and could not give a certificate; but that as far as he can say, it was death from natural causes. Now, poor people do not like inquests, but still they court every inquiry from their neighbours as to why their children die. I do not think you could inflict a greater hardship upon a poor mother than to say that her child has not been properly cared for; enormous sacrifices are made by the poor, which are quite unknown to any except those who live amongst them. A mother has frequently to go out and do a day's washing and leave her little one at home, not because she does not love it, but because she could not afford to be stopping at home and administering to her child all that is necessary; the circumstances of her life prevent it. Then, as to the insurance covering the cost of the funeral, I know a case at the present moment where the insurance was considerably below the cost of the funeral, and where the parties owe 7 *s.* 6 *d.* for the doctor's bill at the present moment, and where they have had to run themselves into debt to get the other necessaries attending the funeral. It seems to me that a man or a woman who is very poor, who has taken the trouble to insure against those risks, at least should have some say as to how the money should be spent. I have thought over the matter carefully, and I talked it over with other people. We say that if there is a bad case which we know, and where the coroner and the
O   jury

Chairman—continued.

jury think there is reasonable evidence to suppose the child was neglected, but where it was not possible to convict before a court of law, the coroner should have discretion to say, "We will bury this child for you." Under those circumstances it might be good, but under existing circumstances what is proposed is very bad, and it will mean that the insurance companies, in this instance, will recoup themselves to an enormous amount for the very reason that hundreds, and I may say thousands, of policies will lapse; parents will refuse to pay that other people may take the money which they have been paying for. The insurance companies, I take it, can afford to look on with indifference as far as this Bill is concerned, but we cannot. It will raise up this question again. The pest of society is the tallyman: it will give him an opportunity of coming round and offering to supply black for the little ones, and so the wife would run into debt again with the tallyman; the insurance companies have rescued us from that position. I do not doubt for a moment that the insurance companies are making a profit; but, since there is no other go-between, we have no alternative but to insure to secure ourselves from these expenses in such times of trouble.

2276. Is there anything else that you would wish to say?—I do not think there is anything.

2277. You say you know thousands of the working classes, and do not know a single case of a bad father or a bad mother?—That is so.

2278. If, on the other hand, you were to read the evidence which has been given before this Committee, and to find that it showed clearly that there were a great many bad fathers and bad mothers amongst the working classes, generally, you would not be disposed, I suppose, to say that all that evidence was false?—Certainly not; but I should say it was no criterion because those gentlemen who have given evidence only meet one case here and there, the same as the judges who try these cases, whereas we meet the whole of these people; the vast majority.

2279. Would you say it was speaking ill of the working classes if I were to say there might be as many as one in a 1,000 of them bad men?—I should say, before I read your Lordship's speech, that I had come to that conclusion from what I had read, that it was possible there might be one in a 1,000, but I said, "Would it be fair to punish 999 in the endeavour to find this one?"

2280. As a matter of fact, have you considered; supposing there were amongst the working classes that one man in a 1,000 who was capable of putting away his child, how many would that come to all over England?—I have read your statement upon that.

2281. But have you considered the question at all as a matter of figures?—I take your figure for it that it was 600.

2282. Supposing there are 15,000,000 working people in England; are there as many?—I scarcely think so.

2283. Take it that there are 10,000,000, if you take one man in a 1,000 who is capable of doing this evil thing, it would come to a great many out of 10,000,000?—I would beg to direct

Chairman—continued.

your attention to the fact that all of those are not insured.

2284. But I was speaking of the one man in a 1,000 who is a bad character amongst working men; do you say that one man in a 1,000 is about your idea of the proportion of bad men to good men amongst the working men?—I should not say that; I should say the proportion of bad men might be greater, but that the want of paternal affection is even less than that. Even a bad man may be, and probably is, very fond of his children.

2285. Will you take my calculation. I put it that there are 600,000 children now insured in Great Britain. I believe the number of policies amounts to 2,000,000. Now, if you take it that one child in 1,000 is put away by foul means that would give 600 on that 600,000, would it not?—Yes.

2286. It would be a great deal more on the 2,000,000, would it not?—Of course it would.

2287. Then, without any libel on the working classes, I might have said that there are 1,000 children put to death foully in England. I am taking now the insured cases; if I had said that there were 1,000 children probably put to death every year for the sake of their insurance you would regard that, probably, as a great libel upon the working classes; yet it would only come, upon your own showing, to one child in 1,000 being foully dealt with; would that be a foul libel upon the working classes?—Yes, certainly it would; you might as well say of the criminal classes that the whole public should be punished for the exceptional case.

2288. What I want to get from you is this: you say it is not a libel on the working classes to say that one in 1,000 would be capable of putting away his child?—I have no knowledge of that; I take your Lordship's figures for that.

2289. What I want to point out to you is that in that case, taking it only at one in 1,000, and taking the number of children insured at 2,000,000, or allowing for double policies at 1,500,000 children, that one in 1,000 children done away with in the whole number of 1,500,000 would give a very large number of children done away with every year; yet you yourself admit that to say that there is one bad man in 1,000 of the working men would be no libel upon them?—Admitting that it might be so, is not the criminal law effective enough to find this one in 1,000, rather than punish the whole of them?

2290. Quite so, if that were possible; but I am only dealing at this moment with the complaints of those who impute it as a foul libel on the working classes, whereas you yourself would admit that one in 1,000 of them may be capable of doing this?—I say it is possible, but I have no means of finding that out, such as your Lordship would have.

2291. If I were right, as a matter of fact it would not be a great libel upon the working classes, on your own showing?—You must not take it in that way; the working classes say the exception is the one, and that they are the 999.

2292. Is it any imputation upon 999 if I say the odd one is a man capable of doing evil?—But

Chairman—continued.

But when there is a suspicion thrown out, and no particular person is singled out, every individual man feels as if he were accused.

2293. May I ask are you acquainted with the provisions of the Friendly Societies Act?—I cannot say that I am.

2294. I daresay you know this: that the Friendly Societies Act imposed certain restrictions upon child insurance. It said that a child under a certain age should not be insured for more than a certain sum, and it required very careful provisions about the doctor's certificate, and the registrar's certificate. Why do you think the Legislature, when it was passing the Friendly Societies Act in the interest of the working classes, put in all those safeguards and protections; was it to prevent crime, do you think; could there have been any other object? —As we at present work, taking the existing state of affairs under which we live, we take the construction of your Bill to be fairly good, with the exception of how the money is to be spent. I say nothing as to the amount.

2295. You do not object to the amount?—Certainly not.

2296. It is only as to the one provision of the money going to the undertaker?—Exactly. I think your Lordships should know I was the cause of a certain resolution being adopted by the representative body, which I will have much pleasure in handing in.

2297. We will deal with that presently. The Friendly Societies Act contains a number of provisions which you yourself think were provisions against a person making a profit upon the death of his child. Do you consider those provisions were a libel upon the working classes generally?—I should think not.

2298. Then, if they were not, and if you feel that it was right that there should be restrictions to prevent crime, there was no libel upon the good working man in that?—But we look upon it in this way: we want that the law shall be a terror to evil-doers, and no restriction upon the law-abiding man.

2299. The Friendly Societies Act contains a number of restrictions to prevent crime; did the Friendly Societies Act in making those restrictions take it for granted that every working man would be a bad man, or only that some of them would be bad men?—Undoubtedly they took it for granted that some would.

2300. Then when the Friendly Societies Act made a number of restrictions to prevent bad working men doing wrong, they passed no libel upon all the good men, who would not do wrong? —It would not injure the good men.

2301. I am not speaking of injury; I am speaking of the libel. The Act was framed upon the principle that a certain number of working men might do what was wrong, and therefore those restrictions were put in to prevent their doing what was wrong; was not that so?—Yes.

2302. Passing restrictions to prevent people from doing wrong is no libel upon those good men who would not do wrong, is it?—Certainly not.

2303. Supposing for the sake of argument that those restrictions were not sufficient, is it any libel upon the working man to make those

(142.)

Chairman—continued.

restrictions sufficient, observing all along that they only apply to bad working men?—It comes in here; you are asking the good working man to suffer equally with the bad working man.

2304. That is another question altogether from what I am asking you to consider. Whether it is right or just that good men should suffer for the bad is another question, but what you and others have dwelt very strongly upon is the supposed libel upon the working-man. Is not every restriction an imputation upon somebody. If every man were good there would be no need for restriction?—I should not take it that way. I should not take it as a libel upon me that you made the present Criminal Law Amendment Act touch persons which the present law would not touch; but I should object to being punished for the sake of others.

2305. But taking the present law as it stands, would you consider it a libel?—I should say it did not libel me, but I am here to speak of the second clause of the proposed Bill.

2306. You say it would compel you to pay all the money now insured for to the undertaker?—That is so.

2307. That is to say, if you had insured your child for 5 *l.* or 6 *l.*, and this Act were passed, the whole of that would have to go to the undertaker?—Yes.

2308. But that would only mean as regards insurances already effected; it would not affect the insurances afterwards, because you need not insure in that case for more than the cost of a respectable funeral; the balance which you assume would go to the undertaker would only apply to those policies already existing?—But the difficulty that would occur is, that the existing insurances, I take it, are for very little more than are laid down in your Bill, and for under 12 months they would be practically less.

2309. But I want to put it to you that this idea of enriching the undertaker, would only apply to policies now existing for considerable sums. Supposing the Bill were passed and the payment of the money would go to the undertaker, then the working man would not insure for more than would pay for a respectable funeral; he would not be so foolish as to insure to put money into the pocket of the undertaker in excess of the cost of the funeral?—I think the poor would not insure at all under those circumstances.

2310. Now, upon the question of payment of the doctor; how is the doctor paid where the child does not die, but recovers?—That is a labour of love; one would rather spend a sovereign to get his child's health restored than he would spend a shilling to help to bury it.

2311. But you were speaking of the doctor's expenses as being amongst the things for which parents insure?—Not necessarily.

2312. I thought I understood you to say that it was greatly objected, that if you were to pay the money to the undertaker only, there would be nothing over to pay to the doctor?—I did say so.

2313. I want to know from what funds is the doctor paid now, if the child does not die?—It has to come out of the weekly wage of the men.

O 2   2314. Are

Chairman—continued.

2314. Are there no such things as sick clubs or club doctors?—For children, I do not know of any.

2315. In friendly societies a man can get medical attendance for his whole family for so much a month, can he not?—I do not know that he can.

2316. When a child dies is the doctor paid in some other manner?—In poor neighbourhoods he very rarely, never, except isolated cases, allows a bill to run, but is paid at the time, and this money is frequently borrowed from a poor neighbour.

2317. In the case of a child dying the doctor's fee is no heavier, is it, than in the case of a child recovering?—No.

2318. Then if a doctor is paid from some other source than the insurance when the child recovers, can he not be paid from the same source when the child dies?—The usual plan is that the woman goes to her neighbour and says, "When my child gets better Mrs. Brown or Mrs. Jones I will pay you off the money you have been kind enough to lend me to pay the doctor."

2319 Would that not be the same thing when the child died; could not Mrs. Brown lend and be repaid in just the same way?—That might be so; but here is the fact; poor people have insured themselves against possible loss, and, having paid 3 *l.*, 4 *l.*, or 5 *l.* as the case might be, to know that the undertaker would get the money which would have paid that debt, is doubly hard upon the poor.

2320. I could understand that objection if my Bill were retrospective, but if you observe that my clause as proposed is entirely prospective and not to apply to the past at all, would not that make a very great difference in your mind?—Supposing it does not affect me at all, but only affects those who may have children in the future, I would ask would not the hardship be as great upon those who may have children in the future as upon those who have children at the present moment? Of course we, who are now insured, should say this has nothing to do with us; let those who like fight it out.

2321. Your point was that the money would go to the undertaker, and that the money would practically be confiscated?—Yes.

2322. But if I made it to apply only to insurances hereafter to be effected, then as I have said, the parent would not insure for 4 *l.* or 5 *l.*; he would insure only for what would pay for the funeral and what would pay the doctor; in that case the confiscation of the money would not take place, it would not be there to confiscate?—It would not be there, neither would the poor people insure.

2323. You say if the Bill were passed the working classes would be so offended that they would cease to insure?—Yes.

2324. Supposing for the sake of argument that it were made clear to the working man that the passing of this Bill was the only way of preventing a considerable amount of child murder, would they say, rather than that our feelings should be hurt we would prefer that a considerable number of children every year should be murdered; would that be the thing you would think that the honest, kindly, respectable working man

Chairman—continued.

would say?—He would still oppose it; he would say, let those who commit the crime be punished, not those who do not.

2325. But this is a question not of punishing but of preventing crime?—But will it?

2326. I want to ask you this: Supposing the great majority of working men of whom I think as highly as you do, and of whom I have spoken highly, were told that by giving up certain privileges which they now possess, they would ensure not the punishment but the prevention of child murder, do you really mean to say that the working men are so selfish and so indifferent to crime that they would be willing that a large number of children should be murdered rather than that they should lose these privileges; do you think that would fairly represent the feelings of the working classes of whom you are the representative?—If I were to put that to my fellow workmen they would say, what are our legislators about that they do not make a law to punish those who commit the crime.

2327. But I am speaking of legislation, the object of which is to prevent, not to punish?—My argument is that the crime would be the same, that taking the Bill as it is, it would not reduce the amount of crime.

2328. Except the working man is willing there should be this prevention?—The working men contend that it would not prevent it.

2329. My point is this: do you think if it could be shown to the working classes that it would prevent crime, they would still say, whether it can be shown to prevent murder or not, we still object to it? Do not you think that would be a greater libel upon the working man than anything I have said?—But they would answer, show me that it would prevent murder.

2330. Then you and I are quite agreed that if the working men could be shown that, they would be willing to give up some privilege?—But as I said before, will it prevent? You would have some difficulty in showing that it would prevent.

2331. But if it could be shown that it would prevent?—But I am of opinion it will be extremely difficult to show that; in fact that you could not do it.

2332. Finally, as I understand, the only clause in this Bill to which you take serious exception is the clause as to paying the undertaker?—That is so.

2333. You do not object to the other part?—No; but I may remark that the Bill, as it stands, would not prevent collusion between the undertaker and the bad parent, not even excepting that part of the sixth clause relating to punishment, which deals with articles supplied, because necessaries might be in the shape of "black," and it would not prevent a bad mother or a bad father from selling those things to get drink.

Earl Spencer.

2334. You do not belong to any insurance company as an official in any way?—No.

2335. Not as a collector, or anything of that sort?—No.

2336. Have you ever belonged to one in that way?—Never.

2337. I understand from what you have answered

Earl *Spencer*—continued.

answered to the Right Reverend Chairman, that you do not object to the present law on friendly societies relating to infant insurance?—No.

2338. And you would not object to those clauses which refer to that subject being modified to meet the case, if it be that they give an incentive to infant crime?—I think I told his Lordship that the only way in which it seems to me to be possible to make them preventive, would be that the coroner should have power, where he thought there was neglect, to take the whole of the money away from the parents and bury the child himself.

2339. You said that you thought the proper way was for the law to punish the evil-doer?—Yes.

2340. Are you not aware that sometimes there is very nearly moral proof of guilt without legal proof?—Yes.

2341. Would you not think there being some cases of that sort, that it might be desirable to take measures to prevent them? — I would endeavour to prevent them in the way I have just said,

2342. We have had various suggestions made. Of course there is the suggestion of the Bill, which I understand you object to, as to paying the insurance money direct to the undertaker; but there have been other suggestions made, such as doing away with the insurance of children under one year; and some people have gone even further than that. Would that be very much of a detriment to the honest working classes, who are no doubt in the very large majority?—Coming to that, I gave it very serious consideration, and I find that the sum for which children are usually insured, if only one policy is in existence, is so small that it would not cover the expenses, so that it would not be necessary to limit the age to over 12 months.

2343. Do you mean the sum is so low that it hardly pays the funeral expenses?—It hardly pays the funeral expenses.

2344. Then you would not object to doing away with the insurance of children under the age of one year?—I should object to abolish it. I have lost a child under three months old, but I have never had any money out of an insurance company since I have been insured. I had lost three children before then. My first child cost me 2 *l.* 3 *s.* to bury it, although we did it in the plainest possible manner. I had to pay the 2 *l.* 3 *d.* out of my earnings, so that I was not likely to do it in an extravagant manner; and seeing that I had no home, and that I was living in furnished apartments, it was very necessary for me to exercise very great care; but that three months' child cost me 2 *l.* 3 *s.*, and the insurance company would not give anything like that for a three months' child, not for the penny a week.

2345. How was that amount made up?—I cannot give you the particulars, but I could send you the bill; it all went to the undertaker.

2346. We have had evidence given before this Committee that a child could be buried for about 1 *l.*, or under?—They must have been very fortunate parents, and it could not have been in London.

(142.)

Earl *Spencer*—continued.

2347. Do you think that the usual charge for the burial of a working man's child would be more than 1 *l.*?—Yes, in most places. All I know is that in Liverpool, where I was then, I lost one of my children; we ordered the coffin from the undertaker; the undertaker brought a cab and took the wife and a friend to the cemetery; they carried the coffin to the grave, and the total cost was 27 *s.* 6 *d.*; but I ought to say nothing would shame me more than to have such a funeral as that at home, at my house. Being in a country place I did not think it so very hard, but I did feel it very hard, although I should have been still more ashamed if I had been surrounded by friends who knew me.

2348. You would be surprised to be told that the Committee have had pretty clear evidence that it could be done with the carriage to convey the body, and all for about 15 *s.*?—I cannot believe it; I would say it could not take place in London.

Chairman.

2349. You would not believe it if we produced to you the list of undertaking firms from more than one part of London, in which they advertise that they will do it for this sum?—I would be glad to ask the undertaker if he would be willing to undertake it as he puts it in his window without any incidentals. I think you would find the contrary would be the fact.

Earl *Spencer.*

2350. In your opinion it would be a serious detriment to working men, if they could not insure the funeral, and other expenses of children under one year?—I do not take it that way. Children under a year for a penny a week are not insured for a sufficient amount to cover the funeral expenses.

2351. Is it within your own knowledge that they are not insured for sufficient to cover their own expenses?— I think I qualified that by saying, " If there was only one policy in existence for a penny a week." The difficulty is to get a man who can afford to pay more than a penny a week; I could give many instances which came under my notice during the dock strike, but that is beyond the question of whether they could afford to pay more.

2352. In your opinion it is desirable to keep up the possibility of poor men insuring the lives of children under a year?—Yes, seeing that under the circumstances I have mentioned they could not make a profit upon it.

2353. You would be against their making a profit, I presume?—I think the existing state of affairs is good.

2354. Do you think they often do make a profit under the existing state of things?—If you take it that the man's wife gets an old black skirt and a black hat, and the man himself gets a pair of black trousers and a black hat; if you call that making a profit, I would admit that they get a profit.

2355. No, I mean money that they can spend in drink?—My contention as to that would be, not that I have found any such cases, but that people who would be inclined to do that would have still greater opportunities of doing so if this Bill

O 3

Bill

Earl *Spencer*—continued.

Bill passed, because they would go back to the old practice of the "friendly lead," and then be likely to go in for a thorough good drunk.

2356. Then another suggestion is that in infant life insurance the sum paid should be applied as in a fire insurance, on the principle of indemnity, where only an amount equivalent to that which is actually lost is paid: that would prevent any profit being made?—The question would be what was the actual loss. I have now a suit of clothes on, which cost 1 *l.*, as a workman. I cannot get any more consistently with attending to my wife and six children. I am glad to get those. If I lose my little one I must change my brown suit for a black suit, and I must come upon the insurance company, and say, "You must indemnify me."

2357. Granting that that might be covered by insurance, and the medical expenses might also be covered, provided you could prove you have been out of pocket, would you object to that?—Although I may pay my doctor, still in that case it does not cover the expenses I am put to. He walks into my house, and says that my child must have Liebig's extract, or sherry or champagne; I must then go hawking about to charitable institutions, or go begging or borrowing to supply these things.

2358. That would be covered by the proposal that the legitimate expenses will be paid out of the insurance?—If all the legitimate expenses were paid then we would not have any objection to the Bill at all; but the weak point of it comes in here; that this very bad fellow, whom the Bill aims at, would still have the opportunity of getting rid of these things which would be looked upon as necessaries by the good man.

2359. You have spoken, first of all, which I understand perfectly, about the difficulty that would ensue when they took the hat round, of going to the public-house and drinking, but I did not quite understand the further objection you made about the tallyman; what is a tallyman; it is ignorance on my part not to know; you might explain what you mean?—I think the Committee ought to know that. He is the man who knocks at your door, and wants to know, "Whether you want any drapery?" "Can we supply you with any black? "Can we do this dress for you; anything in my line?" He offers to sell a suit of cloths, such as I have on, for 35 *s.*; if I were a man who had nothing whatever to do at all, I should jump at the opportunity of having a suit and paying him, say, 6 *d.* a week or whatever I could.

2360. What do you object to in him?—I object to his prices, and also, if my wife were a bad woman, there would be nothing to prevent her taking this cloth to the pawnshop, leaving me to fight the battle out. Your Lordships have known, no doubt, cases of men being summoned to the county court for goods which have been supplied to the wife by the tallyman.

Lord *Kinnaird.*

2361. Do the doctors want, as a rule, immediate payment?—Yes; in poor neighbourhoods.

2362. And the usual charge would be about sixpence or one shilling?—If the doctor sees you

Lord *Kinnaird*—continued.

at the dispensary it is sixpence, but coming to your house he usually wants 1 *s.* 6*d.*

2363. Do we understand, then, that the friendly leads at public-houses have practically come to an end?—Yes, I do say so ; in isolated cases they do take place now, but practically they are unknown.

2364. How long have they been unknown, do you think?—It might be possible for me to walk about Limehouse and Poplar and find a friendly lead taking place on a Saturday night, but years ago every "jerry shop," as we call it, had a friendly lead on ; now you might go round the parish and only find one going on; I think they are putting a stop to it.

2365. How long ago has it gone down?—Practically, I think, I may say ten years.

2366. Among shoeblack boys, of whom I know something, it was very common, and whenever one member of their families died they did that?—It might be that they did, but I was taking it as a general thing, speaking as a man who walks about the street on Saturday night, and sees nearly everything that is going on.

2367. You think good has come of insurance?—Yes.

2368. Then, with reference to the proportion of working men who insure, could you give the Committee any idea of that?—I should say rather more than half, to my knowledge ; we have 89 working at my place ; I do not know any man who is not insured; we look upon it as a kind of stigma amongst us if a man has lost his child and is not insured, and he comes round with the hat to get something for him.

2369. If it happened once it would not happen a second time?—Certainly not.

2370. You think it has distinctly made people rely upon their own resources rather than to be continually sending round the hat?—Yes ; there has been a spirit of independence growing up amongst our men, particularly of late years, that they do not like asking anybody for anything.

2371. It has been suggested that possibly one way of preventing bad people from doing what everybody wants to stop, would be if we had compulsory registration of societies in which the children were insured, so that it must be a public document, thereby preventing the parents from going to two or three societies; do you think that would be objectionable?—There would not be the slightest objection to its being known they were insured; the idea seems to have got abroad that one woman collects the whole of the money. I do not know of any instance where a woman in our street, or anybody else's street, has been going round collecting. I was on the relief committee of the dock strike, and therefore have an intimate knowledge of these people, and I do not know any case where a woman collects insurance money from a lot of people, and hands it over to the insurance agent.

Chairman.

2372. Where have you seen the statement made?—I have seen it in the newspapers. I
saw

Chairman—continued.

saw it in " The Star " and in " The Evening News."

Chairman.] You may take it from me, as Chairman, that no such statement has been made before this Committee.

Lord *Kinnaird.*

2373–4. How is the money usually collected? —The collector calls.

2375. I take it that there is somebody who will have charge of a district do you know whether occasionally someone else will be working for him, and will get some of his commission? —I have heard of cases where the agent, having a very large book, employed a sub-agent, but that agent is responsible to him; it is not done with a view of covering up, or making secret the fact of insurance.

2376. I only wanted to know correctly how the money was collected; are there many of your workmen who are agents?—No one in our works collects for insurance.

2377. You have touched upon this point indirectly once or twice. Could you tell the Committee what you would consider would be the cost of a funeral for a child under one year old? —As regards the cost of a child's funeral under one year, I should be glad to get it done for 2 *l.*

2378. That would include what; a carriage and a hearse?—I should not expect a hearse. I should expect one carriage. I should like your Lordships to see the bill I had for the first little one I lost, you would see how the account is made up.

Chairman.

2379. Will you kindly send it in?—Certainly; I should be pleased to do so.

Lord *Kinnaird.*

2380. That would be the kind of feeling, I take it, among men who were in receipt of good wages, that any other funeral than that which you have described as costing 2 *l.* would not be thought a proper one?—No; I think the contrary feeling prevails among the workmen; they like to have a respectable funeral, but these glass hearses are not very popular amongst my class.

2381. If the Committee have had evidence presented to them to show that in many cases people are insured in three or four societies, which they ought not to be under the present law, you would think that something ought to be done?— I should say stop it at once; I should have no hesitation whatever in stopping such a thing; three or four policies have no business to exist upon the life of any person unless they merely amount to the sum laid down in the Act. If you would allow me I can give an instance of one adult who was insured for 10 *l.* by a man who took the whole of that 10 *l.* away and enjoyed himself with it; he was not even related to the person upon whose life the sum was insured. I think such a thing should be stopped.

2382. If there is any feeling that we are desiring to promote a Bill which is contrary to the feelings of the best of the working men, do you think there are any people who would come and give evidence before the Committee, because we (142.)

Lord Kinnaird—continued.

should be glad to see them?—It is not every workman who has an employer like my own; I explained matters to him and gave him the Bill to read, and told him I wished to give evidence before the Committee, and he said, "By all means go and state what you know about the matter." Other workmen would probably be put to serious inconvenience, and their masters could not spare them; but I do know that relieving officers in poor parishes, and also chemists above all men, could prove that poor mothers do try very hard to do the best with their children when they are ill; and to save the doctor's fee, not for the sake of economy, but because they have not the money to pay. I was speaking to a man last night whom I had known for years before he became relieving officer, and I asked him what he thought about child insurance. He said, "You know I have been 20 years relieving officer, and I never yet met a mother who ever caused me to raise a suspicion as to putting the child away for the sake of insurance." I said to him, "I am going to appear before the Committee of the House of Lords; do you object to my saying that to the Committee?" He said, "Certainly not; but, mind you, we do not want to work any case up; we do not want to make any sensational statements, we only want to say the truth. I have no knowledge of any case which has caused me to have suspicion of any poor person having put her child away for the sake of the insurance."

Lord *Norton.*

2383. You seemed to convey that any check upon child insurance would be practically a punishment upon honest parents?—Yes; without doing any good whatever.

2384. You look upon it as a punishment upon honest parents that they should not be able to insure?—For more than the actual funeral expenses, yes.

2385. Is there no other way in which an honest parent could provide against the casualty of a child's death except insurance?—There may be many ways if one employed his wits to find out a method, but the principal thing aimed at by this Bill is prevention; our contention is that it would not prevent evil.

2386. What do you say to the honest and thrifty parent laying by money in the Post Office Savings Bank?—As to that I might say that the money is so frequently wanted for bread that it would not very frequently go to the Post Office Savings Bank, and that, even if a shilling or two a week were put into the savings bank, it would very soon be drawn out to buy a pair of boots for the children, or anything of that kind; it would be ever so much better for parents in those circumstances that they should not be able to get hold of these pence.

2387. If, in practice, the parent could fairly trust to his prudence not to draw it out, it would be a much more economical way of providing for these casual circumstances, would it not?—Yes; but the difficulty is to bring it about. Take a poor dock labourer whose children were wanting bread; what would his neighbours think of his having a shilling in the savings bank?

2388. Is not the chief profit of the insurance offices

Lord *Norton*—continued.

offices lapsed policies?—I have no experience of that.

2389. Do not you suppose that a great number of policies are lost by neglecting to pay the premium?—It is not neglect to pay; they always pay when they can afford to do so, but there is inability to pay.

2390. By inability to pay do not you suppose that there are a good many lapsed policies?—I know that many lapse.

2391. By inability to pay?—Yes.

2392. Is not that a loss to the insurer, and an inferior mode of insuring against a casualty compared to the safe payment into the Post Office Savings Bank, which is not liable to any such lapse?—It might be so; but under existing circumstances it would never be so; as you have already said, the opportunity of getting out the shilling or two would be seized by the needy poor. When they begin to insure it is their impression that they will be able to continue it.

2393. Then the only alternative to insurance would be to resort to what you call a friendly meeting, that is, taking the hat round?—That would come about.

2394. That is the only alternative, you think, to this insurance?—Yes; there is only one way, as I said before, in which I have thought how to prevent this crime, or to inflict a penalty upon those people who neglect their children, namely, to give power to the coroner, where he thought there had been neglect, to say, "We will undertake the funeral of this child, so that there will be no profit whatever to you."

2395. That you propose as a possibly better way, to punish those who are found guilty of neglect rather than honest parents?—Undoubtedly.

2396. But are they not liable to criminal punishment now?—Yes.

2397. Unfortunately the criminal law is found insufficient to check the crime, and therefore the object before us is to ascertain whether we can check it in any other way more effectually?—We find, those amongst us who read these things, that the chances are that a mother or a father, who was tired of his child, would get it out of the way just the same whether this Bill became law or not, or would fall back upon the parish to bury the child; if it was a burden it would be a burden under any circumstances.

2398. It would appear that you would not have the premium limited to the mere expenses of the burial, because you say it would be felt a disgrace by any working man to have the mere minimum cost of the funeral, because there are other expenses that would have to be met?—Yes.

2399. I have a good deal to do with mendicity in this City, and I find there are innumerable instances among the richer class who insure for a large policy at death for the benefit of the widow, but in which the widow has spent the whole of the sum, say 20 *l.* or 30 *l.*, or 40 *l.*, upon the funeral, and has come next day to ask as a pauper for assistance for herself; do you think that is a good sort of pride?—No; I consider that is a disgrace.

Lord *Norton*—continued.

2400. You would not increase the insurance to cover a pride of that sort?—Certainly not.

2401. Then you spoke of 2 *l.* 3 *s.* as being the cost of the funeral of one of your own children, and I think you stated that that was merely the cost of the funeral itself?—Yes.

2402. Could you tell the Committee at all what the amount of the incidental expenses might be, taking it roundly, in addition to the 9 *l.* 3 *s.*?—No, I could not tell; as a matter of fact, at that time I only had the clothes in which I went to work: a pair of corduroy trousers and a rough coat. The circumstances were peculiar; the wife had to use the tallyman to get the necessary black to follow the child to the grave, which I, as the father, did not do because I had not the clothes to go in.

2403. The incidental expenses you have described as the doctor's fee and the mourning dress?—Yes.

2404. And, as I understand, something like a funeral feast?—I do not exactly consider that the doctor would be paid out of the insurance; he would be paid beforehand, and if the child recovered he would have to be paid; but there are various things which are always thrown into the expense; clothes have been pawned, and things have been taken away; practically given away it would be if this Bill becomes law, because there would be no means of fetching them back; parents part willingly with those things because they know they may restore the child to health, but if they knew they were going to get 5 *l.* which would go to the undertaker when the child died, when they had parted with everything they had to keep the little one alive, that would be hard indeed.

2405. It is extremely difficult to understand what you mean by incidental expenses?—It would be exceedingly difficult to pick out what is necessary from what is not; and you could do nothing to prevent those people, after they have got these things out of this money, from parting with them; the people would sell them if they were so minded.

2406. Talking quite vaguely with reference to the expense you were at yourself for this same child whose funeral cost 2 *l.* 3 *s.*, supposing you were to double it, and say 4 *l.*; would that cover all the incidental expenses?—In that instance, yes.

2407. I think you said that after you had lost three of your children you began to insure the rest?—Yes.

2408. Would you tell me, having lost three children without insurance, what led you to insure the others?—The extreme difficulty I was placed in to bury them, having had to go round to beg from my friends to give me something to enable me to follow them to the grave; to help me to cover the expenses, and to get a little black for the survivors, and for the wife and myself. I thought, why should I lumber myself in this manner when I can protect myself for a trifle a week out of my wages; I have not always got 2 *l.* a week; a cooper, as a rule, works piecework, and his work fluctuates; a good workman would get hold of a good round sum sometimes, and

Lord *Norton*—continued.

and sometimes very small sums, so that it would be necessary for him to insure so as to get this sum if he should unfortunately come to require it.

2409. You seem, from your evidence, to be a very exceptionally shrewd and sensible man; could not you trust to your own control with reference to the insuring of the remaining children in the Post Office Savings Bank, which would be, as you allow, upon much more economical terms, and the safest possible security?— No, I could not.

2410. Could not you trust yourself not to draw the money?—No; my love for my children is too great. When I see my children running about the streets with the uppers of their boots with no soles to them, I would be tempted to go to the Post Office Savings Bank and buy them a pair.

2411. You prefer a possibly lapsing insurance to a greater security, because you are afraid that you will not be able to trust yourself?—The difficulty with the workman is this : if he knew he would be always able to supply his children with the common necessaries of life he could save, but he does not know that; he is the victim of circumstances over which he has no control. It is not because he is not steadfast enough, or does not love his children; it is necessary that his children must have it; he may lay up a penny or twopence for his children in the way of insurance, when he could not buy a pair of boots.

2412. When you were asked, with reference to a contract of indemnity like fire insurance, I suppose the objection to that is the uncertainty as to what would be indemnified?—Yes.

2413. It would be almost as impossible as your own statement of incidental expenses, to say what they would amount to, or what they should cover?—Yes.

Lord *Bishop of Ripon.*

2414. You tell the Committee you have a child who is insured now?—I have six.

2415. Do you find it very costly to keep up the insurance?—No; I pay 6 *d.* a week; a penny on each.

2416. Is it fair to ask what office or company they are insured in?—They are insured in the " Prudential."

2417. Are there not what are called " burial clubs" amongst the working classes?—I have heard of them. I have no experience of them.

2418. Would it be considered a hardship, supposing that insurance were allowed to take place only in a burial club?—The same thing would occur there; they would hand the money over to the parent.

2419. It seems to me that a burial club is a sort of mutual society; all the members of the club who pay in their penny a week have, as it were, a common interest with reference to the money, and if any death occurs the money is paid out to the person whose child has died. The result of all this is that the profit remains in the hands of the club; but when you go to one of these societies the profit does not go to the members, it remains with the society?—Yes; but what is the force of that? The burial club

(142.)

Lord *Bishop of Ripon*—continued.

pay out a certain sum; it does not prevent a parent doing what he likes with it.

2420. It has occurred to some that we might meet the difficulty by saying that the insurance should be effected only with mutual benefit clubs, and not with insurance societies?—It might be a very good plan, but may I ask, would not the same thing occur there? Would it not be necessary to employ a staff of clerks, and so on, as it is here in the case of these insurance companies?

2421. I am only suggesting that that would be an economy to working men?—I do not know about that, but I should prefer it, speaking as a workman. I should probably get an easy berth there.

2422. Would it not be the interest of everybody in that burial club to frown down anything like ill-treatment of children?—I do not think so; you cannot very well judge what your next-door neighbour is doing.

2423. But I thought you had such a good knowledge of your neighbours that you did know?—We were taking it before this Committee as if it were that those people were so careful that people should not know what they were doing. The same thing would occur if it were in a burial club. The temperance societies, as I understand, are already framing a petition against this Bill. I do not belong to any temperance society myself, but I know it is so.

Lord *Brougham and Vaux.*

2424. It is your opinion, as I understand, that a child cannot be respectably buried for less than 2 *l.* 3 *s.*?—In Liverpool I gave the instance of my child having been buried for 1 *l.* 7 *s.*, but that was buried in a manner which I should not like to see repeated.

2425. In answer to Question 2252, we were told by a witness of three undertakers who would agree to bury a child for 15 *s.*, 17 *s.*, and 18 *s.*, and to supply a coach on the condition that the coffin was to go under the front seat; that answer would surprise you, would it?—I do not know of any such cases. I have passed undertakers' shops and seen their advertisements in the window; but they are so pleasantly vague that it would leave the undertaker the opportunity of charging what he liked afterwards in the shape of incidentals.

Lord *Poltimore.*

2426. Could you tell the Committee whether the agent of the insurance office always sees the children before he insures them?—I think not; with reference to adults, it is so. I know the insurance agent, in my case, has been to see the children, and he makes constant inquiries whether they are healthy; but I should say that it was not always so. My children were insured and the policies issued without the agent actually seeing them, because the insurance agent came to the works, but he found an opportunity of going to the house to see the children afterwards.

2427. I understood you to say just now that you did not object to this Bill, except to that clause as to the money being paid to the undertaker; do you think that if that clause were

taken

P

Lord *Poltimore—continued.*

taken out the Bill would be good enough?—Yes.

Lord *Thring.*

2428. You are a journeyman cooper?—Yes.

2429. Have you had special facilities for obtaining the opinions of your fellow workmen?—Yes.

2430. Therefore you think you fairly represent the feelings of the artizan class in the East End of London?—Yes.

2431. I understand you to say that that feeling is, that giving the money over to the undertaker would be a reproach to that class, inasmuch as it would indicate that the Legislature would not trust the parents with it?—Yes.

2432. You think the reproach might be called a libel upon them?—Yes.

2433. Then, with reference to the vexed question of funerals, would you just tell the Committee what sort of a ceremony a respectable working man would have for his child; will you just describe what it is; do you have a hearse?—No; for my children, and speaking from my experience of those funerals that I see amongst my neighbours, it is usually a coach, and the cost is considerably reduced by the fact that the undertaker can do two or more funerals upon the same afternoon. For instance, he has a better class of funeral, probably, to go to at four o'clock, and he will send a coach and pair to your house for your funeral at two o'clock; whereas, if it were only for yourself, he would only have been able to send one horse for that price.

2434. Then, with reference to your dress, I understand that, not unnaturally, a respectable artisan and his wife would desire to attend the funeral in black clothes?—Yes.

2435. Therefore, the expenses of the funeral would have to include those black clothes, unless the artisan happens to have them himself?—Yes; my point is, that at least he would have to find a black hat, and a little black for his children, even if he did not do it for himself, whereas this Bill would not supply what the man could spend in fair and honest necessaries, which he would not be ashamed for any man to know that he had bought for the funeral of his child; it would not cover that.

2436. You would consider it necessary that you should have good black clothes for yourself and your children?—Yes.

2437. Therefore, to have a funeral that you would not think a disgrace, you would put your family into black?—Yes.

2438. You are insured in the Prudential Company, I think?—Yes.

2439. The Committee have had a good deal of evidence that there are a great number of collectors, and that those collectors are very importunate, that they come round and bother people to subscribe; is that your experience or not?—It is not my experience. I have heard of such cases, but I do not find any fault with that.

2440. Then, with reference to the question that my Lord Bishop asked you, I will put it differently; in a collecting society such as the Prudential the profit that is made goes to the

Lord *Thring—continued.*

agents and to the managers; the agents are paid and the managers are paid; the expenses of some of these societies are extremely great; now, with reference to burial societies we are told that the expenses are not so great, because the members themselves collect the contributions, and that the whole of the profits go to the insurers themselves and not to outside people, as, for instance, the managers; the question I want to ask you is, whether you can give an opinion as to whether it would not be an advantage to poor men that something should be done to encourage burial societies, as I have defined them, as against the collecting societies, as you have defined them?—I should say yes.

2441. Then, with respect to the deaths, of course there are some crimes committed, and some children put away; can you give me an opinion as to whether it would be an advantage to make the evidence of the cause of death more strict; for instance, supposing it were made essential that before the Prudential Company paid the money they should be satisfied by some evidence, of doctors if possible, or else by sworn evidence, that the child died a natural death and was properly treated?—Certainly; I should see no objection to that whatever.

2442. Then, with respect to the question which one of the noble Lords asked you, we are told that the natural deaths (I am not talking of violent deaths of children) are extremely numerous under the age of one year, and also that neglect is much easier under the age of one year; that a child is more frail, and also that the expenses of burial are much less. I wish to ask you the question whether, having regard to the fact that a child is so easily put away under one year of age, and that the expenses are very small, it would be a great hardship upon the thrifty man if he were prevented from insuring a child under one year, leaving children above one year of age as they already stand?—I think it would be reasonable to allow it to stand as it is, namely, that a child dying under one year, the amount of money to be drawn shall be less than the actual cost of burial. I do not think there would be any hardship in that.

2443. Your remedy would be to diminish very materially the limit to insurers; you would allow them to insure for very little, for a child under one year of age?—I would allow them to insure at a penny a week, for the sum which the Prudential Insurance Company already allows, which is considerably less than what one's expenses would be.

2444. But you adhere to the opinion that it would be a considerable detriment to the men you represent if they were not allowed to insure children under one year of age?—I do not think it would be a great disadvantage, not so much as it would when they got older.

Earl *Beauchamp.*

2445. I think you told us that, as far as your experience goes, the thrifty poor always insure their children?—Yes.

2446. Would the contrary be true; do the cruel parents, or parents of dissolute habits, equally insure their children?—No, I think that parents of bad habits, as a rule, do not; my experience is that a man, who is what we may call

Earl Beauchamp—continued.

call a loafer, does not go to much trouble to find his children bread, much less to find the money to insure them; that is my experience of that class.

2447. Then if you were told that exactly contrary evidence to what you have just stated had been given before this Committee, that would not in any way shake your opinion?—No, it would not shake my opinion, inasmuch as I should think they were only isolated cases.

2448. You do not believe that parents put their children out of the way for the sake of the insurance money?—I do not.

2449. Then such a charge, especially against the working classes, would be resented by those whom you represent?—Yes.

2450. There is such a thing, I suppose, as public opinion on the part of the neighbourhood?—Yes.

2451. If any parents were guilty of cruel neglect, their conduct would be marked with disapproval by their neighbours?—Yes, whether insured or not.

2452. It would be contrary to the public opinion of the class in general?—Yes; I think that the neighbourhood would be made so uncomfortable to such people that they would be glad to move out.

2453. Did I understand you to say that you calculated there were 10,000,000 working men?—No, I was taking the Bishop of Peterborough's opinion of that; that probably there would be 10,000,000 of working people.

2454. Do you know that the total population of the United Kingdom may be taken at 37,000,000?—I have been always under the impression that it was between 33,000,000 and 34,000,000.

2455. If you take 10,000,000 as working men, and 10,000,000 women, and perhaps 2,000,000 children, whom we are told are insured, that would bring the number up to 22,000,000?—I took it that working men meant working people.

Chairman.

2456. I meant, of course, when I spoke of ten millions, the working classes, men and women, and not men only?—That is what I understood your Lordship to mean.

Earl Beauchamp.

2457. Referring to incidental expenses in connection with funerals, do funerals take place in London on Sunday?—Yes.

2458. To any great extent?—Not so largely as they did ten or fifteen years ago.

2459. When a funeral does not take place on a Sunday that implies the loss of a day's wage to the parents?—Yes, but you will find the workingmen as a rule stop away from their child's funeral and allow their wives and others to go to such funerals rather than lose a day's work.

2460. You were asked whether the only alternative to the present system of insurance was the "friendly lead" that you have described to the Committee. There is the other alternative, is there not, of coming upon the rates?—Yes, they either have a friendly lead or come upon the rates.

(142.)

Earl Beauchamp—continued.

2461. There is the alternative of coming upon the parish?—Yes.

2462. But the honest working classes very much resent a pauper funeral, do they not?—Yes.

2463. And the sacrifices which they make are to avoid that necessity?—Yes.

2464. Did you ever hear of a case of the insurance of children before they were born?—No, but I was asking about that the other night, and the remark was made that an agent had knocked at the door, and asked if Mrs. Somebody, whom he was personally acquainted with, a friend of his, was confined yet, as he was anxious to get the business; that was only reasonable; I do not see anything unreasonable about that.

2465. But you never, yourself, heard of unborn children being insured?—No.

Chairman.

2466. With respect to your suggestion that it would be a check upon crime if the coroner had the power of impounding the money that a child was insured for, if there was proof before him that the child had been done away with; that of course would only apply to cases which came before the coroner?—Yes.

2467. It has been proved again and again in evidence before this Committee that a great many very suspicious cases do not come before the coroner at all, therefore your check would not apply to all those cases?—I took it that the gentleman who gave that evidence before this Committee said that he had sent fifty cases before the coroner, out of which the coroner only tried six.

2468. In that particular instance; but supposing, as a matter of fact, it were proved that there were a great many cases in which there was every reason to think the children had been done away with, yet which had not, for various reasons come before the coroner; your check would not apply to those cases so far as they exist?—It would necessitate that the doctor should not falsify the certificate, but should be more careful.

2469. Those cases would, to a very small extent, come before the coroner?—Yes; but they would be the suspicious cases.

2470. Would you allow the coroner to impound the money if there was not legal proof, supposing the coroner had suspicion?—Not unless the coroner's jury were in agreement with the coroner.

2471. That is to say you would only allow the coroner to impound the money when there was clear legal proof that the child had been done away with?—I would not take it that way, because that would not meet the case.

2472. Then, what is your proposal?—There might be cases come before a coroner in which, morally, there was proof that those people had not given that amount of attention to the child which one had the right to expect from the parents; it would not be possible to convict those people before a court of law, because medical jurisprudence and law would get to loggerheads; but if the jury and the coroner held the belief that the parents had not paid the attention to the child which it had the right to expect, then the

P 2   coroner

Chairman—continued.

coroner should have the right to impound the money.

2473. That would not apply to any cases which did not come before the coroner?—Certainly not.

2474. There is only one more question I wish to ask you; supposing the money had been received from the insurance company before any suspicion, and before the child was brought before the coroner, there would be no money in that case for the coroner to impound?—But may I ask, how could that happen? The Prudential Company, or any other company, would not pay the money until they got the certificate of death.

2475. Are you sure of that?—They ought not to do it.

2476. But you are speaking of the coroner's investigation; in many cases the company pay upon the production of a certificate of death; the certificate may be very loosely given, and there might be guilt; we have had evidence that the money has been paid without the child ever coming before the coroner?—Would not better registration meet that?

2477. I am asking for your suggestion. I think I am right in saying that your proposition would not touch any of the cases that would not come before the coroner?—That is so.

2478. And it would not touch any of the cases in which the money had been previously paid, in which there was a coroner's inquest?—I never heard of a case of that kind.

2479. Do you mean to say that the insurance companies never paid unless there is a coroner's inquest or unless there is a certificate?—How is it possible for me to know? I should say the insurance company ought not to pay.

2480. Then your proposal would go to this, that the insurance company should never pay any money unless there was a coroner's inquest?—The cases that have come within my own knowledge have been these, that before you can get any money from an insurance company you must get a certificate from the registrar, and he would not issue a certificate if there was going to be an inquest.

Lord *Clifford of Chudleigh.*

2481. What is the usual amount for which a child under one year is insured?—I cannot say; I think it would be under 2 *l.*, or not more than 2 *l.*

2482. Your opinion is, that in most cases that would be sufficient, or that that is the usual thing?—I should say that the amount insured, to be got on the death of a child under one year, would be quite inadequate to defray the funeral expenses, and therefore, as far as that went, it would not be necessary to alter that.

2483. According to law, the amount that can be got up to five years of age is 6 *l.* I want to know what is the amount which is usually got? —I do not know any instance in which such an amount has been got, and I should even say that this Bill as it stands, giving 4 *l.* in the case of the death of a child up to five years, would give the opportunity of getting 4 *l.* for a child under one year; there are various sums allowed for children up to certain ages; I think it is 1 *l.* 5 *s.* for the death of a child at six months; for 12 months probably it would be 2 *l.* 10 *s.*

2484. That is under the rules of the insurance company?—Yes, as I know them.

Lord *Kinnaird.*

2485. Might I take it as your opinion that, if there was a case of ill-treatment, somebody in the house, where there were several people living in the house, would know it?—Undoubtedly.

2486. You think the public sentiment would be sufficiently strong to make them tell their neighbours?—Yes.

2487. We have had some evidence that the ill-treatment has gone on, and that the feeling of the people was, that they did not like to get their neighbours into trouble; do you think that is not the case?—In answer to that, I may say that I have known a case where the father has come home the worse for drink, and the children have been crying, and a woman rushed up and got them out of the room to take care of them, to prevent them from crying; how much more would they do so to prevent them being ill-treated.

The Witness is directed to withdraw.

MR. A. A. DOBSON, is called in, and Examined, as follows:

Earl *Beauchamp.*

2488. YOU are the secretary to the Amalgamated Conference of Family Friendly Burial Societies of the Manchester and Salford district? Yes.

2489. Of how many members do those amalgamated societies consist?—We have at present about 280,000 members directly, but I find, since I have been in London, that there are very many more societies in different parts of the country which are very anxious to join our organisation. I wish to present an opinion with reference to the evidence which has been already given. I had a letter from the secretary of the Blackburn Burial Society, in which they have drawn attention to the evidence of Dr. Barwise.

Earl *Beauchamp*—continued.

2490. Is that a letter from Mr. Culshaw?— Yes.

2491. Who is he?—He is the secretary of the Blackburn Burial Society.

2492. Have you followed at all the evidence which has been given before this Committee?— I have.

2493. Have you read the evidence given by Dr. Thompson, who was the coroner of Oldham? —I have. May I be allowed to hand in a letter from the secretary of the Amalgamated Burial Societies in Oldham, calling attention to what the Chief Constable of Oldham has said before his Watch Committee. (*The letters are handed in.*)

2494. Can you provide the Committee with the

Earl *Beauchamp*—continued.

the rules of the various societies which you represent?—I have already supplied the Right Reverend Chairman of the Committee with a bundle of rules, but I have a few more here. (*The same are handed in.*)

2495. The societies you represent, though differing among themselves in detail, are, speaking generally, family friendly burial societies?—They are.

2496. Will you describe their object as distinguished from those of an ordinary life insurance company?—Their object is more of a mutual description.

2497. When you say "mutual," you mean that the benefits resulting are divided amongst the members; they do not become a matter of gain to shareholders or managers?—No; the accumulated funds of all the burial societies go as a contingency against future events.

2498. Who manages those family friendly burial societies?—The members of them.

2499. Are they confined to any locality?—They are more circumscribed in their operations than are the industrial insurance societies, simply because they are more of a family character. In some districts the members almost all know each other, so that that brings it within the term of a local society, and that is the reason why we claim the word "local" society from being circumscribed.

2500. Anything which takes place among the families of the various members would be known to a great number of persons in the neighbourhood?—Generally so.

2501. Therefore, public opinion is formed and brought to bear upon the members of those societies in a manner which does not exist in cases like the Prudential or the Royal Liver, or any of the large commercial undertakings?—Undoubtedly so.

2502. How is the money collected; is it collected by weekly payments?—Yes, by weekly payments; in some cases by fortnightly payments, and in some cases by monthly payments.

2503. By whom are those payments collected?—By officers appointed by the committee of management; those officers are appointed, some half-yearly, and some yearly, and they receive a small sum for their services; but the collection is generally undertaken after they have finished their day's labour or daily occupations.

2504. Those officers have their ordinary day's work to perform, and the collecting is subsidiary to their ordinary daily occupations?—Yes.

2505. How are the officers elected?—They are elected by popular vote at the half-yearly meetings; they are first nominated, and they go through the ballot; they invariably hold office for six or 12 months, according to the nature of the office they are elected for; as a rule, in most of the societies I represent here, the president holds office for six months, and it is stipulated in some societies that he cannot be re-elected for two years; that has been done purposely to bring about a complete change of men to manage the affairs of the society. With regard to the appointment of auditors, societies are a little bit more strict and circumspect, inasmuch as they

(142.)

Earl *Beauchamp*—continued.

invariably try to get hold of the very best men who understand accounts, that they may have confidence in their ability. I have known instances where men who are members of our society, and have been so from childhood, men much older than myself, that are even heads of firms holding a high position in Manchester, take great pride in being members of these friendly societies, from having been connected with them in their infancy.

2506. Are you particularly connected with the Hulme Burial Society?—I am.

2507. How long has that society existed?—I could show you an interesting document connected with the three societies in Hulme. Unfortunately I cannot give this to the Committee, because it is an heirloom to myself. The first society in Hulme was established in 1823, and that made arrangements for making provision for the death of their members. I mention this specially, because it refutes partially what his Lordship said in his speech, that it was only 10 years ago that we had these privileges, and this morning he said it was 25 years; we had also adopted and used extensively, up to the year 1858, the rules that were put in force in 1854, and you will find that in every case we have striven to work out the spirit of the Act of Parliament, under which we work, in its entirety.

2508. What are your rules as to the admission of infants to the benefit of the society?—Children of members only, and they must be two months old; strangers' children we do not take, nor is it possible for any such cases as the so-called baby-farming cases to be admitted members of our local societies.

2509. They would not be admitted members of your local societies; but would it be possible when a parent had insured his children, for him to hand them over to baby-farmers?—No, we should take care of that.

2510. That you would guard against by your rules?—Our officers or inspectors, as they are called in some societies, and collectors, in others, take care to see every child before it is entered.

2511. Have you any medical information as to the state of health of the children admitted?—No, it is not required; being friendly societies, and being respectable, there is no desire to see a medical man, inasmuch as it would require a fee, and a fee means a tax upon the people's savings.

2512. Can a child be insured in more than one society?—It may be entered in two, as the present Act of Parliament allows the opportunity; that is done purposely; owing to the expenses connected with funerals, doctor's fees, and sometimes nurses' fees, it is sometimes necessary to have a child put into two societies, but that is not the real cause of it. The present Act of Parliament admitted the principle from the representation that we made to the late Lord Iddesleigh, showing that the children were in two societies, not through any fault of their own, but from the circumstances of their parents, inasmuch as the parents having been from childhood in these societies, naturally, when a young man gets married, the wife may be in one society, and the husband may be in another, and they are anxious to have their offspring in both societies; that is

P 3   what

Earl *Beauchamp*—continued.

what the late Lord Iddesleigh admitted as a fair thing.

2513. Can you tell the Committee anything about the death-rate of the children insured in your societies?—The death-rate is much lower, and I may add to that this, that two years ago we made a comparative examination of the Manchester and Salford death-rate, as compared with the death-rate of those in our societies. Whilst the death-rate in Manchester was at the rate of 20, we found that the death-rate in our societies was only 16.

2514. Then you think the insurances in your society do not act in any way as premiums upon parents putting their children out of the way?—Certainly not.

2515. Have you any information to give the Committee from Macclesfield upon the same subject?—I have; I hold in my hand a document which gives the facts as to the Macclesfield Amalgamated Society, which is in union with ours; it shows that they provide also for medical aid in connection with their members; they have a membership of 37,793 for the last year, and in the year previous it was a little higher; last year they paid 779 *l.* 15 *s.* 7 *d.* for medical aid; they had 603 deaths.

2516. How many of those were under five years of age?—143.

2517. What is the average death-rate in the Macclesfield Society?—They place it at 15, but I think it is a little lower than that; I have not, however, gone thoroughly into the figures.

2518. That is lower than your own in Hulme?—It is.

2519. Can you tell the Committee anything about Salford?—I have here the report of the Salford Society.

2520. How many members has that?—This society has a membership of nearly 40,000 members.

2521. What is the death-rate there?—The average is 20; their secretary gave me a list a few days ago, in which he put it at 22, but he corrected that, and he made it appear as 20 to me, he having been misled by some figures.

2522. Is there any special precaution in respect of paying money in your Hulme societies?—We adopt a very safe plan, and I think it would be well if this plan were adopted universally; before any money can be obtained from any society, we first of all require a notification from the parent or guardian; a form has to be filled up, and that has to be given to the secretary; the secretary examines it, and compares it with his books, and if they have already produced a certificate of death, that is transferred then to the treasurer, who makes an appointment as to when the money shall be paid.

2523. Speaking generally, what is the average sum insured?—It varies from the date of entrance up to two years; there is what we call a classified scale; three months is one, six months another, then 12 months, and then we go to two years, and after that it goes according to the age again.

2524. The sum increases in proportion to the age?—Yes.

2525. Does the payment made by the parent

Earl *Beauchamp*—continued.

increase too?—No; it is only one penny a week.

2526. Have you a balance sheet that you would lay before the Committee?—I have here a model one which it gives me great pleasure to lay before the Committee; it is one which ought to be adopted by every society in the country (*handing in the same.*) Then this, the Hulme Funeral Branch; this is in accordance with the provisions of the Act of Parliament. It is called " Annual Return," but there is a larger and more detailed return of the income and expenditure connected with it.

2527. How many members has that?—3,439.

2528. What was the number of deaths in that society in the last year?—There were 69 deaths.

2529. What were the ages of those who died?—Those particulars are not classified here, but I may add, being connected with it as a member, that the number of those dying under five years of age is very small compared with the returns of other insurance societies. The secretary of this society and myself have had many conversations with regard to the death-rate, and it is most singular that in this society the death-rate is much lower at times than even in the other two societies in Hulme.

2530. What happens in the event of a member failing to keep up his payments?—We make provision for that in two ways; we have remodelled the rules this year, and they are being accepted by the Chief Registrar. We have what we may call suspension for non-payment and exclusion; we re-admit them as members if in good health; we make a special note of that; they have to be seen; or, if they reside outside the boundaries of our operations, they have to send a medical officer's note of health.

2531. You are referring to children, are you not?—I am referring to children and adults; and with reference to allowing those who have been members of the society the privilege of re-entering, we give them shortly after their re-entrance half the benefit they were entitled to when they lost their membership.

2532. Speaking generally, the description you have given the Committee is a very fair sample of what are commonly called local clubs?—Yes.

2533. What is your rule about medical aid?—As far as medical aid is concerned, we, in Hulme, do not provide that, because we have in our midst a provident dispensary, and many of our members pay a penny or twopence a week, according to their means, to the dispensaries, and obtain medical assistance.

2534. Does that obtain in Macclesfield as well?—Yes, it obtains in Macclesfield and also in the Hyde township.

2535. Is there anything special in Hyde which you wish to explain to their Lordships?—No further than that their operations are similar to ours; they manage theirs exactly on the same principle as we manage ours. There is one very large society there with 17,000 members, and they also have medical aid, and their trustee told me on Tuesday night that they paid over 500 *l.*

Earl *Beauchamp*—continued.

500 *l.* for medical aid in connection with their society.

2536. Then it would be true to say, would it not, that the societies you represent encourage thrift to a very great degree, keeping their members from parochial relief?—Undoubtedly so; that is their main object. I may add to that, that the members thoroughly appreciate it.

2537. You consider it does not in any way tend to promote infanticide?—Oh, dear, no.

2538. What have you to say upon the subject of infanticide?—The question we have to put before the Committee on the subject of infanticide is this: I have been asked by the executive to ask the question, "What is infanticide?" There have been a number of sensational statements made. I may add, that there was one, a very curious one, in "The Daily News," three weeks ago. I and a friend of mine had an interview with the editor of that paper with reference to it, but we could gain no information, only that it came from a source which he was not allowed to divulge; but the information we got was sufficient for us to say that the whole story, which would create a feeling of sympathy in the minds of the upper classes against these societies, was that it was a concoction. The question of infanticide is a very painful one.

Chairman.

2539. Is this a story which you meant to say was brought before this Committee?—No; it was merely one that was published in "The Daily News."

Earl Beauchamp.

2540. Was that the case of a child being insured?—It was a case of a supposed conversation between a child and a stranger. The stranger got into conversation with the child, and the child told him innocently he had got a new suit of clothes. The stranger said, "I hope those clothes are paid for;" and the child said, "No; but when Sarah dies we shall have 4 *l.* on Sarah." We point to that to show that, on the face of it, this was a sheer story; there is improbability and untruthfulness upon the face of it.

2541. You have taken pains in stories of that kind, particularly that story you have mentioned to the Committee, to ascertain what foundation there was for it?—We did our best.

2542. You did not get any information which enabled you to test its accuracy?—No further than that the editor of "The Daily News" said there was plenty of information to be got from the Rev. Benjamin Waugh, the honorary secretary of the Society for the Prevention of Cruelty to Children.

2543. Have you any observations to make as to the alleged connection between insurance money and infanticide?—We have, as I said before, to ask what is infanticide? Are we to be stigmatised because there are children found in public places, on railway stations, and in out-of-the-way places such as ashpits, as children have been found, and those that have been washed up in the river and from the sea? Are we not to take those as meaning infanticide pure and simple, and not for club money?

(142.)

Earl *Beauchamp*—continued.

2544. In those cases parents would not claim the insurance money?—Because there are no owners.

2545. What do you take to be the cause of infanticide?—Immorality.

2546. And you think that parents who would commit infanticide would not be stimulated by the very small benefit that would accrue to them from insurance money?—No; rather the reverse of that; it would be done to be without the trouble of bringing up the child for the future.

2547. Now, with reference to the cost of funerals, can you tell the Committee at all what the cost of funerals is?—I have here a document to hand in. This, too, is a very valuable one and a very important one as representing a large centre in Lancashire. It is what I asked special permission from the seretary of the Manchester Carriage and Tramways Company to have a copy of. This is a copy of their list of charges for coaches for funerals. It is one which had hung in the office for a number of years, and it is the last they had there; but he cheerfully gave it me, as I told him that I might want it in London, knowing that there would be some requirement for it, and upon those conditions I had it. The cost of opening the grave in the Manchester Southern Cemetery is 15 *s.*, the minister's dues are 3 *s.*, and the cost of a coach is 1 *l.* 2 *s.* In this scale that I am now going to hand in the prices have been revised and increased.

2548. I suppose it is true to say that the funerals in Manchester and the district you represent must be conducted by coach, the cemeteries being so distant from the centres of population?—The nearest cemetery to us is three miles, but where they have to go over the boundary to Salford they have to make an additional charge for that.

2549. So that a carriage is not a luxury but a necessity in that case?—That is so.

2550. Besides the fee to the minister, the grave, and the cost of carriage, what other expenses are there?—There is the cost of the coffin, which depends upon the age of the child. I had a case before me only a few weeks ago: the child was only 11 weeks old, and the cost of the coffin in that case was 1 *l.*; the doctor's bill, who had attended the child, was 30*s.*; that leaves the parents nothing; that is 4 *l.* 10 *s.* for the cost of a child's funeral 11 weeks old.

2551. Do the societies which you represent attach great value to interring a child with decent marks of respect?—They do. I may add to that, that we thoroughly appreciate the assistance we received from the late Dean of Manchester. I have his words here where he expressed, "We have respect and have affection for the dead; they are only the natural and justifiable instincts of true mourners."

2552. In reference to Sunday interments in Manchester and the neighbourhoood, are they allowed to take place on Sunday?—No.

2553. Then that means the loss of a day's wages if the parents have to attend the funeral upon a working day?—It means sometimes a loss of two days, and I have known cases where it means a loss of three days. The difficulty of our people in the township of Hulme rests upon this, which

Earl *Beauchamp*—continued.

which causes sometimes serious delay, through the action of the registrar of births and deaths; he only attends for a few hours for four days a week, from 11 to 4, and then he goes to the out-township of Moss-side, and those in our township have to follow him to Moss-side or wait till the next day; that means sometimes waiting three hours, and I have known them to have to wait four hours before they have been able to obtain a certificate of death.

2554. The expenses being so great, you would deprecate any diminution of the amount at present allowed by law for the insurance of children's lives?—Undoubtedly we should. I may add to that this, that I have taken an active part for years in connection with this subject, and the alterations of the various Acts of Parliament. I spent some considerable time in 1874 and 1875 in procuring and coaching the present Act through Parliament, having many interviews with the late Lord Iddesleigh, then the Chancellor of the Exchequer, when we placed in his hands documents showing the cost of a child's funeral in our district; he saw at once that it was only a fair equivalent to allow us the privileges that we had had hitherto. The 6 *l.* we are now allowed to receive for a child under five years is barely sufficient for a decent funeral.

2555. To what point in the Bill besides the restriction in the amount to be received do you more particularly object?—I object to the undertaker question.

2556. Will you explain why?—Because it is such a stigma upon the working classes; they resent it with the greatest indignation. Last night we had a public meeting to denounce it, and that will be the course throughout the length and breadth of the country. I may say that the working classes of Lancashire feel that statement so keenly that they will agitate the whole country upon it.

2557. Do you think that the clause, supposing it became law, would be liable to evasion?—I would not like to suggest that, but the very principle which underlies that clause will be a temptation to the undertaker to commit a crime; it is a temptation to the undertaker to do wrong.

2558. In what way?—Simply this: at present he is to be the recipient, according to that clause in the Bill, of the money; there is no clause in the Bill to ask him what he has done with the money; the parent has no remedy, the society has no remedy; the Bill provides nothing; it simply allows the undertaker to receive the amount, and he is to do what he likes with it.

2559. You think it does not impose upon the undertaker any obligation to carry out the funeral?—Undoubtedly he would carry out the funeral, but he would do it in his own way; the parent would have no control over the funeral.

2560. The ceremony would be conducted without the parent having any voice in the matter?—Undoubtedly it would, and there would be no provision made for a respectable funeral, because the funeral being given over to the undertaker he could please himself whether he would give a respectable coffin or an orange box.

Earl *Beauchamp*—continued.

2561. Would it be possible for the undertaker and the parent to act in collusion to evade the Act?—There would be opportunity for the parent and the undertaker to do that; and I think your Lordship will find that any Act of Parliament which puts temptation in the way of the people ought to be thoroughly condemned.

2562. It implies the inference that the amount for which the insurance can now be made is too great?—It is not too great; but we should further ask, what has the respectable working man done that such a measure as this should be endeavoured to be forced upon him? We are not compelled to be members of these societies; it is a voluntary contribution, and being a voluntary contribution this measure strikes at the very ground of our liberties.

2563. You further object to the Bill as it stands because it interferes with existing contracts?—Yes.

2564. But I will not ask you more on that subject, because I think it will be arranged that existing contracts will in all probability be preserved if the Bill passes into law?—I would hope so.

2565. So far your objections upon the question of existing contracts would be met, would they not?—I think not. I think there is a doubt in the Bill itself; there is an ambiguity there which wants clearing up; it is in reference to the provision for existing contracts; there seems to be a doubt in the ninth clause. It goes on to stipulate in the third paragraph, "is payable by a society to the parent of the child, or to the personal representative of such parent, shall, subject to the provisions of this Act, be payable to the person to whom payment would have been due under a contract made in accordance with this Act, after such commencement." The first part says, "provision for existing contracts," and then it qualifies that by bringing the same contracts within the scope of this Bill.

2566. You have heard that it has been suggested in the proceedings before this Committee that money laid by in the Post Office Savings Bank would answer the same purpose as these insurances; is that borne out by your experience?—Certainly not.

2567. First of all, I suppose the money would not be put by with the same regularity as when the collector calls for it?—There is no provision at the present time for the reception of a payment so small as 1*d.* a week, and if there were, people would not trouble themselves to go to the Post Office Savings Bank; they prefer to have the officer under the name of a collector or inspector to call at their houses; and the reason of that is this, it creates a feeling of sociability; they know him, and there is a feeling of respect amongst the members, whereas at the Post Office it would be a cold reception even if it were 6*d.*, and the lowest they take now is 1*s.*, and even that has a cold reception compared to what exists between the collector and the people.

2568. Besides that, the money put into the Post Office Savings Bank could be drawn out at any moment, and would not be earmarked for the purpose of a funeral?—That would lead to many careless

Earl *Beauchamp*—continued.

careless parents, or those who might unfortunately get on the spree, drawing it out; however small the sum is, if it be only 5 *s.*, it helps them when they are on the spree, and I am afraid the sum in the Post Office Savings Bank would very often be melted away.

Chairman.

2569. Are you acquainted with the provisions of the Act of George III. which governs insurance ?—Yes.

2570. That Act was aimed at preventing any profit on death, was it not ?—Yes.

2571. Do you agree with the principle of the Act ?—Yes ; we agree so far as this goes ; but the times have changed, and what was convenient at one time is not so at the present time.

2572. I am not speaking of what has happened since the Act passed, but I am asking you whether you agree with the principle of the Act, that there should be no profit upon the death money ?—The question is, what is profit upon the child's burial ?

2573. I am asking you whether you agree with the principle of the Act of George III., that no person should be in the position to make a profit out of the death of the person he insures ; is not that contrary to public policy ?—I agree so far as this, that any provisions in any Act which may be passed, which restrict my freedom of doing what I wish with my own, I should resent.

2574. I will ask you as to that presently. Now I am asking you as to the principle which governs the Act which regulates insurance among the upper classes as well as the lower classes : is not the principle a sound one, that no person should be permitted to make a profit by the death of another ?—I am afraid there is a difference of opinion there. The upper classes you name have a right to insure for any amount they like.

2575. Do you mean to say they have a right to insure for any amount, whether they have an insurable interest or not ?—They can insure for any amount they like so long as they can pay the premiums.

2576. Have you looked at the Act ?—I know there are insurances effected by people in good positions for very large sums.

2577. Is it not the case that the statute of George III. forbids any insurance upon a life unless the insurer can show an insurable interest ? —It does.

2578. Then that provision of the Act of George III. was repealed in the case of child insurance in the interest of friendly societies?— Undoubtedly it was.

2579. Then members of friendly societies were allowed to insure the lives of children, although they could not show an insurable interest in such lives; I am speaking of the matter of fact?—That is the fact.

2580. When the framers of the Friendly Societies Act repealed the statute of George III., so far as regarded child insurance in friendly societies, they imposed certain restrictions and checks as to the amount for which the child might be insured, and also as to the production of the registrar's certificate ?—That is so.

(142.)

Chairman—continued.

2581. Have you formed any idea of what was the object of those restrictions?—Simply as a safeguard.

2582. Against crime or improper insurance ? —Rather against improper insurance than against crime.

2583. How would the doctor's certificate be a safeguard against improper insurance; the doctor's certificate was surely intended to be a safeguard against crime; what do you suppose is the object of requiring that the doctor should certify as to the cause of death ?—Simply to know the cause of death.

2584. Only as a matter of statistics, and not as a matter of protection to guard against fraud or crime ?—It is simply to show that the document is sufficient to account for the cause of death ; that document is then useful——

2585. Merely for statistical purposes ?—Not merely for statistical purposes, but as an acknowledgment that the death has taken place and the cause of it.

2586. If the doctor withholds the certificate there must be a coroner's inquest?—Undoubtedly there must be.

2587. What is the object of that ?—To ascertain the cause of death.

2588. To ascertain the cause of death with the view of preventing crime. There would not be a coroner's inquest unless the doctor's certificate were withheld. All I want to get from you is, that these provisions of the Friendly Societies Act were inserted with a view of preventing either fraud or crime; which do you say ?—I would hardly use the word "crime," because, at the time when that restriction was repealed, very little was thought about that. There were certain rumours, but when they came to be sifted they were found to be false.

2589. Supposing the restrictions in the Friendly Societies Act are proved to us to be insufficient for the purpose for which they were intended; is it any libel upon the respectable working classes to make them sufficient?—It is the way in which the charge is made which creates the libel against the working classes.

2590. I am not speaking of any charge whatever: I am only putting to you that if those restrictions are proved to be insufficient for their purpose, is there anything offensive in making them sufficient; if they were not offensive when they were made, how is it offensive to make them sufficient for their purpose ?—In the first place, they have not been proved to be inefficient, and not having been proved to be inefficient, the charge that they are——

2591. Will you kindly observe the form in which I put the question; it is a question of fact whether the restrictions have been proved to be sufficient or not, but I am putting it to you thus : assuming for the sake of argument that they have been proved to be insufficient, is there anything objectionable in making them sufficient; is there more objection to that than there is in the restrictions themselves ?—I shall believe that when they have been proved to be insufficient.

2592. Is there anything more offensive in making the restriction sufficient than in making

Q   it

Chairman—continued.

it at all?—It is not offensive to make the restriction.

2593. If it is not an offence to make the restriction, then it is not an offence to make a sufficient restriction; is that so or not?——

2594. Then I will pass from that point. You stated (and I have no doubt with perfect truth) that your society is a highly respectable one, and composed of the respectable working classes; nobody, I presume, would dispute that fact; I, at all events, have not heard anyone say that the great majority of the working classes are not highly respectable and incapable of crime; you would never go so far, however, as to say that there would not be a minority of the working classes who are not respectable; you would not say that every working man was respectable?—I may say, in answer to that, that there are black sheep in all ranks of society.

2595. These restrictions or safeguards are not imposed against the respectable working people, but they are intended to operate against this minority of black sheep?—And I say that, when the working classes come to look at the restrictions that you put upon them in the way it is intended to put them in this Bill, they will believe and feel that it is a libel upon them, and that they are to be made to suffer for the misdeeds of those who cannot conduct themselves.

2596. Is it a libel for the respectable majority of any class to make laws against the disreputable minority of that class?—Certainly not, if you put it in that sense.

2597. I put it to you in this way: you are aware that there has been a great effort made to put down sweating of late?—Yes.

2598. To state that sweating is practised by certain evil-disposed employers is no libel against the well-conducted employers?—I know nothing whatever with respect to the general body of employers in England.

2599. You would not maintain that the general body of employers were sweaters?—I know nothing at all about the process of sweating, not being connected with any trade in which there is any sweating. I have not taken the trouble to go into it, because my time has all been occupied with my own business, and with what I do for these societies.

2600. There are Acts, as you know, against the adulteration of goods as by grocers or chemists, or other salesmen?—Yes, I am aware of that.

2601. Does that imply that the great majority of the grocers and salesmen are other than respectable salesmen?—It is just in the way that it is put.

2602. I ask, is the law against adulteration a stigma, or is it not a stigma, against the great majority of respectable tradesmen?—No, it is not a stigma against them.

2603. The Archbishop of Canterbury introduced into the House of Lords this year a Bill for dealing very sharply with black sheep amongst the clergy; would you say that that was a libel against the great majority of the clergy, as if they were all black sheep?—Undoubtedly not.

2604. Then you would admit that it is quite possible to pass a law to prevent malpractices

Chairman—continued.

against any class of people which will not be an imputation against the great majority of that class?—It could not be an imputation against those who were innocent, because they would know nothing about it.

2605. To make the registration of friendly societies efficient, for the purpose of preventing fraudulent practices amongst the minority of the working classes, cannot possibly be a libel upon the respectable majority of the working classes; surely that is so?—The nature of these restrictions, as put in your Bill, they look upon as nothing less than a libel upon their position.

2606. The repeal of those provisions of the Act of George III. by the Friendly Societies Act was a special concession to the working classes, was it not?—I think you will find there was an Act before that. We had the privilege in this society of insuring the same as we have to-day, in some cases, more than 100 years ago.

2607. Child insurance?—Yes.

2608. Where you could show no insurable interest, was that legal; could that possibly be done under the statute of George III.?—I was insured when I was three years old, and my father was insured before me.

2609. The statute of George III. was passed in the year 1768; could it possibly have been legal under that statute to insure a life in which there was no insurable interest on the part of the insurer?—I may point out that the Act of 1858 gives the same privilege, and there was one previously to that.

2610. Does it not do so by repealing the provision of the statute of George III.; if that provision had not been repealed it would not be lawful now to insure children?—Certainly not.

2611. It was a special privilege to those who wished to insure their children?—I do not know that it was a privilege; it was simply a confirmation of what had been done before.

2612. If the statute of George III. made it impossible to insure a child, that provision of George III. must have been repealed in order to make it lawful, and it is repealed in the Friendly Societies Act, and it may be in other Acts; and I would ask you, was not the Friendly Societies Act principally passed in order to enable the thrifty people of the working classes to insure against loss in the event of their children's death?—Yes, undoubtedly it was.

2613. I am right in saying, am I not, that that repeal was a special privilege to the working classes with the view of encouraging thrift?—If you put it in that way, it was a privilege to the working classes.

2614. In every case in which any persons, or class of persons, have an exceptional privilege, they are bound at any time to show cause why they should have that exceptional privilege?—It is their right to do so.

2615. In point of fact the Friendly Societies Act was a piece of class legislation, and intended mainly for the benefit of one class?—It was a piece of legislation for the benefit of the working classes.

2616. That being so, and the power of the working classes to insure their children being a pure creation of law which did not exist before,

there

Chairman—continued.

there is no such thing as the natural right to insure a child, is there?—There is the right of the parent to make provision for it.

2617. But this is not a natural right; it is a provision of law entirely?—It is a natural desire on the part of the parent to make provision for death, and the law protects the natural right.

2618. But the law never admitted the right of the parent to provide against the death of his child?—It was a very bad law, then.

2619. You have admitted that the Friendly Societies' Act was an Act passed in the interests of working men?—Yes.

2620. That Act created a legal right, which had not existed before, to insure the lives of children? —But they have a right to protect their savings.

2621. The parent, under that Act, had a right which he would not have had before the Act was passed; if he could not do it before the Act was passed, but could do it after the Act was passed, then the Act gave the parent a power which he had not before?—I suppose it did give him that power.

2622. The working classes having a special privilege created by law, the onus lies upon them to show that that privilege is a safe one in the interests of the public, does it not?—It shows the right of it.

2623. Now, as regards your own society, you have given us very clear and satisfactory evidence that it is conducted with great caution, and on very sound lines; that it admits only respectable parents, parents whose respectability is proved to the satisfaction of the society?—Exactly.

2624. You observe these safeguards very carefully and very stringently?—We do.

2625. You find it necessary to have those safeguards, and to enforce them?—We do.

2626. Then in any case in which those safeguards did not exist, or were not enforced carefully, there would be the very risk and danger that you wish to prevent; you must have a reason for enforcing those safeguards?—Because it is imposed us by the Act.

2627. But you say that you take greater care as to the character of the parents than other societies do; in the case of any society which was not careful as to the character of the parents, there would not be the same safety, and there would not be the same respectability as there is in your society?—Not as far I know, but I do not speak of other societies.

2628. As regards the payment of your officers, do they receive any commission upon the moneys they collect?—They are called inspectors principally with our family burial societies, as the word " collector" is misleading.

2629. Yours is not what is called a collecting society?—Certainly not.

2630. May I ask why you are not a collecting society?—Simply because the members manage their business themselves.

2631. They think that the best and safest way of doing it?—That is so.

2632. How are what you call the collectors or inspectors paid; do they get a percentage on all the moneys they receive?—Some are paid by percentage; some are paid so much a visit, and some are paid an even sum at the end of

(142.)

Chairman—continued.

the year. I know in some societies that we represent, they go so far as to provide their members with extra clothing for the winter time.

2633. In point of fact, those servants of yours have no special interest in running up the number of insurances, or evading the law, or getting disreputable people to insure their children?—They are not allowed to go from door to door.

2634. That makes a very important difference between yours and what are commonly called collecting societies and your societies?—Yes.

2635. Therefore all that you say about the respectability of your society and the low death-rate and so on, would apply to such a carefully-conducted society as yours, but would not necessarily apply to a carelessly - conducted society?—It would not.

2636. You have been speaking of medical aid; your society, I believe, does not supply medical aid?—It does not.

2637. I think the reason you assigned was that there existed a provident dispensary?—Yes, there is a provident dispensary.

2638. At which your subscribers could obtain for a small sum medical assistance?—Yes; and we recommend it; in fact, I was one of those who commenced the work of inaugurating it.

2639. Then it is not necessary for your members to insure for the payment of the doctor because they could get medical aid from the provident dispensary?—But we cannot persuade all our members to do that, because many members who have joined these provident dispensaries owing to the mismanagement or some other thing, have been rather inclined to give them up, and that is why you have so many failures in branches already in existence.

2640. Still the more thrifty of your members would keep up those payments for that purpose?—No; because in that case they can get medical assistance for adults.

2641. Children can be admitted members of your society?—Yes.

2642. Under what age?—None less than two months old.

2643. In a provident dispensary, where a man takes up membership, he gets medical assistance without additional payment?—His subscription is his payment.

2644. Now, I will ask you, is the parent given the money to hand to the doctor, or is the doctor paid from the dispensary?—The dispensary is founded upon the terms of collecting subscriptions, in small sums, from working people; those go through the secretary's hands, and the doctor is paid so much out of that; the remainder goes to providing medicine.

2645. The question it through whose hands is it that the payment to the doctor passes; is it the parent or the secretary of the institution?—It goes through the hands of the officers of the institution.

2646. In that case it is the doctor as distinguished from the undertaker; the parents who secure the attendance of the doctor, do not pay the doctor themselves, but the money passes through the hands of the secretary or the officers of the club?—That is so; it cannot go through any other source.

Q 2

2647. If

Chairman—continued.

2647. If that is the case as regards the doctor, is there any greater stigma upon the poor in making it the same case as regards the undertaker?—There is a wonderful difference between subscribing for medical assistance, through a provident dispensary, and subscribing money in a friendly society for a contingency of your own, and you not to receive the same.

2648. Supposing the friendly society to pay the undertaker as the provident dispensary pays the doctor, is there any greater stigma in the one case than the other?—The parents prefer to pay the doctor, if they can, themselves.

2649. But I am speaking of the cases where the parents secure the attendance of the doctor by the payment of a penny a week; in that case the money does not pass through the hands of the parent; is there any stigma in that case upon the parent?—No, certainly not, because the money is their own; they hand it to the officer to pay to the doctor.

2650. The money they pay to the funeral club is their own, is it not?—Yes.

2651. If there is no stigma in the money not going to the doctor direct from the parent, how is there any stigma when it does not pass direct from the parent to the undertaker?—There is no analogy between the two cases; none whatever.

2652. As regards the cost of the funeral, that which has been said, and I have no doubt with perfect truth, as to the cost of a funeral in the case of a man who wishes to give his child a respectable funeral and to provide respectable mourning, all that applies to a parent who wishes to do that?—Yes.

2653. Is there anything in the law which compels a parent to spend the whole of the insurance money upon those things?—No.

2654. Then if you are calculating the profit not of a good man, but the death profit that a disreputable man wants to make out of his child's death, you cannot possibly count any expense except what he is compelled to incur; I suppose a man who wishes to make money from his child's death will not incur any more expense upon his child's funeral than he can help?—Certainly not.

2655. Then all you say as to the expense of a respectable funeral would not apply to death or funeral expenses in the case of disreputable or dishonest people?—Because there is no compulsion.

2656. In point of fact, under the existing law, there being no compulsion and no power of making the parent spend the whole of the money upon the funeral and death expenses, there is no provision whatever against the misuse of the balance which a disreputable parent may draw from his insurance fund?—I may answer that question by pointing out what we do; we take great care to see the money expended, and if we have any doubt at all about the providence of the parents, I myself have instructed our officer not to pay the money, but have simply paid the undertaker and the doctor, and then paid the difference to the mother of the child rather than let the father touch a penny piece.

2657. You take great care to prevent an improper use of the balance?—Certainly.

Chairman—continued.

2658. You do not consider you are stigmatising decent parents by doing that?—It is a protection to the parents.

2659. Then, as to the cost of the funeral and the age of the child, you are aware that a child under the age of five may be insured for 6 l., which you say does not do more than cover the expense of the funeral and other expenses. When a child reaches the age of five years and six months it may be insured for 10 l., may it not?—Yes, the section of the Act allows it, but we have a graduated scale; we only go up at the rate of about 1 l. a-year.

2660. I am not speaking as regards your society; I am speaking as regards the law, and the law is that if a child is five years of age, he may get insured for funeral expenses for 6 l., but if he is five years and six months the parent may make it 10 l.; do you think that is a reasonable difference as between a child of five years and a child of five years and six months, the difference being 4 l.?—I cannot say how that would be.

2661. Under the law he may do so, if he insures only in one society, that is clear. Then, I ask again, supposing a parent had insured his child at the age of five years for 6 l., you surely do not mean to say that at the age of five years and six months the funeral of the child would cost 10 l., whereas at the age of five years it would only cost 6 l.; you do not mean to say that a difference of six months in the age of a child would make a difference of 4 l. in the cost of the funeral?—I do not suppose it would, putting it in that way.

2662. As regards the registrar's certificate, have you found generally not only as regards your own society, but as regards registrars generally, that they are very careful about giving their certificates?—Undoubtedly very careful indeed; they are very strict.

2663. Then, as regards the agitation and excitement of the working classes that you speak of, you say they are very much agitated and very much excited upon this subject, and that this measure will be very unpopular; is it your opinion that a particular measure, supposing it to be a good measure, and supposing it to be necessary, is to be given up because a number of persons dislike it; do you think that is reasonable?—We do not look upon it as a good measure.

2664. I am quite aware that you do not; but you dwell very much upon the agitation and excitement of the working classes. Supposing this were a measure which affected the upper classes, and the upper classes were very angry with it, and got up an excitement against it, would that be a reason for giving up the measure?—Certainly it would, if they objected to it.

2665. Am I to understand that if any class in the country objects to any measure, whether it be good or bad, it should not be passed?—I mean to say they would do their best to resist it.

2666. I ask is it a reasonable thing to refuse to pass a measure simply because a great many persons dislike it?—If there was no objection to a measure, there would be no order in some things.

2667. Laws

Chairman—continued.

2667. Laws are passed for the good of the general public, not for classes, are they not?— Laws are passed for the general good of the community.

2668. Then if the community comes to be of opinion, whether rightly or wrongly, that the passing of a particular law is for the good of the community, should the Legislature be stopped from passing that law because some class does not like it?—Certainly not, and that is the reason why so many bad laws are repealed.

2669. Do you think that laws are repealed because persons dislike them?—They are repealed because they have been found to be wrong.

2670. Do you think that if this Bill should be passed, and the money should pass into the hands of the undertaker, he will take it and do what he likes with it?—It gives him that opportunity.

2671. Might not the parent go to the undertaker and ask him, "What will you bury my child for?"; he will be left to choose any undertaker he pleases; the clause does not name any undertaker?—It says the money shall be paid to the undertaker actually conducting the funeral of the child.

2672. The parent may choose the undertaker. may he not?—I think your Lordship has hardly thought it all through. The clause implies that the parents are not competent to know best what to do.

2673. Will you kindly answer the question : would not the parent have the power of choosing the undertaker?—He would please himself.

2674. Then, if he pleases himself he will choose the undertaker, who will give him the kind of funeral he wants at the most reasonable price, will he not?—He will; he would make his own bargain.

2675. He would have the power of making his own bargain then, would he not?—The clause is very indefinite.

2676. Supposing a parent has under the Act the power of making his own bargain, and choosing his own undertaker, how can the undertaker possibly take the money and do what he likes with it; surely the undertaker cannot ask the parent to pay him for anything but the funeral as agreed upon?—But your Bill says the society shall not pay any money upon the death of a child except to the person conducting the funeral, and we look upon it in this light, that there is no provision that if there should be a balance over the parent shall receive it, because you put a heavy penalty to that.

2677. That, as I said to another witness, would be the case if the Act were retrospective; but if the Act be prospective, could not the parent say to the undertaker beforehand, "I wish if my child should die to have a funeral of a certain character for a certain sum;" would that still be objectionable to you?—You would have to remodel the rules of all the societies in the country before you could do that.

2678. Do you not think it would be better to alter the rules of all the societies in the country, or of all the societies in the world, than that a certain number of children should be killed?— But I think that would have to be proved.

(142.)

Chairman—continued.

2679. Do you think it would be a sufficient reason against preventing child-murder, by a certain Act, to say, this Act will compel the remodelling of the rules of certain societies?— Under the principle that you have embodied in this Bill of yours you would have to remodel the rules of all the societies in the kingdom.

2680. I ask you whether it is not better that the societies should be put to the trouble of remodelling their rules than that children should be murdered?—We do not admit that children are murdered.

2681. I have only one more question to ask you; do you not think it would be quite possible for your society to engage or contract with a certain number of respectable undertakers, and to say to the parents you shall employ this or that undertaker; just as a sick club employs its own doctor? — I would not recommend our members to do anything of the kind; I think the working classes are quite competent to do what they want to do without combining together to pay the undertaker. I think that the very spirit of competition in the trade itself is sufficient to convince the Committee that it is enough to control that which might be wrong.

2682. In point of fact you think that the spirit of competition amongst undertakers is so great that they will supply funerals as cheaply and respectably as they can?—They do now.

2683. Therefore in point of fact the undertaker under that spirit of competition, supposing this Bill were passed, would not exactly be able to do what he likes with the money, because some other undertaker would compete with him and do it more respectably?—We differ with you upon that assumption; we do not believe your assumption. In this Bill there is no provision for a controlling influence even over the money; you take it out of the hands of the parent and put it in the hands of an irresponsible person, and we object to that.

2684. Is it not the proposal of the Bill that this money should be paid by your society?—We should be forced to do it.

2685. Would you not be the controlling influence?—But you do not give us that privilege.

2686. Supposing it were passed, if your society paid this money to the undertaker, would not the society then be the controlling influence?— We should, but we should want something put in your Bill to give that qualification.

Earl of *Derby.*

2687. Whether your reasons are good or bad you come here to testify that, as a matter of fact, there is a very strong feeling against this undertaker clause amongst the working men?— There is a very indignant feeling.

2688. If that clause were struck out of the Bill, do you think there would be any general objection to a further limitation of the amount for which a very young child's life may be insured?—We should still consider that the privileges we now have, which were settled by the present Act of 1875, are only fair and just, and any interference with that we shall resist strenuously, because we consider that we are intelligent enough and honest enough to do right.

Q 3   2689. You

Earl of *Derby*—continued.

2689. You admit that there is a certain amount of infanticide?—I have already explained that that is so; but we do not admit that there is infanticide to any appreciable extent for club money. If we take and dissect the meaning of "infanticide," we find that a very large number of dead children are found that are not connected with any society, and we resent the interference of those who pose as friends, by implying that that is done for club money.

2690. In fact you consider that insurance and infanticide are not in any way connected?—Not at all.

Marquess of *Lothian.*

2691. Do you know whether any members of your society are insured in any other society?—In two; we admit it.

2692. Are members of your society allowed to insure in other societies beyond your own?—Adult members can insure in two or three societies, and children up to two or three years of age we allow to insure in two societies; but it is impossible to insure in more under the present Act; it is illegal if they do.

2693. You say you have a graduated scale; one scale for six months. another for one year, and another for two years?—Yes,

2694. Where is that scale given; that is not fixed by law, is it?—No; we fix it for ourselves, according to the funds we save.

2695. Could you tell us what that scale is?—This is a copy of our rules (*handing a copy of the Rules to the Committee*). This is our latest scale; these rules were passed at our last half-yearly meeting. The scale runs thus: supposing a child enters at two months, having been a member for eight weeks, the parents may receive 1 *l.* 10 *s.*; after twelve weeks, 2 *l.*; after eighteen weeks, 2 *l.* 10 *s.*; after twenty-six weeks, 3 *l.*; after forty weeks, 3 *l.* 10 *s.*; after fifty-two weeks, 4. *l*; after two years, 5 *l.*; after five years, 6 *l.*; after ten years, 8 *l.*; after fifteen years, 9 *l.*; after twenty years, 10 *l.*; and after twenty-five years, 11 *l.* We have done this simply from the money that we have saved from the time the society has been established; that gives us the opportunity of paying this amount.

2696. I gather from what you said about the cost of a funeral, that the sum which a parent would be paid upon the death of a child would not cover the cost of the funeral?—Not at the young ages.

2697. I think you said the cost of a funeral for a child about six months old would be about 4 *l.* 10 *s.*?—Yes.

2698. Is it the case that more than one child is ever buried in one grave at one time? I do not mean to say a grave belonging to one family, but supposing several young children belonging to different families die, and are buried upon the same day, are they buried together?—There are in some cemeteries what are called public graves, in which they can be buried, but the working classes of Lancashire more particularly, prefer to have their own grave, where the whole family lie together, and they will save their money even independently of what they pay to the Society in the case of death. I have known instances in which the working people will save their money

Marquess of *Lothian*—continued.

until they are able to have their own grave, and in that case the cost of re-opening the grave to put a single body in helps to swell the cost of a private funeral. Every time a grave is re-opened is 15 *s.*, and that, I may say, does not at all come in with the cost which has been given you. Moreover, first of all, they have to buy the grave.

2699. What you put down is 15 *s.* for re-opening the grave?—Yes; for the cost of re-opening.

2700. Do the fathers, as a rule, accompany the funerals of their children?—Almost in all cases; if they do not it is probably because of sickness, or that they are not able to get permission to leave their work.

2701. Are the parents, as a rule, particular about having some decent mourning at the burial of their children?—They are very particular indeed; they like to be respectable.

2702. Are there no Sunday interments in Manchester?—Never.

2703. Therefore the father would, of course, lose a day's work in attending the funeral of his child?—Yes.

Earl of *Selborne.*

2704. Has your society made any profit by its insurances?—No; it has not made any profit because the money is lying in the bank for the use of members for future contingencies; the Act of Parliament compels us to have a certain amount by us.

2705. Your society is in the nature of a friendly family society?—It is in the nature of a friendly family society.

2706. Are you able to tell the Committee anything about the proportion borne by children who die within the period of insurance to those who do not?—No; but we find that the death-rate is greater amongst children who are not insured than it is amongst those that are insured.

2707. I think I heard you say that before insuring any child the child is seen by your officer?—Yes.

2708. And do you take any steps in doubtful cases after death to ascertain whether there is any suspicion of malpractice?—We are very careful so far as exercising care over the payments of those who may be of dissolute character.

2709. What are the precautions which you do take in cases where you find it necessary to diverge from the course ordinarily taken?—In this way; sometimes there may be an application made to me as secretary by parents to know how they stand; they may have been a little bit backward in their payments and want to make themselves right on the books; in that case we are always careful to know something about the child, and if there should be a death take place shortly after that we send down one of our officers to ascertain the full particulars.

2710. I think I understood you to say, in answer to one question that was put to you, that in some cases you see to the application of the money?—We do.

2711. Will you state to the Committee how you do that?—In case there may be a death, and there

Earl of *Selborne*—continued.

there is any dispute in the family in connection with the question of who should receive the money ; sometimes it may arise between brothers ; the eldest invariably tries to have the right to receive the money ; the sisters may object, because they have been paying the subscriptions, while the brothers have been paying nothing, and then when they come to receive the money we refuse to pay either. We engage the undertaker, with their consent ; they have the right to nominate the undertaker, and we see the funeral conducted and carried out, and whatever balance there is we divide amongst the parties.

2712. The balance in those cases, I suppose, is generally small, is it not ?—Very small indeed.

Lord *Kinnaird.*

2713. Your rules are very carefully worked out ; but do you think there is a need for strengthening the law as worked by certain societies ?—We believe there is no need for any alteration of the present Act ; the safeguards in that are sufficient if they are efficiently carried out.

Chairman.

2714. Do you mean that as regards your society ? — I mean as regards all friendly societies.

2715. You would not mean that remark to apply to all collecting societies ?—I know nothing about collecting societies.

2716. Your remark is only intended to apply to friendly societies ?—Certainly.

Lord *Kinnaird.*

2717. If it were proved that certain societies did not take the same precautions as you do, do you think there would be any strong feeling against strengthening the law ?—If we found that it was so we should go in ourselves to ask for a strengthening of the law.

2718. What proportion of the workpeople do you think insure ?—Nearly all of the working classes insure ; there are very few exceptions.

Lord *Norton.*

2719. You would not say that there are no cases of what you call dissolute parents or stepparents neglecting a sick child, allowing it to die, partly to get rid of the burden, and with the still further object of getting the insurance money ? — There are dissolute parents it is true.

2720. Then, do I understand that you think it more the object of the law to punish such cases than to check the use of insurance by a better class of parent ?—That is the object of the law.

2721. If the law is not sufficient now in punishing them ; if there is difficulty in getting convictions, and in inflicting adequate punishment, how would you strengthen the law in the way to carry out your view ; would you propose that there should be severer penalties ?—For those who break the law there ought to be stringent penalties ; I think the law is sufficient now if it is carried out.

(142.)

Lord *Norton*—continued.

2722. You allow that there is a considerable number of cases of heartless parents neglecting their children ?—I do not admit anything of the kind ; there may be a few cases ; there may be many cases which have not come within my knowledge.

2723. Do you agree with the suggestion made in the debate ; that to say there was one case in a thousand would be an exaggeration ?—I should doubt even that.

2724. In making the distinction of investigation in what you call dissolute cases, who is the judge of what is a dissolute case ?—The officer of the society.

2725. Has any offence ever been taken at that distinction when cases have been selected by the officer, and specially investigated in the way in which other cases are not now investigated ?—We have had very few cases to deal with where there could be any offence, excepting the offence upon the part of the parent feeling indignant at not being able to get the money.

2726. You say that in a town like Manchester 6 *l.* is no inordinate sum to insure for ; that would not be the case in the country, would it ?—It varies a little in some country districts ; there are a few where the habits are quite different to what they are in town, because you find in one or two country villages the churchyards are still open, and they have not the distance we have to go, and there the custom is to carry more than it is in the towns.

2727. Should I be beyond the mark if I said the expense of a funeral in a town was double what it is in the country ?—It is not quite double ; you might say safely that it is two-thirds more.

2728. Do you think there ought to be any distinction between the law relating to friendly societies in town and friendly societies in the country ?—None whatever.

2729. You seem to think that it is impossible for any careful parent by laying by money in a Post Office savings bank to provide against contingencies, such as the death of a child, so safely or economically as by insuring in a society ?—It would be simply unworkable in connection with the Post Office savings bank, and I am surprised that the question has been raised in the House of Commons and other quarters with reference to the Post Office ; the staff employed at the post offices would be inadequate.

2730. Surely, if the business increased, the staff would increase ; is that all the objection that the staff is not sufficient ?—No ; there is an antipathy amongst the working-classes against going to a Post Office savings bank with ver small sums.

2731. There are penny savings banks, are there not ?—Yes.

2732. Is there any objection on the part of working men to going there ?—No. In our School Board district we have one in connection with every school, they work from one centre in Manchester in connection with one society ; they are all from one source.

2733. Is there any objection to laying by against casualty in a savings bank, except that a parent may not have self-control enough to prevent

Q 4

Lord *Norton*—continued.

prevent himself drawing upon it from time to time ?—I may add, in answer to that, that we have a number of what are called tontine societies, those are societies in which they can lay by a small sum of money weekly, and at the end of the year they receive a dividend over and above the working expenses, either for death, or sickness, or for what they call the summer " out." We find many who provide for all three things independently of being members of our own societies, but that is only in the case of adults.

Lord Bishop of Ripon.

2734. May I ask what class of people they are who insure with you ?—They are the working classes, and we do not refuse to take even those who are very wealthy.

2735. You take in anybody ?—Yes, we take in anybody.

2736. But as a rule they are all of the respectable class, I presume ?—We exercise a care in this way, that we do not take those who are known to be unhealthy.

2737. But as regards their position you find that your constituents, so to speak, are drawn from the thrifty and well-to-do artizan classes?· — Yes, undoubtedly the majority ; but we have many in the lowest strata, who have been brought up as members of the society from childhood.

2738. Have you any of that class of people commonly called " loafers "?—We could not resist them if they came in.

2739. But would you admit them ?—There would be many that we might not know of because the officer would not go round prying into their domestic circumstances.

2740. But your experience is that those who support your society are mainly the thrifty and well-to-do artizans in fairly good work ?— Exactly.

2741. Therefore your evidence goes to the state of opinion amongst what may be called the really working classes of the well-to-do kind ?— I represent the working class as a body as they are to-day, including the intelligent and better class of the working people, with even some of the lower strata ; if they come to join the society as members, we make no distinction ; we take and judge them from their appearance as to whether they are fit to become members or not.

2742. You know where they live ?—Yes ; we know where they live ; we have all their addresses.

2743. Do you know where they work ?—No, we have nothing to do their work ; sometimes we have cases where the members do not want us to know where they do reside, and if we do accidentally get to know we keep it private ; and I may add to that this, that I have been round with our collector on several occasions, and I have gone to certain houses, and I have seen a peep at the window, and they would not acknowledge that they were in, because they did not know me ; they have their own private reasons for that, so that we do not inquire into that at all.

2744. You cannot speak with reference to the very lowest stratum of society ; your operations do not extend quite to them ?—Not that we know anything at all about ; we do not admit loafers, as far as we know them.

Lord Thring.

2745. You have a graduated scale, distinct from the scale allowed by the law ; you graduate your scale yourselves ?—Yes, we graduate our scale from age to age.

2746. Do you think it would be an advantage to put your graduated scale into the Act of Parliament, instead of the existing scale ?—What may suit our societies would not suit others ; they might not be in a position to do that, from not having been established for so many years ; we have been established 57 years. Other societies, not quite so old, would not have the money put by. The interest upon the money in one society that I am connected with pays the whole of the working expenses ; in that case we have raised the scale of benefits.

2747. I did not quite understand this ; what I was asking was, instead of the maximum of 10 *l.* which covers the ages between five and 10, would you think it wrong to put in the graduated scale you have read to the Committee, and make that the Parliamentary scale ?—I would have no objection to that in one sense, though that would be trespassing upon the interests of other people.

2748. I understand that you do not insure children before they are two months old ?— No.

2749. What is the reason of that ?—It was originally three months, but we reduced it to two months because we considered it safe from this fact that the death-rate of those under one year was so small that we could afford to give even a higher sum of money for the earlier age than what was in proportion to those who had been in longer for benefit.

2750. But I thought more children died under one year than at any other age ?—Our death-rate shows the contrary ; our death-rate is higher amongst adults than amongst children.

Chairman.

2751. Then, speaking of your death-rate, you say it is lower than that of the town generally ? —Yes, generally.

2752. You say you take no child under two months ?—Yes.

2753. But every child that died under two months would appear amongst the general death-rate ?—Yes ; it would be amongst the death-rate of the city.

2754. Then your death-rate is collected from a smaller area than the general death-rate ?— Yes.

2755. You also say that, generally speaking, you are extremely careful as to the persons you admit to your society ?—Yes.

2756. Of course you admit thrifty and respectable people in preference to others ?—Yes.

2757. And there are many of them ?—Yes.

2758. The thrifty, well-conducted man would take care of his children, whereas the loafer would not ?—That is our experience.

2759. In point of fact, your lives of children would be, what are called by an actuary, picked or selected lives ; the lives of the better and more respectable portion of the working class ? —We find it is in the mind of many of our members when they are insured to take a greater interest in their children ; they are more careful
with

Chairman—continued.

with them, and that has a tendency in itself to protect life.

2760. To come back to my question, you do take care first of all that you shall have no child under two months, and next you know, as a matter of fact, that your members are respectable, and also you state, with great truth no doubt, that there is this important difference between your society and others, that your inspectors know the people and the people know them. They can look after the people, and the people are acting under the eyes of their other brother members?—They are under the eyes of their brother members.

2761. All those considerations go rather to indicate that the lives in your society are what would be called picked lives, and safer lives than those of the general community, which includes loafers and drunkards, and a good number of disreputable and wicked people?—They do.

2762. And very poor people also, paupers?—No; not that we know of.

2763. My point is, that if we are to take two sets of statistics, they must be taken over equal areas and under like conditions, otherwise the comparison is no good. What I want to point out to you is that upon your own statement your statistics of the death-rate are not taken over the same area as those of the Registrar General; firstly, by reason of the two months, and secondly, that the lives of many of your children exist and are passed under more favourable conditions for life than those of the worthless, disreputable, and drunken?—I hold in my hand a tabulated statement of 59 societies; those extend over a wide area, and include Stockport, Hyde, Oldham, Manchester, and other places; the average death-rate is 16·11.

2764. Those societies you are speaking of are all friendly societies?—Yes; they are all friendly societies.

2765. The friendly societies, as a rule, represents the better class of artisans?—Yes.

2766. The children of the better class of artisans will be better cared for; they are a better class, of course, than the children of the drunkards, and loafers, and tramps?—Yes.

2767. If the statistics of the Registrar General include the children of loafers, drunkards, and tramps, and yours do not, is it not clear that he will have a higher death-rate than yours?—Yes.

2768. That will considerably vitiate the table you have put in?—This is a comparison mainly between our table and the local death-rate.

2769. But I was pointing out that your statistics are liable to a considerable discount?—I quite understand your Lordship's point.

Lord *Clifford of Chudleigh.*

2770. I did not understand your answer to a question put by Lord Thring about the exclusion

Lord *Clifford of Chudleigh*—continued.

of children under two months. Lord Thring asked you why you excluded children under two months?—As a rule you can hardly tell what they are until they get two months old, the liability to death is so much greater; we take that as the general persuasion.

2771. The cost of the funeral of a child under two months, and of a child of one year, is appreciably different?—There is a wonderful difference between the cost of the funeral of a child of two months and of one of 12 months; a child who dies under the age of two months might be carried by one or two people.

2772. And not under one year?—Certainly not.

Earl *Beauchamp.*

2773. May I take it as the result of your experience that when artizans join your society that rather tends to increase their respectability? It does: it makes them feel that they are members of a friendly society, and they respect themselves more than when they have no such feeling.

Earl of *Selborne.*

2774. Is that the reason which makes you think they take more care of their children when they are insured than when they are not insured?—I cannot say that, but that it makes a man think when he joins a friendly society; he is more careful himself, and of those under him.

2775. But I thought just now you said that those whose children were insured took more care of their children (if there were any comparison to be made) than those whose children were not insured?—I did.

2776. I want to know what was your reason for saying that, because, supposing they do not take less care, and I do not see why they should take less care——?—It makes the insurance more profitable if they take more care of themselves and their children.

Lord *Kinnaird.*

2777. Do we understand that nobody gets any advantage from insuring until the children insured have been two months on your books?—In one society they have to be three months before they are entitled to anything, in another eight weeks, and in another six weeks.

2778. But infants just born you do not take?—We do not take any until they are two months old.

2779. Then your answer to Lord Thring was correct that you do not insure a child before it is two months old, and then it must have two months of membership before it gets any benefit?—Yes; they cannot get anything under four or six months old.

The Witness is directed to withdraw.

Ordered,—That this Committee be adjourned to Wednesday next, at Twelve o'clock.

Die Mercurii, 16° Julii, 1890.

LORDS PRESENT:

Earl of DERBY.
Earl of HARROWBY.
Earl BEAUCHAMP.
Earl of SELBORNE.
LORD BISHOP OF PETERBOROUGH.
Lord CLIFFORD OF CHUDLEIGH.

Lord KER (*Marquess of Lothian*).
Lord POLTIMORE.
Lord BROUGHAM AND VAUX.
Lord KINNAIRD.
Lord NORTON.
Lord THRING.

THE RIGHT REV. THE LORD BISHOP OF PETERBOROUGH, IN THE CHAIR.

THE *Chairman* proposes that the notes for evidence tendered by James Grahame, Chairman of the Committee of the Scottish National Society for the Prevention of Cruelty to Children, be entered upon the Minutes as a written communication upon which no examination was held :—

CHILD LIFE ASSURANCE.

NOTES for Evidence to be tendered by *James Grahame*, Founder and a Vice-President and Chairman of Committee of the Scottish National Society for the Prevention of Cruelty to Children, and J.P. for the County of Lanark, to the Select Committee of the House of Lords, July 1890.

1. The society was founded in 1884.
2. It has for its President His Royal Highness the Prince of Wales, and for its Patron Her Royal Highness the Duchess of Fife.
3. Its head offices are in Edinburgh and Glasgow, and there are affiliated societies in Dundee, Greenock, Paisley, Dumbarton, Hamilton, Motherwell, Dumfermline, Dalkeith, Portobello, Melrose, Corstorphine, Leith, Galashiels, Burntisland, Aberdour, Moffat, Alloa, Brechin, Bridge of Allan, Cupar Fife, Innerleithen ; and there are branches being formed at present in Ayr, Falkirk, Kilmarnock, Stirling, Helensburgh, Hawick, Aberdeen, Inverness, St. Andrews, Peith, Peebles, Coatbridge, and Montrose. In five years ending October 1889 (independent of cases in Edinburgh and other towns in Scotland) the society investigated in Glasgow alone 4,931 cases of cruelty to children, involving 7,363 children ; 4,466 children were sheltered, 1,545 were clothed, 32,112 meals were given, and 5,965 children were sent by the action of this society to industrial schools, day schools, training ships, homes, or domestic service, or placed under the supervision of the school boards. The total number of prosecutions for this period was 4,305. In 3,766 of these cases

the parents were cautioned, in 157 were punished and in 382 were convicted and admonished.

4. The Bill at present before your Lordships' House affects the whole United Kingdom, but its promoters did not consult the Scottish National Society as to its provisions before bringing it in.
5. It is many years since the subject of child life insurance first arrested my attention.
6. Nearly two years ago, in November 1888, I brought the subject specially before the notice of the Scottish Society at a meeting in Glasgow, at which I said a few words upon the subject in connection with the work of the society as one which I had studied, and upon which I made a special effort to return from London to speak to them. I said—

" It is a subject of very great importance to " the community, and one which you, like myself, " must view with painful interest.

" Mr. Marr, our Director, who is Manager of " the Scottish Amicable Life Assurance Society, " with which as a director I have long been con- " nected, is aware that many years before " this society was thought of the subject of " child life insurance engaged my attention, and " that, with his assistance, I investigated into the " practice and business of many of the chief " friendly and benefit societies, and of the indus- " trial insurance companies, who prosecute that " kind of business amongst the poorer classes.

" The work of this society revived my interests " in this inquiry, and the result now, as then, is " to establish the conviction in my mind that a " vast deal of useful, honourable, benevolent, " and wholesome work is done by these bodies.

" There is a proper and laudable desire on the " part of the poorer classes to provide out of " daily income for times of sickness and the cost " of medical attendance and decent duties to " their dead which it would be impertinent to " deal with, and which ought rather to be en- " couraged than repressed.

" But, on the other hand, I am convinced now,

" as

16 *July* 1890.

" as I was convinced then, and know by sad
" experience, that there are people in our great
" cities who have no such provident aim ; who
" have no desire to procure medical attendance
" for their sick children ; who exhibit nothing
" but heartless indifference to their health and
" morals and life ; and who can have no aim in
" insuring the lives of their infants except the
" rational expectation that the life may end, and
" the sooner the better, and be followed by the
" payment of the sum which they can assure by
" the payment of so small a sum as 1 *d.* per
" week.

" Within the last two or three months two
" startling cases came before our notice in Scot-
" land.

" The father and the stepmother of a child
" were convicted and sent to prison for a year
" for the slow starvation to death of a young
" daughter of the male prisoner. That it would
" have died without care or notice by either of
" them is undoubted. The neighbours, how-
" ever, intervened, but too late. When the
" child reached the shelter, the film of death was
" on its eyes, and in a few hours its sufferings
" were at an end. The child was insured for
" 3 *l.*, and the money was paid.

" The other case was at the last circuit court,
" where a wretched old woman, now under
" reprieve of sentence of death, was convicted
" on the clearest evidence of having hastened out
" of this life a delicate child by the aid of a pair
" of scissors. Here, again, but for the observa-
" tion of neighbours, no one might have been a
" bit the wiser That child had been insured by
" her for 30 *s.*

" Now, ladies and gentlemen, there ought to
" be some instant consideration and action with
" regard to this great and obvious evil.

" It is clear that the present system of child
" life insurance presents a direct temptation to
" those parents and guardians who belong to the
" lapsed and criminal classes, when they know that
" without troublesome questions they may acquire
" a pound or two at the expense of a few pence,
" and by merely letting a poor child pine away
" to a death of neglect and starvation.

" There ought to be, and I am sure there will
" be, some legislative security provided against
" the improper insurance of the lives of children,
" and of their insurance by worthless and depraved
" parents.

" I feel sure that all the respectable societies
" and insurance companies are as alive to this
" abuse as we are, and that they would welcome
" such legislation, and co-operate with us in
" obtaining it, so as to put their business beyond
" doubt or reproach.

" That, ladies and gentlemen, is the chief sub-
" ject to which I desired to call your attention,
" as well as the attention of the public, in the
" earnest hope that while we take care to say
" nothing harsh, or to do anything unjust, we
" may assist those societies to clear their
" hands of what is, without doubt, a grievous
" blot and stain."

7. I am convinced that legislation is necessary,
but I do not personally approve of the present
Bill, for the following reasons :—

(*a*) It deals with the whole mass of prudent
provision by the poor for casual heavy charges
in the event of death as if that proceeding was in
itself of a doubtful character, not because the
system is wrong or doubtful, or anything but
proper or laudable, but because it has been and
is being abused by depraved people.

(*b*) Because it has been introduced without
being first considered by the many respectable
and useful benefit societies and insurance companies and their members, who constitute the bulk
of the industrious working population, and
without whose co-operation no such Bill should
have been introduced, and which, thus introduced,
is calculated to defeat its own object by arousing
their natural indignation and hostility.

(*c*) Because it would be found in practice to be
unworkable. For example, upon what scale is a
funeral to be performed, mourning provided, and
medical attendance paid ? There must be a
fixed scale of charge in order to establish a fixed
rate of contribution. Who is, for instance, to
select, say, the undertaker, and who is to dictate
the manner in which he performs his duty or
makes his charge ? Is it to be to the satisfaction
of the parent, or is it to be to the satisfaction of
the office or the society ? I have here an estimate furnished by eight well-known undertakers
in Glasgow of the lowest rates quoted for the
interment of children under five years of age.
These rates are as follows : in common ground
and at the lowest price, 1 *l.* 1 *s.* 6 *d.* ; this
includes ground, coffin. and coach only. If to
this is added doctor's account and two days' loss
of work, say 15 *s.*, it would make in all
1 *l.* 16 *s.* 6 *d.* Where a special grave or lair is
needed the lowest price would be 2 *l.* 13 *s.* 6 *d.*
to 3 *l.* 17 *s.* 1 *d.*, according to the place of interment. to which add doctor's account, and two
days' loss of wages, bringing it up to 3 *l.* 8 *s.* 6 *d.*
and 4 *l.* 12 *s.* respectively.

(*d*) Because there are infinite grades in the
population. I mean there is a perfect succession
of minute steps from the highest to the lowest
person in the great mass of our population, each
of whom has the right to form his own idea of
what his social position demands, and what in
family matters his expenditure should be. It
would be absurd to fix the cost of a child's
funeral who is insured at the same amount in the
case of a working man earning 2 *l.* a week, and
who has a small family, and in the case of a
labourer earning 18 *s.* a week and having a large
one.

(*e*) Because the provisions of the Bill could
not prevent connivance between an unscrupulous
undertaker and a depraved parent. Anyone
could be an undertaker, and there would be no
great difficulty in a criminal getting one of his
own stamp to fulfil that duty, make his charge,
get the money from the insurance company, and
then divide the spoil. The only result would be
to make two transgressors in place of one, and
produce a cover for crime under the sanction and
the appearance of observing the Act.

8. The check I should propose is one of compulsory legal registration (the register to be open
at all times to public inspection) of every child
life insurance within one week of that insurance,
with a statement by the society or company, or
by its agent, as to the following facts :—

First, That the child is born in wedlock.

Second,

Second, That the condition of the child's health when insured and the apparent condition and character of the family are satisfactory.

Third, The name of any other society or company in which the child is insured to the best knowledge of the society or of its agents; and it should also be provided that every claim in respect of child life insurance should be entered in the register of the locality where the insurance was registered; such entry to be made by the society or company within one week after the death of the child, accompanied with a medical certificate of the cause of death.

It should further be provided that no such insurance should be valid, or any payment of claim lawful, which had not been so registered and so notified to the registrar, and that a penalty should be attached to the transgression of this rule, either by individuals, societies, or companies. In such regulations as I suggested there would be no hardship to any individual or society, for in all ordinary life insurance policies, questions much more stringent are matters of every-day occurrence. Such regulations would only compel the societies or companies to protect the public and themselves from abuse of their privileges, and from the competition of unscrupulous agents, and by such regulations the natural wishes and provisions of individuals would not be tyrannised over; but the knowledge that the eyes of public authority and of such societies as ours would always be vigilantly fixed on any abnormal infant mortality in a family, would deter any but those whom nothing would deter from abusing the system.

We must not forget that infanticide has in itself no connection with life assurance, but prevails and has prevailed without it. What we have to do is to check an additional inducement to its commission by the heartless and debased. The primary inducement to infanticide is to get rid of a burden or of a source of personal shame, but that may be accentuated by the temptation of making money.

9. I am also of opinion that the large benefit societies and insurance companies ought even at this late hour to be invited to suggest to Parliament some practical means other than the present Bill of meeting what is an undoubted evil against which we have at present no proper protection, failing which suggestion legislation ought to proceed in default.

10. The suggestions I have made have been considered by the committees of the society in Edinburgh and in Glasgow, and cordially approved as a proper and adequate means of preventing the abuse of Child Life Assurance.

11. The suggestions I have made have been approved by the directors of the Scottish Legal Life Assurance Society, the largest society in Scotland, and the third in rank as regards business in the United Kingdom. Its membership is over 400,000, and they have assured me that they will cordially co-operate in supporting a measure drawn on such lines as I suggest.

12. We have no coroners or coroners' inquests in Scotland; any case of suspicion is reported to the Crown procurator-fiscal, who is bound to investigate.

Ordered, That the said Notes be entered on the Minutes.

(142.)

The *Chairman* hands in the two following letters :—

In re The Children's Life Insurance Bill.

To the Chairman and Members of the Commission on the above Bill.

May it please your Lordships,

We most respectfully desire your attention, as the Committee is now sitting, that at a number of meetings of members and representatives of societies forming the Macclesfield and Congleton Amalgamated Association of Family Burial Societies, the above-named Bill and portions of the evidence given before the Lords Committee have been considered and discussed, the result being a strong feeling is evidenced against portions of the Bill, considering it to be an unwarrantable and unnecessary interference in the management, more particularly of such societies as those composing this association.

It appears to us that the chief reason given for further restrictions being placed upon these societies is the existence of infanticide. Amongst these societies it is not known to exist. Again, it is here considered that the amount to be paid on the death of a child is sufficiently restricted by the Act of 1875, and does not leave a margin, after the most economical funeral expenses are paid, sufficient to induce infanticide. And, further, it is an acknowledged fact that the large majority of members join these societies to secure for themselves and children the services of the medical aid, that is medicine and attendance in case of sickness, provided at a cost shown in the enclosed printed summary. Clause 2, reference to payments of premiums to undertakers, is considered particularly obnoxious, and would have the effect of preventing many from making provision, as at present, resulting in many cases a call upon the rates for parochial aid. Clause 1 would not materially affect these societies (*see* rules enclosed, page 4, No 4). Clauses 3 and 4 are invariably the practice with our local registers, also Clause 5.

Having now respectfully placed before your Lordships our objections to the projected Bill, entitled, "An Act to amend the laws relating to insurances of the lives of children," we humbly pray that these vetoes may be duly considered; we are induced to place these views before your Lordships, having noticed that no evidence has been taken or placed before you from societies based or constructed on such lines as our, the family, burial societies.

I remain, on behalf of the Macclesfield and Congleton Amalgamated Burial Societies Association,

Yours, &c.

(signed)   *Jos. Jas. Mason*, Secretary.

155, High-street, Macclesfield.

The representation of the Leeds Committee of the Society for the Prevention of Cruelty to Children.

My Lords,.   Leeds, 5 July 1890.

We are of opinion that amendment of the law relating to the insurance on the lives of children is needed, but while we approve of the

16 *July* 1890.

principle, we see grave objections to certain details which appear to us ineffective and harsh in Bill proposed.

Clause 1.—We think that the amounts under (*a*.), (*b*.), and (*c*.) are inadequate. After careful inquiry, our own opinion is confirmed, that the cost of the coffin, conveyance, and cemetery fees would barely be met in cases of children of from three to five years of age by 4 *l.*, or from five to 10 years of age, by 6 *l.*, and then only if such a child was interred in a "public grave." No margin whatever is left for—

(*a*.) Medical attendance.

(*b*.) Mourning.

(*c*.) Such minor expenses as necessarily occur.

(*d*.) Any kind of tombstone or record over the grave.

No doubt funerals are often extravagant, and the money spent on mourning lavish ; still, aware of this, we think it dangerous to destroy entirely an instinct, which is in the main good ; nor do we think that it should be dealt with by Act of Parliament, and least of all by this Act.

Moreover, we think that facilities for the calling in and payment for medical advice should be encouraged. We think that children's lives under two years of age should not be insured at all, and though we feel that this is a hardship on many parents, it is one which the demands of the case require. Life is so much more easily destroyed before 24 months have passed, while after that age the child can, as a rule, walk, talk, and become a reality to brothers, sisters, and neighbours. We also think that foul play generally takes place before this age, and that the cost of the burial of a child so young is far less than that of a child above two years of age. We would therefore suggest that in place of (*a*.), (*b*.), (*c*.), in Clause 1, we read—

(*a*.) On the death of a child above two and under five, 5 *l.*

(*b*.) On the death of a child over five and under 11, 7 *l.*

(*c*.) On the death of a child over 11, and being a boy, &c., or a girl, &c., 10 *l.*

We suggest 11 years under (*b*.), in preference to 10, because about that age, or soon after, the child commences work.

Clause 2.—We regard this clause as very objectionable.

(*a*.) It treats our thrifty and prudent working people with unfounded suspicion.

(*b*.) It interferes with the outlay of money which should be entirely at the disposal of the owner unless there is some ground for suspecting foul play, neglect, or the sacrifice of life for the sake of money.

(*c*.) It offers direct inducements for the violation or evasion of the law, and, by giving undue power to the undertaker, creates a new danger to child life, and places the parent in a false position.

(*d*.) It ignores the expense attending the last illness of the child, and discourages medical advice.

In conclusion we think—

1. That no child under two years of age should be insured.

2. That parents only or recognised guardians should insure a child's life.

3. That under no circumstances should a child be insured in more than one office, and that the registrar's certificate should be the legal receipt for this one payment.

4. That the registrar's certificate should be made out for the one office in which the child is insured, and should specify the office and amount.

5. That the registrar should not give more than one certificate for an insurance society.

6. That the same precautions as are used in cases of children dying with money in the Post Office Savings Bank should be used before the parent or guardian can draw the insurance money on the death of a child.

We are fully alive to the danger to child-life which exists in the present state of the law, but we are equally alive to the fact that nearly all our best working people insure their children's lives, and so while we wish to protect those in danger, we also wish not to discourage thrift or prudence on the part of parents.

Yours, &c.
(signed)   *Edward S. Talbot*,
President of the Local Branch of the Society for Prevention of Cruelty to Children, on behalf of the Committee of the Branch.

Mr. THOMAS CHARLES DEWEY, is called in ; and Examined.

Chairman.

2780. YOU are the Manager of the Prudential Assurance Company ?—I am.

2781. You have attended to give evidence with respect to the matters in this Bill ?—I have.

2782. You have made, in a letter to myself, and I believe you are also prepared to make in your evidence, strong objections to Clause 2 in this Bill ; that is what is commonly called the Undertakers' Clause ?—Yes.

2783. Then, I think, it may save trouble to yourself and to all of us, if I state to you that

Chairman—continued.

the Undertakers' Clause has been withdrawn, and, of course, all evidence or examination on that point will no longer be necessary ?—I am obliged for your Lordship's intimation.

2784. You have been in the service of the Prudential Assurance Company, for how long ?—For over 30 years.

2785. And you have been manager, for how long ?—For 16 years.

2786. Are you a member of the Council of the Institute of Actuaries ?—I am.

2787. Can you give us any information as to the

Chairman--continued.

the constitution of the Prudential Assurance Company ?—The Prudential Assurance Company is a joint stock company, incorporated under the Joint Stock Companies' Act, and is regulated by the Life Assurance Companies' Act of 1870 ; under which Act returns and accounts are rendered to the Board of Trade.

2788. Could you inform us what is the extent of the company's business ?—It has two branches, with a total premium income of four-and-a-half million pounds; one million representing ordinary assurances payable by annual, half-yearly, and quarterly premiums, and with funds exceeding eleven millions of money.

2789. You spoke of two branches, I think ?—The two branches are the industrial and the ordinary. The ordinary has an income of one million, and the industrial has an income of three-and-a-half millions.

2790. Is that gross income ?—A gross premium income.

2791. Could you tell us what proportion of that, first as regards the number of policies, and secondly as regards income, is infantile insurance ?—I have had a table prepared giving that information (*producing a table*).

2792. You put in this table in answer to my question ?—Yes; I should like just to read it, because there are some remarks I should like to make upon it. The number of children under 10 years of age in England and Wales, at the census of 1881, was 6,668,260. The number of children under 10 years of age assured in the Prudential in England and Wales was 2,099,369. That, I think, would show that one-third of the families in England and Wales are assured in the Prudential.

2793. You do not include Ireland in your returns ?—Not in these returns.

2794. Do you do any business in Ireland ?—We do a little business in Ireland, but not to the same extent.

2795. This return refers to England and Wales ?—Yes.

Lord *Kinnaird.*

2796. You do not include Scotland ?—We separate Scotland, because the census returns are entirely distinct, and we are not able to separate them in the same way as in regard to England and Wales.

Chairman.

2797. Will you continue what you wish to say about this table ?—The number of children under 10 years of age was 6,668,260, as I said. Then I have deducted 25 per cent. for children belonging to classes who would not insure ; I have taken 25 per cent. because I believe that is the usual per-centage deducted by the Educational Department from the population of a district to ascertain the sufficiency of school accommodation. That would be reckoning 75 per cent. to be of the working classes, and 25 per cent. of the middle and upper classes.

2798. Your calculation is based on the deduction that the education authorities make as regards education ?—Yes.

2799. And you think that the cases are analogous ?—I fancy so.

(142.)

Earl *Beauchamp.*

2800. Speaking broadly, the classes who attend the public elementary schools are the classes you insure ?—Yes ; in our industrial branch. Deducting that 25 per cent., which amounts to 1,667,065, that would leave 5,000,000 of children who could be insured. Then I take the number of children that we have insured in the Prudential, which is 2,099,369, and the number insured in other companies, affiliated and registered societies (in which I include the Odd Fellows and Foresters), which I believe would be about 1,300,000.

Earl of *Selborne.*

2801. That is conjectural, I presume ?—That is taken on their income in the same way as on ours ; I think we can ascertain that fairly accurately. Then, taking the number of children under 10 years of age assured in local clubs and unregistered societies, I estimate that at about 750,000. Those are estimates, but I can show from the figures that they are fairly reliable. That makes a total of 4,149,369 children assured today out of the 5,000,000 which I mentioned previously.

Chairman.

2802. Are you making any allowance in these returns for children on which there are double policies ?—I am not.

2803. That would to a certain extent vitiate your statistics, would it not ?—That applies only with regard to other societies. I can tell you with regard to the Prudential.

2804. You give credit to other societies for a certain number of children ; it might be the case that a child was insured in more than one ?—Very probably.

2805. To that extent it would vitiate the statistics ?—To that extent it would. These figures, I think, show that infantile assurance is almost universal amongst the industrial classes ; and, therefore, when a death takes place, surprise should rather be expressed when the child is uninsured than when it is insured.

Lord *Kinnaird.*

2806. Can you tell how many of that number that you give as insured in your company are insured in another society when they come to you ? —I can only say that we do not effect an insurance with a child if it is already in a society.

Chairman.

2807. That is if you know that it is already insured in a society ?—Yes, and we ask the question.

Lord *Kinnaird.*

2808. Would it vitiate the policy if the child was already insured ; is it part of the terms of the contract ?—It would not vitiate the policy ; or, if I may correct myself, technically, probably it would vitiate the policy, because the declaration made on the proposal by the father would not be a true one. But it is not a matter that we should take advantage of. The parent has to state that the child is not insured in any other company, and therefore to that extent it is the basis of the policy and the contract. (*See* Appendix.)

R 4   2809. Is

Lord *Kinnaird*—continued.

2809. Is it a written statement?—It is a printed statement which he has to sign. I was going to observe that some doctors and coroners appear to think that the fact of a child being insured at once suggested a suspicion of foul play; but the evidence I have just given shows that as regards the statement which has been made many times in this room that in cases where inquests have been held, 50 per cent. of the children have been insured; that percentage is very much below the average of children insured as compared with the total number of children in England and Wales. Then, continuing my remarks upon this table at the bottom of the page, you will see the population of England and Wales is given. I had this printed to show that there is no undue proportion of insurance of infant life; for the proportion of infantile to adult business is practically the same as the proportion of children to adults in the general population. The population of England and Wales at the census of 1881 was 25,974,439; and the number of children in England and Wales under 10 years of age was 6,668,260, giving a percentage of children to population of 25·67. The total number of policies in force in the Prudential Assurance Company in 1889 was 8,693,513, including both adults and children; and the total number of policies in force in the Prudential on the lives of children under 10 years of age was 2,336,527; giving a percentage of children to the total number of 26·88. Therefore the proportion of children to the general population is practically the same as the proportion of children insured in the Prudential to the total number of policies.

Chairman.

2810. You say the number of policies in force in the Prudential on the lives of children under 10 years of age is so many; have you any statistics as to the number of policies in force in the Prudential on the lives of children under 5 years of age?—On the other page of this table you will see they are set out for each year. " The following shows the number of policies existing on 31st December 1889 in the Prudential Assurance Company on lives under 10 years of age," giving the number in each year.

Earl of *Selborne.*

2811. Each year of age?—Yes, each year of age, male and female.

Chairman.

2812. Will you hand in that table?—Yes.

[*The same is handed in, and is as follows :—*]

PRUDENTIAL ASSURANCE COMPANY, LIMITED.

The number of children under 10 years of age in England and Wales at the census of 1881 was - - - -	6,668,260
The number of children under 10 years of age assured in the Prudential in England and Wales is - - -	2,099,369

Chairman—continued.

The number of children under 10 years of age in England and Wales at the census of 1881 was - - - -	6,668,260
Deducting 25 per cent for children belonging to classes who would not insure - -	1,667,065
	5,001,195

The number of children under 10 years of age assured in England and Wales is—	
Prudential - - -	2,099,369
Other Companies, Affiliated and Registered Societies (about) -	1,300,000
Unregistered Societies, Local Clubs, &c.(about)	750,000
	4,149,369

The population of England and Wales at the Census of 1881 was - - - - -	25,974,439
The number of children in England and Wales under 10 years of age was - -	6,668,260
Percentage of children to population - - - —	25·67
The total number of policies in force in the Prudential on 31st December 1889 was	8,693,513
The total number of policies in force in the Prudential on the lives of children under 10 years of age was -	2,336,527
Percentage of children to total number - - - —	26·88

The following shows the Number of Policies existing on 31st December 1889 in the Prudential Assurance Company, on Lives under 10 Years of Age.

Age.	Males.	Females.	TOTAL.
0 — 1	135,773	134,311	270,084
1 — 2	130,865	129,763	260,628
2 — 3	126,089	125,237	251,326
3 — 4	124,382	122,889	247,271
4 — 5	117,895	117,813	235,708
5 — 6	114,423	113,637	228,060
6 — 7	111,622	112,243	223,865
7 — 8	106,961	107,063	214,024
8 — 9	102,270	103,651	205,921
9 —10	98,713	100,927	199,640
	1,168,993	1,167,534	2,336,527

2813. Looking

Chairman—continued.

2813. Looking at that table taking the number of children insured at various ages under 10 years of age, it would appear that the number of children under the age of one (if I am not mistaken) is the largest number, there being 270,000 policies on children under one year of age?—I believe that is according to the population; there are more children living under the age of one than between one and two years, whatever the cause may be.

2814. That is the fact, is it not, that the largest number of policies in your list is on children under the age of one year?—Yes.

Earl of *Selborne*.

2815. And the number diminishes as you get on, year by year?—Yes; that would follow the population.

Chairman.

2816. The number of policies regularly drop from year to year?—Exactly.

2817. Do I understand you to say that the population diminishes in the same ratio?—I think you will find that the diminution in the population is very similar, but not exactly in the same ratio, probably.

2818. What I mean is, we are generally told that the rate of mortality of children is very high in their earlier years, and that up to a certain age child mortality is greater than adult mortality; you will tell me if I am wrong?—That is so.

2819. And the chances of longevity increase as the child gets older?—The chances of longevity increase after the age of seven.

2820. These two statements would be correct, would they not; first of all, the mortality of childhood is greater in the earlier than in the later years of childhood?—It is.

2821. I think the percentage of children dying under one year old is something like 48 per cent.?—I have the printed statistics showing our mortality for each year, if the Committee would desire to see them.

2822. It is also the case, is it not, that infant mortality within these years of childhood is greater in proportion than adult mortality?—It is.

2823. Then it would not be quite correct to say, would it, that these successive falls in the number of children insured exactly correspond to the diminution in the total population?—I have here a table of the census returns for England and Wales, and if you will look at that table, you will find it follows very much the course of these figures.

Lord *Kinnaird*.

2824. Before we leave the table, may I ask why does not the total of 2,336,527 at the bottom of the table agree with the total of 2,099,369 at the top?—The total at the top is for England and Wales; and in the other total at the bottom we were obliged to include all assurances in the United Kingdom, because we cannot give the figures for each age from our own books as regards England and Wales separately.

(142.)

Chairman.

2825. You are subject to Section 28 of the Friendly Societies Act, are you not, for all of what you call industrial insurance business?—For infantile insurances only.

2826. The Friendly Societies Act repealed the Act of George III., which forbade all insurances except where an insurable interest could be shown, as regards insurances under the Friendly Societies Act?—It did.

2927. In so doing it conferred upon the working classes, did it not, a very great privilege and boon; or what they regard as a very great privilege and boon?—Yes.

2828. In that respect the working classes have an advantage over those who are not in their class or order of life; because those who are not working men cannot insure a child's life at all, unless they have an insurable interest?—It is so for everyone.

2829. That is to say, there was a valuable privilege conferred upon the working classes by this Friendly Societies Act, which those who are commonly called their betters, that is, those in another class of life, do not possess?—Yes; I should like to add, that I believe in all mutual societies they had that privilege before, because they were made members.

2830. The Friendly Societies Act confirmed and finally settled that privilege?—It did.

2831. You speak in the notes of your evidence which have been furnished to me of an infantile table, and regulations for infantile assurance; what are we to understand by that?—I thought your Lordships would like to have a copy of our existing tables, and the regulations under which the infantile business is transacted; the table is on the form I am just about to give you.

2832. The table shows the scale of payments?—Yes.

2833. As regards this scale of payments you take a premium payment of 1 *d.* weekly?—We do.

2834. Am I right in saying that you do not accept more?—Yes; it is printed at the top of the table, "No higher premium will be taken."

2835. According to this scale a child aged, we will say, two years on its next birthday, that is, a child between the age of one and two, may be insured, and the parents will get, if it dies at the end of six calendar months, the sum of 3 *l.*?—In the case of a child aged two next birthday they will have 3 *l.* if it died at the end of six calendar months.

2836. Then for that the parent would have paid the sum of how much in weekly payments?—Two shillings and twopence.

2837. Then for the sum of 2 *s.* 2 *d.*, spread over six calendar months, the death of that child would bring in a sum of 3 *l.*?—Yes.

2838. Assuming for the moment that the child was also insured in another society for the same amount, then for the payment of 4 *s.* 4 *d.*, spread over six months, the whole sum accruing to the parent on the death of the child would be 6 *l.*?—£.6 at death.

2839. For 4 *s.* 4 *d.*, then, a parent might get 6 *l.* at death, from which would have to be deducted

S   ducted

Chairman—continued.

ducted funeral expenses, medical attendance, and so on ?—Yes.

2840. But in the case of a disreputable parent, who simply wished to profit by the child's death, we may fairly take it for granted that the parent would not be likely to expend much either upon medical attendance or the funeral ?—Probably not in such a case.

2841. In such a case the amount of profit to an ill-disposed parent, upon the death of a child of between one and two years of age, would very much exceed all the expenses, of the funeral, and of medical attendance?—For such a parent, yes.

2842. Can you tell us what is the average amount for which parents do insure children's lives under five years of age in your society ?—£. 2. 13. is the average amount we paid last year upon all infantile assurances.

2843. That being the average amount which thrifty and respectable parents pay, the amount of the premium being small, may we not fairly assume that that average payment represents all death expenses?—I think you may take it so.

2844. Then anything over that which the law might allow would practically be unnecessary ; I mean as regards the funeral expenses ?—The 2 *l.* 13 *s.* probably would not cover mourning and many other incidental expenses; the 2 *l.* 13*s.*, I take it, would be expended upon the actual funeral.

2845. You think so ?—I think so.

2846. At all events parents do not insure for more than that as a rule ?—That is the average amount we have paid.

2847. Therefore, if the amount obtainable upon the death of a child, which is now either 6 *l.* or

Chairman—continued.

10 *L*, were reduced to something like what is the average amount the parents insure their children for, there would be practically no hardships upon the parent; he would still be practically as well off as he is now ?—He would.

2848. Therefore a reduced scale of premium, provided it did not fall below what the parents now insure for on the average, would be practically no hardship?—It is so; I have a graduated scale here.

2849. I am aware of that; I will ask you for that presently; I am merely at the moment wanting to bring out that the allowance by law of 6 *l.* for a child under five years of age, and 10 *l.* for a child who may be, we will say, five years and six months, is unnecessarily large; a parent would not surely require 10 *l.* in such a case, seeing that on the average they do not insure for more than 3 *l.* ?—Every parent would not require it, but in some cases it might be necessary.

2850. I mean in the majority of cases; it is clear, is it not, that even supposing that 6 *l.* would be the sum required for the death expenses of a child of five years old, 10 *l.* is unnecessarily large for the death expenses of a child only six months over the five years ?—I may say that in fact one-third of our working classes take our table and consider it sufficient.

2851. Therefore, if there were such a reduction in the limit as would bring down the amount obtainable on death to that sum which the working classes now obtain on the average, they would be in no different position on the average from what they are in now ?—They would be in no different position in some respects.

2852. Will you put in that table ?—Yes.

[*The same is handed in, and is as follows :—*]

TABLE C.—Whole Life Assurance (*Infantile*).—Sums payable for a Premium of ONE PENNY Weekly.   No higher Premium will be taken.

Age next Birth-day.	Amount payable if the Child should Die after the Policy has been issued for											
	Three Calendar Months.	Six Calendar Months.	One Year.	Two Years.	Three Years.	Four Years.	Five Years.	Six Years.	Seven Years.	Eight Years.	Nine Years.	Ten Years.
	£. s.	£. s.	£. s.	£. s.	£. s.	£. s.	£. s.	£. s.	£. s.	£. s.	£. s.	£. s.
1	1 10	2 10	3 –	3 10	4 –	4 10	5 –	6 –	7 –	8 –	9 –	10 –
2	1 15	3 –	3 10	4 –	4 10	5 –	6 –	7 –	8 –	9 –	10 –	
3	2 –	3 10	4 –	4 10	5 –	6 –	7 –	8 –	9 –	10 –		
4	2 5	4 –	4 10	5 –	6 –	7 –	8 –	9 –	10 –			
5	2 10	4 10	5 –	6 –	7 –	8 –	9 –	10 –				
6	3 –	5 –	6 –	7 –	8 –	9 –	10 –					
7	3 10	5 –	7 –	8 –	9 –	10 –						
8	4 –	5 –	8 –	9 –	10 –							
9	4 10	5 –	9 –	10 0								
10	5 –	5 –	10 –									

If the child should die within three calendar months from date of policy no amount will be payable.

Chairman—continued.

2853. I think you have also a form of proposal which you wish to put in ?—Before putting in the form of proposal I should like to state that we have always construed the Friendly Societies Act to mean that parents, if alive, are the only persons who can insure. But that reading, I am afraid, is not general; and no penalty is incurred under the Act by non-relatives insuring a child's life. (For form of proposal, *see* Appendix).

2854. You think that is a defect in the Friendly Societies Act ?—I do; I think it should be penal for any person to insure a child who is not the parent, or the personal representative of the parent.

2855. Still more so, if the person is in charge of the child is not a relation ?—I should say it would be better for the insurance not to be effected then.

2856. You decidedly think that that part, at least, of the Friendly Societies Act is a defect, and needs amendment ?—I do; and I made the same suggestion to the House of Commons Committee last year. I may say that the proposed Bill permits any person to insure the lives of other people's children, which the present law forbids. The new Bill, therefore, is not so strong as the present law.

2857. That would be a purely accidental defect in the Bill, and would be certainly remedied; that could not possibly be the intention of the Bill; at any rate, that is a point in which you think the proposed Bill needs amendment in the direction of greater stringency ?—Yes.

2858. In fact, you think my Bill is too indulgent in that respect ?—I think your Bill creates in one or two respects a somewhat dangerous variation in legislation.

2859. You think it errs in point of leniency ?—In that respect.

2860. Will you put in regulations for infantile insurance, and the form of infantile proposal ?—Yes.

2861. That form of proposal is the basis of the policy ?—It is.

2862. A number of questions are put here on the back of the form of proposal, which the Committee will have before them, and I therefore need not go into them; whose duty is it to ask all these questions ?—It is the agent's duty.

2863. By the agent, do you mean the collector ?—We call him the agent; the term "collector" is hardly known with us.

2864. You are aware that in some societies there is a distinction between collectors and agents ?—Yes.

2865. In your company it is not so ?—No; the men who act for us are agents, and receive their appointment and are controlled direct from the chief office.

2866. Now, as regards these agents who obtain for you these proposals, there are, I presume, a very great many of them ?—Yes.

2867. Can you tell me how they are paid ?—They are paid a salary based on a commission, averaging from 17½ per cent. to 20 per cent. for collecting.

2868. For collecting alone ?—For collecting alone.

2869. Is that percentage based on the amount

(142.)

Chairman—continued.

of the weekly premiums they receive ?—On the amount of the premiums actually collected.

2870. I think you saw in your tables that it is something like 5 d. on 2 s. 6 d., a little over 16 per cent.; you put it at 17½ per cent ?—Seventeen and a-half per cent.

2871. In addition to the 17½ per cent. upon the moneys received, do not your agents receive a bonus upon every new case ?—They do.

2872. How much is that ?—That is 4 d. for a penny case; that is to say, it would be four times the premium; and, in addition to that, we pay them ten times the premium, which amount they have to repay us directly the policy has lapsed; our object being to prevent a lapse of the policy.

2873. The total amount you say that your agents receive is very little under what I observe Mr. Lyulph Stanley calculates it at, namely, 30 per cent.; you put yours at 25 per cent., I understand ?—Seventeen and a-half per cent., and the amount of the additional premium.

2874. Which additional premium would run it up considerably, I presume ?—It would only amount to 30 per cent. upon the first year's premium; not afterwards.

2875. It would amount to 30 per cent. upon the first year's premium, you think ?—Probably it would.

2876. It is clear that the agents have a very strong pecuniary interest in increasing the number of policies ?—They have a pecuniary interest.

2877. And a very considerable pecuniary interest ?—Yes, you may take it that they have a strong pecuniary interest.

2878. Therefore, to put it conversely, it is not their interest to be too exacting as to all these questions that it is their duty to put ?—Yes, it is to their interest; because we are frequently obliged to have an inspection in the district, and if we find one of our agents tripping in this way he loses a good position with us.

2879. Of course in that sense it is to their interest; but I am speaking of their pecuniary interest at the moment, and not of the risk they may run; the pecuniary interest to them is greater the larger the number of cases they can get ?—It is.

2880. Has your attention been drawn to an expression of opinion upon this point of agents by the House of Commons Committee of last year ?—Yes.

2881. I will read to you a passage from their Report: "The competition between these societies" (that is, the collecting societies and the friendly societies) "is very acute, and seems to have conduced to some dangers against which, in the interest of the general public as well as of the members, additional safeguards are required, or at least the existing Acts should be administered with greater stringency." Then the Committee go on to say: "Collectors paid by commission are naturally anxious to make as much profit from their business as possible; they are liable to temptation to be unscrupulous as to the methods by which this end is attained; it is, therefore, no matter for surprise to find that assurances for sums at death are effected which are

s 2   not

Chairman—continued.

not recognised by the Friendly Societies Acts, and are otherwise distinctly opposed to the law." That opinion of the House of Commons Committee was come to, I presume, after hearing your own evidence and that of the representatives of other societies?—I believe that does not refer to infantile assurance. I think the reference to the necessity of an amendment of the Act related to the question of insurable interest. It is a question I brought before the Committee myself with regard to the assignment of policies. Policies were too freely assigned, and it was desirable some alteration of the law should be made.

2882. I am not referring at this particular moment to cases of one kind and another in which collectors may have shown themselves unscrupulous, but simply to the fact that, in the opinion of the Committee of the House of Commons, collectors paid by commission are exposed to great temptation and have shown themselves unscrupulous. That would apply, I presume, to all assurances?—That would apply to all assurances.

2883. Infantile as well as adult?—Yes.

2884. The Report says that the collectors are liable to temptation to be unscrupulous, and they are accused by the Committee of the House of Commons of being sometimes, at least, unscrupulous?—There are good and bad agents, no doubt.

2885. Of course we may take that for granted. It would appear that your society depends upon these agents for their information about the cases and for the answers given in the proposals; you are, therefore, very much at the mercy of your agents, subject always to your power of dismissing them if you catch them; is not that so?—It is so.

2886. To take an illustration from a case of which you may have seen an account in the paper yesterday, where the agent of the Victoria Legal Friendly Society deliberately broke one of the rules as to the parent being the only person who could insure, and wilfully and knowingly insured a child where the person insuring was not a parent; the name of the child was M'Kay. I dare say you saw an account of the case?—I did.

2887. I take that as one case only, and it goes to show what the Committee of the House of Commons here says, that the agents are not to be altogether depended upon, and, as you have said, you are greatly dependent upon the agents, and must necessarily be so?—There is a great difference between the Liverpool Victoria Legal Friendly Society and the Prudential as to the way in which they manage the agents.

2888. I merely point out that the agent in that way is tempted to be unscrupulous and might be sometimes unscrupulous?—He is.

2889. Would you have any objection to any restriction or check which made it penal for an agent so to deal with the society he represents and with the insurer?—Taking this very case you have mentioned with regard to insuring baby-farming cases, I should like the law to make it penal against the agent, and against the proposer, and against the society, who knowingly accepted such a proposal.

Chairman—continued.

2890. In every case of a proposal that is illegal, do I understand that you would have all the parties engaging it, the parents or agents, or (as regards other societies) the collectors, made subject to severe legal penalties?—I should very much like to see a change in the law in that respect.

2891. That would be a change directly in the interests of the society you represent?—It would.

2892. You would not object to any such change?—No.

2893. I am afraid you will not answer my next question in the affirmative; would you agree to the proposal that, in order to prevent carelessness on the part of a society or its agents, and to quicken their zeal in catching up or looking after its agents, the society should be subject to a monetary payment in case it granted such a policy?—I should undoubtedly answer your question in the affirmative, understanding you to mean if they knowingly granted such a policy. We are quite prepared to do that.

2894. Of course the word "knowingly" would be put into any provision of that sort. If I gather rightly, as regards the matter of agents and policies effected by agents, you would be in favour of severe penal restrictions on the agent and parent engaged in any wrong transaction of that sort, and also in favour of a pecuniary payment attaching to the society which granted the policy so carelessly obtained?—I should be very glad indeed to see such a law.

2895. You do not object to that part of my Bill?—No. With regard to the alleged carelessness on the part of the companies, I could have brought samples of proposals that have been rejected by us. I have not taken them out recently but two or three years ago, and I have sufficient to fill one side of this room. We have rejected people because they are already insured; we have rejected them because of their indifferent health; we reject them, under a certain age, because they are illegitimate; and we reject them also when they are in unhealthy districts. We have printed lists of proscribed districts in large towns, and in those districts we do not take insurances at all.

2896. That is to say, that is the rule of the society?—Yes; and we see that it is observed, because we check the address in every proposal that comes up from those towns.

2897. It has been given in evidence that a great many disreputable people living in low-class neighbourhoods do succeed in insuring their children; that has been given very largely in evidence?—They do.

2898. Many of the very disreputable class, and many who are living under unhealthy conditions, do insure their children; are we to understand that none of those are insured in your society?—I should say not knowingly.

2899. The evidence, you may take it from me, is very extensive to the effect that a very considerable number of disreputable people, living vicious lives, and living under very unhealthy conditions, do succeed in getting their children insured?—Yes, I have no doubt they do.

2900. Therefore either such children are not insured

16 *July* 1890.]   Mr. DEWEY.   [*Continued.*

*Chairman—*continued.

insured in your society, but in other societies, or else those of them who are insured in your society are insured either through the carelessness or corruption of your agents, or from want of detection on your part?—That is so.

2901. Therefore all your checks, though they may be excellent so far as they go, do not succeed in preventing these improper insurances being effected?—I believe they do.

2902. Entirely?—Almost entirely.

2903. There have been a considerable number of cases in which there was evidence that a very low class of people succeeded in insuring their children?—I should like to say our agents are drawn from all classes. They are men who are fairly educated and able to keep accounts. Our agents collect each year more than four millions of money. Their accounts are always rendered most accurately. I have had acquaintance with a large number of them now for many years, and I hardly think that the charges which have been freel made against them are warranted by the facts.

2904. This charge I quoted to you was made by the Committee of the House of Commons, which was very friendly disposed to insurance in general, and on which there were several well-known Members representing the working classes themselves?—Quite so; but I do not want all to be tarred with the same brush, so to speak.

2905. But they did give you a little tar all the same, did they not?—They included us in that way.

2906. I see in your notes you speak of your system of paying infantile claims; what do you mean by that?—We only pay claims to the parents or the personal representatives of the parents, and we only pay on the production of the registrar's certificate under Section 28 of the Friendly Societies Act, and the amount authorised on that certificate never has been exceeded by the company in any case.

2907. Now with regard to these registrars' certificates, you are of course familiar with the form that the registrar's certificate must take?—I am.

2908. He must certify that there has been a doctor's certificate?—Either a doctor's certificate, or that an inquest has been held, or he must be satisfied that there has been a death.

2909. It is the last word or two of the requirement in the Friendly Societies Act about the registrar that I wanted to direct your attention to; he must have the verdict of a coroner's inquest, a doctor's certificate, or some other satisfactory evidence; to whom is that evidence to be satisfactory? It is to the registrar, I presume?—Yes.

2910. Then the registrar is allowed to go beyond or dispense with the doctor's certificate or the coroner's inquest, if there is what he thinks or chooses to say is satisfactory evidence to him?—I believe it is so.

2911. The registrar receives a fee for every such certificate, does he not?—He does.

2912. It is not, then, his interest to be too particular or to refuse a certificate?—I should

(142.)

*Chairman—*continued.

not like to say that every one who receives a fee thinks only of getting his fee.

2913. I do not say for a moment it would be so; I am not asking what they do, but what they may be tempted to do. It is not the registrar's pecuniary interest to be too particular?—The amount is very small, it is about a shilling. It is hardly a sufficient temptation to a man to do wrong.

2914. At all events the granting of the certificate depends upon his judgment?—Yes; but I do not think there has been such a case reported anywhere.

2915. Do you see any objection to striking out those last words as giving too great a latitude to registrars, so that the result would be that they could never give a certificate except on the strength of a doctor's certificate, or of an inquest; would not that be an additional protection to your society?—I think in some country districts it would be felt as a very great hardship, for the doctor cannot give a certificate unless he has seen the child. In the event of any sudden illness, the doctor does give his report now, but then he would be unable to do so, and an inquest would follow as a matter of course.

2916. Do not you think that a doctor's certificate and a coroner's inquest would be sufficient guides to the registrar, without leaving him what may be at least a dangerous discretion of satisfying himself in some other way, which might be a very insufficient way, as to the cause of death?—I should hardly like to offer an opinion upon that.

2917. If such a restriction were passed it would not be against the interests of your society?—We do not receive doctors' certificates at all.

2918. I am aware of that; but as regards the registrar's certificate it would be, I presume, rather a help than a hurt to your society if he were not allowed to exercise this very wide discretion?—I can hardly see how it is to be worked.

2919. But supposing it could be worked, you would not object to it?—No, we should not object. I should like to say in regard to this matter, that I do think it is most important that there should only be one insurance upon a life. The Committee of the House of Commons strongly recommended that in this very Report. I understand that in your Lordship's Bill, if you will pardon my saying so, you anticipate there being more than one insurance. I would suggest that in any legislation there should be one insurance only allowed; and that one insurance will never come to the statutory account at all, because no company or society could afford to give up to the present limit or even up to the limit in your Lordship's Bill for a penny a week; and therefore that system of a single insurance would keep the amount down to what you yourself would recommend.

2920. That is a recommendation which has been made, and is, I think, about to be made to day, by representatives of other societies than yours, and it seems to me to be a very important one?—

B 3

Chairman—continued.

one ?—That is the recommendation I made to the Committee last year.

2921. Assuming, as I think we should all do, the value of the suggestion, how would you enforce it; how would you obtain proof that a child under 10 years had not been insured in any other society?—It could be easily done by forbidding the registrar to give more than one certificate. A registrar is not infallible, and I have had instances, and I have two or three with me, where registrars have certified to us more than the amount now required. We have had communications with registrars, and some were not even aware of the limit. If it was very plainly put to them that they were only to give one certificate, I think it could be worked.

2922. Would you make it a misdemeanour on the part of a parent if he were to insure a child in a second company, knowingly after the publication of a law on the subject. That is a suggestion which has been made to me by the representative of an insurance company, that not only should a second insurance not be allowed, but that any parent effecting a second insurance on a life should be held guilty of a misdemeanour?—I think forbidding the registrar to give more than one certificate would be the best way.

2923. You see no objection to a second insurance being forbidden ?—I see no objection.

2924. Would you enforce your requisition upon the registrar by payment or fine?—I should have a fine inflicted if he issued more than one certificate.

2925. Would you heavily fine him if he gave more than one certificate?—We are fined if we pay more than we are allowed, and therefore, I think he should be fined if he gave more than one certificate.

2926. A sharp fine upon the registrar in such cases, and making it a misdemeanour on the parent, are the two things you would approve of?—I should approve of anything to carry out that suggestion of only one insurance.

2927. Those checks, at any rate, you do approve of?—Yes.

2928. Now, as regards the limit of benefit in infantile assurance, will you explain that?—The limit of benefit is that we do not pay for three months after the policy has been in existence. Local clubs, on the other hand, as a rule, pay without any limit.

2929. I understand you to refer to what is called coming into benefit?—Yes.

2930. The child does not come into benefit till after three months?—Quite so.

2931. Those cases in which a child has not come into benefit in consequence of the non-payment of premium are what you call lapses, I presume?—They would be strictly; but there are cases where representations are made to us, and we do make a present of the premiums paid, or grant something to the parents if the cause of death is a satisfactory one; but in the event of death from marasmus, for instance, we should not do so.

2932. Those are what you call grants of grace? —Yes.

2933. Practically, as a general rule, you give

Chairman—continued.

nothing unless the child has been in benefit for three months?—Quite so.

2934. When the parent fails to pay the premium, the policy lapses?—The policy lapses.

2935. In the case of a policy lapsing, do you take any pains to trace sufficiently the history of the child to know what becomes of it?—When a policy has lapsed we have notice of it, and it comes off our register.

2936. But have you any power of knowing whether the child dies soon or immediately after? —Not after the policy has lapsed.

2937. Those lapses do not appear upon your books as deaths, but only as lapses?—They pass off our books directly the policy has lapsed.

2938. Then, as I said, they do not appear on the books as so many deaths?—No.

2939. Only as so many lapses?—As so many lapses.

2940. Are you able to tell the Committee what the proportion of lapses is to the rest of your infantile insurances; how many cases of lapse have you during the year?—About one-third, probably, of the first year would lapse. It depends entirely upon the length and duration of the policies. Of policies 10 years in force not 5 per. cent would lapse.

2941. The longer a policy lasts the less tendency there is to lapse; that is obvious, because the parent has more to lose in the way of premiums?—Yes.

2942. Within the first year you say that one-third of the cases are lapses?—One-third are lapses.

2943. In that case, the company has received the premium, and (I do not put at all as an objection) incurs no liability?—It incurs liability so long as the policy is running.

2944. But I mean when the policy lapses?— When the policy lapses the liability ceases.

2945. Then all the weekly pennies received by the company in the meanwhile are so much clear gain?—No. I hope I may be allowed to deny in the most emphatic manner that there is any profit attaching to lapses on infantile insurance. In order to give your Lordships trustworthy information upon this subject, which I know has been frequently alluded to in this room, I have submitted a case to four leading actuaries, and as their opinion is very short, I would ask your Lordships just to allow me to read it. The case which was submitted was this: "The Prudential Assurance Company has for several years granted a large number of assurances on the lives of children under 10 years of age, and had in force on the 31st December 1889, 2,336,527 of such assurances. It has been frequently stated, and is apparently believed in many quarters, that the company derives a large profit from the number of these policies that are allowed to lapse. A prospectus showing the terms upon which these assurances are granted is sent herewith, together with a copy of the last valuation returns to the Board of Trade. Your opinion is requested as to whether the lapsing of these policies is a source of profit to the company, or the reverse." The opinion is as follows: "We have examined the terms and conditions upon which assurances

on

16 *July* 1890.]　　　　　　　　Mr. DEWEY.　　　　　　　　[*Continued.*

Chairman—continued.

on the live of children are granted by the Prudential Assurance Company. The peculiarity of the mortality among children is that it is greatest during the first year of life, diminishing afterwards for some years. Assurances on the lives of children therefore, unlike those on the lives of adults, are decreasing risks, and must be regarded as assurances for short terms, and the risk estimated in the same way as in marine, fire, or accident assurances. No reserve is needed for the liability under children's assurances; the weekly premiums provide for the week's claims and expenses, and if there be any surplus after these latter have been paid, such surplus is profit; and as the amount of this profit increases with the number of the assurances, it is to the interest of the company that policies should not lapse. We are therefore clearly of opinion that the lapsing of these policies is a cause of loss and not of gain to the company." That is signed by Mr. Bailey, the actuary of the London Assurance Corporation, who has been one of the Presidents of the Institute of Acutaries; by T. E. Young, actuary to the Commercial Union Assurance Company, who is now a Vice President of the Institute of Actuaries; by Mr. Augustus Hendriks, actuary to the Liverpool and London and Globe Assurance Company, who is also a Vice President of the Institute of Actuaries; and by Mr. Ralph P. Hardy, who is a well known actuary.

2946. I think you have something to say about the Registrar General's return as compared with the company's mortality return?—I should like the Committee to refer to the Registrar General's 51st Annual Report (which is the last one published), where he quotes the figures of infantile mortality. On page 44 will be found the annual death-rate per 1,000 of children under five years of age, and between 5 and 10; it will be seen that although the insurance of infants is much more general amongst the working classes than it was formerly, yet the death-rate among infants has improved in greater proportion than among the other groups of ages.

2947. Since when?—On this table I have taken from 1841 to 1850, and the mortality under five was 71 per 1,000 against 59 per 1,000 for the last five years published, that is, from 1881 to 1885. It will be seen from the Registrar General's Returns (of which we have the full volume here if it is required), that infant life has improved 15 per cent., while adult life during the same period has only improved 10 per cent. The figures are as follows:

Period.	Group of Ages, 0–5.		Group of Ages, 5–10.	
	Males.	Females.	Males.	Females.
1841–1850	71·2	61·1	9·2	8·9
1881–1885	59·6	50·5	5·8	5·6

Chairman—continued.

This Report also states that the death-rate has increased from premature birth, for instance, in infantile mortality, while the death-rate from tubercular diseases, which includes marasmus, has diminished. Then I would also submit the following extracts from a paper read before the Statistical Society by Mr. Noel Humphreys, of the Registrar General's Office, showing how the mortality is gradually diminishing under the age of 10, while, of course, insurance has been rife among infants:—

MALES.

Age.	Annual Mortality at each Year of Age.	
	English Life Table (founded on Census Returns, 1841–51).	Corrected for Years 1876–80.
0	·18326	·17046
1	·06680	·06213
2	·03624	·03371
3	·02416	·02247
4	·01799	·01673
5	·01369	·00959
6	·01088	·00762
7	·00920	·00644
8	·00767	·00537
9	·00649	·00455

FEMALES.

Age.	Annual Mortality at each Year of Age.	
	English Life Table (founded on Census Returns, 1841–51).	Corrected for Years 1876–80.
0	·14749	·13536
1	·06436	.05907
2	·03603	·03307
3	·02450	·02249
4	·01785	·01638
5	·01337	·00895
6	·01061	·00711
7	·00912	·00611
8	·00771	·00516
9	·00664	·00445

Chairman—continued.

The Prudential rate is obtained from the experience of ten years, 1879–88. The number of policies passing under observation during that period was 9,236,920.

Ages.	Annual Rate of Mortality per 1000.		
	Prudential.	Dr. Farr's English Life Table, No. 3. (From Census Returns).	Carlisle Table.
*0–1	99·46	165·59	153·90
1–2	63·24	65·59	80·61
2–3	32·39	36·14	64·92
3–4	18·62	24·33	37·94
4–5	13·48	17·92	28·72
5–6	10·03	13·53	17·80
6–7	7·61	10·75	12·28
7–8	5·72	9·16	8·79
8–9	4·89	7·69	6·58
9–10	4·28	6·57	5·08

* For the first year after birth the Prudential figures present a too favourable comparison, from the fact of the company having no experience for the first two weeks of life. There are no means of making an absolutely accurate comparison, but eliminating the first month's deaths from Dr. Farr's English Life Table (a severe comparison), the rate is reduced from 165 per 1,000 to 108, being still 9 per 1,000 in excess of the Prudential experience.

The mortality rate of the Prudential is obtained by us from a series of books which we have kept now for many years. I have the books here, if your Lordships would like to see the method upon which they have been worked; they have been worked by our actuary, Mr. Schooling, and I am sure his system would be confirmed by any actuary in London.

2948. I do not propose to dispute that?—We take off from the number at risk every policy as it has lapsed, and, therefore, in calculating our mortality we do not disregard the lapses; every policy as it lapses comes off from the number at risk as these tables will show.

2949. Your point, as I understand, is that infant mortality among insured children is very much below; I think you put as much as 7 per cent. below the general rate of infant mortality? —Not so much as that; one per cent. was the difference between the mortality of the country in 1850 and now; in our rate of mortality for chil-

Chairman—continued.

dren between one and two years of age there is simply a difference of two per thousand.

2950. You mean a difference of two per thousand in your favour?—Yes; it is not very much, but it is in our favour.

2951. You claim that the ratio of mortality shows something in favour of your society to the amount of two per thousand as against the general rate?—At the ages of from one to two; it varies at different ages.

2952. That is the age at which the mortality is highest?—Yes.

2953. You would admit, I presume, being an actuary, that any calculation of two sets of life statistics must be taken over equal areas and under equal conditions?—Yes.

2954. Now as regards the area of life from which these two sets of statistics are taken, I think you stated in the first place that you do not accept illegitimate children?— We do not accept them, as a rule, under three years of age.

2955. We are now speaking of children under two years?—Yes.

2956. Within the years we are referring to you accept no illegitimate children?—That is so.

2957. You also, I presume, accept only the children of those whom your agent may think likely to be able to pay these weekly payments?—Yes.

2958. You would not encourage your agents to take, hap-hazard, everybody who offers?—No doubt the selection is in favour of the company.

2959. I want to bring out the extent of it; that selection is also in favour of the company?—Yes.

2960. Then again the Registrar General's Returns are credited with the death of every child who may have died in a few hours or moments after its birth?—Yes.

2961. Those would appear in the Registrar General's Returns and not in yours?—Those would be at age 0.

2962. We all know that the mortality of children in the very early days of their life is a very much greater proportion than in the later days? Yes.

2963. And that the ratio of mortality decreases the longer a child lives?—It is so.

2964. Therefore all, or the majority, of those cases of death that occurred in that most unfavourable period for child life would appear upon the Registrar General's Returns and not on yours?—I quoted the age of 1 to 2 intentionally, because at the ages of 1 to 2 the cases in the Registrar General's Returns would compare with ours; at age 0 they would not compare; but at the ages of 1 to 2, we take it that they do compare.

2965. There are, of course, a great many parents who are so miserably poor that they cannot even pay a penny a week, and cannot assure at all; those cases would not appear among your deaths?—No.

2966. The case of the death of those children would appear upon the Registrar General's Returns?—Yes.

2967. Those extremely poor people who are hardly able to keep body and soul together, the poor children starving, and living under unhealthy

Chairman—continued.

healthy conditions, are a class of persons among whom you would expect a considerable rate of infant mortality ; is not that so ?—That would be so.

2968. All those cases would go to the credit of the Registrar General's Returns and not to yours ? —Yes.

2969. So far as they go, again your returns are vitiated ?—Yes.

2970. On the Registrar General's list would also appear all the children dying in union work-houses, who presumably are not insured ?—Yes.

2971. Is it not clear, that comparing his general area, and the area from which you draw your cases, the statistics are not taken over equal areas ?—Not perfectly equal.

2972. I should say it very imperfectly ; but at all events you admit that the statistics are not taken over equal areas ?—Against that there is something to be said on the other side ; all the upper and middle classes are included in the Registrar General's Return ; and the mortality we know is heavier among the working classes than among the upper classes.

2973. Making allowance for all that, you admit the area is not equal ?—It is not equal.

2974. The margin of difference between the Registrar General's figures and yours is very small, namely, only two per thousand ?—It is.

2975. Now, let us take the case of the condi-tions of life ; it has been given in evidence by nearly every witness here, and I for my part fully believe it, that the very great majority of the working classes are not only persons who would not abuse their privileges of insurance, but also, generally speaking the great mass of insurers are thrifty people of the better class ; otherwise they would not insure ?—It is so.

2976. Is it not clear that such a parent being thrifty and careful and affectionate would take care of his child ?—Yes.

2977. That would go to show, would it not, that taking the ground that is often put forward by insurance societies, namely, that it is the respectable and thrifty parents who insure, on that very ground those lives of yours are to a certain extent what you would call picked lives ? —Yes, we may take it they are selected lives.

2978. Then are not your statistics vitiated in two important respects : firstly, that the area from which they are taken is not equal, and secondly, that the conditions of life are not the same ; do not you think that those two facts very considerably vitiate the force of your argument from the statistics ?—I think your Lordship is right as to the first ; but the conditions of life I think would tell the other way, because our cases come from the lower three-quarters of the popu-lation, and in that respect the Registrar General would be in a much better position.

2979. At all events those statistics are liable to very considerable discount, and you are aware that the House of Commons, before whom you put the statistics, declared that they did not attach much importance to the statistics on either side ?—Yes, I am aware of that.

2980. You have something to say as regards local societies, I understand ?—It has been stated, I think, in evidence, that local societies

(142.)

Chairman—continued.

are managed in a better manner than companies. I should like to draw your Lordship's attention to the last Report of the Chief Registrar of Friendly Societies referring to local societies. By that term, I mean local societies entirely distinct from affiliated societies, like the Foresters and the Odd Fellows. I mean simply local clubs like the Leek Burial and the Hulme Burial Society. It will be seen here that the total number of valuations of which particulars are given is, 3,472 of local clubs.

2981. Do all those refer to children ?—I do not suppose that the clubs confine their operations to children. There are 2,705 out of the 3,472, or nearly 80 per cent., which show a total deficiency of three millions. Therefore, 80 per cent. of the local clubs are declared by the Chief Registrar to be insolvent at the present time. The question of statistics was referred to by Dr. Ritchie, from the Leek Burial Society. He spoke about the rate of mortality falling from 150, I think, to 109 during the year 1877. He attributed that to the cessation of infantile assurance business ; but it will be seen from the Registrar General's Return that in the year 1877 the infantile death-rate was lower all over the country than it had ever been before, the rate per 1,000 being 63·9 for males and 53 for females ; and in 1878 the rates all increased again very largely. That, I think, would account, or partly account, for the diminu-tion in the town of Leek, of which Dr. Ritchie spoke.

2982. I think you say that there are four mil-lions of policies issued for children ?—Yes.

2983. You are a better statistician than I am ; could you give me any idea of what number of deaths would be required to raise the per-centage of death among four million persons by 1 per cent. ; it would be a very large amount, would it not ?—It would be a considerable number.

2984. I have calculated that to raise it 1 per cent. on one and-a-half millions (supposing that to be the amount), would require 15,000 deaths ; that, I think, you will find to be correct ?—Yes.

2985. Taking the number as four millions, it would be much more than that ?—Yes.

2986. Taking the case figure, which put in the House of Lords, of one in every 1,000 children being done away with every year, and taking the same number of insurances at one and a-half millions, one per thousand upon that would give 1,500 who received foul play in the course of the year ?—On your figures it would be so.

2987. That would appear in your returns as only one per thousand, or 00·1, would it not ? —Yes.

2988. One thousand five hundred children might be annually done away with out of one and a-half millions, without raising your death-rate more than that fractional decimal ?—It would raise the death-rate one per 1,000.

2989. It would raise it an almost imperceptible amount, which no one but a very skilled actuary would detect the meaning of even upon one and a-half millions, and, of course, on four millions it would require a very much larger amount to raise the death-rate even one per 1,000 ?— Yes.

2990. Therefore, your death-rate might be raised

T

Chairman – continued.

raised by one per 1,000 and till produce a favourable contrast to the Registrar General, and yet there might be 1,500 cases of children done away with as I have described ?—Yes.

2991. It comes to this, that there might be a very large amount of foul play to children, larger than I put it at which would make a difference of a very small decimal in your returns ?—Yes.

2992. Do not you think that goes someway to vitiate all you have been saying about the returns ?—I do not think it upsets the Registrar General's Returns.

2993. It seems to upset yours, does it not ?—It may have interfered with ours to a certain extent.

2994. Have you any further amendments to suggest in the proposed Bill now that the undertakers' clause is gone, and that the one or two omissions which you mentioned have been dealt with ; have you any objection to the rest of the Bill ?—I attach very great importance to one person not being allowed to insure another person's children, because in the Swindon case, for instance, which was mentioned here by Mr. Justice Day, under your Lordships' Bill the insurance could go on just the same and would have been legal, whereas it was an illegal assurance under the present law.

2995. We may take it for granted that it is a mere slip in the Bill ?—Yes.

2996. Do you object to the first clause in the Bill which extends the protected age to 14 ?—I would like to suggest that the age of 12 would be the best age, for this reason : The mortality diminishes gradually from the age of one to the age of 12, and then it turns round and goes up again from age 12 ; that is the turning point in the English life table, Dr. Farr's table.

2997. Are what you have mentioned in fact all your objections to the Bill ?—Yes, I think so, now that the undertakers' clause has gone out.

2998. Have you anything further to say as to the undertakers' clause ?—If your Lordship has omitted that from the Bill I need not refer to it further.

2999. You have something to say as regards baby farming, I understand ?—The Bill, I thought, rather encouraged than discouraged it ; because it left it open for one person to insure the lives of another person's children, and in the Swindon case those baby farmers would have been able to insure under this Bill.

3000. That again comes under the head of this mere slip we have already referred to. I understand you wish to make some remarks upon the evidence already given here ?—Merely as regards cases in which the Prudential has been referred to ; they are only two or three cases. The first case I was going to mention is the Deptford case. I believe your Lordships had a letter put in at the end of the second day's Minutes from Mr. Wood, the Coroner of Deptford, which was put in as showing the evil of child insurance. I am afraid your Lordships have been misled upon that point ; because with regard to the names of the persons mentioned, who are supposed to be all children taking the first name, I find that William Sutton was aged 74 ; the next, Elizabeth Jane Frost, was aged 53 ; and the last case, Sidney Bolton, was aged 11. The

Chairman—continued.

recommendation of the coroner was really with regard to insurable interest, and had nothing whatever to do with child insurance.

3001. Is there anything else you wish to refer to ?—Then the Strand case was also mentioned, and was the only case mentioned, by Dr. Troutbeck. Those children were insured in the Prudential. The house was insured for 600 *l.*, and the two children insured one for 9 *l.* and the other for 5 *l.* That was taken by Dr. Troutbeck as evidence of the evil of child insurance. But that man was tried for arson. His children were burnt, and he was tried for murder as well ; but he was acquitted of murder : and any account of the trial will show that he was convicted simply of arson and not murder. So that child insurance did not come into the case. It was for the 600 *l.* fire insurance, and certainly not for the 14 *l.* child insurance. The other case was a case at Arlsey, and Dr. Pullen Burry gave evidence, and said that the only company he knew doing business at Arlsey was the Prudential. In his evidence he stated that he was constantly called to see moribund children, just in time to get a certificate, where medical aid would have saved their lives. The parents of those children he described as "most profligate, adulterous, drunken, and dirty ; everything is abominable and filthy in those people's places." He said that all them were more or less intemperate. He said " the people used to live together as man and wife and have children, any number of them ; I came across cases in which people had lived together as man and wife and then got married." That statement has roused the utmost indignation in the village, and I have had a letter from the vicar, I have had a letter from the clerk to the School Board, and a letter from the present medical officer, and a letter from the registrar, all calling very serious attention to the statement that has been made. I may say that the vicar states " So far as Arlsey is concerned I do not believe that the children are neglected or allowed to die in order that the insurance money may be claimed. No doubt many mothers do not attend to their children as well as they ought, and there is neglect and mismanagement ; but it is not wilful or done with any ulterior view of benefiting by its possible death, but arises simply from stupidity or ignorance. When a mother does realise that her child is seriously ill I have always found her bestowing all her care upon it, and though her treatment may very likely be not the most judicious, at any any rate it seems to be her best."

3002. That is the opinion of the vicar ?—Yes, I will hand your Lordship the letter. He speaks very strongly about it. Then the School Board officer has written about the illegitimacy of the parish to which the doctor makes very strong allusions. He says : " In August last a census of children in Arlsey was taken for school purposes, 687 were scheduled as being 13 years and under. Of these, 10 I believe are illegitimate, and perhaps five or six more may be so. Of the 10 I have named four belong to one family," and he goes on to say the statements made are very unwarrantable. The registrar has

16 *July* 1890.]   Mr. DEWRY.   [*Continued.*

Chairman—continued.

has also sent me a list of all the cases certified by Dr. Pullen Burry. He certified to 25 cases; 16 of them were uninsured, six were insured, and three we are unable to trace. Even taking those we were unable to trace as insured it would only make nine insured; so that it is not quite the proportion he stated.

3003. There are one or two other questions which I wish to ask. I observe in your directions to your agents that you desire them to be very careful in the matter of certificates, because it is not to the credit of your society that you should dispute a policy?—Yes.

3004. Then, in point of fact, your agents must know that you are not very much disposed to dispute policies; have you disputed many?—. We have disputed them in our time.

3005. Are there many cases in which you have disputed policies?—We do not dispute many; there is no reason for disputing.

3006. Then with regard to additional checks and safeguards; some you have proposed seem to be very valuable; I am very much disposed to affix an age limit to child insurance, and to enact that a child shall not be insured under a certain age, say 12 months; do you, as representing your society, object to that?—No.

3007. You would have no objection to raising the age higher?—No; anything that is required in the interests of public policy we should be willing to fall in with.

3008. You would not object, in the interests of public policy, and the preservation of human life, to raising the age limit?—No.

3009. To what age would you raise it?—I would make it the age put by your Lordship, under the age of one year; because it is impossible to tell whether a child in arms is really healthy or not; and therefore we should not object to have it put at under one year.

3010. You have no medical examination at that age?—Not at that age.

3011. You depend upon the judgment and practised eye of the agent?—Yes.

3012. You would not object to the time of 12 months?—No.

3013. Which would be practically 15 months, because the child would not come into benefit till then?—Yes.

3014. An ill-disposed parent would naturally keep the child alive in order to get the money; he presumably would not kill the child for the love of killing it, but would keep it alive until it got your money; however, you do not object to the age limit I have proposed?—No.

3015. And, as you have said, you do not object to some reduction in the amount of the policy?—No.

3016. Have you any objection to a register of insurance policies being kept which would be open to public inspection?—No, we should not object to that as affecting our interest; but there might be difficulties in carrying it out.

3017. You also said that there should be no second policy on children under the age of 10 years?—Yes.

3018. Should you object to extend it to the age of 14?—No; that would be almost our common practice now.

(142.)

Chairman—continued.

3019. I want to ask you, with regard to another check of very great importance, which has not been mentioned yet; the suggestion is, that where a child is insured by its parent, in the case of a conviction of the parent before a magistrate for wilful neglect or cruelty, that should *ipso facto* void the policy he has effected upon the child's life and so punish him for his cruelty and neglect; that is to say, if the fact of his cruelly treating a child whose life he has insured is proved and a sentence recorded against him, that policy should lapse?—I do not see how it would work, unless the child died.

3020. It would work in this way, that if the parent was convicted and sent to gaol the policy would lapse and he should pay no more premiums?—He might take out another when he came out.

3021. I will come to that in a moment; you see no objection to that in principle?—I do not see, at the present time, any great objection.

3022. I would propose it should *ipso facto* void its policy, and void the policy on every other child the parent had, on the ground that he would have shown himself an unfit person to have charge of a child; I propose to make him incapable of insuring any child in his family, on the simple principle that a parent capable of wilfully ill-treating a child is not a person to be entrusted with the child's life, having regard to the temptation of the money coming in upon the child's death; the check of parental affection would not exist in such a case; therefore, what I would contend would be, that a brutal and depraved parent who was brutally and savagely treating his child is not a fit person to have a policy upon his child's life at all?—I think it would, to a certain extent, depend upon the particular case.

3023. It must depend upon the particular case, and discretion would, of course, be given to the magistrate; the object of this Bill is to prevent crime quite as much as to punish; as the law stands a parent may commit a crime and take the chance of escaping punishment for the sake of the insurance money; but if he knows that culpable neglect will lose him the money the temptation is gone?—He might be fined twice for the offence.

3024. The whole or the larger part of the inducement to commit crime for the sake of the money is gone if the parent knows that if he is found out he will not get the money; otherwise he might take the chance, first, that he may not be found out, and secondly, if he is found and sent to jail, if the child dies he would get the money when he comes out of jail; you see my point?—Yes.

3025. It has been suggested by a working man that, in the case of a coroner and jury having reason to believe there has been foul play or gross cruelty, they should have power to impound the policy, and pay the money to the rates; do you see any objection to that?—It would depend a great deal upon the kind of cruelty that had been practised.

3026. We should give the coroner discretion?—Of course, he would want a full discretion.

3027. As regards your interests, as a society,
T 2   you

Chairman—continued.

you see no objection?—I should be only too pleased to remove any scandal that now exists.

3028. You admit that there is a scandal?—Unfortunately there is in these illegal assurances.

3029. You would be very glad to put an end to all that?—Yes.

3030. As regards yourself and your own society, quite apart from the question of whether these things are practical or not, you see no objection to what I have suggested?—I hardly see how it is to be worked.

3031. That is a different point; you see no objection, so far as you are concerned?—We should not object.

3032. You also said, I think, that you would

Chairman—continued.

approve of penal clauses against parents and agents, and fines against companies?—Yes.

3033. Then, as to the certificate of the doctor or registrar, you would be glad of any alteration in the form of the doctor's certificate, or the manner of giving the registrar's certificate, which would tend to make them less lax, and diminish crime?—If it would diminish crime, undoubtedly, yes; but we have had no experience of that.

3034. In fact, as regards all these restrictions which I have named, you make no objection as affecting your society, but you express a doubt or uncertainty as to their being workable; that is all?—Yes.

The Witness is directed to withdraw.

Mr. FRANK HENRY TAUNTON, is called in; and Examined, as follows:

Chairman.

3035. You are Secretary of the Royal Liver Friendly Society?—I am.

3036. You have sent us particulars of the evidence which you propose to give before this Committee?—I have.

3037. Is the society you represent the largest of the collecting friendly societies?—It is.

3038. What do you mean by collecting societies?—A collecting society is one where the weekly payments are collected by men who go from house to house.

3039. When was your society established?—In 1850.

3040. What is the amount of their invested funds at the present moment?—Its accumulated funds are 1,065,000 *l.*

3041. What is its premium income?—Over 384,000 *l.*

3042. Last year, 1889, how many policies did you issue?—We issued policies to the number of 215,637.

3043. Of those policies how many were for children between the ages of one next birthday and 10 next birthday?—83,433.

3044. I think you produce specimens of proposal forms without which no policy is issued? Yes (*see* Appendix). I may add that about two-thirds of our policies, that is, two-thirds of the 83,433, are children between the ages of one and five.

3045. When you say "one," do you mean children who have passed one year old?—No; I mean from birth to age one next birthday

3046. What was the number of deaths of children in 1889, between one and five, and again between five and ten?—The number of deaths between one and five years was 5,813, and the number of deaths between five and ten was 488, making a total of 6,301 deaths.

3047. Then the immense majority of deaths were of children between one and five?—Yes; at the age of one, perhaps.

3048. What is the amount you paid in claims? —On children from one year to five years of age the amount was 13,211 *l.*; from five to ten it was 2,964 *l.*, or 16,176 *l.* altogether.

3049. I understand you paid a certain amount in grants: what do you mean by grants?—

Chairman—continued.

Grants are given to what the board consider deserving cases, where the children have either not arrived in benefit or have lapsed through circumstances over which the parents had no control.

3050. You mean what have been spoken of by another witness, and what are perhaps known to you as grants of grace?—Yes, grants.

3051. Can you state the amounts you have paid in grants?—On the death of children from one year to five we paid about 353 *l.*, and on the death of children from five to 10 years, about 11 *l.*, making an average altogether of 10 *s.* per head.

3052. Were those grants in cases of lapse?—Yes; they would be in cases of lapse sometimes, not always.

3053. Where the policies lapsed, as a matter of favour you made this grant of 10 *s.* or whatever it might be?—Yes; sometimes more and sometimes less, the average being 10 *s.*

3054. You say in your particulars of evidence that you produce a list of grants and claims refused owing to suspicious circumstances attending death; what is the number of those cases?—I have not counted them. These run from about the 9th May 1888 up to date.

3055. That would be about a year and nine months, or not quite two years?—Not quite two years; some in the list of grants date from 1877. I have got the list of the cases here if you would like me to read them.

3056. I am not asking at present about the cases; I want to ascertain the number?—I have not counted them up.

3057. Could you tell us roughly what it would be?—I would prefer not doing so; but I could put the papers in.

3058. You say the grants and claims were refused owing to suspicious circumstances attending deaths; how did you arrive at the knowledge of those suspicious circumstances?—From statements made on the copy certificate of death brought in or from paragraphs in the newspaper as to the coroner's inquests and so on, and sometimes from other information.

3059. You do not expect to get much information

16 *July* 1890.]   MR. TAUNTON.   [*Continued.*

Chairman—continued.

tion in that respect from your own agents?—Sometimes we do, but not often.

3060. If I understand you rightly, there are a good many suspicious cases with respect to which your agents have not informed you, and as to which you have derived your information from other sources? — Yes; chiefly from the facts stated on the certificate and from the newspapers.

3061. But not mainly from your own agents? —Not mainly from our agents.

3062. You state in these particulars that the principal causes of infantile disease are pulmonary, cerebral, and zymotic; could you say how much those cases average?— About 90 per cent.

3063. Have you included in those causes what is known to doctors as marasmus or atrophy? —Yes.

3064. Under what head do you put it?—I should put it under the first.

3065. Pulmonary?—Yes.

3066. You say those are the cause of "infantile diseases," that obviously is a different thing from the causes of infantile death?—Yes

3067. You are simply speaking now of the principal causes of infantile disease. There might be causes of infantile death, of course; for instance, over-lying, which would not come under those heads at all?—Yes, there are other causes, which I should classify as preventable causes.

3068. Your distinction here, then, is that there are certain diseases to which every child is subject, and there are certain other causes of death that are preventable?—Yes.

3069. The others being not preventable, but coming in the course of providence?—Yes.

3070. What would be the number of cases of deaths due to preventable causes among insured children on the average?—Under 10 per cent.

3071. As regards the cases which constitute the remaining 90 per cent., supposing a child suffering from one of those diseases you refer to, pulmonary or zymotic as the case may be, the certificate would indicate of what disease the child died?—Yes.

3072. But the disease might be very much aggravated by neglect or cruelty or improper feeding, might it not?—Certainly.

3073. Would you not call those cases instances of preventable causes?—Not if the doctor gave a certificate that it was only the ailment of the child that caused death.

3074. The doctor's certificate would not necessarily go to show that the child's ailment had not been aggravated in the way which I suggest? —No.

3075. And the aggravating of the child's disease is presumably a preventable thing?—Yes.

3076. Therefore, when you put down the amount of preventable causes as being only 10 per cent., you are omitting to take account of all this preventable neglect, cruelty, and improper feeding, you do not take that into account, do you?—Yes, I do; because where the doctor gives a certificate that the child dies of a natural complaint, we would include it as non-preventable.

3077. That is assuming the doctor knows the history of the case?—Yes.

(142.)

Chairman—continued.

3078. We have had it in evidence that in many cases the doctors do not know the history of the case; I am merely mentioning the fact; I am not asking you whether it is right or wrong; I understand you have something to say as regards doing away with infantile insurance?— Yes.

3079. I think it is hardly necessary for us to dwell upon that, because I do not think anybody proposes to do away with it, and certainly this Bill does not?—I would emphatically object to having infantile insurances done away, even at age one next birthday.

3080. On what ground?—On the ground that all arguments in favour of infantile insurance are equally applicable to the period ranging from birth to 12 months old. The cost of funeral and the expenses of mourning have to be borne for a child under 12 months just the same as for a child over 12 months.

3081. The facilities for crime are not so great in the case of a child under 12 months, are they; it is easier, is it not, to do away with a child a few weeks old than a child some years of age?—An actuary of some renown, Mr. Ansell, shows that two-fifths of the deaths of children occurred in the first six weeks after birth.

3082. Therefore, there would be greater facilities for crime; for instance, you cannot quite easily overlie a child over a couple of years old, but the mother can easily overlie a tiny infant? —Yes.

3083. Therefore, though the expenses might be the same, yet the facilities for crime and the danger of neglect would be very much greater in the case of a child under a year than in the case of a child of two years, we will say?—Yes, I should assume so.

3084. You have something to say, I understand, about reducing the amounts payable on the deaths of children, as to a reduced scale of policies?—Yes. As long as infantile assurance was not done away with, so far as any age is concerned, I would not object to seeing the amounts payable on deaths of very young children reasonably reduced, so as it allows of a reasonable charge for interment.

3085. Would you object to seeing them reduced to the average amount at which parents do insure children; there is, I presume, something like an arrangement for which parents insure their children under five years old?— Yes.

3086. Do you know what it is?—Our claims at these ages would average about 2 l. 10 s. per head.

3087. That is all the parents insure for on the average?—Yes.

3088. If you brought the amount down to 2 l. 10 s. or 3 l., that would meet all the requirements of the case, would it?—For very young ages.

3089. Do you mean children of from one to five years?—I mean children of from one to three years.

3090. Do you think the death expenses of a child between children of three and five years would be very different. I suppose the attendance of the doctor, and the mourning and the coffin would be all very much the same between three and five, would they not?—I should take

T 3   it it that parents are put to more expense the older the child is.

3091. Do you think the difference of those two years would make any considerable difference as regards the death expenses?—Those are questions the parents themselves ought to answer. So far as it affects the societies we ought to be in favour of reducing the amounts, because it would lessen our liability; but that is a question which the working people who insure ought to answer.

3092. I understand, as regards your interests as a society, it would make no difference to you?—Very slight.

3093. Whether it would make much to the people who insure or not is a question you do not think it your province to discuss?—No; it is for themselves to say.

3094. You state in these particulars that the Royal Liver Friendly Society would be only too glad to assist and co-operate with the Society for the Prevention of Cruelty to Children in detecting and tracing out cases where a child has died from improper treatment whilst insured with you; it is your interest to do so, I presume?—I have personally offered to the Liverpool secretary to the Society for the Prevention of Cruelty to Children to give any assistance, but they never sought it; I never heard of their having sought information or assistance from us.

3095. You would be willing to co-operate with them entirely?—It is to our interest to find out these bad cases, because we do not consider we ought to pay them.

3096. The next point you notice in your particulars is with regard to precaution; you say that, "If proper precaution was taken in the initial stage after the death of a child, there would be no possibility of insurance money being paid in improper cases;" what would be "proper precaution," in your opinion?—I think the proper precaution should be found in the registration of the death of the child.

3097. You think people do not take proper precaution in the registration of the death of the child?—Quite so.

3098. In what class does the precaution fail?—There are four classes of evidence that the Registrar General allows the registrar to take and issue his certificate upon; there is the coroner's certificate, the certificate of the doctor who has attended the case, the certificate of the doctor who has not attended the case but has satisfied himself of the nature of the case, and then there is the fourth class of evidence (which is the most common in cases of this kind), which is "any satisfactory information."

3099. Do you say that this is the most common class?—I should take it to be so; and that it is at the option of the Registrar himself to take.

3100. Do you think it altogether a wise or safe thing to leave a matter of such importance to the option of the registrar?—Not in the case of insured children.

3101. If I understand you rightly, you would be disposed to get rid of the fourth condition altogether?—I would to this extent, that all coroners or doctors who were applied to give the necessary papers or certificates to the registrar should be obliged to ask the question whether the

child was insured or not. If the child was not insured it should be marked on the certificate, " Not insured," and if it were insured it should be marked upon the certificate " Insured."

3102. On the doctor's certificate?—Yes; and also this information should be copied on the registrar's certificate of registration of death, viz., whether it is "insured" or "not insured."

3103. This discretion which is left to the registrar in the fourth case that you spoke of, though it is in a great measure undesirable, is still, you say, the most common of the four?—I should take it to be so.

3104. There is obviously room for an amendment of the law in that particular respect?—In that respect there is, in my opinion.

3105. You say that if proper precautions were taken "there would be no possibility of insurance money being paid away in improper cases;" is not that putting it a little too high; as to the doctor's certificate, we have been told by a great many doctors, that they often cannot know much of the history of the case?—The doctor's certificate is often worthless in my opinion.

3106. If the doctor's certificate is often worthless, and if the registrar's certificate is often very carelessly given, is it not clear that there is a very large opportunity for evil practice under the existing law; because you have now mentioned the two chief securities, for the coroner's certificate would only come in where the case was so bad that it came before the coroner; and the majority of cases do not come before the coroner; it appears from your evidence that the doctor's certificate is often worthless and the certificate of the registrar is frequently very carelessly given, therefore in the present state of the law there is a great possibility of crime being undetected; is not that so?—I think that has always been so and always will be so.

3107. You say that you experience great difficulty in cases of suspicion in getting information, from whom do you mean?—From coroners and from doctors sometimes.

3108. Do you seek their assistance very much in those suspicious cases?—I can give you cases. There is for instance the coroner in Birmingham, Dr. Hawkes; we have tried so often to get information from him, that we have given up seeking for it altogether now. I might take also the case of our own Liverpool coroner; not long ago we wrote and asked him for information; but we get no information, because I believe it is the coroner's clerk whose business it is to give that information, and he objects to give us information unless we pay a very large fee, a fee which is sometimes more than the sum at issue might be.

3109. As to the mode you adopt, you state you seek for information from coroners; is that before or after the coroner has given his certificate?—It would be after the coroner has given his certificate, because we would only judge from the newspaper reports, which are very scanty sometimes.

3110. In point of fact you would be asking the coroner to correct and go behind his own certificate?—No; but the coroner's certificate does not sometimes say very much.

3111. But on that certificate and on the certificate

       Mr. TAUNTON.

Chairman—continued.

certificate of the registrar, you are bound to pay, no matter what information you get, are you not? — No, we are not bound to pay upon the certificate unless the committee consider the claim is all right.

3112. You mean you may dispute the policy? —We may dispute it.

3113. As to the next point you notice, of handing the money to the undertaker, it is not necessary to question you because that has been withdrawn from the Bill?—I am very glad to hear it.

3114. As to the class of people who mostly insure with collecting societies and industrial companies, what do you wish to say?—I have heard or read that Mr. Justice Day said that it was the very lowest of the working-class who insured. If he said that, he is very wrong in that respect; it is the respectable · classes who do insure.

3115. I think you are mistaken as to the evidence; the evidence was rather that a great many of the lowest class insured, not that the majority who insured were the worst class, but that a considerable number of the worst class did insure?—I would almost challenge that statement.

3116. That a great many of the lower classes do?—I would challenge the statement that a majority of the most depraved classes do insure.

3117. I do not say the majority; the evidence given is that a very great many of the low and depraved class do insure, or rather it was actually proved a great many of the insurances were cases of the depraved and bad class; that is what the evidence has gone to, I think; I suppose as regards the condition of the poor and what they do about their children, the evidence of the relieving officers, who have a great deal to do with the very lowest class, would be of considerable importance, would it not; they would be likely to have a knowledge of the worst and lowest class?—Yes; but I do not think their knowledge would extend to infants at all; it would be more the poor old people who would come within their actual knowledge.

3118. But a very poor man with a large family would come to the relieving officer for help, would he not?—Yes, but then the relieving officer would not come and examine the child.

3119. I mean that the relieving officer must have a very large acquaintance with a number of very poor people?—With poor people, but not with children.

3120. But he would know the parents?— Yes.

3121. The parents of those children might be needy and distressed people; the fact of a man having a large family would tend to make him more distressed and needy?—Yes.

3122. It is natural to suppose that the relieving officer would know a great deal about the poor, and especially the lowest class of poor. We have had it in evidence from relieving officers that parents who have insured their children have nevertheless after getting the insurance money left the parish to bury the child; have you ever known a case of that kind?—No, not in the case of a child; we have known it in the case of an adult.

(142.)

Chairman—continued.

3123. It has been largely proved that parents of the worst class have insured their children and got the insurance money and then left their children on the parish?—I should doubt that.

3124. That has been actually given in evidence, not as a matter of opinion but as a matter of fact. For instance, one of these relieving officers declared that he was able in two cases to compel the parents to pay for the funeral by threats?— I do not doubt that has occurred, but I do doubt that it has occurred very largely.

3125. Your doubt whether it has occurred largely would not, I presume, stand against the fact that a person said it actually had occurred; you would not set your doubt against their positive assertion, would you?—Against positive proof I would not; but against assertion I would.

3126. On what ground do you base your impression, because we have had a good many instances given to us?—Because I think we should have heard of it. If it occurred so often as that we should have heard of it.

3127. That is all. That is your only reason? —That is my only reason.

3128. You produce a list of unregistered collecting societies and burial clubs; what do you say about that?—That it is the unregistered collecting societies and local clubs that very often do things which are against the Friendly Societies Act, and when classified under the names of societies people do not distinguish between those which are registered and those which are not registered, and we get blamed for their actions.

3129. You think a good deal of misdeed and wrong goes on in connection with these unregistered societies?—Yes, they ought all to be registered.

3130. Will you produce a list of those. (*The same is handed in.*) I see you make certain suggestions; you suggest that in all cases of inquests on children, something should be done?—In all cases of inquests the coroner should, on the certificate given by him to the registrar, state whether the child is insured or not, which question should be always asked on inquests, and the registrar should so endorse any copy certificate of deaths furnished by him.

3131. In every case of inquest the coroner should be bound to inquire whether the child is insured or not?—Yes.

3132. What power has he of extracting the truth from the parent who may be denying it, and saying the child is not insured?—If the parents were to say that it was not insured when it was, and the registrar marked on the certificate of death that it was not insured we should not pay the claim.

3133. Supposing you knew the fact?—The copy of the certificate that was presented to us would show on the face of it that the child was not insured.

3134. Whereas you would know from the books that the child was insured?—Yes, and we should refer it back again for something more.

3135. Then you wish to suggest something about doctors' certificates?—If people answered that question as to whether a child was insured

T 4   by

Chairman—continued.

by saying it was not insured they would prevent themselves getting the money.

3136. I am speaking of the doctor's certficate? —I think the doctor should, before giving a certificate, ask the people whether the child is insured or not.

3137. The doctor's certificate could only run to this; that the parents state that the child was not insured?—He would just put on that, it was not insured, and the registrar would copy that on the certificate itself.

3138. Then you wish to speak as to the amount of benefit given in assurances increasing; what do you say on that subject?—Owing to the great competition with the industrial insurance companies the benefits given at the death of children now have increased in comparison with what they used to be.

3139. The amount of the policies have increased?—Yes.

3140. Has the amount of weekly payments increased in the same proportion?—No, the weekly premiums would remain about the same.

3141. The weekly payments remaining the same, the amount of benefit to be obtained is on the increase?—That is owing to the competition chiefly of the industrial companies.

3142. On the other hand, the price of most things is now a good deal cheaper than it was when the Friendly Societies Act was passed;—Yes.

3143. Mourning is cheaper; clothing of all sorts is cheaper?—Then on the other hand, the cemeteries are further out of town, involving carriage often where it would not be charged before.

3144. With regard to mourning, you have a large knowledge of the habits of the poorer classes; do you think they like to spend so much on mourning?—The respectable portion of the working classes, I think, are very fond of mourning.

3145. You would not say that spending money largely upon expensive mourning is, upon the whole, tending to thrift. Do you not think that men of all grades, high, low, rich and poor, spend a great deal too much money on mourning?— Yes. If your Lordship is asking me my own opinion, I am against mourning myself.

3146. If this Bill had indirectly the effect of lessening the extravagant expenditure on mourning and funerals, it would have a good effect?— Granted the cause existed.

3147. I think you then wish to suggest another check, but you do not state what it is?—That agents and collectors should be licensed. Agents and collectors mean the same. The companies call their men agents, and we call ours collectors. The work they do is practically the same, so that there is no distinction between them; but I think they all ought to be licensed. That is my own individual opinion.

3148. You mean to say that no agent should act as an agent for any society or company unless he was licensed?—Yes.

3149. Licensed by whom; by some authority having the power and authority to issue licenses? —That is a matter of detail. That has hardly been worked out, but I should think it would be by the Inland Revenue. They should be merely licenses of half-a-crown or 5 *s.* a year.

Chairman—continued.

3150. To whom would you give the power of depriving the licenses on the ground of any misconduct?—To any bench of magistrates.

3151. What would you regard as misconduct on the part of an agent justifying the taking away of his license?—Well, any improper collusion with anybody, or aggravated breach of the Friendly Societies Act. Of course I am referring to this also as regards adult insurance as well as child insurance.

3152. You mean any breach of the law?—Yes.

3153. Or any breach of the company's regulations?—You might endorse his license for the first time, or the second time, and take it away if he persisted in it.

3154. I suppose you would have a penalty, then, for any person acting as an agent who had not a license?—Yes, it would improve the tone of the men, because there is no doubt that unfortunately often a very low class of men become agents and collectors, and those are the men who would be doing harm, and it would tend to check that.

3155. This low class of men you speak of, of course obviously, having a considerable pecuniary interest in getting cases, and being a low class of men, might be indulging in practices against the law, and against the interests of your society?— Yes.

3156. You think then it would be an improvement if there were legislation on this subject, so as to do what the Legislature could to raise the character of the agents?—Yes.

3157. It has been asked of a witness here to-day, whether he saw any objection, in principle, to making it a penal thing, not merely a matter of license, but a penal thing for an agent or a parent insuring, to transgress the law. Would you punish him penally?—To what extent?

3158. In the discretion of the magistrates?— But to what extent would the transgression be considered such as that your Lordship is speaking of?

3159. I mean if any agent knowingly insured a child in any way which was forbidden by law, do you think that he should suffer penally?— Any agent who knowingly did it?.

3160. Yes?—Certainly.

3161. How are your agents paid; by commission?—By commission.

3162. Do you know what it amounts to?—25 per cent.

3163. Do they also get a premium in new cases?—They do.

3164. Do you give them, as the Prudential does, besides that, a quarterly remuneration or premium?—No, we give our men better terms than the Prudential gives, but we do not give them the same terms.

3165. Has it ever occurred to you that you might pay your agents fixed salaries and so avoid all this competition and touting and illegal practices?—That would be impossible, I think.

3166. Why?—First of all, there would not be the same incentive to work.

3167. But the incentive to work is, of course, at the same time, a strong incentive to work irregularly and illegally?—I hope not my Lord. I do not believe it is, myself.

3168. I am speaking of the lower class of agents that you have spoken of?—Well, admittedly,

Chairman—continued.

tedly, if your Lordship is speaking of a low class of man, you do not know what he would do.

3169. I am speaking of that class. You do not see your way to paying them by fixed salaries?—No. It would have been adopted long before now, had it been feasible.

3170. Are those the only checks that you suggest?—No, I would suggest the compulsory use of proposal forms.

3171. What do you mean by that?—That all societies and companies who were transacting industrial insurance business, should be compelled to use proposal forms before insuring any children; that is to say, the proposal form should be filled up. In many societies and companies they do not use them.

3172. That is a question I was going to ask you. In many cases no proposal forms are used or filled up?—No; we use them in all cases, but in many societies and companies they do not use them.

3173. You propose that not more than one insurance should be permitted of children under 10 years of age. That is one of your proposals, is not it, in your note, " Also more than one insurance should not be permitted of children under 10 years of age "?—In any one or more institutions.

3174. That no child should be insured, (whether in one or two societies does not matter), for more than one policy?—No.

3175. That is what you propose; no child under 10 years of age should be insured for more than one policy?—Of course this would not be retrospective.

3176. Not more than one insurance should be permitted of children under 10 years; that is your proposal?—Either in the same society, or company or in any other

3177. In fact that there should be but one insurance of that child's life, no matter whether it is in one or three societies?—Yes.

3178. Would you punish that if that were done. I see you suggest that in your paper?—I would make it illegal.

3179. It would be a misdemeanour?—It would.

3180. And that misdemeanour should be punishable legally?—Yes, where it was a matter of doing it knowingly.

3181. Suppose the parent chose to run the risk of this misdemeanour, and the punishment for doing it, in the hopes of getting money out of you, would it not be a good and an additional precaution to say, that in every such case the policy should be void; that you should not have to pay anything?—I do not think that is necessary, because we should make it void ourselves if we found it out. But perhaps it would be well to make it so. Others might not be so particular as we are.

3182. You might make it void yourselves, but it would be better to make it one of the conditions of the society?—Yes.

3183. Would not you prefer instead of having to fight this out in all these cases, that the law should be, that the policy should be void, no matter what you did?—I think I would; because the industrial companies might not be bound so much as we are by the Act, and they

(142.)

Chairman—continued.

would obtain a sort of favour or preference among people by ignoring this law.

3184. Then to prevent this competition and one society fighting, more or less, another society in the easiness of its dealings, it would be in your opinion a very desirable thing that the law should do whatever is necessary, and not the society itself, it is better that it should be done by the law?—It is better done in some way so as to make it compulsory on all societies and companies doing this business.

3185. Then your idea is that not only should the parent be punished, because he might take the risk of punishment for the sake of the money, but that his policy should be void *ipso facto*?—Yes.

3186. That would tend very much to check a parent from doing this thing?—Yes; and it would check the competition which your Lordship refers to.

3187. I was going to ask you whether you thought that a parent who had been sentenced by a magistrate for very brutal cruelty to a child, should be allowed to continue a policy on that child's life?—Certainly not.

3188. He would have shown himself a person totally unfit to be entrusted with any child's life?—Yes.

3189. Then it would be also in your opinion desirable that if any parent was convicted of brutally illtreating a child, the policy on that child's life should be void, and that it should be settled that he should get nothing on it. The policy would lapse to you then?—Is your Lordship assuming that the child died.

3190. No, I am assuming that the child is so brutally illtreated that the magistrate sent the mother, or father, or both, to gaol for three months with hard labour. You would think it a right thing that in that case the policy should be void?—It should be, I think.

3191. Would you allow that parent then, after that was done, and his policy had become void by sentence of law to go and take out a new policy for that child?—Not if we knew it.

3192. Therefore there would be no harm, in your opinion, if the law also enacted that the parent who had done that, and had been proved to be so unfit, should be incapable of insuring his child's life again?—Yes, but I do not know how the law is going to stop it.

3193. But if it could it would be a good thing?—If it could, it would be a good thing. I would like to add, while your Lordship is on this question, that I think it should be made a misdemeanour for any person, other than the parent or guardian, or *bonâ fide* foster-parent, to insure any child under 10.

3194. Parent or guardian?—Or *bonâ fide* foster-parent; because I think that foster-parentage is a thing that is more common amongst the working classes than amongst better classes. They adopt children, and bring them up as their foster-children; really *bonâ fide* foster-children.

3195. That is another precaution that you would take?—Yes.

3196. Then you speak as to altering copy certificates of death. What do you mean by that?—Very often people alter the copy cer-

U   tificates

Chairman—continued.

tificates of death that they bring to us. We have often found them scratched out, and by holding them up to the light you can see that they have altered the age or duration of illness or something like that.

3197. Would you have a penalty for that?—I believe I am correct in stating that under the present Registration Act there is no provision as to whose duty it is to undertake the prosecution in these cases. We have ourselves referred cases of that kind to the Registrar General, and his invariable reply has been, that it is our place and not his to undertake the prosecution; but the Act does not specify who is the person to prosecute.

3198. You yourselves have not prosecuted in those cases. Is there any case in which you have prosecuted?—I do not think, my Lord, I can think of any case at present. We would prefer this to be done by the Registrar General, because we do not want to be made unpopular.

3199. That fear of unpopularity appears not only in your evidence, but in the directions given by another society to its agents. They say it is not creditable to a society to contest policies, and in point of fact, that fear of being unpopular operates to a certain extent on your own society in all these cases?—We would prosecute, perhaps, in a case if we were certain of winning, but if the case went against us, it would be very damaging to us.

3200. And therefore you do not like to run the risk of defeat because you would be damaged for no good?—They would think that we were trying to void the policy wrongfully.

2201. Naturally you would be reluctant to prosecute, and you would prefer the prosecution to be carried on by somebody else?—By the Registrar General.

3202. From what funds would you have the prosecution provided for. Where is the cost of the prosecution to come from?—From the Treasury.

3203. The Registrar General would not have any power to draw from the State the cost of the prosecution?—No, but I think the Treasury finds funds for prosecutions, through the Public Prosecutor. I am not conversant with the method.

3204. But you say that the cases should be prosecuted in other ways than at the risk and cost of the societies?—Yes.

3205. Then you state that the affiliated orders have an influence on the indirect insurance of children and have not been free from child murder cases. Will you explain that?—I am an Oddfellow myself of many years standing, and it is often forgotten in speaking about the affiliated Orders, that the affiliated Orders do insure children.

3206. What do you mean by an affiliated Order?—Such as the Manchester Unity of Oddfellows, which I belong to; or the Foresters. They do insure children although they are popularly supposed not to do so. They pay on the death of the child to the parent a certain sum. .

Earl of *Selborne.*

3207. You do not mean by the words "affiliated Orders" orders of affiliation?—·No, no.

Chairman.

3208. Will you explain it a little. I do not know what you mean by affiliated orders?—The affiliated Orders are such as the Foresters or Oddfellows.

3209. You are speaking not of orders for payment, but the orders?—The affiliated societies.

3210. I understand now. I was confounding, as the noble Earl did, the affiliated Orders with orders for affiliation?—No, it has nothing to do with that.

3211. You mean the societies?—Yes.

3212. You say that they insure children, and that they have not been free from child murder cases?—No, but not very often; the affiliated Orders are held up, and in some cases justly so, as superior to the collecting societies and industrial insurance companies, but it should not be forgotten that they do insure these children though indirectly, I mean without any fund for child insurance; and there was a case, I believe, the case of Mary Ann Cotton, in No. 370 of the Fourth Report of the Royal Commission that occurred years ago, which clearly showed that the child in that case, though not insured with a collecting society or company was done away with, and that the funeral money thereon was paid by an affiliated Order, the Oddfellows, I believe it was in that case.

3213. It has been contended very strongly, that in any legislation on this subject a broad distinction should be drawn between these afiliated orders that you speak of, and societies like yours and the Prudential Society. That does not seem to be your opinion?—No, not at all, because the affiliated orders do insure children indirectly. If you were to forbid to us the insurance of children altogether, what is to prevent their insuring them indirectly, the same as they do now.

3214. You think that in any legislation on the subject no such distinction should be drawn between you and these affiliated societies; you think you should all be treated alike?—I merely mention this to show that we, ourselves, the collecting societies and industrial insurance companies, are not the only ones who insure children. Although it is popularly supposed that the others do not do so they do, but it is in an indirect manner.

3215. You state that the mortality among children is decreasing. What do you wish to say upon that subject?—I only wish to point out that it is decreasing while the facilities for insurance are increasing. The mortality among children is well known to be decreasing to what it used to be; and I would like to add that the mortality of children in various parts of the Continent is far in excess of what it is in England. At the same time the insurance of children is, as far as I am aware, practically unknown there. Therefore, we would point out that insurance does not affect the question.

3216. I pointed out to a witness that a considerable increase of criminal child mortality might occur which would scarcely appear on the death rate of the Registrar General at all?—I understood your Lordship's remarks.

3217. You understood my point. I need not trouble you with it. Do not you think that this decrease of mortality among children may be, at least, in part owing to the much greater care **and**

Chairman – continued.

and attention given to children generally in the way of providing children's hospitals and better sanitary conditions, and a better understanding of the way of feeding and taking care of children?—No doubt; but at the same time the increased facilities for insurance would be set against that if that were so.

3218. You would not argue, I suppose, that because the mortality amongst children has lessened, it necessarily follows that there is no crime in connection with insurance?—No.

3219. Then you have something to say as to the evidence of former witnesses, and the manner in which that has been obtained. Before you answer this question, let me say to you that I think anything you say upon it should be matters entirely within your own personal knowledge, and that you should not give us here what you hear or have heard from others as to the evidence of former witnesses, or as to the manner in which their evidence has been obtained. If you have any particular case in which you know personally, as a matter of fact, that the evidence of any witness has been obtained in such a way that you think it necessary to bring that fact before us, please speak of it, but not otherwise?—I am afraid that is for your Lordships to say after I have told you.

3220. No, pardon me; it is for us to say it before. I mean to say if you know of any case within your own personal knowledge please speak of it, but you are not to give us here any hearsay, that you may have heard, that somebody has said about some witness, or the way in which his evidence was procured. If you know anything of your own personal knowledge in any particular case, please give it to us?—I only know by correspondence.

3221. Correspondence with whom?—One of our agents.

3222. Is this one case, or a number?—Only one case, my Lord.

3223. Would you then state what is the case. Before you go into the correspondence, give me the name of the witness that you refer to?—William Taylor, I think it is.

3224. Of what place?—Sheffield.

3225. What was he?—He was summoned here.

3226. Alfred Taylor was summoned, but he did not appear here?—He did not appear, my Lord.

3227. Then it is no use going into the question further?—It was, as to the manner in which the evidence was said to have been obtained.

Earl of *Derby*.

3228. I suppose that every case of a child put out of the way after being insured involves to your society a payment which you would not otherwise have to make?—No.

3229. It involves a loss?—Certainly.

3230. A payment which you would not have to make, not a payment to you?—It is not a gain to us, it is a loss to us.

3231. Therefore you have a strong interest in lessening the number of such cases?—Yes.

3232. Although a society might not like to make itself unpopular by refusal to pay in sus-

(142.)

Earl of *Derby*—continued.

picious cases where they have not sufficient evidence to dispute the payment?—My lord, in all suspicious cases we do not pay. We examine further into it, and if we get any corroborative proof that it was a bad case or an improper case we do not pay; but the evidence is so slight that sometimes we feel obliged to pay.

3233. Take the case of insurance of a child under 12 months old; if that were entirely prohibited would it cause you any loss? I will put it in this way, suppose such children lived over the year, probably they would then be insured, and if they died within the year, their not being insured would be a gain to you and not a loss; is it not so?—No, my Lord. I think that people should insure shortly after the birth of the child. When the child is born they have the fear before them that they may be called upon perhaps (knowing how precarious child life is) to go to the expense of a funeral, and they should provide early for those things.

3234. Do you think that, as a fact, the practice of insurance would be much discouraged if it were limited to children over 12 months old?—I think it would be somewhat discouraged.

3235. Then I did not quite understand what you said about agents or collectors often being a low class of men. How does that come about? Are they found to be more efficient, or are they cheaper; or why is it that they are so?—Well, I hope I did not give the impression that they often are a low class of men. I think I said that they are sometimes a low class of men.

3236. I took it down that a very low class of men became agents or collectors?—Perhaps your Lordship will allow me to qualify that, and say sometimes they do become collectors, for instance, a man who is given to drinking or dissolute habits himself, I dare say he would lose employment of any other kind, and he might then turn to insurance.

3237. That would be to the disadvantage of the society who employed him?—Yes, we would not employ him if we knew it. We always ask for references.

3238. Therefore, in point of fact, is not the suggestion that a license should be required as a certificate of character simply asking some public authority to do for a society what it ought to do for itself, namely, to exercise proper care as to the persons whom it appoints?—No, I think it would make a man more careful for fear of losing his license, and thereby losing his ability to work. If a man loses his situation he can get another one sometimes.

3239. Even if there were no licenses, if you found him to be a disreputable person, you would cease to employ him?—We should get rid of him after a time, but then the injury might be done.

Marquess of *Lothian*.

3240. With reference to the question asked you as to the reduction of the scale of amounts payable to 2 *l.* 10 *s.*, I think you said you would not see any very great objection on the part of your society if that was the scale under three years old?—Under three years of age.

3241. With reference to that, can you give me a certain

Marquess of *Lothian*—continued.

a certain amount of information passed over by the Chairman with regard to the charges of undertakers in Liverpool?—Yes; I think the very lowest funeral expenses would be about 25 *s.* For a child three months old, it would be about 20 *s.* That does not include the cost of the grave or the burial fees.

3241.* It would not include those charges?—No.

3242. Then the charges would go considerably higher than that?—Yes.

3243. The cost to the parent would be considerably higher?—Yes.

3244. Can you give an idea what it would be?—About 2 *l.* altogether.

3245. Then what is it above three years old, say from three to five years old?—I would not like to say. It would depend on various other matters; and perhaps a doctor's bill. You see there would be more friends attend the funeral of a child of five or six or seven years than there would be an infant.

3246. You would rather not give an opinion as to whether such a limit below the age of three years would be popular with your people?—I know it would not be; and if such a Bill were passed, it would raise a great agitation; that I am confident of.

3247. Do you think it would make any difference in the amount of insurances in your society; do you think they would decline to insure for so low an amount?—I suppose they would insure, but the premiums would perhaps be less.

3248. Your society charges less than a penny a week for some insurances?—Yes, we have some halfpenny insurances.

3249. In your opinion is there any great objection to the limit of 6 *l.* under five years old?—No, I do not think there is any great objection; but on the other hand I could not see any very great objection to it being slightly reduced.

3250. But above three years old you think 2 *l.* 10 *s.* would be too little?—No, I do not think so.

3251. Up to five years?—No, 2 *l.* 10 *s.* up to three years.

3252. Between three and five years, what should it be?—Between three and five say 5 *l.*; I am not arguing in favour of the reduction, I am merely saying if it is reduced.

3253. When you make inquiries after coroners' inquests, with what object do you make inquiries?—To ascertain whether the case is an improper one to pay.

3254. If the case appears to you to be an improper one, you invariably withhold the payment of the insurance money?—Yes; I offered to produce a quantity of cases in which we had done so.

3255. Do you object to insure in all cases of illegitimacy?—I would object.

3256. You do not insure in any case of illegitimacy?—I would not. We only recently refused to pay a claim in Stirling, where the foster parent, or the person who called himself the foster parent (he was really the baby-farmer), insured the child, and we refused to pay, and

Marquess of *Lothian*—continued.

also another Scotch society refused to pay on the same death when they found out the facts.

3257. Have you extensive operations in Scotland?—Yes, we have many agencies in Scotland, going as far as Caithness in the north.

3258. Is it your impression that the proportion of insurances on child life in Scotland is greater or smaller than it is in England or Wales?—I do not think so, taking it on the whole, taking town and country together, I do not think so. It is about the same.

3259. Then you spoke, I think, of the insurance of what were called the depraved classes. What is your experience of that; do you think the proportion of insurances in the depraved classes is greater or less than it is in the classes a little better to do?—It is only a matter of opinion, but I should say it is decidedly less. If people are so depraved as that they do not save much money at all, either for insurance or anything else; they spend it in drink.

3260. By the depraved classes, you mean the vicious classes?—Yes.

3261. The very poor classes, for instance, who are not depraved at all, do they insure as much as the classes a little better to do?—Yes.

3262. You think that the actual poverty of a family would not prevent their insuring the lives of their children?—No, I do not think so. I think very often they stint themselves in food and clothing so as to pay the insurance money.

3263. As a general rule, you think, as to the 75 per cent. that we have heard of as the class who generally insure, the insurances are pretty evenly spread over the whole number?—Yes.

3264. At what age do you admit insurance at all?—At any age; as soon as the child is born.

3265. Immediately after birth?—Yes.

3266. But there is no payment immediately?—No; the first payment would not be due for some little time after that.

3267. Would you pay on a child dying under three months; when would the first payment become due?—The first payment of premium by the child's representatives.

3268. The first payment of the insurance on death; not the premium. I mean, suppose a child died under three months?—We might give a quarter benefit, the same as the Prudential Society gives a quarter benefit. All societies give about the same.

Chairman.

3269. Supposing a child to be insured immediately after its birth, how soon would he get any benefit?—In 13 weeks.

Marquess of *Lothian.*

3270. There would be 13 *d.* paid before the parents would become entitled to have any money paid?—Yes; but if it was a deserving case, and the child died, we might make a small grant.

3271. That would be a grant; there would be no right to it?—No.

3272. Then what is the rule of your society as to those who insure; do you admit any except **parents**

Marquess of *Lothian*—continued.

parents and guardians?—No, only the parents or *bonâ fide* guardians.

3273. Do you ascertain whether a child insured has been insured in any other society before you admit its application to be insured ; do you take any steps to find out whether the child has been insured otherwise or not?—No, we do not, as long as the limit allowed by the law is not exceeded.

3274. You ascertain that?—Yes.

3275. Do you ascertain what amount the child was insured for before it comes to you ?—No, it is a matter of indifference to us.

3276. The limit is 6 *l.* ; how do you ascertain that it has not been exceeded?—The law does not allow us to pay more than 6 *l.* on the death ; but we do not ask (so far as I am aware) any question as to whether the child is already insured in other societies or companies. I do not think any of them do.

Lord *Kinnaird.*

3277. Will you explain to the Committee what you mean by the payment of grants, because the object of the insurance is this, that the moment a child is born the parent wants to be sure of a decent burial of it. How does he procure that?—How does he procure the insurance?

3278. Yes?—There is no claim arising until the child has been 13 weeks paying, but it is generally known amongst members that in certain cases they can usually depend on getting grants from the societies or companies.

3279. How much will that grant be?—It will range from 5 *s.* up to a higher amount ; the average would be about 10 *s.*, perhaps. Because it may be a case of parents having a large family of children, and all insured and paying for years, and then the youngest child might die before deriving any benefit. In that case the people have been paying for years, and never getting anything, and it would be only reasonable for the society to give a grant in that case.

3280. So that, practically, a child in three months, if the parents are respectable, and they have other children insured, gets the full cost of burial?—Not the full cost, they would only get a grant. We only give grants to a quarter of the sum assured.

3281. Have you many contested cases?—Yes.

3282. Can you tell us at all the proportion ?—In the case of children do you mean?

3283. Yes ; with regard to payments, I mean ?—Well ; we had one case recently where the full amount had been paid by another society. The parents insured in our society, and they wanted us to pay them. We saw that the limit had been exceeded already, and we refused to pay.

Chairman.

3284. Is that a case of child insurance?—Yes; I am speaking " off the book " ; I think it was a child's case.

Lord *Kinnaird.*

3285. Would it be one case a month?—No ; very seldom.

(142.)

Lord *Kinnaird*—continued.

3286. Would it be one in a year?—There might be be two or three cases a year, perhaps.

3287. Then you mentioned the altered certificates. Is that at all a common thing, do you think ?—Yes, but more with adults; more as a feature of altering the age of adults. I think that is more especially done in Ireland where the age is very often understated.

3288. Do you, of your own personal knowledge, speak of many cases of ill-treatment of insured chidren?—No ; I do not know of many cases of ill-treatment, except what I have read in the newspapers.

Earl of *Selborne.*

3289. I see in your form of proposal there are only three questions asked in substance. Omitting the formal one, with which it begins, to relate to the health of the person proposed, and the other relates to his being already insured in this society ?—Yes.

3290. Are the answers by the person proposing upon the subject of health taken in all cases, or do you ever make investigation?—We very often make investigation.

3291. Is the child seen?—Yes, it is supposed to be, by our agent or collector.

3292. It is the duty of your agent to see the child?—Yes ; to see the child before it derives any benefit.

3293. What are the instructions with regard to the verification of the answers on that subject. Supposing for instance, the answer is that the proposed member is in good health, and has never been afflicted by any of the disorders mentioned ; if that is so, is anything done, and if so, what is done ?—If a person made a wrong and untruthful answer?

3294. For instance you say the agent always sees the child ?—Yes, he is supposed to.

3295. When he sees the child, supposing he doubts the truth of those answers, what is done ?—His duty would be to tell us.

3296. Does he often perform that duty ?—I do not know of many cases where they have told us. It is very difficult to judge of the health of an infant. The parent is the best one for that.

3297. Is his inspection of the child more than formal ?—No ; in the case of an infant I should say it was merely a formal inspection, unless the child had something the matter with it that was apparent, such as scrofulous diseases of any kind.

3298. That might be visible ?—That would be visible ; and I have known cases where it has been mentioned, and we have refused to insure them.

3299. With regard to the other point, I see it is your opinion that it would be desirable that only one insurance should be permitted on children under 10 years ?—I think that is only right.

3300. Your society has not hitherto taken that view apparently. It has not asked a question on that subject ?—No, not as to whether it be insured in any other society.

3301. These is no qustion asked as to whether it is insured in any other society ?—No.

u 3   3302. And

Earl of *Selborne*—continued.

3302. And the omission to ask that might result, I suppose, in insurances exceeding the limited amount, might it not; for instance, if it was insured in your society for 3 *l.* 10 *s.*, and in another society for 3 *l.* 10 *s.*, under the age of five, the limited amount would be exceeded, would it not?—Yes, but there is nothing in the Act at present limiting the amount of premium that shall be paid upon a child. It merely limits the amount of claim that shall be paid; and there the amount of claim would not be paid in excess.

3303. I am speaking of the amount for which the child is insured, which of course, if the child died, would become a claim?—It would not be paid in excess.

Earl *Beauchamp.*

3304. Will you refer to Rule 51 of your instructions to agents?—I have not our instructions to agents, but your Lordship may take it they are practically the same as the instructions to the agents of the Prudential.

Earl of *Selborne.*

3305. That is an important statement. We have had those instructions, and I have referred to the one which the noble Lord mentions, 51: " If the child is assured in another company or society, and all the assurances inclusive of the amount proposed to be effected by this company do not exceed 6 *l.*," the proposal may be taken, which of course implies that if they do it would not be taken. I do not see in your form of proposal any question which would bring out the facts as to that?—No, my Lord, that being in the instructions, it was not necessary to repeat it on the proposal form.

3306. Those instructions do not say positively that the agent is to ask questions which are not on the face of the proposal?—No. I said that our instructions to our agents were practically the same as the Prudential instructions, but I did not say that they were actually the same word for word. I will send your Lordships up a copy of the instructions given to the agents by ourselves.

3307. The answers in the form of proposal enter into the contract between the society and the person who is assured, but anything said outside does not enter into the contract, unless it is something volunteered to induce a contract which otherwise would not have been made. Of course, if you tell me that it is the practice of your agents to ask all the questions which are contemplated by these rules, then I can understand it; but there was produced to us the other day the form of proposal from the Prudential Society, containing a great many questions which are not in your proposal?—Certainly.

3308. Amongst others, one as to insurance in any other society?—I can explain that; people are averse to do more writing than they possibly can help, and they grumble very much at unnecessary questions being on the proposal form, and so we try to reduce it down to the lowest possible number of questions.

3309. Is the Committee to understand that it is the duty of your agents to ask the question

Earl of *Selborne*—continued.

about insurance in another society, and the amount of it, which is not asked in this form of proposal?—He should do everything in his power to see that no improper insurance is effected. I would send up a copy of the instructions to our men if required.

3310. You have been asked several questions as to the amount paid in grants. Now, under the age of, say, one year, any amount paid in grant is necessarily a loss to the society, is not it?—Yes.

3311. And what is the reason for this practice of giving them voluntarily what they are not entitled to by the terms of the insurance?—I tried to explain, my Lord, that parents with large families may have been paying in, for years to the society, money; and their youngest and lately born child may die. It would be only reasonable that we should, in that case, give them something.

3312. Are we to understand that that is only done in very exceptional cases of that kind?—In very exceptional cases of that kind. It is not done in every case.

3313. At the head of your form of proposal there is written, " If immediate benefit is required state whether quarter, half or full "; will you explain that?—Yes, these forms are used for all assurances, adult and infantile and everything, and where an immediate benefit is required we ask them to state so.

3314. It is only applicable to adult assurances?—Not only to adult, but mostly to adult assurances. In exceptional cases we extend it to children such as where the parents join also.

3315. To children of any age?—To children of any age. If the family join as in many cases: the parents and children of years for instance 12, 10, 8, 9, 7, 6 ; we should insure them.

Lord *Kinnaird.*

3316. Do you post date any?—No.

3317. Or ante date?—No ; we do not encourage immediate benefit. The immediate benefit has arisen out of the competition between the collecting societies and industrial companies of all classes.

3318. Under the competition do you practically ante date?—No.

3319. Will you put them back three months in order to begin immediate benefit?—No.

3320. May your agents do that?—No.

3321. Because they will get at once a pecuniary advantage?—No, they do not do that, besides it is not an advantage to the agents at all to insure for immediate benefit because they do not get the 12 weeks which we otherwise give them.

Earl of *Selborne.*

3322. We understood you to object to any limit of age. Now, under one year, whenever the death occurs, it is necessarily, so far as it goes, a loss?—Yes.

3323. And the evidence from the Prudential Society was, that upon the average of insured lives 99, or, we will say, 100, in every 1,000 died. That would be a necessary loss on the average of deaths under that age. Is that much the same experience that you have?—I should say that the evidence of the Prudential would
be

Earl of *Selborne*—continued.

be the experience of all industrial societies or companies.

3324. Then, we may take it, upon every death under one year there is a loss?—Yes.

3325. On the average?—Yes, certainly.

3326. And that to that you have to add the personal commission of your agent?—Yes.

3327. So that when you object to a limit of age, it is not in the interests of your society but, according to your view, in the interests of the classes who insure?—That is it, my Lord.

3328. I should like to ask a question upon the subject of lapses. Some witnesses before us have been under the impression that the societies derive large profits from lapses; is that the fact? —No, my Lord; it is impossible to derive any large profit from lapses of young children.

3329. Then, I presume, the real source of profits, is the large number of cases in which, either by the continuance of the insurance beyond the age at which there is an average practical risk, or by the continuance beyond the whole full age, there is a gain to the society?—Yes.

3330. That is the source of profit relied on. It depends upon the number of insurances?— The risk being spread over a large number.

3331. And the small proportion of deaths to the total number of insurances?—Yes.

3332. I should like to ask you about the premium. I suppose the premium varies according to the amount assured, does not it?—The premium varies taking it through the society as a whole.

3333. When it is said that the premium is a penny a week that would not be the same whether it was 3 *l.* or 6 *l.* that was insured would it?—Oh, no. I have known cases where people insured for ½ *d.* a week when in poor circumstances, particularly in Scotland where they go in for ½ *d.* insurances.

3334. That is the lower rate of insurances, but what I want to know is whether, according to the practice of your society, the premium of 1 *d.* a week is paid upon an insurance of 3 *l.* or 6 *l.*?— Yes, it is. We have a sliding scale that rises with the age of the children.

3335. Is not that an inducement to everybody to insure for the highest amount?—I am afraid I do not understand your Lordship's question. There is our sliding scale (*handing in the same*). That is an infantile policy.

3336. Then I suppose you do charge more for the higher amount than for the lower?—A child of one year of age paying a penny, is only insured for the amount your Lordship says, 3 *l.*, but when the child increases in age, the amount increases also, but the premium of a penny remains the same.

3337. By law, up to five years of age the amount may be 6 *l.*—Yes.

3338. And if there is no insurance in other companies it may be 6 *l.* with you?—Yes.

3339. I should like to know what premium you would charge in the case of a 6 *l.* insurance? —A penny, just the same. The premium does not rise at all.

3340. Then I should like to repeat my question. Is not that an inducement to the persons

(142.)

Earl of *Selborne*—continued.

always to insure for the greater, and not for the lesser amount, if they say the same?—Yes; I suppose it is.

Lord *Clifford* of *Chudleigh.*

3341. I understand that they always insure for the same amount. They always pay the same premium, but they get different amounts according to the age of the child?—Just so.

3342. So that it is impossible to insure a child for 6 *l.* when it is only one year old?—Yes.

3343. What instructions do your give your agents as to finding out the position that a person making an insurance holds to the person who is insured?—Your Lordship will see no person may insure except those having an insurable interest. That is in bold type on the proposal form.

3344. Is that all the instructions you give them?—Beyond what is in the instruction book.

3345. What is the nature of those instructions; that is what I want to know?—That only persons having an insurable interest can insure.

3346. For instance, taking the form which has been handed in by the Prudential Company, they require that the person signing the form shall be the father or mother of the child?—The phrase which your Lordship sees is that he must have "an insurable interest," which is not precisely the same. It is well understood, I think, and I think our precautions are just as effective as the Prudential precautions.

3347. We have heard a good deal of cases of baby farming being insured; would that be quite contrary to the instructions given to your agents?—Certainly. There would be nothing to prevent a baby-farmer signing his name as the parent of the child on either the Prudential or our proposal form. If a person came and said his name was John Brown we could not tell whether he was or not.

3348. But the agent might?—He might if he had a knowledge of the people, and lived there some time. If he collected in the locality he would have a greater knowledge.

3349. In addition to that it would prove this, would not it, that the baby-farmer fraudulently and not by mistake, signed his name to the paper?—Not by mistake; fraudulently.

3350. If the baby-farmer signed his or her name as the father or mother of the child, when they were not either the father or mother of the child, surely that would naturally be a fraudulent act?—That would be done fraudulently.

3351. But the baby-farmer might rightly or wrongly, and without any fraud, think that he had an insurable interest in the child?—No, I think not.

3352. Why not?—It is well understood I think now-a-days that an insurable interest in a child is only confined to its parents or legal guardians. Our agents would know that well enough.

3353. The agent would ask that question?— He should do.

3354. There is nothing in your instructions to provide for that?—Yes, I think there is, only I have not a copy with me, I will send one up.

U 4   3355. You

Lord *Norton.*

3355. You say that you cannot ascertain whether the person insuring is a parent or baby-farmer?—I say that they can impose upon us sometimes.

3356. You do not feel certain at all that the parent is applying?—Yes, we take it for granted that what they say is correct.

3357. You cannot tell whether it is the parent or step-parent, for instance?—No we cannot. If they describe themselves as the parent we take it for granted that it is so.

3358. You ascertain the age and health of the child?—Yes.

3359. But you take no steps to ascertain the character of the parents?—No.

3360. Suppose you knew the applicant to be a dissolute, drunken fellow, would you insure his child?—We should probably reject it.

3361. On the ground of the character of the the parent?—On the ground of the character of the parent.

3362. Does that often occur?—Not often.

3363. Do you think, generally speaking, we may say that dissolute and drunken parents cannot insure their children in your society?—No, not with our knowledge.

3364. Do you think your knowledge is generally accurate?—Fairly so.

3365. For what amounts can a parent insure a child under the age of three years old?—They vary.

3366. They are not all for the same amount?—At one year they can assure for 3 *l.* for a penny, and the same penny will give 3 *l.* 10 *s.* at two years, and the same penny will give 4 *l.* at three years, and so on.

3367. At a particular age must it be one particular sum?—One particular sum.

3368. At that age?—At that age.

3369. You said that the average cost of burial for the younger age was 2 *l.* 5 *s.*, I think?—£.2.10 *s.* about.

3370. Does that mean merely the burial expenses, or does it include doctor's expenses and other things?—No, I should say merely the burial expenses.

3371. Does that amount cover the whole of the expenses of a parent on the death of a child?—It cannot.

3372. Can you say at all whether that 2 *l.* represents about one-half of the expenses which the parent must incur, taking it very loosely?—Taking it very loosely, I daresay it is, if they have had a doctor attending the child.

3373. In average cases the expenses of the parent on the death of a child would be 4 *l.*?—Not quite so much as that, but there would be the loss of labour, the loss of a day's pay, and so on, which must be taken into consideration; perhaps there would be more than one day's loss of pay.

Lord *Brougham and Vaux.*

3374. Is a lapsed policy a source of profit or loss to the society?—A loss in the majority of instances.

3375. Do you mean to say that they are an actual loss?—An actual loss.

Lord *Norton.*

3376. Your society includes country districts as well as towns?—Yes, all over England, Scotland, Ireland, and Wales.

3377. What is the difference of expense of burials in towns and country, taking it very loosely and roughly?—I cannot give it.

3378. Would the minimum expense in a town be double what it is in the country?—I should think it would be about the same, because in country districts there would be less competition among tradesmen to get cheaper funerals.

3379. You think it would cost 2 *l.* as a minimum in the country?—Yes; everything included.

Earl of *Harrowby.*

3380. I see in your paper that there are four different agencies connected with the Proposal; there is an agent, a canvasser, a collector, and the committee; will you tell me what is the course which the proposal has to go through with regard to all these various authorities?—Those names are put down, although they are not always used; sometimes there is no canvasser, but it is only put down there as a contingency, if there should be a canvasser employed, so as to have the form adaptable for all circumstances.

3381. What is your usual course in regard to a proposal?—It comes from the parent to the collector, who is practically the same as the agent.

3382. He is the same as the agent?—Practically the same as the agent, there is a very slight difference.

3383. Who does it go to after that?—The agent, to forward to the committee.

3384. Then the committee consider whether it should be accepted or not?—No, sometimes it is referred to another agent.

3385. There is only one person concerned, the collector, and then it goes to the committee?—The collector and the committee, and they refer it back sometimes to another collector or agent to go and examine, to have a check.

3386. Your experience in Liverpool has been a long one?—Not so very long myself.

3387. What sort of time?—I have been in Liverpool seven years.

3388. You are in possession of all the traditions of the office of course?—Yes.

3389. Do you find that there is a considerable increase in the number of labouring classes that insure now compared with what there was 10 years ago; is it a larger proportion who insure?—Yes.

3390. A very large proportion?—Very large.

3391. There is a great increase?—A great increase.

3392. Can you give us any idea of the increase; is it 10 per cent. more than what it was 10 years ago?—I should not like to enter into any figures as to the increase, but it is a very large increase.

3393. You are confident that that increase is very large?—Yes it was a very difficult thing to get workpeople to insure sometime ago.

3394. That condition of things represents a considerable change in the habits of the working population?—Yes.

3395. How did they meet the expense of the funerals of their children before in Liverpool?—There

Earl of *Harrowby*—continued.

There were various methods; sometimes by collecting from neighbours. It sometimes used to be the practice to put the corpse out in the street with a plate on the chest, and people would throw coppers in, or give contributions, until they raised enough, and sometimes they would have singing and drinking parties.

3396. Are you talking of the English population as well as the Irish?—I am speaking of all.

3397. Have those habits disappeared?—Almost entirely.

3398. You attribute that to the growth of insurance which has created a more thrifty habit?—Yes.

3399. You have considerable knowledge of the habits of the working people in Liverpool?—As far as that is connected with insurance.

3400. Should I be right in saying that, quite independently of anything wrong or of negligence or of anything criminal, it is a well known fact that in Liverpool, as in other large cities, the working population unhappily lose a considerable number of their children in early infancy owing to the crowded condition of their houses and other necessary conditions of their lives?—Yes.

3401. Owing to the condition of the houses or lodgings or work in which they are engaged?—I think the factory districts are much worse than Liverpool in that respect.

3402. But it is unfortunately a condition of the ordinary life of a labouring man in Lancashire that he must look to the probable loss of a good number of his children in infancy?—I should say that, as to the children of the poorer working classes, naturally there is a higher rate of mortality among them than there is among others.

3403. Therefore it is a matter of great importance to them to have some means of meeting the expense of funerals and the other expenses of death?—It is. It would cripple them still further if they had not.

3404. Did you hear that suggestion which was made that we should get rid of some of the admitted evils of the present system if the registrar was obliged to give only one certificate?—Yes. He could only be required to give one certificate if there was only one insurance.

3405. I wanted to know whether, in your opinion, that would not be a security against there being more than one insurance if he was only allowed to give one certificate?—Yes, because any society or company paying the claim would retain that copy certificate, and no one could get another.

3406. Would you attach importance to that?—Yes. I think it follows it should be a security.

3407. Have you reason to know from your own personal knowledge that many insure in more than one society?—I believe they do.

3408. In Liverpool?—All over the country, London as well.

3409. With regard to your suggestion of a uniform Proposal form, do you think that the Government should lay down by legislation a necessary form of Proposal?—There should be one universal form.

3410. Who is to lay down this universal form?—I think that the Act should define the form itself.

3411. You wish that there should be laid down

(142.)

Earl of *Harrowby* – continued.

by legislation a universal Proposal form?—Yes.

3412. Drawn up by the Registrar of Friendly Societies, I suppose?—By the Registrar of Friendly Societies. I only hope that it will be taken into consideration that it should not be made too cumbersome.

Earl Beauchamp.

3413. Referring to your proposal form, I do not quite understand about "immediate benefit," what does that mean?—It means the same system with these industrial societies and companies as is in force at present with all the ordinary life insurance companies.

3414. At the present moment a person cannot obtain the benefit of the insurance until he has been 13 weeks a member?—Yes.

3415. Then if immediate benefit is required, does he pay 13 weeks' payment down?—No.

3416. Then what is immediate benefit?—The fact is that where a person enters into immediate benefit a more stringent examination is made of the person's health and the surroundings, and if all is satisfactory he is placed in such a position that should death occur immediately after the granting of the insurance the claim would be paid. I should like to qualify what I have said by adding that immediate benefit ought rather to be a safeguard than anything else, because the inquiries being more stringent with regard to the admission of people for immediate benefit, it should imply that more care was taken then. It should be, if anything, more of a safeguard.

3417. Then in your paper you draw a distinction between preventable causes of death and causes not preventable?—Yes.

3418. I think I understand you to say that you thought that over-lying was a preventable cause of death?—It is a preventable cause of death, Over-crowding leads to over-lying of children in a great measure. Sometimes it arises from the drunkenness of the parent, but in a great measure it arises from the over-crowding of families in small tenements.

3419. But it may so happen that quite irrespective of over-crowded apartments or lodgings, a child of tender years may be sleeping in the same bed with its parents?—Certainly; I have known cases where two children of tender years were sleeping together, one being an infant, and the infant was suffocated by the other little child accidentally throwing its arm over the infant's mouth.

3420 You consider overlying a preventable cause of death, just in the same sense as accidents, such as being run over, or any casualty of that kind preventable?—Certainly.

3421. What is your rule with regard to payment of insurance money to persons other than the parents of the child?—We do not pay the money to other persons than the parents. We have a form of application for the money which the parents have to fill up, and they must state on it that they are the parents of the child.

3422. In the event of a person claiming the money, who is not a parent of the child, what steps are taken?—It might happen occasionally that a parent was incapacitated from illness from

X   coming

Earl *Beauchamp*—continued.

coming for the money and she would then give a letter of authority to someone else to receive the money, and if it was all *bonâ fide* the claim would be paid to that person.

3423. We have had before the Committee a great many cases of baby-farming where the insurance appears to have been either effected or the money received by persons who were not the personal representatives of the parent. Do many of such cases come within your knowledge in connection with your society?—Not many, and in any cases that do come to our knowledge we do not pay them at all. We repudiate such cases at once.

3424. You think that that is a valuable security with regard to any abuses that might spring up in connection with the insurance of children?—Yes, the money should not be paid to anybody but the parents, except as I have mentioned.

3425. Do you allow in your society the insurance of unborn children?— No; you cannot insure an unborn child. You cannot give it a name.

3426. Did you ever hear of such a case. Has that ever come within your personal knowledge? —The nearest approach to it?

3427. I did not ask the nearest approach to it. Did you ever hear of such a case that you could investigate, the case of a child being insured when it was unborn?—If your Lordship will permit me, I should say that the nearest approach has been. where the mother of a child, shortly expecting to be confined, may have promised the agent of any society or company that she would, when the child was born, insure it with him in preference to any other agent or collector. That is the nearest approach to it.

3428. A child that is not born could not be insured?—No.

3429. Any agent insuring an unborn child would be reprimanded?—It is a fallacy. It has never been done. It could not be done.

3430. An agent insuring an unborn child would be reprimanded?—Certainly; he could not get a policy without the name of the child.

3431. You do not believe such a thing ever happened?—No, I do not.

3432. I understood you to say that you had never been invited to afford assistance to the Society for the Prevention of Cruelty to Children, or any other body, in tracing out suspicious cases?—I offered the secretary of the branch in Liverpool of the Society for the Prevention of Cruelty to Children, to give any assistance in

Earl *Beauchamp*—continued.

ferreting out what you may call suspicious cases, in which we were, or might have been, the society who had insured the children, but he has never come to me with any claim for assistance. Whether he did not require it because the Royal Liver does not do these things, I do not know, but the fact is we have not an application.

3433. Has any benevolent or philanthropic person applied to you for assistance?—A Mr. Agnew, of Liverpool, once came to see me about a proposed Bill of two or three years ago.

3434. Those gentlemen who make philanthropic speeches with regard to the treatment of children have never applied to you for co-operation in dealing with the question of insurance? —I am not aware of any case, with the exception of Mr. Agnew, that I am speaking of, and then it would be merely as to what would be well to put in a Bill for the prevention of cruelty to children.

3435. You mentioned the name of Mr. Hawkes?—Yes, the coroner near Birmingham.

3436. He has never applied to you?—We cannot get any information. In fact we have given up applying to Mr. Hawkes as a bad job.

3437. You have an agency in Birmingham?— A large one.

3438. Is it within your knowledge that Mr. Hawkes has frequently denounced the practice of child insurance?—Yes, I daresay many people denounce it, but they will give us no assistance to find out these cases. They may denounce it publicly, but they do not do anything else.

Chairman.

3439. Suppose that the parties that Earl Beauchamp has referred to did apply to you, it would appear that in most cases you could really give them no information? — We would try.   If they produced a specific case before us we should certainly try and get information.

3440. The only information you could give would be whether the child was or was not insured?—We should get the collector or agent to give all the information he could respecting the case.

3441. What information could he give?—It depends on what he could find out.   We take all cases as good cases when they come before us. If there was a suspicious case to our knowledge we should make searching inquiries from the neighbours, and other people.

[The Witness is directed to withdraw.

Ordered,—That this Committee be adjourned to Friday next, at Twelve o'clock.

Die Veneris, 18° Julii, 1890.

LORDS PRESENT:

Earl of DERBY.
Earl SPENCER.
Earl of HARROWBY.
Earl BEAUCHAMP.
Earl of SELBORNE.
LORD BISHOP OF PETERBOROUGH

Lord CLIFFORD OF CHUDLEIGH.
Lord POLTIMORE.
Lord BROUGHAM AND VAUX.
Lord KINNAIRD.
Lord NORTON.

THE RIGHT REV: THE LORD BISHOP OF PETERBOROUGH, IN THE CHAIR.

MR. THOMAS CHARLES DEWEY, is again called in; and further Examined, as follows:

Chairman.

3442. THERE is a point in your evidence which you gave on our last meeting, which appears to me to require a little clearing up; I should be glad if you would give the Committee some explanation about it; it is with reference to your objections to my Bill. In your answer to Question 2856, on page 139, you say that my Bill permits any person to insure the lives of other people's children which the present law forbids. Now, at the moment you said that I had not my Bill before me, and I answered you that that might be an accidental defect in the Bill; however, on looking over the Bill carefully since you made that statement, I have been unable to find any clause in my Bill which permits any person to insure the lives of other people's children; would you kindly point out which the clause is that you had in your mind?—Your Lordship's Bill, I believe, repeals the 28th Section of the existing Friendly Societies Act, which forbids the insurance of any child except by the parent, or the personal representative of the parent. Section 28, Sub-section 1, of the existing Act, says, "No society shall insure or pay on the death of a child under five years any sum of money," that, we take it, means, that by law we are prohibited from allowing any guardian to insure a child at all; that is proposed to be repealed by your Lordship's Bill, and therefore if it is repealed it will be considered that it is now legal.

3443. The proposed Bill substitutes the provisions of this Bill for the provisions of Section 28 of the Friendly Societies Act?—Yes.

3444. Your point is that by repealing Section 28 of the Friendly Societies Act, we repeal the law upon that particular point which prevents any person insuring another person's child?—We have always considered it so.

3445. You have always considered it so, but at the same time you say in another passage of your evidence that the section is not generally so

(142.)

Chairman—continued.

construed?—I take it that it is not, because I have seen instances where baby farmers have insured children, and I say those insurances are illegal under the existing law.

3446. That is your impression?—That is my impression.

3447. That is your impression, but you state that it is not the general interpretation of the Act?—There is no penalty attaching to this clause in the Friendly Societies Act.

3448. But you state in answer to Question 2853, that your reading you are afraid is not general, that is to say, that that view of the law is not generally taken?—That is so, it is not generally taken.

3449. Then it would not be the general interpretation that the repealing of that portion of the Friendly Societies Act would have that effect?—I think it is simply a question of ignorance.

3450. In the same section of the Friendly Societies Act there is a Sub-section 9, which says that it is not to apply to any person having an insurable interest?—Yes.

3451. Then any person even under the Friendly Societies Act, who could show an insurable interest in the life of another person, would have a right even under that Act to insure, would he not?—Yes, he would; but, I think, it has also been held that a guardian has no insurable interest in law.

3452. That is another question; the question might be raised, might it not, that a baby farmer receiving so much a month for a child, would have an insurable interest?—It might be so held.

3453. Sub-section 9, which you have quoted now against me, excludes all persons except those having an insurable interest in the child insured?—That is so.

3454. The whole sum of this matter therefore is, that you object to the Bill, not because it makes

x 2

any

Chairman—continued.

any absolute variation in the present law, but because you are of opinion that a certain interpretation by you of the present law which is not apparently held by others, is affected by it?—It is not generally held by others, because of ignorance only. I take it that it is the intention of the Legislature in putting in the word " insure," to mean what it states.

3455. You would propose that the law should be altered so that it should come to this, that no persons should under any circumstances insure any other person's child?—But the existing Act says that the insurance must be effected by the parent or the personal representative of the parent.

3456. But you would amend this Bill, so far as your proposed clause would go, to the extent of preventing any person insuring any other person's child, for the purpose of preventing baby farming?—Yes.

3457. You are aware that there are perfectly innocent cases of insurance of other people's children; for instance, where a guardian, say the guardian of a minor under the Court of Chancery, is receiving a large sum during his guardianship; would you forbid that?—Yes, I would.

3458. You would forbid cases of innocent insurance in order to prevent cases of guilty insurance?—If you refer to Sub-section 2, you will see that under the existing Act it is impossible for us or anyone to pay such a person as your Lordship mentions the amount of the policy in case of death, because there is a penalty if we do.

3459. Then, if I understand you rightly, you would, for one reason or another improve the law in this way, that you would forbid any person insuring another person's child?—Exactly so.

3460. Have you considered what a very extensive effect that would have upon insurance generally?—We have considered it carefully for many years.

3461. Then, may I put this question to you: you said a person should be forbidden to insure any other person's child; would you allow a man to insure his own life?—Certainly.

3462. Is he his own child or another person's child?—A man has a perfect right to insure his own life.

3463. But I am asking you what would be the effect of your clause; you say you would forbid a person insuring another person's life; at the same time, you say you would not object to his insuring his own life; now, I ask, is a man his own child or another person's child?—He is as his own child, I take it, for insurance purposes.

3464. Do you mean to say that a man is his own child?—In the eye of the law I take it to be so.

Lord *Kinnaird.*

3465. Might I ask what latitude you give your agents in paying without consulting the head office?—They have to send in a paper to the head office for the payment to be made or to our district offices; we have district offices all over the kingdom.

3466. How soon after the claim can they get

Lord *Kinnaird*—continued.

the money?—They can get the money within 24 hours after the death.

3467. The whole of the money?—The whole of the money, but there must be the registrar's certificate.

3468. There is sometimes delay in getting the certificate; may they pay a portion on account?—No.

3469. I was going to ask you one other question. You were asked whether the average that you paid was about 2*l.* 13*s.*, and you assented to the question; then you do not think, I presume, that there would be any hardship in making that average the maximum; that is to say, in reducing the 6*l.* to somewhere about what the average is now?—I think I answered that 2*l.* 13*s.* would be the expenses, but that that did not include the expenses of the mourning; the average amount now paid in our office is 2*l.* 13*s.*

3470. You would not approve of the amount being reduced from 6*l.* to, say, 3*l.*?—I think it is a question for the working classes. We only pay the reduced sum, because, for a penny a-week, we cannot afford to pay more.

3471. Would you tell the Committee if you have any table which would show what the proportion of lapses is, and then re-insuring the same life?—I have no statistics with me, showing that.

3472. Would there not be a considerable number of cases in which a man gets out of work, and omits to pay his penny?—In such a case we allow him to revive his policy within 12 months, on paying up the arrears, without any charge at all.

3473. But there is no benefit to you in his dropping it?—Within 12 months he may pay up his arrears without interest, and revive the policy.

3474. You say you often have to refuse; have you any proportion of cases in which the claims are disputed?—No; pardon me; I say there is no reason for disputing any claim. You will find that in my answer to Question 3005.

3475. Have you any percentage of the children by your tables who are insured in two or three offices?—I can give the Committee information upon that point; out of 100 claims we pay on the deaths of children, 94 are insured with us only, the remaining six have second insurances; that is on the average.

3476. With reference to the table you gave the Committee of the number of children insured in your different offices, the same children would count two or three times over, would they not?—I mentioned, I think, that that did not include double insurances, and that we might take off 200,000 or 300,000 from the total number.

3477. Have you many double insurances in your own office?—No.

3478. Do you allow it?—We do not. We should be infringing the Act by allowing it ourselves.

3479. Then I will ask you this as my last question, do you consider that the poorest people insure less than the rather better-to-do people?—It is the thrifty artisan who insures. As a rule, the dissolute and intemperate people have

no

Lord *Kinnaird*—continued.

no idea of paying a weekly premium for some weeks, which they would have to do for an infantile life, before they could obtain any money.

3480. We have already heard from a witness that collections on death have very much decreased owing to facilities for insuring with you and others?—I think you may take it so. I heard a working man say here last week that these companies have rescued the working man from the necessity of sending round the hat, and friendly leads.

3481. How do the children of the poorest and most dissolute parents have to be buried?—They have to be buried by the guardians.

3482. A considerable number get buried by the guardians, do they not?—Yes; if they are unable to pay, the sanitary authorities compel the parish to get the body buried.

Earl of *Selborne.*

3483. You just now said that you, charging a penny a week only up to 10 years, restrict the amount of insurance in your society?—Yes.

3484. To what sum is it restricted?—Ours is a graduated table, and your Lordships will see that the policies have the tables printed upon them, and if we issue two policies, taking it as if the policy had been paid up for six years, that would give 12 *l.* at risk, whereas the Act says only 10 *l.*; therefore, we should be infringing the present Act, and should be liable to a penalty.

3485. Do I understand that you do insure upon single lives up to 6 *l.*?—No; this is a case of having been insured six years; the rate is, under one year, after three months, 30 *s.*; after the policy has been in force one year, 3 *l.*; after two years, 3 *l.* 10 *s.*; after three years, 4 *l.*; after four years, 4 *l.* 10 *s.*; after five years, 5 *l.*; and after the policy has been in force six years, 6 *l.*

3486. Then, according to that scale, you insure up to 10 years for a penny a week?—Yes.

3487. Then you fix the scale so that the person insuring has nothing to do with the amount for which he insures, but, on insuring, he accepts those terms?—Yes; it is a uniform premium and an increasing amount.

3488. Now, I wish to ask you a few questions next upon the form of proposal you put in; the first six questions relate to the parents; are they sufficient to inform you whether the child is an illegitimate child or not; you do not ask the question directly, but would the answers to those questions sufficiently inform you on that point? —The answer to the first question, which gives the name of the father, does that; the surname of the father would not be the same as that of the mother if the child were illegitimate.

3489. You find, in practice, that it is enough for that purpose?—Yes.

3490. I see your 53rd rule is, that "illegitimate children will not be accepted until they have attained the age of three years"?—Yes.

3491. That is founded, I presume, upon the greater risk of their being ill-treated, is that so?— It is so; we have found that it is advisable to do this, but, as I mentioned on a former occasion, in some cases we have to make an exception, and we do make an exception; for instance, if the parents are living together, married, but have an

(142.)

Earl of *Selborne*—continued.

illegitimate child, we should not regard that as an illegitimate child.

3492. But your general practice is that which is indicated by these instructions?—That is so; we should not take a single woman's baby.

3493. With reference to the instances which you put in upon the last day you were here, of refusals, which were numerous, I rather collected from looking cursorily at them, that the grounds of refusal are usually one or other of these; either that the child was an illegitimate child, or that it was not in the actual care of its parents? —Yes, that is so.

3494. Sometimes even where there was a certificate that the child was in good health and everything else seemed right, you refused upon those grounds?—We did.

3495. I see, in your 39th and 40th instructions, that you direct your agent, in some cases, to have the medical examination which is defined by the 39th instruction, and then you say by the 40th, "The fact that a medical examination is to be made in no way relieves the agent from the responsibility of obtaining all available information as to the health of the proposers;" do your agents, in all cases, give the result of their personal observation or inquiry into those matters? —They do upon our forms of proposal, that refers merely, however, to adults. Your Lordship has an infantile policy also before you.

3496. Then in your form of proposal you require information from the person proposing to insure?—We do.

3497. In addition to that, does your agent take any steps to satisfy himself?—He does. In the adult form of proposal there are questions to be answered by the agent.

3498. I infer from the table you put in upon the former day, that all deaths under the age of three are a greater or less loss to the company upon the percentage of deaths to the thousand?— Yes.

3499. And all above that are a gain to the company?—Yes.

3500. I presume the profits of the company arise upon the insurances which do not become losses before the age of three, and those which never become losses at all?—That is so.

3501. And that they are so great a proportion of the whole, as to produce a satisfactory profit? —Yes, our margin of profit on our business is 2 per cent. upon the amount received, that would be one-fiftieth; and out of a 4 *s.* 4 *d.* policy (52 pennies) two per cent. would be a penny per annum upon each policy; that is our last ascertained profit.

3502. It has been stated by some witnesses before the Committee, as their belief, that the principal, or at least a great part of the gains, of these societies arose from lapses; I think you have put in an actuarial opinion to the contrary? —I have.

3503. That, as I understand it, does not so much deny that a lapse when it occurs is a gain, so far, of the premiums which have been paid, but that it will be more for the interest of the company that a policy should go on and not lapse; is not that the fact?—I do not read it so. Infantile assurance is the same as fire, marine, and accident insurance, where, so long as the risk is

X 3   running

Earl of *Selborne*—continued

running, premiums received, even when the policy ceases, are not profit.

3504. Is not that rather technical; as a matter of fact, you have received in such cases of lapse a certain amount of premium which you have not to return?—That is so.

3505. No loss has occurred upon those cases, therefore it is, so far as it goes, a gain to the company, is it not?—No, it is not.

3506. A less loss in comparison with what you might have sustained if it had gone on?—No, it is no gain at all.

3507. It is so much the less due to pay, is it not?—No; that is not the way I should put it. If there are ten policies in hand to-day which will lapse between to-day and next Christmas, the premiums which would accrue would be 10 times 2 *s.* 2 *d.* for the six months, which will be 1 *l.* 1 *s.* 8 *d* During that time we may assume we shall have a claim which will absorb the one pound of that amount, therefore, all the premiums we shall have received upon the policies which are going to lapse will have been taken to pay the claim upon the policy then claimed.

3508. Not a claim upon a lapsed policy?—No, it will be a claim upon one policy running, and we shall require the premiums upon the policies that are to be lapsed to pay that one.

3509. That, I take it, means that the average losses more than balance the profit upon the lapses within the same period of time?—I take exception to your Lordship's expression that there is any profit at all upon the lapses.

3510. I do not repeat the word "profit" if it is objected to; but is that your meaning that there was not a profit because in point of fact, within the same period of time, the average losses exceed the average lapses?—That is so.

3511. I understand you to say that not only do the companies not gain by lapses, but that they have actually a practice which is intended, so far as may be, to prevent them?—That is so for my company.

3512. I think you said that there is a certain sum, I forget the amount, which is left in the hand of the agent, which in case of a lapse he has to return?—It is so; the agent suffers a direct loss for every policy which lapses.

3513. Therefore the company promotes its desire to prevent lapses by making it the interest of the agent to do all he can to prevent them?—It is so.

3514. I will now ask you a question upon the point you have just referred to, namely, your actuarial opinion which says, that the risk is estimated in the same way as marine, fire, or accident insurances. I am not sure about accident, but marine and fire insurances as you know are paid, not upon the amount insured, but upon the loss which is proved to have been actually sustained by the fire or by the casualty at sea?—That is so.

3515. Would there be any objection, in your opinion, to adopting the same rule as to these insurances of children, and to say that the company is not to be bound to pay the exact sum for which the insurance is made, but that it is to receive proof in every case of that which is claimed as lost by the insurer. For example, to show what I mean, the funeral expenses, the undertaker's bill, that is to say, paid or not paid,

Earl of *Selborne*—continued.

the bill for mourning, if there is mourning, and the doctor's bill, if there is a doctor's bill, to be paid. That would be the way in which the principle of marine and fire insurance would be applied. The amount of loss has to be sufficiently stated, and the society to be satisfied that it is correctly stated. Would you see any objection to applying that principle to child insurance?—I think there would be a great objection to such a contract of indemnity; it would be impracticable altogether in this class of insurance; persons require payment immediately. there would be all the bills; the undertaker's bill, and the doctor's bill would all have to be submitted to us, and, I think, we should require to keep a staff of assessors the same as fire insurance companies do, to prevent fraud upon the company.

3516. You think the transactions would be too numerous, and too small to make the work possible?—I think so; our claims altogether now exceed 500 a day, and it would be a very important alteration.

Lord *Poltimore.*

3517. I think you said on the last occasion that your agents were paid by commission varying from 17½ up to 20 per cent.?—That is so.

3518. Surely, is not that rather an objectionable system?—It is the only system which would work satisfactorily, I think.

3519. You do not think any other system could be adopted which would meet the necessity of the case, and yet answer equally well?—I think in every walk of life it is necessary to pay men on results, in order to be successful.

Earl of *Harrowby.*

3520. Do you agree that there has been a very large increase in child insurance in the last 10 years?—There has been.

3521. Have you any figures to show that, during the last 10 or 20 years?—Insurance has grown almost entirely within the last 25 years.

3522. That is to say, child insurance?—Yes.

3523. Your experience is in the rural districts as well as in London?—It is.

3524. Is there the same growth in the rural districts as there is in London?—Yes quite.

3525. Has there been a great increase in the number of companies which insure children's lives?—No, there are not many companies which insure children's lives now.

3526. Can you tell the Committee how many companies there are which insure children's lives?—I should not think there are more than six.

3527. Except the local companies?—Yes, I am talking of companies registered under the Joint Stock Act, and amenable to the Board of Trade; excluding collecting societies, new companies before they could embark on infantile business would have to deposit 20,000 *l.* in the Court of Chancery.

3528. You say there are six of those companies?—Yes, speaking off-hand; there are certainly not eight.

3529. Will you tell the Committee what are the actual officers of your company concerned in a proposal; I see in another company there was a canvasser, an agent, a collector, and the committee mentioned?—That is a collecting friendly society we have the agent to obtain the

Earl of *Harrowby*—continued.

the business, then we have a superintendent in each district who is paid by salary to see that all our regulations are strictly carried out. Then we have clerks inside the office to also check the outdoor staff.

3530. You have agents, superintendents, and clerks?—Yes.

3531. The clerks are mainly kept for the clerical work, I suppose?—Yes, and to examine all fresh forms as they come in to see if they are correctly filled in.

3532. What is the next step?—The next step is management.

3533. The form goes before the committee, does it not?—No, there is no committee, there is a board; the board of directors.

3534. And they settle whether it is to be accepted or not?—Yes.

3535. Then I see that in the proposal form the agent has to certify that the child is either in good, indifferent, or bad health; what qualification has the agent for giving that opinion?—He has no special qualification.

3536. What does he base his opinion upon?—His intelligence.

3537. That is to say, his general intelligence?—Yes, his general intelligence.

3538. It is difficult to ascertain what the health of a child, under 12 months, is; is it not?—It is, as I stated on the last occasion.

3539. Then I see, you say, you fill into the form the first class rate, or second class rate, or third class rate, as the case may be; what do those different rates mean?—The rate is to enable us to tell what the agent means by the previous entry as to the state of health.

3540. If he states "good health," does that mean that he recommends the first class rate?—The first class means where everything is satisfactory.

3541. Where the highest amount of insurance can be given?—Yes.

3542. Then taking it for a child, the first year next birthday, 30 *s.*; that would be given in the case of a child certified to be in good health?—Yes.

3543. But if the child were in indifferent health?—Then we should not take it.

3544. Then why should you make a second rate?—That is for the higher ages.

3545. Do you ever pay anything if a child dies before the age of three months?—Yes, we do; as the noble Chairman put it, we make a grant of grace.

3546. You think that is important?—We have a strong appeal frequently made to us when a child dies, say by accident or from scarlet fever, or anything of that kind; but that is always done at the head office, upon the receipt of medical evidence.

3547. And when many children in the same family have been insured before, I presume?—Yes; we take all the circumstances into consideration.

3548. It has been suggested by some witnesses that they regard it as a matter of considerable importance that there should be a general form of proposal laid down by the Legislature; would you attach importance to that suggestion?

Earl of *Harrowby*—continued.

—We should not object to that, if it were not less stringent than our own.

3549. In your experience, would you think it an improvement?—I think not.

3550. It is suggested to me to ask whether you would object, if it were made more stringent than your own form of proposal?—No; we are open to consider any alteration.

3551. There is a great difference between the forms: yours is very searching; whereas another that we have seen does not ask many questions. Does not it seem to you that if your form is necessary, it would be desirable to enforce the same precaution upon all?—Yes, there is reason in that.

Earl *Beauchamp.*

3552. You told the Committee that out of 100 claims made to your office 94 per cent. were insured in your office alone?—Yes.

3553. Does that apply to all your insurances, or to those of children only?—It applies to children only.

3554. May we take it that those who insure in other offices besides your own would be the well-to-do artisan?—Probably they would have a larger income coming in, and could spend more on insurance.

3555. If they were restricted to one policy of insurance, and the amount payable under the policy was limited to 2 *l.* 13 *s.*, that would be a great hardship upon the more thrifty and respectable poor?—That is so.

3556. I think you told the Committee that you did not object to a reduction of the amount of the policy; were you speaking of the effect of the limitation upon your own company, or upon the habit of the people?—It was more as to the effect upon our own company.

3557. Then, with reference to lapses, do lapses with you include proposals declined?—No; lapses simply mean that the policies have been issued, and then dropped afterwards, whether premiums paid or not.

3558. Are you aware whether that practice is universal in other companies?—If they issue a policy, I take it that it is so; but, in some cases, in local clubs, they do not issue policies.

3559. You think it better for your society to exercise care before a policy is granted rather than to grant a policy easily and dispute it afterwards?—That is so.

3560. You regard that as being in the interest of your company as well as in the interest of public morality?—It is in the interest of every one, I think.

3561. And in consequence of the care exercised you dispute very few policies?—We dispute very few policies.

3562. Have those precautions been adopted recently?—No; they have been adopted for many years.

3563. Were those precautions adopted at the time the company was formed?—No; the company was not formed for this class of business at all; we have a very large business in other insurances.

3564. But were these precautions adopted concurrently with the adoption of this class of business?—No; we have gone by our experience.

3565. Were

Earl *Beauchamp*—continued.

3565. Were they the result of external advice?—No; I think they were the result of our experience.

3566. Has your society in any way been invited to co-operate with the Society for the Prevention of Cruelty to Children in cases where the insurances have been said to be an incentive to crime?—We have been often in communication with them; we have in recent cases, and we have always given information to them, but, at the same time, I am bound to say that I do not think it has been fairly used.

3567. Will you explain that a little more?—I could explain that in a very recent case, alluded to by Mr. Waugh in his evidence, which is known as the Wandsworth case.

3568. Could you give me the reference?—I could not give you the reference. He stated that during that very week there were ever so many convictions, and that this was one of the convictions that he had obtained. In this case an inspector of the society came down as they usually do, to obtain information, and we gave him all we could. The father was insured and paid annual premiums for 100 *l.*, and all the children had been insured; the child upon which the cruelty case arose has been insured for 10 years. The information was very strong that the family had been all insured for at least 10 years; then a step-mother appeared upon the scene and things changed in the family; and we pointed out to the inspector, that we did not think it was proved at all that this insurance had anything to do with the crime, the inspector made a remark, which I thought was a very ominous remark, that he agreed with us that it did not, but that they were obliged to introduce the point of the insurance in order to induce the magistrate, before whom the case was coming that day, to commit; that they had a special magistrate who they thought would be up at the court, and that if they did not throw in the insurance they would probably not get a conviction. In that case, therefore, we sent on full particulars to the solicitor defending the family. We read the Act passed last year to mean that the insurance was to be brought in only in the way that previous convictions are brought in, those are the words of the Act, I think, and not to be brought in, in the form which it was brought in, in this case; but we never withheld the information; the information was given all the same. That is what I mean by its not being fairly used. In that very case at Wandsworth Police Court the counsel prosecuting for the society withheld all reference to the insurance, as no doubt he felt his duty compelled him to do, but when the case came before the quarter sessions, the solicitor or barrister defending the family had to leave the court and left his brief in the hands of another man. Then the counsel for the society brought out the insurance. The Act did not mean that; the information which we had given, of course, as we think, prejudiced that case; at the same time we had not refused the information.

3569. You have been always ready to afford assistance whenever you have been requested to do so?—Yes, I think Mr. Waugh would bear

Earl *Beauchamp*—continued.

that out; I told Mr. Waugh of this case at the time, so that he could trace the inspector, and he says the inspector exceeded his duty.

3570. A great deal has been made in this Committee-room, and elsewhere, of what is known as the Deptford case; the Committee have been told that there were three persons who died in the Deptford case, one of them a boy of 11 years of age; another, a person of the age of 74; and another, a person of the age of 53. Has that fact ever been mentioned in the reports of the Society for the Prevention of Cruelty to Children?—No; one of the leading London newspapers contained an article condemning infantile insurance, and quoting this very case.

3571. Quoting the case of the three persons put out of the way, supposing they were put out of the way?—There was not one of them which came under the Friendly Societies Act in any way.

3572. You think that a prejudice has been created against infantile insurance, by the dexterous use of sensational statements?—I can assure you there is, and I can give your Lordships the most recent case of all—that was in the newspapers last week—I refer to the case at Newcastle, of which a sensational statement was made in Court; we had the magistrate condemning infant insurance, and we had the recorder condemning it. The man came before Mr. Justice Charles last Saturday. I ought also to say that the preacher in the Cathedral on Sunday also condemned infant insurance. When the case came before Mr. Justice Charles he saw at once that the child would not be in benefit for two months, whereas the other children were in benefit; and he told the jury that the child, in fact, was not insured; and that, therefore, they were to discard that point entirely, before they gave their verdict. That case has been in all the London newspapers, headed "Insurance and Child Murder." The facts of the case show that the mother could not have had any intention to murder the child for the sake of the insurance, else she would have kept it alive for the next two months.

3573. Do you know anything about the Swindon case?—I do.

3574. Was that life insured in your office?—No; it was not.

Chairman.

3575. You say, and no doubt quite truly, that you never refuse information to the Society for the Prevention of Cruelty to Children?—We do not.

3576. Whether that is asked from yourself personally, or from your board of management?—From the office.

3577. But you do not mean to say so when asked from the agent; I presume you would not take upon you to say, that you know, as a matter of fact, that the agents are always ready and willing to give information?—The agents would not be allowed to give information at all; we consider the insurance is a private matter. We know that charges have been made, that the agents have not given information; all I have to say in reference to that is, that the agents are not

in

Chairman—continued.

in bad company, because Mr. Waugh told me that not a single clergyman in London had ever given him any such information.

3578. You would admit, would you not, that an agent would be more likely to be possessed of the information than a clergyman ?—I am not prepared to say that.

3579. You may take it from me, I think, that that would be so ; you could tell the Committee, however, that the agents are not allowed to give information ?—Yes, the insurance is a private matter, and they are not authorised to state it at all to their neighbours.

3580. The only case in which you could give information would be a case in which your agent had already privately informed you to that effect ? —The ordinary course would be, that the secretary of the Society for the Prevention of Cruelty to Children would write to our office, and we should give information. I do not wish to say anything against the society. I know it has done an immense amount of good. I am a vice-president of the Church Society, and I would do everything I could to assist their objects legitimately.

3581. You think, however, that their inspectors have exceeded their instructions ?—There are two such cases in which they have exceeded their instructions within the last six weeks.

3582. And there might be cases in which your own agents would exceed their instructions ?— Yes ; no doubt they do sometimes.

3583. Then, with reference to the evidence given before coroners; you have seen the evidence given by Mr. Taunton before this Committee, that it would be highly desirable in every case of a coroner's inquest that the coroner should ask a question about insurance ; what do you say as to that suggestion ?—If it is to prejudice the inquiry, I should say that he should not.

3584. I am only pointing out that persons in your own occupation have recommended that this question of insurance should be introduced upon coroners' inquests, and that the coroner should be bound to ask it ?—I should differ from them.

3585. The fact that a question about insurance was asked by the coroner does not necessarily show a very violent prejudice against insurance societies, if the secretary to one of the greatest insurance societies recommends that that should be done ?—I am not prepared to father everything that Mr. Taunton has recommended.

3586. But there cannot be a very violent prejudice against child insurance when the secretary to a very large institution of a similar nature to your own so strongly recommends that ?—I cannot admit it, but I am aware of the suggestion.

3587. Then, with reference to the Deptford case ; there was a distinct opinion expressed by the jury, was there not, as to the lax manner in which children insurance societies conduct their business ?—I think not; there was no child before them. I think you will find in the House of Commons' Report it is put under the head of Infantile Insurance, with a note, " The following letter has been forwarded by the Secretary of State since the close of the evidence." There-

(142.)

Chairman—continued.

fore, the compiler put it there, thinking it referred to infantile insurance, though the Committee did not.

3588. But this was a letter forwarded to the Chairman of the Committee by the Secretary of State ?—Yes, but that was a Committee beyond merely child insurance.

3589. This was the opinion of the jury who heard the case : " The jury are of opinion that the facilities given by the loose system of life insurance practised by some companies is an incentive to wilful murder for the sake of the insurance money "; that was the opinion of the jury who tried the case, not the opinion of any prejudiced or excited person ?—That was the opinion of the coroner's jury.

3590. The jury had some evidence, I presume, as to the manner in which life insurance was conducted by some society or other, and gave it as their opinion, " that the loose system of life insurance practised by some companies is an incentive to wilful murder " ?—That was in reference to the assignment of policies.

3591. Was it in reference to the assignment of policies that they complained that " the loose system of life insurance practised by some companies is an incentive to wilful murder " ? –Yes.

Earl Beauchamp.

3592. In reference to the ages of the insured——

Chairman.

3593. One of the insured was a child of eleven years of age ?—Yes, which had nothing to do with child insurance.

3594 The child in this case, Sidney Bolton, was induced to sign the application upon his own life ?—He would be obliged to do that.

3595. If it were the opinion of a magistrate (I do not know whether he tried the case, but at all events he knew all about it), expressed to me, that in case the child signed his own death-warrant, that would be very much your own opinion, would it not ?—I think not.

3596. You have mentioned Mr. Justice Charles as having said that in the case he tried, there was no incentive to murder arising from insurance ?—He simply said there was no insurance, therefore the jury must discard it.

3597. Are you aware that Mr. Justice Charles is one of the witnesses who has expressed a very strong opinion about child insurance ?—That makes that remark all the stronger.

3598. You would agree that Mr. Justice Charles who gave that instruction to the jury was not influenced by his hostility to child insurance, because, notwithstanding that instruction to the jury, he has expressed a hostile opinion to child insurance ?—Yes, so I understand.

Earl Beauchamp.

3599. Has he expressed that opinion subsequent to the trial ?—No.

Chairman.

3600. Do you think the influence of that one case, in which there was that evidence, would induce him to change the opinion which must

Y   have

Chairman—continued.

have been founded upon a number of cases?—I expect that remark which your Lordship refers to was made to the grand jury before he had all the depositions before him.

3601. But it is a general opinion founded upon his experience of child insurance. He did not say, " This is a case I strongly condemn," but he spoke in very strong terms of the effect of child insurance generally. You would not surely contend that the fact that he discovered afterwards that that particular case had nothing to do with child insurance had altered, or could possibly have altered, the general opinion he expressed which doubtless must have been founded upon a large experience?—With all deference the learned judge might have founded his opinion upon articles he had read in the newspapers. There are many articles which have appeared in the newspapers which have influenced public opinion we know.

Earl of *Derby.*

3602. You told us on the first day of your examination that you had no objection to the prohibition of child insurance up to the age of 12 months?—As far as my company is concerned, we should see no objection to it; it is a question entirely for the working classes.

3603. As far as the interests of your company were concerned, you saw no objection to it?—I saw no objection to it.

3604. Do you think there would be any material objection, so far as the interests of your company are concerned, in raising the limit of age a little higher, say up to two years?—The company would do everything they could if it were deemed public policy to conform to the suggestion, but at the same time we think from the evidence of the working man who was examined last Friday, that the working classes would regard it as a hardship.

3605. That is to say, if they were not allowed to insure their children under two years old?—The greater the prohibition, the greater the hardship they would consider it; but I would venture to suggest that, if any change of the sort were recommended, the best way would be to prohibit the company from paying anything during the first year, but let the working man still insure, because by insuring he could get some future benefit.

3606. You mean that he should insure upon the terms of not receiving anything if the child died under 12 months old, but might begin his payments?—He could have the money that he had paid as premiums back again, but beyond that nothing; letting it be for some future benefit.

Chairman.

3607. Would you explain that proposal a little further, because it seems a very valuable suggestion; if I understand you correctly, you propose that the working man should be allowed to insure his child at a given age, and that it should be understood that if that child died within a year, the company should not pay that money to the parent, but should carry it on to his credit or benefit, say for the benefit of other children?—I would have the premiums returned,

Chairman—continued.

if the child died, but if it lived I would have the money applied to its future benefit.

3608. If the child died you would have the premiums returned to the parent?—Yes.

3609. Would you not also have the policy carried on for the parents' benefit?—No; the policy must cease; but in the event of the child living, we would give some future benefit.

3610. In the event of the child dying the premiums would be returned?—Yes.

3611. In the event of the child living the policy would be continued for its benefit?—Yes.

3612. Then, supposing the child dies shortly after it is one year old?—Then, of course, we should pay whatever amount should be specified, and we should specify it clearly upon the policy. What I mean is, that the money which is paid during the first year we could carry on for some future benefit, so that it would be advisable not to prohibit insurance but to prohibit the companies paying claims during the first year. Then, might I add this: you mentioned the question about the agents being licensed; I think there would be a very strong objection to that; I think they have done nothing for which a ban should be placed upon them in the way of a license.

3613. Do you know of any proposal which has been made with reference to this matter of child insurance which has not appeared objectionable to somebody, whether agent, society, or parent?—No doubt that is right.

3614. If nothing is to be done because some one does not like it, would anything be done?—That would be so, no doubt. Then, I would like to make this suggestion; your Lordship has suggested that infantile insurance is a privilege conferred; I think that the friendly societies which do that class of business should all be registered; there is a great difference now between registered friendly societies and unregistered friendly societies; the interest of the friendly societies office is to get every one registered; this would make them register if infantile insurance were forbidden in societies which are not registered.

3615. That would bring certain societies which are not now registered under the operation of the Friendly Societies Act?—Yes, but unless your Bill is very strongly worded, the local societies would get out of it as they do out of the present Act.

3616. You would compel all societies having to do with the insurance of children in any way to come under the Friendly Societies Act?—I think it would be very much better for all societies doing this class of business to be registered, and all their operations to be conducted in the full light of day.

3617. That would be the case if they were registered under the Friendly Societies Act?—That is so, and that is what we want.

Earl of *Derby.*

3618. What do you conceive the advantage of registration would be?—The advantage of registration would be that a society's constitution must be known; it must deliver its accounts; it must deliver a proper valuation; all that information

Earl of *Derby*—continued.

information would have to be given by the society, and would be laid annually before Parliament; whereas, now, there are societies in existence which no one out of them ever hears of at all; societies such as that which the inspector for Rochdale, who was before your Lordships, alluded to.

Chairman.

3619. There are what are called, in my diocese, slate clubs; have you ever heard of them by that name?—Slate clubs do not, I think, insure children, as a rule.

3620. Do they not?—I believe they do not; they are clubs in which the money is divided every year.

Earl of *Derby.*

3621. I suppose it happened to one of the unregistered societies, that its constitution was wrong, and its accounts were not to be depended on; who has the power of interfering?—That is a question for the Friendly Societies Office; but, at the same time, they are not under the penal clauses of the Friendly Societies Act, and, I think, they should be brought under it.

Earl of *Selborne.*

3622. Is registration at present merely voluntary?—Registration is simply voluntary under the present law.

Earl *Spencer.*

3623. How do societies escape being registered; I thought it was under some new Act? —That is the Rochdale Friendly Society; at present a society must be registered or unregistered, or come under the Joint Stock Act. This Society at Rochdale has evaded the Friendly Societies Act; it does not issue policies, and therefore does not come under the Life Insurance Act. It simply means that some clever lawyer has managed to find out how he can evade the existing Acts.

3624. How many societies done the same thing?—I think there are thousands of unregistered societies about.

3625. You think that is an undesirable thing? —They are not stopped even now within the 6 *l.*, they are not stopped, because there is no law to touch them.

Lord *Norton.*

3626. Although registration is voluntary, are there not advantages dependent upon it?— The advantages are so slight (investing the money at 2½ per cent. I believe) as to be not sufficient inducement.

3627. I do not quite understand your suggestion, that insurances falling due upon the death of children might be held by the insurance company for future objects; did you mean at the option of the insurer, or how?—We have the confidence of the working classes so far, and we should not wish in any way to abuse their confidence; we should not like to take the premiums under one year without giving them some benefit, and if we did not pay the amount at death we should have to increase it in some other form; there are many ways in which it can be done.

Earl of *Selborne.*

3628. You mean you would increase it in case the child did not die?—Yes; for instance, if the amount was reduced, under the existing scale, for under one year, we should still charge a penny a week, but we could give, perhaps, a free accident policy for 10 *l.* which would be payable at any time during life.

Lord *Poltimore.*

3629. I understood you to suggest that the premiums should be returned, if the child died under one year of age?—Yes.

3630. Would you suggest that that should be done in all cases; whether the death was suspicious, or whether it was not?—It would be merely returning the man his own money; I suggest that that should be done, in order that it should not appear that the company or society was making a profit by it; the man would think that as the child was dead the society ought to return the money.

3631. Therefore you would do that in every case, whether it was a suspicious case or not?— I would.

The Witness is directed to withdraw.

MR. DAVID FORTUNE, is called; and Examined, as follows:

Chairman.

3632. You are the president of the Scottish Legal Life Assurance Society?—I am.

3633. That society was established in 1852, was it not?—Yes.

3634. The membership and business of the society are almost exclusively confined, I believe, to the working classes?—That is so.

3635. Is your society what is commonly called a collecting society, a commercial society, or is it a mutual society?—It is a collecting society; it is mutual in the sense that the entire profits of the society are the property of the members.

3636. The chief offices of your society are at Glasgow?—That is so.

(142.)

Chairman—continued.

3637. Has it agencies in the leading centres of Scotland and England?—Yes, that is so.

3638. And also in Belfast, Londonderry, and Ballymena?—Yes.

3639. And it has upwards of 400,000 members? —Yes.

3640. Of which 38,771 are under five years of age?—Yes.

3641. And 37,731 are between five and ten years of age?—Yes.

3642. Then the Committee understand that the numbers of children under five and over five years of age insured with you are very nearly the

Chairman—continued.

the same; roughly speaking, about in equal numbers?—Within 1,000.

3643. Your premium income for last year was how much?—£.100,405. 7 *s.* 5½ *d.*

3644. And you paid in claims on children under five years of age, how much?—£. 3,394. 10 *s.* 6 *d.*

3645. On how many children was that sum paid?—One thousand three hundred and sixty-six.

3646. And on 241 children between five and ten years of age you paid 1,064 *l.* 10 *s.* 8 *d.*?—We did.

3647. And on 6,610 adults you paid upwards of 49,000 *l.*?—Yes, 49,772 *l.* 12 *s.* 2½ *d.*

3648. Does the word "adult" in that return of yours mean every life above 10 years?—It means the entire remainder above 10 years.

3649. That is to say, every life above 10 years you count as an adult life in that return?—Yes, we do in this return.

3650. You state, as a matter of opinion, that you do not think that infantile insurance leads, as has been said by some, to infanticide, or even to neglect of children by parents, to any appreciable extent?—That is my opinion.

3651. There has not, to the knowledge of any of the officials or yourself, been a single case of a parent or guardian charged with the crime of infanticide, whose child was insured in your society?—That is so.

3652. In what sense did you use the word "guardian," in answer to my last question?—It is the legal term which is implied in the section of the Act, which says "personal representative."

3653. That is to say, the person legally qualified to represent the child?—Exactly.

3654. The sum for which children under five years of age can be insured is not such, in your opinion, as to prove a strong temptation to parents to ill-use their children, even where all true parental feeling has been eradicated by a course of vice?—That is so.

3655. You think the cost of interment, in Scotland at least, is such that little, if any, margin is left after all the expenses connected with the cheapest interment are defrayed, even where the child is insured in those societies and companies giving the largest benefits in their infantile class?—That is so.

3656. You say that you do not think that infantile insurance leads, as has been alleged, to infanticide; may I ask in what sense you use the term "infanticide"?—Child murder.

3657. Do you mean actually putting away the child by violence or simply neglecting it?—By neglecting it as by starvation, or not giving it proper medicine.

3658. You include all things incidental, not actually violence, but dangerous to life?—Yes, not natural death.

3659. And intended to produce that effect?—Yes.

3660. What lawyers in England call criminal neglect?—Yes.

3661. You do not think it leads to that?—We have had no such experience to any appreciable extent.

Chairman—continued.

3662. I ask how you would ascertain that; I wish to draw your attention to the fact that the Report of the Committee of the House of Commons states, that it is in the majority of cases almost impossible to obtain a conviction for neglect and cruelty to children, that the thing is done in the privacy of home; if, therefore, the opinion of the Committee was that it is impossible to ascertain it, how do you ascertain it?—Our collectors are instructed very strictly to be very careful not only at the time of the child joining the society, but from week to week when they visit the house for the purpose of lifting the subscriptions to see to the general character and tone of the domestic life.

3663. That is the general direction you give to your agents?—That is so.

3664. That does not appear as far as we have had it given in evidence already, to be a feature of other societies?—It is in this way that we make it a general understanding with our agents.

3665. It is not a public feature of your rules, but you give it as a general instruction, as I understand?—Yes.

3666. You say in your notes of evidence that there has not to the knowledge of the officials or yourself been a single case of a parent or guardian charged with the crime of infanticide; you mean I suppose charged in some court of law?—Yes, or at the instance of the Fiscal even where the crime may not have been proved.

3667. You are speaking altogether of legal accusation?—By some legal authority. Further I may say that we are always open to receive any communication from the Scottish National Society for the Prevention of Cruelty to Children, and therefore we should have learnt from them if any such case had arisen. I am referring to that source of knowledge as well as to criminal procedure, on the part of our Procurator Fiscal.

3668. That is to say your word "charge" includes both moral and legal charge?—Yes.

3669. In no case have you had any complaint or any charge made to you with respect to cruelty; neither in the shape of a legal charge, nor in the shape of a moral charge, have you any reason for supposing that any one of the parents of the children insured with you has been guilty of cruelty or neglect?—That has been our experience.

3670. Your opinion, therefore, is that insurance in no way tends to infanticide?—In no way, speaking of our own experience; and I had better at this stage indicate that that is largely our Scotch experience, because our business is almost four-fifths confined to Scotland.

3671. Your opinion, therefore, would conflict with that of persons having considerable means of judging, without having reference to the judges who have given evidence before this Committee. You are probably acquainted with the name of Mr. Ludlow in Scotland?—Yes, he is the Chief Registrar of Friendly Societies.

3672. You are aware that he has given to the House of Commons Committee evidence to the effect that he considers that the association of the

Chairman—continued.

the insurance with the death of a child in the mind of an insuring parent has an ill effect in tending to evil?—I heard words something to that effect coming from Mr. Ludlow.

3673. When he was asked if it were possible to put an end to the evils connected with child insurance he said it was impossible; that would imply. would it not, that he thought there were evils connected with child insurance?—Yes, no doubt.

3674. Therefore upon that point the evidence of a witness so experienced as Mr. Ludlow differs from yours?—Mr. Ludlow is probably speaking from general experience, whereas I am speaking from special experience, which may account for my being at issue with him, but it may not necessarily involve both or either of us being wrong.

3675. I am not supposing that at all; but then, we have this again, you may have heard the name of Mr. Lyulph Stanley?—I have.

3676. He is, as I understand, the referee of one of the greatest of our English societies, the Royal Liver?—He is a trustee.

3677. He has expressed the distinct opinion before the House of Commons Committee that the insurance of children is a direct incentive, or a strong incentive, to murder?—I know he has spoken strongly upon the point.

3678. That is evidence referring to England?—Yes.

3679. Your evidence, on the other hand, would refer to Scotland?—Yes, specially.

3680. Your evidence would, therefore, seem to go to this, that, either from some creditable peculiarity in the Scotch character, the nature of their family affection, or from the greater precautions which, very much to your credit, are taken in your society, these cases do not arise in Scotland within your experience?—That is so.

3681. That would not any the more invalidate the opinion of Messrs. Ludlow, Stanley, and others, than that their opinion should be taken to invalidate yours?—Certainly not; but I should hesitate to say that they were correct in making that general statement, basing my view upon the experience of our society.

3682. I see you say in your statement that an interment in Scotland costs at least from 2 *l.* to 4 *l.*, and that in few cases can the highest infantile insurance claim allowed by the present Act cover even the barest expenses connected with the death and funeral of a child; that I take as your opinion?—It is my opinion; that opinion is based, of course, upon the actual amounts for which alone interments can be obtained.

3683. When you speak of the "bare expenses," do you mean the bare expenses connected with the funeral, the coffin and the cemetery expenses, or do you also mean the expenses of the doctor and the mourning?—Not the doctor and the mourning, but I do include the expense of the father or parent of the child attending the funeral and going to the registrar, and so on, being necessarily absent from work at least a day.

(142.)

Chairman—continued.

3684. That is to say, being out of pocket?—Yes.

3685. Therefore it is the parent being out of pocket, and the undertaker's charges, and the charges at the cemetery, that you have alone in view?—Yes.

3686. Several witnesses have stated to this Committee that parents have received insurance money after the death of their children, and then left the parish to bury their children, have you ever known a case of that kind occur in Scotland?—I have never to my knowledge heard of such a case, neither in connection with our society's experience nor yet from any public report of any case recorded in the Scotch newspapers. At the same time, I do not wish to say that such cases have not, and may not occur; I am not making a broad statement of that kind; I am not speaking dogmatically, but from my own knowledge. I cannot call to mind a single case.

3687. Are you in a position to know of such a case; would it be likely to come before you? It would be the business of the relieving officer, or the parish officer, to know of such a case; it would not be your business, would it? In what way would you become cognisant of it?—We might know through the officer of the parochial board, who corresponds to the relieving officer of an English union

3688. But unless you had any special reason for asking him, you would not of course become cognisant of it; you have no special reason for asking him. and you never do ask him, I presume?—No; but I can tell you how I think we would know when a child would be buried at the expense of the parish. The question would necessarily be asked whether their means were exhausted, or no means existed for burying that child, except by means of the parish, the officer would put that question to the parents, and would get an answer, yes or no. If they answered yes, they had received the insurance money, but had drank it, or disposed of it in some illegitimate way, that would lead to some inquiry, and I would be almost certain to get some knowledge of such cases.

3689. In the Scottish Legal Society the highest amount which can be obtained for a child under one and two years, is 3 *l.*?—Yes.

3690. Under three years, 3 *l.* 10 *s.*; under four years, 4 *l.*; and under five years, 4 *l.* 10 *s.*?—Yes.

3691. And those sums are payable only after a child has been entered 12 months upon your books?—Yes.

3692. There is a very important difference there, between your society and a great many of the English societies in which payment for a child may be made, after the child has been three or six months on their books; do I understand you to say, that you never pay in respect of a child who has not been 12 months on your books?—No; if your Lordship looks at the 8th clause of my notes, you will observe an explanation of that very point I am speaking now of the maximum sums which can be secured, not of the quarterly and half-yearly amounts which may be paid, which are indicated in the first clause of the 8th section of my notes: "We give no

Chairman—continued.

payments on children's deaths, unless they have been in our society at least three months, and then only what is termed 'quarter benefit.'"

3693. How much would quarter benefit, in the case of a child between one and two years, be?—Three months at a halfpenny would come to about 15 *s.*, a mere nominal sum; that is at a halfpenny a week; and in the case of a penny a week it would come to say 30*s.*

3694. That would be after the child had been insured three months?—Yes.

3695. That is a very much lower scale of payment than some we are acquainted with in English societies?—That may be.

3696. And being smaller amounts of course the temptation to ill-deeds for the sake of the amount would, as regards many at any rate, be less than in the case of an English society, because the parent would get much less?—Naturally one would conclude so if we admit at all that the money is an object, which I am not prepared to say just now.

3697. Assuming for the moment that the money is a temptation; the money temptation with you is much smaller than it is with many societies?—That is so; they give larger benefits than we do; that may be to their credit or otherwise.

3698. Assuming that the money has anything at all to do with it, that would go so far to account for the comparative or the entire paucity or entire absence of crime in connection with your society?—It would be an important factor.

3699. Your highest insurances in the infantile department are under the sums provided by the Act, which shows, you say, that you have no desire to strain your Parliamentary limit with the view of placing an artificial premium on infantile mortality?—That is borne out by your Lordship's own view of the case as stated just now.

3700. You say further that you believe that intemperance, overcrowding, defective sanitation, lack of proper nourishment, the necessity for maternal labour, and the various ailments incidental to child life, are the chief factors in the high rate of infant mortality, and I should be inclined to agree with that; but I pointed out to a witness the other day, and in this you might perhaps be disposed to agree, that there might be a considerable amount of infant death which would not perceptibly raise the rate of infant mortality as appearing upon the tables; it would take, over the whole number of children, a considerable amount of death, would it not, to raise the infant rate of death even by one per cent.?—It would.

3701. Therefore, a considerable amount of criminal death of infants not owing to those causes you have spoken of, and not appearing upon any table of mortality, nevertheless might exist?—That is quite possible.

3702. Now you give certain statistics; you have, I believe, had a statement prepared showing that your average rate of mortality over the five years ending 1889 for children under five years of age was 3·81, and for children between five and ten years of age 0·71; or taking the average of the two combined, 2·72, which is considerably below the general infantile death-rate

Chairman—continued.

as shown by the Registrar General's returns?—That is so; that is our experience.

3703. I have no wish to occupy the time of the Committee by going into these statistics, but I think if you look at the evidence which was given by a director of one of our English societies, in which he and I discussed this subject, you will see some statements of mine, and I think some admissions of his which would go far to affect the value of these comparative statistics?—I will refer to the evidence.

3704. The Committee of the House of Commons before whom parallel statistics to yours were produced, gave it as their opinion that they could lay very little stress upon figures either way?—That is a very old discovery, at the same time we are asked to give them, and I am simply giving our experience.

3705. You have also a carefully prepared return of the experience of six representative agencies of your society in Scotland and England for the last five years, which shows that in Preston the ratio of deaths to membership under 10 years of age is 10·29; Blackburn, 1·96; Paisley, 2·38; Greenock, 2·00; Lanark, 1·73; and Blairgowrie, 1·02?—That is so. (*The Tables are handed in, see Appendix.*)

3706. The Preston rate is very much higher than the Blackburn rate which follows it; how do you explain that?—Yes, that is so. I may say that is another outcome of our experience; so much so that within the past year or two we have almost closed up our direct agency in Preston; we found that it was not profitable, and we began to feel that it was not perhaps so safe as it should be; we have now ceased taking on any new lives in Preston.

3707. Have you formed any opinion as to why you were obliged to do that in Preston?—One opinion I formed was that the social life was not perhaps as good as in some other centres, and also that there was possibly a good deal of maternal neglect, not intentionally, but from the fact that a great number of female operatives, married women, are employed in the factories in Preston; I attributed the very high infantile death-rate in our Preston agency to that, although I may have been mistaken.

3708. Glasgow is also a place where female operatives are very largely employed; you do not find the same result in Glasgow as in Preston?—No, we do not.

3709. That would again also go to show that the Scotch people are more careful of their children than the English?—I should not like to draw the comparison; we have a high respect for our English friends.

3710. I believe in 1886 you instituted a system of children's endowments, by which, on payment of a small weekly or monthly premium, sums varying from 9 *l.* to 36 *l.* are paid at the age of 14?—That is so.

3711. And sums varying from 15 *L* 15 *s.* to 63 *L* on a child attaining the age of 21?—Yes.

3712. Thus making the life, rather than the death, of a child the basis of contract for payment?—Yes.

3713. That is a very admirable arrangement, if you will allow me to say so; that arrangement of yours would necessarily have this effect, that the

parents

Chairman—continued.

parents insuring in your society would be strongly inclined to keep their children alive rather than to do away with them?—Yes.

3714. In that respect your society contrasts very advantageously with any society that we have as yet had any evidence from?—I do not know what other societies you have had before you, and I do not know what their evidence has been.

3715. Your society contrasts very advantageously in this respect with all other societies that I know : do not you think that this very remarkable and excellent arrangement of yours would have a tendency to preserve the lives of the children in connection with your society?—We wish to do that.

3716. I am taking that for granted; I am only pointing out that your society is, as far as I know, an exceptionally good one?—I am proud to hear your Lordship say so.

3717. You say in your notes that this scheme has been most successful, a much larger number of juvenile endowment policies having been issued than the directors anticipated?—That is so.

3718. That is to say, to a very large extent these juvenile endowment policies are taken out by parents?—They are very extensively adopted by the parents; very largely beyond our anticipations.

3719. And they are also adopted by parents, I presume, who have insured their children's lives on the ordinary terms with you?—In some cases ; the majority of the cases, however, are entirely new juvenile lives; and I may add that this system is striking at the very poorest class. I may say that, from the fishing districts of the north-east coast of Scotland we are receiving a large number of these juvenile endowment proposals.

3720. You say, again, that nearly all the friendly orders now give benefits, some even larger than your society, on the death of children from three months and upwards?—Yes.

3721. By "friendly orders," you mean what we would call Foresters, and similar societies?—Yes.

3722. I believe that three months and upwards is the period fixed by your rules; and you say that you are not aware that any evil results are alleged against this system in those organisations?—I have not heard of any specially.

3723. I believe in your society you have never known of a single case in which a child was insured by any person save the parents or guardians?—That is so.

3724. Have you any rule to the contrary effect that you will not insure a child who is insured by any but the parent or guardian?—We simply instruct our agents in the terms of the Act; and, even in any case, if there were such over-assurance, we would not pay the claim. If, inadvertently, a second policy of insurance came up to be paid, we would ascertain whether this was the parent or only a relative ; and, if we found it was not the parent, we should dispute the claim.

3725. Have you had to dispute a large number of claims?—No.

3726. But you would have no hesitation in doing so, if the case arose?—No.

(142.)

Chairman—continued.

3727. In point of fact, you would have no such motive, because you are not a commercial society?—That is so.

3728. Therefore, you would probably dispute a claim under those circumstances?—Certainly ; but I may say our collectors are so careful that we do not require to dispute a claim but very seldom.

3729. You employ a high class of agents, I take it?—Yes ; we must have certificates from the former employer ; we interview them personally, and are very careful in selecting people of moral character as our agents.

3730. How do you pay those agents?—We pay them the first eight times as collected ; that is to say, they take the first eight payments, and we give them 25 per cent. upon the industrial business, and 12½ per cent. upon the endowment business.

3731. Are there many infant assurance societies in Glasgow, besides your own?—There is only one large society which is local; the City of Glasgow Friendly Society does exactly the same business as ours; it is more local indeed than ours, but it is principally Scotch.

3732. Then there is no very strong competition going on between you and the other societies, I presume?—Yes, there are our English friends who compete very strongly and very successfully with us.

3733. I do not know whether it is a fair question to ask, and you need not answer it unless you wish, but do you think their agents are as careful as yours?—I hope so; I would almost go as far as to say, I think so.

3734. Then you go on to say that you believe that there is far less speculation on children's lives than there is on the lives of adults, either in industrial or general assurance societies or companies?—That is so.

3735. When you speak of speculation on the lives of adults how can that arise under the statute of George III., how can there be speculation on the lives of adults?—Take such a case as we had very widely reported in Belfast about two years ago ; there were certain prominent citizens including certain town councillors, and others who were insured wholesale, at the instance of a number of needy persons who had got policies upon them, and the people themselves were not aware of it. They had therefore speculated upon the deaths of those people. These men were brought up before the assizes, and you may remember to have seen that they were punished by three years' imprisonment ; one of them was a town councillor, another an eminent doctor of Belfast; he I think got 12 months' imprisonment for that speculation upon Mr. Finlay M'Ance, a justice of the peace, and some other prominent citizens of Belfast.

3736. Those must have been insured in some society?—That society was an American society.

3737. That society could not have been careful to see that those insurances were made within the statute of George III., under which you may not insure unless you have an insurable interest?—I believe in this case the doctor was a party to the whole thing.

3738. But it was a violation of the statute?—

Y 4   It

Chairman—continued.

It was a violation of the statute, and the parties suffered accordingly.

3739. But nevertheless, the society insured them?—They did for a large sum.

3740. Apparently the society never took the pains to find out whether the parties insuring had an insurable interest or had not?—They had the means, but they did not find out or wish to take the trouble.

3741. That goes to show, with reference to the country I have the honour to belong to, that it must be the fact that in Ireland insurance is very laxly and carelessly done, and moreover, wickedly done?—Yes; but it may relieve your Lordship's mind to know that one of the principal actors was either a Scotchman or an Englishman.

3742. I am quite prepared to believe that. Now I believe it is the rule with your society to make no payments on children's deaths unless they have been in your society at least three months, and then only what is termed "quarter benefit;" six months insuring, half benefit?— That is so.

3743. Your society never makes grants or gives gratuities out of the funds in the case of children not in benefit?—Never.

3744. That is another important distinction between your society and the English societies? —That is evident.

3745. Do you ever make what are called grants of grace?—Never.

3746. You say that your directors would welcome any legislation aimed at making child life more secure, which did not unduly interfere with the legitimate rights and privileges of the industrial classes, or place such obstacles to, and restrictions on the system of infantile assurance as would virtually suppress what has proved a great benefit to the members of your industrial and friendly societies, who, you state, are amongst the most provident, honest, and independent classes in the community?—That is so.

3747. Have you any suggestions to make to the Committee upon that point?—There are one or two lines, I think, upon which there could be an attempted reform of that kind provided you allow that infant assurance is permissible, and is in fact commendable. If the evidence which has been laid before your Lordships' Committee (of which I have no knowledge) goes to establish the money temptation, even if these small sums are too great for certain frail parents to resist, then, of course, your remarks would imply that a reduction of those sums might prevent a good deal of that speculation.

3748. I understand you to mean that assuming, merely assuming, that small sums have proved a temptation, it is obvious as you say that a reduction would lessen that temptation?— It might. If, however, you think that in a question of this kind it would be a good thing, as perhaps it might to have a consensus of opinion from the leading societies, I am quite sure they are very desirous of doing anything to meet the views of your Lordships' Committee in any suggestions they could offer. There might be, perhaps, a graduated scale of payment, instead of that block payment of 6 *l.*

3749. Suddenly jumping up to 10 *l.*?—Yes;

Chairman—continued.

I must say that I think that is rather clumsy, and I think there could be some gradation by which that necessity would be met, and at the same time, perhaps, there might be a reform brought in by such a scale.

3750. You would recommend a new graduated scale in place of this clumsy lump sum, as you call it, jumping from 6 *l.* to 10 *l.*?—Yes.

3751. That would tend to reduce the danger which may exist?—Yes; you might have a graduated scale, but not so as to reduce the maximum amounts payable at the various ages.

3752. I quite understand that what you would recommend is a better graduated scale?—Yes; and possibly quarter and half benefits might be introduced; you might say three months was too early, and that there should be no benefit given until they had been six months in the society. Then, my friend, Mr. Grahame, who is the chairman of the Scotch Society for the Prevention of Cruelty to Children, laid before me a few days ago a scheme of registration; I think there may be some merit in it, but it would require to be very carefully looked at before it was adopted; I am not prepared to say that, perhaps, a better system of registration, whereby it would be impossible for the parent to get more than the Act permitted, even though the child was insured in more than one society, might not be arrived at; I think that difficulty might be obviated which now may exist, but that laxity is on the part of the registrar; we, ourselves, would not pay a penny more than the Act allowed.

3753. You work in Scotland under the registrar's certificate?—Yes.

3754. And there the provisions are the same as here?—Yes.

3755. You may remember that the registrar's certificate has to recite first the doctor's certificate, and then the coroner's certificate, if any, and then he is to have "such other evidence as may seem to him to be sufficient"; does not that seem to give a very large discretion to the registrar?—Yes, too large a discretion.

3756. Then one amendment would be, of course, to strike out those words?—Yes, and to make it arbitrary.

3757. Another suggestion which has been made is that there should be a public register kept, open to inspection, of all children insured; does that strike you as desirable?—No, the working man does not wish every transaction of that kind publicly advertised, and I think the great body of working men would feel it a slur put upon them that the working man must publicly advertise the fact that he has insured his child.

3758. But it would not be a discredit to him that he had insured his child, it would be rather a credit would it not?—Still, they do not wish that these facts should be compulsorily made public; yet, I do not think that the great bulk of the working classes would object to a system of that kind.

3759. The working classes would, you think, be very anxious to join in any legislation which did not deprive them of their existing rights and privileges?—I quite think so.

3760. And this proposal would not interfere with

Chairman—continued.

with their existing rights and privileges ?—Not with their existing rights and privileges, but it would be a little delicate.

3761. We are all obliged to register things about ourselves which are often a little delicate ; a lady has to register her age in the census returns, and so on ?—Yes.

3762. Then the last clause of your paper has special reference to the payment to the undertaker ; that has been withdrawn from the Bill, so that it is not necessary to discuss it ?—I noticed a paragraph to that effect in yesterday's newspaper.

3763. To sum up the whole matter it appears that your society is not a commercial society, but a mutual benefit society ?—That is so.

3764. That it is conducted with very great care, that its agents are highly respectable, that it adopts certain provisions which are not amongst the provisions of other societies, and that on the whole your society is a most favourable specimen of an industrial association ; that would sum up the whole of your evidence ?—That is your Lordship's summing-up, and it is very gratifying to me.

Earl Beauchamp.

3765. You state that the chief factors of the high rate of infant mortality are intemperance, overcrowding, defective sanitation, the lack of proper nourishment, the necessity for maternal labour, and the various ailments of child life ?—I believe them to be so.

3766. Have you any sufficient familiarity with the habits of those who insure their children which would enable you to tell the Committee how far you have found them intelligent in the management of their children ?—We believe that the class who insure their children with us are a provident, and although not perhaps strictly abstinent, yet a very temperate body of parents, taken as a whole ; we believe that.

3767. I am speaking rather of their intelligence and their understanding of the proper methods of bringing up their children ?—I daresay it is on account of the very good system we have in Glasgow in connection with our sanitary department, male and female officers going amongst the poorer people day by day and instructing them in the elementary principles of housekeeping and domestic economy, that in that way a great deal is being done in Glasgow specially for the purpose of teaching the working classes how to maintain a better and a higher social life, and we are reaping the advantage of that very largely in connection with our membership and the insurance of children.

3768. I was not drawing your attention so much to the matters of sanitation and overcrowding as to the proper method of rearing children ?—These female sanitary inspectors or visitors have that as one of their special functions.

3769. If it is found necessary to employ those persons to instruct the working-classes in the proper methods of domestic economy and rearing their children, that fact shows, does it not, that they are deficient in knowledge in that respect ?—It shows, at all events, that they are none the worse for having a little more knowledge. Our

(142.)

Earl Beauchamp—continued.

sanitary institution in Glasgow has been a marked feature in our municipal life, and it has helped us in Glasgow very much.

3770. Defective intelligence as to the proper method of bringing up children would not necessarily indicate criminal neglect, would it ?—Certainly not.

3771. Are you able to say at all whether the employment of mothers away from home has any serious influence on infant mortality ?—I have a very distinct opinion to that effect. Where the mother has to attend at the factory, I believe, that does militate against the healthy growth of the child life.

3772. Would it be true to say that where mothers are absent from their children there is an increase in the rate of mortality ?—I would be inclined to say that that was a predisposing cause.

3773. Do I understand you to say that you would be in favour of restricting insurances to one alone, that only one insurance should be effected on the life of a child ?—I think that would be an improvement upon the present system, and would obviate the possibility of any mistake being made in respect to the registrar's certificates, for we think there may be more than one insurance above the amount allowed at times.

3774. That is, assuming that the legal maximum would be left at present ?—Yes.

3775. The legal maximum being 6 *l.* in the case of a child dying at five years old ?—Yes ; but I would not give 6 *l.* on the death of a child dying under twelve months ; that is where I think there may be some improvement. I would have a graduated scale, not so fixed that all children under five years of age should be able to get the maximum sum of 6 *l.*

3776. But practically, leaving the maximum as it is, you would prefer a graduated scale ?—Yes.

3777. You think there would be no inconvenience in the working of such a system ?—I do not think there would, because, as a matter of fact, all the societies or companies at the present time have a graduated scale which they work upon. The Royal Liver, the Prudential, and other societies work upon a graduated scale from a twelvemonth up to five years, and so on ; and therefore it would be simply making statutary what we at present find expedient and desirable.

3778. I understand you to say that you believe that it is the superior class of artisans who insure, and not the idle and dissolute ?—Certainly not ; we do not place any premium upon that class at all ; we do not wish to get the business of that class, and we preclude our collectors from going at times to certain districts which we proscribe by reason of the fact that they are inhabited by that class of people, and that they are fever-dens, and in other respects unhealthy and undesirable places.

3779. You see, in fact, no connection between the insurance of the lives of children and the crime of infanticide ?—I have not seen any such connection in my experience.

3780. If a parent is heartless enough to wish to put his child out of the way, there are sufficient motives for doing so already, without the miserable

Z

able

Earl *Beauchamp.*—continued.

able motive of the few shillings which would be gained by taking out an insurance policy?—There is the primary motive of getting rid of the burden of the child's support, apart altogether from that afforded by an insurance policy.

3781. And what would be a far larger incentive to child-murder in the case of a parent who was not restrained by any moral considerations than the mere payment of the sum that would be gained by any insurance that was taken out?—Certainly; the one would last for years, whereas the other would be a very small sum at the best, and would last but for the moment.

Earl of *Selborne.*

3782. Did I understand you to say that you saw no great objection to registering the insurances which are made?—I do not see any objection myself to that; but I would say that it should be very carefully done, so as not to take away the natural feeling of pride from the working classes.

3783. Would it not be the best way of doing that if it were done, to require the insurance societies to make a return to some public officer?—Perhaps to the registrar.

3784. Not requiring the people who insure themselves, and who in all probability would be likely to make a good many mistakes about it, or not to like it at all, but to throw that burden upon the societies?—Yes, it would be a considerable addition to our work; but I have no doubt, if it were thought practicable by your Lordships, we would endeavour (I think I may speak on behalf of most of the societies interested), or would be willing at all events to endeavour, to meet any such requirement for registration.

3785. You have local agents in all your districts and these local agents could report to the local registrar, could they not?—Certainly.

3786. I have only one other question to put to you; you have given some specimen places in order to show the rate of deaths, and you have explained the circumstances with reference to Preston; I do not see Glasgow in your list of those places. You mention Paisley, Greenock, and Lanark; are you able to tell the Committee why you did not mention Glasgow?—I can only say in reply to that, that the reason why I did not take Glasgow was simple inadvertance. What I wished to get was six typical cases; two in England, two large urban centres in Scotland, and two suburban or agricultural centres. Greenock is, to all intents and purposes, a lesser Glasgow; it has the shipbuilding class, it has the shipping, it has the same other industries, the same kind of municipal and social life, and you may take it that it would fairly represent Glasgow.

3787. May we take it that the same average would hold at Glasgow as holds at Greenock?—I am prepared to say that it does so with very little variation.

Earl of *Harrowby.*

3788. Has the increase in the practice of child insurance been very great in the last few years in Scotland?—It has not increased beyond the ordinary ratio of the increase of our membership.

Earl of *Harrowby*—continued.

3789. Are you speaking with knowledge of the other societies as to that, or only of your own society?—I am speaking from incidental statements given to me by the leading officers of other societies as well as our own.

3790. Might I ask you whether one might say roughly that the whole of the working classes insure their children's lives now in Scotland?—I think I should be safe in saying, at all events, that two-thirds of the entire number of the working classes are insured either in friendly benefit societies, or in industrial assurance societies, or such societies as our own.

3791. It has been the habit for some time in Scotland, has it not?—It has.

3792. There is nothing abnormal in the increase?—There is nothing abnormal in the increase.

3793. Are there many local societies in Scotland which insure children's lives?—There are not many societies there which insure children's lives other than those that I am aware of; there are a considerable number of what are called yearly friendly societies, but in those there is no insurance; it is merely that, upon the death of a member's wife or child, he, as a matter of consequence, gets a certain amount, but, as I say, there is no insurance there.

3794. Should you think it a matter of importance that all societies which can insure children's lives should be registered under the Friendly Societies Act?—I think that would be a safeguard as compelling them to give regular returns which would be extremely useful.

3795. Have you a copy of your proposal form?—I have.

3796. I should wish that to be put in as we have the proposal forms of other societies before the Committee?—Then I have much pleasure in handing it in. (*The same is handed in*, see *Appendix.*)

3797. Then with reference to the proposal form should you be in favour of having a proposal form laid down by the Legislature as necessary to be adopted by all societies, a uniform form?—I would be quite willing to accept that form.

3798. Should you think it would be advantageous or otherwise?—Unless it was too detailed. If it were merely a form containing the ordinary queries, which could be answered in a fair and reasonable manner, and which did not entail too much responsibility on the collectors and agents of the societies, I think it would be desirable to have a uniform draft.

3799. You are aware, probably, that there is considerable difference between the practice of some of the large societies; one putting into its form many detailed questions as to health, and so on, and others seeming to have very few?—Yes; a uniform schedule, I think, would be very advantageous and acceptable to the great body of societies.

3800. Both to the societies and to the insurers?—Yes, to both.

3801. It has been suggested to us that one way of dealing with the matter would be that no insurance should be payable, say, under the age of 12 months or two years, but at the premiums should be repaid upon the occasion of the child's

Earl of *Harrowby*—continued.

child's death; have you ever thought over that scheme, and can you give us an opinion upon it? —Yes ; I have incidentally answered that question. In reply to my Lord Bishop, I stated that it might possibly minimise the risk of child neglect if there were no payments made until the child was at least six months upon the books of the society ; that is to say, that there should be no quarter benefits. The principle would be the same whether it was 12 or six months.

3802. I heard you speak of that, but I do not think you alluded to this question ; it was suggested that the insurance premiums should be repaid, but that the claim should not be paid ?— We have that principle in the endowment clause. If the child dies before the maturity of the endowment, we return half the sum paid ; and perhaps the same principle might be adopted with reference to industrial insurance upon the children's lives ; we have it at present working in the parallel case.

3803. You stated that you had been very closely identified with the working of all sorts of working class institutions and friendly orders ; would it be your opinion, as it is the experience of many people in working class towns, that the working class must almost necessarily look forward to the sad prospect of the loss of one or more of their children owing to the deficiency of sanitary accommodation, and the general conditions under which they live ?—It is most palpable.

3804. Therefore, it would be a most natural thing to insure against the heavy loss which arises on those occasions ?—I do believe so.

3805. I see that you speak of the orders you have been connected with, as the Free Gardeners, the Ancient Shepherds, and the Rechabites ?—Yes.

3806. Are those class of societies very numerous in Scotland ?—Yes, they are.

3807. The Rechabites I am acquainted with; would you give the Committee any idea of the composition of the Free Gardeners and the Ancient Shepherds ? — Taking the Glasgow district, the Ancient Shepherds, of which I am a member, number 12,600 in that district alone. I think the Oddfellows, if I mistake not, have a membership of somewhere about 650,000, and the Rechabites have a very large membership, I think of about 130,000. The St. Andrew Order of Ancient Gardeners have a membership of about 7,000.

3808. So that if we had any witnesses from those associations they would give us a very fair opinion, one might assume, as to the views of the working classes upon this subject ?—I believe they would give the Committee most important evidence.

3809. Because their members are generally taken from the working men of the most thrifty and respectable class ?—That is my experience.

Earl *Spencer.*

3810. I think you stated that your society paid smaller sums particularly for younger children than other societies?—Than some other societies we do.

3811. Were those sums made smaller than is usual on account of the belief that the larger sums offer temptation to crime, rather than for financial reasons ?—The reasons were purely financial.

(142.)

Earl *Spencer*—continued.

We considered how much we could give for the premiums paid.

3812. You have heard, I think, the last witness examined as to whether the insurance could be limited to the sums actually out of pocket, such as funeral expenses, the doctor's fees, and the nurses, what is your opinion upon that proposal ? —I think that is a proposal which is wholly impracticable.

3813. Will you just state why ?—In the first place those accounts would require to be brought together and dealt with, but even then there would be domestic charges that could not be covered by merely the undertaker and the nurse and the doctor and the medicine and so on ; there would be incidental charges such as loss of labour, clothing, and other necessaries connected with the funeral, which I think, would render that proposal rather impracticable.

3814. Would you think it impossible, on account of the expense it would put the societies to in investigating those matters?—I was not aware that the societies were to be expected to do that work; it would certainly be a very serious thing for them to undertake.

3815. The last witness stated that that would be one of the chief objections ?—I should say it would be a very formidable objection on our part if we had to undertake such work, and I do not think there would be any commensurate advantage, supposing we did it.

Lord *Norton.*

3816. I think you have suggested that, under your graduated scale of insurances, the premium should not be altered from what the present amounts are ?—I said so.

3817. Have you stated what you think the minimum should be for the burial expenses in the case of a very young child ?—I have stated already the actual expense, so far as my inquiries have gone , my experience is that the minimum is about 2 *l.*, roughly speaking.

3818. Does that 2 *l.* take in, besides the actual burial, what we may call incidental expenses, the doctor's fees and mourning ?—No.

3819. It is simply burial expenses?—Yes ; it is simply burial expenses.

3820. Do not you think the minimum should include a little more for such incidental expenses as you have alluded to ?—I do.

3821. Would you state, speaking very vaguely, what you think might be the minimum ?—If the suggestion were carried out that there should be no payment made until after six months or 12 months, I think the sum would require to be not less after that age than from 2 *l.* to 2 *l.* 10 *s.*, and even then that would not cover, but would merely meet in some slender way, the total expenses.

3822. In this insurance society with which you are connected, of which, I suppose, the area is not only urban but partly rural, would any such limitation as you suggest apply equally to the two, the urban and the rural part ?—I think the cost would be about the same.

3823. It would not be much more expensive in a town than in the country?—No ; because there is keener competition in a town, which reduces, perhaps, the cost ; whereas in the country there

Lord *Norton*—continued.

is, perhaps, only one hearse and one coach, and the consequence is that there is a sort of monopoly, and the charges there may be made quite as high as they are in a city.

3824. Is it your opinion that if very young children's insurance were done away with altogether there would still be as strong an inducement to an unnatural parent to allow a child to

Lord *Norton*—continued.

die, simply to get rid of the burden of the child?—I think the motive would remain.

3825. So much so, that we may consider the motive in the mind of unnatural parents is not much aggravated by the few shillings that would be gained by the insurance?—That is my opinion.

The Witness is directed to withdraw

Mr. WILLIAM HENRY HAMBRIDGE, is called in; and Examined, as follows:

Chairman.

3826. YOU come here on behalf the Royal London Friendly Society?—Yes.

3827. I believe you have some information and statistics to submit to the Committee as to that society; would you just state what those are, if you please?—I place myself in the hands of the Committee to answer any questions the Committee may put to me. I have no programme, but the statistics I refer to I will hand in.

3828. Would you inform us of what nature are those statistics; are they statistics of deathrate, or of any other kind?—With your permission, I will read them. Royal London Friendly Society, Infantile Assurance. Experience for the year 31st December 1889: The number of children insured in the society under the age of five years on that date was 124,678; that is the number that were insured at the end of 1889. The maximum amount allowed by the Act would be 6 *l.*; the average amount of actual insurance in the society for that number was 3 *l.* 1 *s.* 7 *d.* The number who died, and benefits paid, was 4,997; the average amount of benefit paid was 1 *l.* 13 *s.* 3 *d.*

Lord *Clifford of Chudleigh.*

3829. That is the average on those that died? —Yes.

3830. Not on the larger number?—The average sum assured is on the whole number. Over five years of age, and under 10 years, the total number of infants insured in the society on the 31st of December 1889 was 102,086, and the maximum amount allowed by the Act would be 10 *l.* The average amount of actual insurance in the society was 4 *l.* 16 *s.* 8 *d.* The number who died, and benefits paid, was 408; and the average amount of benefit paid was 4 *l.* 12 *s.* between those ages.

Chairman.

3831. Those are statistics which you hand in? —That is all.

3832. Have you drawn from those statistics yourself any conclusions or inferences that you wish to put before the Committee, or do you tender them only as statistics?—Merely to show the experience of our society. From my own experience, which extends over 30 years, and from the observations I have made, I do not think the sums paid are too high, provided, as has been suggested by previous witnesses, they were upon a sliding scale.

3833. Then if you have no other observations to make, I should like to ask you a question or

Chairman—continued.

two with the view to making those statistics, which you have given us, quite clear, you say the maximum amount of insurance allowed by the Act is 6 *l.* under five years of age?— Yes.

3834. Whereas you find that the actual average amount of insurance is 3 *l.* 1 *s.* 7 *d.*?— Yes.

3835. From that we may gather that probably the considerably greater number of parents who insure with you do not insure up to the full 6 *l.*, but only up to an average of 3 *l.* 1 *s.* 7 *d.*?—We have a very large number of children insured at as low a rate as a halfpenny a week, and there are some who would insure for 2 *d.* a week, and that brings about the mean average of 3 *l.* 1 *s.* 7 *d.* as being the sum insured.

3836. It is quite clear that a great number of the parents do not insure for the whole 6 *l.*, otherwise your average would be higher?— Yes.

3837. The 3 *l.* 1 *s.* 7 *d.* would be what the majority of the parents would go in for?—Yes.

3838. Of course there are exceptions? — Yes.

3839. Now would you explain this: you say the average amount for which parents insure their children is 3 *l.* 1 *s.* 7 *d.*, but the average amount of benefit that is actually paid is only 1 *l.* 13 *s.* 3 *d.*; how does it come to pass that what you pay is so much less than what members insure for?—That is owing to the fact of members dying when they are only entitled to half benefit.

3840. That accounts for the difference?—Yes.

3841. There must be a very large number of children dying who are only entitled to half benefit?—Yes, half benefit or grants, as the case might be.

3842. Now, it is a thing to be noted you would say, would you not, that the number of children over five years and under 10 is only 408, whereas under five the number is 4,997?—Yes.

3843. That goes to show, does it not, that there is an enormous preponderance of mortality under the age of five years?—Yes; every society knows that by experience.

3844. Taking that for granted for a moment, supposing there were any necessity at all for imposing fresh restrictions or safeguarding for the protection of infant life, clearly those safeguards should go more in the direction of children under five years of age than in the direction of children between five and 10 years, because the greatest mortality is in those insured under five years?— Yes.

3845. The

Chairman—continued.

3845. The greatest amount of care to guard against mortality would be required as to children under five years, and not over?—That is so.

3846. Obviously, a child over five years of age is able to speak and tell about itself; it does not run the same risk as a child six months old?—I do not think there is much risk of that.

3847. A child of five years old could not be overlaid?—That is so, but as a matter of fact that very seldom happens after the first year.

3848. Then again a child of five years would, in all probability, have got through its infantile diseases; teething, and so on?—That is so, no doubt.

3849. Then, supposing any amendment of the law were adopted by the Legislature it should rather be with regard to children under the age of five than with regard to children over five, that would be more important, would it not?—No, I do not admit that; the death-rate is heavier, I admit; but I do not think there should be any further protection at the lower age than at the higher.

3850. I do not think I have any further question to ask you upon these statistics. A good many of the witnesses, in fact, speaking apart from the societies, I may say all the witnesses, have expressed their willingness to yield to any amendment of the law which would not restrict the advantages which thrifty parents now derive under the Friendly Societies Act. Your impression would be, would it not, that the societies you represent would be willing to concur in any reasonable and just regulations which would prevent infanticide?—Certainly.

3851. Could you help us at all by saying what are the restrictions which you think the working men would not object to?—I do not know. I should not like to speak for them in that respect.

3582. Then may I ask with respect to your society, is it what is called a collecting society or a mutual friendly society?—It is both.

3853. What do you mean by both?—It is a registered friendly society, and the principles are mutual; there are no shares or anything of that kind.

3854. Yours is not what might be called a commercial society?—Certainly not.

3855. You employ agents, do you not, to collect?—We do.

3856. Could you tell the Committee how you pay those agents?—We pay them by commission principally.

3857. What is the amount of the commission?—It ranges from 12½ to 25 per cent.; there are very few at 25 per cent., but there are a few, very old collectors.

3858. Do you pay them any occasional douceur?—We pay them procuration fees equal to 10 times the weekly premium.

3859. That is a higher remuneration than is paid in other societies, is it not?—I believe not.

3860. Some representatives of societies told the Committee that they only gave as much as eight weekly premiums?—We give ten.

3861. Do you give in addition to that a quar-

(142.)

Chairman—continued.

terly douceur, as some societies do?—We do not.

3862. You are careful in selecting your agents, are you not?—We are as careful as we possibly can be.

3863. You believe they are generally men of good character, respectable, and trustworthy?—Yes, we pride ourselves upon getting as good men as we can.

3864. You have not considered any of those safeguards which have been suggested, and you would not like to speak on behalf of the working men without having considered them?—I think they would be capable of speaking for themselves as to their own interests; but I would venture to make this statement, that the suggestion made by the previous witness, that there should be only one insurance upon the life of a child is a very admirable one, and one that all societies, I think, would be willing to adopt.

3865. Supposing that we adopted that, and made that the law, the representative of one of the societies who was examined here told us that he would have no objection to any infraction of that rule being severely punished; that any parent or agent knowingly allowing a parent to insure for more should be severely punished; do you see any objection to that, or do you think the working classes would object to that?—No; I think it rights itself; when a death occurs, of course our proposals are properly checked.

3866. You see no objection to punishment in addition in order to enforce the law?—I think that any attempt at fraud of that description should be punished.

3867. At present have you any way at all of ascertaining whether a child is insured in any other society than yours?—Yes.

3868. How do you ascertain it?—I have a batch of proposals with me (*producing the same*) which have been submitted to the committee of management, and which have been in those cases rejected where information has been given of their being in another society or where there has been anything of a suspicious character with reference to the cases.

3869. But I want to know in what way did you get at the facts which made you suspicious; who informed you?—The collectors or agents, as the case might be.

3870. They found that the child in that case was insured in some other society?—Yes.

3871. And they told you the child was insured in some other society?—Yes, but that would not prevent our issuing a policy if they were only insured for a very small amount.

3872. But if the suggestion that you propose were made in the law, that would prevent you?—Yes.

3873. And any policy issued in violation of the law then would be void, it would be an illegal policy?—It would be so.

Earl *Spencer.*

3874. I think you would have probably heard if you had been in the room that some societies do not come under the Friendly Societies Act, and do not register; do you think it would be

z 3   desirable

Earl *Spencer*—continued.

desirable that all societies should come under the Friendly Societies Act, and the conditions imposed by it?—Yes, in every case.

3875. You see no objection to that at all?—No, it ought to be done.

Lord *Kinnaird.*

3876. Why do you think it ought in all cases to be done?—Because the precautions taken by the framers of the present Act to prevent over-insurance compel us to demand and retain the registrar's certificate showing the amount for which he has granted the certificate; we retain the registrar's certificate with our receipts for the purpose of auditing or any other purpose that it may be required for, but in the case of those local societies they have have no laws to abide by. The certificate that was given by the registrar to be produced for a society similar to ours is produced. The Act makes use of the expression only "to be produced," and upon sight of such certificate they pay whatever they think proper; there is no one to take them in hand, so that there is a large amount of child insurance in that way paid for in the country of which you get no record at all.

3877. Have you ever considered whether the registration of death is faulty in some way?—Yes; I think it might be improved.

3878. In what way do you think it might be improved?—It is rather a difficult thing to explain; but previous to the present Act under the old system, until 1875, the medical man upon the death of a person in a friendly society or burial society received a fee in proportion; that fee was very often regulated in proportion to the sum which the poor people were about to receive, and the coroner's in the same way; but by the Act of 1875 all those fees were swept away from those gentlemen, and placed in the hands of the registrar, consequently the medical men have, taking them as a body, never given the same amount of information that was given originally, and when the registrar issues a certificate it very often conveys little or no information for the benefit of these societies.

3879. You think since the passing of that Act it has been easier to get the registrar's certificate, or at all events with less information?—It is not very much easier, but they are able to demand it for a certain fee; but with reference to the medical men, under the old system they had to pay whatever the medical man charged them.

3880. With reference to your own society do you confine your operations to a special class, or do you take all classes?—We certainly take care to get as good lives as we can, and we have proscribed certain districts in which we have experienced extra mortality; but I should not like to say with regard to children that we do not think that a criminal's child should be buried as much as other children.

3881. Would you exclude it'—We would

Lord *Kinnaird*—continued.

proscribe certain districts where we knew that drunkenness existed, or where women work upon pit brows, or even at iron works where women have to work, because amongst the children under those circumstances the mortality is certainly heavier.

3882. You would exclude those districts?—We do so as being unfair to other districts.

3883. You have no system of increased payment to meet increased risk?—No, we have uniform premiums up to five years of age, and again between five and ten years of age.

Lord *Clifford of Chudleigh.*

3884. I suppose those cases in which you pay half benefit are generally cases of very young children?—Yes.

3885. I understand you to say that the system of having only one policy taken out would be practically self-protecting without any actual penalty, because the second insurance would not be paid?—That is so.

3886. Do you think there might not arise cases in which a company or society holding a second insurance, although not bound to pay anything, might be inclined to give a grant in order to prevent contention?—No; that would be in violation of the Act. What is done when it occurs is this. Sometimes it occurs that when a claim has been paid, the company find that the child has by the ignorance of the wife or husband, been insured in a second society, and has already received the full amount in the first society; thereupon the premium which had been paid to the second society would be returned, and there would be no payment whatever by that society.

3887. You would have no objection to a penalty upon any society adopting this practice of over-insurance?—I should have no objection if it were made universal, that is to say, if every class of persons throughout the country were brought within the same regulation.

Earl of *Selborne.*

3888. You said just now that there was formerly a system, now abolished, by which the medical man who certified the cause of death, received fees graduated according to the amount receivable by the insured?—Yes, fixed by the medical men themselves. What I wished to explain was that if the child died, and the parents were receiving from 3 *l.* to 5 *l.*, the medical man would perhaps be satisfied with a shilling as his fee, but that if it were a larger amount he would not hesitate to charge 2 *s.* 6 *d.* or even 5 *s.*

3889. Do not you think that that would be a bad system, as giving certain medical men an inducement to certify favourably where they would receive the most?—No, I do not think so, but they could withhold information, and that is what they do now.

The Witness is directed to withdraw.

Mr. JOHN CLENSY, is called in; and Examined, as follow:

Chairman.

3890. You are Secretary to the Liverpool Victoria and Legal Friendly Society?—I am.

3891. May I ask whether you are attending here in answer to an invitation received from this Committee, or are attending on behalf of the society?—I am attending in answer to an invitation.

3892. Your society received a letter from the Clerk of this Committee stating that the Committee desired the attendance of a representative of that society?—That was so.

3893. You have not furnished me with a list of the matters you would wish to state, therefore will you kindly make your own statement?—I would like to preface what I have to say by announcing the fact that our society is the largest collecting friendly society in existence at the present time.

3894. You say your society is a collecting friendly society?—"Friendly society" is its proper name.

3895. Your society is what is called a collecting friendly society?—Yes.

3896. That is as distinguished from a mutual society?—Yes, as distinguished from affiliated orders and industrial assurance companies.

3897. How is your society distinguished from an industrial assurance company?—They make their returns to the Board of Trade, we make ours to the Registrar. They pay dividends to their shareholders; all our surplus goes to our members.

3898. Those are the points upon which you differ from a commercial society?—Precisely.

3899. Would you tell the Committee what the number of your members is?—In round numbers about 1,200,000.

3900. You mean insuring members?—Yes.

3901. Could you tell the Committee how many of those are child insurances, or are they all child insurance?—They are not all child insurances.

3902. What is the number of your child insurances as compared to the others?—Under ten years of age I should say about one-third of the total number.

3903. That would be about 400,000?—Yes, about 400,000 in round numbers.

3904. Of the 400,000 how many insurances are there under the age of five years?—From 0 to four years of age there are 185,000 insured.

3905–9. You have not got the figure from 0 to five years of age?—We take it from 0 to four; everything under five years we call four.

3910. Would you tell the Committee what is the amount of your gross profit return in the year?—Is your Lordship speaking now of saving or profit?

3911. I mean your gross receipts?—Our gross receipts are 390,000 *l.*

(142.)

Chairman—continued.

3912. Could you say how much of those receipts come from children insurance, and how much from adult?—I could hardly tell you that, but I could let your Lordship have the information.

3913. You say you are a collecting society, and I presume you employ agents?—We employ agents.

3914. Do those agents collect subscriptions from week to week?—There is a trifle of difference between what we call agents, and what are called agents in industrial assurance companies. Our agents supervise what we call collectors.

3915. You have both agents and collectors?—Yes.

3916. The duty of those collectors is to receive weekly payments?—Exactly so.

3917. The tables of payments are weekly, I suppose?—We have tables where they receive weekly, and we have tables where they receive monthly, but the bulk of the payments are made weekly.

3918. Is your scale a fixed scale of so much a week, which you do not increase?—No; it is an increasing scale.

3919. I think most of the societies, if not all of them, whose representatives have been here have told us that their scale is a penny a week, and remains a penny a week, but the policy attained rises year by year?—That is our case.

3920. Then when you said that yours was an increasing scale, you meant an increasing scale of policy, not an increasing scale of premium?—Undoubtedly.

3921. Your collectors receive premiums of a penny a week?—Yes.

3922. Do you ever go as low as a halfpenny?—We do.

3923. Have you many weekly payments at a halfpenny?—Not very many.

3924. The bulk of the payments are at a penny a week?—Yes.

3925. How are your collectors paid?—They are paid by a percentage.

3926. What is the percentage?—Twenty-five per cent.

3927. Is that on the premiums paid?—Yes.

3928. Do they get any premium or douceur on first collections?—They have the first six payments, and 25 per cent. on all subsequent premiums received by them; that is our industrial branch; I presume your Lordship refers to that, which is the bulk of our insurance.

3929. Could you put it roughly in the form of so much in the £. what a collector's place is worth, or what he gets in the shilling?—I should think the remuneration of a collector averages something less than 3 *d.* in the shilling; on paper he gets more, but in reality he gets less.

z 4

3930. You

Chairman—continued.

3930. You would say that his remuneration was about 2½ *d.* in the shilling?—Yes.

3931. Then you have both agents and collectors?—Yes.

3932. What are the duties of an agent?—The duties of the agents are to supervise the collectors and to see that they do their duty in a proper business-like manner; the collectors hand their money to the agents, who enter it on a return and forward it on to the chief office of the society.

3933. You do business outside Liverpool, all over England?—We have nearly 400,000 members in London alone.

3934. Those agents you employ are very respectable men, I suppose?—They are very respectable men, and I think they will compare very well with the employés of any commercial institution in England.

3935. That is an important consideration for you, because you must necessarily be very much in the hands of your agents?—That is so.

3936. If they felt inclined to do anything against the law they have the opportunity of doing it?—Yes; I should like to take this opportunity of saying for myself and my board that we are very proud of our staff.

3937. In your directions to your agents, do you give them directions as to ascertaining the health of children who are proposed to be insured?—Yes, we do, very stringent directions.

3938. Do you give them any directions as regards the character of the parents whose children they insure, and to take care that they are people of good character?—I cannot exactly say that; but we specially instruct them not to take low-class or unhealthy business.

3939. You mean disreputable parents?—Yes.

3940. There are a good many of them, I suppose?—Undoubtedly; and we have, in common with a large number of other societies like ours, proscribed certain streets in which we prevent our men doing any business at all.

3941. I suppose if they did go into them they would get plenty of business there?—Undoubtedly.

3942. The reason I ask the question is that it has been stated that under such circumstances people would not insure at all; is that your opinion?—Our agents could get plenty of business in those streets, simply because they have not been canvassed for a long time; but I do not think the proportion of business that would be got in those streets would compare favourably with the amount of business to be got in other streets.

3943. They would get some business?—They would get some business.

3944. You said just now plenty?—Yes, because they have not been canvassed for some time.

3945. You would not send your agents into any one of those streets to canvass; would they refuse voluntary applications?—The large bulk of our employés collecting would object to take business in streets like that; these instructions, I ought to say, are more for the newer people than for the established staff.

Chairman—continued.

3946. These instructions do not appear in any list of orders, do they?—We issue lists of streets, which we send out to every collector.

3947. And those streets the collector would understand that he was desired to avoid getting business in?—That is so.

3948. Are there any observations that you yourself wish to tender to the Committee?—I have just one or two observations to make. I should like to say for my committee, and for a very large body of our employés, and the people with whom they do business, that they have a very strong opinion against any interference with infant insurance as it at present stands.

3949. Do you mean against any interference whatever?—Yes, any interference whatever, if that interference is in the direction of the amount which they are at present entiled to receive.

3950. That is to say, any interference in the direction of curtailing the amount of the policy for which a child may be insured?—Undoubtedly.

3951. What would you call curtailing? It has been shown to the Committee that the majority of parents do not go up to the 6 *l.*; would you call it unduly curtailing the privilege if they were limited to the average for which they now do insure?—I do not think the "average" argument is a good one, because our connection extends from the second-class artizan to the second-class shopkeeper; we have some very good people belonging to our society, and what would satisfy the second-class artizan for the burial of his children would hardly satisfy the second-class shopkeeper, and although there are more of the poorer class of funerals than of the better, because our second-class artizans are more in numbers, yet, I think, it would not be right to restrict the rights of those who patronise such a society as this.

3952. Then your conscientious objections do not go entirely to the working classes, but apply to the upper class as well?—No; there are many of the working classes who are just as particular as to the manner in which they bury their dead as any class of society.

3953. Notwithstanding that, you say the working class do not insure, as a rule, up to 6 *l.*?—They do not average up to 6 *l.*

3954. Therefore they must be below it; have you, as a matter of fact, many who do go up to 6 *l.*?—Yes.

3955. What would be their number?—I could not exactly tell you the number, but I know we have a very large number who insure for 6 *l.*

3956. I am sure you will say for these men what others have said for them, that they would gladly join in any checks or restraints, which did not interfere with those rights and privileges, which might be thought necessary for preventing evil practices?—I think the general opinion is that murders are murders outside insurance, that a mother murders her child not because of the insurance but in spite of it; I think that is the idea.

3957. You think that there are probably a considerable number of parents who would, merely for the sake of getting rid of their child, in

Chairman—continued.

in order to avoid the expense of bringing it up, let it die?—No, I do not think so.

3958. Not even those disreputable people whom you would not insure?—I have not a large enough experience with them to speak with any degree of certainty.

3959. You would admit, probably, as we would all admit, that there is a certain amount of cruelty to children; parents have been convicted before the magistrates of that offence?—Undoubtedly, but I think that cruelty existed before child insurance.

3960. You would say that to those disreputable or cruel people the insurance money is no temptation, and that they would do just the same thing out of wickedness?—If a mother makes her mind up to kill her child I do not think the fact of receiving 3 *l.*, 4 *l.*, 5 *l.*, or even 6 *l.* would be any incentive one way or the other.

3961. That if they do murder their children, they do it without any money incentive?—Yes, that is what I say they do.

3962. Is not there something more than that in reference to those children; you say they would put away their children for the purpose of saving trouble; I say they might do it for the purpose of the insurance money, would you not admit that?—I do not think that. The struggle for existence is a very terrible thing amongst these people, and they do not attach much value to life, and if they do not attach much value to life themselves they do not think anybody else is relinquishing much in giving it up.

3963. You do not think there would be any objection except if you in the slightest degree interfered with their rights and privileges?—I think not.

3964. I give them credit for being sufficiently well affected, intelligent and kindly people to say, We would give up a little of our privileges if we could be quite sure that it would lessen the danger of crime to those poor little children?—I think you would have to prove to them that the insurance was a cause of danger to children.

3965. I should like to point out that I am as ready to believe that those working men are so regardful of life that if it could be shown that giving up a little of their privileges would save the lives of these poor dear little children they would be willing to do so; do you think they would?—I think they would, but you would have to prove to them that insurance was a cause of crime.

3966. You think they would not be ready to give way?—I hold the opinion that they would think it would be rupturing their privileges, which they think are already low enough.

3967. You remember that a few years ago there was a great and just indignation at the wickedness of those shipowners in the matter of insurance who sent rotten ships to sea and destroyed poor sailors' lives in order that they might get money, and there were laws introduced to prevent that; that would have been a very serious restraint upon the respectable shipowners; would you have thought it quite a proper and decent thing of the respectable shipowners to say, We see these things may save life, but we have our rights and privileges, and we will not give up a shadow of them in order to save life?—No;

Chairman—continued.

but I think it only right for me to ask what privileges those shipowners did give up; I am not sure that they gave up anything.

3968. But do you think it would have been a nice attitude to take up to say, We will not give up a shilling or the least privilege to safe the life of the poorest of these poor sailors?—Certainly not.

3969. I understand this much from you, at all events, that the working man would be willing to submit to or approve of any restrictions which do not interfere with his privileges?—With what he considers his privileges.

3970. You think they would approve of them to some slight extent?—I am afraid they have got to the end of their tether, and I think they were hardly dealt with the last time by being limited to 6 *l.* and 10 *l.*

3971. Do you think that the restrictions which exist in the Friendly Societies Act are hard upon them?—I think they believe so.

3792. You know there is a sentiment amongst some people that these restrictions are pressing upon the working classes and are very invidious; that they love their children as much as the rich do, which I believe is perfectly true, and I have said so, but you are aware that, speaking generally, a rich man cannot insure his child's life at all, and that he is forbidden to do it?—I was not aware of that.

3793. Nobody can insure his child's life unless he can show an insurable interest; that is to say, for the purpose of making money by it, unless he happens to be in one of these industrial societies; that is to say, that he is a poor man; if I wanted to insure the life of my child and make a profit by it, I could not do it by law. I mention that to show that the law as it now exists is harder upon the rich man than upon the poor man?—I think not.

3974. It is hard upon a man to say, You shall not insure your child, for that if you do, it shall be only for a limited sum?—If a rich man insured his child it would be a pure speculation on his part.

3975. That goes to show, does it not, that the legislation under the Feiendly Societies Act is a legislation in the working men's favour?—It is, in strict logic, I have no doubt.

3976. It is really what may be called a piece of class-legislation?—But the working men insure from necessity.

3977. I quite admit that; I only point to the fact that they can do that. You have been in the room and heard the other witnesses examined, have you not?—I have.

3978. You have heard the various suggestions made by various gentlemen representing insurance companies, and so on?—Yes.

3979. Have you formed any opinion upon them?—I have formed a strong opinion with reference to abolishing insurance under one year or two years. I think it was my Lord Derby who mentioned that.

3980. You would be in favour of that, would you?—No; I would be against that; I heard one gentleman giving evidence about fireside clubs and friendly leads; as a working man I know something about that practice, and I am afraid it would lead to the resuscitation of those clubs,

(142.)   A A

Chairman—continued.

clubs, and it would be very injurious to the morality of the working classes, I am sure.

3981. Did you hear the suggestion made that a man should be allowed to insure his child at any age, and that if the child died within one year he should get back his premiums; on the other hand, it was suggested that the money for which a man had insured his child should be carried on to the credit of the other children, or if the child did not die within one year, that it should be carried on to its credit; how does that strike you?—It is ingenious, but it is impracticable, I think; I do not think it would work.

3982. Do you think that the working classes would resent it?—I do not think they would take any notice of it; the working classes would want something definite; they do not understand bargains of that sort.

3983. They would not consider they were wronged or injured in any way?—I do not think so; but I do not think they would accept that as a compromise, or in lieu of the insurance between the age of one and two years.

3984. You think they would object to any reduction of the money to be received or any alteration in the age?—I think so; they might consent to the variation, but I do not think they would consent to the reduction.

3985. You think they would object to reduction?—I think they would; I do not think a graduated scale is fair to our clients; one mother would think she was doing all honour to her little one by spending 2 l. upon its burial, and another that she was spending too little in spending 6 l.

3986. Now it has been alleged that insurance tends to thrift; do you think that a great expenditure upon funerals and upon mourning tends to thrift?—No; but I think there is an idea above that altogether, and that is sentiment.

3987. Are you aware that many people now, both rich and poor, hold that we spend a great deal too much upon funerals?—Yes.

3988. That there is a great deal of wasteful expenditure both upon mourning and funerals?—Yes.

3989. You would not call it a thrifty thing, would you, for a man who had saved a lot of money when he had got it saved up, to spend it on an unwise thing?—It depends upon what we call thrift; the ordinary British working-man would rather put his children away in a manner becoming his position and creditable to his family than he would have that money in the bank; it is part of his religion to lay his child away decently; he attaches great importance to that.

3990. You do not think it would be a good thing in the long run if this Bill or any other tended to reduce the funeral expenses?—I do not think so.

3991. Do you think it is a good thing to spend a great deal of money upon funerals?—No; but I think the effect of insuring has been to inculcate thrift to an extent amongst the working classes which they never knew before.

3992. You think the effect of insurance has been to inculcate thrift?—Yes, I do.

3993. Have you anything more to say to the

Chairman—continued.

Committee?—I would like to remark that I do not think that you or your colleagues can take seriously Mr. Taunton's idea of registering the collectors. I do not like to characterise that suggestion as absurd, but I regard it as totally impracticable.

3994. Why do you think it impracticable?—In our society we have considerably over 3,000 collectors; out of the 3,000 there is a usual number of what I may call floating collectors, some going out and others taking their places, and that is bound to be so with such a large number; and the changing of licences, the transfer of the licence from one to another would mean no end of confusion; and I cannot see that the end to be gained by it is good.

3995. The end that Mr. Taunton thought would be gained by it would be that now if an agent or collector misconducted himself you might or could dismiss him and he would be able to get employment in another society, whereas if his licence were endorsed or taken away he would not be able to get employment?—I think it rather an uncharitable view to take.

3996. You think that?—I do.

3997. What is your opinion about it?—I have a very strong opinion against it.

3998. What do you think about the restriction that a child should not be allowed to be insured in more than one society?—I think that would be a very good regulation.

3999. How would you enforce that regulation?—I think that would want a trifle of thinking about.

4000. Is there any other suggestion that you can make to the Committee?—The best suggestion which I can make is to have a uniform table. I think most of the evils which attend industrial insurance are the result of rivalry or competition, I might say, and if every office in existence were compelled to use the same or a similar table, I think a great many of the evils which are complained of to-day would be done away with.

4001. Would you kindly explain that; do you mean if all the societies had exactly the same scale of premium or policy?—I am speaking purely of child life.

4002. Supposing half-a-dozen societies in the same place all had exactly the same scale of premiums, and the same amount of policy, how would that prevent them from touting for custom all the same; they would be competing with one another still, would they not?—They would be competing with one another, but they would be on one platform.

4003. Supposing we made a law that every grocer in London should sell his sugar at the same price per lb., they would still compete, would they not?—They would.

4004. Then I do not see how your proposal would prevent competition?—I do not say it would prevent competition, but the competition would be of a genuine and natural character.

4005. It has been suggested that if a parent is convicted before a magistrate of gross and wilful cruelty, the parent should be punished by not getting the policy upon the child's life?—You are supposing, I presume, that the child is dead.

4006. No;

Chairman—continued.

4006. No: I am not supposing that the child is dead ; that would be a question for the coroner ; that was proposed by a working man to the Committee, and I thought it was a very good suggestion indeed. Supposing a child was very nearly dead, but not killed by such cruelty so that the magistrate would send the parent to gaol for three months' hard labour; do you think that a parent who is sent to gaol for three months' hard labour should be entrusted with the care of the child's life?—No, I do not.

4007. Now, would you see any objection to the magistrate saying to that person, you are not a fit person to have a policy?—No ; but I think it would be more satisfactory that the magistrate should be allowed to transfer the policy to another person.

4008. You think that the working men would not object to that?—I think they would not object to that.

4009. Then, in point of fact, they would not object to an amendment of the kind that I have just suggested to you?—I think not.

4010. Have you anything to add to the evidence you have already given?—I have one or two more items before me as to statements by coroners; they are simply as to matters of opinion; they are not as to statements of facts.

4011. You are putting your opinion against the coroner's opinion?—Yes ; Dr. Thompson makes a statement that his opinion was that the effect of child insurance was of a prejudicial character: He founded that opinion upon his experience as a medical man of cases in which he was not summoned until the child was beyond all medical treatment; in answer to that I say, it is not the custom of the working classes to call in medical treatment until such time as the ordinary remedies have been found to fail entirely, because the ordinary English mother has unlimited faith in her own resources, and because of the dread of incurring a doctor's bill, which would take them months of privation to pay. It is an established fact, and one admitted by the faculty, that women having had large families are better qualified to deal with the ordinary ailments of children than a medical man himself. And I know from personal experience, that the ordinary British working woman has a sentimental horror of calling in the parish doctor, as anything savouring of pauperism is a cardinal objection to her adopting anything connected with the parish in any way. He further says that the average death-rate of children in Oldham is higher than that for all England. In answer to that I say, this is not singular, as the death-rate of the adult population in Oldham or in any congested district will be found larger than that of all England. He further says, he thought the insured child was less cared for than the uninsured child. I have here with me private letters from Mr. Wynne Baxter, a coroner at the East-end, whose opinion is diametrically opposed to that of this gentleman ; his opinion is that an insured child is cared for and loved more than an uninsured child.

4012. Is there anything more that you wish to point out?—According to the evidence the post-mortem showed the body in a particular case cited, to be in a very emaciated condition; and the

(142.)

Chairman—continued.

medical man said the life would have been prolonged with care and nourishment. My answer to that is that nourishment requires money.

Earl *Beauchamp*.

4013. You were referring to the evidence of Mr. Carter, coroner, in his answer to Question 772 ?—Yes. Then Dr. Troutbeck states, that parents came to the inquest drunk on the proceeds of the insurance. That statement is ridiculous, as none of the insurance money is paid until the coroner has given his certificate, and the registrar's certificate has been presented to the company.

Chairman.

4014. That is the law ?—Yes.

4015. It might possibly nevertheless happen that as a matter of fact such a thing was done ?—I could hardly suppose they would pay unless the coroner had issued his certificate.

4016. Is there anything else you wish to say ?—With regard to the statement as to the flower-girl, the examination showed that the infant had suffered 36 hours from inflammation of the lungs. The father was a porter, and the mother who was a flower-seller had taken the child out with her, and denied all knowledge that it was ill. I should only like to say that I do not see what the flower-seller could have done with the child except to take it with her.

Earl *Spencer*.

4017. I am not sure whether you gave the number or children under one year who were insured in your society ?—No, I did not.

4018. Can you give the number ?—No, I have not the figures with me at present.

4019. You do your business, not only in Liverpool, but in other places ?—Yes, all over England.

4020. You have head offices in Hull and London ?—We have district offices in every large town in the United Kingdom.

4021. Do you find any difference in your business when it is removed from the principal office, and merely under the charge of these collectors and agents ?—No.

4022. You do not find that they are more lax in the lives that they take ?—No we have district managers or agents (the terms are synonymous) attached to each district office ; those are all tried men, who have been in our employ many years, and in whom we have confidence.

4023. You do not have local committees ?—We do not have local committees.

4024. We have had the evidence from other witnesses; but could you state what the cost of the poorest funeral would be of the people that come to your society to be insured ?—The lowest cost in Liverpool would be, I should think, about 2 l. 5 s., and that would be a very poor one.

4025. Do you know what it would be in London ?—I should think in London it would be 15 per cent. more, but I am now speaking a little off the book, because I am not acquainted with the prices in London.

4026. What do you include in the charge; the funeral and the grave?—No, not the grave ; I have known many working-men in my time

A A 2   when

Earl *Spencer*—continued.

when I was an apprentice, to buy a grave, but it is a very expensive thing to do.

4027. You include the opening of the grave?—Yes; the opening of the grave, a pall, a mourning coach, and, when they can afford it, the mourning and the fees for the service.

4028. We have had it in evidence that a funeral can be conducted for from 15 *s*. to 1 *l*.; do you believe that to be possible?—I believe it to be possible.

4029. We have had it stated in evidence before this Committee that certain streets or places were proscribed by insurance companies; for what reason do you proscribe streets?—Streets in bad sanitary condition.

4030. Where the mortality would be very high?—Yes; where the mortality would be very high.

4031. Not on account of the poorest class living there?—Not necessarily.

4032. Do you have those proscribed streets in nearly every town?—Yes; in nearly every town we do business with.

Lord *Kinnaird.*

4033. I think you said that the number of insurances under five years in your office was 185,000?—I think that was the exact number.

4034. The total insurances of those under 10 years was about 400,000; could you give the Committee any figure between the 185,000 and the 400,000?—In the period from 0 to 4 there are 185,000, and in the period between 5 and 9 there are 155,000, making the total number under the age of 10, 340,000.

4035. You mentioned the question of a friendly lead, is that still practised in Liverpool, or is it practically abolished there?—They are now abolished; I do not know one. I have heard our men repeatedly state that the greatest enemies to their advancement in business were the slate clubs, friendly leads, and fireside clubs.

4036. What are slate clubs?—Slate clubs are simply putting down a certain amount of money at certain periods, and it being paid either for the funeral or for drink, or both, at the public-house. The fireside club is exactly the same thing; they go there once a week and sit round the fire with long pipes, and they pay a certain amount to the publican for the same purpose.

4037. What effect has industrial insurance had upon those institutions?—Industrial insurance has simply wiped out altogether the slate clubs, the fireside clubs, and the friendly leads; I am speaking of course only of Lancashire.

4038. You think that if men were improvident, and went into their workshops or mills and wanted subscriptions for the burial of their children, they would find great difficulty in raising the necessary amount?—No, I think not; I think they would find it very easy to raise it, but the natural independence of the working man comes in here; he would prefer to pay it himself; he has a chronic objection to going round with his cap and asking for subscriptions.

4039. Do you think there is any truth in the charge that the policies are paid before the death has legally been proved?—No.

4040. Do you ever have advances made upon your policies?—No.

Lord *Kinnaird*—continued.

4041. Are they assigned?—No, we are not a trading company; a friendly society could not assign a policy, it is not a legal document; if anybody were to assign a policy we have no legal means to receive it in the ordinary way and register it, so that it is not worth the paper it is printed upon. The Friendly Societies Act provides for nominations, which can be revoked at any time after they have been given.

4042. You stated, I think, that you considered it better on the whole for the working man to join a friendly society, rather than one which paid a dividend to its shareholders?—No, I do not remember saying that. I said that our surplus money went for the benefit of the members connected with it, whereas the industrial companies' surplus moneys went partly to pay the dividend to their shareholders.

4043. So that they would get better terms by joining one of your societies?—One would think so; but we are hedged round with so many restrictions that we have not the numerous chances that the industrial societies have; we work under the Friendly Societies Act, but they are not under the same restrictions.

4044. Do they pay their collectors at the same rate?—I think we pay our collectors a trifle better than they do in industrial assurances.

4045. You think the working classes would not mind a strengthening of the law against the criminal element; provided it did not affect the question of the intelligent working man doing what he could to insure?—Yes; for the respectable working men have no incentive to murder afforded by insurance, the murder would take place exactly the same if the insurance were non-existent.

4046. You say that insurance does not tend to crime?—I have a very strong opinion in that direction.

Lord *Clifford of Chudleigh.*

4047. I want to ask you a question about your table; I see that according to the table that I have before me, by paying a premium of 2 *d*. a week for a child from one week old to one year and six months, they can after twelve months of insurance get a claim of 5 *l*.; and then lower down I see that in the case of children insured for 1 *d*. a week premium the claims increase from 2 *l*. 10 *s*. to 10 *l*. 6 *s*.; and for 2 *d*. per week premium, from 5 *l*. to 20 *l*. 12 *s*. according to age; what does that mean?—It ranges according to age; beginning at 2 *l*. 10 *s*. for 1 *d*., the 10 *l*. 6 *s*. is the amount to which under that table they will be entitled when they become practically adults; that is to say after they pass the age of 10 years

4048. What is the scale for a child that is 12 months old up to five years; does it only increase by 1 *l*.?—No, it increases from 2 *l*. 10 *s*. to 6 *l*.

4049. I am assuming that by paying a premium of 2 *d*. a week at the end of one year I can get an insurance of 5 *l*.; how much can I get at the end of five years?—How old is the child supposed to be?

4050. A child just born?—£. 6.

4051. If I insure for only a penny a week at the

Lord *Clifford of Chudleigh*—continued.

the end of one year I can get 2 *l.*, and at the end of four years only 3 *l.*?—Yes.

4052. Is not that rather a small increase?—It is half what we are entitled to give according to law; it is half what we give for 2 *d.*

4053. Taking the case of another society, if I insure a child at its birth for a penny, at the end of one year I can get 3 *l.*, and at the end of five years I can get 5 *l.*; is not that a much more favourable table?—Yes, I think it is much more favourable than ours, but all tables differ, not so much in detail as in degree.

4054. Now can you tell me why you give such a considerable advantage to the insurance of infant life under one year as against succeeding years?—I suppose it is because of our experience. Our experience as collated by the actuary would show that we could afford to give a larger amount; but in a matter of this kind I should very much like your Lordship to refer to our actuary, he would be able to give you a very much more intelligent reply than I could.

4055. If I were to judge by your table of insurance, I should come to the conclusion that the risks within the first year were rather less than the risks in the subsequent years?—I should think the reverse is the fact; the risk of the first year of life is very great.

4056. Then I should have very little inducement to insure my child after the first year, seeing that I get much worse terms than if I had insured my child under one year?—You must have an inducement to join.

4057. For that reason you give more favourable terms in the first year?—I presume it is for that reason.

Earl of *Selborne.*

4058. Some witnesses have suggested that there should be a graduated scale; have you any objection to that?—Yes; I would object to a scale graduated so that it would interfere to any extent with the amount as at present allowed by law.

4059. The suggestion was that the maximum amount should be as now allowed by law, but that that should be only payable when a certain age had been reached?—Yes.

4060. And that for the lower ages you would have a graduated scale of less amount. Do you think it a good thing that children under 12 months' old should be insured for 6 *l.*?—If it takes 6 *l.* to bury it in a proper way, I should.

Earl *Beauchamp.*

4061. If the parents of the child are dead, who receives the money?—The next-of-kin.

4062. Do you ever, in the lifetime of the parent, pay the money over to anyone else?—Yes, under exceptional circumstances, we do; for instance, if the parents are away long distances, say, in Africa or in India, and the child happens to be with an aunt or guardian, we would then pay the money to that person.

4063. The Prudential Society, in their instructions to their agents, have this; it is the 134th: "The Friendly Societies Act provides that when a death takes place of any child under 10 years of age, one of the parents only of the child can receive the money; should the parents

(142.)

Earl *Beauchamp*—continued.

be dead, an application must be made to the chief office." Have you any corresponding rule in the instructions to your agents?—Yes; that instruction simply means that there are certain people authorised to pay claims under certain conditions, but if those conditions are not complied with even in the smallest degree (and this is one of them), then the claim must be sent to the chief office for them to say to whom the money is to be paid.

4064. Do I understand you to say that in all cases where the parents do not put in an appearance the payments are made upon the responsibility of the chief office?—Undoubtedly.

4065. Referring to the Deptford case, how came the money in that case to be paid over?—I have not the facts of the Deptford case just now by me.

4066. In what is known as the Deptford case the persons whose deaths were investigated were insured in your society; is not that so?—I believe that is so.

4067. When did the Deptford case occur?—I should think it was about two years ago.

4068. How long have you been connected with the society?—For nearly 21 years.

4069. Was not the Deptford case a matter of considerable discussion?—It was.

4070. But you can give the Committee no special information upon that point?—I can only give a general statement that we pay a large number of claims, and you can quite understand from prudential motives, and from other motives that we are very glad if we can to pay the money as soon as possible. There are people, of course, who would be unscrupulous enough to make false statements occasionally, and we are often, or at all events occasionally, let in to pay things that we have hardly any right to pay.

4071. Do you think that the evils which are attributed to child insurance are very much aggravated if the payments are loosely made to persons who are described as baby-farmers?—Yes; the great difficulty is to discover when they are baby-farmers. Often we have children insured in our society, and it is not likely that men or women would make any statement to the effect that they were farming those children. They are very often entered as, and are supposed to be, the children of the parents in whose house they are staying.

4072. In your form of proposal do you require the proposers to state that they are the parents of the children?—We do not rely so much upon the proposal, we depend more upon house to house visits; we have what are called testers in some cases, that is to say, not in the case of our old employés who have too large a stake in the society to do anything irregular, and those testers go and visit and initial every case.

4073. Do those testers derive any commission from the cases they pass?—None whatever.

4074. Are they paid by fixed salary?—They are paid by fixed salary.

Chairman.

4075. I wish to ask you only one question about baby-farming, have you ever known that you have actually paid money to baby-farmers?—We have never known such a case.

A A 3   4076. There

*Chairman—*continued.

4076. There have been instances, have there not, of baby-farmers having insured the children placed in their charge ?—Undoubtedly.

4077. In those cases the societies, I quite assume, were deceived, and were not aware of it ; but nevertheless whatever the precautions of the societies have been, the baby-farmers have succeeded in getting the children insured ?—Sometimes.

4078. Have you any suggestion at all to make as regards preventing baby-farmers insuring the children in their charge ?—It is a very difficult thing indeed ; we see no way out of it at all, but when we find any of our agents entering insurances with people who are known to be baby-farmers, we quash the insurances, and do not allow the policies to be made out.

4079. You have never knowingly paid to a baby farmer, but you have known of cases of baby-farmers applying for insurance ?—Yes, I think that people who are paid a small weekly sum to keep children should be exempted from the benefits of life insurance.

4080. You are aware that all that subject is before a Committee of the House of Commons ? —Yes. With regard to the Deptford case, I should like to say that the woman represented herself to be the mother.

The Witness is directed to withdraw.

Ordered, That this Committee be adjourned to Tuesday next, at Twelve o'clock.

Die Martis, 22° Julii, 1890.

LORDS PRESENT:

Earl SPENCER.
Earl of HARROWBY.
Earl BEAUCHAMP.
Earl of SELBORNE.
LORD BISHOP OF PETERBOROUGH.

Lord KER (*Marquess of Lothian*).
Lord KINNAIRD.
Lord NORTON.
Lord THRING.

THE RIGHT REV. THE LORD BISHOP OF PETERBOROUGH, IN THE CHAIR.

The Chairman hands in a letter and presentment of the Grand Jury at the General Quarter Sessions of the Borough of Great Yarmouth (see Appendix).

MR. EDWIN HOOPER, is called in; and Examined, as follows:

Chairman.

4081. YOU are Coroner for a district of Staffordshire?—I am coroner for what is called the West Bromwich District of Staffordshire.

4082. I believe that you have held the office of coroner for 30 years?—That is so.

4083. Your district is one of the largest in England?—It is.

4084. I believe that you have no interest, either directly or indirectly, in any insurance company or friendly society?—None whatever.

4085. In your opinion is the industrial insurance of the working classes a distinct and great benefit?—That is my opinion.

4086. Both with regard to infantile and adult insurance?—Just so.

4087. You say in your *précis* of evidence that from your long experience you have no hesitation in stating that you do not consider infantile assurance is conducive to the neglect of children by their parents, in order to put them out of the way with a view of obtaining the insurance money?—That is my opinion.

4088. Your observation leads you to state that upon the average a sum of 50 s. is the amount generally paid by insurance companies upon the death of a child?—That I find, as a rule, is about the amount.

4089. As a rule, you think the whole of this sum is expended upon the funeral?—So far as I am able to ascertain. I have taken some interest in this matter, and perhaps I may have gone rather beyond my duties as coroner, but I have done it with the anticipation that this question would arise sooner or later; therefore I have taken some little trouble, outside the actual inquiry as to the cause of death, to ascertain the facts, and that is the result of my inquiries.

4090. You wish to put before the Committee first of all that the average sum generally insured for is 50 s., and that so far as your knowledge and inquiry go that sum is generally expended upon the funeral?—Yes; and more than that is expended upon the funeral. The parents' friends

(142.)

Chairman—continued.

generally make a subscription towards the expenses of the funeral beyond the amount of the insurance.

4091. With regard to insurance upon the lives of children between the ages of one and three years you are of opinion that there is necessity for it, as the children must either be buried by the parents or the parish authorities; is that your view?—That is my view.

4092. If it be by the parents the money expended must be provided from a source outside the family?—That is so.

4093. That is the sum and substance of your evidence?—It is.

4094. I want in the first place to make quite clear what it is you mean in paragraph 3 of your statement, in which you say, you "have no hesitation in saying that the infant insurance is not conducive to the neglect of children by their parents in order to put them out of the way with the object of obtaining the insurance money;" do I understand you to mean by that that it is your belief that the parents do not insure with that object?—That is what I mean.

4095. But you would not mean to assert as a matter within your own knowledge that although the parent may not have insured with that object, yet that nevertheless the presence to his mind constantly of the profit to be made by the insurance might not have an injurious effect upon a child's death?—Quite so.

4096. You are referring, of course, to parents who insure their children with the intention, in the first instance, of putting them away, or in order to put them away?—I have never had a case come under my notice in which that has been clearly proved.

4097. You state that you have never had reason to think that insurance operated upon the parents' mind as an inducement to criminal neglect of a child?—I have not.

4098. But you had formed an opinion at one time as regards the effect upon the minds of parents

A A 4

parents of money in death clubs. May I draw
your attention to the letter dated, Harbourne,
5th October 1877; it is a letter addressed to
R. Williams, Esq., chairman at a lecture delivered by Dr. F. E. Manby, of Wolverhampton, by yourself, and you say: " Dear Sir,—I am
glad to find this subject (which in my opinion is
one of the most important questions of the day)
is occupying the attention of the Wednesbury
Local Board "; may I ask what that subject was?
—It had reference rather to the improper feeding of infants than to their insurance, as well as
I recollect.

4099. You say next, " I am quite certain that
the lives of numberless children are thrown
away through the administration of insufficient
or improper food when young, and also through
the parents and midwives neglecting to call in
the aid of duly qualified men where necessary ";
that opinion you still entertain, I presume ?—
I do.

4100. Then follows this sentence : " The
great object with the parents seems to be ever
to obtain the club money, for in nine cases out of
10 the mother is in the death club "?—Yes.

4101. That seems rather to conflict with the
opinion you have just now expressed, that insurance has no evil effect. That would seem to
go to show that the great object of the parents
was to obtain this club money ?—It always is the
first object immediately after the inquest is
held.

4102. You say further, " I do not see how the
evil can be checked, as long as death certificates
are given and received in the loose way they are
at present "; what was the " evil " you were
referring to?—The improper feeding of these
children, that was my great object.

4103. You did not at all imply, then, that there
was any evil in the way of temptation to crime
connected with insurance ?—It has never been
my opinion that there has been any direct
criminal intention on the part of the parents, or
direct incentive as far as that goes, arising from
insurance.

4104. That of course, not speaking disrespectfully, is a question of opinion ; that is the
opinion you have formed ?—That is the opinion
I have formed ; it is a matter of opinion, as you
say.

4105. Then you go on to point out the defects
in the registration, upon which you say, " I
know that unqualified persons have no difficulty
in getting deaths registered, and I am constantly
coming across cases where midwives take children
to the sexton, and get them buried as stillborn,
when they have lived many hours and sometimes longer "?—That is so ; I have had many
exhumed for the purpose of examination.

4106. " And perhaps have been lost through
the neglect of the midwives in not calling in medical aid." And then you say, " or through more
serious causes which I shudder to think of " ; what
are the more serious causes of this malpractice
beyond the burying of stillborn children ; what
are the more serious causes of neglect that you
shudder at ?—I had in my mind when that letter
was written this fact, and it is a very extraordinary one, that there are more deaths of infants

reported to me which take place upon a Sunday
morning than at any other time; bodies are found
dead on Sunday morning in bed, no doubt through
the excessive drinking of the parents on the
Saturday night, and that continues to the present
day.

4107. By the " serious causes " you mean
overlaying from drunkenness ?—That is what I
had in my mind at the time I wrote that letter.

4108. Then you say in conclusion. " I have
acted as coroner for nearly 20 years, and am
sorry to believe the practices to commit crime
without detection are quite as great now as they
were on the day I held my first inquest." That
opinion you still entertain ?—That opinion I still
entertain.

4109. When you speak of the power to commit
crime without detection I suppose you would be
of opinion that the power of effectually committing
crime without detection is very much greater in
the case of infant life than it would be in the
case of an adult ?—Undoubtedly.

4110. Therefore, supposing the parent were
for any reason inclined to criminally neglect or
put away a child, he might do with far greater
impunity than in the case of an adult ?—That is
so.

4111. Are you acquainted with Mr. Thorneycroft, deputy coroner for Wolverhampton ?—No,
I do not know him personally ; I know his principal, Mr Phillips, very well.

4112. It is in rather a neighbouring district to
yours, is it not ?—His district touches on mine.

4113. It marches with yours?—Yes.

4114. Therefore he would have to do with
very much the same class of people as yourself?
—He would.

4115. Now I will direct your attention to what
he states in a letter dated the 8th of July this
year. He says, " For a time I was in some doubt
as to whether the insurance of children was for
good or evil, on the whole, for the working
classes, even the most thrifty, in many cases do
not get the means to save in this part of the
country, and in case of death the insurance money
comes in most usefully, for the better class of the
people have the greatest horror of seeking the
aid of the parish." You will observe that
Mr. Thorneycroft fully recognises, as you do, the
value and usefulness of child insurance to the
respectable portion of the community; but he
goes on to say, " I came to the conclusion however,
long since, that the insurance, as the system at
present prevails, is bad and wrong, and ought to
be prevented." That is Mr. Thorneycroft's
opinion ?—Could you tell me the length of experience Mr. Thorneycroft has had ?

4116. I cannot say ; perhaps you could tell
the Committee?—It has been rather short, I
think, in comparison to my own. Then he concludes, " Why should people desire to insure
their children at all ? In my opinion it is with
an object of personal gain in many cases, and a
hope of one day receiving the money. I would
prohibit such insurance of all children under five
years old, and then only to be in one insurance
office, and on strict conditions for the benefit of
the child at certain stages of age. A policy of
this description should be under a very small
premium."

Chairman—continued.

premium." Whatever that opinion may be worth I suppose you would say it directly conflicts with your own?—It does. I do not quite see in that case how the children are to be buried; it does not matter what age they are.

4117. I am not asking whether Mr. Thorneycroft's proposals are wise or otherwise, but I am merely pointing out that a coroner who takes the district which marches with your own, holds a directly contrary view to yours?—All I can say is, that he has not had the same experience as I have.

Earl *Spencer.*

4118. What is the class of the population you have principally to deal with as coroner?—Mining and ironworks; I have what is commonly called the black country.

4119. Is it the same kind of country as Mr. Thorneycroft's is?—Mr. Thorneycroft has more of a rural district than I have.

4120. I do not understand from your evidence that you have not had cases of criminal neglect of children where the children have died, but that you have had cases of that sort before you?—I have; I had a case of that sort a little time ago, when I committed the parents for manslaughter; that was at the latter end of last year.

4121. What were the particulars of that case?—The children were not insured.

4122. It was a case of neglect?—It was simply a case of neglect.

4123. You have not yourself noticed, though you have had those cases of neglect which have ended fatally, that the death has been accelerated in any way by reason of the insurance?—I have not; I have gone carefully into all those cases.

4124. And have you asked the question?—I never hold an inquest without asking the question; it always appears upon my depositions. I have adopted the practice for years.

4125. Could you give at all an idea of the number of cases which come before you in which death is caused by neglect?—I had only one case last year, and they were two children in one family; the parents had been summoned previously for neglecting their children; the children were taken away from the parents; then they were brought back, again they were neglected, and the children died.

4126. Have you had any considerable number of such cases?—Not that I have been able to trace clearly to neglect; a great number of deaths have been caused undoubtedly by improper feeding. The medical evidence shows that.

4127. Is that from ignorance or neglect?—From ignorance, undoubtedly.

4128. Then so far as your opinion goes, you do not think the present laws need to be altered with reference to infant insurance?—I see no need for it myself.

4129. Not even with the youngest children a year old?—No; my reason for saying that is that however young a child may be, or however old, it has to be buried, and the money the parents get in this way is for the burial of the child; I do not see what benefit the parents can get when it is all expended for the funeral.

4130. But it is possible there might be a profit?—There might be a few shillings balance.

(142.)

Earl *Spencer*—continued.

I have heard of cases of this kind where the family consists, say for the sake of argument, of seven children, and one of the children has died, and when I have made inquiry about the insurance, I have found that all the family has been insured except this one child, that has happened; and in one or two cases on the other hand I have found that the children have been insured, but that they have not been on benefit, the policies have lapsed.

4131. Do you know whether it is the general practice among the workers in your district to insure their children?—It is.

Earl of *Selborne.*

4132. When you spoke of improper feeding, I suppose neglect is also a frequent cause of children dying?—What might your Lordship mean; neglecting them in what way?

4133. Not feeding them enough; not taking care to keep them clean and so on?—I have not had many cases of that kind; as I said before, the majority of the cases are from improper feeding. I have had cases such as that which I have referred to where the parents were committed for manslaughter where the children were literally starved, no doubt; but that was not a case of insurance, because the children were not insured.

4134. You think that in cases of unnatural parents, insurance might prove an additional motive for neglect; that they would gain something by it?—It might be certainly.

4135. But you think they do not generally gain by it?—I do not think they do so generally; that has been my experience.

4136. Do not you think that the power to insure up to 6 *l.* at five years of age as far as the law goes, so that it might be done even in the first year of the child's existence, might be used so as to bring in a profit beyond the expenses of burial?—That is quite possible.

Lord *Thring.*

4137. I understand that infanticide, or rather the death of children is very common, but you attribute it usually to improper feeding?—I do.

4138. And you attribute that improper feeding not so much as a general rule to negligence, or parental misdoing, as to ignorance?—I attribute it to ignorance, as a general rule, but you will find exceptions, of course.

4139. Then with respect to the application of the insurance money, are you aware of any cases in which parents have received the insurance money and not applied it to the funeral expenses?—They do not come under my knowledge.

4140. Do you believe, as a general rule, that such would be the case?—I believe, as a general rule, that the money is applied for funeral expenses.

4141. Then it follows, as a matter of absolute certainty, that if the money is applied to the funeral properly, very little profit or surplus can, as a general rule, remain?—Very little.

4142. Therefore the incentive to crime is a very small one?—In many instances subscriptions are made afterwards. I have known it myself; my juries often contribute.

B B   4143. When

Lord *Thring*—continued.

4143. When you speak of subscriptions, do you mean that in many cases where a child dies the neighbours subscribe to help the parents with the funeral?—They do.

4144. Then you say that people very properly object to a pauper funeral; do they not also wish that the mother and the children should have some black to go to the funeral in?—I think that they perhaps atttribute more importance to that than people in a better station of life do.

4145. They attribute more importance to it than you or I should do?—Undoubtedly.

4146. Then in point of fact your opinion is that insurance, practically speaking, is not an incentive to murder?—I have not found it so in my experience.

4147. How long do you say you have been coroner?—For 30 years this month, and for four years previously as deputy coroner.

4148. That is 34 years' experience in a mining district? — Yes; in the mining district of West Bromwich.

4149. I suppose your mining people include people who make very good wages, and also poor people?—There are more poor, I am afraid, in late years; their wages have been very low indeed.

4150. What is their character, as a rule, are they what we have had called dissolute poor, or are they well conducted?—Thay are a mixture.

4151. Then with regard to Mr. Thorneycroft, do you know how long he has been a coroner? —He is a deputy coroner, and I should say he has been so about six or seven years, but I am not quite clear as to that.

Earl of *Harrowby.*

4152. In the 30 years you have been coroner has there been a great increase in the habit of children's life insurance in your part of the country?—I should say there has; but I am not clear upon that point.

4153. Can you tell the Committee what societies the working people of your district they generally insure in?—I find that the Prudential Society is their great office.

4154. Do they insure in small local societies besides?—No, I think not; they are generally insured in large offices, well-known offices.

4155. I think we should be right in describing the part of Staffordshire with which you are connected as having a great deal of poverty in it?— An immense amount.

4156. Therefore, you would consider it a very great help to those people, poor and struggling with great privations, to be able to meet the expenses of a child's death by insurance?—That is my opinion.

4157. Apart from that, do you think it is a great boon to them?—I do.

4158. You would say, I imagine, that, as a general rule, there is a warm affection for their children amongst the mining class?—I should say so; there are, of course, exceptions.

4159. But you have no reason to suppose that generally they are defective in family affection?— Not the slightest. I believe the people in the Black Country are not nearly so black as they are painted; there is a great deal of sympathy amongst them and heartiness of character, more

Earl of *Harrowby*—continued.

particularly amongst neighbours, they help each other more than people in the middle station of life would, I have no doubt.

4160. I am afraid the condition of the dwellings of our people in that part of the country are anything but advantageous to the health of children?—They are anything but advantageous; how many of them manage to exist there I do not know.

4161. So that I am afraid a working man in that part of the country, taking a careful view of the future of his family, must expect that he will unfortunately lose a good number of his children in early childhood?—Certainly; I have formed that opinion from what I have read of the medical evidence in that district and from my experience.

4162. It is therefore of extreme importance to him to provide for these expenses?—It is.

Chairman.

4163. You state that you think that only a profit of a few shillings, if any profit, could remain to a parent upon the balance of his insurance money after burying the child?—It could not be much out of the 50 s.

4164. In saying that, you refer to a child insured for 2 *l.* 10 *s*?—Yes.

4165. You are aware that under the law he might be insured to the amount of 6 *l.*?—Yes.

4166. And that if he were a few months over five years of age he might be insured to the amount of 10 *l.*?—Yes.

4167. You would not call the difference between that amount and the cost of a child's funeral "a few shillings," would you?—No, I was referring to the burial of an infant.

4168. Will you take it from me that a parent could, for a cost of 4 *s.* 4 *d.*, spread over six months, obtain 6 *l.* on the death of his child under five years old?—No doubt.

4169. Taking the funeral of the child to cost 3 *l.*, which has been shown to be about the average, you would not call that balance " a few shillings "?—No, certainly not, but I was referring to a child under two years of age.

4170. The younger the child the cheaper the funeral, as a general rule, is it not?—Yes, that is so.

4171. And therefore the cheaper the funeral the greater the balance between the amount received and the amount expended?—Certainly.

4172. And, therefore, also the greater the advantage of putting the child away?—That is so; but I speak of the great bulk of the insurances being for the amount I have stated, namely, 2 *l.* 10 *s.*

4173. That is what you are informed?—Yes.

4174. But the parent might not wish to state to the coroner the exact amount?—But the depositions are taken on oath.

4175. Then as to the case of a parent having insured a child and leaving it to be buried by the parish, such a case has not come within your knowledge?—Such a case has not come within my knowledge.

4176. What opportunity would you have of tracing the money afterwards?—I have made it
a point

Chairman—continued.

a point for the last two or three years of asking the police to trace the expenditure of the money for me, for this reason: that I was quite certain that this question would crop up sooner or later.

4177. I understand you to say that the police under your directions have made inquiries in order to trace the expenditure?—That is so.

4178. With regard to this question of the application of the money for the funeral only, and not applying to the parish to bury, the Committee have had before them certain relieving officers; and their evidence, which I have just now looked at, goes distinctly to the effect that in cases within their knowledge this very thing has happened, namely, that parents have insured their children's lives for funeral expenses and then left the children to be buried by the parish?—They would have a better opportunity of finding that out than I would, no doubt.

4179. You would say that a relieving officer from his station and occupation would have better opportunies of finding that out than you would?—He would.

4180. Therefore you would give considerable weight to the evidence of such persons?—I would.

4181. Then as regards your experience as coroner, which no doubt is considerable, you state that you have been a coroner for 30 years?—Yes.

4182. One coroner who appeared before this Committee, and who gave evidence in a directly opposite sense to yours, had been a coroner for 36 years. He also put in written statements I think, speaking from memory, of 10 (if not 10, of nine) coroners who all declared that they agreed with him; and there were also two coroners who gave evidence to the same effect before this House of Commons Committee on Friendly

Chairman—continued.

Societies; that would make, if I am correct, somewhere about 17 coroners, some of whom have a considerable length of experience giving evidence opposed to yours?—That I cannot help. I can only speak from my experience. I hope it will be quite understood that I have no interest whatever in this matter.

Earl of *Selborne*.

4183. You stated that it was quite the exception with reference to very young children that they were insured for above 50. *l*; you also said, I think, that in your district the chief insurance company was the Prudential?—I think, no doubt that is the favourite office.

4184. You are aware that the Prudential Society has a fixed scale, and do not undertake insurances which depart from that scale?—I really do not know their rules; I have never gone into the question not being connected with it in any way.

4185. Where any sinister motives exist, of course, those cases would be exceptional, would they not?—They would.

4186. Therefore, if it be a rare thing to insure for more than 50 *s.*?—I say, I find that 50 *s.* is the amount that the majority of these parents pay for.

4187. Then if a greater insurance than that is rare, as that the cases in which it is done are exceptional, should you see any great objection to amending the law by introducing a scale so as to prevent insurance within certain ages above that amount?—I should not.

4188. And that would meet the exceptional cases where a sinister motive might possibly exist?—It would

The Witness is directed to withdraw.

MR. JOHN EDWARD CLEVELAND, is called in; and Examined, as follows:

Chairman.

4189. You are the secretary to the National Independent Order of Odd-fellows?—Yes.

4190. You also represent to-day the Conference of Affiliated Friendly Societies?—I do; that conference was held 12 months since.

4191. You are also an *ex-officio* member of the Parliamentary committee appointed by the Affiliated Friendly Societies?—Yes.

4192. And you represent how many adult members?—By the figures of the last conference 2,012,969.

4193. And you represent how much capital?—14,064,447 *l.*

4194. And the number of affiliated orders contained in the union you refer to, is how many?—Seventeen.

4195. You attend here to state certain objections to this Insurance Bill?—I do.

4196. Would you kindly state them?—I do not think there has been anything which has been suggested as regards legislation in the interests of friendly societies which has created so much disturbance amongst the affiliated orders as this suggested Bill has. The reasons why we object are that the principle of the Friendly

(142.)

Chairman—continued.

Societies Act, as applied to the affiliated orders, has been found to be all that is desired to support or protect them in carrying out the business which they have instituted on behalf of the working classes of this country. We consider it would be a considerable limitation also of the freedom which we have enjoyed, and consented to be protected by legislation, as witness our acceptance of the Act of 1875, and our support of its enactments.

Lord *Thring.*

4197. Am I right in suggesting that these societies have a conference to-morrow?—They have; I am secretary to the conference which meets to-morrow.

4198. Therefore after to-morrow you will be able to tell the Committee the result of the various opinions expressed at the conference?—Quite so; but what I have to say upon the subject of infantile assurance was discussed at the last conference.

The Committee-room is cleared. After a short time the Witness is again admitted.

4199. The

Chairman.

4199. The Committee being aware that a conference of friendly societies is to be held to-morrow, have decided to postpone hearing your evidence until after that conference shall have been held. They think it on the whole fairer to the societies you represent that you should give your evidence after that conference has been held than to-day; therefore the Committee have decided for the present to postpone hearing your evidence until after that conference has been held?—May I explain that the infor-

Chairman—continued.

mation I have to present to you has been conveyed to me by the various executives of the societies, and I have some statistics that they have favoured me with to give the Committee to-day.

4200. But there will be nothing to prevent your giving these when you come again?—Certainly not.

Chairman.] The Committee will sit on Friday, and can hear all that you have to say then.

The Witness is directed to withdraw.

MR. WYATT SARGENT, is called in; and Examined, as follows:

Chairman.

4201. WHAT are you?—My profession is a manufacturing stationer's foreman.

4202. Where is your residence?—No. 40, Baring-street, Islington, N.

4203. You wish to make some statement with reference to this Bill?—The society which I represent is the United Order of the Total Abstinent Sons of the Phœnix; it is a temperance organisation. I represent one section, which numbers 12,000 members; there are several sections of the society.

4204. Are you deputed by this society to appear here to-day?—I am; I have a petition here from the society against the Bill. We have upwards of 7,000 juveniles attached to our society ranging from the age of five to 16. Our benefits are 8 *l.* upon death.

4205. In every case of death?—In every case of death.

4206. From what age?—From five to 16 years.

4207. Have you any benefits under five years of age?—None; that is the age of admission, from five to 16.

4208. Do I understand you to say that in your association no child under five years of age can receive any benefit?—None whatever; we have no members under five. We object strongly to this Bill for the reason that it will interfere materially with our work. I have here the number of deaths which have occurred from February 1887 to June 1890, which are 33, and the various diseases of which they died; amongst them are several hospital cases owing to injuries either by machinery or falls or various other things; the amount of money which is expended by our society does not cover the funeral expenses, which comprise the medical attendance and other incidentals attached to the death. Large numbers of our members also pay their own contributions. We are undoubtedly almost the lowest rung in the ladder of societies, we take in the very poorest.

4209. You say that a number of your members pay their own contributions; I do not quite understand what that means?—That means their subscriptions towards their benefits; they are lads of an age to pay their own contributions or subscriptions towards the benefits which the society holds out to them.

4210. You mean that some of the young

Chairman—continued.

people in your society are not subscribed for by their parents, but subscribe for themselves?—That is so.

4211. With reference to those contributions and the payment of them, to whom are they made; are they made to collectors or agents on behalf of your society, are they made to any central office of your society?—The payments are made to branches of our society.

4212. Does that mean offices?—We call them lodges. That is an institution which is, as it were, a wing of an army; of the central body; which we have attached to this society, and as a rule to all societies of that description, and the money is collected by the secretaries of each branch.

4213. Then, if I understand you rightly, you are not what is commonly called a collecting or commercial society?—We are not. I may also say that the work, or the bulk of the work, is of a voluntary nature; the subscriptions are received by a committee who do their work on the voluntary principle.

4214. And have no pecuniary interest whatever in obtaining contributions?—They have no pecuniary interest, although of course the general secretary has a small stipend which he receives from the management fund, but on the whole the working of the juvenile society is conducted on the voluntary principle. Our object is to promote the better condition of our fellow working men, and those who are depending on them; to inculcate temperance, thrift, and self-dependence; and we consider that if this Bill is passed it will be a great detriment to the work of our society; it will cast, as it were, a great shadow over the past 50 years' work, which will take a great deal of time and trouble to overcome; in fact our societies are as a rule educating societies, not only to the juveniles, but to the adults as well. We seek to uplift the working classes as we are of their number, and therefore we repudiate and disclaim the assertions in some of the evidence which has been put before your Lordships with reference to the work in which we are engaged.

4215. You say you repudiate statements made to this Committee or to the House of Lords with reference to the work that your society is engaged in; what statements are you referring to?—I have before me the statement of a witness of the name of Dr. Barwise, medical officer of

Blackburn,

Chairman—continued.

Blackburn, and formerly parish doctor of Birmingham. I do not, for my own part, say personally that I can find anything in the way of any facts to which to hold on, but his expressions were more of a general character. We entirely repudiate, for instance, the assertion that there is no maternal affection amongst the working classes.

4216. Has Dr. Barwise stated that there is no maternal affection amongst the working classes? —So I see it stated in the report in the "Daily Telegraph" of the 28th of June 1890. He is reported as saying, "but very little exists in the lower orders," or, "very slight," is his term. He makes use of two expressions there which also we distinctly say have no bearing upon the fact; and if your Lordships will just permit me, I would state them. "It would be a blessing if the child were dead," or, "if the Lord would take it." Those expressions or exclamations you may hear from John o'Groat's House to the Land's End, not only in the society of working people, but of many others who are above them; that expression is made use of out of pure sympathy; perhaps it is not a right term for them to make use of, but certainly it is not a term made use of for the purpose of wishing a child to die; I have myself personally had experience of work amongst the working classes in connection with mission work, and I think I may say with safe assurance that I can speak with some experience, perhaps just as important as that of a medical officer who would not perhaps be so likely by a curt or imperious manner to be able to get experience from his connection with the working classes; I have free access amongst large numbers of the very poorest in London, and I find their feelings are very much touched by each other's circumstances, and likewise that they have a great feeling towards their children, so much so, that they would do anything for them; in my mind's eye I have a very poor depraved creature indeed, as to whom, if I were to make use of a term strong enough, you would hardly perhaps allow it; but yet she has a great feeling towards her child, and when some friends of mine desired to take the child, and put it away from her, because she was not in a condition, as usual, to look after it, being as she is a great drunkard, the poor woman's feelings were very acute indeed, and in consequence of this, no action was taken in the matter. That is generally the case amongst the poor; they have a strong feeling of love and sympathy for each other, and when any case of distress or death arises, there is always a ready hand amongst them to help one another. Then our societies have a very large number of men who are very ignorant; they cannot write their own names; we have done our utmost to take away from the petitions those names which have been repeated, but their signatures show that they are very poor and very ignorant; still the statistics of our societies warrant us in asserting that the insurance with our society is purely for burying, in a decent manner, their children; and not with a view to making any profit, because they have no opportunity of doing so; the amount of money which doctors charge for their fees, and the various other in-

(142.)

Chairman—continued.

cidental expenses attached to the sections in connection with our society, we find are all expended, and more than that, in the funeral arrangements.

4217. When you say that all the money arising from the insurance is expended upon the funeral and the doctor's expenses, you say that, I presume, within your own knowledge; you know it to be the case?—Yes, I do.

4218. Will you continue your statement?— Therefore the work* which we are engaged in, if this Bill should pass, would be affected considerably to our detriment; in fact, until this Bill came in, or the draft of this Bill came before your Lordships, we had been considering the question of adding to the benefits which the society at first offered, from the very simple fact that our society is a rapidly growing society, and the money has accumulated far beyond our expectation; and it is but right and just that we should return some increased benefit to those who paid in those moneys, as we hold that they are the proper persons to receive it. The consequence is, that in order to pay back this money again, we must do it in some shape or form, either in higher benefits or in some other shape.

4219. I do not understand about paying back; under what circumstances must you pay something back?—In reference to the rights which are attached to this penny a week which they pay, a halfpenny of this sum goes to form the fund which pay their benefits; that is accumulating so fast that we hardly know what to do with it unless we pay it back to them in benefits; the natural consequence will be that we shall have to raise the benefits in some shape or other.

4220. I understand you to mean this, that you have so large an accumulated fund in the shape of the weekly premiums paid by your members, that you feel it desirable and right, in consideration of that, that you should increase your benefits to them?—Yes; quite so, that is our desire; whereas if this Bill should pass we should be entirely blocked out from doing so. It would, in fact, reduce the benefits, and the consequence would be that we should be losing our members, because our membership would not be so extensive if the members or their friends were to suffer a reduction in their benefits; under these circumstances we strongly object to this Bill, and we would ask your Lordships to consider that as we have been members of organisations which have a single object in view, namely, the uplifting of our fellow working men, you will see, in your wise and just consideration, that we are carrying on a work of philanthropy, kindness, and sympathy to our fellow-creatures with the sole desire of brotherly love extending to all mankind. This may be perhaps somewhat of a sentiment, still it is a sentiment of a true character which we feel; and if I were to show your Lordships that feeling which does exist amongst the working classes for each other you would perhaps readily then see that my views are not too strong. There is an old adage that an ounce of experience or practice is worth any amount of theory, and, as your Lordships have been in-

B B 3   formed

Chairman—continued.

formed by your servant that I have had experience, I can only reiterate these words which I have found borne out in mission work and society work for nearly 30 years; it is my experience that the health, wealth, and strength of society has been caused by the educating principles inculcated by friendly societies generally.

4221. Is there anything else that you would like to say in the way of a statement?—That is all I wish to say.

4222. You say that the Bill, as it now stands, would very much interfere with your work; I think, if I mistake not, that the only instance of such interference you adduce, would be that it would prevent your giving the increased benefit you wish to give to your members?—That is so.

4223. You now give up to 8 *l.*?—Yes.

4224. The law at present allows you to go up to 10 *l.*?—Yes.

4225. To what extent do you think the Bill would interfere with you?—We should desire to go up to 10 *l.*, as the law now permits.

4226. In cases of children over five years of age?—Yes.

4227. Therefore, to that extent you say the Bill would interfere with your operations?—That is so.

4228. You say you give no benefits under five years?—No.

4229. Therefore, any part of this Bill which applied to the insurance of children under five, would not touch you at all?—Exactly so.

4230. It has been very clearly proved in evidence, and I think is admitted by everybody who has considered this subject, that the great danger to infant life and the time when it especially needs protection, is under five years, therefore, any provisions in this Bill which went to protect the lives of children under five would not affect the children in your society?—My sole desire is that the friendly societies should take up that insurance of infant lives, especially in connection with their own families.

4231. But I am now speaking of your own society; at the present moment this Bill, so far as it related to any protection for the lives of children under five, would not touch your society at all?—It would not.

4232. Your society is a temperance association?—It is.

4233. Therefore, it naturally includes the temperate, those who desire to avail themselves of it, and to become thrifty and respectable?—That is the tendency, that is our teaching.

4234. Naturally your experience in your society; and the working of your society would not lie with the drunken and disreputable, what we call the residuum of the working classes, but it would lie with the improving class, and the temperate class of the working people?—It does so, we have experience amongst the people in the working classes.

4235. But I am talking of your experience of this matter of insurance, it would lie naturally and necessarily with the members of your own society, your benefits are only for those?—Yes, and our object is to extend those benefits among persons in our immediate neighbourhood, and

Chairman—continued.

those are of the poorest class, and drunkards amongst others.

4236. The object of joining your society is that they may become temperate and teetotallers? —Yes, and make provision for their future.

4237. No one proposes to take that away altogether, but if you somewhat diminished the money benefit which your society can give, would you say that the persons who desire to be temperate and teetotal would not join your society because they would not get quite so much money as they would otherwise?—You must always understand that we are also a benefit society, you must disassociate the one from the other, and to all intents and purposes the motive in joining our society is to get the benefits; there are temperance societies which give no benefit. Those who have this object in view only would not join our society, but joining our society must be allied with temperance.

Earl *Spencer.*

4238. When you speak of benefits, are there only benefits for burial, or do you give other benefits to your members?—We give sick benefit as well. May I remind your Lordship that that would not be included in the penny-a-week contribution; that is another scale altogether. In addition to the penny-a-week for burial you have to pay a penny a week for sick benefit.

4239. When you speak of the penny a week being divided into two halfpence, one going for the burial, and the other for other benefits, what do you mean?—That is for management expenses.

4240. What kind of benefit would the halfpenny, which did not go for burial, procure for the members?—It would be for the conduct of the work of the society.

4241. In your burial benefits have you a graduated scale at different ages between five and 16?—We have not.

4242. You said you wished to extend the benefits of the society; do you mean that you wish to go lower than five years old?—If the society was advanced or educated to that point, I should say yes. I believe firmly it is our duty as friendly society men to look after our own children and hence that we ought to insure them ourselves instead of allowing the insurance to go into industrial societies.

4243. All the members of your society who receive those benefits are total abstainers, are they?—Yes, in our society.

4244. And not in any other?—Two.

4245. Do you take any under five years old for other benefits?—No, not for any other benefits.

Lord *Norton.*

4246. You say that you have no graduated scale between five and 16; there is no such point as 10, is there?—No, there is no graduated scale for the burial fund; there is for the sick fund.

4247. Is the sum for insurance at death 8 *l.* always; neither more nor less?—It is neither more nor less.

4248. And no payment is made under five years old; when does the subscription begin for insurance?—

Lord *Norton*—continued.

insurance ?—It commences when they join the society, from five years upwards.

4249. But for the infant, when does the penny a week begin?—We have no infants ; none less than five years of age can join the society.

4250. Do you mean that the subscription begins at the age of five years ?—Yes ; when the child joins the society.

4251. How soon would the 8 *l.* be due if the child died very soon after the age of five ; would the 8 *l.* be due at once ?—In six months.

4252. Although the penny a week had begun only six months before?—That is the good of combination amongst the working classes ; that comes from helping one another.

4253. It is a very large liability for so small a subscription compared with that of other societies ?—It is ; but the very fact of its being a temperance society gives us that advantage.

4254. Do you think it reduces the mortality, the children being more cared for?—I think so.

4255. I suppose it is impossible that you should ever have a member of a dissolute and disreputable character?—Quite so.

4256. So that there could hardly ever or never be any suspicion of foul play in the case of child death in your society ?—None whatever.

4257. When you said that the sum subscribed for was not only for burial, but for incidentals, what did you mean by "incidentals"?—The doctor and the nurses.

4258. And for mourning?—Yes, and mourning too.

4259. And anything like a funeral feast ?—None whatever, there is nothing for that. I have a list of a large number of items.

4260. Eight pounds is a large sum for that, is it not ?—No, it is not a large sum.

4261. Does your society comprise a large area both town and country ?—We are not so extensive in the country ; we are more so in London. We have about 30,000 members in London.

4262. Would there be much difference between the burial expenses in the country as compared with those in London?—I should say there would be very little difference.

4263. The 8 *l.* may on the average be supposed to cover all their expenses though they must be very different, must they not, as between a child of five and a child of 10?—There is of course a difference, and there will be a difference in the burial ' of it ; the undertaker himself would charge more for the elder child, still that would not reduce the feeling which exists towards the assistance of one as well as the other.

4264. Does any part of the subscription of your society go towards the doctor for medical attendance ?—They have to pay in addition to that, they cannot join the sick fund without having a medical certificate.

4265. Then the 8 *l.* would not be required to pay the doctor because that is provided for by the extra subscription?—Yes, where it is taken out.

4266. I thought you said amongst the incidentals which the 8 *l.* covered, was the doctor's attendance ?—I will explain that. I said that the amount of money which we pay is 8 *l.*, and that the amount of money which a person would

(142.)

Lord *Norton*—continued.

receive to pay for the funeral, if they had a reasonable undertaker who may be able to do the matter for a little less than others, that goes towards paying for the expense of the doctor which they may have incurred during the sickness of the child of two or three months, or a shorter period if it be so; the money is wholly expended which is received, either upon the funeral or including the doctor, for the child.

4267. I thought you said there was a sick fund ?—If the child was connected with the sick fund then the doctor would be paid for separately ; but all members do not belong to the sick fund, which is voluntary, and I am speaking now of the society as a burial society only, as our sick fund members are very small in numbers.

4268. I did not gather whether you stated what were the actual expenses of the burial and nothing else of a little child of five years old?—That would depend upon the desire of the parent to have one or more of the coaches which are thought necessary. Rightly or wrongly, and I think it is a feeling which exists, not only in the working classes, but in a large number of those who are above them ; there is always a desire to bury a child as decently as possible ; the consequence is that they do perhaps expend the whole of their money, or very nearly so, in the arrangements for the funeral.

4269. Even the 8 *l.* ?—Yes ; even the 8 *l.*

4270. You cannot tell us at all what you think the minimum expense of burying a child of five years old would be ; would it be 2 *l.* out of the 8 *l.* ?--In our society it would be fully up to the 8 *l.* I have a list of three or four before me in our branch, and the average is about 8 *l.*

4271. A good deal of that arises from what you would call the very natural desire of having a decent funeral ; but it is not actually a necessary expense ?—Personally I should not like to indulge to that extent myself, but then we cannot help the feelings of all our members, they desire to have as decent a burial as possible, they have great objections to being connected with or buried by the parish, very strong objections indeed.

4272. Do you suppose a child of that age could be buried for 2 *l.* ?—I should say not, I should say the practical experience of persons familiar with the cost of undertaking, in London especially, is that there is no sum so low as 2 *l.* ; it is generally from 2 *l.* 10 *s.* to 2 *l.* 15 *s.* at the lowest.

4273. Do I understand you to say that this Bill, if passed, would only restrict your society to the limit of 8 *l.*, or have you in your mind any other restrictions which would be put upon your operations by the Bill?—The undertaker clause having been withdrawn I take it that the Bill, as it now stands, would reduce our benefits by 2 *l.* at a certain age.

4274. But there is no other restriction that you see upon the operations of your society ?—As far as I see, none.

Earl of *Selborne.*

4275. You just now spoke of some instances which you had collected and brought with you of of the actual expenditure upon funerals, should you object to put them in ?—I should have no

B B 4   objection

Earl of *Selborne*—continued.

objection whatever ; I produce certain letters (*producing the same*), but I have not tabulated them.

4276. Could you tabulate them ? — I could do so.

4277. How many examples are there altogether ?—About six.

4278. Perhaps you would kindly tabulate them and put them in ?—I will do so.

At a late period of the day the Witness hands in the required tabulation.—The same is as follows :—

United Juvenile Order of Total Abstinent Sons of the Phœnix—Cost of Funeral Expenses and Incidentals arising therefrom in Six Cases.

	Funeral.	Doctor.	Various Minor Expenses.	Amount of Benefit.
	£. s. d.	£. s. d.	£. s. d.	£.
1	4 10 -	2 6 6	1 3 6	8
2	5 5 -	Not known	· - - -	4 half benefit. 8
3	7 15 6			8
4	8 5 -	These are given as the entire cost of all expenses. Their ages being between 14 and 18 years.		8
5	8 15 -			8
6	6 10 -			8

4279. I understood you in answer to Lord Norton to say in effect that the only clause in the Bill to which you object is the first ; that is the one which limits the amount of the insurance ?—So far as I have read the Bill now, I think the most obnoxious portion of the Bill has been taken from it, that is to say, the undertaker clause. I take it that several of the incidental portions of this Bill will likewise follow No. 2 Clause ; that would be natural.

4280. Whatever is necessarily incidental will follow it ?—No doubt.

4281. Have you then any strong objection to a graduated scale such as some of the societies have, according to age, without having a jump to a very large sum all at once ?—No, I see no objection personally to it ; I rather approve of that scale being adopted.

Lord *Thring.*

4282. As I understand it, your society includes the poorest people in your opinion in London ?—The very poorest I believe.

4283. Then with reference to drunkards, I presume that one of the objects of your society is to reform the drunkards ?—Yes, quite so.

4284. In your opinion, have you many members who have been originally drunkards ?—Yes.

4285. A considerable proportion or not ?—A very large proportion.

4286. Therefore, in effect, your society does include people who have been previously dissolute ?—It does.

4287. Then, with reference to the benefits, as I understand it, of the penny subscription, half goes to the fund for burials and half goes to the establishment expenses, as we should call them ? Yes.

4288. I understand you to say that the fund for your insurances has accumulated to a great extent ?—Very largely.

Lord *Thring*—continued.

4289. Do not you think that, with reference to the establishment expenses, it is rather heavy to have 50 per cent. attributable to establishment expenses ?—That money. partly goes back as presents, as an incentive to the children in carrying on the work of the society, and partly in rent ; a proportion of it is also paid to the secretary for keeping the accounts. The children themselves receive back again that other portion of the money with the exception of rent and other small expenses.

4290. Then it is not, strictly speaking, 50 per cent. for establishment expenses, but a certain portion of it is returned in the shape of presents? —Yes, in presents to the lads for their services ; they meet weekly, and they are taught as soon as possible temperance principles, and the various modes of carrying on the work, for which they are granted allowances out of this halfpenny, which is their own.

4291. Then you have a sick fund which is distinct from the burial fund, which has distinct subscriptions ?—Yes.

4292. But with reference to the burial fund, the money is, as far as you know, applied either to the burial itself, which may or may not be too great, or to the payment of medical expenses in cases where they are not subscribers to the sick fund ?—That is so.

Earl of *Harrowby.*

4293. With reference to the expenses of the funeral, the position I gather from you is that a child could be buried for a smaller sum than 3 *l.*, but that there is such a very strong feeling that the child should not be considered as having a pauper funeral ; that the parents like to have the funeral rather of a higher character ?—I take that to be the general feeling throughout.

4294. It is an honourable wish to spend rather more money, which is after all their own saving, upon the funeral of the child, so that there might be no question of its being buried at the public expense ?— That is so.

4295. So that it is an honourable feeling which leads to what is called a grander funeral than is necessary ?—That is so.

4296. What was the date of the establishment of your society ?—February 1887.

4297. Has there been a great increase in the number of members since then ?—Yes, there has been a large increase since then.

4298. From your intimate knowledge of the habits of working people in London, do you find that there is a great increase in the habit of insuring the children's lives ?—I think so.

4299. That is one of the signs of the growing tendency to thrift ?—I think it is indeed.

4300. Have you not found that amongst the poorest of the poor whom you have had to do with in your mission work, there is just as strong affection for their children as there is in the respectable artizan class ?—It is so.

4301. It is not poverty or comfort which account for more or less affection ?—It is not.

4302. You would say that unless their feelings were blunted by drink or vice, the poorest of the poor have very strong parental feelings ? –They have.

4303. And

Earl of *Harrowby*—continued.

4303. And make greater sacrifices for their children than many in a higher position?—Yes.

4304. Supposing it were found that, blunted by drink or vice, a considerable number of parents were led to this crime against their children, would you agree to some such provisions as are in the Bill?—Whilst my feelings are strong against those who would commit evil, I cannot conceive that the good should be made to suffer for the bad, as there is, I think, a very large percentage of the good over the bad.

4305. Still you would wish for some power to deal with those cases?—Yes, that those should be punished.

4306. You would consider that the number of those cases is small as far as your experience goes?—Very small.

4307. I wish to ask you a que-tion with reference to a suggestion which was made by an important witness, that infant insurance should be permitted up to 12 months' with this restriction, that if the child died under 12 months, no insurance money should be paid, but that the money actually paid should be returned to the parent; would you see any difficulty about adopting this plan?—I presume you mean the money they had paid for the 12 months' insurance.

4308. That the parent should not be able to get any advantage, but get his money paid back if the child died under 12 months?—I do not agree to that. I think that owing to the number of disadvantages under which the working classes labour, they, generally speaking, cannot find the money even to decently bury their dead without assistance; what with the high rent they have to pay and other things, I do not see how they can bury their children in a decent manner, without they have assistance; the effect of it would be, as it were, to throw them back upon the rates; because I claim, that we help considerably in reducing the rates by our action and combination; I think that would to a very large extent, take away the feeling and the desire for thrift, the honourable feeling which I think exists among the working classes generally; I am speaking now in answer to your Lordship's question which I take to be in reference to industrial insurance.

4309. You only insure after five years of age? —That is so.

Earl *Beauchamp.*

4310. As I understand it, your objection to this Bill generally, is that it tends to discourage thrift among the working classes?—It will do so.

4311. And that any legislation which discourages and discredits thrift, would be a great injury to the working classes?—It would.

4312. You think that cases of evil doing should be punished?—Yes.

4313. But any legislation which tended to inflict hardship upon the innocent would not be the form of punishment that you would propose? —Certainly not.

4314. May I ask, have you ever had occasion to withhold the payment of any insurance money in consequence of suspicious circumstances?— None whatever.

(142.)

Earl *Beauchamp*—continued.

4315. Therefore you have never been invited to give any assistance to any society for investigating such cases?—I have not.

4316. You have said that you would approve of a graduated scale of insurance; would you explain why?—Yes; this is my own personal view. I have been connected with a friendly society for upwards of 30 years, and their system is by a graduated scale, which is by far the best, and my views are therefore in favour of that, but a society like ourselves now, are not so far advanced, therefore I cannot give you the views of our society.

4317. But I ask you your own personal reasons for preferring a graduated scale?—Because it is more advantageous, and perhaps more just.

4318. Advantageous to whom?—To the members, and likewise to the society.

4319. How is it advantageous to a member? —He would pay more in proportion to his liability.

4320. Surely you mean less, because we have had it in evidence before the Committee that the payment by members remains the same though the benefits they receive may be greater?—Now I gather what your Lordship means; you mean with reference to receiving. I was taking your Lordship as meaning paying towards the society.

4321. I understand you to approve of a graduated scale of insurance; that is to say, the payment should be graduated according to the age; that is so, is it not?—It is so in this way: that it should not be less than 8 *l.*

4322. You would approve of a graduated insurance above that amount, but not below it?— Yes.

4323. Should that graduated insurance be paid for by a higher weekly premium than at present, or not?—Not at present; not under our existing constitution.

4324. But you do not contemplate any extra legal or illegal payment; you contemplate working within the limit of the law?—Quite so.

4325. You have told the Committee that you have never had to withhold payment in consequence of suspicious circumstances, therefore, you have never had any difficulty with regard to the registrar's certificate?—None whatever.

4326. That has not happened within your experience?—It has not.

4327. The society with which you are at present connected deals only with members above the age of five?—That is so.

4328. But in your connection with the other society, you have mentioned you dealt with children of all ages, I suppose?—No; but I think I had better leave that portion of the evidence to those who will be called before you, because they will be better prepared to answer it. There are very few friendly societies which do take in children under five years of age.

4329. Then your experience has been friendly societies as distinguished from collecting societies? —Quite distinctly.

4330. You say friendly societies, as a rule, do not take in very young children, but that that branch of the business is undertaken by the collecting societies?—That is so.

C o   4331. You

Lord *Norton.*

4331. You say that the effect of this Bill would be to restrict the amount of insurance to 8 *l.*; how high would you go?—As high as it is at present.

4332. Would you make it as high as 10 *l.* throughout without any gradation, so that there should be 10 *l.*, either for a child of five or a child of 15; a fixed sum for all?—At present, that was our contemplation.

4333. You would have it 10 *l.* for all?—Yes.

Lord *Thring.*

4334. Why does your society not insure children under five years of age?—We generally take our experience from those who have had greater experience than ourselves; and their experience is that five years of age is the age at which juveniles are not so liable to fall off by infantile diseases, and the consequence is that it is a safe age for us to adopt as a friendly society.

4335. It is safer for the society?—Yes.

4336. But do you, or do you not, disapprove of the principle of insurance under five years of age?—No, I would rather approve of their being insured at birth.

Marquess of *Lothian.*

4337. I think you said that this insurance did not bring any benefit to the subscribers?—No.

4338. But in the case of children five years old dying, surely there must be some surplus in some cases out of the payment of 8 *l.*; the funeral expenses and other expenses would not all come to 8 *l.*?—Rightly or wrongly, it is all expended in the funeral expenses, or the incidental expenses connected with the child's illness.

4339. Supposing the expenses do not come to 8 *l.*, in what way is the surplus expended; it is all handed over to the parent, I take it?—Yes; and expended in the way of purchasing decent dress for the child or children or for themselves as well.

4340. Is there any question of a funeral feast?—None whatever. I most emphatically deny that there is anything in the shape of a funeral feast in any shape or form amongst our members.

4341. I think you stated that the society in some cases conduct the funerals for the parents; is that so?—They do sometimes.

4342. The society is quite ready to do so in the case of a parent wishing it?—Yes, they are.

4343. In that case does the society expend money for the parents?—No, they only add to it for the purpose of conducting the funeral; it is extra money given to them by those attending or assisting in the burial.

4344. Do the members attend in these cases?—Yes, they do.

4345. Does your society, although you do not insure children under the age of five, ever give assistance to members of the society whose children may die under that age?—They do not.

4346. Do you know whether any members of your society are members of industrial societies; do they insure with industrial societies, their children under five years of age?—Personally I cannot say, but I think they do.

Chairman.

4347. You have given evidence in which I think, we all concur, that your society tends very much, and desires to tend to the cultivation of thrift amongst the working classes; now is it your opinion that a very great expenditure upon a funeral is a thrifty thing?—That is not my personal opinion.

4348. I gathered as much from your evidence that you yourself think we all of us spend too much money upon funerals?—Yes.

4349. You would not say that a person saving up money for some time, for the purpose of spending it in an unthrifty way when he has got it all together in a lump, is really practising thrift; he is spending his money very wastefully, is he not?—In the form in which your Lordship puts it, but I cannot see how this will agree with our view of carrying out the work of the burial portion; you put it in rather a peculiar way; if a man saves up his money for the purpose of making use of it in any other than a proper way he would certainly be doing wrong.

4350. I was speaking not of an improper way but of an unthrifty way, indicating an unnecessary expenditure. I think you agreed that we all of us spend too much upon funerals?—Yes.

4351. If a man saved up money in order to spend too much upon a funeral he is not putting the money to a thrifty use, he might put it to a better use might he not?—But he does not save it up for that purpose in the form in which you express it, he would not get the benefit if he did not combine with others, it is the combination with others which gives him these benefits. Were a man to save by himself he could not save sufficient to get a decent funeral, it is only the combination with others which enables him to do so.

4352. He invests his money at a penny a week with you in order to get 8 *l.* in the end. We will call it investing, if a man invests money from week to week in order that at the end of a certain period he may have a lump sum and then spends it wastefully he is not really learning thrift, is he?—That is entirely a matter of opinion.

4353. But your proposal to add 2 *l.* to your benefit beyond the 8 *l.* is solely for the funeral?—Yes.

4354. Adding 2 *l.* to that would give 10 *l.*?—Yes; making up the amount which the present law allows.

4355. Although you consider a wasteful expenditure upon a funeral undesirable, do you think it desirable to increase the expenditure upon the funeral from 8 *l.* to 10 *l.*?—My point is that they do not spend the whole amount of the money on the funeral, but it gives them a sum of money which enables them to pay the doctor, and the nurses where they have them.

4356. But I thought you said that the money was required in order to give a handsome funeral?—I did not say that the money was required in order to give a handsome funeral; I said a decent funeral.

4357. I think you said that the doctors and other expenses would be so great as only to leave
sufficient

Chairman—continued.

sufficient margin to give a decent funeral?—That is so.

4358. You stated that you would have no objection to persons guilty of wilful neglect being punished?—No.

4359. But when they were punished it would be after the commission of this wilful cruelty and neglect?—That is so.

4360. Meanwhile there might be a great deal of very horrible cruelty although the persons who commit it might afterwards, or some of them, be punished; do you not think that it is desirable if it can be done that legislation should tend to prevent crime as well as to punish it?—Yes.

4361. Any provisions in a Bill which tended to prevent crime would if they were not unjust and unreasonable in themselves have your approval?—Yes.

4362. Then it would be desirable not only to punish wilful cruelty to children but to prevent it?—Yes.

4363. Would you then say that depriving innocent people of a certain part of the privileges which they now enjoy, is unfair, even if it is in order to prevent a supposed crime; you would not consent that innocent parties should suffer any diminution of their rights and privileges even although that diminution could be shown to tend strongly in the direction of preventing crime?—For the simple reason that I do not see that there is any percentage of crime which sufficiently warrants us in having an Act which would, to a large extent, bear burdensomely upon those who are thrifty, and likewise well disposed and well inclined.

4364. Your idea is that there is not a sufficient amount of crime to warrant legislation?—That is so.

4365. But assuming that there were a sufficient amount of crime to warrant it, you would not say that the innocent might not and ought not to give up some of their privileges to prevent crime?—If it were sufficient I would say they should.

4366. You probably remember two or three

Chairman—continued.

years ago a great deal of sensation was created in the country in the case of marine insurance; owners of ships were accused of sending ships to sea in a very shocking condition, and destroying human lives in order to make money; but I am sure you would not say that was the case with the great majority of shipowners?—I should say not.

4367. Nevertheless it was proposed that the Legislature should to enact certain restrictions upon marine insurance with the view of preventing the minority committing crime; would you say that was an injustice or a wrong to the great majority of respectable shipowners?—So far as my knowledge extends of that matter, I should say no.

4368. And you would think it would have been creditable for the decent and respectable shipowners to have said, We do enjoy these rights and privileges at present; but we find that the enjoyment of them tends to crime, therefore we willingly submit to the restriction, that would have been to their credit if they had said it?—Yes.

4369. Would it not be also very much to the credit of the respectable working classes if it could be shown that certain restrictions prevented crime to say, We accept those restrictions for the sake of preventing crime?—Yes, if it could be shown.

Earl Beauchamp.

4370. Have you paid any particular attention to the question of marine insurance, and do you know how far the statements that were made about shipowners some years ago in the public newspapers were correct?—This is a question which comes upon me somewhat by surprise, and perhaps I should really have to work up my memory to refer to a number of things that have occurred; I know there were a great number of ships which did not sail out of London and other ports in a fair condition.

4371. Your recollection is rather vague upon the subject?—Yes, at present.

The Witness is directed to withdraw.

MR. M. J. CUNNINGHAM, is called in; and Examined, as follows:

Chairman.

4372. YOU are Secretary to the London Industrial Co-operative Clothing Manufacturing Society?—I am.

4373. You attend here as deputed from a meeting of delegates of the working classes which met, I think, last week in Farringdon Hall?—That is so.

4374. You have certain statements to make on their behalf. You state as regards yourself that you have had more than 20 years' practical experience and knowledge as a collector, agent, and superintendent of agents, and as secretary of a friendly society?—That is so.

4375. May I ask what you mean by a friendly society?—A friendly society is not exactly a company; it is established under an Act of Parliament, the Friendly Societies Act.

Chairman—continued.

4376. Was this friendly society of which you were secretary what is commonly called a collecting or commercial society?—It has a broader meaning than that; the one I was connected with was a collecting society, but there are an immense number, some thousands of others which are not collecting societies, but are friendly societies, such as the Foresters, the Odd Fellows and so on.

4377. Which was yours?—Mine was a collecting society.

4378. What was its name?—The London and Kent United Friendly Society, registered with the late Mr. Tidd Pratt.

4379. You did employ collectors and agents?—Yes.

4380. Were they paid by percentage upon the

Chairman—continued.

sums they obtained?—They were paid by commission, and partly by a small salary.

4381. Are you able to inform the Committee what was the number of annual policies you had?—At the commencement of a society, of course the number of policies issued is small, but as it progresses the numbers then progress in proportion, and very rapidly in proportion too, because the name of the society becomes more known amongst people.

4382. Does the society with which you were connected exist still?—No.

4383. How long is it since it ceased to exist?—About 20 years ago.

4384. Your experience then dates back 20 years?—It dates back anterior to that.

4385. But it is not later than that?—It is not later than that.

4386. And you cannot tell the Committee at all what the amount of business the society did was?—I could not say now, because it has been amalgamated with another friendly society.

4387. From your experience and knowledge of it, you could not tell the Committee how much of it turned over every year in the way of premiums?—I think at the time I ceased when the society had been transferred, the number of policies issued was about 5,000.

4388. I presume the payments in the society were made weekly?—Yes, they were made weekly.

4389. Were they made on a scale such as the Prudential and other societies have now?—On a similar scale.

4390. Where did your society principally work?—In London the chief office was; but we had branch offices, that is to say agencies, in very many of the principal towns all over England.

Lord *Thring.*

4391. Your society was amalgamated with another society 20 years ago?—It was.

4392. What was that society?—The Integrity.

Chairman.

4393. The next statement you make is, that you believe certain statements made are untrue and slanderous, as applied to the industrial classes, who would be mainly affected should this Bill become law; what are the allegations which you regard as untrue and slanderous?—I regard it that if legislation is made under this bill, it will affect the working classes very much;

Chairman—continued.

the fact that legislation being attempted under the Bill would imply that there was a necessity for it; and I do not believe there is.

4394. That is not an answer to my question. You state in your proof that certain statements were made. By whom were those statements made, and what were they?—I have read them in newspapers.

4395. If you have read them, of course you can quote them; what were they, and by whom were they made?—I think it was an extract from an article which appeared in the "Contemporary Review," by the Rev. Mr. Waugh, and the newspaper in making a comment upon that article, stated that it was a horrible thing that this state of things should exist in the nineteenth century.

4396. What you mean to say, is that some newspaper said, that the things described by Mr. Waugh were horrible things; do you know what Mr. Waugh said; could you mention any allegations?—I must confess I did not read the article; but I have read comments in the newspapers.

4397. At the meeting you attended how many delegates were present?—Somewhere about 40.

4398. At this meeting a resolution was passed; were you present?—I was.

4399. You appear here in support of a resolution which is to this effect: "That this meeting solemnly protests again the sweeping, untrue, and slanderous statements made in the House of Lords and elsewhere"; upon what grounds do you support that resolution?—I have seen leading articles in the newspapers, and I have seen comments in smaller paragraphs, and the public mind has been impressed from the newspapers that such statements emanated from the House of Lords.

4400. Then that is all the evidence you can give in support of your resolution; have you anything beyond newspaper paragraphs which you can adduce?—The public mind is impressed that they are correct.

4401. Have you anything beyond the impression upon the public mind to produce. The public mind is not always right in its impressions; can you give any definite statement; can you prove anything; have you anything further to say upon the subject?—So far as I can interpret the public mind, they are impressed that such a feeling has been manifested in the House of Lords.

The Witness is directed to withdraw.

Ordered,—That this Committee be adjourned to Friday next, at Twelve o'clock.

Die Veneris, 25° Julii, 1890.

LORDS PRESENT:

Earl SPENCER.
Earl of HARROWBY.
Earl BEAUCHAMP.
Earl of SELBORNE.
LORD BISHOP OF PETERBOROUGH.

Lord KER (*Marquess of Lothian*).
Lord POLTIMORE.
Lord KINNAIRD.
Lord NORTON.
Lord THRING.

THE RIGHT REV. THE LORD BISHOP OF PETERBOROUGH, IN THE CHAIR.

THE *Chairman* hands in the two following letters :—

" Infant Life Protection,
Guildhall, Nottingham,
" Sir,   20 February 1890.
" I HAVE this morning received a copy of the Infant Life Protection Bill brought in by yourself and Mr. Stuart-Wortley.

" Enclosed I send you a copy of a letter written by me in December last to the Local Government Board, at the instance of my health committee, pointing out the need for legislation with regard to the insurance of children.

" It seems to me that clauses to deal with this matter might be appropriately inserted in the above Bill, and my committee will be glad if you will take the question into consideration.

" I am, &c.
(signed)   " *Samuel George Johnson*,
" Town Clerk.
" To Her Majesty's Secretary of State
for the Home Department."

" Town Clerk's Department,
Guildhall, Nottingham,
" Sir,   11 December 1889.
" I AM requested by my health committee to ask you to call the serious attention of your Board to a great and growing evil, viz., the insurance of the lives of young children.

" Some notice of this has been taken in the recent Act for the protection of children, by which the penalty for wilful neglect is doubled where the person having charge of the child has insured its life.

" A bad case has recently occurred here, and proceedings have been taken under the Act, and both parents imprisoned.   One child died and was found to be insured as well as other children, who had been all shamefully neglected.

" It appears to be the custom with the insurance companies not to require medical examination where the amount insured does not exceed 50 *l.* ;

and the result is that children who are weakly or actually seriously ill are often insured, and no care taken of them, and no medical assistance obtained, and in the case before mentioned the children are frequently wilfully neglected.

" The views taken by parents of the question of insurance may be gathered from the following facts: A woman living in this town was recently asked by a medical man why the only child insured was one who was ill and delicate.   The reply was, ' Why the others are well and strong; why should I insure them ? '

" I am credibly informed that this is not an isolated case, but represents the feeling of many parents of the poorer classes who insure their children.

" My committee suggest that your Board should introduce into Parliament a Bill—

" 1. To make it compulsory on the insurance company to give the local authority public notice of the insurance of every child of tender years, and of any change of residence.

" 2. To make it compulsory to give full particulars to the local authority of the death of every child a certain time before any money is paid over, that the local authority may have time to make inquiries.

" 3. To confer on the local authority and their officers, including sanitary inspectors and police, authority to enter any house in which any insured child is kept or has died, for the purpose of making inquiries and ascertaining such information as may be necessary as to the condition of such child.

" I enclose a copy report of the case.

" My committee will be glad to hear that your Board will take the matter into consideration.

" I am, &c.
(signed)   " *Samuel George Johnson*,
" Town Clerk.
" To the Secretary, Local Government Board,
Whitehall, London, S.W."

Mr. JOHN EDWARD CLEVELAND, is again called in ; and further Examined.

THE previous evidence of this Witness having been read in his presence,—

Chairman.

4402. Will you inform the Committee in what position you appear before them now subsequently to this Conference of the friendly societies; do you now represent that Conference? —Yes; and by a resolution of the Conference two other friendly societies have had representatives elected in conjunction with myself.

Lord *Thring.*

4403. Is there any resolution making the appointment ?—This is the resolution : " That the corresponding Secretary of the National Independent Order of Odd Fellows ; Mr. T. B. Stead, Permanent Secretary of the Ancient Order of Foresters ; and Mr. Thomas Walton, Senior Director of the Manchester Unity of Friendly Societies, are elected on behalf of this Conference to appear before the House of Lords' Committee in reference to the Children's Life Assurance Bill."

Earl of *Harrowby.*

4404. Might I ask if that is in answer to a formal invitation sent by this Committee to the Conference ; did the Conference receive a formal invitation from this Committee ?—Yes.
4405. Therefore in consequence of a direct invitation from the Committee delegates are sent to this Committee from the Conference ?—Yes.

Lord *Thring.*

4406. Of whom you are one ?—Yes.

Chairman.

4407. Representing your Order and certain other Orders ?—Yes.
4408. The Committee wish to be clearly informed first, whether you appear here as delegated from this Conference, and secondly, whether the two other gentlemen also appear as delegated from this Conference, and thirdly, whether all three appear in consequence of a letter of invitation addressed by this Committee to the Conference ?—That is so.
4409. You have heard your evidence read ; would you kindly take it up at the point at which the shorthand writer's notes leave off, unless you wish to go back upon anything that is stated there ; do you present any resolutions to the Committee as passed by the Conference ?— I do.
4410. Perhaps you will kindly read them?— " That this Conference representing, the affiliated orders and friendly benefit societies protests against the prohibitive provisions of the Bishop of Peterborough's Bill relating to insurances on the lives of children being made applicable to our orders and societies, either as regards the age of those insured or the amount to be insured, such provisions being in the opinion of this meeting, an unwarranted and unsupported attachment of suspicion against our societies." I may mention that there were 20 societies represented by 33

Chairman—continued.

representatives, the number of members whom they represented amounting to 2,199,178, and the capital represented by them being 15,100,860 *l.* There was an unanimous expression of opinion from those who spoke at the meeting as to the provisions of your Bill being completely inapplicable to our societies, inasmuch as we believe that the privileges we now enjoy covered by the provisions of the Act of Parliament, cannot be in any way abused by the affiliated orders or friendly benefit societies ; that is to say, that no case of infanticide has been proved against any of our societies, and from figures, which I will ask you to listen to, I think it will be clear to you that so far as I have been able to provide you with information upon this point a very low death-rate indeed exists amongst the children who belong to us. I have here, my Lord, some returns given by 13 affiliated friendly societies ; the number of members contained in them are 218,652, the capital is 192,484 *l.* I have only the death-rate in four of those orders possibly in consequence of the fact that just at this time of the year the returns are being compiled by the various corresponding secretaries, but those four societies contain 126,642 members, and the death-rate of 623, which is the figure, is not a half per cent. upon that number.
4411. May I ask whether this 126,642 includes both adults and children, or children only ?— They are children only, under 16 years of age.

Earl *Beauchamp.*

4412. When you say the " death-rate," you mean the actual number of deaths, do you not?— That is the actual number of deaths ; but the death-rate would be under a half per cent.

Chairman.

4413. Is that the death-rate per cent. or per thousand ?—Per cent. The Bill makes no classification as to its applicability. If it were passed in its present form a part of the business that we have lately been giving very great attention to would be considerably hampered. In the first place, the insurance of the children of members, a principle which has been instituted in the affiliated orders recently to a greater extent than it has been in any other previous part of their history, would be prevented, supposing that any limitation of age beyond what we now enjoy was enforced against us. I know that in some of the societies of this particular character of which I am speaking, the members will insure their children amongst themselves at the earliest age. Others will, by the direction of their general rules, suggest a time of three months ; but it is being generally accepted as a very wise provision that the members should be permitted to insure their children at the earliest age. We are aware that infanticide in some cases has been proved, but probably not in any greater degree, in proportion to other crime, than circumstances in the courts generally prove ; and we believe

Chairman—continued.

believe that the excessive infantile mortality is not due to a desire of the working classes to put aside their children. We believe that, irrespective of insurance, the idle and the dissolute will endeavour to get rid of the incubus. So long as this condition of things exists we feel that it is unnecessary that the Friendly Societies Act should be in any way amended to limit the freedom which we now possess, and that we should not be prevented from indulging in those courses of thrift and providence which are absolutely necessary to the existence of the working classes of this country, so long as nothing is brought home to our doors to incriminate us. We believe that infantile mortality is due to many reasons, to the fact of insanitary dwellings, congested districts, the absence of parental care, to the fact that the mother has to attend, in large centres of industry, in a factory, and is also at work in a factory during pregnancy which will produce unhealthy children; the experience of infantile mortality wherever it has been excessive has generally been brought home to these particular facts. The sums of money, supposing that greater precautions were taken by the registrars in the future, are totally apart from the inducement to murder. Your Lordships have had evidence before you that it will take a certain sum of money to bury a child, and I can assure you that in many cases, especially in Manchester, the undertaker does not receive sufficient, relying upon the insurance money to bury the child, and that the insurance money is generally handed over to the undertaker and a settled bill given before the corpse is taken out of the house; so that the statements with reference to the drinking and levities of such a character which undoubtedly, where they occur, are to be regretted, are not borne out; those things do not happen in the majority of instances; nor is it possible to attach them to the funerals of the working classes of this country with reference to their children. If we could get rid of the peculiar feeling created by custom amongst the working classes with reference to "respectable funerals," I do not think that even then there would be any balance between what a parent might generally receive on the death of his child and the expenditure. If this insurance principle is in any way interfered with, or if you place a limit on the age, especially at about 12 months, the poor rates of large centres will undoubtedly be considerably increased, and that independence, which the working classes of this country so much value, will be seriously sapped; and you will either require to have recourse to the old principle of taking round the hat, as it were, which now has come to be looked upon as a disgrace in their social lives; or recourse must be had to other equally undesirable means. The Post Office Savings Bank has also been suggested as a means whereby the difficulty might be overcome. Now, to make provision to bury a child at an expense of 2 *l.* 10 *s.* by saving a 1 *d.* per week in this way, it would take 600 weeks or over 11 years to make it; how is it possible that that sum of money at the ordinary rate of infantile mortality in a large centre could be saved? An unfortunate incident would arise,

(142.)

Chairman—continued.

when the money would be required, and there would not be sufficient to bury the child; it is only by the principle of co-operation in friendly societies, the accumulation of reserves, and the production of interest, that those liabilities per cent. can be met; therefore it is in consequence of having started this principle, and being at this moment in a fair way to carry it to a successful issue as regards the insurance of the children of the working classes of this country, that we think that this Bill would be a serious interference. It is possible that some suggestion is desirable upon this particular matter. If the criminal law of the country is not sufficient, let it be made so to those against whom crime is proved; but the societies represented at the Conference were undoubtedly in favour of insurance being effected amongst ourselves at birth, if we think fit. It might be desirable that a limit of insurance money be imposed; it might also be desirable that the children under 12 months of age should not be insured in more than one office, and that a child under that age should not be insured in an unregistered society. I had occasion to attend for a policy of insurance at the Cheetham Town Hall, near Manchester, some time ago, to identify a man as belonging to one of our branches, it being registered before the registrar, and whilst in the room a person applied for a certificate to procure the money from an insurance society. The registrar of course asked for the card and the rules, and found that the society was not registered. I thought it was a very interesting case, and I waited to make some further inquiries by the aid of the man who was with me, and I found there were three policies on this life for an amount which was very much above what I consider should be at the use of some people for the burial of their children. That is a case in point: this life was insured in three unregistered offices.

4414. And could you state what was the total amount of the sum insured for?—I could not; it was, I think, something under 10 *l.*; but it was a very young child.

4415. Under five years of age, I suppose?—Yes, it was that fact which struck me. There is a very great feeling upon this point, that if there is any alteration of the Act of Parliament it should be in our cases in the direction of the assimilation of the age at which a child may be entered in all societies. A society registered previously to the passing of the Act of 1875, may take in children at birth, whilst ourselves, in the management of our societies throughout the kingdom, are absolutely not permitted to take in the general public into them, being restricted at the present moment solely to the children of members for insurance at the earliest age.

4416. Do I understand you to say that in the juvenile societies of your society you only take in children of three years of age and upwards?—Yes.

4417. Do I gather that is a regulation of your own, or in obedience to an enactment of Parliament?—That is in direct touch with the provisions of the Act of Parliament. That Act which

c c 4   permits

Chairman—continued.

permits us to take children over three years of age, and to insure for benefits in sickness and death, also permits us to establish what is called a Children of Members' Insurance Fund, and my order admits them at three months; but it is to be amended by the resolution of the annual meeting, and made one month, and we further desire permission to insure the children of the public. The benefits which we assure for 13 monthly payments of a penny, from which we only permit the sum of 15 per cent. to be deducted for management expenses, are as follows : After they have been members three months they are entitled to 30 *s.*; after one year from the date of insurance they are entitled to 2 *l.*

4418. Could you say how much after six months; have you any scale for six months?— They would then take 2 *l.*

4419. It is 30 *s.* for three months, 2 *l.* for six months; and for a year, what is it?—It is the same up to 12 months; after a membership of three months 30 *s.*, and thence to the limit of 12 months 2 *l.*, and after 11 years' membership 8 *l.* The principle that we desire to inculcate amongst the societies is one similar to that ; and it would be preferable, if we were permitted to do so, in consequence of the fact that our members themselves manage these societies We designate them " agents " or " collectors " to conform to the Act of Parliament, but we do not pay them excepting some small acknowledgment which may be voted quarterly for what might be considered an out-of-pocket expense for visiting parents and seeing the children who desire to be insured ; our societies are managed particularly in the interests of members and not of the officials.

Earl *Spencer.*

4420. I understood you to say there was some Act of Parliament which prevented your insuring children under three years old ; now you have been giving us various rates that you give, say three months, 30 *s.*; up to 12 months, 2 *l.*; up to 11 years, 8 *l.* ; these appear to be inconsistent with the first two items ?—You understand those are two distinct societies ; that in our juvenile societies we cannot take a member under three years of age ; that is particularly laid down in the Act of Parliament, but we are permitted to form what are called Children of Members' Insurance Funds, by which we may take them in at the earliest age we think fit; they are two distinct classes of insurance societies.

Chairman.

4421. I think you do not mean two distinct societies, but two distinct branches of your society ?—Two distinct characters of the society.

4422. But they are both what we may call " Odd Fellows " ?—Yes.

Lord *Thring.*

4423. They are formed under different Acts of Parliament?—No. Under different sections of the Act of Parliament, Sections 8 and 15.

4424. But are they distinct in law ?—Yes; the Act of Parliament will not permit us to take in children of the public for insurance.

Earl *Beauchamp.*

4425. How long must a member be enrolled before his child is eligible to come into the Children's Insurance Fund ?—Three months in our society, and I think that principle is generally extant in most societies.

Earl of *Selborne.*

4426. What Act of Parliament was it that you mentioned ?—The Act of 1875.

4427. You mean the General Friendly Societies' Act ?—Yes.

Earl *Spencer.*

4428. Is that the one which prevented your insuring children under three years of age ?— Yes, except the children of members.

Lord *Thring.*

4429. Then what is the Act which enables you to insure children of members under three years of age ?—The same Act.

4430. But you told the Committee they were formed under different Acts ?—Under different sections. All the business of friendly societies derives its impulse from the Act of 1875 and its subsequent amendments, and is guided by those conditions.

Chairman.

4431. Would it be in one of the subsequent amendments to the Act that the clause you refer to, which permits you to insure children at three months or one month. would be found; would you refer us to the section ?—No, with reference to the juvenile societies, it is Section 15, Sub-section 8 (a): " Societies and branches consisting wholly of members of any age under 16 years, but exceeding three years, may be allowed to register under this Act, subject to such regulations as may be made in that behalf;" the insurance of children of members under Section 8. The other part of the Act refers to the admission of members into the parent society and the limits.

4432. As I understand, you say there are two descriptions of the society which are formed under different sections of the same Act?—Yes.

4433. Then I understand you to say that in one description of these societies, which I think you called the children of members insurance society, you can insure children under three years of age ?—Yes.

4434. But that under the other section which you read, the 15th, you cannot ?—That is so.

4435. Then what is the difference between those two societies ?—In the juvenile society over three years we take in the general public outside our own members ; but the children of members' insurance is confined to the business implied by the distinctive title; it is confined to the children of members solely.

4436. What you mean is that you are allowed to insure the children of members of that your societies under certain conditions, under three years of age ?—Yes.

4437. But then you also become what you may call an outside general insurance society ; if you perform that description of general in-

surance,

Chairman—continued.

surance, then you cannot insure any child except he is three years of age ?—No.

4438. The general public society may be termed a branch of the parent society, may it not ?—Not a branch at present, in the affiliated orders, in consequence of the fact that we do not wish to mix up the "Juvenile" with the "Parent."

4439. But could you by law ?—Yes, we could by law under the same management; they are under the same management now.

4440. I am not yet quite clear as to these two different forms or conditions of insurance. You have informed the Committee that you not only admit to the benefits of your insurance, children of members: but under certain conditions, and under a certain clause of the Act of Parliament, the general public; are you then as regards the outside public, what may be called a general insurance society ?—No, only by establishing a general insurance society of members over three years of age and under 21, we can admit the general public, not in the other case.

4441. That is the point I want to ascertain clearly from you, whether those stricter conditions, which prevent your assuring children under three, apply to the general insurance of the public, as distinguished from your insurance of children of your own members under the other branch ?—No.

4442. Then so far as you are a society, acting generally for the public, you are, under a particular clause of the Act of Parliament, now within the three years' limit ?—Yes. If our policy of insurance was more generally adopted we should have greater supervision over the insured, in consequence of being in close contact with the parents. Now they have generally to be introduced by a member, and inquiry is made as to the character of the parents, and, in some cases, as to the health of the children, before they are admitted.

4443. When you say inquiry as to the character of the parents, do you mean the general public, or the parents of the children insuring under that section you have referred to ?—That statement applies both to the general public and to the children of members. Both of the societies, or their principles, are managed by members of the parent order. The management is not deputed to any stranger, consequently, knowing each parent, and having some knowledge of the children, it would be almost impossible for any infanticide to take place under such supervision: for if it did it would be impossible to cloak it. That is to say, there would be no possibility of their recovering the money.

4444. I think I understood you to say, that if infanticide occurred in connection with any member connected with your society, the circumstances of your society are such, and the care you exercise is such, that it would be impossible to conceal the act of infanticide ?—Yes; and if at the present moment there is any doubt existing in the mind of the public as to the prevalence of infanticide, the principles we have established we believe are the very best that it is possible to surround questions of this character with. If it were possible by any recommendation or otherwise that the affiliated friendly societies and all

(142.)

Chairman—continued.

the friendly benefit societies of this county where registered, were permitted to have a free hand in this direction, I am satisfied that all suspicion would be set at rest in the course of very few years in consequence of the complete success which has followed our efforts since we have established the juvenile societies.

4445. You speak of your societies having a "free hand" in this direction; would you kindly explain what you mean ?—I omitted to say that we think we should be permitted to enter a child at any age.

4446. You think it would be desirable that this restriction of the three years limit which operates against your society should be repealed ? —Yes; and also that that portion of the Act which only permits us to insure our children amongst ourselves, should be repealed, and then we could admit the general public; in fact, as far as I am able to gather from inquiries made in the district surrounding a neighbourhood like Berwick-on-Tweed, the societies in which the children have been previously insured are losing their insurances and they are registering in the Foresters and Oddfellows of the neighbourhod. An institution connected with my own society, which has only been established a little over 12 months (their rules were registered on the 10th May 1889), started with a juvenile membership of something under 50. I cannot remember the exact number at this moment, but they now have nearly 500 members.

4447. Is this in Berwick-on-Tweed ?—In Berwick-on-Tweed and the surrounding neighbourhood, so that you will see that the feeling of the people, the feeling of security, is extending towards us. I do not know that I have anything more to say, except to press upon the Committee the desirability of the terms of the resolution of the conference, that we do not desire to be interfered with in any way; we believe the present Act is all sufficient for our requirements, with the exception I have mentioned, and that the suspicions which have been supported probably in rather an indifferent manner, to my mind, before this Committee, so far as the assertions have gone, are not borne out in any way with reference to our orders.

4448. Is there anything else you would like to add to your evidence ?—No.

4449. You have drawn a distinction, the force of which I fully admit, and have always admitted, between your affiliated societies and what are commonly called commercial and collecting societies ?—Yes.

4450. I think you have hardly done full justice to your societies yet in bringing out all the points of difference which are in your favour. Would you state distinctly to the Committee what are the points in which you think your affiliated societies essentially differ from those other societies I have spoken of ?—I have purposely avoided making any comparative remark, but as you ask me the question I must do so. The collecting societies are not managed in the first instance in any particular locality in the same way as a juvenile branch is, or a children of members' insurance fund. The members of a collecting society have rarely or never any

D D   opportunity

Chairman – continued.

opportunity of attending a meeting of the society. The affiliated orders in nearly every instance do make provision for either a half yearly or annual meeting of the parents and guardians at which they may be present and discuss the business of the previous year, the accounts, and other matters. The expenses of management are distinctly different in amount as between the two principles. In ours, as I read to your Lordships, from the rule, we do not permit more than 15 per cent. to be taken for management, and that must include everything, salaries, books, and rent ; whereas it is well known from various publications that the management expense of other societies is very much in excess of that. Whatever profit there is or would accumulate in our societies, would remain in the general fund, and would be used either in enhancing the value of the benefits or in the reduction of the contributions, providing that after a valuation had been made it disclosed a surplus ; the members manage this themselves, and there are no strangers to the members engaged in any of the offices. Our societies are generally established at our own doors in connection with the lodge, but in all cases of juvenile branches in connection with our own society, and I believe in the majority of other societies, they are carried on outside the place ; the main lodges are generally held in public-houses, but the juvenile lodges are generally held in a schoolroom ; consequently, therefore, they are in touch with each other, and any abuse can be stopped ; whereas in the case of societies, not friendly societies, the members have not that opportunity.

4451. You mean in what are termed collecting societies ?—Yes.

4452. Those are the points of difference that there are between you?—Yes, those are the principal points of difference.

4453. I think you have omitted one difference. Do not you make some inquiry into the characters of those whom you would admit to your society, before you admit them ?—As I have stated previously, not only the character of the parent, but the condition of the children is inquired into, and also medical examination is made.

4454. Have you a medical examination always before you admit the child ?—Not always.

4455. There is another point to be brought out as a difference between your society and a collecting society ; do you employ any paid agents ?—No ; I told your Lordships in the previous part of my evidence, that the members do it as a labour of love.

4456. May I sum up the distinction between yourselves and those societies thus : you have local control ?—Yes.

4457. And you have personal knowledge of the members one by another ? ··· Yes.

4458. Then you have self-management ?—Yes.

4459. And inquiry as to character before you admit to membership?—Yes.

4460. You have no paid collecting agents, and there are no profits accruing to shareholders ?—No, and further than that, at 21 years of age, it is becoming a generally acknowledged principle,

Chairman—continued.

and in fact the registrar has been drawing our attention to the necessity of having inserted in our juvenile society's rules, as at age 21 liability ceases as regards a member, that there shall be a surrender of that part of the capital which has accumulated to a person living to 21 years of age who is not able to get entrance into one of the parent lodges of the affiliated orders.

4461. If I understand you rightly, a kind of deferred payment accruing ? — No, it is a surrender of part of the profit which has been made, of the capital.

4462. A return of capital ?—Yes, but usually it happens that a juvenile of 16 or 18 years of age according as the rules provide, has his initiation money paid from the juvenile branch into the parent order.

4463. Then one other question upon this point ; you speak of careful inquiry as to character ; now supposing that any member or members of your society were to turn out afterwards bad characters, becoming dissolute or depraved, have you any provisions in your order for their expulsion on the ground of their change of character ?—I have never met a case of that description, and I do not know that we would punish the children for the sake of the parent, but we would probably exercise some greater supervision.

4464. All those points you have now stated, which seem to me important, are points of distinction between yourselves and these other societies ?—Yes ; and further, I might add, that the members year by year as they approach the age for transference, have been transferred into the various affiliated societies, so that we get a continuation of thrift and providence from the earliest moment ; in five societies during last year, there were 9,775 young people transferred to the adult lodges.

4465. Naturally, therefore, in the case of societies so carefully managed and with such careful safeguards against evil as yours, it will be expected that the evils, if there were any, resulting from insurance, should be much fewer than in societies less carefully managed ?—Undoubtedly ; our experience is that there is a total absence of them.

4466. Your point is, that on that ground your society should not be dealt with in the same way by Act of Parliament as other societies ; supposing them to be dealt with at all, you would maintain, would you not, that there should be a distinction made in any legislation between the affiliated orders and other societies ?—There should be a distinction.

4467. Then as regards one point, you stated that in the event of a case of infanticide occurring ; I presume by "infanticide" you would not merely mean death by violence, but death by criminal neglect ?—Death by intent.

4468. You say it would be quite impossible to conceal such a death ?—I am satisfied it would be.

4469. You have probably seen the Report of the Committee of the House of Commons on the subject of Friendly Societies which reported, I think, last year, that in the majority of cases it would be impossible to bring conviction home of
a deed

Chairman—continued.

a deed done in the privacy of the home; that opinion would go rather against yours?—I do not think that that privacy exists.

4470. Let us take the case, which is not an uncommon case, of a mother over-laying her child; do not you think it would be quite possible to conceal the fact that she had done that on purpose instead of accidentally?—Undoubtedly it would be; but the fact remains that suffocation is so easily distinguished, and the inquest would bring out that verdict.

4471. What verdict?—Even supposing the woman lay upon the child ever so lightly, but sufficiently to suffocate it, the impression made by the weight upon the corpse would have such a marked effect that it would be discovered.

4472. Undoubtedly the fact of the over-laying would be discovered, but we are now speaking of the crime of infanticide; the proof of the parent having done that on purpose would not be easily procurable?—I cannot say; I think it would be quite possible to decide by appearances whether it was done by accident or design.

4473. That is a matter for medical opinion, and that I need not trouble you further about. Then you say that the mortality in your society is low, which I do not for a moment intend to dispute; but have you considered what a very small percentage of increase in all the numbers of insured children, death by intent would amount to on the whole?—I am aware that, numerically, it would be a very serious amount.

4474. We will take, if you please, this calculation; we will suppose that one child in 5,000 comes to its death by criminal intent on the part of its parent, whether father or mother. Now there are 4,000,000 child-life policies issued. I think you may take it from me, you may correct me if I am wrong, that if only one of those children in 5,000 met with foul play it would come to 800 cases of death by foul play in the year?—You say "if," I presume.

4475. I do not pretend to be a skilful arithmetician, but I have worked it out, and if I am wrong you or some other person I take it will correct me. If one in 5,000 is improperly dealt with, it would come to 800 cases in the year; and you will admit that 800 cases of infanticide in a year would be a very serious thing to deal with?—Yes, it would.

4476. And yet that number might be produced by one child in 5,000 being so dealt with; now if I or any one were to say that one child in 5,000 has been so dealt with foully, or putting in other words, that the chances or probabilities of a child of the working classes being dealt foully with, were 5,000 to one against, I suppose you would hardly call that a very serious imputation against the working classes; 5,000 to one in their favour?—We do consider it is an imputation, because we do not consider the working classes can be charged with infanticide, but it is the residuum of the population amongst whom those unfortunate cases occur.

4477. You say you have admitted of late years an increasing number of the general public to the benefits of your insurance?—The juvenile branch.

4478. I am speaking of that; to that extent you (142.)

Chairman—continued.

are becoming a general insurance society as distinguished from a society for the benefit of your own members, still speaking of the juvenile branch?—Yes.

4479. In the case of the admission of the general public to those benefits in your juvenile societies, would you have the same facilities of testing the character and looking after the cases that you have in the case of your societies where the members are all known to one another?—Yes, it would simply be an enlargement of the management and provided for by registered rules.

4480. But would you have the same power of checking them?—Decidedly; we should have more inquirers.

4481. You would require more careful inquiry?—We should.

4482. You would insist upon that?—Yes, we should have 12 if they were required, but five have been sufficient in the early stage of the society.

4483. You would have what would be necessary in consequence of the greater precaution taken?—I do not consider there will be any greater risk that we should engage in.

4484. The sum of your statement is, that you maintain that your societies are essentially distinguished from certain other societies whose case has come before the Committee, and you claim in consideration of that, that you should be differently dealt with in any legislation upon this subject of child insurance?—Yes.

4485. Assuming for the moment that increased precautions were to be adopted by the Legislature for preventing crime, would you suggest any mode in which your society should be, or could be, excluded from the operation of such additional safeguards. To put it briefly, could you suggest any way in which your societies could be dealt with by Act of Parliament differently from other societies?—Yes. I apprehend that there would be no difficulty at all about it. The Select Committee of the House of Commons last year, which sat to inquire into the management of collecting friendly societies generally, has reported in favour of separating the Act into its component parts.

4486. Would you be in favour of making two distinct Acts?—Yes, sub-section 30 and its amendments would be taken as applying to collecting societies, and that portion which belongs to affiliated orders, that is to say, orders with central bodies and branches, would be taken by itself; and I believe when that opportunity occurs we shall have some representation to make as to the advisability of doing what we require.

4487. In point of fact your suggestion comes to this: if the subject of child insurance is to be dealt with by Parliament, it should be in the form of two Bills; one Bill dealing, if it is necessary to deal at all, with the affiliated orders; and another Bill dealing with the collecting societies?—Yes.

4488. Have you considered at all the question whether it would be desirable to adopt a graduated scale of payments; not of premiums, but of policies such as has been suggested to the

Chairman—continued.

Committee by several of the witnesses?—Our principle is by a graduated policy.

4489. Was your attention drawn to the terms of these graduated scales ?—No ; I do not give any attention to graduated scales except they have special application to the affiliated orders.

Earl *Spencer.*

4490. Do I understand that it is your opinion that if the scale which now prevails for permitting child insurance were altered, it would materially affect your business, and that it would affect what you consider the good influence you have amongst the working classes ?—Yes.

4491. Do you apprehend that you would lose a great number of insurers ?—I apprehend that in the possibility of the continuation of the restriction with reference to the affiliated orders being permitted to admit the general public, we should suffer.

4492. That is to say that in the new legislation, supposing that were passed upon the lines you wish, and were brought under separate Acts, you would be inclined to extend the facilities for child insurance to the lower age in the friendly societies ?—Yes.

4493. Rather with a view of increasing your business and carrying on a more successful competition with the collecting societies ?—Yes.

4494. You said something as to your society having taken the place of some of the collecting societies on the border, at Berwick ?—Yes, at Berwick and its surroundings, where they are severely competing with us.

4495. How was it that you successfully competed there with them ?—I cannot answer that question excepting that it is in consequence of the popularity of the affiliated orders at the present moment amongst the working classes in this country.

4496. Do you know of any return which shows what the number of the people using these insurance societies for children in the affiliated orders is, as compared with the commercial societies ?—I have made no comparison of the figures, but I stated at the commencement of my evidence that in the 13 orders we have 218,615 juveniles.

4497. I understand that you would be in favour of altering some of the conditions now imposed ; you used these words at one part of your evidence : " Supposing greater care were taken by the registrars in future." I am not sure that you explained that exactly. What would be the greater care taken by the registrars ?—They are not careful enough to ask in all cases as to how many societies is this child insured in, and for what amounts, I believe, but it is possible that there is more general care being taken at this present time in consequence of the evidence that has been given in this direction, and if it were made penal that a child should be insured in an unregistered society, the registrar then would be in a very much better position than he is at the present moment, with so many of these unregistered societies in various localities.

4498. You are aware, are you not, that there are a great many unregistered societies now insuring lives ?—Yes, there are.

Earl *Spencer*—continued.

4499. And that system has been in existence many years?—Yes, it has been in existence a long time.

4500. Before the Act of 1875 ?—Yes.

Chairman.

4501. The Act of 1875 then did not succeed in bringing all these unregistered societies within its provisions ? — No, because registration was voluntary.

Earl *Spencer.*

4502. I have a return put in by the Prudential Society, which shows that the number of children insured in England and Wales is, in the Prudential, 2,099,369 ; in other companies, affiliated and registered, about 1,300,000, and in unregistered societies and local clubs about 750,000 ; have you anything to say about that ?—I have not.

Lord *Kinnaird.*

4503. You think that would be about the figure?—I should think that possibly it might be.

Earl *Spencer.*

4504. You said that you thought that possibly there might be some limit to the insurance of children under a year ?—I meant in respect to amount.

4505. Would you explain that a little more? —I think that in the present state of public opinion it is advisable that respectable societies of the character that I represent, should be wishful to give every assistance they possibly can in stamping out what undoubtedly is a great evil; and as the greater proportion of deaths occur at about that age, it probably would be wise to limit the amount. I would not like to see the amount too limited, because, from inquiries I made in Manchester before I came here, I find that undertakers will charge 2 *l.* 5 *s.* to bury a child when it is taken in the coffin on the knees of the parents, in one coach ; it would cost that in that case. Now it is an impossibility that any black can be bought; there would be nothing to pay the doctor's bill with, and there would be nothing to make up for the little necessaries that have had to be provided during the illness.

4506–7. Then do you think now there is possibly too much profit on children under a year in their insurance ?—No; I say I would not fix it too low, as I find that 2 *l.* 5 *s.* is the cost of a child's burial, where it is possible to take the body in the coffin on the knees of the parents, in one coach to the cemetery.

4508. I understand that; but when you say that you like to see some alteration in the limit, I presume you think that possibly the amount may be too large now ?—I do not think the amount is too large.

4509. Supposing some limit were imposed to meet public opinion, do you think then that the parents would have to find part of the expenses ?—Yes, undoubtedly they would.

4510. Then you would come across what you object too, namely, having the hat go round sometimes ?—Decidedly ; it would come to that, I have not the slightest doubt.

4511. Following

Lord *Kinnaird.*

4511. Following that question, do we understand that you rather are for increasing the limit or for decreasing the limit of 6 *l.*?—I have not suggested 6 *l.* I was speaking with reference to a limitation being placed upon that age, where the greatest mortality is proved to occur.

Earl of *Selborne.*

4512. You mean under one year?—Yes, under one year.

Lord *Kinnaird.*

4513. You think that those you represent would not mind, for that age, the limit being made rather less; do I understand that?—I think that fact is established; our scale, which I read to the Committee upon that particular matter, says that after admission at three months of age it will be 30 *s.*, and after a year 2 *l.*

Earl of *Selborne.*

4514. What is the next amount?—After two years, it is 50 *s.*; after three years, 3 *l.*; rising 10 *s.* per year up to 11 years of age.

Lord *Kinnaird.*

4515. I wish to ask you a question or two with reference to the amounts that you pay; did you say that 15 per cent. is the maximum amount of commission?—No; that is the maximum amount which is allowed by the rule, to be deducted from the contributions for the whole expenses of management.

4516. One would have expected that that would leave a larger sum to be paid as benefit to the parents, since the Prudential Society will pay more for the same money than most of the friendly societies, either the Royal Liver Friendly Society or the Liverpool Victoria Society?—I have no doubt they have reasons for doing so; I cannot compare that company with my society.

4517. People joining them will?—Probably they will, but we have the preference at present.

4518. But your point was that you were rather better to insure with, because you did not incur those expenses?—Decidedly.

4519. Whereas the figures show that you are worse to insure with?—That may be, taking the difference of benefit; but the people are beginning to prefer us.

Lord *Norton.*

4520. You spoke of cases in which the insurance was generally handed over to the undertaker; what sort of societies are those which you referred to?—I was speaking of the practice of undertakers requiring to be paid before entering upon a funeral.

4521. Is that a usual thing?—It is with undertakers amongst the working classes.

4522. I understand you to maintain that no cases of infanticide have ever occurred in any of your affiliated societies, but that you acknowledge that cases have been proved elsewhere?—Yes.

4523. And to meet such cases your suggestion is that the criminal law should be made more stringent?—Undoubtedly.

4524. Is that your notion; in the way of increased penalties, or in the way of facilitating

(142.)

Lord *Norton*—continued.

conviction; in which direction should the alteration of the law be?—That the punishment should be increased.

4525. Do you think there is a difficulty of conviction now which enables such cases to escape?—I cannot answer that question.

Earl of *Selborne.*

4526. What limit is there to the punishment now; the punishment may be capital in a bad case, may it not?—It is.

4527. You cannot increase that?—No. I forget what Act it is under, but the penalty is six months for anything that would tend to it; but of course if the infanticide be murder there is but one punishment for it, and that capital.

4528. Do you know the exact offence which is punishable by a maximum of six months?—Parental neglect.

Lord *Norton.*

4529. Do you know how far the fact of insurance is admitted as evidence in a case of infanticide?—I do not know how far, except that occasionally the question is asked, but very seldom is it proved that a child which has been set aside has been insured.

4530. You do not know whether the fact of the insurance aggravates the penalty for neglect of a child?—I do not know that; I could not answer that question; that is a question for the judges.

4531. You made use of the expression, "If we could get rid of the idea of respectable funerals;" do you think there is a vicious sort of pride in that respect in making funerals more costly by way of a notion of respectability?—It is not a vicious sort of pride, but it is an unfortunate custom.

4532. You look upon it as an unfortunate custom, and a thing not to be encouraged?—Yes.

4533. You have stated that the collecting societies do not meet as affiliated societies do; what is the difference as to the general regulations for meetings in those two different classes of societies?—I cannot give you the management or any of the rules of the collecting societies, excepting in this particular, that I believe that the parents of members and the guardians of members do not have the possibility of meeting annually with such conveniences as those who belong to the juvenile societies of the affiliated orders have.

4534. There was no other distinction in your mind when you said that collecting societies did not meet as the affiliated orders do?—That is the distinction.

4535. Then you spoke of the calculation of the surplus; how could a valuation be made without ascertaining the surplus beyond liabilities?—It is made by the actuaries taking the mortality at certain ages, and what is required to meet the insurance promised to members.

4536. Including all deferred liabilities?—Yes.

4537. I do not think you completely gave the Committee your idea of the privileges which might be given to affiliated societies by a statute distinguishing between them and collecting societies?—In what direction; do you mean with reference to juvenile societies?

D D 3   4538. You

Lord *Norton*—continued.

4538. You said that the Committee of the House of Commons proposed that the two classes of societies should be differently dealt with in the way of legislation ?—Yes.

4539. You did not state in what sort of way such a distinction should be made, whether it should be by higher privileges being given to the affiliated societies or otherwise ?—I have stated that the friendly societies are satisfied with the Friendly Societies Act as at present passed ; but suggest that we should have a free hand with reference to the admission of members into the society, whether as children of members or the general public.

Marquess of *Lothian.*

4540. Do you know, or have you ever heard, of any case, not necessarily in your own society, in which there has been reason to suspect foul play, and no prosecution has followed ?—No.

4541. Have you never heard of any ?—No.

4542. Then, with reference to another question ; would you not rather propose, in place of increased penalties, that there should be greater facilities for prosecution ?—I should have thought that that already existed.

4543. I think the Committee have had evidence that there was some difficulty in getting a prosecution in cases where foul play has been suspected ?—In cases of that kind there is generally an inquest ordered, if there is an absence of medical testimony with reference to the death.

4544. But a witness examined before the Committee told us that when cases were referred to the coroner he could not get the coroner to take any steps ?—That is not the fault of the societies, it is the fault of the officers ; but no doubt it would be desirable to have increased facilities.

4545. You would desire that in such a suspicious case a prosecution should necessarily follow ?—Yes.

4546. Do you think that would be preferable to an alteration of the present law ?—Yes, or to the interference with the amount of the insurance at present existing.

Lord *Norton.*

4547. There are variations in the form of insurance upon children ; for instance, there is such a thing as provision for a child on coming of age or putting out to a trade ?—We have nothing of that sort ; we only insure for funeral expenses in our case ; for sick benefits and funeral allowances ; in no other form.

Lord *Thring.*

4548. With respect to the custom of funerals, what I suppose you would say is, that it is a good thing that the poor should wish to give their children a decent burial, but that it is a question of degree whether it is not now wished for a little too much ?—That is what I think.

4549. Then with reference to these unregistered societies, do you happen to know why they do not register ; do you know what objection they have ?—If they were registered they would have to comply with the provisions of the Act, that is

Lord *Thring*—continued.

to say, making annual returns and valuations, and other matters, which they consider irksome ; and in some cases, in the majority of cases, they resent any, what is called Government interference with their societies, which have been in existence for many years.

4550. Upon that point, let me ask, do you wish that all societies which do the same business as you do, should be registered ?—Yes.

4551. Then with respect to collecting societies, has it occurred to you how you could prevent the evils which either more or less you think attach to them ?—No ; I could make no suggestion with reference to the collecting societies.

4552. Would you go so far as to prohibit them ?—No.

Lord *Poltimore.*

4553. What is your great objection to allowing a child to be insured in an unregistered society ?—Because there is no supervision which can be exercised by anyone ; no one knows how much is paid.

Earl of *Harrowby.*

4554. Do the members of your society, as a rule, insure all their children from birth ?—In some cases they do not ; because, previously to the establishment of our societies, they had some of their children insured in others, and they have not thought fit to drop the elder one, but in some cases they have taken the younger ones away, insuring them in the children's insurance branch, the elder ones being transferred to the juvenile societies.

4555. So that now it is becoming very much the habit of your members to insure their children ?—Yes.

4556. And there is a great increase, is there not, in the habit amongst the working people ?—I feel quite sure that there is, and I hope that nothing will be done in any way to interfere with the tender plant of thrift, which undoubtedly appears to me to be in a very fair way to not only assert the independence of the working classes by their own means, but to reduce the curse of poverty and pauperism.

4557. When did your societies begin their work ?—My order had some juveniles in connection with it nine years ago ; three years ago model rules were drawn up, printed, and sent to the various lodges, but at the time of which I speak there possibly were not more in our society than a few over 1,000 members, and in three years we had increased that number to 7,241.

4558. Then the habit of child insurance is quite a recent one amongst the affiliated societies ?—Yes, in its general application.

4559. I mean amongst their own members ?—Yes.

4560. I think you said just now that the societies were most willing to assist the stamping out of what is most undoubtedly a great evil ?—Yes.

4561. This "great evil" you suppose to exist amongst the class of immoral, dissipated, and the thriftless ?—Yes.

4562. Those are just the people whom you would not admit into your society, would you ?—I think

Earl of *Harrowby*—continued.

I think that their chance of admission would be very small.

4563. Because it is generally a very high standard that your members maintain?—Yes, that is one of the reasons why we have arrived at our present position.

4564. But with respect to child insurance, which you want to have set up, would you allow that class, that is to say, what you call outside members, to insure their children?—I would allow every man to insure his children.

4565. But even in your societies?—We would exercise considerable discretion after inquiry.

4566. But it is just those classes that you would be shy of having to do with in your association that we have to deal with?—I cannot but see that the Bill being so general applies to all, and that when a person asks for the admission of his children into the societies we cannot discriminate much by appearances; those unfortunate conditions develop.

4567. But this "great evil" you admit to exist undoubtedly exists with that class?—Yes.

4568. That is what we have to handle?—Yes.

4569. Therefore if we attempt to deal with that we are not throwing any slur upon the character of the working class, whom we all suppose to be as affectionate to their children as any other class. Then supposing that a law were made that the registrar could only give one certificate of death, would that, do you think, meet the evil?—Under a certain age. If you begin with a limitation, let us have it all through the societies by having no age of limitation of entrance but penalties for entering a child under 12 years in more than one society upon both parents and societies, especially unregistered ones.

4570. That would tend to check insurance in unregistered societies; but you wished to check that?—I cannot say anything about it checking insurance in unregistered societies, but it would prevent the possibility of children being insured at the age at which there is a greater possibility of death occurring, for a greater amount than is necessary, which possibly may in some cases lead to the crime of infanticide.

4571. From your knowledge of the habits of the population generally, should you have thought that the dissipated and the immoral were largely insurers of their children?—I should not think they were.

4572. That is a fact that we wish to ascertain?—I do not think that the class you have mentioned have anything to spare for any purpose outside what will bring them the necessaries of life.

Earl *Beauchamp.*

4573. Do I understand you to say that you see no objection to children over 12 months being insured?—There certainly would not be as much objection over that age to the full amount of insurance.

4574. Would not the means of investigation be very much facilitated if the insurance were limited to one office, or one society?—Decidedly it would.

4575. You were asked a question which was based on the assumption that one child in 5,000 was treated with criminal neglect, have you any

(142.)

Earl *Beauchamp*—continued.

knowledge whether that assumption has any foundation other than conjecture or assertion?—I said, if that were the case, it would amount to a certain result. I made no assertion that one child in 5,000 was foully treated.

4576. Have you any knowledge whether one child in 5,000 is treated with criminal neglect?—I have no knowledge of that, and I would imagine by the results shown by the general population that no such percentage exists.

4577. And, therefore, you have no reason to believe that 800 children are annually put aside?—No; I take it that the fact of a child being put aside would be discovered.

4578. Therefore, you think that any such statement if it be made is exaggerated?—Yes.

4579. And you do not know of any evidence which would warrant such an assumption, if it were made?—I do not.

4580. Is it not possible that by surrounding child insurance with precautions based upon exaggerated statements as to child murder, great difficulties would be thrown in the way of the operations of your societies?—Yes.

4581. Your affiliated societies exercise a very educational and elevating influence upon the members?—Yes, undoubtedly, in consequence of being permitted to share in the management.

4582. Any legislation which thwarted or hampered these elevating influences of your societies would be very injurious to the working classes?—Yes.

4583. Such legislation then ought to have better foundation than calculations based only on conjecture and assertion?—Undoubtedly so.

4584. If the development of the self-respect and independence of the working classes is stifled and prevented by heedless legislation, the finer feelings of parental affection are not likely to be promoted?—Undoubtedly not; and further than that, you will drive the registered juvenile societies out of the Act altogether, and you will lose all control over them whatever.

4585. You think that the degradation of the lower orders in respect to parental affection, thrift, and independence of character would be a national calamity?—It would.

4586. Then may I ask whether you agree with the public writer, who said last week, "There are some expedients for removing a particular ill which involve ills of a more disastrous order"?—Undoubtedly so; this is one of that particular character.

Chairman.

4587. I wish to ask you just one or two questions arising out of your evidence; you stated that the mode that you would suggest for preventing, what I think you spoke of as an admitted evil, to a certain extent at any rate, namely, infanticide, would be in the way of increasing the penalties?—I did; but "increased facilities of prosecution" would be the best way to put it.

4588. All legislation in the way of facilities of prosecution would be more punitive than preventive; but I was rather on the point of preventive, than of punitive legislation?—Anything that will prevent crime we most undoubtedly subscribe to.

4589. Your answer at first seemed to go

D D 4   simply

Chairman—continued.

simply in the direction of penal legislation, whereas this Bill, and I think all Bills relating to insurance, go always in the direction of preventive legislation; you see no objection to that, I presume?—I see, no objection beyond the statements I have made.

4590. I wish to direct your attention to one or two suggestions which have been made in the direction of prevention; I speak, of course, of the actual prevention of infanticide, or of such criminal neglect or cruelty, as very nearly approaches infanticide, and have ended in infanticide, if the person committing it had not been stopped. Now with a view of preventing that, one working class witness offered the suggestion in any case in which the coroner and jury thought the case a suspicious one, although they did not actually convict of infanticide, the coroner should have the power of impounding the policy and spending the amount on the funeral; have you considered that suggestion? —Yes; I have; I considered that the great principle that prevails in this country that a man is considered innocent until he is proved guilty, is a sufficient set-off against any such proposition as that.

4591. Taking the case of a person brought before a magistrate in one of those cases of shocking and sickening cruelty, which have come before us, and being convicted and sentenced to imprisonment, that would not be a case of a person being presumed to be innocent, because he would have been found guilty and sentenced; do you see any objection that in that case the policy of the person so convicted should become *ipso facto* void?—I think the principle of that question was answered by stating, as I have already done, that I would not punish the children for the sins of their parents, and if a man or a woman had been proved guilty in this particular case, surely you would not throw the onus of the burial upon the parish.

4592. I am not speaking of the burial?—The withdrawal of the policy would amount to that.

4593. In the case of the child's death it would?—Decidedly.

4594. But that would be no punishment to the child?—It would be punishing the family.

4595. It would be punishing the parents?—Yes.

4596. Then you said the dissipated and the immoral class do not insure as a rule?—I do not believe they do.

4597. Do you found that opinion upon what you know, or upon what you have heard, because the dissipated and the immoral class do not insure with you?—I say so from my experience, not exactly with that particular class, but from observations I have made, and from persons I have come in contact with on former occasions.

4598. You say it would be unlikely that the dissipated and immoral classes should insure, because you say they could not afford to do so; now are the dissipated and immoral amongst the workmen always the very poor, and receiving very low wages; are there no instances of the dissipated and immoral receiving very good wages?—I have no doubt that dissipation and immorality lead to poverty; on the other hand I have no doubt there are such cases as your

Chairman—continued.

Lordship mentions of people receiving good pay being dissipated, but I do not wish to attach that charge to the working class.

4599. I was not attaching any charge or speaking of any individuals: I am not implying, nor have I ever thought, the working classes, or any but a very small minority of them, are dissipated or immoral; but every class in life we may take it as a witness has said, has its proportion of black sheep. Now those dissipated and immoral persons may be persons in receipt of fairly good wages. It has been proved distinctly, at all events I am prepared to assert it, that the sum for which such immoral person could obtain a sum of 6 *l.* by insuring in two societies upon his child's death; the sum he would have to pay to obtain that upon the death of a child of six months would be only 4 *s.* 4 *d.* spread over that period of time; would that be a very heavy demand upon a workman receiving 2 *l.* and sometimes 3 *l.* a week?—No, it would not; but people of that character have no foresight, and I do not think except in a case where criminality could be proved, that any such insurance would be effected.

4600. Then you have spoken of it as being an imputation upon the working classes to say that any portion of them insure their children with the intention of putting them away. May I ask whether that is the opinion you have formed of this Bill, that it proceeds upon the assumption that a parent would insure his child with the intention from the very first of putting it away?— Yes, it is proposed as a preventive to a crime, and the smallness of the proof with reference to the crime of infanticide we consider completely puts aside the necessity for this Bill being made applicable to the providence of the working classes.

4601. That I quite understand; but I think you are hardly taking in my question. I may say for myself, and I think for most others who support this Bill, that this is not the assumption upon which we proceed, namely, that the parent will in the first instance insure his child for the purpose of putting it away for the sake of the insurance money. The assumption which lies at the bottom of my own mind in respect of this Bill is that a parent may insure a child and being hard-hearted, careless, or cruel, the association in his mind constantly for weeks, and it might be for months, of the child's death with the means of making money by the insurance, might be a strong inducement to him to do away with it, although he may not have intended to do it in the first instance?—I am perfectly satisfied that in 99 out of 100 insurances effected by the working classes in this country there is no conception of infanticide.

4602. You mean when making the insurance? —That is so; I have kept the residuum as small as I possibly can.

4603. I was asking you whether in the case of the residuum the constantly present thought, that not only would money be saved by the child's death, but that money might be made by the child's death, would not be a powerful inducement to bring about the child's death?—I do not think there is that inducement in the case of the working classes neither has it ever been so.

The Witness is directed to withdraw.

25 *July* 1890.

MR. THOMAS BALLAN STEAD, is called in; and Examined, as follows:

Chairman.

4604. YOU are permanent secretary to the Ancient Order of Foresters?—I am.

4605. Which possesses a membership of how many adult benefit members?—Six hundred and seventy-five thousand nine hundred and eighteen.

4606. How many honorary members are there? —Sixteen thousand nine hundred and sixty-six.

4607. You have in funds 4,392,662 *l.*?—We have.

4608. And also 1,360 juvenile societies; by which you mean, I presume, juvenile societies in connection with the Ancient Order of Foresters? —There are 1,360 juvenile societies in connection with the order.

4609. With 83,180 members?—That is the total of the societies, of which number 79,000 are in Great Britain.

4610. And the rest are in the colonies?— Yes.

4611. I think that their capital is 102,069 *l.*? —That is the capital of the juvenile societies.

4612. Do you mean the sums for which the juveniles are insured?—No; the savings.

4613. I believe you have taken an active interest in friendly societies; for how many years have you done so?—Thirty-two years.

4614. I believe you have lived in Leeds and Sheffield, and you are now residing in Hull?—Yes.

4615. Have you always taken an active part in working-class movements?—I have.

4616. Have you been a member of the Leeds School Board for three years?—Yes.

4617. I believe you were also visitor to five schools in the poorest districts?—I was.

4618. May I ask if you were present, and have heard the evidence given to the Committee by the last witness?—I was.

4619. Do you agree with that evidence?—I agree with that evidence thoroughly and entirely.

4620. Then, that being so, is there anything in addition to that evidence that you would wish to say, or would you be satisfied that we should accept your statement that you would agree with the entire of that evidence?—We accept it entirely, except that I should like to say that we regard ourselves in respect to juvenile societies rather as the guardians of our juvenile members than as carrying out a commercial transaction. Mr. Cleveland alluded to it, but he did not put it in that light.

4621. I believe you are prepared with statistics to show the experience of your juvenile societies? —Yes.

4622. Would you wish to put in those statistics now?—I am prepared with statistics to show the mortality of our societies, and also the most important branch in this juvenile society work which has some bearing on this question, that is the sickness. I may say that our mortality experience is borne out by Mr. Cleveland's figures, which he gave for the four large societies. Of course, I am speaking now of the Ancient Order of Foresters.

(142.)

Chairman—continued.

4623. Do you include that order in the four large societies?—I suppose Mr. Cleveland would, but these figures I give are our own.

4624. I understand you to say that you accept Mr. Cleveland's statistics as fairly representing your society? — They are rather above our figures.

4625. Do you mean too favourable?—No, unfavourable. In the year 1886 our number of deaths per 1,000 was 4·43; in 1887 it was 4·37; in the year 1888 it was 3·84, showing a reduction; and last year, 1889 it was 3·94; the average over the four years was 4·12, which is somewhat less than Mr. Cleveland gave for the four societies.

4626. Last year your mortality returns are slightly more favourable than Mr. Cleveland's? —Yes.

4627. Then I understand that you have sent out queries to your juvenile societies in Great Britain respecting this Insurance Bill, and you have invited answers to a series of questions, and you have received back 873 replies from as many societies; that is to say, 873 societies representing 59,000 members?—Yes.

4628. Will you inform the Committee what were the queries and what were the replies; perhaps you will put in the queries and the replies? —I will (*handing in the same*). (See *Appendix.*)

4629. It would be impossible to go all through these queries; could you give any analysis of them which would show the result?—I may say the only variation which appears in the answers of the 873 which have come back, is with reference to Question 9; in all the rest the answers are unanimous.

4630. Perhaps I need not trouble you upon that Question No. 9, as it refers to a clause no longer in the Bill?—It might interest you to know the number of those who thought your proposal would not injure the societies. Out of 873 societies who sent answers to Question 9, 834 of the societies, representing 56,462 members, said that the undertakers' clause would be the ruin of the societies; they put it in various ways, but that was their answer; 39 societies, representing 2,538 members, thought the Bill would not affect them, but all the 834 societies answered Question 8, which asked whether there were any grounds for including the societies under the Bill, and they all agreed there were none.

4631. Would you kindly put in your analysis of those questions and answers if you have it?— It is merely what I have read.

4632. I think you are prepared to show what the juvenile societies do for their members in the shape of medical attendance and medicine; that point was not touched upon by Mr. Cleveland? —It was not; the reason I wish to put that in is, to show your Lordship that we are not anxious to shorten the lives of our members, but to make them live to a longer age by providing them at the earliest age with medical attendance and medicine.

E E   4633. Is

Chairman—continued.

4633. Is that what you include under the head of what are commonly called "sick benefits"?—The sick benefits are money benefits; that is to say, a certain allowance per week at a certain age according to the rules, at which a money payment begins when the child is ill.

4634. How do you distinguish between that and the money paid to the doctor?—In addition to money benefit during sickness at any time if the child is ill it has doctor and medicine found by the society.

4635. That is to say, the effect of all this in your society is, that the doctor is found?—The doctor is found.

4636. And the medicine is found?—Yes, the medicine is found.

4637. Are there any medical comforts supplied?—Anything that a surgeon would order ordinarily is found for the member.

4638. And in addition to that a certain sum always upon death?—Yes; that is a funeral benefit.

4639. I think you have prepared figures to show how many inquests have been held upon members of your society?—Would you allow me to put in figures with reference to medical attendance? We have medical associations; that is to say, unions of our friendly societies, both juvenile and adult, for the purpose of securing medical aid and giving it with the greatest efficiency.

4640. Are those what would be commonly called club doctors?—Yes, they are what would be commonly called club doctors, except they are solely in the service of the society, and have no other practice.

4641. There would be a doctor probably to each lodge, or to two or three lodges?— To many. It is the custom now, in the large towns chiefly, for the affiliated orders to unite together and engage surgeons at an annual salary whose whole time is devoted to their service; they put up surgeries and provide their own medicine, and the children who belong to the various juvenile societies are entered as members of this medical association, and also facilities are given to members of the societies, who may not be members of the juvenile societies, but who are simply the children of adult members; they also are received into the benefits of the medical association by a small annual payment, from 1 *s.* per year.

4642. I was going to ask you what is the annual payment which obtains the gratuitous attendance of the club doctor?—Do you mean to the children?

4643. Yes?—It varies from 1 *s.* to 1 *s.* 6 *d.* or 2 *s.* per year in the cases of members of the juvenile societies.

4644. And you have stated that the doctor has an annual salary?—Yes.

4645. Now will you put in the figures that you are referring to?—I have a list of the societies: there are about 56 of them; the total membership is 175,340, out of which 53,004 are children under 15 years of age; I simply put this forward to show the care we take to preserve the lives of children.

4646. Have you any statistics to show what proportion of children under five years of age

Chairman—continued.

there are in that number?—No, I have not; but I have a list which shows in our order, the Ancient Order of Foresters, the age at which members are admitted to the juvenile societies.

4647. At what age is that?—I have them all tabulated.

4648. Would you read it?—In our Foresters' Juvenile Societies, out of the 1,279 societies in Great Britain, I find that only 11 societies admit members at one day old; only six admit at one week old; only two admit at one month old; only two admit at three months old; only one at six months old; 18 at one year; and nine at two years, so that out of the whole of the 1,279 societies only 49 of them admit children under three years, which, of course, the Friendly Societies Act lays down as the limit for the registered societies.

4649. Then in point of fact, if I understand you correctly, you really have no such thing in connection with your order as what is commonly called "infant insurance," unless by an "infant" you mean a child of three years old?—We have only 49 societies which admit members under three years of age out of the 1,279. That means that we have 1,230 societies whose membership only begins at three years and upwards, and only 49 whose membership begins under three years.

4650. Then, with the exception of the 49 societies, any legislation forbidding the insurance of children under the age of three would not affect your society?—Apparently not. This is an accurate compilation.

4651. Then, speaking strictly, as regards the interest of your society, you would see no objection, except as regards these 49 societies, to an Act limiting the assurable age of children to under three years?—I should, personally.

4652. But I mean as regards the interests of the society?—But our society might suffer if that limitation was enforced. By the law at present we have freedom, and we wish to extend that freedom.

4653. You think it would be desirable to have that freedom extended?—I think we should have the power to take them in at any age, because I think we have shown our capacity for taking care of them at a higher age, and we should look after them at the younger age.

4654. Then you agree with Mr. Cleveland that this limit which now prevents your insuring children under the age of three should be repealed?—You will find that the greatest bulk of our societies admit members about the ages of three years, four years, five years, and six years, because I find that out of the whole number (I stopped, if you remember, at under three years) 56 admit at three years; 302 at four years; 329 at five years; and 316 at six years. Then we begin to decline, only 85 admit at seven years; 89 at eight years; 23 at nine years; 62 at 10 years; six at 11 years; 47 at 12 years; nine at 13 years; three at 14 years; one at 15 years; and two at 16 years; yielding the total of 1,279.

4655. Would you say which of all those various ages has the highest number?—Between three and six years.

4656. The majority of your insurance cases are

Chairman—continued.

are between three and six years of age?—That is so; that is the great entrance age.

4657. Then I understand that you have prepared figures to show how many inquests have been held upon members of your juvenile societies, and the verdicts; would you state that?—Yes; I thought it would be of interest to the Committee to know that seeing if there were any case of infanticide it would have been before a coroner, so I asked the question in that list of questions, whether it "has ever come to your knowledge that a coroner's inquest has been held?" I find that from the beginning of our societies we have had 92 inquests, and in every case the verdict has been either "accidental death," or "death from natural causes." I may say that of "accidentally drowned," out of the 92 cases there were 37 drowned while bathing; nine were colliery accidents; nine were killed on the railway; 17 were street accidents, and one was a suicide, out of the 92; but each case is detailed in this list. (*The Witness hands in a detailed list of the result of 92 inquests.*)

4658. Amongst your queries, did you ask whether there ever had been any cases of criminal neglect or cruelty to children, as distinguished from death followed by inquest?—No, I have only the deaths.

4659. You are prepared to show the advantages resulting from your method of management of your juvenile societies; upon that subject we have had Mr. Cleveland's evidence, and you accept his statement, I presume?—Yes, with this addition, that our committees of management which manage our juvenile societies, in addition to looking after the material benefits which are paid to the members, contribute in no small degree to their instruction and amusement. I know many of our juvenile societies where every year competitions are arranged for amongst the members only, in the way of writing competitions, and competitions in various ways, where prizes are given by the adult members to the successful competitors.

4660. Are they money prizes?—They are books, generally, or that sort of thing.

4661. You spoke of the age at which sickness benefit begins; that is to say, a child must be a certain time a member before the sick benefit begins?—Yes.

4662. How long is that?—I have a list for the whole number of the 873 societies which answered the question as to the age at which they begin to pay sick benefit.

4663. Could you tell the Committee the average age?—No, I could not, and that would not be of any value, perhaps; but I only find one society out of the 873 which begins to pay sick benefit at the age of one year, only one at two years; two societies begin at two and a-half years, only one at three and a-half years, and 32 begin at the age of four.

4664. Does that rule apply also to death benefits; is there any limitation of the age at which you pay death benefits?—No; there is generally a short probationary period of a few months, and then they begin.

4665. Could you state how long the period is?—Sometimes it is three months, and sometimes

(142.)

Chairman—continued.

it is six months; it varies in the various societies, because we do not put any restriction upon them, there is no general limit at all.

4666. But in your society, as I understand you, there is a limit which has this result, that the children are not generally insured in death insurance in some of your societies before three months, and in others before six months?—There are some limitations of that sort; that is to say, if a member joins upon the 1st of January, in some of our societies it will perhaps be April, and in others it may be July, before he would be entitled to funeral benefit if death occurred, that being the probationary period.

4667. Is not that the same rule as there is in the collecting societies, that children must be so many months insured before they come into benefit?—I understand so, only in the other case our members come into medical benefit at once; that is to say, as soon as they join they are entitled to medical benefit and doctor from the day they insure.

4668. A man may insure for medical benefit for himself and all his children, may he not?—Yes.

4669. Up to the age of 13?—There is no limit to age, only when they get to the age of 18 they are generally charged as adults.

4670. What are the number of your societies which are registered?—Out of our total of 1,360, which includes the colonies, only 452 of our societies are registered under the Act; that is to say, practically one-third of the whole.

4671. Are the other societies what are called "unregistered"?—Yes.

4672. Evidence has been given to the Committee by Mr. Cleveland, I think, certainly by others, that there is a strong objection to any societies being unregistered?—Yes; Mr. Cleveland said so.

4673. He expressed it as his opinion that all societies having to do with death insurance should be registered; is that your opinion?—Yes, I think so.

4674. You would have no objection to your own societies being all of them required to be registered?—Speaking personally, I think they are better for being registered; but I do not wish to say officially that I think they ought to be.

4675. What has been the rate of sickness of the members for the last five years?—In 1885 the average of the sickness experienced amongst our juvenile members was 2·61 days per member for the year. In 1886 it was 2·78 days, in 1887 it was 2·62, in 1888 it was 2·61, and last year, 1889, it was 2·45; showing the lowest average sickness over the five years to have been that of last year.

4676. Will you state the amount of contributions paid and the benefits received by the juvenile members?—They vary in every case; we put no restriction upon our societies with reference to the amount of benefits or contribution. The only restriction with reference to benefit is that imposed by the Friendly Societies Act, so that it would be almost impossible to state what would be the average amount. During the course of our inquiries many of them sent up a return of their contributions and benefits, which I have here,

E E 2

and

Chairman--continued.

and I will hand them all in if you do not object. I have in my hand those of the Juvenile Branch of Court Windsor held at Great Yarmouth; in that case their entrance fee, from 5 to 9, is 1 *s.*, and the contribution paid by a child of that age would be 4 *d.* per month. From 9 to 12 the entrance fee is 1 *s.* 6 *d.*, and the contributions 6 *d.*; from 12 to 15, 2 *s.* entrance fee and 8 *d.* per month contribution; from 15 to 17 the entrance fee is 2 *s.* 6 *d.*, and 10 *d.* a month contribution. The benefits would be, from 5 to 9 years of age during sickness, medical attendance and medicine; from 9 years till 12 years of age the sick benefit would be 2 *s.* per week; from 12 to 15 it would be 3 *s.* per week; and from 15 to 18 it would be 5 *s.* per week. In the case of death, from 9 to 12, the amount payable would be 1 *l.* 5 *s.*, from 12 to 15, 2 *l.*; and from 15 to 18, 3 *l.*; there are a number of others here; they all vary a little, more or less, from the figures I have given.

4677. Then in all other matters about which you have to give evidence we may take Mr. Cleveland as fairly representing your views and those of your society?—You may.

4678. Is there anything that you would like to add further to what Mr. Cleveland has said?—There is nothing. Mr. Cleveland has covered the ground to our satisfaction.

Marquess of *Lothian.*

4679. I think you mentioned that of the 1,279 societies, there were only 49 which allowed membership under the age of three years?—Yes.

4680. Can you give the Committee an idea at all what is the number of membership of those 49 societies?—I could not give you that; I have not added the membership together, but speaking from memory, they are only small societies; they are not the largest societies in numbers.

4681. Do none of the largest admit members under the age of three?—Not the large societies.

4682. As a matter of fact some of the other societies admit members in large numbers under that age?—Yes, they do.

4683. Then, in reference to your Query No. 10, I do not think that has been referred to in your evidence; the question is, "Have you any objection to reducing the amount payable at death?" Could you tell me at all what the answers to that question were?—A large number said they had objections; but in no case at present does the amount that we give at death, reach the limit, or would it reach the limit suggested by his Lordship in his Bill.

4684. What is the amount you generally pay?—It varies. I should think that out of 20 or 30 societies there would not be two alike in regard to amount.

4685. What would be the maximum?—I should say the maximum would be about 8 *l.*

4686. What would it be at five years of age?—It cannot be more than 6 *l.*, and I should say the average would be 3 *l.*; some might be 4 *l.* and some only 2 *l.* I think 3 *l.* would be the average.

Earl of *Harrowby.*

4687. Does your society insure all the members' children on birth?—No.

Earl of *Harrowby*—continued.

4688. I thought you took the children of members, and not the children of outsiders?—We have not that distinction which Mr. Cleveland drew; it has not obtained much in our order to do what Mr. Cleveland said he had done, namely, to make any special benefit for the children of members. Ours are societies separately registered and separately managed, but still belonging to our order.

4689. This is not a feature of your order?—No; we have only 11 societies which take them at one day old out of 1,279.

4690. Your association has specially in view the raising of the whole moral condition of the working classes?—Yes.

4691. Therefore, you are very watchful of anything that would dissuade the young from joining you?—Yes.

4692. Because you think that if you get them young they are likely to be embarked in the whole thing as they grow up?—That is so; we receive between 4,000 and 5,000 every year, who are transferred from the juvenile society into the parent order as members, and we think that by enlarging our scope with reference to our juvenile members a still larger number would be added to the parent body.

4693. You look to enlarging your parent body by still further enlarging your work amongst the younger members?—Yes.

4694. Mr. Cleveland told us that the societies he represented would cordially co-operate in stamping out what is admitted to be a great evil?—Yes.

4695. I suppose your society takes that view?—Yes, when the existence of the evil is proved.

4696. He said "undoubtedly," so that there is something that we have to struggle against in this matter; I want to know what that meant, "stamping out what is undoubtedly a great evil"?—I say we should be very anxious to stamp out an acknowledged evil; as to whether this particular matter is an acknowledged evil that is another matter.

4697. I am not supposing it affects the great bulk of the working classes?—We are anxious for the advancement of the working classes by any means.

Earl *Beauchamp.*

4698. You think that anything that tended to check thrift would act very injuriously upon the working classes?—It would.

4699. And you think that any serious restrictions, as at present proposed by law, in respect of child insurance, would tend to discourage thrift?—I think they would.

4700. Insurance for funeral expenses is not perhaps the highest form of thrift, but it has a very educating effect; is that your view?—We have found it so.

4701. Those who begin to insure for the burial expenses of their children are led on to practice thrift in other respects?—Yes, and to provide in many ways by co-operation for their wants.

4702. And

Earl *Beauchamp*—continued.

4702. And the benefits which accrue to the working classes by the practice of thrift are largely in excess of any benefits that may be derived by the ratepayer in the mere keeping down of the rates?—Yes.

4703. No doubt it is an advantage to keep the rates at a very low point?—It is, to the rate-payer.

4704. But the development of the independence of the working classes is a far higher object?—Yes; we believe that that is the object of our society; that is the doctrine we teach.

The Witness is directed to withdraw.

Earl *Beauchamp*—continued.

Mr. THOMAS WALTON, is called in; and Examined, as follows:

Chairman.

4705. YOU appear here as one of the deputation on behalf of the affiliated orders?—Yes, I may say that I am the senior director of the Manchester Unity of Odd Fellows, and I am a member of the Town Council of Southampton.

4706. Have you heard the evidence which has been given by those who join you in this representation. Mr. Cleveland and Mr. Stead?—Yes.

4707. May we take it that you agree with all that they have said?—I thoroughly agree with the opinions they have expressed.

4708. And also with the facts and statistics which they have furnished so far as you are acquainted with them?—Yes, I think that they very fairly represent my own society.

4709. I suppose we may take you as accepting their evidence; is there anything you would wish to add to what those witnesses have stated? —There was a question with reference to benefits at respective ages. Speaking for my own particular district of Southampton and the neighbourhood, I find the funeral benefit varies, beginning at eight years of age, and going as low as three years of age, and we have in the Southampton district some 22 of those societies

4710. I do not quite understand your answer; you say it begins at eight, and goes down to three?—Some of the societies give funeral benefit not before eight years of age, and some as early as three years.

4711. Will you tell the Committee what proportion there are which give it at eight, and how many of them give it as low as three years of age?—There is only one that gives it as low as three years of age, and one at eight; the rest of them are at six years of age.

4712. The average do not give funeral benefits until six years of age?—That is so.

4713. There is only one that goes as low as three years of age, and only one that goes as high as eight?—Yes.

4714. Out of how many societies?—Out of those 22 in and about Southampton.

4715. What is the amount of funeral benefit, generally speaking, taking the highest and the lowest; what is the amount given in the case of the death of a child three years of age?— £. 1. 10 *s.*, increasing by increments of say 10 *s.* per year, till it attains a maximum varying from 3 *l.* 10 *s.* to 10 *l.* at the age of 18.

4716. But what is it up to 10 years of age, which is the limit fixed in the Act?—Up to 10 years of age the highest that we have had is 10*l.*, but that is one solitary example; in the others it is 2 *l.* and 3 *l.*

(142.)

Chairman—continued.

4717. Upon the funeral benefit 3 *l.* you said was the average?—£. 3 would be the average funeral benefit that we pay at 10 years of age.

4718. What is the average funeral benefit that you pay at three years and six months?— £. 1. 10 *s.*

4719. That funeral benefit, I presume, is for funeral expenses?—It is paid to the relatives.

4720. It is paid to the relatives for death expenses?—Yes.

4721. As a rule, are the members of your society satisfied with that amount?—I think so, because, as I say, they get medical attendance and medicine and sick pay as well.

4722. And they are satisfied when they receive for all these purposes 30 *s.* funeral benefit?— I am not quite prepared to answer that question as to whether they are satisfied; at any rate, there has been no attempt to alter the rules.

4723. Your societies are governed by the members generally, are they not?—Yes.

4724. Consequently, if they were generally dissatisfied with the rules, they would alter them?—It is clear they do not join with any mercenary object.

4725. They have not asked to have the amount raised?—No; but I think there is every probability that they will ask to do so as they get into better circumstances.

4726. During your past experience you have not formed any movement in that direction?— The society I am more particularly acquainted with was established 28 years ago.

4727. During that time you are not acquainted with any great movement for increasing this amount?—No; I think I may explain why: that there is the idea of keeping money more particularly in the society, because, when they arrive at the age of 18, from that time until they arrive at 21, we pay a portion of their subscriptions or contributions into the parent society.

4728. Then, in fact, your society is rather more in the direction of what we may call life insurance than of death insurance?—They cease belonging to a juvenile society at the age of 18 years.

4729. The operations of your society rather tend to the preservation of life?—Exactly. We look upon the juvenile societies as moral nurseries for the juveniles. We look upon it that the earlier we can inculcate habits of thrift and providence, the better it will be, not only for our society, but for society at large. I may say that last year we brought in 3,397 of the juvenile members into the parent soceity.

E E 3

4730. In

Chairman—continued.

4730. In the case of a child insured for death benefit who lives on to the age of 18, and then becomes, if I understand you, an adult in your society, what do you do with the policy; the child does not die: does the child, when it reaches the age of 18, get the policy paid to it, or is there any payment made to the child when he does not die, but lives to the age of 18?—He is drafted into the parent society in any lodge he desires to enter; his entrance fee is paid for him, and a portion of his contributions is also paid to his credit to the lodge which he joins till he reaches the age of 21; so that that materially reduces the amount which he has to pay during those three years which may be possibly the last three years of his apprenticeship.

4731. Then he or his family receives certain advantages by his life being insured up to the age of 18?—Yes; and the society also gains in like manner.

4732. What is the weekly contribution you receive from your members?—It varies; beginning (on the rule I have here) at the age from eight to 12, it is 8 d. a month; that will give a benefit of 2 s. per week for the first six months' sickness, and 1 s. per week for the next six months; 6 d. per week for the rest of the sickness, and 1 l. 10 s. at death. Taking the next class, when he arrives at the age of 12, from 12 to 14, his contribution is 10 d. per month; he then receives 3 s. per week in sickness for the first six months; 1 s. 6 d. for the next six months; and 9 d. for the remainder of the sickness, and 2 l. in the event of death. When he arrives at the age of 14, from 14 to 16, his contribution is 1 s. per month, and he then receives 4 s. per week in sickness for the first six months; 2 s. per week for the next six months; and 1 s. for the remainder, and 3 l. at death. Then when he gets to the age of 16 he gets to the maximum, his contribution is 1 s. 4 d. a month, and he receives for sick benefit 6 s. for the first six months; 3 s. for the next six months; and 1 s. 6 d. for the remainder, and 4 l. at death.

4733. Do you find that those children begin making payments by themselves out of their own earnings early in life, or are those payments made for them by their parents generally?—I should imagine in great measure the payment is made by the children themselves; this particular one is the largest juvenile concern in the whole county; there are about 1,500 members belonging to it, and from the noise they kick up on their contribution nights, I should imagine that most of the children come and pay themselves, and not their parents.

4734. With regard to these contribution nights, are there places or offices were those contributions are paid?—The school-room is used for that purpose.

4735. You agree with Mr. Stead in saying you do not employ collecting agents?—We employ no collecting agents; the business is managed by the parent committee, who give their services gratuitously. The question has become an extremely oppressive subject with us who have been connected with this particular concern for the last 28 years; we look with apprehension at the step which has been taken, although in a

Chairman—continued.

monetary point of view it will not make any difference to us.

4736. What step do you refer to?—I refer more particularly to the undertaker clause.

4737. But the undertaker clause, as you are aware, has gone out of the Bill; it is some days since the undertaker clause was withdrawn from the Bill?—I may say that we are endeavouring, as far as we possibly can, to promote habits of thrift, beginning at very early ages, and that we do deprecate any undue interference which may be made with our efforts.

4738. But it would appear that the scale of payments proposed in the first clause of this Bill would not practically touch your members, inasmuch as the scale, if I am not mistaken, is rather higher than your average scale?—It is so.

4739. Then that same clause extends what is called the protection age up to 14; the law now protects by limitation of death benefit, up to 10 years, and the Bill proposes to extend it to 14; that, I presume, would in no way touch your society?—Not in a monetary point of view, because, as a matter of fact, our scale is lower than the minimum that you have put in the Bill.

4740. In point of fact, if my scale were adopted it would be a higher scale than the one you now work upon?—Yes.

Marquess of *Lothian.*

4741. Do you agree with what I understand Mr. Cleveland's opinion to be, that you desire in your society to alter the conditions imposed by the Friendly Societies Act, so as to be able to insure children under three years?—I think that would be very beneficial.

4742. You would then be in a position of being able better to compete with some of the collecting societies or commercial societies?—I have not the slightest doubt of it.

4743. Have you many of them in your district?—A large number, more especially the Prudential and the Royal Liver.

4744. Are they more or less supported than your society?—There is this to be said about them, that their collectors go from door to door, and it is less trouble for the parents to pay when called upon than to take it to some central place.

4745. That plan enables them to compete to your disadvantage?—Yes.

4746. Can you hold your own when this competition takes place?—Speaking for my own town I should say that we do well hold our own against the collecting societies.

Earl of *Selborne.*

4747. You spoke of Southampton and the neighbourhood; do you include Portsmouth?—No, except so far as this, that part of the Southampton district takes in one of our lodges in Portsmouth.

4748. Is there much difference between your terms of insurance and those which prevail in the other societies which insure in the neighbourhood?—As regards the affiliated societies there is very little difference indeed.

4749. So

Earl of *Selborne*—continued.

4749. So that one may take it that so far as the affiliated societies go, your experience represents or nearly represents that of the whole district we will say, and perhaps all the considerable towns in the county?—Exactly so.

4750. Is there much insurance in the rural parts of the county?—So far as my own society is concerned, which takes in the southern part of Hampshire, we have 11,000 adult members and 33,000 juvenile members.

4751. I suppose your knowledge may not extend to other parts of the southern counties of England, does it?—I should say the south of England would compare very favourably indeed with any of the other parts of the country for thrift and providence.

4752. As far as your knowledge goes, may one say that your figures would probably agree with those of other friendly societies in other parts of the south of England?—Yes, I think so; the Foresters, ourselves, and the Hampshire Friendly Society, I should take it, are the three leading friendly societies in the south of England.

4753. You spoke just now of the tendency to increase the amount insured with the improvement of the circumstances of the insuring class; may I infer that, according to your observation, the circumstances in that part of the country of the working classes are improving?—I should think so; the wages have increased to some appreciable extent, and also, more than that, the habits of thrift and providence which have been inculcated have led to an improvement in the condition of the people. I may tell the Committee in passing that our own society, and the Foresters also, have only been established there 50 years, and there has been scarcely time yet to educate the working classes up to the necessity of making due provision.

Lord *Thring.*

4754. Would you recommend any legislation with respect to collecting societies to restrict them?—I scarcely feel competent to express an opinion upon that matter; it is outside our scope. What I would suggest, and I think Mr. Cleveland suggested it also, was that if any legislation takes place at all it should be to separate the two classes of societies, because they are entirely distinct. In ours and the Foresters, and all affiliated societies, the societies are managed by the members themselves. In collecting societies they are managed for the members; a very wide difference.

4755. What would be the good of separation unless you had some particular law which applied to you which did not apply to others?—That would be necessary, I suppose, if the present Act were divided or a fresh Act made.

4756. What would you suggest?—We think it very unfair that we should be subject to the same kind of odium which often attaches to collecting friendly societies.

4757. But what legislation would you suggest?—I think that point was dwelt upon last year by a Committee of the House of Commons, which sat with regard to this very point, and I am under the impression that they went very exhaustively into the subject.

(142.)

Lord *Thring*—continued.

4758. They did; but they did not make, so far as I can recollect, any very explicit suggestions as to what should be done?—I think, as far as we are concerned, we are very well satisfied indeed with the Act of Parliament; there are some minor matters that we should like to see remedied.

4759. You would wish for an Act of Parliament without any special legislative provisions applying to the one or the other?—Yes.

Earl of *Harrowby.*

4760. Your very remarkable success has been owing to the extremely hard work done during those 50 years by those who are interested in the success of these societies?—That is so.

4761. So, naturally, you would be very jealous of anything that would interfere with the results of your work?—Our societies have been remarked upon in such complimentary terms during those 50 years in respect of the manner in which we did our business that we are naturally jealous of any imputations which we do not deserve.

4762. But, putting aside any consideration of that kind, you are interested in watching very narrowly anything that might check this great effort at self-help which you have been carrying on?—It is in response to that that we are here to-day.

Earl *Beauchamp.*

4763. I understand you to say that the adoption of the scale proposed in the Bill would not affect the monetary position of your society?—It would not affect the monetary position of our society.

4764. Would it affect it in any other way?—Yes, I am afraid it would have an injurious effect upon our members, as implying that we are not competent to attend to our own business, and that we have to be legislated for in a way that we think unwise.

4765. May I take it that societies like yours object very much to what you would call "grandmotherly legislation"?—Yes, that has been the stock phrase with us; when Members of Parliament have attended our annual gatherings, and the question has been put to us, what do you want? the reply we have given has been, " To be severely left alone."

4766. The place to which your juvenile members bring their contributions is usually a school, but your meetings are not held in a school; where would they be held?—Sometimes they would be held in a room attached to a public-house to which there is a private entrance, so that the members would not have to go through the house.

4767. And in other cases?—That would cover it all, I think.

4768. Do I understand you to say that in all cases where the meeting would be held at a public-house, it would be in a public-house to which there was a separate entrance, and not in the public-house itself?—That is so; we should not tolerate children having to pay in in a public-house.

Chairman.

4769. In the event of any persons joining your society, and afterwards becoming disreputable,

E E 4   have

224   MINUTES:—SELECT COMMITTEE ON CHILDREN'S LIFE INSURANCE BILL [H.L.]

25 *July* 1890.]   Mr. WALTON.   [*Continued.*

Chairman—continued.

have you no power of weeding your society of such persons; could you expel them?—Yes, anyone guilty of disgraceful conduct subjects himself to expulsion.

4770. Any person becoming a drunkard, or leading an immoral life?—That would be a matter of degree, unless the charge were brought against him for committing some offence against the rules for which he could be punished.

4771. An offence against the rules would be probably some offence with reference to payments, and so on; but I am speaking of a person originally respectable and turning out, as unfortunately some persons will, disreputable; have you any power of turning him out as a person can be turned out of a club?—That only can be done by a charge being preferred against him that he had been guilty of conduct disgraceful or disreputable.

Chairman—continued.

4772. Who would bring the charge?—Generally his brother members.

4773. And the matter would have to come before the committee?—It would.

Earl of *Selborne.*

4774. Is it likely that such a charge would be preferred unless it had been a matter of judicial inquiry?—I do not think it would, unless it was a matter of notoriety.

Chairman.

4775. I am speaking of such a thing as drunkenness; would that be a matter for expulsion?— I scarcely think it would.

The Witness is directed to withdraw.

Ordered,— That this Committee be adjourned *sine die.*

A P P E N D I X.

F f

LIST OF APPENDIX.

A P P E N D I X.

APPENDIX A.

PAPERS handed in by Mr. *William Crooks*, 11 July 1890.

BILLS OF FUNERAL EXPENSES.

London, 26th February 1873.

Mr. Crooks, *Dr.* to G. Westbrook, Furnishing Undertaker, 12, High-street, Poplar, opposite North-street.

Funerals at stated Charges.

Monuments, Head and Foot Stones, &c., erected in a superior manner.

For the funeral of the late Matilda Faith Crooks, died 20th February 1873, aged three months.

	£.	s.	d.
Inch elm coffin, covered white, neatly furnished, lined bed and pillow, winding sheets, fittings, and pall; mourning coach with one horse, and attendance to the Tower Hamlets Cemetery - - - - - - - - - -	1	8	—
Fees at the cemetery - - - - - - - - - - - - -	—	15	—

Settled, 29th March 1873, *G. Westbrook.*

12, Hardy-street, and

26, Great George-street, Liverpool, October 1873.

Mr. Crooks, *Dr.* to George Bowring, General Undertaker.

Superior Hearses and Mourning Coaches.

	£.	s.	d.
Car to necropolis, oak coffin, gown, pall - - - - - - -	1	10	6

Settled, same time, *George Bowring.*

London, March 1882.

Mr. Crooks, *Dr.* to Alfred Burridge & Co., Funeral Furnishers and Carriage Masters, 56, Robinhood-lane, Poplar, and 233, High-street, Stratford.

Distance no object. Orders by post and telegrams immediately attended to.

	£.	s.	d.
To the funeral of the late Ada Caroline Crooks, who departed this life 7th March 1882, aged one year six months, as agreed, cemetery fees, &c., at Bow - - - - - - - - - - - - - - -	2	7	—

Received the above, *Alfred Burridge.*

APPENDIX B.

PAPER handed in by the *Chairman*.

BOROUGH OF GREAT YARMOUTH.

THE Presentment of the Grand Jury at the General Quarter Sessions of the Peace for the Borough of Great Yarmouth, holden at the Town Hall in the said Borough on Monday the 7th day of July 1890.

The Grand Jury is of opinion that in the case of insurance with Herbert Twitchett, an imbecile, which has been before them, it would be a good opportunity to make a presentment to the Recorder, that lunatics and imbeciles should be included in the Bill now before the House of Lords, and that the Recorder should convey this presentment to the proper quarter.

A. S. Hewitt.	Joseph Rant.
W. P. Fulcher.	James Leggett.
W. E. Sacret.	S. J. Ramsey.
H. S. Lane.	J. Hastings.
W. Johnson.	Geo. Baker.
W. J. Denew.	Robt. H. Cooper.
H. W. Turrill.	George H. Self.
W. Fitch.	Thos. V. Doughty.
G. C. Kew.	H. V. Brand.

APPENDIX C.

PAPER handed in by the *Chairman.*

LETTER of *E. B. Thorneycroft,* Deputy Coroner for Wolverhampton.

25, King-street, Wolverhampton,
8 July 1890.

Dear Sir,

I HAVE read the Children's Life Insurance Bill, which you were good enough to send to me, and if passed into law it would, I think, do much towards decreasing the insurance of infants, and as a consequence, in my humble opinion, death among children.   Insurance is not so much traceable to the desire of parents generally to insure their infants as to the manner in which the insurance companies, who lay themselves out for this class of insurance, conduct their business.   As the law now stands, these companies are free to continue their present mode of touting for the insurance ; local men are employed thickly on the ground, and immediately a child is born, and, to my personal knowledge, even before birth, the parent is canvassed and shown the advantages of insurance, and is generally found quite willing to pay the small weekly contribution of, say one penny, and thereby secure a small sum on the death of the child.

I have many times thought, and said, that parents in such circumstances of life as these people are should not be permitted to make a gain, not even the smallest, by the death of a child; but the money is undoubtedly too great a temptation in many cases, especially in times of bad trade, and more especially when either parent may be of intemperate habits or of a disposition tending to evil.

It is difficult to detect as cases come before the coroner when systematic neglect or slow starvation have been adopted, and it is more difficult still to obtain such conclusive evidence as the judges require to put a parent upon his or her trial for manslaughter. The Act of last year for the prevention of cruelty to children is doing good work, and when one considers that it is the commonest occurrence to find that a woman among the lower classes has borne 10 or more children, it is time that more stringent legislation for the protection of infant life were adopted.

For a time I was in some doubt as to whether the insurance of children was for good or evil on the whole, for the working classes, even the most thrifty, in many cases do not get the means to save in this part of the country, and in case of death the insurance money comes in most usefully, for the better class of the people have the greatest horror of seeking the aid of the parish.   I came to the conclusion, however, long since, that the insurance as the system at present prevails is bad and wrong, and ought to be prevented. Why should people desire to insure their children at all?   In my opinion it is with an object of personal gain in many cases, and a hope of one day receiving the money. I would prohibit such insurance of all children under five years old, and then only to be in one insurance office, and on strict conditions for the benefit of the child at certain stages of age.   A policy of this description should be under a very small premium.

I would encourage burial clubs established on sound bases (as these may be open to great abuse), but under which no money would pass to the parent, but with, however, some provision for small articles of slight mourning.   I have not taken statistics, but I should say that there are many more suspicious deaths of insured infants than uninsured.

A great many deaths of careless but innocent overlying occur, and also where the parents do not send for the doctor in time; this, however, very often occurs through lack of means or ignorance.   An offence, in degree short of manslaughter, and which the Act for the prevention of cruelty to children does not touch, might be created with much advantage to the protection of child life.

I am, &c.
(signed)   *Edward B. Thorneycroft.*

Rev. Benjamin Waugh,
Society for Prevention of Cruelty to Children,
7, Harpur-street, Bloomsbury, London, W.C.

APPENDIX D.

PAPER handed in by the *Chairman*.

LETTERS from the Town Clerk of *Nottingham*.

Infant Life Protection.

Sir,   Guildhall, Nottingham, 20 February 1890.
I HAVE this morning received a copy of the Infant Life Protection Bill brought in by yourself and Mr. Stuart-Wortley.

Enclosed I send you a copy of a letter written by me in December last to the Local Government Board, at the instance of my health committee, pointing out the need for legislation with regard to the insurance of children.

It seems to me that clauses to deal with this matter might be appropriately inserted in the above Bill, and my committee will be-glad if you will take the question into consideration.

                                        I am, &c.
To Her Majesty's Secretary of State   (signed)   *Samuel George Johnson*,
    for the Home Department.   Town Clerk.

                          Town Clerk's Department, Guildhall, Nottingham,
Sir,   11 December 1889.
I AM requested by my health committee to ask you to call the serious attention of your Board to a great and growing evil, viz., the insurance of the lives of young children.

Some notice of this has been taken in the recent Act for the protection of children, by which the penalty for wilful neglect is doubled where the person having charge of the child has insured its life.

A bad case has recently occurred here, and proceedings have been taken under the Act, and both parents imprisoned. One child died and was found to be insured, as well as other children, who had been all shamefully neglected.

It appears to be the custom with the insurance companies not to require medical examination where the amount insured does not exceed 50 *l.*; and the result is that children who are weakly or actually seriously ill are often insured, and no care taken of them, and no medical assistance obtained, and in the case before mentioned the children are frequently wilfully neglected.

The views taken by parents of the question of insurance may be gathered from the following facts: a woman living in this town was recently asked by a medical man why the only child insured was one who was ill and delicate. The reply was, "Why, the others are well and strong; why should I insure them?"

I am credibly informed that this is not an isolated case, but represents the feeling of many parents of the poorer classes who insure their children.

My committee suggest that your Board should introduce into Parliament a Bill:—

1. To make it compulsory on the insurance company to give the local authority public notice of the insurance of every child of tender years, and of any change of residence.

2. To make it compulsory to give full particulars to the local authority of the death of every child a certain time before any money is paid over, that the local authority may have time to make inquiries.

3. To confer on the local authority and their officers, including sanitary inspectors and police, authority to enter any house in which any insured child is kept or has died, for the purpose of making inquiries and ascertaining such information as may be necessary as to the condition of such child.

I enclose a copy report of the case.
My committee will be glad to hear that your Board will take the matter into consideration.

                                        I am, &c.
To the Secretary,   (signed)   *Samuel George Johnson*,
Local Government Board, Whitehall,   Town Clerk.
    London, S.W.

APPENDIX E.

PAPERS handed in by Mr. *Dewey*.

PRUDENTIAL ASSURANCE COMPANY, LIMITED (INDUSTRIAL BRANCH).

REGULATIONS for INFANTILE ASSURANCE.—EXTRACTS from Printed Instructions issued to each Agent of the Company.

CLAUSE 49.—All infantile assurances are effected under the provisions of the Friendly Societies Act, 1875, and the clauses relating to infantile assurance must be strictly adhered to.

Clause 50.—Under this Act proposals cannot be entertained on the lives of children under 10 years of age unless they are proposed for assurance by one of their parents ; but if both parents are dead, an assurance may be effected by a relative, provided such relative has undertaken the support of the child.

Clause 51.—Children under five years of age cannot be assured for more than 6 *l.*, and this sum must include assurances in all companies or societies. If, therefore, a child is proposed to be assured with this company, and it is assured for 6 *l.* in another company or society, the proposal cannot be entertained. If the child is assured in another company or society, and all the assurances, inclusive of the amount proposed to be effected by this company, do not exceed 6 *l.*, the proposal may be taken, and the names of the companies or societies, and amount assured in such companies or societies, must be entered on the proposal in reply to the question therein asked.

Clause 52.—Children of five years and under 10 years of age can be assured for 10 *l.*, but this sum must include all the assurances effected in this and other companies or societies, as explained in the previous clause.

Clause 53.—Children may be proposed for assurance when 14 days old, but illegitimate children will not be accepted until they have attained the age of three years.

Clause 54.—One penny per week is the highest premium that can be taken until the child is 10 years of age.

Clause 124.—Policies issued under the infantile table must be three calendar months in force at the time of the death of the assured before any claim can be admitted ; for instance, no claim could be made on a policy issued on 1st January until on or after 1st April. The payment of 13 weeks' premiums does not entitle the parents to a claim under a policy.

Clause 134.—The Friendly Societies Act provides that when a death takes place of any child under 10 years of age, one of the parents only of the child can receive the money ; should the parents be dead, an application must be made to the chief office.

Clause 141.—By Clause 28 of the Friendly Societies Act, 1875, no sum can be paid on the death of a child under 10 years of age until the registrar's certificate has been produced to the company.

Clause 144.—You should examine the certificate and see that the registrar has entered the name of the company, the correct amount payable, and also whether the certificate is the " first," " second," or " third " form issued, or delay in the payment of the claim may occur. If the certificate is not the " first," the name of the company, society, or club to whom the previous certificate or certificates were given, together with the amount for which they were granted, should be stated on the claim form.

EXTRACTS from Printed Instructions on Form of Claim.

If a child, was it assured in any other company or society ? If so, give the name and amount to be received.

This question need only be answered when deceased is under 10 years of age, and the registrar's certificate is other than the first.

C.—As to policies issued under the infantile table, if the child should die within three calendar months from date of policy, no amount will be payable ; for instance, no claim can be made on such a policy issued on 1st January unless death occurs on or after 1st April. The payment of thirteen weeks' premiums does not give a right to claim under an infantile policy.

I.—The Friendly Societies Act provides that when a death takes place of any child under 10 years of age the parent only of the child can receive the money ; should the parents be dead, an application must be made to the chief office.

L.—By Clause 28 of the Friendly Societies Act, 1875. no sum can be paid on the death of a child under 10 years of age until the registrar's certificate has been produced to the company.

L Division.—LONDON.

INDUSTRIAL BRANCH.
[*Form No. 4.*]

No.

Agent at   under the Superintendency of Mr.

PRUDENTIAL ASSURANCE COMPANY, LIMITED, Chief Office:—HOLBORN BARS, LONDON.

INFANTILE PROPOSAL.—All Infantile Policies are issued subject to the provisions of the Friendly Societies Act.

The Policy to be issued on this proposal will contain a condition that it will be rendered absolutely void if it be in any way assigned, sold, mortgaged, or otherwise parted with.

DECLARATION TO BE SIGNED BY THE PARENT.

Being desirous of effecting an Assurance on the life of my child in the Industrial Branch of the Prudential Assurance Company, Limited, in accordance with this proposal, and upon the terms to be contained in such Policy as shall be granted in pursuance thereof, I declare that all the answers to the questions on the other side hereof are strictly correct, and that I have withheld no material information, and I agree that such answers shall be the basis of the contract for such Assurance.

I certify that I saw the parent duly sign this proposal.

Dated this   day of   189

The father or mother of the } child must sign here   }

Agent

No one must sign the proposal for or on behalf of the father or mother, one of whom must sign it personally. If unable to write, the father or mother must make his or her mark, which must be attested in the same manner as a signature.

CERTIFICATE OF AGENT.

I have this   day of   189   , personally seen the child mentioned on the other side, and am of opinion that   he is in*   health, and that h   appearance indicates that   he is of the age which is stated, and I recommend the Directors to accept the proposal, at   † class rates.

(Signature of Agent)

* State whether good, indifferent, or bad, as the case may be.
† Fill in at first-class rates, or second, or third, as the case may be.

Approved{

For use at Chief Office.

TABLE OF SUMS PAYABLE FOR ONE PENNY WEEKLY.
(No Higher Premium can be taken.)

	Amount payable if the Child should die after the Policy has been issued for										
	Three Calendar Months.	Six Calendar Months.	One Year.	Two Years.	Three Years.	Four Years.	Five Years.	Six Years.	Seven Years.	Eight Years.	Nine Years.	Ten Years.
AGE AT ENTRY:	£. s.	£. s.	£. s.	£. s.	£. s.	£. s.	£. s.	£. s.	£. s.	£. s.	£. s.	£. s.
1 year next birthday -	1 10	2 10	3 –	3 10	4 –	4 10	5 –	6 –	7 –	8 –	9 –	10 –
2 years „ -	1 15	3 –	3 10	4 –	4 10	5 –	6 –	7 –	8 –	9 –	10 –	
3 „ „ -	2 –	3 10	4 –	4 10	5 –	6 –	7 –	8 –	9 –	10 –		
4 „ „ -	2 5	4 –	4 10	5 –	6 –	7 –	8 –	9 –	10 –			
5 „ „ -	2 10	4 10	5 –	6 –	7 –	8 –	9 –	10 –				
6 „ „ -	3 –	5 –	6 –	7 –	8 –	9 –	10 –					
7 „ „ -	3 10	5 –	7 –	8 –	9 –	10 –						
8 „ „ -	4 –	5 –	8 –	9 –	10 –							
9 „ „ -	4 10	5 –	9 –	10 –								
10 „ „ -	5 –	5 –	10 –									

If the child should die within three calendar months from the date of the policy no amount will be payable.

IT is essential to the VALIDITY of the ASSURANCE that the QUESTIONS be truly and correctly answered.

QUESTIONS.	ANSWERS.
1. Name of father? (In full.)	
2. Is he alive?	
3. Name of mother? (In full.)	
4. Is she alive?	
5. Residence of parents? (Fill in the town as well as the street.) Note.—The full postal address where the parents actually reside must be given.	
6. Occupation of parents?	
7. Name of child? (In full.)	
8. What is the child's age next birthday? (The greatest accuracy is necessary in answering this question.)	Exd. { } For use at Chief Office.
9. Day, month, and year of birth of child?	day of 18
10. Amount of weekly premium to be paid?	One Penny.
11. Is the child now in good health?	
12. Is the child ruptured or deformed in any way? If so, give particulars in full.	
13. Have either of the parents, or any of the brothers or sisters, died from consumption, or is any relation at present suffering from that disease?	
14. Have any of the brothers or sisters of the child died? If so, state ages and the causes of death?	
15. When and from what complaints has the child at any time suffered?	
16. Has the child's life been proposed before to this Company?	
17. Was the proposal accepted or declined?	
18. Is any policy now in force on the child's life with this Company?	
19. Is the child assured in any other company or society?	Names of companies or societies (To be answered if child is already assured.) Amount of assurance, £. : : (To be answered if child is already assured.)

EXTRACT FROM FRIENDLY SOCIETIES ACT, 1875.

No Society shall insure or pay on the death of a child under five years of age any sum of money which, added to any amount payable on the death of such child by any other Society, exceeds six pounds, or on the death of a child under 10 years of age any sum of money which, added to any amount payable on the death of such child by any other Society, exceeds 10 pounds.

PAPER handed in by Mr. *Taunton*.

Y.

If Immediate Benefit is required.	Time and place (Surgery or otherwise) for Medical Examination if required by the Committee.
State whether Quarter, Halfs or Full.	Time
	Place {

ROYAL LIVER FRIENDLY SOCIETY, Chief Offices—Prescot Street, Liverpool.

PROPOSAL FORM FOR INDUSTRIAL TABLES.

District of   Agent

Canvasser   Collector

Table.	Date Entered. Monday's Date.	Age next Birth-day.	Pay Weekly.	Sum Assured.			If an Increase, insert the word "Increase."	Policy Number (to be filled in at Chief Office).	Initials of Policy Writers.
				£.	s.	d.			

QUESTIONS.	ANSWERS BY PROPOSER.						
1. What are the full Names of the proposed Member? (The correct spelling of the names must be given.)							
2. Full Postal Address and Residence of proposed Member { (A) No. of House (B) Name of Street (C) Name of Town	(A) (B) (C)						
3. Is the proposed Member now in good health?							
4. Is proposed Member now, or has proposed Member ever been, afflicted with Asthma, Cough, Disease of Lungs or Heart, Dropsy, Fits, Gout, Palsy, Rupture, Spitting of Blood, or any other complaint tending to shorten life?							
	Date.	Age.	Pay.	Amount.		Table.	Collector.
				£.	s.	d.		
5. Is proposed Member already insured in this Society? If so, state full particulars.							

☞ DECLARATION. (This Declaration must be read over to the Proposer before the Form is Signed.)

Being desirous of effecting an Assurance under the Industrial Tables of the Royal Liver Friendly Society, in accordance with this Proposal, I declare that all the above Answers are strictly correct, and that I have withheld no material information with which the Committee of Management should be made acquainted. I agree that such Answers shall be the basis of the contract between me and the said Society, for effecting the Assurance hereby proposed, and that any misstatement of the above facts shall render void any policy issued there. And I also agree that such Assurance shall be subject in all respects to the rules (present and future) of the Society.

Signature, or mark of Proposer,

Address in full,

Witness to Signature

(A neighbour in preference, but Agent, Collector, or Canvasser may sign) }

Address   Date   18

I certify that I have recently seen proposed Member, that the above Answers were made by Proposer, and that the life is a good one and fit for acceptance.

Signature of Collector,

☞ Not more than one month's contributions (from date of entry) must be received for above Assurance until this Proposal Form has been accepted by the Committee of Management.

☞ Only those having an insurable interest therein may effect an assurance on the life of another.

☞ To be filled in at Chief Office. Checked by and Date Checked,

The Report of Doctor or Life Inspector (when same is required) must be attached here.

Agents and Collectors must not write Memorandum on these documents   Their remarks or observations on the lives proposed must be written on the Official Stationery provided for the purpose.

☞ TO BE FILLED IN AT CHIEF OFFICE ONLY.

Date received at Chief Offices

Acceptance or Rejection Stamp

APPENDIX G.

PAPER handed in by Mr. *Fortune.*

FORM OF POLICY.

Industrial Branch.—Policy Form (A) No. 15.

Table B.—Infantile.—Benefit commencing after 13 weeks.

THE LONDON, EDINBURGH, AND GLASGOW ASSURANCE COMPANY (LIMITED).

Head Office : Insurance Buildings, Farringdon-street, London, E.C.

Policy No. 896421.

WHEREAS one of the Parents (hereinafter called the Proposer) of the Child (hereinafter called the Assured) whose name and age appear in the First Column of the First Schedule hereto has proposed to effect an Assurance upon the life of the Assured with the London, Edinburgh, and Glasgow Assurance Company, Limited (hereinafter called "the Company"), in such sum as may hereafter become payable according to the duration of the life of the Assured, and the provisions and terms hereinafter contained, and has undertaken to pay to the Company, as the consideration of such Assurance, the weekly premium or sum mentioned in the Second Column of the said First Schedule, and has warranted that the Assured is of good health, sound constitution, and free from all infirmity or disease. AND WHEREAS the Company has, in faith of the said warranties (which are hereby declared to be the basis of the contract of Assurance hereinafter contained), and in consideration of the said undertaking, agreed to accept such proposal and to effect such Assurance upon the terms and subject to the provisoes and conditions hereinafter contained and endorsed hereon (it being also hereby expressly declared that the acceptance of and compliance with which said terms, provisoes, and conditions by the Proposer and the Assured shall be a condition precedent to the commencement of any liability of the Company hereon). NOW THESE PRESENTS WITNESS that, in pursuance of the said agreement, and in consideration of the payment on or before the handing over. or transfer hereof, and during the good health of the Assured, of the sum or premium mentioned in the Second Column of the First Schedule hereto, and of the payment of the like premium or sum by the Proposer or the Assured to the Company on the Tuesday now next, and on every succeeding Tuesday during the life of the Assured, the Company (subject to the said terms, provisoes, and conditions) doth hereby undertake to, and shall and will, upon the death of the Assured, and after proof to the satisfaction of the Directors of the Company of the death and cause of death of the Assured (including, in the event of the death of the Assured under 10 years of age, such certificate as is required by Section 28 of the Friendly Societies Act, 1875) has been received at the Registered Office of the Company, pay, if the Assured shall die under 10 years of age, to the Proposer or other Parent, or if the Assured shall die after attaining the age of 10 years, to the Executors or Administrators of the Assured, such sum as shall, regard being had to (1) the age of the assured at death, (2) the said weekly premium payable and paid hereunder, and (3) the period which shall at the death of the Assured have elapsed since the date of this Policy, appear to be payable according to the scale or table set forth in the Second Schedule hereto. PROVIDED ALWAYS AND IT IS HEREBY EXPRESSLY AGREED AND DECLARED that if the Assured shall die after attaining the age of 10 years, the production of these Presents, together with a receipt for the sum hereby assured and made payable, and made by any person being or having been an Executor or Administrator, Widower or Widow, Relative by Blood, or connection by marriage of the Assured, shall, notwithstanding that the Company shall have received notice that the benefit of and interest in this Policy has become vested in any person or persons other than the Assured, be final and conclusive evidence against all persons whatsoever that the sum hereby assured has been duly paid unto and received by the person or persons lawfully entitled to receive the same, and that all liability whatsoever of the Company upon this Policy has been fully discharged and satisfied. AND PROVIDED ALSO that this Policy shall become void, and the Company shall not be liable to pay any sum whatsoever on account of the Assurance intended to be hereby effected, and all premiums paid by the Proposer or the Assured hereon shall be forfeited to the Company, if the Assured shall not be in a good state of health and free from infirmity or disease at the time when these Presents are handed over to the Proposer, or if the Assured shall die within three calendar months from the day of the date hereof, or shall die by or in consequence of the act or neglect (whether intentional or otherwise) of any person or persons interested hereunder, or who would be entitled to receive any of the benefits hereof on the death of the Assured, or if the Assured shall go out of the United Kingdom

of

of Great Britain and Ireland without the previous consent of the Company under the hand of the Manager of the Company endorsed hereon, or if a Policy or Policies effected with the Company, previous to the date hereof, on the life of the Assured (whether by the Assured or by any other person or persons whatsoever) shall now be in force, or shall hereafter be renewed, unless this and each such other Policy or Policies shall have endorsed hereon and thereon under the hand of the Manager of the Company an express permission and consent that two or more Policies (to be specified by their numbers) may be in force at the same time, although the omission to obtain such endorsement shall be by reason of oversight or negligence, or otherwise howsoever, or if the Proposer or the Assured shall in any way sell, assign, or otherwise part with this Policy. AND PROVIDED ALSO that neither the Proposer nor the Assured shall participate in the profits of the Company.

First Schedule above referred to.

First Column. NAME AND DESCRIPTION OF THE (CHILD) ASSURED.	Second Column. Amount of Weekly Premium.	Third Column. Sum or Amount *ultimately* Assured (as per Second Schedule below) subject to the foregoing Conditions and to those endorsed hereon.
		£.
George Price · · · · · · · · · · · 5 H 10, Court Westgate, Rotherham. Age at entry, Two years, next Birthday.	One penny · · · · ·	10

Second Schedule above referred to.

Age of (Child) the Assured at Death.	Amount payable (for One Penny per Week) if the Child shall Die after the Policy has been issued for			Amount payable (for Three-halfpence per Week) if the Child shall Die after the Policy has been issued for			Amount payable (for Twopence per Week) if the Child shall Die after the Policy has been issued for			Age of (Child) the Assured at Death.
	Three Calendar Months.	Six Calendar Months.	One Year.	Three Calendar Months.	Six Calendar Months.	One Year.	Three Calendar Months.	Six Calendar Months.	One Year.	
	£. s. d.	£. s. d.	£. s. d.	£. s. d.	£. s. d.	£. s. d.	£. s. d.	£. s. d.	£. s. d.	
Under 3 years	1 10 -	2 5 -	3 - -	2 5 -	3 7 6	4 10 -	3 - -	4 10 -	6 - -	Under 3 years.
Over 3 years	1 15 -	2 12 -	3 10 -	2 7 6	3 11 3	4 15 -	3 - -	4 10 -	6 - -	Over 3 „
„ 4 „	2 - -	3 - -	4 - -	2 10 -	3 15 -	5 - -	3 - -	4 10 -	6 - -	„ 4 „
„ 5 „	2 10 -	3 15 -	5 - -	2 15 -	4 2 6	5 10 -	3 - -	4 10 -	6 - -	„ 5 „
„ 6 „	3 - -	4 10 -	6 - -	4 - -	6 - -	8 - -	5 - -	7 10 -	10 - -	„ 6 „
„ 7 „	3 10 -	5 5 -	7 - -	4 5 -	6 7 6	8 10 -	5 - -	7 10 -	10 - -	„ 7 „
„ 8 „	4 - -	6 - -	8 - -	4 10 -	6 15 -	9 - -	5 - -	7 10 -	10 - -	„ 8 „
„ 9 „	4 10 -	6 15 -	9 - -	4 15 -	7 2 6	9 10 -	5 - -	7 10 -	10 - -	„ 9 „
„ 10 „	5 - -	7 10 -	10 - -	7 10 -	11 5 -	15 - -	10 - -	15 - -	20 - -	„ 10 „
The Policy may be continued for the same Weekly Premiums at										
Over 10 „	5 - -	7 10 -	10 - -	7 10 -	11 15 -	15 - -	10 - -	15 - -	20 - -	Over 10 „

IN WITNESS whereof the Common Seal of the Company is hereunto affixed by order of the Directors of the Company, this 17th day of June 1890.

Entered (*E. D.*)

Examined (*B.*)

Spencer Gregory,} Directors.
Richard North,

L. S.

Countersigned, *C. Weeding Skinner*, Secretary.

Wilfred A. Bowser, Manager and Actuary.

CONDITIONS referred to upon which this Policy of Assurance is granted.

1. ALL statements made and acts done by any person other than the Proposer in connection with the proposal and warranties within referred to, or otherwise in connection with this Policy, shall be deemed, as between the Proposer and the Assured on the one part and the Company on the other part, so far as the same shall be relevant hereto, to have been made and done by such person for and on behalf of the Proposer and the Assured, and not the Company. This condition applies equally, although such person be an agent of the Company, the authority of such agents being hereby expressly declared not to include the acceptance of proposals, declarations, or warranties, and all such as are received by any such agent shall be deemed to have been received by him as agent for the Proposer and the Assured for the purpose of submitting the same to the Company.

2. If any warranty within referred to is untrue, or if any untrue statement shall have been made to the Company in the within-mentioned proposal, or if any information material to be known to the Company in determining the acceptance or rejection of the said proposal shall not have been truly and fully stated (whether the same shall have been specifically asked for or not), this Policy is void, and all premiums paid hereon shall be forfeited to the Company.

3. The Assured shall not become employed as a Soldier or Sailor, or in any seafaring occupation, without the previous permission of the Company, to be endorsed on this Policy ; and as a consideration for the grant of such permission, it shall be lawful for the Directors of the Company to require, and compulsory on the Proposer and the Assured to submit to, such increase in the amount of the premium or such reduction in the amount of the sum assured as the Directors shall decide upon.

4. It shall be lawful for the Directors to give the Assured permission to follow the occupation of a Sailor, or any seafaring occupation, in time of peace, without any increase of premium or deduction from the sum assured, provided he serves on a British or Irish ship regularly sailing to or from a British or Irish port, and provided also that such permission be endorsed on this Policy.

5. The premiums payable in respect of this Policy shall be paid as within provided, and in case of default the Assurance hereby effected shall (subject to the provisions of the Friendly Societies Act, 1875, Section 30) become void, and all the interest and benefit of the Proposer and the Assured shall be forfeited. If, however, such premiums shall have been duly paid for 26 weeks from the day of the date hereof, those subsequently payable may be paid within 90 days after they have respectively accrued and become due, and during such 90 days the Assurance shall be and remain in force, and the Company shall (subject to their rights to such premiums) be and continue liable in the same manner and to the like extent as if such premiums had been paid on the days when the same became respectively due and payable.

6. The agents of the Company are not authorised to receive, and are strictly prohibited from receiving, any renewal premium after a Policy has lapsed, as provided in Condition 5 above.

7. No payment of money to any person shall be held to keep this Policy in force unless such person is an authorised agent of the Company, and shall forthwith give to the Proposer or the Assured a receipt for such premium in a printed receipt book issued from the Head (Registered) Office of the Company.

8. The receipt books in which are entered the periodical payments made in respect of the premiums shall at all times, upon the application of the agent, collector, or other authorised officer of the Company, be produced and exhibited to him, and in case of a new receipt book being at any time required, the sum of 1 d. shall be paid for the same to the Company.

9. The Directors may require this Policy and the receipt books containing the receipts for the premiums due to be delivered up to them, and the Probate of the Will or Letters of Administration to the estate and effects of the Assured, or other evidence of title, to be produced to them at their Head (Registered) Office, before the sum assured or any part thereof is paid by the Company.

10. If any of the considerations or conditions on or for which this Policy is granted have not been or shall not be complied with, and the Policy and all premiums paid thereon be thereby forfeited, the Directors may remit or waive the forfeiture on such terms as they in their absolute discretion shall think fit.

11. Any sum payable by the Company under this Policy shall not carry interest against the Company, and the Company shall cease to be liable for such sum if the same be not claimed by or on behalf of the party or parties entitled thereto within six years next after the same shall have become due.

12. That any alteration or erasure in or addition to this Policy shall render it absolutely void. No change or alteration whatever can be effected, except by endorsement, made and signed by the Manager at the Company's Head (Registered) Office.

Pursuant to the Act of Parliament, 38 & 39 Vict. c. 60, s. 28 (the Friendly Societies Act, 1875), it is hereby declared that this Company will not pay on the death of a child under five years of age any sum of money which, added to any amount payable on the death of such child by any other company or society, shall exceed 6 l., or on the death of a child under 10 years of age, any sum of money which, added to any amount payable at the death of such child by any other company or society, shall not exceed 10 l.

Appendix H.

PAPER handed in by Mr. *David Fortune,* 25 July 1890.

SCOTTISH LEGAL LIFE ASSURANCE SOCIETY.

STATEMENT showing RATE of AVERAGE MORTALITY for last Five Years, with the Membership as at 31st December 1889, of CHILDREN under Ten Years of Age.

AGES.	Membership at 31st December 1889.	Average Deaths for Five Years at 31st December 1889.	Ratio of Deaths to Membership or of (2) to (1).
	(1.)	(2.)	
From 0 to 5 Years - - - - -	38,771	1,479	3·81
From 5 to 10 Years - - - - -	37,731	265	0·71
For both Periods together - - -	76,502	1,744	2·27

STATEMENT showing MORTALITY of CHILDREN under Ten Years of Age, in the following DISTRICTS, during 1889.

DISTRICTS.	DEATHS FOR YEAR 1889.		
	Under 5 Years.	Between 5 and 10 Years.	Total for both Periods.
Blackburn - - - - - - - - -	1	—	1
Blairgowrie - - - - - - - - -	4	1	5
Greenock - - - - - - - - -	58	6	64
Lanark - - - - - - - - - -	3	1	4
Paisley - - - - - - - - - -	48	7	55
Preston - - - - - - - - - -	1	1	2

STATEMENT showing RATIO of MORTALITY of CHILDREN under Ten Years old, with the Membership, in the following DISTRICTS, as at 31st December 1889.

DISTRICTS.	Under 5 Years.			Between 5 and 10 Years.			Total for both Periods.		
	Membership as at 31st December.	Deaths for 1889.	Ratio of Deaths to Membership.	Membership as at 31st December.	Deaths for 1889.	Ratio of Deaths to Membership.	Membership as at 31st December.	Deaths for 1889.	Ratio of Deaths to Membership.
Blackburn - - - -	28	1	3·57	23	—	·0	51	1	1·96
Blairgowrie - - - -	191	4	2·09	200	1	·50	391	5	1·27
Greenock - - - - -	1,430	58	4·05	1,613	6	·37	3,043	64	2·10
Lanark - - - - -	111	3	2·70	120	1	·83	231	4	1·73
Paisley - - - - -	1,313	48	3·65	1,246	7	·56	2,559	55	2·14
Preston - - - - -	28	1	3·57	40	1	2·50	68	2	2·94

136, Ingram-street, Glasgow,
15 July 1890.

APPENDIX I.

PAPER handed in by Mr. *Stead*.   *See* Question 4027.

Questions sent to Juvenile Branches.

Ancient Order of Foresters' Juvenile Societies.

QUESTIONS.	ANSWERS.
1.—Name of Society - - - -	
2.—Number of Members - - -	
3.—Name of Town - - - - -	
4.—How many Years established ? - -	
5.—During those Years has it ever come to your knowledge that any Member has been deliberately done to death for the sake of the Funeral Benefit ?	
6.—Has it ever come to your knowledge that at any time a coroner's inquest has been held over any of the Members of your Society ? - - -	
7.—If so, state how many, why they were held, and what were the verdicts of the jury ? - - . - -	
8.—In your opinion are there any grounds for including your Society amongst those whom the Bishop of Peterborough has condemned ? - -	
9.—If the proposal to compel Societies to pay the Funeral Benefit to the undertaker instead of the parent is adopted, what influence do you think it will have upon the future of your Society ? - - -	
10.—Have you any objections to the reducing of the amounts payable at death ? - - - - -	
11.—Do you pay Sickness Benefits to your Members ? - - - -	
12.—State the age at which Sickness Benefits begin - - - -	
13.—Do you provide your Members with a Medical Man and Medicine during illness ? - - - -	

1,278 sheets sent out to 79,272 members.

873 have been returned up to date, representing 59,000 members.

834, representing 56,462 members, say the proposed " Undertaker's Clause " would be the ruin of the societies, and they strongly object to the Bill.

39, representing 2,538 members, think the Bill would not affect them, but agree they ought not to come under the Bill.

APPENDIX K.

PAPER handed in by Mr. *A. A. Dobson*.

BALANCE SHEET of the *Hulme* Friendly Burial Society.

THE income for the year has been 2,490 *l*. 15 *s*. 10 *d*., viz.. 2,042 *l*. 13 *s*, 6 *d*. paid in by the collectors, and 448 *l*. 2 *s*. 4 *d*. interest from investments. The accumulated capital now amounts to the sum of 13,008 *l*. 10 *s*. 2 *d*. The following statement will show the result of the past year's work :—

	£.	s.	d.	£.	s.	d.
Funeral Fund Income - - -	1,867	15	7			
Paid on Deaths - - -	1,501	10	–			
				366	5	7
Management Fund Income - -	623	–	3			
Paid Working Expenses - -	549	7	11			
				73	12	4
Increase for the Year - - - £.				439	17	11

Number of Members, December 1888 -	10,273	New Members - - - - -	520
Exclusions - - - - - -	284	Present Number of Members - -	10,330
Deaths - - - - - -	179	Increase of Members - - - -	57

		£.	s.	d.
Worth per Member, 1888 - - - -		1	4	5½
„ „ 1889 - - - -		1	5	2½

Scale of Payment at Death for the undermentioned periods of Membership :—

		£.	s.	d.			£.	s.	d.
6 weeks' membership - - -		1	–	–	10 years' membership - - -		8	–	–
13 ,, ,, - - -		3	–	–	15 ,, ,, - - -		9	–	–
1 year's .. - - -		4	–	–	20 ,, ,, - - -		11	–	–
2 years' ,, - - -		5	–	–	25 ,, ,, - - -		13	–	–
5 ,, ,, - - -		6	–	–	30 ,. ,, - - -		15	–	–

N. B.—The Entrance Fee has been reduced to One Penny.

FUNERAL FUND.

FIRST QUARTER.

INCOME.		£.	s.	d.	£.	s.	d.	EXPENDITURE.		£.	s.	d.	£.	s.	d.
Balance last Report - - -					11,609	7	7	Funerals (*see* Summary) - .. - -					417	10	–
Subscriptions - - -		347	2	3				Invested Capital - - -		11,592	11	8			
Interest - - - -		132	14	11				In Treasurer's hands - -		79	3	1			
					479	17	2						11,671	14	9
£.					12,089	4	9	Gain, £. 62. 7 *s*. 2 *d*. £.					12,089	4	9

SECOND QUARTER.

INCOME.		£.	s.	d.	£.	s.	d.	EXPENDITURE.		£.	s.	d.	£.	s.	d.
Balance last Quarter -					11,671	14	9	Funerals (*see* Summary) - - - -					379	10	–
Subscriptions - - -		358	6	9				Invested Capital - -		11,613	2	8			
Interest - - -		20	11	–				In Treasurer's hands - -		57	19	10			
					378	17	9						11,671	2	6
£.					12,050	12	6	Loss, 12 *s*. 3 *d*. £.					12,050	12	6

(142.)   H H

FUNERAL FUND—*continued.*

THIRD QUARTER.

INCOME.					EXPENDITURE.				
	£. s. d.	£. s. d.			£. s. d.	£. s. d.	
Balance last Quarter - - - -		11,671 2 6		Funerals (*see* Summary) - - -		359 10 -	
Subscriptions - - -	435 11 1			Invested Capital - - -	11,800 - -		
Interest - - - -	82 4 11			In Treasurer's hands - -	29 8 6		
		517 16 -					11,829 8 6
	£.	12,188 18 6		Gain, £. 158. 6 s.		£.	12,188 18 6

FOURTH QUARTER.

INCOME.					EXPENDITURE.				
	£. s. d.	£. s. d.			£. s. d.	£. s. d.	
Balance last Quarter - - - -		11,829 8 6		Funerals (*see* Summary) - - -		345 - -	
Subscriptions - - -	391 5 2			Invested Capital - - -	11,972 15 2		
Interest - - - -	99 19 6			In Treasurer's hands - -	2 18 -		
		491 4 8					11,975 13 2
	£.	12,320 13 2		Gain, £. 146. 4 s. 8 d.		£.	12,320 13 2

MANAGEMENT FUND.

FIRST QUARTER.

INCOME.					EXPENDITURE.				
	£. s. d.	£. s. d.			£. s. d.	£. s. d.	
Balance last Report - - - -		959 4 8		Working Expenses (*see* Summary) - -		126 1 2	
Subscriptions - - -	115 14 -			Invested Capital - - -	967 8 4		
Interest - - - -	44 5 1			In Treasurer's hands - -	25 14 3		
		159 19 1					993 2 7
	£.	1,119 3 9		Gain, £. 33 17 s. 11 d.		£.	1,119 3 9

SECOND QUARTER.

INCOME.					EXPENDITURE.				
	£. s. d.	£. s. d.			£. s. d.	£. s. d.	
Balance last Quarter - - - -		993 2 7		Working Expenses (*see* Summary) - -		123 9 11	
Subscriptions - - -	119 2 3			Invested Capital - - -	974 5 4		
Interest - - - -	6 17 -			In Treasurer's hands - -	21 6 7		
		125 19 3					995 11 11
	£.	1,119 1 10		Gain, £. 2. 9 s. 4 d.		£.	1,119 1 10

MANAGEMENT FUND—*continued.*

THIRD QUARTER.

INCOME.				EXPENDITURE.			
	£. s. d.	£. s. d.			£. s. d.	£. s. d.	
Balance last Quarter -	- - -	995 11 11		Working Expenses (*see* Summary) - -		157 2 1	
Subscriptions - -	145 3 8			Invested Capital - - -	1,000 - -		
Interest - - -	27 8 4			In Treasurer's hands - -	11 1 10		
		172 12 -				1,011 1 10	
	£.	1,168 3 11		Gain, £. 15. 9 s. 11 d.		1,168 3 11	£.

FOURTH QUARTER.

INCOME.				EXPENDITURE.			
	£. s. d.	£. s. d.			£. s. d.	£. s. d.	
Balance last Quarter -	- - -	1,011 1 10		Working Expenses (*see* Summary) - -		142 14 9	
Subscriptions - -	130 8 4			Invested Capital - - -	1,007 11 9		
Interest - - -	33 6 7			In Treasurer's hands - -	25 5 3		
Sale of Old Door - -	- 15 -					1,032 17 -	
		164 9 11					
	£.	1,175 11 9		Gain, £. 21. 15 s. 2 d.		1,175 11 9	£.

SUMMARY.

FUNERAL FUND.

INCOME.			EXPENDITURE.				
	£. s. d.	£. s. d.		£. s.	£. s. d.	£. s. d.	
Balance, December 1888 -	- - -	11,609 7 7	3 Funerals at - - 1 -		3 - -		
Income, 1st Quarter -	479 17 2		1 „ - - 2 10		2 10 -		
„ 2nd „ - -	378 17 9		29 „ - - 3 -		87 - -		
„ 3rd „ - -	517 16 -		2 „ - - 3 10		7 - -		
„ 4th „ - -	491 4 8		17 „ - - 4 -		68 - -		
			13 „ - - 5 -		65 - -		
		1,867 15 7	13 „ - - 6 -		78 - -		
			12 „ - - 8 -		96 - -		
			22 „ - - 9 -		198 - -		
			20 „ - - 11 -		220 - -		
			24 „ - - 13 -		182 - -		
			33 „ - - 15 -		495 - -		
						1,501 10 -	
			Invested in Widnes Local Board, at 4 per cent. - -		2,000 - -		
			Ditto - at 3½ per cent. -		1,000 - -		
			Invested in Birkenhead Corporation, at 3½ per cent. -		4,000 - -		
			Invested in Chorlton Board of Guardians, at 3½ per cent.		2,000 - -		
			Invested in Wallasey Local Board, at 3½ per cent. -		1,500 - -		
			Invested in Bradford Corporation, at 3½ per cent. - -		1,000 - -		
			Invested in Savings Bank, at 2½ per cent. - - -		472 15 2		
			Invested in Treasurer's hands		2 18 -		
						11,975 13 2	
	£.	13,477 3 2			£.	13,477 3 2	

	£. s. d.
Funeral Fund Gain - - - - - -	366 5 7

SUMMARY.

MANAGEMENT FUND.

INCOME.			EXPENDITURE.		
	£. s. d.			£. s. d.	£. s. d.
Balance, December 1888 - - - -	959 4 8		Office Rent and Taxes - -	31 5 6	
	£. s. d.		Gas and Coal - - -	11 5 8	
Income, First Quarter - -	159 19 1		Office Repairs, &c. - - -	1 17 4	
„ Second Quarter -	125 19 3		Meeting Room, Christ Church -	2 - -	
„ Third Quarter -	172 12 -				46 8 0
„ Fourth Quarter -	164 9 11				
		623 - 3	Books, Stationery, and Reports -	18 9 -	
			Post Cards and Postage -	2 16 5	
			Exchanging Stamps - - -	- 17 6	
					22 2 11
			President's Salary - -	14 - -	
			Committee and Trustees -	6 18 -	
			Auditor's Salary - -	20 - -	
			Treasurer's Commission, at 1 per Cent. - - - -	20 8 9	
			Treasurer to Savings Banks -	1 10 -	
			Secretary's Commission, at 5 per Cent. - - - -	102 2 8	
			Friendly Societies Conference -	6 6 -	
					171 5 0
			No. 1 Collector's Commission, at 15 per Cent. - - -	98 6 1	
			No. 2 Collector's Commission, at 15 per Cent. - - -	73 10 3	
			No. 3 Collector's Commission, at 15 per Cent. - - -	134 11 9	
			Supplementary Collector - -	3 3 -	
					309 11 1
			Invested in Widnes Local Board, at 3½ per Cent. - - -	500 - -	
			Invested in Savings Bank, at 2½ per Cent. - - -	507 11 9	
			In Treasurer's hands - -	25 5 3	
					1,032 17 -
	£.	1,582 4 11		£.	1,582 4 11

	£. s. d.
Management Fund Gain - - -	73 12 4

I N D E X.

ANALYSIS OF INDEX.

LIST of PRINCIPAL HEADINGS in the following INDEX, with the Pages at which they may be found.

I N D E X.

[N.B.—In this Index the *Figures* following the names of Witnesses refer to the Questions in the Evidence.]

A.

AFFILIATED SOCIETIES:

Distinction drawn between affiliated friendly societies, such as Oddfellows or Foresters (or the Manchester Unity of Friendly Societies), and collecting friendly societies, such as Royal Liver (or Liverpool Victoria Legal and Friendly), *Taunton* 3205. See *Friendly Societies.*

Age. The Royal Liver insure from birth, *Taunton* 3264——Child comes into benefit after thirteen weeks' insurance, *ib.* 3269 ;—but grants of grace given in deserving cases, *ib.* 3270——The same in Prudential, *Dewey* 2928——In Liverpool Victoria Legal and Friendly, from one week, *Clensy* 4047.

Quite untrue that children are insured before birth, *Taunton* 3425-31.

Sons of the Phœnix do not insure till five years, *Sargent* 4207. 4251——Friendly societies generally do not, *ib.* 4328——Hulme Burial Society only takes children of members, and not under two months, *Dobson* 2508 ;—and must have from nine to three months' membership before they get anything, *ib.* 2779-9—- -Age was formerly three months, but has been reduced, as society found they could afford it, *ib.* 2749—— Scottish Legal, at any age, *Fortune* 3689 ; – give half and quarter benefit after three and six months' insurance, *ib.* 3692 ;—and full benefit only after twelve months, *ib.* 3691——Below these limits they give no grants of grace, *ib.* 3692——Better class of parents do not insure their children till about five years old, *Tasker* 1614——Friendly societies registered under the Friendly Societies Act may not grant insurances on children, except those of their own members, *Cleveland* 4417. 4420. 4435—--Oddfellows admit these at three months old ; but friendly societies may establish juvenile branches for insuring children from three to sixteen, *ib.* 4416. 4431.

In twenty-two Oddfellows' Societies in Southampton district insurance begins generally at six, in one case as low as three, in one as high as eight years old, *Walton* 4709-14.

Out of 1,279 Foresters' Juvenile Societies 49 only admit children under three, 56 at three, 302 at four, 229 at five, and 316 at six, 85 at seven, 89 at eight, and remaining 167 at various ages to sixteen, *Stead* 4654.

Insurance should be prohibited under one year, or sum made so small that there could be no profit, *Browne* 1154-1161 ;—or sum paid direct to undertaker, *Carter* 875 ——If children were not allowed to be insured till one year old they would have a chance of getting better able to take care of themselves, *Tasker* 1589 ;—two years better still, *ib.* 1590 ; *Hartop* 1731-32——If so, dissolute parents wishing to make profit out of death would not then insure, *Tasker* 1592-5——Should be forbidden under two years, *see* letter of Leeds Society for Prevention of Cruelty to Children, *page* 134—— Prudential has no objection to insurance under one year being forbidden, *Dewey* 3006-14 ;—which would practically be fifteen months, as no benefit till after three months' insurance, *ib.* 3013 ;—or to age, at which only one policy could be issued, being raised from ten to fourteen, *ib.* 3017-8——Better plan would be to allow insurance at any age, but if death occurred below one year, that only premiums actually paid should be repaid ; out of the gain to them on this the insurance companies could give some other benefit to survivors, *ib.* 3605-12. 3628-31——Might be forbidden under one year, and profit applied to endowment for children attaining a certain age, *Hartop* 1730-2——Amount on deaths under three years might be diminished, *Taunton* 3088-9. 3240——Strong objection to insurance under one year being abolished, *ib.* 3079 ; *Crooks*

Age—continued.

2344——Hard on respectable parents, *Ritchie* 1447 ;—as sum now insurable is not enough to cover expenses, *Crooks* 2342-4. 2352, 2482——Hardship, and would lead to revival of "friendly leads," *Clensy* 3980 ——Hardship, as all children of any age must be buried, *E. Hooper* 4129 ;—and expense would be thrown on the rates, *Sargent* 4307-8.

For scale of insurance at different ages, see *Amount of Insurance Money.*

Agent. See *Insurance Agents.*

Amount of Insurance Money. Average amount paid in Royal London Friendly Society is 1 *l.* 13 *s.* 3 *d.* under five years, *Hambridge* 3828 ;—4 *l.* 12 *s.* between five and· ten, *ib.* 3830 ;—2 *l.* 10 *s.* average paid under five in Royal Liver, *Taunton* 3086 ;—2 *l.* 13 *s.* in Prudential, *Dewey* 2842——As one-third of whole working classes are content with this, no detriment to them in most cases if legal amount were reduced to this, but there would be exceptions, *ib.* 2843-51——Sons of the Phœnix give a uniform sum of 8 *l.* from five to sixteen, *Sargent* 4204. 4207. 4247.

Scale of insurance money in Royal Liver, *Taunton* 3366 ;—in Liverpool Victoria, *Clensy* 4047, *et seq.* ;—this is less than some offices, but more favourable in the first year, probably to attract entry, *ib.* 4053-7 ;—in Prudential, *Dewey* 2852 ; *App.* E., *page* 232 ;—in Scottish Legal, *Fortune* 3689-91 ;—in London, Edinburgh, and Glasgow Assurance Company, *App.* G., *page* 236 ;—in Hulme Burial Society, *Dobson* 2695—— These sums enabled to be given because, being a mutual society, it has from time to time invested money to increase benefits, *ib.* 2497. 2746——Oddfellows give 30 *s.* at three months, 2 *l.* at one year, rising 10 *s.* a year to eleven years, *Cleveland* 4513-4——Average in Foresters is 3 *l.* at five years, *Stead* 4686——Average amount now paid, in witness' experience, is 50 *s.*, which is all spent on funeral, *E. Hooper* 4088-90.

Amount of insurance money has been gradually increased by competition of societies, *Taunton* 3138-41.

3 *l.* 4 *s.* 7¾ *d.* was average amount received on each insured child dying in Hospital for Sick Children, Pendlebury, Manchester, *see* Report read by the Chairman, *page* 55——Case of six children in family insured for 28 *l.* 17 *s.*, *Burnett* 1280-7 ; *Waugh* 2054——One of these children much neglected, and would probably have died if not rescued, *Burnett* 1277-8——Case of young child insured in three unregistered societies for 10 *l.*, *Cleveland* 4413-5——Legal limit can be exceeded in unregistered burial clubs who do not insist on death certificate, *Leach* 1772. 1791——Case of child beggar insured for 20*l.* 12 *s.*, *Waugh* 2269.

Should be limited to 1 *l.*, the cost of a decent funeral, *Carter* 833·4. 850-5 ; *Hooper* 1241——Might be limited to 2 *l.* 10 *s.* or 3 *l.* under three, and 5 *l.* under five, *Taunton* 3088-9. 324C——Limitation to actual lowest cost of funeral would be a hardship, as working people insure to get mourning, 1447. 1449-1501——£. 6 now allowed by law hardly enough for funeral of child of five; sum given not enough at younger ages, *Dobson* 2696 ——Children under two should not be insured ; hardship to parents, but required by necessities of case ; between two and five burial money ought to be 5 *l.*, between five and eleven 7 *l.*, over eleven 10 *l.* ; some margin should be given for medical aid and mourning ; scale in Bill too low ; *see* letter of Leeds Committee of Society for Prevention of Cruelty to Children, page 134.

Instead of going from 6 *l.* below five years to 10 *l.* after, there might be a graduated scale ; there would be no inconvenience in this, as almost all insuring societies have a graduated scale of their own, *Fortune* 3775-7 ;—no great objection, and would meet the exceptional cases where bad motive might exist, *E. Hooper* 4186-8 ;—no objection, *Sargent* 4281——Graduated scale not fair, one mother might think 2 *l.* enough, another 6 *l.* too little, *Clensy* 3985.

If only one policy were allowed on a child, the amount a society could afford to pay for one penny a week would be lower than limit in Friendly Societies Act, *Dewey* 2919-20.

Scale in Bill framed by Mr. Ludlow, Chief Registrar of Friendly Societies, and approved by Committee of House of Commons, *Waugh* 2214-7.

Arlesey. Population here engaged in brick-making and straw-plaiting, *Burry* 493 ;— was very wretched and depraved, and many suspicious deaths took place, *ib.* 547 ;— children largely insured, *ib.* 503 ;—a large proportion of children here illegitimate, *ib.* 514. See *Burry. Mr. H. B. P.* (Analysis of his Evidence).

Letters from registrar and School Board officer that child-neglect, though it exists from carelessness, is not for insurance money ; that only ten for certain, or perhaps sixteen children, out of 687 on school census, are illegitimate ; that of twenty-five cases certified by Dr. Pullen Burry sixteen were uninsured and three more doubtful, which is not the proportion he stated, *Dewey* 3001.

B.

Barwise, Mr. Sidney. Letter from Mr. Culshaw, secretary of the Blackburn Burial Club, criticising the evidence of Mr. Barwise, handed in, *Dobson* 2489-91.

Barwise, Mr. Sidney, M.B. (*London*), M.R.C S. (Analysis of his Evidence.)—Is Medical officer of Health for Blackburn, and was formerly parish doctor in Birmingham, 3-7 —— His evidence relates principally to Birmingham and to pauper classes there, as he had no private practice, 9. 106. 206 ;—to lowest classes, 182.

Believes that insurance of children leads to their neglect, 20, 21, 49. 53. 91 ;—was led to that by inquiries he made, whether children he saw neglected were insured, 10-12. 37 ;—and by anxiety of parents to get death certificate, 34, 35——Children died from marasmus which means wasting, from improper food, neglect to call in doctor in time, and from exposure, 25-31.

All his experience of insured people were people on the parish, 86-69 ; very common for them to insure, 179 ;—perhaps 25 per cent., 190 —— Sometimes parents denied children were insured, and he afterwards found out they were, 14. 36 ;—sometimes said they did not know, but thought some relation might have put them in a club, 38.

Many dissolute parents unwilling to bear burden of supporting children, but insurance an additional inducement for getting rid of them, 19-21. 51. 106-8. 202-—— To these a few shillings a temptation, 51 ;—but not, of course, where there was any natural feeling for child, 203——This is often very slight in the lowest class, 201.

Difficult to prove neglect intentional, though strongly suspected, 23 *et seq.*, 53-62. 82 ;—nothing except history of case can prove it to doctor, 30. 58-62. 105 ;—and doctor is therefore obliged to grant certificate, 53.

If doctor has seen patient alive he may give certificate, 134 ;—he is not obliged to, but must report fact to the coroner, 136. 142 ;—under penalty if he refuses without cause, 146 —— There is no fee for death certificate, 147——Certificates are sometimes given without proper care, by doctor whose unqualified assistant has been attending patient, 137 ;—but apart from that every doctor has inducement not to refuse certificate, for peace and quiet, and unpopular if he refuses, 168-9——Certificate to get insurance money can only be given by registrar, 120 ;—if it had to be given by doctor he would then know and could watch all cases of insurance, 123.

Has sent cases to coroner, who makes inquiries, but generally does not hold inquest, 63-6 ;—when he does, he often advises jury not to return verdict of manslaughter on account of the doctor being unable to give positive evidence, 67-9 ;—and difficulty of getting conviction at assizes, 69-74. 80-85——Death, where intentional, more generally procured by neglect than by actual violence, 67-9.

Insurance companies pay even in suspicious cases, as it is the agents' interest they should, though not theirs, 126——Insurance need not be for the purpose of paying doctor, 95 -100——All applicants can get medical aid, 102,—from the parish, 109,—or from gratuitous dispensary, 112——One-third of the population of Birmingham receives free medical aid, 183 ;—more than in almost any town, 184.

Illegitimate children have furnished most cases of suspicion, 163. 173 ;—but witness, as parish doctor, had to do with more than normal proportion of illegitimate children, 174.

Benefit. Children, though insured, do not come into benefit till a certain age, or a certain time after insurance ; three months after insurance in Prudential, *Dewey* 2928 ; —same in Royal Liver, *Taunton* 3269.

Practice of insurance companies where a child dies not yet in benefit, to make parents a grant of portion of sum insured ; of 15 *s.* or 1 *l.* ; *Browne* 1075-7 ; *Dewey* 2931-2 ; *Taunton* 3049. 3270-1 ——This grant averages 10 *s.*, *ib.* 3051-3 ;—not invariably given, but especially where many in a family are insured, *ib.* 3278-80. 3311-2 ; —makes them popular, *Branson* 273——Case where man was convicted and got a grant of 10 *s.* from insurance company, though nothing was due, *ib.* 223. 272. 292—— In Scottish Legal children do not come into full benefit till after twelve months' insurance ; below that society pays quarter benefit after three months, half benefit after six, but never makes grants of grace otherwise, *Fortune* 3692. 3743-5. 3742.

In Royal Liver some children are insured for immediate benefit after a more stringent examination ; this is really a safeguard, *Taunton* 3416.

Grants of grace or quarter, or even half benefit, might be made illegal, *Fortune* 3752 ; —perhaps with return of premiums actually paid, *ib.* 3802.

Birmingham. One-third of population receives gratuitous medical relief, *Barwise* 183;—more than any other town, *ib.* 184.   *See* Evidence of Mr. Barwise, *passim.*

Branson, Mr. John, M.R.C.P., Edinburgh. (Analysis of his Evidence.)—Is Medical Officer of Health at Rotherham, 210 ;—previously in private practice there, 212.

Insurance of children demoralises parents, 221 ;—connection of death with profit tends to neglect, 229. 259 *et seq.* 332 ;—they look on death as a natural sequence to insurance, 222 ——Amongst miserable surroundings parents seem rather to wish children to die, and in these cases insurance is a powerful inducement, 232——There is a great deal of parental affection amongst the poor; witness is only referring to the dissolute classes, 269.

The better of the working classes do not insure in insurance companies; it is generally the most improvident, 218. 223. 269. 318. 337——The more respectable have their own clubs, which give a sum on death of a child, 319 ;—either friendly societies or burial clubs, 319–21.

Cases of neglect mentioned, 223 *et seq.* 316——There is no necessity to give drugs to cause death, milk allowed to turn sour quite sufficient, 266–8 ;—doctors' orders often neglected, 262–4,—case mentioned, 267——In one case a woman caused death of child (and was convicted), who had previously been warned, but had certificate granted, on the death of another child, 227 —— Case where coroner refused to hold inquest, but witness prosecuted before magistrates for neglect and got conviction, 300–4.

Coroner investigates when certificate is refused by doctor, but, generally finds no evidence, and grants a certificate, 251—— Witness refuses his certificate in doubtful cases, 251 ;—but often gives it where, though he is morally certain, he can get no proof, 236. 336——Doctor cannot be certain unless he knows the past history of a case, 237. 252 ;—this is the experience of all doctors, 256–7——A doctor has no wish to become prosecutor, has no time for attendance at inquest and assizes, and if he fails to get a conviction becomes unpopular, 239 ;—and so certificates given that ought not to be, 258——Doctor may always refuse certificate, stating his reasons to the coroner, 335–6——Police take up suspicious cases, but they have even less power of getting proof than the doctor, 246–8——Neighbours refuse to give evidence, 322 ——In case of death husband and wife cannot give evidence against one another, 249.

Illegitimate children afford most suspicious cases, 314.

Lapses of policies often occur, as these insurances are by careless people, and are very profitable to insurance offices, 229. 270–2. 308–10.

Insurance companies must know of these suspicious cases, but witness has never known them prosecute, 294–5 ;—it would be their gain not to pay, 293 ;—but sum so small that it would be disadvantageous to their business, 331——They refuse in suspicious cases to pay full sum, but give a small grant, 272. 278. 295 ——They also give a small sum if child dies before coming into benefit, before three or six months' insurance, and this is useful to them as an advertisement, 305. 323–5.

Medical relief can always be obtained gratis, either from club, dispensary, hospital, or parish, 284–7 ;—so it is not necessary to insure for this, 288.

Amount of insurance money is greater than necessary to cover funeral expenses, which would be 2 *l.*, insurance generally being about 3 *l.* 10 *s.*, 333–4——Sunday is a favourite day for funeral with thrifty people, as otherwise they lose a day's work, 343.

The best check would be that every insurance of a child should be registered, as in case of vaccination, and child should be seen by a doctor before insurance, 277——Agents now insure children they do not even see, 278.

Brighton. Opinion of House Surgeon at Hove General Hospital quoted, that many children there are starved for the insurance money, *Hodson* 586.

Browne, Mr. Arthur. (Analysis of his Evidence.)—Is a solicitor, and has been Deputy Coroner of Nottingham for fourteen years, 1048——Believes that insurance money is often the final cause of allowing children to die, 1058 ;—not only by neglect but by violence, especially by suffocation, 1059. 1130–3——This is only true of dissolute parents, 1062. 1127——Not sufficient alone but as an additional motive to dislike of burden of children felt by some parents, 1123–5—— Sometimes earning good wages; instance given, 1065–7. 1122 ;—in this case father and mother were convicted of neglect and sentenced, 1067–75 ;—another instance of death by improper feeding, 1088–93 ;—other cases, 1099, 1100——A large number of suffocations take place on Saturday night, 1129 ;—probably on account of drunkenness, 1136.

It can always be ascertained from registrar if children are insured, as he must give certificate, 1081–2.

Does not encourage his juries to find verdict of manslaughter, 1098 ;—on account of difficulty of getting a conviction on trial, as judge and juries seem unwilling to convict, 1099 ;—even when medical evidence is strong, 1106 ;—prefer to convict, when

possible,

Browne, Mr. Arthur. (Analysis of his Evidence)—*continued.*

possible, of concealment of birth, 1108——His practice is to recommend jury to censure mother, and advise guardians to prosecute for neglect, 1100 ;—details of specimen case, 1101——Jury at sessions disagreed (a new trial now proceeding), because doctors admitted that children would sometimes die in spite of all care, 1110——Want of funds no obstacle to prosecution, as police take up any case where conviction seems probable, 1126 —— Believes that medical men do not give certificates too easily, at any rate in Nottingham, 1118——They are not liable to penalty for refusing unless without reasonable cause, 1116 ——Thinks it better simply to refuse in doubtful cases, when it then goes before the coroner, than to attempt to encumber certificate with additional particulars, 1113-7 —— When doctor refuses to certify the registrar enters what the coroner or, in case of inquest, the jury find to be the cause of death, 1175–80 ——This satisfies the provision of law that insurance money cannot be paid without certificate of cause of death, 1175——If the verdict of the jury is unsatisfactory, murder, for instance, the money would probably not be claimed or paid, 1181. 1184.

Illegitimate children, in his experience, nearly all insured, 1134.

Sunday interments are not the practice in Nottingham, probably not by law or bye-law, but because ministers of religion have made a rule against it, 1169–73.

Cost of funeral in Nottingham for child under one year about 1 *l.* or 30 *s.*, 1143——Insurance money would be from 30 *s.* to 2 *l.* 10 *s.*, 1144.

Agents put great pressure on parents to insure, 1166 ;—difficult to say if their registration would be beneficial, as it must be very easy to be registered, 1167 ;—has never received any assistance from agents, 1185–6.

Insurance premiums are so high that there is profit to the company even where many deaths occur, 1162–3——When children are not old enough to be in benefit, companies make parents a grant of portion of sum insured, 1075–7.

Thinks insurance of children ought to be prohibited under twelve months, as expense of funeral then very small, 1149–1158 ;—and children after a year have a better chance of living ; or perhaps under six months, 1156 ;—or at any rate limited to a very small sum, 1149. 1154 ;—so that no profit could be made, 1155——A proportion of the working classes would resent the interference, but not very reasonably, 1139, 1157.

Burial Clubs and Societies. Local friendly burial clubs are preferable to collecting societies, *Ritchie* 1431, 1441, 1518–20——Even exercise beneficial effect, on account of publicity, and the committee inquires in suspicious cases, and does not pay insurance money if neglect proved, *ib.* 1437, 1478——All profit in them goes to the members, *ib.* 1439, 1490-1——Profit in societies in Manchester and Salford Amalgamated Conference of Family Friendly Burial Societies goes to form a fund to increase benefits, *Dobson* 2497 ;—which now amount to sums stated, *ib.* 2695.

Better than insurance companies, but the evidence of Dr. Ritchie not altogether favourable to them, *Waugh* 2255–62——All members almost know each other, and thereby a strong public opinion is formed, *Dobson* 2501——Balance-sheet of Hulme Burial Society handed in; it is a model one, and ought to be adopted by all societies, *ib.* 2526——Burial clubs ought to be encouraged, but so that no money should pass into hands of parents except a small provision for mourning, *Thorneycroft, App.* C., *page* 229.

Payments are collected by members, who are paid a small sum and collect after their day's work, *Dobson* 2503.

Frequently pay immediately after insurance, *Dewey* 2928.

There are many local clubs which issue no policies but give members a certain grant on death of wife or child, *Fortune* 3793.

Are, as to eighty per cent. of them, bankrupt, *Dewey* 2980-1.

See *Friendly Societies.*

Burnett, Captain Lindsay Robert. (Analysis of his Evidence.)—Is now Chief Constable of Rotherham, formerly of Wolverhampton, 1261–3——Has a strong opinion that child insurance is an incentive to neglect and murder, 1267. 1391——The population in his district are miners, ironworkers, &c., 1268 ;—now earning good wages, 1269—— His remarks only apply to the dregs of the population, 1270 ;—a very small fraction of the whole, 1271.

Only a small proportion of cases of cruelty to insured children came to his knowledge, 1316. 1369 ;—only hears of them by chance, 1293——As many uninsured (as far as he knows) children are treated cruelly as insured, 1346. 1384. 1393 ;—but character of cruelty different ; in the cases of insured children, deliberate slow starvation, 1394–1400.

Particulars of case of gross neglect of six children by parents, all insured, one three times ; policies were found in the house, or fact might have been difficult to discover ; agent, whose name was on policies, summoned as a witness; admitted he asked

Burnett, Captain Lindsay Robert. (Analysis of his Evidence)—*continued.*

no question as to health of child, and that he got a shilling commission when the penny a week insurance money had been paid twelve weeks, 1277——One child was almost dead when insured, but is recovering ; parents were committed for three months' hard labour, 1277–79——The aggregate amounts for which the children were insured was 28 *l.* 17 *s.*, 1280–7,—for a total weekly payment of 7 *d.*, 1286.

Magistrates have expressed a strong opinion on the system of infant life insurance, 1290——Has no difficulty in getting convictions for neglect, 1386 ;—has had no cases of child manslaughter or murder, 1388–90 ;—but in above-mentioned case if neglect had not been stopped it would have ended in murder, 1405–6.

There are many sick clubs by which a working man can get medical attendance for his family, 1329–33.

There ought to be a system of registration of insurances, 1297–1301 ;—produces a form of certificate drawn up by Dr. Cobban, police surgeon, 1301 ;—to be drawn up by agent, to be signed by doctor as to health of child, and sent to registrar ; and in case of death a special certificate should be issued by registrar to justify payment of insurance money, not only a copy of the usual death certificate, 1302. 1359——All lapses of policies to be entered on register, 1339–41 ;—this register to be kept by parochial authority, 1338 ;—and paid for at the public expense, 1360–5——With this publicity any suspicious cases could be watched and traced, 1352–56——Insurance offices bear very different characters, 1350 ;—they get large profit from lapses of policies, 1340. 1351.

Has never received any assistance from agents, 1307–9——There is great competition between them, 1304. 1306 ;—if one agent rejected a case another would take it ; midwives are in the employ of agents to give them earliest information of birth, 1305. 1310–2——Agents are struggling men of rather good education, living by their wits, 1372–78 ;—or in a small way of business, so that they would be injured if they were too strict, 1401–3——Registration of agents might increase their responsibility and check ill practices, but doubtful, 1407–10.

If insurance were prohibited under two years it might perhaps have some good effect, 1334–8 ;—but publicity would be attained by registration of insurances, 1335 ;—except registration, knows no remedy but prohibition of insurances under five or six, 1379–80——It would be hard on honest poor to prevent them, 1342–3, 1366–8 ;—they insure to cover medical expenses and mourning, as well as funeral expenses, 1344 ;—restriction might be a serious hardship, but the evil is great, 1381.

Burry, Mr. H. B. Pullen, M.R.C.S (Analysis of his Evidence.)—Is a general practitioner at Liphook, and previously in Hertford and Bedfordshire, 492——There his population was engaged in straw plaiting, brickmaking, and malting ; at Liphook entirely agricultural, 493–4——Unfavourable evidence applies exclusively to Hertfordshire and Bedfordshire, 547.

Has a strong unfavourable opinion of infant life insurance, 498–9 ;—had many moribund children brought him that care in time could have saved, 502 ;—of whom most were insured, 503–8 ;—brought just in time to get a certificate, 505 ;—all classes were insured, but neglect only amongst dissolute people, 513 ;—some of them earning good wages, 515 ;—many illegitimate children, 514——Believes insurance money was a temptation, 521–4. 544 ;——Had a case in which one delicate child was the only one insured of many in family, 559——Had great difficulty in getting fees for medical attendance, 529.

Custom for doctors to have private sick clubs, 532 ;—in which labourers paid so much a year, 533 ;—never had a suspicious case amongst these, 535–6.

Most of the insurances were with the Prudential Society, 563——Agents were constantly going round to get new business and collect fees, 562.

Did not refuse certificate unless for some absolutely certain reason, 537——Difficulty of proving anything wrong before coroner, 538—— Injurious to private practitioner if he had reputation of refusing certificates, 539——Believes many cases of neglect escape the law, 541.

C.

Carter, Mr. Maurice Frederick. (Analysis of his Evidence.)—Is coroner and clerk to guardians in Gloucestershire, 753 ;—a mining, manufacturing, and agricultural district, 755–757.

Believes insurance of children is prejudicial to them, 765——Gives instance where child was insured for a sum not entirely payable till age of ten, and who died in an emaciated condition soon after that age, 768–772. 869–871——Cross-examined as to this case, 887–880——Another case where several children in a family died insured, 774–779 ;—one child insured when in bad state of health, 779, 798——Parents do not
often

Carter, Mr. Maurice Frederick. (Analysis of his Evidence)—*continued.*

often deny insurance, 786—— Idea of profit in connection with child's death has tendency to deprave parents, 796 ;—is an additional temptation to get rid of burden of child, 814-816.

Doctors in Gloucestershire certainly do not give certificates in suspicious cases, 784.

Has never sent a case for trial, 805 ;—not being able to get the jury to give a verdict of criminal neglect, 806-815. 842——They take the most charitable view, 809, 886-9 ——Necessary to prove means to convict parent of neglect to provide nourishment, 843—or medical attendance, 899 ;—though parents can apply to parish if necessitous, 900-902—— Insurance not effected to pay doctor, 818. 900-910 ;—but is of opinion that application to the parish for medical relief has a tendency to bring people on the list of paupers, 892-3.

Agents make no inquiry as to health of child to be insured, 844——Has never received any assistance from them, 845 —— The society with which he is the most familiar is the Prudential, 890.

Guardians could not easily recover if they buried an insured child, but does not think this occurs in his district, 822-827 —— Is of opinion that either insurance of children should be stopped, or that it be limited to amount necessary for decent funeral, 829 ;—not to the absolutely lowest rate of funeral, 834 ;—but might be paid to undertaker direct, 835 ;—cannot fix any sum as proper, 851 ;—but thinks 1 *l.* sufficient, 854 ;—thinks it would be a hardship to forbid insurance of children under one year, 862——It is parents' duty to do so, 861——Thinks it possible, but not probable, that payment to undertaker might tend to his acting in collusion with parent, 872-875.

In suspicious cases police make inquiries and report to coroner, and, when registrar is informed that doctor will not grant certificate, he reports to coroner, who then investigates and holds inquest if he thinks necessary, 846, 865——Witness always holds inquest in such cases of illegitimate children, 865——This and his announced decision to hold inquests, when circumstances are suspicious, has had a good effect in district, 867, 868.

Cases of Suspicious Death or Neglect. Cases mentioned : (Pritchard's case), *Branson* 223, 226, 229, 267——(Teresa Smith), *Waugh* 2041, 2044, 2054, 2055——Case dismissed (before Mr. Justice Wills) because of want of proof of means, *ib.* 2079-82——(Ernest Bastan), *ib.* 2083——Deptford case (Sydney Bolton), where thirty-five policies on lives of two children were found in the house of a baby farmer, *ib.* 2093-2102, 2120; *see* also page 52——But report of jury in this case was not directed against child insurance but against assignment of policies, *Dewey* 3587-94.

Birkdale case, *Waugh* 2103-10, 2117, 2136-7, 2153, 2164, 2184, 2185-7.

Strand (or Serné) case, *Troutbeck* 968——In this case man found guilty of arson, which was really committed for insurance money, 600 *l.*. not for few pounds of child insurance, *Dewey* 3001.

Case where child only came into full benefit after ten years old ; died then of emaciation, *Carter* 772——Another case where child died without proper medical aid, and mother said she had insured it, as the money would be acceptable, *ib.* 774 ; *Browne* 1065-70, 1079, 1088, 1103 ; *Grahame* (par. 6), page 132.

Case at Leicester, *see* page 53 ;—another at Leicester, *see* pages 103 and 104 ;—at Rotherham, *Burnett* 1277 *et seq.* ;—at Newcastle, *see* page 79.

Swindon baby-farming case, tried at Wells, *Day* 1952-4, 1963 ;—in this case insurance was by baby farmer, not by parents, *ib.* 1908-2011 ;—out of seven children on four no more payments for keep were due ; these were insured ; on three further payments were due ; these were not insured, *Waugh* 2179-83—— Case where money was paid by an Affiliated Order on death of a child made away with, *Taunton* 3212.

CERTIFICATE, DEATH :

        1. *Registrar's Certificate.*
        2. *Doctor's Certificate.*
        3. *Refusal of Certificate.*
        4. *Suggestions.*

(1.) *Registrar's Certificate :*

Required to be given by registrar under the Friendly Societies Act before insurance money may be paid, to the effect that cause of death has been certified by doctor or coroner, *Cleaver* 450-5 ;—or found by coroner's jury, *Browne* 1174-80 ;—doubtful how this is got over in cases where doctor has refused to certify, and no inquest has been held, *Cleaver* 457 ;—words of Act quoted, Question 454——Registrar has option, when doctor has refused, to grant certificate, on satisfactory evidence of cause of death, of

(225—IND.)   K k   which

CERTIFICATE, DEATH—continued.

1. *Registrar's Certificate*—continued.

which he is the judge, *Dewey* 2908–10 ;—no objection on part of Prudential to this option being taken away, *ib.* 2915–9 ;—but cases of hardship might then arise where doctor had not been called in in time, *ib.* 2915——This option should be taken away, *Taunton* 3103 ; *Fortune* 3752–6.

Registrar alone, not doctor, can under Friendly Societies Act grant certificate for insurance money, *Barwise* 120.

Registrar receives a fee of 1 *s.* 3 *d.* for each certificate, *Thomson* 648——Though it is his interest therefore to grant it, fee is so small that it is no temptation, and no case of impropriety has ever been reported, *Dewey* 2911–3.

Registrars are very strict about giving certificates, *Dobson* 2662 ;—give them carelessly, *Taunton* 3096 *et seq.*; 3106.

Certain societies, Newbold Friendly Society for instance, not registered under the Friendly Societies Act, have power in their rules to dispense with registrar's certificate, *Leach* 1760 *et seq.*—Statement that certain societies do this, *ib.* 1760–1.

Registered societies, for their own protection, retain registrar's certificate ; unregistered societies are sometimes content to see it, so that any amount may be paid upon it, *Hambridge* 3876.

(2.) *Doctor's Certificate :*

Often given by doctor in suspicious cases, as he knows difficulty of proving neglect, *Barwise* 53 ; *Thomson* 638–656 ; *Cleaver* 381 ;—on account of difficulty of proving guilt, *Branson* 336 ;—often given carelessly or in improper cases, because doctor has no means of distinguishing culpable from ignorant neglect, *Cleaver* 385 ;—without knowledge of previous history of case, *Branson* 237–9——Certificate very easily got from cheap dispensary doctors, *Hartop* 1696–7 ;—from some doctors, *Branson* 332.

Applications to witness for certificate have diminished since he began to question mothers before granting it, *Cleaver* 363 ;—or mothers sent children by someone else, to avoid answering, *ib.* 366–7.

Refusal of certificate makes doctor unpopular, *Barwise* 167–9 ;—especially if he fails to get a conviction, *Branson* 239 ;—injurious to his practice, if known to be apt to refuse certificate, *Burry* 539–40——Loss of time attending trial a very serious matter for medical man, *Branson* 239.

Not given by doctor in suspicious cases, *Carter* 784 ; *Branson* 251 ; *Browne* 1118.

Case where insurance agent has asked witness to falsify certificate, *Thomson* 671–3 ; —to post date beginning of disease till after date of insurance, *ib.* 672 ;—such applications come more commonly from parents, *ib.* 737.

Doctor may always refuse to give certificate, stating his grounds to the coroner, *Branson* 335——Sometimes give certificates in doubtful terms, which ensures inquiry, *Barwise* 125——Is only subject to penalty for refusing without reasonable cause, *Browne* 1116.

Better for doctor to refuse certificate, when case is inquired into, than to fill up certificate more fully with his opinions and comments on case, *Browne* 1115–7.

Anxiety of parents to get certificate aroused witness' suspicions, *Barwise* 34.

Can only be given by doctor who has seen patients alive, *Barwise* 134——Is given gratis ; there is a penalty on doctor for taking a fee, *ib.* 147–8——Hospital doctors do not necessarily see out-patients dead, but give certificate if their death was not unexpected, *Cleaver* 426 *et seq.* ;—but registrar requires besides a statement from some one present at death, *ib.* 438——Unqualified medical men call in qualified practitioner at the last moment to see patient they have been attending, *Barwise* 137.

Necessity of sending for doctor to get certificate has sometimes resulted in saving moribund child, *Wills* 1884.

Death certificate simply records medical cause of death, not that that was caused by neglect, *ib.* 42 ; *Branson* 252 ;—no mention of how cause of death was brought about, *Browne* 1183.

(3.) *Refusal of Certificate :*

When refused by doctor, registrar reports to coroner, *Carter* 846 ;—or gives certificate himself, *Cleaver* 394 ; *Taunton* 3098—— Parents often when it is refused communicate with police ; they make inquiries, and often send to doctor to say there is no ground for his suspicions, *Thomson* 639–44——This is too great a responsibility to be left on police, *ib.* 659——Coroner on hearing of refusal from registrar makes inquiries, and if he thinks necessary holds inquest, *Carter* 845.

Doctor

CERTIFICATE, DEATH—continued.

(4.) *Suggestions:*

Doctor or coroner should always be obliged to ask if child was insured, answer to be marked on certificate ; if denied, insurance society should not be allowed to pay money, *Taunton* 3130-7.

Any alteration of certificate to be made illegal and punishable ; at present there is no provision who is to prosecute, *Taunton* 3196-204.

A special form of certificate should be issued on which only insurance money should be payable, *Burnett* 1302.

Only one certificate for insurance should be given, which should be legal receipt for insurance money, *Taunton* 3404-6 ;—specifying name of office and amount payable ; letter of Leeds Society for Prevention of Cruelty to Children, page 134 ;—only one certificate under penalty on registrar, *Dewey* 2921-6.

If it had to be given by doctor attending case, instead of registrar, he would then know all cases, and could judge better of neglect, *Barwise* 123——Formerly certificates for insurance money were given for a fee by doctors, but Friendly Societies Act abolished this, and only allowed registrar to give them ; since then doctors' death certificates are less full, *Hambridge* 3878-9, 3888-9.

Certificate of Health. If certificate of health were required on insurance of child, it would diminish evils, *Hartop* 1715-17 ;—many thriftless parents would not insure at all, as they wait till the child is sick, *ib.* 1723.

In Prudential agent has to certify on the proposal as to health of child; he has nothing but his general intelligence to guide him, *Dewey* 3535-40——In friendly societies, which are respectable, there is no need of a medical certificate, which would cost money, *Dobson* 2511.

Charles, Mr. Justice. In charge to grand jury at Newcastle, at trial for causing death by culpable neglect, said it was a question whether some legislation ought not to take place ; not to prevent the insurance of children's lives, but to prevent the proceeds getting into the hands of parents, *see* page 104.

Children's Life Insurance Bill (H.L.). Undertakers' clause is the chief objection to Bill, *Dobson* 2555-7 ; *Crooks* 2273, 2232 ; *Dewey* 2782-3 ; Letter of Macclesfield Amalgamated Burial Societies, page 133 ; Letter of Leeds Society for Prevention of Cruelty to Children, page 134.——See *Undertaker.*

Though it concerns Scotland, the Scottish National Society for the Prevention of Cruelty to Children was not consulted, *Grahame,* par. 4, page 131——Nor even the principal insurance benefit societies, *ib.* par. 7 (*b*), page 132.

No objection to scale of amount in Bill, *Crooks* 2294——No objection to Clauses 1, 3, 4, and 5—Letter of Macclesfield Amalgamated Burial Societies, page 133.

Scale in Bill drawn by Mr. Ludlow, Chief Registrar of Friendly Societies, and approved by Committee of the House of Commons, *Waugh* 2214-7——Is too low ; Letter of Leeds Society for the Prevention of Cruelty to Children, page 134.

Would allow other persons than parent to insure children; this should be altered, *Dewey* 2855-9, 2999——Discussion as to how far this is accurate, *ib.* 3442-9

Cleaver, Mr. W. J., M.D. (Analysis of his Evidence.)—Is surgeon at the Child's Hospital, Sheffield, 348—— Used formerly to give certificate without question, but for the last few years has had his suspicions aroused and makes inquiries, 351 ;—and in doubtful cases refuses certificates and sends a note to registrar, 362 ;—especially in cases where children are only brought to him just before death, 352.

No cases where witness has refused certificates have been brought before the coroner, 394 ;—probably registrar gives a certificate himself, 394-6 ; perhaps after consultation with coroner, 445—— Has refused certificate about half-a-dozen times a year for the last few years, 482—— Since inquiries have been made fewer suspicious cases have been brought to the hospital, 363, 413 ; — children often brought by someone other than mother, to avoid answering questions, 366-7.

Certificates often given without proper inquiry, 373—— Doctors have little time to give to each case, 374 ;—are unwilling to put parents to trouble of inquest without strong grounds, 434——Difficult or impossible to distinguish cases of culpable neglect, 381 ;—by medical symptoms, 388 ;—without evidence from neighbours, 382 ;—which they will not readily give, 468——Difficult to check statements of parents which are often the only evidences doctor can get, 359, 393——Asks parents if child is insured, but has only their statement, 401-4 ;—of which he is often suspicious, 409-10—— Does not think mothers generally ignorant of the proper way of treating children, 469-72 ;—pains have been taken at Sheffield to teach them, by distributing leaflets, 472——The ignorance sometimes existing affords a convenient excuse for neglect, 484.

Cleaver, Mr. W. J., M.D. (Analysis of his Evidence)—*continued.*

Hospital doctors have little means of knowing about the cases they certify, 376, 400.

Certificate of doctor only states medical cause of death, 440, 480——Hospital doctors do not necessarily see patient after death before giving certificate, 426, 432;—but registrar further requires a statement from some person present at time of death, 438.

Under Friendly Societies Act insurance companies may not pay without certificate from registrar, that the cause of death has been certified by doctor or coroner, 450–5 ; witness does not know what happens in cases where doctor has refused certificate, 457.

There is a common opinion in medical profession that there is much criminal neglect in connection with life insurance, 397.

Clensy, Mr. John. (Analysis of his Evidence.)—Attends by invitation of the Committee 3891——Is secretary to the Liverpool Victoria and Legal Friendly Society, 3890 ; —which is the largest collecting friendly society in existence, 3892——It is a mutual society, as all profits go to the members, 3897——But a friendly society is hedged in with so many restrictions that an industrial society is able to do as well or better, though they pay a dividend to shareholders, 4042–3.

Has 1,200,000 insuring members, 3899–900 ;—185,000 children below five insured, 3904 ;—155,000 between five and ten, 4034——Usual premium is 1 *d.* a week, but there are a few of ½ *d.*, 3917–24.

Their agents are a most respectable body of men, 3934, 3936 ;— they are paid by commission of 25 per cent. on premiums and the first six payments, 3925–6 ;—in practice they get rather less than 25 per cent , though more nominally, 3929.

Insurance has no connection with cruelty or neglect of children, 3964–5 —— This existed before, and outside insurance, 3959——Struggle for life is a very serious matter to very poor people, 3962 ;—if mother wishes to kill her child it is not done for the insurance money, 3956, 3960–1——Criticises Dr. Thomson's remark that doctor is often called in too late, if so from dread of doctor's bill or parish doctor ; if death-rate for Oldham is higher than that for all England, so is that of all crowded towns ; and dissents from opinion that insured children are less cared for than uninsured, 4011—— Mr. Troutbeck's statement that parents came drunk, out of insurance money, to inquest, is absurd, as money would not be paid till coroner has given a certificate, 4013——Not true that money is paid before death is legally proved, 4039 ;—or that advances are made on policies, 4040 ;—such an assignment would be a worthless security, 4041—— Society would always rather pay money without discussion, and as people make false statements they sometimes pay when they ought not to, 4070——Great difficulty in discovering baby farmers ; children in their charge are often entered as their own, 4071——If discovered, insurance is cancelled, 4078——In Deptford case (insured in Liverpool Victoria), the woman represented herself as mother, 4080— —Knows nothing more about that case, 4065–70.

Working classes have a very strong feeling against interference with infant insurance as it stands at present, 3948 ;—in the direction of curtailing amount, 3949——Their privileges are already low enough, 3966, 3969——The Friendly Societies Act dealt hardly with them in restricting the amount to 6 *l.* and 10 *l.*, 3970–1——Is aware that the Friendly Societies Act was a piece of class legislation, in favour of the working man, 3975 ;—and gives him privileges it denies to the rich man, 3792–4——But the poor man insures from necessity, 3976 ;—if the rich man insured his child it would be a speculation, 3974.

Agents and collectors are stringently instructed to inquire into health of children they insure, 3937 ;—and to avoid low-class business, 3938 ;—and are restricted from insuring in certain unsanitary districts or streets at all, 3940, 4029 ;—where they could get plenty of business, as they have not been canvassed for a long time, 3941–7.

Claims paid average much less than legal maximum, 3953 —— But it would be hardship to restrict insurance to average claim, as there is a great variety in the class of insurers, 3951 ;— a graduated scale would not be fair, as one parent might think 2 *l.* enough for a funeral, another 6 *l.* not enough, 3985 — There may be wasteful expenditure on funerals, 3988 ;—and many people may think it ought, in all classes, to be reduced, 3987 ;—but it would not be a good thing if this Bill reduced it, 3990 —— British working man attaches immense importance to a becoming and creditable funeral, 3989 ;—which is a question of sentiment, 3986 —— Cost of a very poor funeral in Liverpool would be 2 *l.* 5 *s.*, 4024 ;—only actual funeral expenses, 4027.

Scale of payments and premiums in Liverpool Victoria, 4047–53 —— In some other offices more is given after first infancy but less in first year ; this is probably as an inducement to join, 4054–7.

Insurance has had the effect of wonderfully inculcating thrift in working men, 3991–2 ;—and interference with it would resuscitate " friendly leads " and be prejudicial to thrift, 3980——Friendly leads and slate clubs are now extinct, 4037——
These

Clensy, Mr. John. (Analysis of his Evidence)—*continued*.

These clubs were held at public houses, 4036——A man could still get money sub-scribed at his workshop for funeral, but working men now have a horror of this form of begging, 4038.

Money is only paid to persons other than parents in exceptional circumstances, 4061-62;—which would be settled not by agent but by head office, which is the same rule as in Prudential, 4063.

A parent who is convicted of gross cruelty to a child is unfit to be allowed to insure any child, 4006——Rather than declare the policy void it would be better to allow the magistrate to transfer it to some other person, 4007;—working classes would not object to this, 4008;—or to any strengthening of the law to prevent murder, 4045.

Is strongly opposed to prohibition of insurance below one year or two years, 3979-80;—and thinks it would be impracticable in actual working to pay no insurance money if child died below one year, but only return the premiums, 3981;—and any scheme of employing the saving to the insurance companies in some endowment would be unintelligible to the working classes, 3982-83;—objects to any graduated scale that would reduce present legal maximum, 4058.

Impracticable, as Mr. Taunton proposed, to license agents. 3993——In Liverpool Victoria Legal there are over 3,000 agents, and a certain proportion of them are always shifting, 3994.

Desirable that a child should be insurable only in one office, 3998.

There should be a uniform table of insurance money for all societies, 4000——They would still compete for business, 4004;—but a great many of the evils complained of would be removed, 4000;—and the competition would be of a healthy character, 4004.

Cleveland, Mr. John Edward. (Analysis of his Evidence.)—Is secretary to the National-Independent Order of Odd Fellows, 4187;—and appears by invitation of the Committee, as representing, with Mr. Stead and Mr. Walton (*see* their evidence), the conference of Affiliated Friendly Societies, 4402-5;—which represents 2,012,969 members, 4192.

Conference passed a resolution that the limitations as to age and amount of insurance in the Bishop of Peterborough's Bill were quite inapplicable and unjust to the Friendly Societies, inasmuch as the privileges now enjoyed by them cannot be, and are not, abused, which is proved by the fact that four societies of 126,642 members (the only ones of the conference whose figures are ready), only had a mortality of one-half per cent., 4410——This is of children under sixteen years only, 4411.

The popularity of friendly societies is much increasing, and they gain many members for collecting societies, 4446——They have great advantages; members of friendly societies meet together in yearly or half-yearly meetings, 4450;—which share in the management has an elevating effect on them, 4581;—they are in touch with each other, and any abuses would be stopped, 4450——The profit in them belongs to members, 4450;—and they are managed by members gratis, or for a very small gratuity to cover expenses, 4419. 4460——The expenses of the collecting societies are known to be very great, whereas in the Odd Fellows they are limited to 15 per cent. of receipts, 4450; —and when members survive and have to leave the juvenile societies at twenty-one, a return of a portion of the profits is made them, or their entry money into parent society is paid, 4460-2;—also advantage that more and more members of juvenile branches are passed on to parent society, and the habit of thrift is made continuous from youth up, 4464.

It may be that some collecting societies give larger benefits, but, nevertheless, people are beginning to prefer the friendly societies, 4519.

Societies registered prior to 1875 may grant insurances at any age, 4415——But friendly societies registered under the Friendly Societies Act, 1875, are not allowed to grant insurances on children, except by (Section 8) on children of members, 4417. 4420, 4435;—but by Section 15 of the Act of 1875, societies or branches are allowed to be separately registered for the insurance of any children over three and under sixteen, 4416. 4431;—and the friendly societies have under that power established juvenile branches, 4421-2;—not mixed up with the parent society, but under the same management, 4439——The effect of these provisions is that friendly societies cannot insure infants from birth to three, except those of their own members, 4435;—not children of the outside public, 4424. 4440.

It is very desirable that these restrictions should be abolished and friendly societies allowed to insure children at all ages in one society, 4446. 4539——They would certainly so extend their insurances if it were allowed, 4492;—with a view of carrying on a more successful competition with the collecting societies, 4492-43——If they did, the same careful supervision would continue, simply requiring more inquirers, 4479-82 ——The habit of infant insurance is very much increasing, and children of members are now generally insured in parent society, 4554-49.

Report, 1890—*continued.*

Cleveland, Mr. John Edward. (Analysis of his Evidence)—*continued.*

It might be desirable that children under twelve months could only be insured in one office, 4413 ;—whether registered or not, 4569-70 ;— which would much facilitate investigation, 4574 ;—quotes a case where, to his own knowledge, a very young child was insured in three unregistered offices for nearly 10 *l.*, 4413-5.

Registrars are not sufficiently careful to inquire in how many societies a child is insured ; though since this Committee began they may have become more so, 4497.

There are many unregistered societies, 4498 :—they have not registered under the Act of 1875, as registration is voluntary, 4501 ;—if registered they have to make annual returns and valuations, and dislike government interference, 4549 ;—all societies which insure children ought to be registered, 4550 ;—without it there is no supervision and no one knows how much is paid, 4553.

It is possible that it might be well to limit amount of insurance on children under twelve months, 4504 ;—the amount ought not to be too limited, as the cost of the simplest funeral in Manchester, with the coffin carried on the parent's knees in the coach, is 2 *l.* 5 *s.*, 4505-7——If it were too limited the old custom of begging subscriptions would be revived, 4510 ;—the amount paid in the Odd Fellows is, under three months, 30 *s.*, and under one year 2 *l.*, rising 10 *s.* a year till eleven years, 4513-4 ;—which shows that those witness represents would not object to legal limitation to those amounts, 4513.

Inquiry is made as to character of parents, and in some cases, health of children, and under the system of management by members and mutual acquaintance, impossible that any infanticide should take place, 4443-4 ;—and if legislation is necessary some distinction should be made between the affiliated friendly societies and other insurance companies, 4466, 4485-7 ;—as was suggested by the House of Commons Committee of last year, 4486.

Admits that infanticide has, in some cases, been proved ; in the great majority of cases the heavy infant mortality is owing to overcrowding, to unsanitary dwellings, and to mothers working in factories before and after birth of child ; but where it has been proved that idle and dissolute parents endeavour to get rid of the burden of children, insurance has had nothing to do with it, and so long as this is so it is unnecessary to amend the Friendly Societies Act so as to restrict the freedom which friendly societies now possess, 4413.

Admits that a very small percentage of child murders would be a large number in the aggregate, 4473 ;—but does not admit that this exists, 4575-9 ;—but considers the suggestion of even this small percentage is an imputation on the working classes, as if infanticide takes place, it is not amongst them but amongst the residuum, 4476 ;—who do not insure, at any rate in friendly societies, 4562-6, 4571-2 ;—have not sufficient foresight to insure, 4599.

The proceeds of insurance are hardly sufficient to bury a child ;—even if the desire of the poor to bury their children " respectably " (which in excess is not to be encouraged, 4532-4548) were got rid of there would be no margin, 4413.

If insurance is in any way diminished the poor rate will be increased and the independence of the working classes destroyed, 4413.

Impossible to make provision in the savings bank for death ; at the rate of 1 *d.* a week it would take eleven years to make a sum of 2 *l.* 10 *s.*, and besides, some necessity might arise and the money be drawn out, 4413 ;—as some cases of infanticide do exist, though not in witness' society, legal penalty should be increased, 4525 ;—and facilities for prosecutions, 4544-5. 4587 ;—would gladly agree to anything to prevent infanticide, 4588 ;—Objects to coroner having the right to void policy without actual conviction for neglect, 4590 ;—and even if the parent were convicted of cruelty or the child died, does not think policy should be void, as the child must be buried, and the cost would be thrown on the rates, 4591.

Cobban, Dr. Is Police Surgeon at Rotherham, and has drawn up a form for registration of insurances and death certificate, *Burnett* 1310 *et seq.*

Collecting Societies. Scottish Legal Life Assurance Company is both a collecting and mutual society, *Fortune* 3635 ;—also Liverpool Victoria and Legal, *Cleasy* 3893-7 ; —also Royal Liver, *Taunton* 3037-8 :—also Royal London, *Hambridge* 3582-5—— Most of the bad cases are in connection with collecting societies, *Ritchie* 1441-2. See *Insurance Companies* and *Friendly Societies.*

Collectors. Same as agents, *Dewey* 2863-5 ; *Taunton* 3381. See *Insurance Agents.*

Conviction. Difficult to get conviction for manslaughter at assizes, *Barwise* 70-74 ; *Branson* 242——Evidence given before coroner gets weaker before trial, *ib.* 85——Cannot often be got, as doctor cannot swear that the child would have recovered even if properly cared for, *Hodson* 574——Case where conviction failed because doctors said that children might die in spite of every care, *Browne* 1110——Great difficulty of getting evidence other than of parents who cannot give evidence against one another,

and

Conviction – continued.

and of neighbours who always make out the best case, *Troutbeck* 954-8 ;—evidence of other children to be looked upon with suspicion, *ib.* 961-2,

Conviction procured on charge of neglect before magistrates after coroner refused to hold inquest, *Branson* 303 ;—better to prosecute before magistrates than to send to trial for manslaughter, *Browne* 1101-1— Case where magistrate refused to commit for neglect, saying offence was manslaughter or nothing ; public prosecutor examined into evidence, and thought it not sufficient to get conviction for manslaughter at assizes, so case dropped, *Waugh* 2137.

In cases of cruelty (not murder or manslaughter), juries require rather restraining than urging, *Day* 2018-20.

Case of conviction and punishment of fifteen months' imprisonment on mother for neglect, *Browne* 1065-74—-Case at Rotherham for neglect, *Burnett* 1277 *et seq.*—Cases mentioned (Teresa Smith), *Waugh* 2041-4 ; *ib.* 2044 ; *ib.* 2058 ; (Ernest Bastan), *ib.* 2083 ; (Pearson) 2106-9 ; Swindon baby-farming, *ib.* 2179-83.

Society for Prevention of Cruelty to Children got 670 convictions in 752 cases, *Waugh* 2037-8.

Statistics of length of punishments awarded, *ib.* 2040 — Scottish Society for Prevention of Cruelty to Children prosecuted in 4,305 cases ; letter of Mr. J. Grahame, paragraph 3, page 131.

Discovery often only by accident ; in Deptford case father and baby farmer quarrelled over insurance money, *Waugh* 2120— Case at Liverpool, *ib.* 2118—Easier to get in baby farming cases, as neighbours dislike them, *ib.* 2192—-On conviction for cruelty policy should become void ; also person convicted be made incapable of insuring other children, *Taunton* 3187-93 : *Cleusy* 4006 ;—or policy transferred by magistrate to some one else, *ib.* 4007.

Coroners. For opinions of, *see* Evidence of Thomson, Dr. ; Carter, Mr. M. F. ; Troutbeck, Mr. J. ; *Browne*, Mr. Arthur ; Hooper, Mr. H. W. ; Hooper, Mr. Edwin ; and letter of Mr. Thorneycroft, App. C., page 229.

Are often obliged to advise juries not to find verdict of manslaughter in suspicious cases on account of difficulty of getting convictions at assizes, *Thomson* 664 ; *Barwise* 69-74. 85 —— Cannot get juries to give verdict of culpable neglect, *Carter* 806-813. 842 ,—find juries unwilling to give verdict against parents, especially mother of illegitimate child, *Troutbeck* 985.

Investigate suspicious cases reported to them by police, or, on refusal of certificate, reported by registrar, and hold inquests if they think necessary, *Carter* 865——Do not have to in the majority of cases, *Barwise* 65 ;—hold informal inquiry, and if not of opinion that it is a case for inquest, issue form to that effect, on which death is registered, *Troutbeck* 1026—— Good effect of its being known that they will readily hold inquests in doubtful cases, *Carter* 868——Witness always holds inquest on illegitimate children not certified for, *ib.* 865.

Statistics of inquests, *Thomson* 625 *et seq.* ; *Carter* 838 ; *Troutbeck* 977 ; *H. W. Hooper* 1215, 1229.

Letter of Mr. W. Wood, Deputy Coroner for Greenwich Division, to Home Secretary, giving rider of jury, that the loose system of insurance by some companies is an incentive to murder, read by the Chairman, *page* 52——Opinions unfavourable to infant insurance quoted, of coroners of Plymouth, Devonport, Barnstaple, Okehampton, Crediton, Totnes, Honiton, and Stoke Damerel, *H. W. Hooper* 1224.

Crooks, Mr. William. (Analysis of his Evidence.)—Is a journeyman cooper, living at Poplar, E., 2270-1——Is well acquainted with the working classes, 2274. 2429-30 ;—and was on the committee of the late dock strike, 2371.

Great objection is to part of Bill making compulsory the payment of insurance money direct to undertaker, 2273. 2332——A great reproach to working class parents, 2431——Has little objection to rest of Bill, 2294. 2333. 2427 ;—none to limitation in it on amount to be insured for, 2295.

Thrifty parents insure, unthrifty do not, 2445-6——Any evidence to the contrary can only refer to isolated cases, 2447——Object of working men who insure is to provide not only for funeral, but also for incidental expenses, 2273 ;—such as doctor's bill, and mourning for the funeral, 2274. 2435——Doctor has to be paid out of wages if child recovers, but says that is a labour of love, and different to payment if child dies, 2310 ;—in case of death money already paid to doctor should be repaid from insurance, 2404 ;—and possibly things taken out of pawn, pledged to pay for illness expenses, 2464——Untrue that parents do not send for doctor in time for want of affection, but on account of expense ; they generally go to the chemist, 2274——Knows no cases of

(225—IND.)   K K 4   bad

Crooks, Mr. William. (Analysis of his Evidence)— *continued*.

bad mothers, 2274. 2277——If they exist they will make away with their children, with or without insurance, simply letting the parish bury for them, 2397——Quotes statement of relieving officer that he has never known a case that raised suspicion in his mind that child was put away by parent for sake of insurance money, 2382—— Opinion of neighbours a strong check against cruelty, 2450-2. 2486-7——Hard that expression of hope that a sick child may die, be attributed to desire to get insurance money rather than to distress at its suffering, 2275——Admits that there may be one bad case out of 1,000; 2279 ;—which would come to a considerable number in the aggregate, 2285 ;—but it would be wrong to punish the whole working class for the sake of this one in 1,000 ; 2279, 2385 ;— the law ought to be able to detect and punish this one case, 2289. 2326.

Has no objection to restrictions already placed by law on infant insurance, 2337—— Thinks if they do not answer their purpose of preventing crime, the remedy should be that where coroner and jury censure parents for neglect, but when they cannot convict, the insurance money should not be paid to parents, but that burial should be provided out of it, 2275. 2338. 2394. 2472.

Serious objection to preventing insurance under one year : the sum now insured is so low that it does not cover expenses, 2342-4. 2350. 2482 ;—and should be retained, 2442 ;—but loss, if forbidden, not so great as when children are older, 2444——Quotes amount of expense in burying his children, in one case 2 *l.* 3 *s.*, though buried in the plainest way, 2344 ;—in another case 27 *s.* 6 *d.*, but this was a funeral he was ashamed of, 2347. 2424——Working men attach great importance to having a respectable funeral, 2380 ;—but agrees that an extravagant funeral is a poor form of pride, 2399. (For details of these bills, *see* App. A., *page* 227)——Believes that a funeral would in most places cost more than 1 *l.* ; thinks that if undertakers advertise to do it for 15 *s.*, this does not cover all expenses, but that there would be extras, 2349. 2425—— Believes funeral for child under one year cannot be done under 2 *l.* ; 2377.

Would have no objection to registration of insurances, 2371——No one ought to be insured more than once unless total insurances only amount to legal amount, 2381.

If insurance only allowed to be for actual expenses question would arise what are necessary expenses ; whether mourning, doctor's bill, or medical comforts should be included, 2356-7. 2413——If mourning included, worthless people could pawn it, 2333. 2358 ;— if not, the tallyman would be brought back, 2359.

If Bill passes, old system of " friendly leads " will be revived, 2275 ;—which are now nearly extinct, 2363-4——Since insurance of children has existed working men expect others to insure, and do not approve of sending round the hat to meet funeral expenses that ought to come out of insurance, 2368——Large sums used to be got at friendly leads, as much as 18 *l.*, 2275——If this Bill passes, and only allows payment of exact expenses of funeral, contributions of insurers will be confiscated, 2306 ;—not if undertakers' clause would only apply to future insurances, 2308. 2320-1 ;—yet believes that working classes would not insure at all under this Bill, 2309, 2322——Possible, no doubt, to save up money in savings bank, but great likelihood of its being drawn out for daily needs, 2385-92. 2409-11.

Bill would lead to collusion with the undertakers, 2333.

Has no opinion on the comparative merits of insurance companies and burial clubs, 2417-22 ;—but on hypothesis put to him that burial clubs are cheaper, and all the profits go to members, admits they should be encouraged, 2440.

His children were insured without the agent seeing them, 2426 ;—but canvassers do not, in his experience, importune people to insure, 2439——Has never heard of a child insured before birth, but knows of a case where agent came to ask if a woman was confined yet, 2464.

Sunday funerals not so common as formerly, 2457-8——Working men, as a rule, stop away from funeral rather than lose a day's work, 2459.

Cunningham, Mr. M. J. (Analysis of his Evidence.)—Was secretary of a friendly society, which issued 5,000 policies, 4374. 4387 ;—and ceased to exist twenty years ago, 4384 ;—being amalgamated with another society, 4386. 4391-2——Was deputed to attend here by a meeting of delegates of the working classes held in Farringdon Hall, 4373 ;—at which about forty delegates were present, 4379.

Appears to support a resolution protesting " against the sweeping, untrue, and slanderous statements made in the House of Lords and elsewhere," 4399 ;—founds this upon an article in a newspaper containing an extract from an article in a review, by Rev. Mr. Waugh, 4395 ;—and upon the impression left in the public mind by articles in newspapers that such statements were made in the House of Lords, 4399-401.

D.

Day, Mr. Justice. (Analysis of his Evidence.)—Has been for eight years a Judge of the High Court, 1945——Has formed a strong opinion as to the connection of crime with infant life insurance, 1947–50——Has tried many cases of neglect of children, some insured, others not, 1953——Thinks that people in a poor condition are tempted, when their children are insured, to get the money as soon as possible, 1963.

Is opposed to child life insurance as carried on by large societies, 1977, 1992. 1997 ; —thinks that no exception ought to be made in favour of any class from the provisions of the Act of George III., which prohibits gambling on human life, 1965 ;—a parent has usually no insurable interest in the life of his child, 1973–5 ;—child insurance tends to deaden the interest of a parent in the life of his child, 1976 ;—and in the case of children, the facilities for malpractices are stronger than they are in the case of adults, 1980——Quotes case tried at Wells of baby farming at Swindon where the caretaker found means to insure the children though she did not to feed them, 1952——The burial expenses of a child ought to be provided against in the same way as other misfortunes, 1983 ;—which are often much more expensive, 1988–9.

Child life insurance is a very wasteful form of thrift, 1957–8. 1970–2. 1985.

Has no objection to local burial clubs, 1992 ;—which ought not to be interfered with ; the members watch one another, as their interests are bound up together, 1994——Has never known of a criminal case in connection with a local burial club, 1994.

Trials have proved to witness that very little care is taken to control agents, 1954 ; —who are paid a large commission on each new insurance they effect, 1954–6, 1959 ——In case referred to above, agent reported lives as good, when some of them were in a desperate state, 1957——The touting of agents must bring before the parents the idea of profit to be got out of deaths, 1962.

Doubt how far baby farmers could be the "personal representatives" of the parents, so as to justify them insuring the children, 2009–10 ;—but they believed in the validity of the insurance or would not have paid the premiums, 2011.

Juries have no hesitation in convicting for neglect of children; the difficulty of a judge is rather to restrain them, 2018, 2020——This does not apply to trials for child murder which raise different questions, 2011, 2020——Difficulty of getting conviction depends on view some judges have taken of the proof required of means of parent to support child, but some judges have held that where there is a workhouse within reach a child may not be allowed to starve, 2019.

Death Rate. See *Mortality of Children.*

Deaths, Suspicious. Difficult for doctor to say if neglect is intentional, *Barwise* 23, 58–62, 104, 105——Children often brought very late to doctor, *Cleaver* 352····—Very easy to kill children simply by improper food, *Hobson* 579.

Do not occur in respectable working men's families although insured, *Troutbeck* 1010 ——Ten per cent. of deaths of children from preventible causes, including overlaying ; this by drunken parents or more generally from overcrowding, *Tauntou* 3062–77, 3417–20.

See *Cases of Suspicious Death or Neglect.*

Deptford Case. Jury added a rider to their verdict that the present loose system of insurance by some companies is an incentive to murder; letter put in by Chairman, page 52 ;—this related to insurable interest, not to child insurance, and persons affected were not children but aged 74, 53, and 11; *Dewey* 3,000, 3587–94——Victims insured in Liverpool Victoria and Legal Society, *Clensy* 4066——Secretary knows no particulars except that the woman insuring pretended to be the mother, *ib.* 4065–70, 4080.

Devonshire. For opinion that at Bovey Tracey children were neglected for the sake of insurance money, see *Hodson, Mr. H. A.* (Analysis of his Evidence.)——Opinions of coroners of Plymouth, Devonport, Barnstaple, Okehampton, Crediton, Totnes, Honiton, and Stoke Damerel, unfavourable to infant insurance, quoted, *H. W. Hooper* 1227. See also *Hooper, Mr. H. W.* (Analysis of his Evidence).

Dewey, Mr. Thomas Charles. (Analysis of his Evidence.)—Is, and has been for sixteen years, Manager of the Prudential Assurance Company, 2780 ;—which is a joint stock company, and is regulated by the Life Assurance Companies Act, 1870 ; 2787——It consists of two branches, one for industrial and the other for ordinary life insurance, 2789 ;—has a gross premium income of 4,500,000 *l.*, and funds exceeding 11,000,000 *l.* ; 2788–90.

Insures 2,099,369 children under ten years, about one-third of children of that age in England and Wales, 2792 ;—about 1,300,000 are insured in other large societies, and about 750,000 in local clubs and unregistered societies ; total 4,149,369 children insured, out of about 5,000,000 children of classes likely to insure them, 2800–1 ;—which is reckoned by deducting 25 per cent. of whole, according to practice of Education Department in calculating necessary elementary school accommodation, 2797 ;—this makes no

Dewey, Mr. Charles. (Analysis of his Evidence)—*continued.*

allowance for whatever children are insured twice, 2802 ;—but the Prudential does not
knowingly insure children insured in other offices, 2803-7 ;—which the parent is asked,
and his answer is part of the contract of insurance, though society would not take
advantage of untruth, 2808——Out of every 100 claims ninety-four are insured in the
Prudential only, 3475 ;—perhaps 200,000 or 300,000 may be taken off for double
insurances, 3476.

There is no undue proportion of children insured, as proportion of children insured to
adults insured is about the same as total children to total adults, 2809——These tables
and number of policies in Prudential for each year of age, set out, 2812——Insurance
of children is a growth of the last twenty-five years, 3520-2.

Insurance so general that no surprise ought to be expressed at a given child being
insured, but rather the contrary, 2805——If 50 per cent. of children at inquests are
insured, it is much below the proportion of whole population, 2809.

Tables of mortality amongst all children generally, and amongst those insured in
Prudential, set out, 2947——Showing that though insurance of children has increased,
mortality amongst them has decreased faster than amongst adults, 2946——Deducting
from general tables deaths under one month, death rate of insured children is 2 per
cent. less than of children in whole population, 2947-51 ;—but Prudential does not
insure illegitimate children, 2956 ;—nor children dying in workhouses, 2970 ;—makes a
selection of parents, 2758——Does not get the most miserably poor, 2965 ;—so that the
comparison is not equal, 2973 ;—but per contra, the Registrar General's tables include
all well-to-do classes, Prudential's only working classes, 2972-8——Is aware that the
House of Commons Committee did not attach much importance to his comparison, 2979.

Estimate of one in 1,000 children killed for insurance money would give 1,500 cases a
year in the total, 2983-4 ;—if this estimate is accurate it would only make a difference of
·001 in the death rate of the insurance companies, which no one but a skilled actuary
could detect, 2988-91.

Refers to two cases mentioned against Prudential ; in Deptford case, instead of being
children the persons were aged 74, 53, and 11 ; 3000 ;—in the Strand case the father
was found guilty of arson, and the crime was committed for 600 *l.* fire insurance, not for
the 14 *l.* child insurance money, 3001——As to Arlesey, referred to by Dr. Pullen Barry,
the vicar has written indignant letter that children there are not neglected for insurance
money, but that neglect that undoubtedly exists is from ignorance, 300 ;—and School
Board officer that out of 687 children on school census only ten are illegitimate, and
perhaps five or six more ; and the registrar writes that Dr. Pullen Barry when at Arlesey
certified to twenty-five cases, of which sixteen were uninsured, and three doubtful,
which is not the proportion he stated, 3002.

Prudential never pay without registrar's certificate, according to Section 28 of
Friendly Societies Act, 2906 ;—where doctors have refused to certify cause of death,
registrar must have coroner's verdict or some other satisfactory evidence of cause of
death, he being judge if evidence is satisfactory, 2908-10——He receives a fee on giving
certificate, so it is his interest to give it, 2911 ;—but it is so small that it is no temptation, and no case of impropriety is reported, 2913-4——Prudential would not object to
option to registrars to give certificate without doctor's certificate being removed, 2915 ;—
but witness does not see how it could be worked, 2918, 3034——On receipt of certificate
insurance money paid at once, 3466 ;—no agent allowed to pay without order from
district office, 3465 ;—never allowed to pay a portion on account before receipt of
certificate, 3468.

Prudential always gives assistance to Society for Prevention of Cruelty to Children,
3566, 3575 ;—quotes two cases where that society has not behaved fairly to them,
where information given them as to insurance was used to prejudice the case against
prisoner without any real charge that the insurance was motive of crime, 3567-72——
The information must be obtained from the Board, no agent being allowed to divulge
private business of people, 3576-80.

Disagrees with opinion of Mr. Taunton that coroner at every inquest should ask if
deceased insured, if this is to prejudice the inquiry, 3583.

Letter to Secretary of State respecting the Deptford case, quoted in Report of
House of Commons Committee, refers not to child insurance but to assignment of policies,
really infringing law about insurable interest, 3587-94.

Illegitimate children not insured in Prudential under three years old, 2954, 3490,
3492——Question as to this not asked directly but can be discovered by father's name
not being same as mother's, 3488——Society insures illegitimate child of married
parents living together, 3491——Illegitimacy most usual ground for refusing policy,
3493 ;—even when child otherwise satisfactory, 3494.

Scale of insurance money at various ages and lengths of insurance, set out, 2852 ;—
no larger sum than a penny a week is taken, 2833-4——The average sum paid on all
infantile claims last year was 2 *l.* 13 *s.* ; 2842 6——As one-third of the working-classes
are satisfied with this, it seems that generally this is sufficient, but in some cases more
might be necessary, 2849——This about covers actual funeral charges, but leaves
nothing for mourning or incidental expenses, 2844, 3469——In the case of disreputable
                                                                              parents

Report, 1890—*continued.*

Dewey, Mr. Thomas Charles. (Analysis of his Evidence)—*continued.*

parents there would be a margin over bare funeral necessities, 2840-1——If statutory limit were lowered to amount for which people now really insure, they would in most cases lose nothing, 2851——But hardship on thriving working man if he were limited to the 2 *l.* 13 *s.*; 3555;—but this is a question more for the working classes; the insurance companies cannot afford to pay more than they do for 1 *d.* per week, 3470, 3556—— If life between one and two was insured in two societies and died after six months, the parent could get 6 *l.* for outlay of 4 *s.* 4 *d.*; 2835-8——The Prudential does not issue more than one policy on a life, because after a certain time the amount payable might then be 12 *l.* instead of 10 *l.* maximum allowed, and society liable to fine, 3477-8, 3483-7——It is not true that lapses are favourable to company, as mortality diminishes yearly for first years of life, and each year child lives more favourable to insuring company; puts in the report of four actuaries to prove this, 2941-5——Not even true to say that where policy lapses the premiums already received are profit to the company, 3503;—because all premiums received have already been taken to pay the usual proportion of death claims, 3503-9——Deaths under three years old are a loss decreasing day by day to the company; on deaths after three a profit remains, 3498-9;—and to prevent lapses agent is made to refund part of commission if policy lapses, 2872——Arrears allowed to be paid up within twelve months, 3473——No statistics of same lives re-insured after lapse, 3471.——One-third of all policies issued lapse in first year, 2940——The profit the Prudential makes is 2 per cent. on gross receipts, 3501.

Puts in the Prudential form of proposal, 2853, App. E., page 231;—which contains many questions to be answered; agent is the sole judge if health of child is satisfactory, no doctor being required under ten years, 3535-9.

Prudential has always read Friendly Societies Act as authorising only parents, if alive, to insure children, but there is no penalty for breach, 2853-4——This Bill allows any person to insure children, but it ought to be forbidden and Bill amended accordingly, 2855-9.

Discussion how far the present law is in this respect altered by Bill, 3442-54—— Witness admits that his view that insurance is only allowed by parents is not generally held, 3448-9, 3454;—and that the Friendly Societies Act in the clause forbidding, as he thinks, this practice, has no penalty for breach, 3447——Observation by Chairman that if a change is made by Bill it is an inadvertence, 2857, 2999——It might be held that under present law baby farmer had an insurable interest in the life of child for whom an income was paid, 3452——Principle should be extended and no person allowed to insure life of other person's child in spite of having insurable interest, 3455- 60;—exception in favour of man's own life, 3461-2.

Agents are paid by commission 17½ per cent. and a bonus, 2870-3;—this would amount to 30 per cent. for first year, 2874-5——It is necessary to pay them by results, 3517-9——Believes strong opinion expressed by House of Commons Committee about agents did not refer to the way they take infantile insurances but to their action with respect to insurable interest, 2881;—they are respectable men, 2903;—but they are subject to temptation, and the society is much in their hands, but there is always the check of the possibility of detection, 2882-5, 2888——It is impressed upon them to be careful in the matter of certificates, as it is not to the credit of society to dispute policies, 3003——They do not dispute many, because there is no cause for doing so, 3005——Case mentioned of McKay, where agent allowed some one other than parent to insure child, was in Liverpool Victoria Legal Friendly Society; the Prudential manage their agents very differently, 2886-7——Would like the law to make it penal against society agent and proposer to effect such an insurance, 2889-92;—and willing that society should be fined if it knowingly granted it, 2893-4——Prudential refuses large number of proposals because already insured, illegitimate, in bad health, or living in unhealthy districts, 2895, 3493-4.

Prudential does not pay till child has been three months insured; local clubs, as a rule, pay at once, 2928;—but Prudential makes grants of grace before child is in benefit if cause of death satisfactory, 2931-2;—such as scarlet fever, accident, &c., but always done at head office on receipt of medical evidence, 3545-7.

Local clubs, which have been compared favourably with large societies, have been declared by Chief Registrar of Friendly Societies to be bankrupt as to 80 per cent. of total number, 2980-1——Only one insurance on a child ought to be allowed; the amount then could never reach the statutory limit, as no society could afford to give that for one penny a week, 2919-20;—could easily be enforced by only allowing registrar to give one certificate, 2921;—under penalty of fine if he did, 2924-3.

Impossible in practice to make insurance a contract of indemnity; Prudential's claims exceed 500 a day and too expensive to inquire into details of such a number, 3515-6.

Should have no objection that age below which there should be no second policy allowed should be extended from ten to fourteen years, 3017-8.

No objection to form of proposal being legislatively settled if not less stringent than that now used by Prudential, 3548-51.

Dewey, Mr. Thomas Charles. (Analysis of his Evidence)—*continued*.

As representing his society, has no objection to insurances below twelve months being forbidden, 3006-14, 3602;—which as a child does not come into benefit till after three months would practically mean below fifteen months, 3013.   •

Has no objection to registration of insurance policies, but sees difficulties in carrying this out, 3016.

Does not see any great objection to forfeiture of policy if parent convicted of wilful neglect or cruelty to child, 3021;—but is doubtful how it could be worked, or whether it would be possible to forbid such parent insuring any child, as being unfit to have the privilege, but does not object to this on behalf of his society, 3022–31.

Working classes would object to limit being raised to two years, 3604——Better plan would be to allow insurance to begin at any age, and if death occurred under one year only to repay premiums actually paid; if child lived over one year company could out of the saving to them give insurer some benefit, perhaps a free accident insurance of 10 *l.* during whole life, 3605–12, 3628–31.

All societies insuring children ought to be registered, 3614–7;—some clubs now escape all observation, 3618——Clause to effect this would have to be very carefully drawn, or it would be evaded as is the Friendly Societies Act, 3615, 3621–5.

Has the strongest objection to undertakers' clause in Bill, but being informed by Chairman that this is withdrawn, gives no evidence on the subject, 2782–3.

Dispensaries. In case of dispensaries payment is made by society direct to doctors without the money passing through the hands of parents, *Dobson* 2544–6;—but argues that there is no analogy between this and money being paid direct by burial society to undertaker, *ib.* 2647–51.——See *Medical Relief.*

Dobson, Mr. A. A. (Analysis of his Evidence.)—Is Secretary of Amalgamated Conference of Family Friendly Burial Societies of the Manchester and Salford District, 2488,—having a membership of 280,000, and many more anxious to join, 2489——These are mutual societies, 2495;—the profits are accumulated as a contingency fund, 2497; —and to add to amount of benefits; sums to which benefits now amount, stated, 2695 ——These societies are managed by the members, 2498;—and are local, so that in some districts the members all know each other, 2499;—and opinion of their fellows brought to bear in a way that does not exist in Prudential or other large societies, 2501;—the payments are collected by members who are paid a small sum, and generally collect after their day's work, 2502–4——The officers of the societies are elected by members, 2505;—collectors are not allowed to go round from door to door, 2633.

Only children of members are admitted, and they must be two months old, 2508—— There is an interval besides of from six weeks to three months in various societies before child comes into benefit, 2777–9——There is a wonderful difference in the expenses of funeral of a child under two months old and one of a year old, 2772.

The death rate of these societies is lower than the general death rate of the population, 2513–21, 2529;—but they do not, as far as they can discriminate, take in "loafers" who might not take care of their children, 2744, 2756–8, 2766;—nor paupers, 2762; – nor children under two months, 2760;—majority of members are respectable artizans in good work, 2736–41; – so that the comparison is not equal, 2767–9.

Is particularly connected with Hulme Burial Society, 2506 (for balance sheet and report of this Society, *see* Appendix K, pages 241 to 244, inclusive)——Pains are taken in the payment of insurance money, 2522, 2708;—on re-admitting lapsed members, their health is investigated, 2530——If parents in arrears apply to know how they stand, inquiries are made about the child, and if it dies soon, full investigations are made, 2709——Pains are also taken to supervise the expenditure of insurance money; if society has doubts about the providence of any member, it pays the doctor and undertaker, and then pays balance to mother rather than to father, 2656, 2710;—so if relations quarrel about the money, 2711,—the society is the sole judge whether they need take these precautions, 2724——When a man joins these societies he becomes more careful and respects himself more, 2773–6.

All these precautions make a difference between these societies and others less carefully conducted, 2634–5——If it is proved that some societies do not take similar precautions, witness' society would be the first to urge strengthening the law, 2717—— Knows nothing about collecting societies, 2715–6.

Hands in and calls attention to letters calling in question the evidence given by Dr. Barwise and Dr. Thomson, 2489–3.

Cost of funeral at Manchester is 15 *s.* for opening grave, 3 *s.*, minister's dues, coffin, 1 *l.*, cost of coach, 1 *l.* 2 *s.* (which is not a luxury as cemetery is far off), total 3 *l.*; 2547, 2550——In a recent case the doctor's bill was 30 *s.*, which left the parents nothing out of insurance, 2551——Sunday funerals not allowed, so there is loss of day's wages also, 2552–3——The 6 *l.* allowed in the Act for insurance of child under five years is barely sufficient, and certainly ought not to be diminished, 2554– —The cost of a funeral after five years would not jump from 6 *l.* to 10 *l.*, the sums allowed by present law, but as a fact societies have a graduated scale rising about 1 *l.* a year, 2657–61, 2695——Working classes in Lancashire very particular about having a private grave, 2698;—and about
                                                                                                    having

Dobson, Mr. A. A. (Analysis of his Evidence)—*continued.*

having mourning, 2701 ;—would object to any further limitation being put on amount for which children's lives may be insured, 2688——Expenses in country districts less than in towns, but does not think any difference should be made, 2726–8.

Insurance in savings bank would not answer same purpose as life insurance, 2566 ;—poor people do not like to take small sums to post office, 2567, 2730 ;—and careless people apt to draw out from bank for other purposes, 2568.

Believes registrars are very strict and careful about giving death certificates, 2662 ——In Hulme Burial Society members are allowed to belong to two societies ; main reason for this, that father and mother both wish children to be insured in the society to which each of them belonged from early youth, 2512, 2691–2.

In some of the amalgamated societies medical aid is provided, 2515——Not in Hulme, as there is there a provident dispensary, 2533 ;—there would therefore be no necessity to insure for medical aid, but that all workmen will not join dispensaries, 2639.

These societies encourage thrift and self-respect, and absurd to say their insurances encourage infanticide, 2536–7——A certain number of children are deserted, but the reason is the trouble of bringing them up, not insurance money, 2538-46, 2689–90.

Recognises that the Statute of George III. was passed to prevent anyone making profit out of another's death, 2577 ;—and that the Friendly Societies Act makes an exception from this, as an exceptional privilege to working classes, 2578. 2612–6. 2621——Though, as insurances of the sort existed before, some similar law must have prevailed before, 2507. 2606 ;—but objects to any alteration of the Friendly Societies Act, because he does not admit that its safeguards are inefficient, and because the allegations in support of charge are unproved and are a libel on the working classes, 2588–93.

Chief objection is to part of Bill making payment of insurance money to undertaker compulsory, 2555 ;—this is a stigma on the working classes, who feel this most strongly and indignantly, 2556. 2687 ;—would be a temptation to the undertaker to commit fraud, 2557 ;—as he would be under no check, 2559 ;—and might lead to collusion between him and parent, 2561——It is true that the payment to dispensary doctor passes only through society's hands, 2544-50 ;—but denies there is any analogy between the cases, 2647, 2551 ;—admits that under the Bill the parent could choose his own undertaker and make bargain with him, but rules of all societies would have to be re-modelled i Bill passes, 2670-9 ;—does not admit that children are murdered, which is the reason assigned for this interference, 2680.

Objects to Bill as interfering with existing contracts, 2563——Hopes that if Bill passes it will be made clear that it does not, 2564 ;—but thinks that there would be possibility of it, under the words of Bill, 2565.

Drugs. Very common to give children harmful drugs, but milk allowed to turn sour is as efficacious as poison, *Branson* 266, 267.

At Nottingham women who work in factories leave their children in charge of other persons, who often give them laudanum to make them keep quiet, *Browne* 1097.

E.

Endowment. If sum payable on death (say 2 *l.*) was reduced to 25 *s.* the saving to the companies, which would be very large, might be accumulated for child's benefit till boy was fourteen and girl fifteen, *Waugh* 2220——If insurance under a year were prohibited the profit might be paid as endowment to child on attaining a certain age, *Hartop* 1730-2 ;—might be applied for benefit of survivors, perhaps by issuing a free accident insurance for whole of life for 10 *l.*, *Dewey* 3612. 3627-8.

Exists to a certain extent in Oddfellows, where entrance money is paid for juvenile members at twenty-one to enter adult societies, *Cleveland* 4460-2 ;—and a portion of their subscriptions from eighteen to twenty-one, *Walton* 4730.

Endowment Policies. Granted by Scottish Legal Life Insurance Company for small weekly premiums, insuring 9 *l.* to 36 *l.* at age of fourteen, and 15 *l.* to 63 *l.* at age of twenty-one, *Fortune* 3710-2——This has become very popular even amongst poorest classes, *ib.* 3717-20.

Evidence. Royal Liver contest all suspicious cases, but after examination are obliged to pay in many cases for want of evidence, *Taunton* 3232. 3254.

Difficulty of conviction, because husband and wife cannot give evidence against one another, *Wills* 1879-81 ; *Waugh* 2237.

In the " Strand case " a man was acquitted of murder or manslaughter, his wife, the principal witness at the inquest, being incapable of giving evidence against him at the trial, *Troutbeck* 968-74.

Opinion in favour of proposed change in the law, that the prisoner should be examined, *Wills* 1917.

See *Conviction.*

(225—IND.)   L L 3

F.

Foresters. See *Stead, Mr.* (Analysis of his Evidence), and *Friendly Societies.*

Fortune, Mr. David. (Analysis of his Evidence.)—Is President of the Scottish Legal Life Assurance Society, 3632;—its business almost entirely confined to working classes, 3634——It is a collecting society ; but also mutual, as all the profits belong to members, 3635——Has 400,000 members; 38,771 under five years, 37,731 between five and ten, 3639–41 ;—paid last year 3,394 *l.* on 1,366 children under five, and 1,064 *l.* on 241 children between five and ten, 3644–6.

Does not believe that child insurance leads to infanticide or even neglect, 3650, 3656–60——There has been no charge against anyone insuring in Scottish Legal, 3651, —neither by legal process nor by information from Scottish Society for Prevention of Cruelty to Children, 3666–70——Without disputing what Mr. Ludlow or Mr. Lyulph Stanley may have said, witness says experience of his society proves no evils in connection with child insurance, at any rate in Scotland, 3670–81, 3779——Do not dispute many claims, but being a mutual society would, without hesitation, if occasion required, 3725–8——There is more speculation on adult life than on children; quotes case, which of course was a breach of the Act of George III., but was nevertheless effected, 3734–41—— Cost of burial such that there is little, if any, margin, 3655 ;—in Scotland from 2 *l.* to 4 *l.* for bare cost of funeral, and the loss perhaps of day's work, 3682-5, 3818——Has never known a case of insured child buried by parish, 3686–9——If parent were heartless enough to wish to get rid of child, burden much greater inducement than few shillings of insurance money, 3780–1 ;—and would remain if insurance totally abolished, 3824——As to difficulty of getting conviction on account of crime being committed in privacy of home, collectors of Scottish Legal are instructed to make careful observation of habits of families, not only at issue of insurance, but from week to week, 3662——Have had no case of insurance by person other than parent or guardian, 3723——Agents of Scottish Legal are of a very superior class ; require testimonials, 3729 ;—are paid a bonus of first eight payments, and 25 per cent. on industrial and 12¼ per cent. on endowment business, 3730.

Insurance is by respectable persons and effort is made to ensure this, 3778 ;—child insurance has not increased more than increase of general membership 3788 ;—two-thirds of working classes insure, 3790.

In Scottish Legal highest amount payable is 3 *l.* under two years, 3 *l.* 10 *s.* under three years, 4 *l.* under four, and 4 *l.* 10 *s.* under five, 3689–90——These amounts only when child has been insured for twelve months; if for three months only, quarter benefit ; if for six months, half benefit, 3692, 3742 ;—this is less than English societies give, 3695—— Scottish Legal never give grants of grace as some English societies do, 3743-5 ;—scale fixed from financial not moral motives, 3811——Therefore, if money is a temptation, less in Scottish Legal, 3696–8——Amounts payable being less than legal maximum shows that Scottish Legal has no desire to place artificial premium on child mortality, 3699 ;—the large amount of which is owing to intemperance, overcrowding, &c., 3700, 3765 ;—though a great deal is being done in Glasgow in the way of sanitation and also teaching of parents how to care for their children, 3767–70—— Admission that a considerable amount in the gross of infanticide might exist without perceptibly raising rate of infant mortality, 3700–1——Whatever qualifications ought to be made, average rate of child mortality in those insured in Scottish Legal less than general infantile death-rate, 3702–3——Death-rate of insured in various towns given, 3705 ; *App.* H., 239——Typical places selected, 3786–7——Preston rate very high, attributable perhaps to fact that mothers work in factories ; so much that Scottish Legal now refuses to take any new insurances there, 3706–7——Glasgow rate much more favourable than in Preston, 3708——Factory work of mothers certainly militates against children's health, 3771——Death-rate in towns necessarily so high, that it is the duty of working classes to insure, 3803–4.

Scottish Legal instituted in 1886 a system of children's endowments, by which, for weekly premiums, sums of 9 *l.* to 36 *l.* are payable at age of fourteen, and 15 *l.* to 63 *l.* at age of twenty-one, 3710–2 ;—making life, rather than death, of children profitable, 3712–5—— This scheme very successful, 3717 ;—even amongst the poorest class, 3720.

Scale of legal payments at death might be graduated, not going as now by large jumps, 3748. 3776——There would be no difficulty in this, as all societies have a graduated scale of their own, 3777 ;—but not reducing maximums now payable, 3751 ;—least sum should be 2 *l.* or 2 *l.* 10 *s.*; 3821—— Expense in country not materially less than in towns, 3823.

It might be well to forbid quarter or even half benefits, 3752. 3802——If child died before benefit, part of premiums might be repaid, as Scottish Legal do in their endowment policies, 3802.

There

Fortune, Mr. David. (Analysis of his Evidence)—*continued.*

There might be a better system of registration, in respect of the action of registrar, 3752;—whose option to give certificates where refused by doctors should be taken away, 3755-6——Only one insurance should be allowed on a child, then with only one certificate there would be no possibility of insurance beyond legal amount, 3773——. Not desirable that insurances should be registered, as it would be unpopular amongst working classes to have private affairs published, however creditable, 3757;—but no objection from point of view of societies, 3782;—and perhaps bulk of insurers would not object, 3758.

All societies insuring children ought to be registered under Friendly Societies Act, 3794.

Proposal form in all offices should be uniform, but ought not to be made too cumbrous, 3797-800——Hands in form used by Scottish Legal, 3796; *App. G.*, pp. 236-8.

Insurance could not be a varying amount to pay only actual expenses, as impossible to know what it was in each case, besides expense of investigation, 3813-5.

" *Friendly Leads.*" Meetings held, generally in public-house, to make a collection for a neighbour who has a death (or some such misfortune) to pay for, *Crooks* 2275;—was the usual custom formerly, but has ceased with prevalence of life insurance, *ib.* 2363-6; *Clency* 3980——Working-men no longer like to contribute, as they expect every one to insure, *Crooks* 2368, 2370——Case of as much as 18 *l.* being raised in this way, *ib.* 2275——If Bill passed, this bad custom would revive, as working classes would no longer insure their children, *ib.* 2322, 2393, 3460.

Friendly Societies. Conference of Friendly Societies, of 17 affiliated orders, representing 2,012,967 members, delegated Mr. Cleveland, Mr. Stead, and Mr. Walton, to appear as witnesses, in answer to an invitation from the Committee, *Cleveland* 4196-4, 4402-8. (*See* Analysis of their Evidence.)—Conference passed resolution protesting against restrictions as to age and amount of insurance in Bishop of Peterborough's Bill being applied to Friendly Societies, *Cleveland* 4410——Their main object is relief in sickness, *Ritchie* 1444——They exist for the purpose of raising the welfare and thrift of working classes as well as for benefits, *Sargent* 4220-1;—and in some cases for propagating temperance principles, *ib.* 4237, 4283——The system on which they work is preferable to that of collecting societies, *Ritchie* 1498.

Only admit respectable people, *Dobson* 2623;—and take great precautions in paying money to dissolute characters, *ib.* 2708——They take such ample precautions, inquiring into character of parents and sometimes health of children, and consist of members knowing each other, that it would be impossible for any abuses of insurance to exist in them, *Cleveland* 4442-4, 4453;—and in their experience there are none, *ib.* 4465 —— But case of child insured in Oddfellows and done away with quoted, *Taunton* 3212.

Anything restricting their insurances would be detrimental to themselves and injurious to the steadily growing independence and thrift of working classes, *Cleveland* 4580-85; *Sargent* 4310——They are content with the present law and do not admit necessity of any change, *ib.* 4413; *Walton* 4758, 4765——If legislation takes place they ought to be dealt with separately from the collecting societies, *Cleveland* 4466, 4485-7; *Walton* 4754-7;—no distinction ought to be made, *Taunton* 3213-4.

The lowest class of the population does not insure in Friendly Societies, *Cleveland* 4562-1——Sons of the Phœnix Society takes in the very poorest, *Sargent* 4208—— Friendly Societies have these advantages over collecting societies, that they meet together and members generally know each other, *Dobson* 2499; *Ritchie* 1437,—so that any abuses would be stopped, *Cleveland* 4450——The profit in them belongs to the members, *Cleveland* 4450;—goes to form a contingency fund, out of which benefits are gradually increased, *Dobson* 2497, 2695——They are managed by members, *Ritchie* 1513-7;—gratis, or for a very small gratuity for expenses, *Cleveland* 4419, 4460; *Sargent* 4213-4—— Payments collected by members after work hours, *Dobson* 2503-4.

The expenses of management of collecting societies are known to be very great; in the Oddfellows, as an example of Friendly Societies, they are limited to 15 per cent. of receipts, which includes rent, *Cleveland* 4450——In Sons of the Phœnix Friendly Society they are 50 per cent., *Sargent* 4219;—but a considerable portion of this is returned to the children in presents and for temperance work, *ib.* 4289-90——The other 50 per cent. put by for benefits; funds are accumulating so fast that they wish to extend operations, *ib.* 4218-20.

Royal Liver is a collecting Friendly Society, *Taunton* 3037-8——So is the Scottish Legal Life Assurance Company, *Fortune* 3635;—also the Liverpool Victoria and Legal, *Cleasy* 3893-8;—also the Royal London, *Hambridge* 3582-4.

When their juvenile members survive, a return of part of the profits is made or their

(225—IND.)   L L 4   entrance

Friendly Societies – continued.

entrance money to the adult society is paid, *Cleveland* 4460-2 ;—and contributions to their subscriptions from 18 to 21, *Walton* 4727-30 ;—and it is a great advantage that their members are passed on to the adult societies, and thus are trained in thrift from earliest days, *Cleveland* 4464.

Scale of benefits and payments in Oddfellollows set out, *Cleveland* 4417-19 ;—in a Hampshire branch of the Oddfellows, *Walton* 4732, 4715-18 ;—in Yarmouth branch of Foresters, *Stead* 4676——In Hulme Burial Society, *Dobson* 2695.

One affiliated society gives about the same benefits as another, *Walton* 4749 —— There is no agitation to increase these benefits, so presumption is that the people are satisfied, as they get medical aid, and in many cases sick pay besides, *Walton* 4721 ;—medical aid often includes anything a doctor may order, *Stead* 4633-8——In large towns the affiliated societies join to pay a doctor for giving all his time to sick children of the juvenile societies, and adult members and their children, *ib.* 4639-41.

It may be that collecting societies give greater benefits, but nevertheless the people are beginning to prefer Friendly Societies, *Cleveland* 4519——These can quite hold their own, *Walton* 4746——Friendly Societies registered under the Friendly Societies Act, 1875, may not grant insurances on children; except (by Section 8) on children of their own members, *Cleveland* 4417, 4420, 4435 ;—but (by Section 15) societies or branches are allowed to be separately registered, and to insure any children between three and under sixteen years, *ib.* 4416, 4431 ;—and Friendly Societies have under this section established juvenile branches, *ib.* 4421-2 ;—not mixed up with the parent society, but under the same management, *ib.* 4439——The effect of this is that Friendly Societies cannot insure infants from birth to three, except those of their own members, *ib.* 4424, 4435, 4440.

Very desirable that these restrictions should be abolished, and that they should be allowed to insure all children at any age in one society, *Cleveland* 4446, 4539 ; *Walton* 4741—— The same careful supervision would exist as at present, *Cleveland* 4479-82 ——They ought, as prosperity of societies increase, to take in their own children instead of letting them go to collecting societies, *Sargent* 4230, 4242——They would certainly take advantage of this to enable them to compete with the collecting societies, *Cleveland* 4492-3 ; *Walton* 4742 ;—who have great advantages in sending round their collectors from door to door, *ib.* 4744 ;—and it would tend to the increase of their adult societies, *Stead* 4692-3.

Registration under the Act of 1875 is voluntary, so that many societies do not register under it, *Cleveland* 4501 ; *Dewey* 3622 ;—out of total of 1,360 Foresters Societies, only 452 are registered, *Stead* 4670——If they register they have to make annual returns and valuations to the Registrar of Friendly Societies, *Cleveland* 4549—— Instance of Rochdale Friendly Society, which not being registered, is not under the Friendly Societies Act, and not issuing policies, is not under the Insurance Companies Act, *Dewey* 3623.

Very desirable that insuring societies should be registered, *Cleveland* 4550 ; *Stead* 4672-4 ;—without it there can be no supervision, and no one can tell how much may be paid, *Cleveland* 4553.

Friendly Societies under so many restrictions that companies, in spite of paying dividends, can give their members equal advantages, *Clensy* 4042-3.

Besides pecuniary benefits in Friendly Societies, committee of adult members look after amusement and instruction of juvenile members, *Stead* 4659-60.

Do not generally insure children till five years old, *Sargent* 4328—— Usually begin at six years, in one Hampshire society as low as three, in another as high as eight, *Walton* 4709-14 ;—only 49 out of 1,279 juvenile branches of the Oddfellows insure before three years, the majority about equally at four, five, and six, *Walton* 4654—— Yarmouth Branch of Foresters begin at nine, *Stead* 4676——In the Sons of the Phœnix at five, *Sargent* 4207——In Hulme Burial Society, children of members only, at two months old, *Dobson* 2508.

The scale of benefits in Friendly Societies is generally below limit of present law, and also below that in Bishop of Peterborough's Bill, *Stead* 4683 :—so that they will not be affected pecuniarily, *Walton* 4738-40 ;—but the Bill is injurious to them, as implying that they are not fit to be entrusted with the insurance of children, *ib.* 4763-6 ;—and they hope to be able, with increasing wages and thrift, to raise their benefits, *ib.* 4753——Sons of the Phœnix now gives 8 *l.* on death in all cases from five to sixteen, and wish to raise it to 10 *l.*, which is present legal limit, and which Bill would restrict, *Sargent* 4223-7.

The mortality in the juvenile branches of the Affiliated Friendly Societies is less than one-half per cent., *Cleveland* 4410-3 ;—in the Foresters it is 4·12 per 1,000, *Stead* 4622-6.

Only

Friendly Societies—continued.

Only 92 coroners' inquests have been held in the case of Foresters since their foundation, and in all cases verdicts of accidental death or from natural causes, *Stead* 4657.

Affiliated Friendly Societies, such as Oddfellows or Foresters, really insure child-life though they are not popularly supposed to; they do not issue policies, but pay a sum to members on death of their children, *Taunton* 3205–12.

Friendly Societies Act, 1875. Makes an exception from the Act of George III., which forbids one person to insure another's life without insurable interest, in favour of infant insurance of the working classes, *Dobson* 2610-5, 2619 ;—but this privilege existed before, *Dobson* 2507—as in mutual societies, insured became members, *Dewey* 2829.

Provides that a child shall not be insured for more than certain sums varying with age. and that the sum shall not be paid without production of registrar's certificate of death and certificate of amounts the society is liable to pay, *Leach* 1791——Certain societies incorporated under the Companies Acts appear to be exempt from this rule ; this may lead to children being insured for more than amount allowed by Friendly Societies Act, *ib.* 1763, 1772, 1783——The object of ceasing to be registered under Friendly Societies Act is on account of difficulty of making out valuation every five years, required by that Act, *ib.* 1788.

Industrial assurance companies and trades unions are liable to provisions of Act as to insurances, *Leach* 1763.

Affiliated Orders (such as Oddfellows or Foresters) really insure children though they are not supposed to, *Taunton* 3205-14.

Funeral. Sometimes paid for by parish though deceased was insured, *Barwise* 45-7 ; *Kirshaw* 1813, 1822 ; *Hartop* 1683-6 ; *Leach* 1796 ; *Tasker* 1537-40——No use for parish to take proceedings to recover amount, as such people have no goods to distrain on, *ib.* 1543, 1601 ; *Burnett* 1321-2 ;—but sometimes amount has been recovered by threat of proceedings, *Tasker* 1542, 1601.

No case of insured child buried by parish known to Royal Liver, but case of adult known, *Taunton* 3122.

Funeral Expenses. Ought to be met as other misfortunes are, without insurance, but no objection to local burial clubs, *Day* 1983, 1988-94.

Amount to be insured should be limited to cost of decent funeral, *Carter* 829, 833, 834—— If not so limited the children will tend to be neglected, *Tasker* 1569.

Cost of :—£.1 sufficient, *Carter* 855——30 *s.* legitimate expense in Westminster for child under ten, *Troutbeck* 1016, 1029——£.2 will cover all legitimate expenses, *Brandon* 333——£.1 for absolutely necessary expenses in Rochdale, *Kirshaw* 1833-5——£.1 or 25 *s.* ample for child under twelve, *Browne* 1143——12 *s* or 13 *s.* cost of pauper funeral in Rotherham, *Leach* 1778—— 12 *s.* expense of funeral to parish in Sheffield, *Tasker* 1546 ;—this is by contract, *ib.* 1639 ;—a decent coffin and coach can be got for 15 *s.*, and burial fees 5 *s.* besides, *ib.* 1640-4.

Cost of coffin 6 *s* to 15 *s.*, *Carter* 854.

£.1 about the lowest at Bradford for inclusive expense of funeral, *Hartop* 1733-6 ; —about 1 *l.*, *Wills* 1885 ;—but cannot say that this is the maximum of legitimate expenditure, *ib.* 16, 1907.

Three undertakers contract to bury children dying at Refuge of Society for Prevention of Cruelty to Children, at Harpur-street, London, for 15 *s.*, 17 *s.* and 18 *s.*, supplying a coach to carry body on front seat, *Waugh* 2252.

Not less than 2 *l.*, *Crooks* 2377—— Statement of exact expense of three funerals, *Crooks, App.* A., page 227 —— If an undertaker advertises to do it for 15 *s.*, believes this does not really cover all expenses, but that there will be extras, *ib.* 2349, 2425.

At Manchester, opening grave 15 *s.*, minister's dues 3 *s.*, hire of coach 1 *l.* 2 *s.* ; total 3 *l.*, *Dobson* 2547 ;—this was in the case of child eleven months old, *ib.* 2550.

Bare expenses of funeral 2 *l.*, *Taunton* 3241-4 ;—or 2 *l.* 10 *s.*, *ib.* 3369——Cheapest at Manchester 2 *l.* 5*s.*, and then only where coffin can be taken in coach with parents, *Cleveland* 4515-7——£.2. 5 *s.* lowest cost in Liverpool, and that a very poor funeral, *Clensy* 4024 ;—not including a private grave, *ib.* 4026.

£ 2. 10 *s.* to 2 *l.* 15 *s.* is the lowest possible, *Sargent* 4272.

Necessary funeral expenses barely met by 4 *l.* under five, and 6 *l.* under 10 years, leaving no margin for other expenses ; Letter of *Leeds Society for the Prevention of Cruelty to Children*, page 134.

£.2 to 4 *l.* bare cost in Scotland, *Fortune* 3682-5, 3818.

(225—IND.) M M Amount

Funeral Expenses—continued.

Amount to 8 *l.* in experience of United Order of Sons of the Phœnix, *Sargent* 4269; —including incidental expenses of doctor, nurse, and mourning, *ib.* 4216-7, 4255, 4355, 4339——Examples set out, *ib.* 4278.

In Glasgow estimates of eight undertakers were 1 *l.* 1 *s.* 6 *d.* lowest price in common ground, and with private ground from 2 *l.* 13 *s.* 6 *d.* to 3 *l.* 17 *s.* 1*d.* ; Letter of Mr. *J. Graham*, page 132.

G.

George III., Act of. See *Statutes.*

Grahame, Mr. James. Notes of evidence which he proposed, but was unable, to give to the Committee ; ordered to be entered on the Minutes, *see* pages 131 to 133.

(Analysis of said Notes.) Is Founder and Chairman of Committee of Scottish National Society for the Prevention of Cruelty of Children, founded in 1884 (par. 1), —which has many branches ; in five years investigated cases of cruelty to 7,363 children ; sheltered, clothed, and fed many thousands, and sent 5,965 to industrial schools, training ships, &c., or placed them under supervision of school boards ; prosecuted in 4,305 of these cases, in 3.766 of which parents were admonished, in 157 punished, and in 382 convicted and admonished (par. 3).

Believes that in connection with life insurance much useful work is done, and that there is a laudable desire of poor to insure against expense of sickness and death, but that amongst the criminal classes there are cases of insurance solely for the sake of the money, where children are made away with, and the present system makes an additional temptation to those who dislike the burden of children ; quotes two bad cases as examples——Believes there ought to be immediate action to put down this evil (par. 6).

Disapproves of present Bill (upon which, though it concerns Scotland, this Society was not consulted, par. 4), because (par. 7) :

(*a.*) It confounds prudent provision for misfortune with its abuse by depraved people ;

(*b.*) It was introduced without consultation with the many respectable and useful benefit societies, &c., and their members ;

(*c.* and *d.*) Because it would be unworkable, as it would be impossible to provide on what scale the funeral and mourning should be provided and medical attendance paid for——Has estimate from eight undertakers in Glasgow showing that 1 *l.* 1 *s.* 6 *d.* is the lowest price of funeral in common grave, and in private grave goes up to 2 *l.* 13 *s.* 6 *d.* and 3 *l.* 17 *s.* 1 *d.* ; it would be absurd with the many grades of population to fix a sum suitable for all cases, for an artizan with a small family earning 2 *l.* a week, and labourers with a large family earning 15 *s.* a week ;

and (*e.*) because the Bill would not prevent collusion between an unscrupulous undertaker and depraved parent.

The remedies he would propose (which have been considered and approved by committees of his society in Edinburgh and Glasgow (par. 10), and also by the Directors of the Scottish Legal Life Assurance Company, the largest society in Scotland (par. 11), are compulsory registration of every childlife insurance within a week, with statement of society that—

(1.) The child is legitimate ;

(2.) The child's health and condition, and character of family are satisfactory ; and

(3.) The name of any other society in which, as far as known, the child is insured.

It should be further provided that every claim should be entered on register within one week of death, and that no insurance or claim be legal unless so registered (par. 8).

The publicity of this would deter all but the worst from abusing life insurance (par. 8).

The large benefit societies ought to be consulted to provide remedies against an admitted evil (par. 9).

Grants of Grace. See *Benefit.*

H.

Hambridge, Mr. William Henry. (Analysis of his Evidence.)—Represents the Royal London Friendly Society, 3826,—which is a collecting and mutual society, 3582-4.

Number of children under five years under insurance in 1889 was 124,678;—average amount of actual insurance, 3 *l.* 1 *s.* 7 *d.*; average amount paid on each death, 1 *l.* 13 *s.* 3 *d.*, 3828;—number insured between five and ten, 102,086; average actual insurance, 4 *l.* 16 *s.* 8 *d.*; average payment on death, 4 *l.* 12 *s.*; 3830;—number dying under five, 4,997: between five and ten only 408; 3842.

Some parents pay ½ *d.* a week, others 2 *d.*, 3835-7;—low sum paid on death accounted for by number of deaths before full benefit, where grants or half-benefit are given, 3839.

Royal London employs agents who are paid from 12½ to 25 per cent. commission, and the first eight weekly premiums, 3855-61——Is very careful in selecting them, 3863.

Royal London takes pains to get as good lives as possible; for that purpose refuse insurances from districts where drunkenness prevails, or where mothers work at iron works or mines, 3880-1——Excludes these as being unfair to other districts, 3882—— Has no system of varying premiums for increased risk, 3883.

Restrictions should be rather on insurances before than after five, 3844;—but does not admit necessity of any further protection than now exists, 3849.

Agrees with suggestion of another witness that only one insurance should be allowed; all societies would be willing to adopt this, 3864——It would work itself, as when claim came to be paid, this would be inquired into, 3865, 3885;—if second insurance were made illegal, no society would violate Act; it sometimes occurs that parent has received full legal amount in one society, and on applying to second company no payment would be made, but only premiums returned, 3886——-Any agent or parent infringing this to be punished, 3866——Royal London rejects many cases where there is already an insurance, 3868;—but not where insurance is very small, 3871——They ascertain if already insured by their collectors, 3868.

All societies insuring ought to be brought under Friendly Societies Act, 3874-5;—because, for instance, societies under it have, as matter of precaution, to keep registrars' certificates; but others only see it, and it can be used again, without any record of the fact, 2876.

Death certificates might be improved; formerly they were given by doctor who charged a varying fee; Act of 1875 abolished this, and authorised only registrar to grant certificate for insurance for fixed fee; since then doctors give much less information in their certificate, 3878-9, 3888-9.

Hartop, Mr W. (Analysis of his Evidence.)—Has been nine years relieving officer of No. 1 District, Bradford, 1666-7;—the lowest part of the town, 1669, 1705—— Insurance of children has a bad influence on debased parents, 1672;—who in general insure their children, 1673;—for the sake of the money, not for thrift, 1674——Entertain their friends on day of funeral, 1700-2——Such parents neglect their children, but the money is an additional reason for doing so, 1678-81——Parents bring children very late to the doctor, probably only in order to get certificate, 1893-4, 1712—— Many cases of neglect escape notice, 1695.

Attempts are made to deny insurance and make parish bury insured children, 1683; —not so much as formerly, as in Bradford the assistant clerk to the parish is also registrar, 1685.

Cases of neglect are perhaps one in fifty, 1688, 1749;—most cases of neglect when children are weaned, 1709, 1753;—no use taking proceedings for neglect, as it is impossible to prove, 1689-91.

Agents make no inquiries as to health, 1676, 1714——Case of twelve policies on an old man with cancer, 1675, 1713;—if a medical certificate of health was required on insurance of children, as on adults insuring with a Friendly Society, it would greatly diminish evil, 1715-17;—would prevent thriftless parents insuring at all, 1724:—as in many cases they do not insure till the child is sick, 1723.

£. 3 is about the most insured on one policy for a child, but they sometimes have more than one policy, 1706-7——A working-man's child might be buried for 1 *l.*, including coffin, burial fees and conveyance to cemetery, 1733-4;—this is about the lowest charge, 1735-6.

A limitation of insurance till after two years would meet with no opposition from respectable poor, especially if combined with some endowment for child if it did not die, 1730-2.

Hodson, Mr. H. A., L.R.C.P., M.R.C.S. (Analysis of his Evidence.)—Is a physician at Brighton, 565 ;—formerly practised in Devonshire at Bovey Tracey, and was Poor-law medical officer, 566, 605 —Population at Bovey Tracey partly agricultural, partly brickmaking, 570——Holds strong views as to connection of insurance and child murder, 567 ;—first suspicion aroused by sick children not recovering as they ought, and found they were improperly fed ; such children were all insured, 572.

Respectable poor did not there insure their children, 584, 590——Insurance and neglect were amongst dissolute people, 581.

Very difficult to be sure of neglect ; improper food quite sufficient to kill, 574, 579 ——Witness refused certificates in suspicious cases, 576 ;—but no use in sending cases to coroner, as it is impossible for doctor to swear that child would have recovered even if properly treated, 574.

Has less knowledge of subject in Brighton, but believes same thing occurs there, 589, 592 ;—quotes opinion to this effect of house-surgeon at Hove General Hospital, 586——Believes mothers in the poorer classes are quite capable of properly bringing up their children by hand when they care for them, 611-2.

From experience in London, Devonshire, and Brighton, thinks infant life insurance is simply a premium for murder, 589,—and ought not to be allowed, 608.

Hooper, Mr. Edwin. (Analysis of his Evidence.)—Has been coroner for West Bromwich Division of Staffordshire for thirty-six years, and deputy for four years previous, 4081-2, 4147-8——His is a mining district with many poor, 4149.

Believes that infantile insurance is not conducive to the neglect of children, 4087, 4146——Though insurance is not effected with object of profit, the idea of profit might afterwards be connected with death, and might have injurious effect, 4095 ; —but not so within his experience, 4096-7——Is confronted with letter written by him in 1877, stating that numberless lives are destroyed by improper feeding and neglect to call in doctor, 4098-9 ;—and that the great object with parents in nine cases out of ten seems to be to get the club-money, 4100 ; —and saying that " I do not see how evil can be checked as long as death certificates are given and received in the loose way they are at present," 4102 ;—and also, " I know that unqualified persons have no difficulty in getting deaths registered, and I am constantly coming across cases where midwives take children to the sexton and get them buried as still-born, when they have lived many hours and sometimes longer, and perhaps have been lost through neglect of the midwives to call in medical aid, or through more serious cases, which I shudder to think of," 4105-6——Acknowledges letter and says he has often had children exhumed for examination, and had in his mind the fact that more deaths occurred and bodies found dead in bed on Sunday morning than at any other time, no doubt through drunkenness of parents on Saturday nights, which continues still, 4105-7——But says this letter referred principally to improper feeding, and not written with the idea that there has been any criminal incentive arising from insurance, 4098, 4102-4.

Detection of cruelty to children much more difficult than in the case of adults, 4109 ——Disagrees with opinion of Mr. Thornycroft, deputy-coroner for Wolverhampton, that the present system is bad and ought to be prevented——He has not had the same experience as witness, 4117 ;—and has only been deputy-coroner for six or seven years, 4151——If seventeen coroners have expressed opinions differing from those of witness, can only say that experience is different from his, 4182.

Has had many cases of death of children from neglect, 4120 ;—but has carefully examined and believes that insurance had nothing to do with them, 4123 ;—really caused by improper feeding ; from ignorance in the majority of cases, 4126-7, 4137-8.

The average amount of claim is 50 s.; 4088 ;—and that sum, and more, is generally spent on funeral, 4090, 4140.

Insurance of youngest children necessary, as they must be buried, and there is the strongest objection amongst working-classes to coming on the parish, 4091, 4129 ;—and they attach more importance to proper funeral and mourning than people in a higher class of life, 4144-5——Practice of insurance is general in his district, 4131——Very necessary as from unhealthy occupations a great child mortality must be expected, 4160-2.

No profit to parents if money is all spent on funeral, 4130, 4141 ;—but in cases of neglect such as he has had, the small gain might be an additional incentive, 4134-6 —— The younger the child the cheaper the funeral 4170 ;—and there might be a surplus if child were insured for legal maxima of 4 l. and 10 l. according to age ;—but not at what is the usual sum of 50 s., 4163, 4172——Has never known case of insured child buried by parish, 4175 ;—but relieving officers would have better opportunities than witness for finding this out, 4178-9.

Most insurances in this district are in Prudential, 4153, 4183 ——Sees no objection,

as

Report, 1890—continued.

Hooper, Mr. Edwin. (Analysis of his Evidence)—*continued.*

as average amount that parents insure for is only 50 *s.*, in legalising a scale to limit insurances within certain ages to that amount, 4184-7 ;—which would meet exceptional cases where sinister motives might possibly exist, 4188.

Hooper, Mr. H. W. (Analysis of his Evidence.)—Is a solicitor and has been coroner for the city of Exeter for thirty-seven years, 1187-9 —— Has volunteered his evidence holding strong opinions, 1227-8.

Believes child insurance very prejudicial to child life, 1199-1201, 1215 ;—thinks that bad cases have increased with the increase of child insurance, 1194-7 —— Has found many cases of neglect, a large proportion of them insured, 1202-7 ;— and having only the parents' word for it, more may have been insured than he knew of, 1207-14— Since his attention has been called to the subject, always asks if children have been insured, 1208, 1215.

Quotes opinions against infant insurance of coroners of boroughs of Plymouth, Barnstaple, Devonport, and of districts of Okehampton, Crediton, Totnes, Honiton, and Stoke, all in Devonshire, 1224.

Only commits for trial where besides being morally satisfied, believes there is legal evidence to convict; finds judges unwilling to convict, but quotes a case tried by Mr. Justice Day where father had fifteen years and mother five years penal servitude for brutal ill-treatment of a child, 1252.

The majority of cases of suspicious deaths occur when children are under twelve months, 1229 - Children are often insured as soon as born, 1234—— Canvassing agents go round and persuade parents to insure, 1252.

Thinks dissolute members of working class insure more frequently than respectable, 1249 —— They are a very small minority,1255 —— Accusations he brings are solely against drunken and disreputable parents, not against the large majority of working classes, 1249, 1253-4. 1255—— Thinks any restriction on insurance would irritate respectable poor, 1245, 1248 ;—but it is impossible to distinguish between proper and improper insurance, 1246 ;—and that the respectable persons would be willing to submit to restrictions, if they understood the evil that goes on under present system, 1257-59.

Thinks that 1 *l.* ought to cover expense of funeral of infant, 1240 ;—and that if insurance were limited to that temptation to neglect would diminish, 1240-41.

States that opinion of coroners of whole county of Devonshire is that no life under six or seven years ought to be insured, 1243.

Hulme Burial Society. Balance sheet and report handed in ; it is a model one, and ought to be adopted by every society in the country, *Dobson* 2526.

See *Appendix* K., pages 241-244, and *Dobson, Mr. A. A.* (Analysis of his Evidence).

I.

Ignorance. Cause of almost the neglect and improper feeding, *E. Hooper* 4098, 4126-7, 3137-8.

Mothers in the lower class are quite able to bring up their children by hand, when they care for them, *Hodson* 611-2.

Ignorance, if not criminal, is very gross, as it is easy for mothers to find out, *Cleaver* 471—— In Glasgow pains are being taken to instruct them, *Fortune* 3767-70 ——In Sheffield leaflets giving instruction are distributed, *Cleaver* 472.

Opinion that in criminal cases the amplest allowance is made for ignorance, *Wills* 1851.

Illegitimate Children. No large proportion of inquests on, in Oldham, *Thomson* 694 ;—of insurance on, *Carter* 863—— Furnish majority of suspicious cases, *Burwise* 163, 173 ;— but being parish doctor would see more of them than the usual proportion, *ib.* 174—— Very numerous, *Branson* 314 ;—a large number, *Cleaver* 416 ; *Burry* 514.

Most illegitimate children insured, *Brown* 1095, 1134.

Not insured in Royal Liver, *Taunton* 3256—— Not insured in Prudential under three years of age, *Dewey* 2954—— Except in cases when father and mother are married and live together, *ib.* 3491.

Juries unwilling to find a verdict against a mother in the case of the death of an illegitimate child, *Troutbeck* 985.

Indemnity. Fire and marine insurances are contracts of idemnity ; no one can recover more than he has lost, *Wills* 1939—— Difficulty to apply this principle to life insurances,

Indemnity—continued.

as opening door to fraud, *Wills* 1886, 1944——Impossible from expense of employing persons to inquire into each case, *Dewey* 3515-6 ;—from variety of each case and expense of investigation, *Fortune* 3813 ;—would be a very serious thing for societies to undertake if it were expected that it should be done by them, *ib.* 3814-5.

Inquests. See *Coroner.*

Insurable Interest. Is required to be proved to enable one person to insure life of another, *Day* 1973.

This is a sound principle, and ought not to be departed from in the case of children who are less able to protect themselves from malpractices than adults, *Day* 1964-6. 1976-82.

Might be construed to allow insurances by baby farmers of children for whose care they get an income, *Dewey* 3452——Bill ought to be amended to stop this, *ib.* 3456 ;—not held by Royal Liver to apply to justify insurance by baby farmers, *Taunton* 3351, 3423.

Is evaded by assignment of policies; it was against this that jury protested in Deptford case, not against infant insurance, *Dewey* 3587-94——Policies are too easily transferable, *ib.* 2881——Cases of evasion of law at Belfast, by an American society, *Fortune* 3735-40——Case of an old man with cancer insured by his friends on twelve policies, *Hartop* 1675——There is a great traffic on adult deaths, *Leach* 1796.

No money is paid by Royal Liver, except to persons having an insurable interest (term used not in legal sense, but as meaning parents and guardians having right to insure), *Taunton* 3343-7, 3352——It has been held that baby farmers adopting child out-and-out are in the place of parents and entitled to insure ; probably right, *Waugh* 2240-1——In Liverpool Victoria payments to other than parents cannot be made except by head office, *Clensy* 4063-4.

Insurance Agents. Are generally a struggling class of slightly educated people living by their wits, *Burnett* 1372-8 ;—sometimes of a low class, *Taunton* 3154 ;—fairly educated and most accurate in their accounts, 2903 ;—chosen with great care in Scottish Legal, *Fortune* 3729 ; in Royal London, *Hambridge* 3863 :—are a most respectable body of men, *ib.* 3934-6 ;—Liverpool Victoria very proud of their staff, *Clensy* 3936.

Do not give assistance to coroners in cases of suspicious deaths, *Thomson* 668-70 ; *Troutbeck* 987 ; *Browne* 1185 ;—have sometimes asked witness to falsify certificate, *Thomson* 671 ;—although it is against interest of society, makes them personally popular not to give trouble, *ib.* 751-3 ; *Barwise* 126 ; *Troutbeck* 988-9——Agents have often a small business which also might be injured if they made themselves unpopular by being too strict about insurances, *Burnett* 1401-3——Do not assist justice, *Burnett* 1307 ; *Tasker* 1658 ;—in only one case did agent give assistance to relieving officer ; witness has had two cases where agent assisted to cheat the parish into burying insured child, *Kirshaw* 1821-3, 1820.

Insure children they have not seen, who may be ill at the time, *Branson* 229, 277 ; —who are ill and neglected at the time, *Burnett* 1291 ;—they make no inquiries, *Tasker* 1625, 1655 ; *Hartop* 1676, 1713-6——Agents are not allowed to give information about private affairs of insurers, but head office is always ready to do so when applied to, *Dewey* 3575-80.

Case of agent satisfied to believe that children at baby farms were children of the baby farmers who were sixty years old, *Waugh* 2113——Society for Prevention of Cruelty to Children has had seven baby farmer cases, in all of which the children were insured, *ib.* 112——In case quoted of McKay, where agent insured child knowing that insurer was not parent, he was agent of Liverpool Victoria Society, who do not manage their agents as the Prudential Society, *Dewey* 2886-7—— Very little care exercised by companies in supervising their agents, *Day* 1954 ——Take insurance regardless of health or condition of child, *Wills* 1858 ;— sometimes certify that children are in good health, when they are really moribund; have no interest except in getting commissions on new insurances, *Day* 1954-7. 1959——Their business is so competitive that, if one refuses a case, another would take it, *Burnett* 1304-11——Complaint of working-man quoted, " that the agents are constantly plaguing us ; they are never off the doorstep," *Branson* 233——Tout very actively as soon as child is born, *Thornycroft, App. C.,* page 229——Put much pressure on the poor to insure, *Wills* 1853 ; *Day* 1996 ; *Browne* 1166——Midwives are in the employ of agents to give them early notice of births, *Burnett* 1305.

Many cases of fraud of agents on their companies, *Wills* 1854,—which are very much in their agents' hands, *ib.* 1858 ; *Tasker* 1663 ; *Dewey* 2885——Royal Liver does not receive information of bad cases mainly from their agents, *Taunton* 3059-61.

Danger of having people going about shewing advantages to be gained in case of death of others, *Wills* 1851 ; *H. W. Hooper* 1252.

Do

Insurance Agents—continued.

Do not importune parents, *Crooks* 2439——Insured witness's children without seeing them, *ib.* 2426——Do not insure unborn children, but has heard of agent calling to know if a woman was yet confined, *ib.* 2464 —— Are under check of fear of dismissal if caught tripping at frequent inspections by managers, *Dewey* 2878.

They are paid by commission; 25 per cent. on industrial and 12½ on endowment business, besides bonus of first eight payments in Scottish Legal, *Fortune* 3730——Same per centage in Royal London, and ten first payments, *Hambridge* 3855–61——25 per cent. and the first six payments in Liverpool Victoria, *Clensy* 3925–9——17½ to 20 per cent., and fourteen first premiums, ten of which they have to repay if policy lapses, in Prudential, *Dewey* 2867–75——Rather better terms in Royal Liver, *Taunton* 3164——Impossible to pay them otherwise than according to results to ensure active work, *Taunton* 3163–6; *Dewry* 3518–9.

Voluntary agents collect payments in the Sons of Phœnix Society, *Sargent* 4213–4 ——In the Manchester Unity of Friendly Societies, *Dobson* 2630 ;—and they are not allowed to go from door to door, *ib.* 2633 ;—done as a labour of love in the affiliated Friendly Societies, *Cleveland* 4455.

Registration of agents would increase their responsibility, but doubtful if it would check evils of child insurance, *Burnett* 1407–13——They ought to be licensed, *Taunton* 3147,—with powers to magistrates to take away license, *ib.* 3150 ——This would make them more careful; now if a man loses one situation he can get another, *ib.* 3238——It would be quite impossible ; Liverpool Victoria alone has over 3,000 collectors, many constantly changing, *Clensy* 3993–4——Has a strong opinion that it would be uncharitable in preventing agent dismissed by one society getting employment from another, *ib.* 3995–7.

Liverpool Victoria employ superior officers to go round and test cases insured by all but very experienced agents, *Clensy* 3072–4.

Insurance Clubs. Insurance clubs paying part of benefit money in drink censured, in Report of General Children's Hospital at Pendlebury, Manchester, *see* page 55.

Are able to evade registration under Friendly Societies Act, and escape all observation, *Dewey* 3614–27.

See *Burial Societies.* and *Friendly Societies.*

Insurance Companies. There are only about six companies registered under the Joint Stock Acts which insure children's lives, *Dewey* 3526–8.

Make considerable profit out of lapsed policies, *Branson* 227 ; *Burnett* 1531. See *Lapsed Policies.*

Often give a small grant when nothing is due under policy, *Branson* 272 ;—which is an advertisement for them, *ib.* 324. See *Benefit.*

Rather pay than have the unpopularity of contesting claims, *Branson* 331;—but get out of payment or part payment in various ways in suspicious cases, *ib.* 278–295.

Case of policy marked outside " immediate benefit;" inside was in usual terms, giving only part benefit till after one year, *ib.* 229.

Verdict of jury in the Deptford case that the loose system of insurance by some companies is an incentive to murder, *see* page 52——This refers not to infant insurance, but to assignment of policies, *Dewey* 3000, 3587–94.

Expense of management very high; 40 or 50 per cent., *Ritchie* 1492——Dividend-paying industrial companies are able to do as well for their members, in spite of the dividend to shareholders, as friendly societies, because of the many restrictions to which these are subject, *Clensy* 4042–3.

Local friendly burial clubs preferable to collecting societies, *Ritchie* 1431–1440—— Bad cases mostly take place in connection with collecting societies, *ib.* 1441–2. See *Friendly Societies.*

Sometimes get themselves incorporated under Companies Acts, and so avoid limitations on child insurance of Friendly Societies Act, *Leach* 1763, 1766, 1783–8, 1792. See *Newbold Friendly Society*, and *Friendly Societies Act.*

Any evils that exist are the result of keen competition, which would be remedied if there were a uniform scale of insurance, *Clensy* 4000.

Insurance Money. Can only be paid on certificate from registrar, *Barwise* 120. See *Certificate, Amount*, and *Benefit.*

Insurance of Children. Prejudicial to children as leading to their neglect, *Thomson* 615–8 ; *Carter* 765 ;—or even death, *Burnett* 1267 ; *H. W. Hooper* 1201 ;—unfavourable to child life, *Ritchie* 1419—·-Is an additional reason for getting rid of burden of support

(225—IND.)   M M 4   of

Insurance of Children—continued.

of children, *Carter* 814–6; *Troutbeck* 922, 935; *Barwise* 20, 21, 106–8, 202; *Browne* 1123;—is a temptation to neglect, *Tasker* 1531——Has a bad influence on debased parents, *Hartop* 1672——Demoralises parents by connecting profit with death of children, *Branson* 221, 261——Death is looked upon as the natural sequence of insurance, *ib.* 222 —— Is thought a lawful speculation, *ib.* 259 ——Two or three pounds, or even two or three shillings, is a temptation to parents who systematically neglect their children, and is enough to upset the balance of motives, *Barwise* 1951——People who have had a child die have been noticed to have money to spend, *Tasker* 1529–30 ——Opinion that there is connection between infant insurance and murder, *Hodson* 567; *Day* 1947–50——This opinion gradually formed during judicial experience, *Wills* 1851.

In spite of the utility of insurance for respectable working people, opinion that, on the whole, the system is bad, as many insure to make money, *Thornycroft, App. C.,* p. 229——Statistics showing rise in infant mortality in district whilst collecting society only insured there, *Ritchie* 1423 *et seq.*——Child neglect has increased with the increase of child insurance, *H. W. Hooper* 1194–7——More suspicious deaths of insured than uninsured children, *Thornycroft, App. C.,* p. 229——Great difference in ill effects of child insurance between different localities, *Burry* 547–8.

Dissolute and improvident insure more than thrifty parents, *Branson* 218–20, 269; *H. W. Hooper* 1249; *Thomson* 621; *Tasker* 1559;—quite as much as respectable parents, *Hartop* 1723——Respectable parents do not insure their children, *Hodson* 584;—but belong to benefit clubs which pay something on death of child, or to friendly societies like the Oddfellows, *Branson* 318–21;—common not to insure till children are sick, *Hartop* 1723;—in the Swindon case baby-farmers found means to insure children, though not to feed them, *Day* 1952;—illegitimate children mostly insured, *Browne* 1095, 1134;—neglected children generally found to be insured, *Burry* 507.

Insured children not so carefully treated as uninsured amongst a dissolute class, *Thomson* 700–1;—but dissolute a very small proportion of whole working class, *ib.* 723.

All classes of working people insure children, but practically no suspicious cases amongst respectable class, *Troutbeck* 1010; *Browne* 1124, 1127, 1145——Bad cases only amongst dregs of the population, *Burnett* 1270; *Tasker* 1533;—amongst drunken and idle people, *Branson* 338–9; *Thomson* 619——Respectable people do not insure their children till they are about five, *Tasker* 1613–4——Dissolute class of people insure their children only for the insurance money, *Kirshaw* 1808, 1827–30——For the sake of the difference between the cheapest burial and the insurance money, *Tasker* 1593; *Hartop* 1683——Common practice for people receiving outdoor relief to insure their children, *Barwise* 986–9.

Opinion of magistrates in a case at Leicester that a woman charged with cruelty could have had no motive in insuring the child except to get a premium on its death, *see* page 52——Opinion of magistrates at Newcastle that insurance in a case before them was a premium on murder, *see* page 79.

Report of Committee of General Hospital for Sick Children, Pendlebury, Manchester, extract from, read by the Chairman; that 184 children, out of 251 who died there, had been insured; that average amount received was 3 *l.* 4 *s.* 7¾ *d.* for each child; that "the influence of the worst form of 'death clubs' is wholly bad;" that these remarks apply principally to clubs which insure children a few months old and give a portion of the benefit money in drink, *see* page 55.

Laudable desire of poor to provide against sickness and death ought to be supported, but there are occasional cases of parents who insure for nothing but to get the money, *Grahame*, page 131——Some evils exist requiring legislative remedy, but present Bill is harsh and ineffective; Letter of *Leeds Society for Prevention of Cruelty to Children*, page 134.

Undue restrictions are very undesirable, but the same restrictions that are put on all classes in the case of fire and marine insurances, and on life insurances (except so far as excepted by the Friendly Societies Act), should be placed on the poorer classes too, and no profit allowed to be made on death, *Wills* 1935–6, 1939–40.

Has no connection with infanticide, which existed before insurances; where parent is heartless enough to be able to kill a child, the burden of its support is a much greater inducement than the small sum of insurance money, *Clensy* 3956, 3959–65—— Opinion of Mr. Wynne Baxter, an East-end coroner, quoted, that insured children are as well cared for as uninsured, *ib.* 4011;—certainly does not promote infanticide, *Fortune* 3650, 3656–60, 3780–1; *Dobson* 2537;—story quoted believed to be fiction, *ib.* 2538–42——Has no connection with neglect, which arises from ignorance, *E. Hooper* 4087, 4116, 4126–7;—confronted with letter by him to the contrary effect, says that he was then referring to improper feeding, and to the fact that most overlaid children were found dead on Sunday morning, from parents drinking on Saturday night, *ib.* 4098–109.

Prudential

Report, 1890—*continued.*

Insurance of Children—continued.

Prudential exercise care in selection of insurances; many proposals rejected, *Dewey* 2895 ;—same in Royal London, *Hambridge* 3868——In friendly societies cannot be, and is not, abused, *Cleveland* 4410, 4465 ;—never been a single case of charge against an insurer in Scottish Legal, *Fortune* 3666–70.

Tends to thrift, *Clensy* 3992; *Sargent* 4308 ;—and any legislation restricting insurance would be a great misfortune for the working classes, *ib.* 4311; *Stead* 4698-704 ;—reduces the curse of pauperism, *Cleveland* 4556——Not effected much by dissolute parents; very poor insure generally and stint themselves to pay, *Taunton* 3114–6, 3259–62 ;—usually by the more respectable classes, *Fortune* 3778 ;—not by dissolute parents, *Cleveland* 4476, 4562–72, 4599 ; *Crooks* 2445–7.

Unavoidably large mortality of children in towns amongst poorer classes makes it a duty on parents to insure their children, *Fortune* 3803–4 ;—immediately at birth, *Taunton* 3233.

Almost universal amongst working classes, so that no surprise should be expressed at inquests if child insured, but rather the contrary, *Dewey* 2805 ;—complains that if fact is mentioned at inquest that child was insured, it prejudices case against parents, *Crooks* 2275——Working-men consider it discreditable when their fellow-workmen do not insure, *ib.* 2368——Certainly two-thirds of working classes in Scotland insure, *Fortune* 3790.

Number of Insurances :

Child insured in three societies, *Burnett* 1278 ;—in four societies, *Leach* 1772 ;—30 per cent. of insured are insured in more than one society, *ib.* 1786——No child knowingly insured in Prudential who is already insured in another society, *Dewey* 2803–7——Six per cent. of claims in Prudential are also insured in other offices, *ib.* 3475——No inquiry as to other insurances made by Royal Liver, but they do not pay if total amounts to more than legal limit, *Taunton* 3273, 3300—— Royal London would grant policy if amount already insured were very small, *Hambridge* 3871——Hulme Burial Society allows two insurances, because father and mother each wish to insure child in the society to which they have belonged before marriage, *Dobson* 2512, 2691–2——Double insurance common in London, Liverpool, and all over the country, *Taunton* 3407–8.

Case of four children in family together insured for 28 *l.* 12 *s.*, *Waugh* 2054 ;—boy insured for 20 *l.*, and four children insured altogether for 25 *l.*, *ib.* 2055—— Beggar child insured for 20 *l.* 12 *s.*, *ib.* 2269——Children in Oldham not generally insured in more than one office, *Thomson* 676.

Objects of Insurance :

Mainly for funeral, but also for mourning and expenses of illness, *Burnett* 1344 ; *Ritchie* 1499-1501——Amongst respectable poor partly for mourning, *Tasker* 1608–11 ;—for mourning, doctor's bill, and medical comforts, *Crooks* 2273–4, 2435 ;—for doctors and nurses, *Sargent* 4355–7.

Fact of insurance difficult to find out, *Barwise* 36 ; *Cleaver* 402–4, 410 ;—especially in London ; parents sometimes deny or say policy has lapsed, or child is not yet in benefit, *Waugh* 2121 ;—especially difficult in unregistered societies who do not always insist on having registrar's certificate before paying, *Leach* 1771–7——Case of agent helping to deceive parish as to burying insured child, *Kirshaw* 1823——Denial common, *Tasker* 1539——Insured children buried by parish ;—See *Funeral.*

Interference, with infant life insurance would be very much resented by working classes, *Troutbeck* 1013——This Bill keenly felt as a libel, *Dobson* 2556, 2589, 2595.

Any check on child insurance would be a punishment upon honest parents, *Crooks* 2383——Would be resented by them, but very difficult to discriminate between proper and improper insurances, *H. W. Hooper* 1244–8——Believes they would not object to certain restrictions if it was made clear to them that much evil goes on under present system, *ib.* 1258–9——Any interference with conditions at present enjoyed under Friendly Societies Act much resented, *Crooks* 2688; *Clensy* 3948–9, 3966, 3969—— Any limitation of amount now legal, would be much resented, *Taunton* 3246.

J.

Judges. For evidence of, see *Wills, Mr. Justice* ; and *Day, Mr. Justice.* Generally agree with evidence of Mr. Justice Wills, *Wills* 1851—— Mr. Justice Charles said, in a charge to grand jury, " It is a question whether some legislation ought not to take place not to stop insurance of children, but to prevent proceeds getting into hands of parents ; *see* page 104——Baron Pollock allowed his opinion to be quoted in support of Mr. Justice Wills, *Wills* 1851, 1924.

A judge has rather to restrain than to urge juries in the case of charges of neglect of children, *Day* 2018, 2022.

Judges—continued.

Judges differ as to proof required of " means " of parent to support child in cases of charge of starvation ; some hold that a workhouse within reach is " means," *Day* 2019 ——Case dismissed at Derby for want of proof of " means," *Waugh* 2080.

Juries (*Assizes and Sessions*). Unwilling to convict for murder or manslaughter, *Brown* 1098-1100——Witness, a coroner, recommends his juries not to return a verdict of manslaughter but to censure for neglect, when guardians prosecute before magistrates, with greater chance of success, *ib.* 1100-1.

Very ready to convict for neglect of children, require restraining rather than urging, *Day* 2018-21 —— Case of murder or manslaughter different ; there is always an unwillingness to convict of this, *ib.* 2022.——See *Conviction.*

Juries (*Coroners*). Do not readily find verdict of culpable neglect, *Carter* 806-883, 842, 886-889 ;—against parents, especially mother of an illegitimate child, *Troutbeck* 985.

Rider to verdict of jury on the Deptford case, that the loose system of insurance by some companies is an incentive to murder, read by the Chairman, page 52.

Juvenile Societies. See Analysis of Evidence of, *Cleveland, Mr.* ; *Walton, Mr.* ; *Stead, Mr.* ; *Sargent, Mr.*, and *Friendly Soceties.*

K.

Kirshaw, Mr. James. (Analysis of his Evidence.)—Is a relieving officer in Rochdale, 1801——The population of his district is 40,000, with only a small proportion of the better class 1802-5——All classes insure their children, 1831-2——Believes that there are cases where parents allow their children to die for the sake of the insurance money, 1809-10——This class cares nothing for being on the parish, 1811-2 ;—insures only to make money, 1808—Has found parents drinking after death, 1827——These were Irish, 1844——It is not a proof of thrift to insure and to give a child a cheap funeral and drink the surplus, 1846-8.

Has had cases where parents have got insured children buried by the parish, 1813-4.

Has only in one case had assistance from an insurance agent, 1821, 1826 ;—has had two agents who helped to cheat the parish, 1822-3.

About 1 *l.* would cover all absolutely necessary expenses of a child's funeral, 1833-5 ——Sunday funerals are forbidden in Rochdale, 1836-7 ;—which would entail loss of a day or half day's work to attend funeral, 1838.

L.

Lapsed Policies. Are very profitable to companies, *Branson* 229, 270-272 ; — very numerous, *ib.* 308 ;—one-third of all insurances lapse in first year, *Dewey* 2940—— Profitable to all insurance companies, but especially when poor people insure, on account of their improvidence or from misfortune being unable to keep up payment of premiums. *Wills* 1851, 1860, 1893-5.

Not profitable to companies, as the ratio of mortality of children becomes less each year in the earlier years ; the first year is the least profitable to them, *Dewey* 2941-5—— There is a loss on deaths under three years after allowing for apparent profit on lapsed policies, *ib.* 3502-10 ; *Taunton* 3374——Every death under one is a loss, *ib.* 3323—— Report from well-known actuaries read, showing that lapses are a loss, not a gain, in infant insurances, *Dewey* 2945.

Not profitable to agent in Prudential Society, as he has to refund part of his commission on lapse, *Dewey* 2872, 3512.

Policy in Prudential allowed to be revived on payment of arrears only, within twelve months, *Dewey* 3472-3.

Leach, Mr. Robert Alfred. (Analysis of his Evidence.)—Is Clerk to the Guardians of Rochdale and Superintendent Registrar, 1755-7.

Several societies pay insurance money on death of infants without production of registrars' certificate, 1760-1——The Friendly Societies Act, 1875, provided that children should be not insured for more than certain specified sums ;—and that a Friendly Society should not pay without the production of the registrar's certificate of death and a certificate from him of the amount to be paid, 1791——This applied to friendly and benevolent societies and industrial assurance companies, and by a subsequent

Leach, Mr. Robert Alfred. (Analysis of his Evidence)—*continued.*
quent Act trades unions which pay money on death of child under ten are brought under Act, 1763.

But some companies, formerly registered under Friendly Societies Act, have now got themselves incorporated under the Companies' Acts, 1762——They did this on account of the difficulty of making out the valuation every five years to the Registrar of Friendly Societies ordered by Friendly Societies Act, 1788——They appear then to be exempt from provisions of that Act, and are not obliged to require a certificate of death to be produced, 1763——The Newbold Friendly Society has a rule that the production of the certificate may be dispensed with, which rule would be illegal if they were still registered under the Friendly Societies Act, 1766——This society has a membership of 25,000 ; 1768 ;—its meetings are held at a public-house, 1769 ;—there are several other clubs of the same sort in Rochdale, 1769-70——The Newbold Society do not insure children under three months, and they must have been insured twenty-four weeks before they are entitled to the money, 1780.

Children are often insured in several societies ; case mentioned of four, 1772 ;—nearly 30 per cent. insured in more than one society, 1786 ;—but parents cannot get certificates from the registrar for more in the aggregate than the amount limited according to age under the Act, and therefore if production of these certificates be dispensed with they can get more than the legal amount, 1791—— No societies should be allowed to get out of safeguards of Friendly Societies Act by being incorporated under another Act, 179-3 ;—all working people insure their children, but the worst class do not, 1796, 1798.

A pauper's funeral for a child costs at Rochdale 12 *s.* or 13 *s.*, 1778.

Insurances of children ought to be registered, 1799, 1800.

Leeds. Letter from the Leeds Committee of the Society for the Prevention of Cruelty to Children, handed in by the Chairman, stating objections to Bill, though in favour of legislation on the subject ;—that amounts limited in Clause 1 are too small, barely meeting actual expense of burial, leaving no margin for medical attendance, mourning, or tombstone——That no child under two ought to be insured at all, as it is before this age that foul play mostly takes place, and burial much cheaper ;—that the scale should be 5 *l.* on a child between two and five, 7 *l.* between five and 11, 10 *l.* over 11 ——Undertaker's clause very objectionable :—

   (*a.*) Shows unfounded suspicion of working classes ;

   (*b.*) Interference with owner's disposal of money only justifiable where foul play or neglect is suspected ;

   (*c.*) Offers inducement to fraud and collusion ; and

   (*d.*) Ignores expense of last illness.

Opinion :

   (1.) That no child under two be insured ;

   (2.) That only parents and guardians should insure child's life ;

   (3.) No insurance in more than one office, registrar's certificate being the legal receipt for the insurance money ;

   (4.) That this certificate should be made out for the one office, specifying its name and amount insured ;

   (5.) That registrar should only give one certificate ; and

   (6.) That same precautions as Post Office Savings Bank uses where child depositors die be used before paying insurance to parents, *see* page 134.

Leek (Staffordshire). A local burial club exists here, and works well, *Ritchie* 1423, 1471—— When it discontinued insurance on children under one year and collecting society took its place, the infant mortality of the town increased, *ib.* 1423-8, 1457-8, 1470-5, 1487.

Leicester. Report of a summary conviction before borough magistrates for ill-treatment of a child aged five years, and their statement that there could have been no object in the insurance except to secure the premium on its death. Read by the Chairman, p. 53.

Report of case before borough magistrates of death caused by neglect of insured child. Read by the Chairman, pp. 103 and 104.

Liverpool Victoria and Legal Friendly Society. Is a friendly collecting society, *Clensy* 3895—— All the profits go to the members, *ib.* 3897——Has 1,200,000 insuring members, *ib.* 3899,—of whom 185,000 are under five, and 155,000 between five and ten, *ib.* 3904, 4034.

Liverpool Victoria and Legal Friendly Society—continued.

Employs collectors at a commission of about 25 per cent., *Clensy* 3928–30——They are a most respectable body of men, *ib.* 3934–5——Are specially instructed not to take low class business, and to avoid certain unhealthy districts in almost every town, *ib.* 3937—47, 4029–32——Case of McKay, where agent deliberately broke rules as to parent being only person to insure, *Dewey* 2886——Their agencies not managed so well as those of Prudential, *ib.* 2887.

Scale of insurances given, *Clensy* 4047–52 ;—is less favourable than some other offices, *ib.* 4053 ;—but gives considerable advantages in the first year, with a view probably of inducing people to join, *ib.* 4054–7.

In the Deptford case, insured in the Liverpool Victoria, the woman insuring said she was the mother, *Clensy* 4080—— Secretary knows no other particulars, *ib.* 4065–4070.

In the Swindon baby-farming case, whether a baby farmer is or is not the personal representative of the parent, who alone, except the parent, can insure, the children were insured in the Liverpool Victoria, *Day* 2008–11.

Case of a boy begging in the street found to be insured in the Liverpool Legal Friendly Society for 20 *l.* 12 *s.*, *Waugh* 2269.

Ludlow, Mr. Is Chief Registrar of Friendly Societies ; said before the House of Commons Committee that he considered association of insurance with the death of a child has an ill effect on the mind of a parent, *Fortune* 3672.

The scale of insurance allowed by Bill was framed by him, and was approved by the Committee of the House of Commons, *Waugh* 2214–8.

Lunatics. Presentment of Grand Jury at Yarmouth Quarter Sessions, recommending that lunatics and imbeciles should be included in the Children's Life Insurance Bill, [H.L.] ; App. B., p. 228.

M.

Macclesfield and Congleton Amalgamated Burial Societies Association. Letter from Secretary of, to Committee on the Bill, handed in by the Chairman, to the effect that the Bill is an unwarrantable interference with such societies as belong to Association; and that infanticide is not known to exist in connection with them ;—that the Friendly Societies Act of 1875 sufficiently restricts amount to be paid on death of child, which leaves no margin after payment of the most necessary expenses, and that the majority of working classes insure also to obtain medical aid ;—that Clause 2 (undertaker's clause) is the great objection to the Bill; and that Clauses 1, 3, 4, and 5 will not affect this Association, *see* p. 133.

Magistrates. Expression of opinion of magistrates at Leicester, that the only object of insurance in case before them was to get the insurance money, *see* page 53.

Expressed strong opinions on subject of child insurance at Newcastle, *see* page 79 ; —at Rotherham, *Burnett* 1290.

Manchester and Salford District, Amalgamated Conference of Family Friendly Burial Societies of the. These societies have 280,000 members and many more societies are anxious to join, *Dobson* 2489——They are all mutual societies ; profits go to their funds ,*ib.* 2496–71—— They are each managed by members, *ib.* 2498 ;—so that in many districts all the members know each other, and a public opinion is formed which does not exist in the Prudential or other large societies, *ib.* 2499–501.

The payments are collected by members for a small sum, generally after work hours, *Dobson* 2502–4.

Only children of members are insured, and not before two months old, *Dobson* 2518 ; —and there is an interval of from six weeks to three months before they come into benefit, *ib.* 2777–9.

Some of the societies give medical aid as well as burial money, *Dobson* 2515, 2534–5.

Manslaughter or Murder. Evil of child insurance not measurable by number of convictions for murder or manslaughter, as charges or convictions often on minor offences, on account of difficulty of getting conviction for greater, *Wills* 1882–4.

Willingness of juries to convict for cruelty to children does not apply to murder or manslaughter, *Day* 2018, 2022.

Prosecution for, being at common law, requires " means " in parents to be proved, *Waugh* 2063–71.

See *Cases of Suspicious Death or Neglect; Conviction ; Evidence,* and " *Means.*"

Marasmus.

Report, 1890—*continued.*

Marasmus. A vague term, meaning wasting, *Barwise* 22 —— If of opinion that perhaps child might have been starved, would simply put "marasmus" on certificate as cause of death ; the registrars have orders from Registrar General to make inquiries in cases of these doubtful certificates, *ib.* 125——Marasmus is properly only a symptom, *ib.* 129 ——- In the well-to-do classes children do not die of marasmus, *ib.* 131 ——90 per cent. of marasmus cases might have been saved, *Branson* 258—— Children properly cared for do not die of marasmus, *Hodson* 602.

Means. "Means" must be proved before a parent can be convicted of neglect to supply food, *Carter* 843 ——Necessary in prosecutions at common law, *Waugh* 2063 ;—but in cases under the Guardians Act or the Prevention of Cruelty to Children Act, power of applying to parish is held to be "means," *ib.* 2066——Difficulty of conviction for starving on account of view some judges have taken of necessity of proving "means" ; other judges have held that where there is a workhouse in the neighbourhood children must not be allowed to starve, *Day* 2019.

In case at Derby, Mr. Justice Wills laid down law that there were no "means," and case therefore dismissed, though he said the parents were poor voluntarily, *Waugh* 2079–83.

Medical Men. For evidence of, see *Barwise, Mr. Sidney ; Branson, Mr. John ; Thomson, Dr. ; Cleaver, Dr. ; Hodson, Mr. ; Burry, Mr. ; Ritchie, Mr. J. J.*—— Often give certificates in cases of suspicious death, *Thomson* 634 *et seq.* ; 702—— Hesitate to refuse except evidence is very clear, *ib.* 725——Knowing difficulty of getting convictions at assizes, *ib.* 679 ; *Branson* 239——Unpopularity would follow refusal, *Barwise* 167-169 ; *Thomson* 726——Loss of time in attending coroner's inquest and assizes very serious, *Branson* 239.

Do not give certificate too easily, *Carter* 784 ; *Browne* 1118——Sometimes asked to falsify certificates by insurance agents, *Thomson* 671, 731 *et seq.* ;—more commonly by parents, *ib.* 737.

Often called in too late, *Barwise* 25——Chiefly but not exclusively in the case of insured children, *Thomson* 616, 682.

Unqualified doctors call in qualified doctor at the last moment to see patient alive so as to sign certificate, *Barwise* 137.

Sometimes when their suspicions are aroused are able to stop neglect, *Branson* 233, 234——Necessity of their being called in to give certificate while child is still alive has had effect of stopping neglect short of death, *Waugh* 1884.

If doctors had to give certificate for insurance money instead of registrar, they would know who were insured, which would act as a check on neglect, *Barwise* 123——Used formerly to be paid a fee for giving death certificate, but this was abolished by Friendly Societies Act ; now they certify without fee to the registrar who has to give the only lawful certificate for insurance money and gets a fee ; since this change doctors' certificates are not so full as they used to be, *Hambridge* 3878-9, 3888–9.

Medical Relief. Not the reason for insuring as it can always be had from the parish, *Barwise* 95-109 ; *Branson* 286 ;—or from gratuitous dispensaries, *Branson* 112 ;—or sick club or hospital, *ib.* 286——Parish doctors can also order medical extras, *Barwise* 110——Many of those who insure are already receiving relief, *ib.* 9, 86–9.

Respectable working men generally belong to sick clubs, which give attendance to themselves and families, *Burnett* 1329-33 ;—or to provident dispensaries, *Dobson* 2533 ——But unfortunately all working men will not belong to them, and some of them have failed through mismanagement, *ib.* 2639.

Custom of medical men to have private sick provident clubs, *Burry* 532—— Witness never knew a suspicious death amongst subscribers to his club, *ib.* 535–6.

No harm in insuring to pay for medical attendance as well as funeral, if it could be insured that doctor should get the money, *Wills* 1908.

To obtain medical aid one of the principal reasons of the working classes for insuring ; letter of Macclesfield Amalgamnted Burial Societies, page 133—— Should be encouraged ; letter of Leeds Society for Prevention of Cruelty to Children, page 134.

One of the great features of friendly societies is that they give medical relief and sick pay in juvenile branches, *Cleveland* 4547 ; *Stead* 4633-8——Pay a doctor for exclusive attendance on members, *Stead* 4639-41——Have a sick fund separate from insurance fund for adult members and their children, *ib.* 4668-9.

Mortality of Children. In Manchester Amalgamated Friendly Burial Society lower than death-rate of whole population, *Dobson* 2513-21, 2529 ;—but as they only take in the children of members, mostly respectable artizans, and "loafers" are not admitted, *ib.* 2756-8, 2744, 2766 ;—and do not insure children under two months old; admits comparison is not equal, *ib.* 2767-9.

Mortality of Children— continued.

Table of death-rate of children insured in Prudential, and general death-rate set out, *Dewey* 2947 ;—is two per cent. less in Prudential than general, *ib.* 2947-51 ;—but in various respects the comparison is not equal, *ib.* 2956-79——In Scottish Legal death-rate is 3·81 per cent. for children under five years, and 0·71 between five and ten, *Fortune* 3702——About four per cent. under five in Royal London, and about 0·4 between five and ten, *Hambridge* 3828-30——In four large friendly societies mortality of children under sixteen years is only one-half per cent., *Cleveland* 4410-3——In Foresters it is only 4·12 per thousand, *Stead* 4622-6. (For Age of Insurance, see *Friendly Societies.*)

Ratio of deaths to membership in specimen large towns, under ten years of age, set out, *Fortune* 3705- 8 ; *App.* H., page 239.

Ten per cent. of mortality of children is from preventible causes, including overlying, *Taunton* 3062-71 ;—overlying arises from drunkenness in parents, but principally from overcrowding in small tenements, *ib.* 3417-20——Does not include in preventible causes cases where they have aggravated or induced natural causes of death, *ib.* 3072-7.

Mourning. One of the great objects of insurance is to procure mourning, *Burnett* 1344 ; —amongst respectable working class, *Tasker* 1608-10 ; *Crooks* 2434-7 ;—is partly to get mourning, *Ritchie* 1500-1 ; *Taunton* 3144——No margin left by scale in Bill for any expenditure on mourning ; letter of Leeds Society for the Prevention of Cruelty to Children, page 1314——Possible that if this Bill indirectly diminished expenditure on mourning it might be well, *Taunton* 3145-6.

N.

Neglect. Neglect of insured children greater than of uninsured, *Thomson* 618 ;—among the dissolute classes, *ib.* 700 ;—very common, *Burry* 505-12.

Difficult to prove, without knowledge of previous history of case, *Barwise* 60-1 ;— from happening in the privacy of the home, *Thomson* 679 ;—neighbours will not speak except in very gross cases, *Cleaver* 468.

Difficult to distinguish, whether neglect intentional or not, *Thomson* 683-685 ;— whether doctor's orders have been carried out, *Branson* 262-264 ; *Cleaver* 359-378 ; *Burry* 580.

Ignorance pleaded to excuse, *Branson* 267 ; *Cleaver* 484.

Children often brought to doctor too late ; *Barwise* 25, 26 ; *Cleaver* 351, 400 ; *H. W. Hooper* 1203 ;—whom care in time could have saved ; *Burry* 502 ; *Thomson* 616.

Children observed not to get well as they should have done, and found that these children were insured, *Hodson* 572.

Suffocation or overlaying very common ; belief of witness that it is often intentional, *Browne* 1059-61.

As many uninsured as insured children neglected, but not so many starved, *Burnett* 1346, 1354 ;—character of the cruelty in the two cases distinctly different, *ib.* 1393-1400.

Suspicion aroused by dissolute parents having a good deal of money to spend after death, *Tasker* 1529

Not true that parent put away or neglect their children for sake of insurance money, *Crooks* 2448 ;—such conduct would be visited on them by their neighbours, *ib.* 2451 ;—if such cases exist they are isolated cases, *ib.* 2447.

See *Cases of Suspicious Death or Neglect.*

Newbold Friendly Society. Is one of the societies that have ceased to be registered under Friendly Societies Act, and got themselves incorporated under Companies Acts, *Leach* 1764 ;—by this it ceases to be bound by limitations intended by Parliament to be placed on child insurance, *ib.* 1783, 1791-2——Has a rule permitting the production of registrar's certificate to be dispensed with, *ib.* 1766.

Newcastle. Case of parents committed for trial for manslaughter of child ; child was insured ; statement made that it costs about 8 *s.* to bury a child insured for 30 *s.* or 2 *l.* See Report of Proceedings, read by the Chairman, page 79.

Nottingham. Letter from the Health Committee of the Corporation of Nottingham to the Local Government Board, handed in by the Chairman ; states that the attention of the Committee has been called to a great and growing evil in the matter of the insurance of young children ; that bad cases have occurred in Nottingham ; that as
children

Nottingham—continued.

children are not medically examined, children seriously ill are often insured and wilfully neglected, and recommends that :

(1.) It be compulsory on the insurance company to give to the local authority notice of every insurance of infants ; and

(2.) Full particulars of the death of every insured child, that they may make inquiries before the insurance money is paid ; and

(3.) That power be given to the local authority to enter into any house where an insured child is kept or has died, for ascertaining its condition.

See page 205.

O.

Oddfellows, National Independent Order of. Allows fifteen per cent. only of receipts for all management expenses including rent, *Cleveland* 4450——Is gaining members from the collecting societies, *ib.* 4446, 4494——Is holding its own in competition with them, *Walton* 4742-6.

Has itself a graduated scale of insurance, and therefore witness is of opinion would not object to such being legalised, *Cleveland* 4413——Its benefits being below scale allowed in Bill would not be pecuniarily injured by it, *Walton* 4738-40——Scale given, *ib.* 4709-18, 4732.

See *Cleveland, Mr.* (*Analysis of his Evidence*); *Walton, Mr.* (*Analysis of his Evidence*); and *Friendly Societies.*

Oldham. Number of inquests from 1887 to 1890 stated, *Thomson* 625——Deaths of children under a year varied from 157 to 187 in the eight years from 1882 to 1889, the average for all England being 147, *ib.* 689.

Opinion as to number of cases in Oldham of children buried without inquiry under suspicious circumstances, *ib.* 635, 702-711.

Insurance of children general here, *ib.* 690 ;—not usually in more than one office, *ib.* 676.

If average death-rate here higher than rate for all England, so it is in all congested districts, *Clensy* 4011.

P.

Phœnix, United Order of the Total Abstinent Sons of. Is a temperance friendly society, *Sargent* 4203 ;—founded in February 1887, *ib.* 4296 ;—having 7,000 juvenile members from five to sixteen years of age, *ib.* 4204 ——Takes no insurance under five, and gives no benefit till after six months' insurance, *ib.* 4207, 4250-1.

Its premiums are collected by voluntary agency, as Order exists for purpose of encouraging thrift and temperance, *ib.* 4212-4.

Gives a uniform sum of 8 *l.* at death, *ib.* 4204, 4241 ——This is not too much for burial and incidental expenses, such as doctor's bill, nurses, and mourning, *ib.* 4217, 4269, 4278, 4338-9——This Bill would at some ages diminish this by 2 *l.* ; 4273——Order wishes, as their funds have increased, to raise benefit to 10 *l.*, as allowed by present law, but this would also be impossible under Bill, *ib.* 4218-25, 4332.

Order has also a sick fund, but quite distinct from burial fund, *ib.* 4238 —-Very few members belong to it ; if they did, they would have no necessity to pay part of funeral insurance money for doctor, *ib.* 4265-7.

Has never had a case of suspicious death, *ib.* 4314, 4325.

Police. Are generally applied to by parents when doctor refuses certificate of death, *Thomson* 639 ;—make investigations and often ask doctor to reconsider refusal, as they can get no evidence likely to lead to conviction, *ib.* 640, 647——Have less chance of detecting criminal neglect than the doctor, *Branson* 247, 248——Have too much power in this matter, *Thomson* 659.

Report to coroner all suspicious cases, *Carter* 846, 865——Take up prosecution in all suspicious cases where there seems to be any evidence, *Browne* 1126——In metropolitan district have had orders to communicate all suspicious cases affecting children to Society for the Prevention of Cruelty to Children, *Waugh* 2105.

Pollock, Baron. His opinion as to the evils of infant life insurance quoted : " Indefensible in theory and bad in practice," *Wills* 1851, 1924.

Report, 1890—*continued,*

Premiums. All insurances on children are at a uniform rate of one penny a week, *Dobson* 2525; *Dewey* 2833-4; *Taunton* 3339, 3366; *Clensy* 3919-21——Sometimes half the amount is insured for one halfpenny, *Taunton* 3333;—in a few cases, *Clensy* 3922-3.

Very high for infant life insurance, *Wills* 1851;—especially considering the number of lapses, *ib.* 1860-11; *Browne* 1162;—but escapes notice on account of the small sums paid at a time, *Wills* 1851; *Day* 1957-8, 1970

Preston. Death-rate of children insured in Scottish Legal so high in Preston that that society has given up issuing new policies there, probably because mothers work in factories, *Fortune* 3706-7.

Prevention of Cruelty to Children, Society for. Was formed in 1884; *Waugh* 1884—— Has had 5,314 cases of cruelty reported to it, *ib.* 2036——Has prosecuted in 752 cases, and obtained convictions in 670, *ib.* 2037-8———Rarely prosecutes; at Cardiff one case out of every seven, but issue warnings, *ib.* 2059.——*See* Evidence of *Rev. B. Waugh.*

Having received all information from Prudential Society in two cases, used fact of insurance to prejudice prisoner, though no serious allegation made that insurance was cause of crime, *Dewey* 3566-72——Received offer from Royal Liver Society of help, but have never applied for it, *Taunton* 3094, 3432.

Profit on Death. No one ought to be allowed to make a profit on other's death, *Wills* 1878——Danger as long as this is allowed, cost of funeral being lower than insurance, *ib.* 1885.——See *Statutes* (George III.), and *Amount of Insurance Money.*

Prohibition of Insurance. Would be a hardship to forbid insurance of children under one year of age, *Carter* 861; *Taunton* 3079-80——Would revive bad old system of "Friendly leads," *Clensy* 3980.

See *Age,* and *Remedies Proposed.*

Proposal. Form of proposal in Prudential Assurance Society, *Dewey* 2853; App. E., page 231; in Royal Liver Friendly Society, App. F., page 234; in Scottish Legal, *Fortune* 3796, App. G., pages 236-8.

No objection to form of proposal being compulsorily framed by law, provided that it is not less strict than Prudential's, *Dewey* 3548-51——Very desirable, but it should not be too complicated, *Taunton* 3170, 3410-2; *Fortune* 3797-800.

Prudential Assurance Company. It is a joint stock company, *Dewey* 2787——Has an income of 4,500,000 *l.,* and funds over 11,000,000 *l., ib.* 2788——Was not originally formed for infant insurances; has a large general business, *ib.* 3563——Insures 2,099,369 children under ten, *ib.* 2810——Tables of mortality of children insured in Prudential, set out, *ib.* 2947——Comparison of this mortality with general death-rate favourable to society, but for various reasons comparison unequal, *ib.* 2947-79——Insurance money at various ages, set out, *ib.* 2852;— average claim last year was 2 *l.* 13 *s.,* therefore presumption that this sum meets general needs, *ib.* 2842-51.

Form of proposal in Prudential set out, *Dewey* 2853; App. E., page 231;—allows parents only, if alive, to insure children, *ib.* 2853-4, 2855-9;—agent is the sole judge of health of child, *ib.* 3535-44 — Does not knowingly insure children insured in other offices, *ib.* 2803-7;—but does not contest policy, if untrue statements as to this are made to them, *Dewey* 2808.

Does not issue two policies on same child, because after a certain time the sum due would exceed the 10 *l.* limit allowed by Friendly Societies Act, *Dewey* 3484.

Agents paid by commission, amounting to 30 per cent. of first year's premiums, *Dewey* 2870-5;—lose part of this commission on lapsed policies, *ib.* 2872, 3512-3 ——Lapsed policies no source of profit to society, *ib.* 2941-5, 3498-9, 3503-9.

Prudential does not pay till child has been three months' insured, but makes grants of grace if cause of death prove satisfactory, *Dewey* 2928-32;—such as accident or scarlet fever, *ib.* 3546.

Profit in Prudential is two per cent. on amount received, *Dewey* 3501.

No objection as far as interests of society go, to:—

1. Option of registrar to give certificate when doctor has refused to do so, being removed, *Dewey* 2915.

2. It being made penal on insurer, agent, and society to allow person other than parent to insure, *Dewey* 2889-94.

3. A child

Prudential Insurance Company—continued.

3. A child being only allowed to be insured in one office, *Dewey* 2919;—the registrar only, under penalty, giving one certificate, 2921-6;—and the age being raised from 10 to 14 years, 3018.

4. No child being insured under 12 months of age, *Dewey* 3006-13;—or, preferably, that insurance may begin at any time, but in case of death under one year, only premiums actually paid to be repaid, *ib.* 3605-12. 3628-31.

5. A register of child insurances being kept, *Dewey* 3016; and—

6. The forfeiture of policy when parent convicted of cruelty or neglect, and perhaps to his being made incapable thereafter of insuring any child, 3019-31.

R.

Registrar. Often asked by police to register deaths after doctor has refused certificate, *Thomson* 646——Belief that registrar often gives certificate when doctor has refused, *Cleaver* 394——Has option, where doctor has refused certificate, of giving one on satisfactory evidence (of which he is himself judge) of cause of death, *Dewey* 2908-10 ——Receives so small a fee that it is not a temptation to give one wrongly, *ib.* 2911-4 ——This option ought not to be allowed, *Taunton* 3100, 3103; *Fortune* 3755-6—— Receives fee of 1 *s.* 3 *d.* for issuing certificate of death, *Thomson* 648.

Should only be allowed to give one certificate of death, *Dewey* 2921-6; *Fortune* 3773——Should be obliged to mark certificate with answer to question if child was insured;—in case of denial, on certificate so marked, society not to pay, *Taunton* 3130-7.

Registration:—

1. *Of Insurances and Claims:*

All insurances should be registered, *Burnett* 1297-1301. 1337——All insurances of children should be registered by society within a week, with statement showing that the child was legitimate and healthy, condition and character of family satisfactory, and setting out if insured in any other society, *Grahame* (par. 8) *pages* 132-3.

Prudential Society has no objection to registration of insurances, *Dewey* 3016;— would be unpopular, *Fortune* 3757;—but societies would not object, and perhaps bulk of insuring class, *ib.* 3782, 3758.

Every claim on death should be registered within one week after it becomes due in register of same district as original insurance, with penalty on society paying without this, *Grahame* (par. 8), *page* 133.

2. *Of Insuring Societies:*

Registration under Act of 1875 is voluntary, *Cleveland* 4501; *Dewey* 3622——Quotes Rochdale Friendly Society, which, not being registered, is not under the Friendly Societies Act, and not granting policies, is not under Life Insurance Act, *ib.* 3623.

All societies insuring child-life should be registered; some that do so really, but do not issue policies, but give grant to member on death of child, escape notice, *Taunton* 3128-9. 3205-14; *Cleveland* 4550; *Fortune* 3793-4——Without this there can be no check on amount of insurance money paid, *Cleveland* 4553; *Dewey* 3625—— Unregistered societies often do things against Friendly Societies Act, *Taunton* 3128.

REMEDIES PROPOSED:

1. *Registration of Insuring Societies.*
2. *Form of Proposal.*
3. *Agents.*
4. *Persons to Insure.*
5. *Registration of Insurances.*
6. *Prohibition.*
7. *Limitation of Age.*
8. *Certificate of Health.*
9. *Limitation of Insurance Money:*
   (a.) *Amount.*
   (b.) *Graduated Scale.*
   (c.) *Grants of Grace.*
10. *Number of Insurances and Certificates.*
11. *Certifying Authority.*
12. *Forfeiture.*
13. *Payment to Undertaker.*

1. *Registration of Insuring Societies:*

All societies insuring children should be registered, *Dewey* 3614, 3626; *Hambridge* 3874-5; *Cleveland* 4550; *Taunton* 3129——Should not be allowed to evade rules of

(225—IND.)   O O   Friendly

REMEDIES PROPOSED—continued.

1. Registration of Insuring Societies—continued.

Friendly Societies Act by getting themselves incorporated under the Companies Acts, Leach 1783–5. 1788. 1792——All societies insuring children nominally or actually should be under the same rules, Taunton 3128–9. 3205–14; Fortune 3794; Hambridge 3874–6.

Any law to effect this would have to be very carefully drawn up, or some societies would evade it, as now, Dewey 3615.

2. Form of Proposal:

All societies should have to use a uniform form of proposal, to be fully filled up, Taunton 3170–2——Advantageous to companies and insurers, but should not be too cumbrous, Fortune 3797–80——Prudential has a very searching form; desirable to enforce the same in all insurances, Dewey 3548–51.

3. Agents:

All agents and collectors ought to be licensed, Taunton 3147——Matter of detail by whom, ib. 3149——Magistrates to have the power of taking away license, ib. 3150.

Impossible to license agents, Clensy 3993—— Liverpool Victoria alone has over 3,000, many of them constantly shifting, ib. 3994——Uncharitable view to take, that agent dismissed by one company should not be able to get employment from another, ib. 3995–7——Have done nothing to justify their being placed under a ban, Dewey 3612.

Agents to be legally punishable for any wilful breach of the Friendly Societies Act, Taunton 3157–60.

4. Persons to Insure:

Only parents or guardians should be allowed to insure child's life, see letter of Leeds Society for Prevention of Cruelty to Children, page 134; Dewey 2856;—breach of this should be made penal, Dewey 2853-9. 2889; Taunton 3193;—should be extended to bonâ-fide foster-parents, a relation very common amongst the poor, ib. 3194.

5. Registration of Insurances:

All child insurances should be registered, Branson 277; Leach 1799–1800; see letter of Nottingham Health Committee, page 205; Burnett 1297 ——Would give publicity and enable suspicious cases to be watched, ib. 1353–6——No objection to this, Crooks 2370——Registration should be compulsory on insuring society within a week, with statement showing that child was legitimate and healthy, and character of family good, and name of any other society in which child may be insured; claims on death should also be registered in the same register as original insurance, under penalty on society paying without these formalities, see letter of Mr. J. Grahame, (par. 8), page 133 ——Notice of claims to be sent by insurance company to local authority that they may inquire before payment is made, see letter of Nottingham Corporation Health Committee, page 205——Register should be open to sanitary and parish authorities and police, Burnett 1298——Form of register suggested, ib. 1302.

No objection as far as companies are concerned, but great practical difficulty in working, Dewey 3016——Might be objected to by insurers as publishing their private affairs, Fortune 3757–61;—and should be done delicately, ib. 3782——All societies would be willing to assist such legislation, ib. 3784.

6. Prohibition:

Infant life insurance should be forbidden, as all other insurances on life of others is forbidden, except where insurable interest can be shown, Day 1964–75. 1997——Life of infants requires even more protection than that of adults, ib. 1976–82——Expenses of death must be provided for as all other misfortunes are, ib. 1983–6—— But local benefit clubs are free from most of the objections against insurance by companies whose sole business it is; members are watchful of one another; they ought not to be interfered with, ib. 1992–6.

7. Limitation of Age:

Insurance under twelve months. or perhaps six months, should be forbidden, or at any rate limited to a very small sum, Carter 829–32; Browne 1139. 1149–52. 1154–61 ——Profit if no insurance under a year allowed, to go to endowment for child on attaining a certain age, Hartop 1730—2——No objection on part of Prudential to prohibition under twelve months, Dewey 3006–12;—which would practically be fifteen months, as insured do not come into benefit till after three months, ib. 3013.

Prohibition under one year good, two years better, and would not be much objected to by better working class, Tasker 1589–91. 1627.

Should be prohibited under two years, see letter of Leeds Society for Prevention of Cruelty to Children, page 134.

Opinion

REMEDIES PROPOSED—continued.

7. *Limitation of Age*—continued.

Opinion of all coroners in Devonshire that no insurance should be allowed under six or seven years, *Hooper* 1243——Except registration, this is the only remedy; would be a great hardship on many, but the evil is great, *Burnett* 1380–1.

Any limitation as to age would press unduly on respectable parents, *Ritchie* 1446-7 ——Should stand as it is now in practice, that amount under one year should be less than cost of funeral, *Crooks* 2442–3 ——Prohibition under a year would not be so great a disadvantage as when children get older, *ib.* 2444——Better that insurances be allowed at any age, but that if child died under one, only premiums actually paid be returned, *Dewey* 3607–8.

Strong opinion against prohibition under one year; would bring back bad old system of "friendly leads," *Clensy* 3980;—and throw burial expenses on the rates, *Sargent* 4308.

8. *Certificate of Health*:

Should be produced when child is insured, *Hartop* 1715-7 —— This would stop insurance by parents who neglect their children and insure them when ill, *ib.* 1723.

9. *Limitation of Insurance Money*:
        (a) *Amount.*
        (b) *Graduated Scale.*
        (c) *Grants of Grace.*

(a) *Amount.*—If insurable sum were limited to 1 *l.*, amount of temptation to get rid of child much diminished, *Hooper* 1241——Should be limited to lowest cost of funeral, which would not prevent well-to-do artizan from adding money of his own to outlay on funeral, *Waugh* 2204. 2213. 2250 ;—to lowest necessary expenses of funeral, so that no profit would arise from death, *Wills* 1897. 1911.

No objection to sum being limited to 2 *l.* 10 *s.* or 3 *l.* on child from one to three years, *Taunton* 3064–9. 3240 ;—perhaps to 5 *l.* on child between three and five, *ib.* 3249-52 - — Some limitation might be put, *Cleveland* 4504 *et seq.*

(b) *Graduated Scale.*—Sum should be a graduated scale fixed by law, instead of increasing by a few large jumps as now; there would be no difficulty in this, as it is already the practice of most societies, *Fortune* 3748. 3776-7 ;—but not reducing present maximums now payable, *ib.* 3751——No objection to this, *Sargent* 4281.— — It is absurd that if 6 *l.* is a proper sum at five years, that 10 *l.* can be got at five years and a few months, *Waugh* 2209 ——Six months would not make this difference in the expense of funeral, *Dobson* 2661.

There is no need for change, but a limitation to the amounts for which parents actually now insure might remove temptation which may exist in a few exceptional cases, *Hooper* 4184-8 ;—would not prejudice insurers in most cases, though it might in a few, *Dewey* 2847 51.

Desirable that all companies should have the same scale, which would destroy unhealthy competition, *Clensy* 4000-4 ;—objects to any graduated scale that would reduce present legal maximums, *ib.* 4058-60.

(c) *Grants of Grace.*—Assuming insurance is a temptation, it would be less if grants of grace and part benefits were not so large or immediate, *Fortune* 3691-8 ——Grants of grace or quarter benefits (after three months), or even half benefits (after six months), might usefully be forbidden, *ib.* 3752. 3801 ;—the actual premiums paid to be repaid in case of death before, *ib.* 3802 ; *Dewey* 3607 -8.

10. *Number of Insurances and Certificates*:

Only one insurance should be allowed, *Taunton* 3173-7 ; *Hambridge* 3864 ; *Cleveland* 4413 ;—whether in registered or unregistered societies, *ib.* 4569-70 ;—either in one or more societies, *Taunton* 3177—— Amount which any company could afford to insure for one penny a week must then be below legal maximum, *Dewey* 2919-20 ;—this would much facilitate investigation, *Cleveland* 4574—— In case of infrigement policy to be declared void by law ; if to be voided by company, more unscrupulous might ignore this, *Taunton* 3181-6.

Registrar only to be allowed to give one certificate, which, being kept by insurance company as receipt for the money, could not be used again, *Taunton* 3404-6 ; *Fortune* 3773.

Coroner in case of inquests should always ask if child is insured ; answer to be marked

(225 —IND.)   O O 2   on

REMEDIES PROPOSED – continued.

10. Number of Insurances and Certificates—continued.

on certificate; if denied, insurance company not to pay, *Taunton* 3130–4——Every doctor before granting his certificate should do the same, *ib.* 3135–7.

Any tampering with certificates to be made penal, and provision made for whose duty it should be to prosecute, *Taunton* 3196–8.

11. Certifying Authority:

Certificates for insurance money should be granted by medical man instead of registrar; protection that he should know which patients were insured, *Barwise* 123—— This was formerly the law, and doctors' certificates were then much fuller than they are now, when they have to certify causes of death to registrar without a fee, *Hambridge* 3878–9. 3889.

12. Forfeiture:

When coroner or jury think there has been neglect on part of parents, even if they are not able to find legal proof, insurance money should not be paid to parents, but funeral carried out for them, *Crooks* 2275. 2338. 2394. 2472——On conviction for cruelty policy should become void, and parent not allowed to insure any child, *Taunton* 3187–93; *Clensy* 4006;—or, preferably, that convicting magistrate might order transfer ot policy to some one else. *ib.* 4007.

Objection to forfeiture, that if child died it must be buried, and cost would fall on the parish, *Cleveland* 4591——No great objection to forfeiture, *Dewey* 3021;—but doubtful, and does not see how it would be worked, *ib.* 3019–31.

13. Payment to Undertakers:

In order to preserve benefits of insurance, and also to remove temptation to weak parents, insurance money should be paid direct to undertaker, *Waugh* 2204;—desirable, as it would prevent any profit being made, *Carter* 835–6——Hulme Friendly Society, where it doubts the thrift of any member, pays the money now direct to undertaker, *Dobson* 2656.

Objectionable; might lead to collusion between undertaker and parent, *Dobson* 2561; *see* letter of Mr. J. Grahame (par. 7), *page* 132——Objected to by Prudential, but clause in this Bill respecting payment to undertaker being withdrawn, no evidence given in support, *Dewey* 2782–3.

See *Undertaker*.

Ritchie, Mr. John James, M.R.C.S. (Analysis of his Evidence.)—Has been Medical Officer of. Health for sanitary district of Leek, Staffordshire, for 31 years, 1414–7.

Has unfavourable opinion of infant life insurance, 1419——At Leek a local burial society discontinued in 1876 the insurance of children under one year; at that time the infant mortality was 156 to 1,000 children born, 1423——A collecting society then worked the district vigorously, and the infant mortality rose in 1884 to 186, the average for England being 147; 1426–7. 1457–64—— Since then the local burial society resumed infant insurance, and the death rate of the town diminished to 145 in 1885, and 135 in 1888; 1470–1——It appears that the increase was coincident with infant insurance by a collecting society, 1428–30.

Local societies are preferable to collecting societies, 1431. 1441. 1518–20;—indeed exercise a beneficial effect, 1487—— Members know each other and there is publicity, 1437;—all profit in them goes to the members, 1439. 1490;—in the collecting societies it goes to the managers, and expenses are very high, sometimes 40 or 50 per cent., 1492——Local societies are managed by very respectable persons, 1443—the operatives themselves, 1513–1517——Bad cases occur much more rarely, if ever, in local societies, 1441.

There are also local friendly sick clubs, 1433, 1445.

In local society sick children would be refused, 1502;—and there is a rule that the committee shall investigate cases of death, and if they find neglect, do not pay insurance money, 1478.

Opinion that it would be a hardship to forbid insurance under one year, 1446;— unpopular to limit amount to lowest expense of funeral, 1449;— insurance being also to provide mourning, 1499–1501;—also unpopular to compel insurance money to be paid direct to undertaker, 145 2 3.

Royal Liver Society. Is the largest collecting friendly society, *Taunton* 3057–8;—has income of 384,000 *l.* and funds of 1,065,000 *l*, *ib.* 3040–41;—issued last year 215,637 policies, of which 83,433 children under ten, *ib.* 3042–3.

Proposal form set out, *App.* F. *page* 234.

Give

Royal Liver Society—continued.

Gives grants of grace, amounting on average to 10 *s.* in each case where child is not yet in benefit, or policy lapsed, *ib.* 3049–53. 3270-1 — Given especially where many of a family are insured; but not invariably, 3278–80. 3311-2——In some cases issues immediate benefit policies, which are a safeguard, as more careful inquiries are made into health and circumstances, *ib.* 3313. 3413-6.

Average claim under five years is 2 *l.* 10 *s.*, *ib.* 3086.

Pays its agents by commission, about 25 per cent. on premiums and a bonus on new insurances, *ib.* 3161-3——Takes pains to get references about them, 3237.

Has offered to assist Society for Prevention of Cruelty to Children, but has had no applications from them, *ib.* 3094. 3432.

Instructs agents to be careful not to insure children already insured, for more than aggregate allowed by law, *ib.* 3304-9.

Does not insure illegitimate children, *ib.* 3256 ;—or allow baby farmers to insure, *ib.* 3351. 3423.

Royal London Friendly Society. Is a mutual and collecting society, *Hambridge* 3582-4 —— Insured last year 124,678 children under five, and paid average of 1 *l.* 13 *s.* 3 *d.* on 3,830 deaths, *ib.* 3,828 ;—and 102,086 children between five and ten, and paid average of 4 *l.* 12 *s.* on 408 deaths ; small sum at early ages accounted for by number of deaths before full benefit, *ib.* 3839.

Is very careful in selecting agents, 3863 ;—who are paid from 12½ to 25 per cent. commission and the first eight premiums, *ib.* 3855-61.

Takes pains to select good lives, and refuses insurances from districts where there is much drunkenness, or where there are unhealthy trades, *ib.* 3880-1.

S.

Sargent, Mr. Wyatt. (Analysis of his Evidence.)—Is a stationer's foreman, living at Islington, 4201-2——Has also been engaged in mission work, 4220——Represents the United Order of the Total Abstinent Sons of the Phœnix, 4203——Has a petition from that Order against the Bill, 4204——Order has 7,000 juvenile members from five to sixteen, many of whom pay their own contributions, 4204-10——Takes in the very poorest classes, 4208——The collection of premiums is by voluntary unpaid agency, 4213——The object of the Order being to better the condition of their fellow workmen and to inculcate thrift and temperance, 4214——That is their object, but members join for the advantages offered, and any curtailment of those would reduce membership ; all members must be abstainers, 4237.

Repudiates the statements that have been made, that the working classes are deficient in natural affection or care for their children, 4214-5——Have it very strongly except where blunted by drink or vice, 4302——If in these cases parents commit evil, does not think that the great majority who do not should be punished for the few, 4304-6. 4312-3. 4363——But those committing crime or neglect should be punished, 4312. 4358——Order has never had to withhold money on account of suspicious death, 4314——There is not sufficient crime to warrant legislation, 4364.

The Order gives 8 *l.* on death in all cases, 4204-4247 ;—no graduated scale, 4241 ;—insures no lives under five, 4207 ;—and they come into benefit after six months' insurance, 4251——Can afford to pay so large a sum on death for a penny a week, being a temperance society, having no dissolute members, 4253-6——Half the penny a week subscription goes to the funeral fund, 4219 ;—the other half to provide for expenses, 4239 ;—not only establishment expenses, but in teaching boys and paying them for their work in propagating temperance principles, 4290.

All the 8 *l.* is expended on funeral, 4269—and expenses connected with it, 4292—doctors' bills, 4216-7 ;—nurses, 4257, 4355 ;—and mourning, 4258, 4339——It is not too large a sum for the purposes required, 4260 ;—has a list of actual expenses, and the average is about 8 *l.*, 4270——These cases set out, 4278——There is no expenditure on a funeral feast, 4340——£. 8 may be excessive ; witness personally thinks there is too much expenditure on funerals, but Order cannot help the sentiments of members who desire to have a decent funeral, 4271. 4347-55 ;—which is an honourable feeling, 4293-5——Believes 2 *l.* 10 *s.* to be the lowest sum for which a funeral alone could be got, 4272.

This Bill will discourage thrift among the working classes, 4310 ;—and will injuriously affect the Order, their funds having increased so much that they are contemplating increasing benefits given up to 10 *l.*, as law now allows, 4218. 4220. 4225——This Bill would prevent increased benefit at death, 4227 ;—and would cut down what they now give, by 2 *l.*, at certain ages, 4273.

Greatest danger to life being under five years, any provisions in the Bill to prevent

Sargent, Mr. Wyatt. (Analysis of his Evidence)—*continued*.

this would not affect Order, who only insure over five years, but they are very anxious to extend insurance to infant children of members, 4230;—instead of sending them for this purpose to the insurance companies, 4242. 4346——Most friendly societies do not at present insure under five, 4328–30.

Order has also a sick fund, 4238;—distinct from the burial fund, but to which comparatively few belong, 4267——If all members subscribed to it, the doctors' bills would be taken out of the expenses at present paid for out of the surplus of insurance money over actual funeral expenses, 4264-7.

Has personally no objection to a graduated insurance, 4281;—more just, as more premiums are then paid for greater death payments, 4320——But the 8 *l.* now paid ought not to be diminished, 4321——Does not approve of prohibition of child-insurance under 12 months; the poor have great difficulty in finding money for burial, and the result would be to throw them on the rates, 4307-9——His Order does not at present insure below five, only because mortality is so much greater, 4334-5.

Savings Banks. Working classes dislike taking very small sums to Post Office Savings Banks, *Dobson* 2567. 2730.

There is not the same objection to Penny Savings Banks, *ib.* 2731-2.

Money in Savings Bank is liable to be drawn out for some emergency, *Cronks* 2386-92, 2409-11——Or for a " spree," *Dobson* 2568.

To save 2 *l.* 10 *s.* at a penny a week would take over 11 years, *Cleveland* 4413.

Scottish Legal Life Assurance Company. Is the largest society in Scotland; approves of Mr. Grahame's suggestions; *see* pages 131 to 133. See *Grahame, Mr. James.*

Is a mutual as well as collecting society, *Fortune* 3635——Has had no case of child neglect or child murder, *ib.* 3651, 3666-72——Sums insured on death not so high as in some English societies, 3695. 3720. 3810;—and have strict rule not to give grants of grace, but after three months' insurance give quarter benefit, and after six months, half benefit, *ib.* 3692. 3742-5.

Form of proposal handed in, *ib.* 3796; *App. G., pages* 236-8.

Figures of child mortality in different towns stated, *ib.* 3702;—*App. H., page* 239 ——In Preston very high, so that Society has given up taking new insurances there, *ib.* 3706-7.

Is very careful in appointment of agents, *ib.* 3729;—who are paid from 12½ to 25 per cent. commission, besides bonus on new policies, *ib.* 3730.

Have since 1886 a children's endowment system, by which, for small weekly payments, they pay from 9 *l.* to 36 *l.* at age of fourteen, and 15 *l.* to 63 *l.* at age of twenty-one, *ib.* 3710-12——This has become very popular, and even amongst the very poor, *ib.* 3717-20.

Scottish National Society for the Prevention of Cruelty to Children. See *Grahame, Mr. James.*

Stanley. Mr. Lyulph (*Trustee of the Royal Liver Society*). His opinion quoted that child insurance is a direct incentive to murder, *Question* 3677;—opinion disagreed with, *Fortune* 3681.

Statistics. 2,099,369 children under 10 assured in Prudential, *Dewey* 2792——1,300,000 in other large societies, and 750,000 in local clubs and unregistered clubs, making total of 4,149,369 insured, *ib.* 2801——There are 6,668,260 children in England and Wales; taking off 25 per cent. for children of classes not likely to insure, leaves 5,000,000 insurable children, *ib.* 2792-800.

Statistics showing that mortality of insured children less than average of England, published by insurance companies, fallacious, because (1) they (at least the Prudential and others) do not insure illegitimate children; (2) children below three months, most fatal period, are not much insured, as they do not come into benefit till then; and (3) so many cases lapse, which therefore only appear amongst lives and not amongst deaths, *Waugh* 2193. 2201.

Death-rate of children insured in Prudential 2 per cent. less than general mortality, but for various reasons comparison not equal, *Dewey* 2947-79—— Less in Scottish Legal, *Fortune* 3702-3;—in Oddfellows, *Cleveland* 4410-2;—in Forresters, *Stead* 4625.

Of inquests, out of 407 from August 1887 to June 1890, 71 on children under one year, half of them not yet in benefit or uninsured; 41 on children between one and five; 22 between five and ten; nearly all those insured, *Thomson* 625-31.

Number

Report, 1890—*continued*.

Statistics—continued.

Number of deaths and amount paid in Scottish Legal under five years, *Fortune* 3644–5;—and under ten years, *ib.* 3646–7;—in Royal London, *Hambridge* 3828–30.

Death-rate of children in various towns, *Fortune* 3705; *App.* H., page 239.

Statutes :

(1.) *Act of George III.* :

Prohibits wagering or gambling on others' lives, *Wills* 1862 ; – forbids insurance of others' lives except where insurer has an insurable interest, *ib.* 1863 ;—ought to be applied universally and no exception made in favour of friendly societies, *Day* 1964, 1969.

Is more often infringed in the case of adults than of children ; case quoted, *Fortune* 3734–41.

See *Insurable Interest.*

(2) *Friendly Societies Act*, 1875 :

Is a repeal of the Act of George III., as a privilege to the working classes, *Wills* 1864–8 ; *Dewey* 2827. 2830 ;—but mutual societies had same right to insure children before for their own members, *ib.* 2829 ;—a similar right existed long before ; the first society was established in Hulme in 1823, *Dobson* 2507.——Lives under a certain age not to be insured for more than a certain sum, *Wills* 1870.

Discussion how far the present Bill modifies the Act as to forbidding insurance by other than parents or guardians, *Dewey* 3442 *et seq.*

Strand Case. A man charged with arson and murder, his children being burnt in the fire; committed by coroner's jury on both charges; acquitted on trial of murder; found guilty of arson, his wife, the principal witness at the inquest, being incapable of being a witness against him at the trial, *Troutbeck* 96-748.

Crime committed for 600*l.* fire insurance money, not 14 *l.* child insurance, *Dewey* 3001.

Stead, Mr. Thomas Ballan. (Analysis of his Evidence.)—Is permanent secretary to the Ancient Order of Foresters, 4604,—(and delegated to appear by the conference of Friendly Societies, *Cleveland* 4403)——Foresters have 695,918 members, 4605 ;—and have 1,360 juvenile societies, with 83,180 members, in connection, 4608.

Agrees with evidence of Mr. Cleveland, but he did not mention that Friendly Societies regard themselves as guardians of their juvenile branches rather than as carrying on a commercial business, 4620.

The mortality in the Foresters is rather more favourable than Mr. Cleveland's figures for all the large societies, averaging for four years 4·12 per 1,000 ; 4622–6.

Foresters sent out a series of questions to all their juvenile branches as to present Bill; out of 873 answers, 834 said the Undertakers' Clause would be the ruin of their societies, 4627–31; *App. I. page* 240—— Is aware that that clause has now been withdrawn from Bill, 4630—— The Foresters have 1,279 Juvenile Societies in Great Britain; out of these forty-nine (mostly small societies) admit children under three years (which is the limit the Friendly Societies Act lays down for registered societies), 4648 ——Fifty-six admit at three years, 302 at four, 229 at five, 316 at six, eighty-five at seven, eighty-nine at eight, and the remaining 167 at various ages up to sixteen, 4659.

These juvenile societies give allowance during sickness, medical attendance (generally including anything a doctor would order, 4637), and a sum for burial, 4633–8——The contributions and benefits vary in each society, central body leaving it to local society to make their own regulations ; the only limitations being those placed by Friendly Societies Act on insurance, 4676——In no society does amount given reach limit under Act, or even limit under present Bill, 4683——The average at five years is about 3 *l.*, 6 *l.* being the legal limit, 4686——Quotes, as specimen case, branch at Yarmouth, where, at ages from 5 to 17, the entrance fee is from 1 *s.* up to 2 *s.* 6 *d.*, and the monthly subscription from 4 *d.* to 10 *d.* ; the benefits are, at all ages, medical attendance and medicine, from 9 to 18, weekly sick pay rising from 2 *s.* to 5 *s.*, and from 9 to 18, burial money rising from 1 *l.* 5 *s.* to 3 *l.*, 4676——In most societies burial money is not paid till after a certain number of months' membership, 4664–6 ; but medical benefit begins at once, 4667.

Besides actual benefits, committees look after instruction and amusement of juvenile societies, 4659–60.

Though so few of Foresters' juvenile societies insure before three, and many not before higher ages, witness would be unwilling that the age for insurance should be put at three years, because the society wishes to extend its infant insurance, 4650–3 ——It wishes to raise the moral condition of the working classes, and therefore unwilling to have anything done which would keep young from entering on insurance

(225—IND.)   O O 4   which,

Stead, Mr. Thomas Bullan. (Analysis of his Evidence)—*continued.*

which once begun, will probably continue through life, 4690-2. 4700-4;—and tend to the increase of the parent society, 4692-3.

Only 92 cases of coroners' inquests on members since foundation; in every case verdict was death by accident or from natural causes, 4657.

The affiliated orders in large towns generally join to pay a doctor for exclusive attendance on sick in juvenile society, and on children of members of adult societies and adult members, 4639–41——Member of adult societies can insure for medical aid for all his family till 18, when they are charged for as adults, 4668-9.

Out of total of 1,360 societies of Foresters (including colonies), only 452 are registered under the Friendly Societies Act, 4670——Agrees with Mr. Cleveland that all societies should be registered, 4672-4.

Suffocation. Very common; most cases found dead on Sunday morning, from drunkenness on Saturday night, *Browne* 1059. 1129. 1136; *Hooper* 4106——600 cases in London in one year, of which 50 per cent. were known to be insured, *Waugh* 2050;—partly by drunken parents, but mostly from overcrowding, *Taunton* 3417-20.

Sunday Funerals. Popular amongst respectable workpeople, as they do not lose a day's work, *Branson* 343;—at Sheffield, *Tasker* 1645-7- --Take place on Sundays, but not so much as formerly, *Crooks* 2457-8——Working men stop away from funerals rather than lose a day's work, *ib.* 2459.

Not the practice in Nottingham, probably neither by law or bye-law, but because ministers of religion do not encourage them, *Browne* 1168-73——Not allowed in Manchester, *Dobson* 2552 ;—not in Rochdale, *Kirshaw* 1837.

T.

Tasker, Mr. James. (Analysis of his Evidence.)—Has been for eleven years relieving officer at West Bar, Sheffield, 1523——Attention called to infant insurance by persons whose children had been neglected having money to spend after a death, 1529-30, 1557 ;—these were the lowest class of the people, 1533-5——In many cases they had their children buried by the parish, 1537. 1540 ;—and denied they were insured, 1539 ——Did not take proceedings to recover the money, as they had no goods that could have been distrained on, 1543, 1601 ;—but in some cases recovered amount by threat of proceedings, 1542. 1601——Very difficult to find out if children were insured, 1556 ;—sometimes heard of it from neighbours, 1596——Opinion that insurance caused children to be neglected, 1531, 1617–19.

Insurances most numerous amongst the lowest class, 1559. 1587-8——Respectable people also insure their children, but not generally till they are about five years old, 1613–14.

Expense of parish funeral about 12 *s.*, so that if parents got 2 *l.* 10 *s.* from insurance company they would have a large profit, even if they were made to repay the parish for burial, 1544–51——Better class also insure to get mourning, 1608-11——A respectable funeral can be got for 15 *s.*, and 5 *s.* burial fees, 1640–4 ;—which would not leave a large margin for mourning, &c., 1642 ;—but this does not apply to disreputable parents, 1651.

The local manager of each society is a very respectable man, 1622 ;——The collectors make no inquiries, 1626. 1655 ;——The societies compete keenly, 1654——Has never known an agent give assistance to justice, 1657-8 ;—it is simply his interest to get as many insurances and commissions as possible, 1659-62——The societies are largely in the hands of their collectors, and have no means of checking their statements, 1663-5.

It would diminish evils if insurance money were paid direct to undertaker and doctor, 1571 ;—as the doctor is paid in sick clubs, 1577 ;—but the better class would be much offended, 1580 ;—the worst class would cease to insure if they could not get a balance over expenses, 1592–5.

If insurance were limited to children over one year it would diminish abuses, 1589 ;—two years better still, 1590. 1627 ;—opinion that respectable working class would not object to this, 1591, 1615.

Taunton, Mr. Frank Henry. (Analysis of his Evidence.)—Is secretary of the Royal Liver Society, 3035 ;-- which is a collecting society, 3037 ;—and has an income of 384,000 *l.* a year, and funds of 1,065,000 *l.*; 3040-1 ;—issued last year 215,637 policies, of which 83,433 on children under ten, 3042-3 ;—two-thirds of these under five, 3044 ; —deaths under five, 5813, between five and ten, 488 ; 3046.

Produces list of claims refused to be paid owing to suspicious circumstances, 3054——
Information

Taunton, Mr. Frank Henry. (Analysis of his Evidence)—*continued.*

Information as to this obtained from newspapers or coroners' inquests, 3058 ;—rarely from society's agents, 3059-61——Contests perhaps two or three cases a year, 3286.

Cases of preventable death of infants, including overlaying, perhaps 10 per cent. of whole, 3062-71——Overlaying arises from drunken parents, but in a greater measure from overcrowding in small tenements, 3417-20——Does not include in preventable deaths cases where natural causes have been aggravated or induced by neglect, 3072-7.

Royal Liver gives grants of grace where child is not yet in benefit, or policy has lapsed, 3049, 3270-1 ;—amounting last year to 364 *l.*, averaging 10 *s.* in each case, 3051-3——Child not in benefit till three months after birth, 3269 —— Quarter benefit is generally given, same as Prudential, 3268 ;—especially where family of children are all insured, and where on the one dying nothing is yet due, 3278-80, 3311 ;—but not invariably, 3312——There are some cases of insurances for immediate benefit, 3313 ; —but this is generally for adults, though sometimes extended to children where parents insure at same time, 3314——This applies to child insurance the universal rule in adult insurance, 3413——Immediate benefit is a safeguard, as more careful inquiries are made, 3416.

Not true that it is the lowest of working classes that insure; it is the respectable classes, 3114 :—nor even that majority of depraved classes insure, 3116 ;—as a rule they do not, 3259 ;—but the very poor do insure largely, and stint themselves to do so, 3261-2——Has never known of insured child left to be buried by parish, 3122-7—— Mortality amongst children is diminishing, in spite of great increase of child insurance, 3215-8——It is to the interest of insuring society not to pay if child is made away with, 3228-30 ;—so it is their interest to diminish such cases, 3231——Royal Liver does not pay in suspicious cases, but sometimes so difficult to get evidence that they are obliged to, 3232, 3254 ——Does not insure illegitimate children, 3256——Rejects application of parents where they are known to agents to be dissolute and drunken, 3360-4.

Insurance of children has much increased, 3389-93——Owing to this thrift, habits of begging for funeral expenses have disappeared, 3395-7——Owing to necessarily greater mortality of children amongst poor people, it is very important to them to have some means of meeting funeral and other expenses of death, 3400-3.

Objects to abolition of infant insurances, even under one year, 3079——Cost of funeral and mourning has to be paid just as well under as over one year, 3080——No loss to Society if forbidden, but people ought to insure as soon as child is born to provide against misfortunes, 3233——Quite untrue that unborn children are insured, 3425-31.

Amounts of claims in Royal Liver average 2 *l.* 10 *s.*, 3066——Lowest cost of funeral of Liverpool would be 2 *l.*, 3241-4 ;—or 2 *l.* 10 *s.*, 3369 ;—for nothing but actual funeral expenses, 3370.

Should not object to insurances under three years being reduced, 3084 ;—say, to 2 *l.* 10 *s.* to 3 *l.*, 3018-9, 3240——Under five years might perhaps be reduced from 6 *l.* to 5 *l.*, 3252——Under competition the amount payable on claims has been increased, premiums remaining the same, 3138-41——Poor people like to have mourning, 3144 ;— expense on which might well be reduced, 3145-6.

But reduction of insurances is not a question for insurance companies so much as for working classes, 3091-3 ;—believes any lowering of the insurance money under three years would be very unpopular, 3446——Deaths under one year leave a loss to the society, 3322-7.

Lapses of young children are not profitable to company, 3328 ;—are an actual loss, 3374——All insurances are on the same scale and at the same premium, except that in very poor cases, especially in Scotland, there are half-scale insurances, ½ *d.* a week instead of 1 *d.*, providing half usual insurance money on death, 3332-42.

Has offered to assist Society for Prevention of Cruelty to Children, but has never been applied to by them, 3094, 3432——Great difficulty in getting assistance from doctors or coroners ; instances Dr. Hawkes, coroner in Birmingham, 3107-8, 3436—— Coroner's clerk in Liverpool refuses to give information without heavy fee, 3108—— Mr. Agnew once applied to him about a Bill he proposed to introduce relative to cruelty to children, 3433-4——It is company's interest to find out bad cases, as they do not consider they ought to pay them, 3095 ;—but does not know of many, except from reading of them in newspapers, 3288.

Not sufficient care taken in giving certificate, 3096-7——Can be given by registrar when doctor has not certified, nor inquest been held, on "any satisfactory information," 3098——Such option ought not to be allowed to registrar in case of insured child, 3100, 3103——Doctor and coroner should be obliged to ask if child is insured, and mark answer on certificate, 3101-2 ;—and registrar should be obliged to mark this on copy certificate for insurance money, 3130——If parents denied insurance and certificate so marked, society would refuse to pay the money, 3132-7——Any alteration of

(225—Ind.)   P p   certificate

Taunton, Mr. Frank Henry. (Analysis of his Evidence)—*continued.*

certificate by insurer to be under penalty, 3196——Under present law it is not provided who is to prosecute; Royal Liver has communicated with Registrar General, who says society, not he, is to prosecute, 3198——Society hesitates, as it would be very unpopular if they failed to convict, 3199——Should be duty of Registrar General at expense of Treasury, 2201–4——Alteration of certificate more common in Ireland, and more common with adults than children, 3287.

Agents in Royal Liver are paid by commission of 25 per cent. and bonus on new cases, 31613——Impossible to have incentive to work otherwise, 3166-9——Agents and collectors (different names for same sort of persons) should be licensed, 3147, 3238 ;–perhaps by Inland Revenue at a small fee of 2 *s.* 6 *d.* or 5 *s.* a year, 3149—— Magistrates to have power to revoke license, 3151——Unfortunately sometimes a low class of men become agents, 3154 ;—though Royal Liver always requires testimonials of character, 3237.

There are many unregistered clubs and friendly societies, who often do things against the Friendly Societies Act; all such ought to be registered, 31289——The great affiliated orders, such as Foresters or Manchester Unity of Odd Fellows, really insure, though they are not supposed to, 3205——They pay to the parent a certain sum on death of child, 3206——These orders have been quoted as superior to collecting societies, but they insure children indirectly ; quotes case where such an affiliated order paid money on death of a child made away with, 3212——All insuring societies should be treated alike, 3214.

All societies should be compelled to use a statutory form of proposal, 3170—— defined by Act or prepared by Registrar of Friendly Societies, but should not be too cumbersome, 3410-2——Agent has to verify answer to question asked in Royal Liver's form as to health, but in case of child this is really formal, 3289-97;—though there have been cases where insurance refused, 3298.

Form of proposal in Royal Liver set out, *App.* F., page 234——Instructions to their agents are substantially the same as in Prudential, 3304-9.

Not more than one insurance of children under ten years should be allowed in either one or more societies, 3173-7——Not of course to be made retrospective, 3175—— Infringement should be made a misdemeanour and policy made void, 3180-1——Better that it should be made so by law, rather than by rule of society, as some companies might not be scrupulous, and gain popularity over others thereby, 3181-6.

Royal Liver now makes no inquiry if child is insured in another society, provided legal amount is not exceeded altogether, 3273, 3300——They never pay more than legal amount, 3276——There is nothing in present law limiting amount of premiums to be paid, but only amount to be paid on death, 3302-3.

Registrar should only give one certificate, which is all that would be required if only one insurance allowed, 3404——Company paying claim would retain certificate, 3405 ; —which would be a security against there being more than one policy, 3406.

If parent convicted for cruelty to child, policy should be void, 3187 ;—should not, thereafter, be allowed to insure any child, if it could be prevented, 3188-93.

No person other than parent or guardian, or *bonâ fide* foster parent, should be allowed to insure child under ten, 3193-4——Agent in Royal Liver is directed to find out relation of insurer to insured, 3343——Policy refused where insurer has no insurable interest (using the words not in the legal sense, but as applicable to a parent or guardian), 3343-7, 3352——Does not recognise that baby farmers have an insurable interest, 3351 ;—and refuses to pay them if they have effected an insurance, 3423—— No insurance money is paid by Royal Liver except to parents, or to persons having a letter of authority from them, 3421-2.

Thomson, Dr. George. Letter from the Secretary of Amalgamated Burial Societies in Oldham to the Chief Constable of Oldham, calling attention to the evidence of Dr. Thompson ; handed in, *Dobson* 2493.

Thomson, Dr. George. (Analysis of his Evidence.)—Is a medical man and Coroner of Oldham, 613, 614——In both capacities has formed opinion that insurance of children is prejudicial to them, 615, 663, 748——Has sometimes found that medical man is not summoned till too late, 616——This principally but not exclusively, in insured cases, 682 ;—and that such children are neglected, 618——This occurs amongst the lowest class of workpeople, 619 ;—who do not insure from motives of thrift, 621——Difficult to say if neglect is intentional or not, 684——Thinks insured children less carefully looked after than uninsured by dissolute parents, 700, 719.

Gives number of inquests on children of different ages; more than half under one year, and almost all over one year insured, 625-31——No large proportion of these illegitimate, 694 *et seq.*——Deaths of children in Oldham for eight years varies from 157 to 187 per 1,000 births ; over all England averages 147 ; 689,

Believes

Thomson, Dr. George. (Analysis of his Evidence)—*continued.*

Believes that many certificates are granted in suspicious cases, 634 *et seq.*, 702——Gives reasons for his estimate of numbers, 703–711;—because a doctor hesitates to refuse unless evidence is very clear, 725 ;—he would become unpopular, 726——Very difficult to obtain evidence of neglect in privacy of home, 679.

Coroner often advises jury not to find verdict of manslaughter, knowing the difficulty of convicting at assizes, 665, 666——When witness has at first refused certificate, he is often advised by police that they have inquired and find no evidence, 639–647——Police exercise too much responsibility in this respect, 659——Has never had assistance from insurance agents in suspicious cases, 668–70——Has had cases where agent has asked him to falsify certificate, 671, 731 *et seq.* ;—to post-date beginning of disease till after date of insurance, 672——This would be against interest of insurance society, but popular for agent, 749–751 ;—but such applications more commonly from parents, 737.

Life insurance of children is general in Oldham, equally amongst thrifty and dissolute people, 690, 718, 724——Proportion of dissolute to thrifty very small there, 721–723——Not usually insured in more than one office, 676–678.

Thorneycroft, Mr. E. B. Letter from, is handed in by the Chairman——Is Deputy Coroner for Wolverhampton ; hesitated long whether child insurance was for good or evil, as in his district it is often difficult for the most thrifty to save enough to pay for funeral ; but now believes that the present system is bad ; it is often done with the object of gain ; the insurance money is too great a temptation.

No child should be insurable under five years, and then only in one office.

Burial clubs should be encouraged ; but so that no money should pass to the parents, except some slight provision for mourning.

Insurance is not so much traceable to desire of parents to insure as to the touting of agents, who easily persuade parents to pay the penny to begin it.

There are a great many cases of careless but innocent overlying which may require some legal penalty. See *App.* C., page 229.

Thrift. Not the reason for insuring children among dissolute parents, *Thomson* 621 ; *Hartop* 1673–4——Does not tend to thrift where funeral money is spent on a wake ; instance quoted, *Leach* 1827, 1841–8——Thrifty parents do not generally insure in insurance companies, *Branson* 218, 233 ; *Hodson* 584, 590——They have burial clubs of their own which insure their children, *Branson* 319.

Infant insurance is a most expensive form of thrift ; premiums are very high, though from the smallness of each payment it escapes notice, *Day* 1957–8, 1970——Insurance a great incentive to thrift, *Dobson* 2536, 2774 ;—and raises a man's self-respect, *ib.* 2773——Members are transferred in large numbers from the juvenile to the parent societies, so that there is a continuance of thrift from the earliest age, *Cleveland* 4464.

Troutbeck, Mr. His statement that parents have come to his inquests drunk with proceeds of insurance money is absurd, as money is never paid till after coroner's certificate has been given, *Clensy* 4313, 4039——Advances are not made on policies, *ib.* 4039——They cannot be assigned, as the security cannot be registered and so is worthless, *ib.* 4041.

Troutbeck, Mr. John. (Analysis of his Evidence.)—Is Coroner of Westminster, 911——His district comprises a very bad part, especially round Clare Market, 932——Believes that infant insurance is prejudicial to child life, 922——Finds children in the dissolute classes badly fed and neglected, 923 ;—more when they are insured than when they are not, 925-6——Always inquires if they are insured at inquest, 928 ;—finds sometimes that parents deny it to inquiring officer, but admit it when on oath, 929——Thinks that though dissolute parents are inclined to neglect children, yet insurance money is an additional temptation, 933–5, 948, 952——Instance where child obviously ill was taken out in the street, and died without medical attendance, 937–43 ;—though hospital quite close, 941——This child insured for 2 *l.* 10 *s.*, 944.

Difficult to get evidence except from parents and neighbours, who are friends, and anxious to make the best case, 954, 963——Evidence of other children unreliable, 961-2——In Strand case, father committed for murder by coroner's jury ; acquitted of murder at trial ; mother's evidence unfavourable to him at inquest, inadmissible at trial, 968-974——Held 51 inquests last year on children under a year, of whom eighteen were suffocated in bed, 977.

Coroner's jury unwilling to find verdict against parents, 978–80 ;—especially against mother in the case of an illegitimate child, 985——Case where mother committed, at trial doctor's evidence not strong enough, 1047.

Troutbeck, Mr. John. (Analysis of his Evidence)—*continued.*

Insurance agents give no assistance, 987— — Though it is the interest of insurance office to prove culpability, the agent might become unpopular if too strict, 988–9.

All classes of working men insure their children, 991, 1006–7 ;—but very rare to get a case of neglect from family of a respectable working man, 1010——They would much resent any restriction on insurance, 1013 ;—and have a strong feeling against being buried by the parish, 1030.

Expense of burial of a child in Westminster about 30 *s.*, 1016, 1029 ——They can get 2 *l.* 10 *s.* for insurance after child is three months old, 1017——Believes that if there could be no profit over burial expenses it would check crime amongst dissolute classes, 993–4.

When doctor refuses certificate it is reported to coroner, who investigates informally ; if he sees no reason to hold inquest he signs a form to this effect, whereon the death is registered, and the body can be buried, 1019–28.

U.

Undertaker   Clause 2 of the Bill (Insurance money to be paid to undertaker), which provides that no society shall pay any sum on the death of a boy under fourteen, or girl under sixteen, except to the person actually conducting the funeral, withdrawn. *See* Report of Committee, page iii; Proceedings of Committee, page viii; and *Dewey* 2782-3.

Satisfaction thereat, *Taunton* 3113.

To preserve benefits of life insurance, and to remove temptation from weak or worthless parents, insurance money should be paid direct to undertaker, *Waugh* 2204 ; *Carter* 835–6——Possible, but not probable, there might be collusion between him and parent, *ib.* 872–6——Might lead to collusion, *Wills* 1886, 1944 ;—Letter of Mr. Grahame (par. 7 (*e*)), page 131; Letter of Leeds Society for Prevention of Cruelty to Children, page 134 ; *Dobson* 2561.

Would be unpopular if money had to be paid direct to undertaker, but might be supported on account of evils of child insurance. *Ritchie* 1452–5 ; *Tasker* 1580;—but could be done, and would diminish evils, *ib.* 1571–86.

Undertaker's clause is chief cause of dislike of working classes to Bill, *Crooks* 2273, 2232 ; *Dobson* 2555 ;——Shows such distrust of them, *Crooks* 2431 ; Leeds Society for Prevention of Cruelty to Children, page 134——They regard it with deepest indignation, *Dobson* 2556, 2687.

If passed would confiscate money insured for to pay incidental expenses of death, besides funeral, *Crooks* 2307 ; but if Bill is not retrospective, admits no one would for the future insure for more than necessary outlay ; but believes working classes would cease to insure, *ib.* 2319–23——Bill interferes with existing contracts ; but hopes, if it passes, that it will be made clear that it is not meant to, *Dobson* 2564–5——Admits that parent will be able to choose his own undertaker and make his own bargain with him, *ib.* 2670–9 - —Prudential Society has the greatest objections, but clause being withdrawn, witness gives no evidence respecting this, *Dewey* 2782–3.

Out of 873 societies of Foresters, 834 said this clause would, if passed, be their ruin, *Stead* 4630.

Impossible to work because it would be absurd to prescribe the same sort of funeral, mourning, &c., for all classes, artizans and labourers ; letter of Mr. J. Grahame (par. 7 (*e*)), page 132.

Ignores all expenses of last illness ; letter of Leeds Society for Prevention of Cruelty to Children, page 134.

W.

Walton, Mr. Thomas. (Analysis of his Evidence.)—Appears as delegate, at the invitation of the Committee, from the Conference of Friendly Societies, and is senior director of the Manchester Unity of Odd Fellows, and member of Town Council of Southampton, 4705.

Agrees with the evidence of Mr. Cleveland and Mr. Stead (*see* Analysis of their Evidence), 4707–8.

In twenty-two Odd Fellow societies in district of Southampton burial benefit begins usually at six years; in one society as low as three; in another as high as eight, 4709–14.

The amount given varies from 1 *l.* 10 *s.* at three years to generally 2 *l.* or 3 *l.* at ten; in one office it is as large as 10 *l.* at ten, 4715–18——Cannot say if members are satisfied with these rates, but there is no agitation to increase them, 4722— —Presumes they are, as they get medical aid as well, 4721 — One reason for being content is that the money remains as profit to the society, and is applied, when juvenile member is eighteen, in paying his entrance into adult society, and contributing to his subscription till he is twenty-one, 4727–30.

The

Report, 1890—*continued.*

Walton, Mr. Thomas. (Analysis of his Evidence)—*continued.*

The payments vary from 8 *d.* at eight years to 1 *s.* 4 *d.* at sixteen; the sick benefits, from 2 *s.* a week for the first six months, 1 *s.* for the next six months, and 6 *d.* for the rest of the sickness at eight years, to 6 *s.*, 3 *s.*, and 1 *s.* 6 *d.* at sixteen years; and the burial money, from 1 *l.* 10 *s.* from eight to twelve years to 4 *l.* at sixteen years, 4732.

Children pay the contributions themselves to a great extent, 4733 — — Their meetings are held in schoolrooms, 4734 ;—never in public-houses, 4768.

Infantile insurance is managed gratis by members of the parent society, 4735—— One affiliated society gives about the same terms of insurance as another, 4749.

The south of England compares very favourably with the other parts of the country in thrift, 4751—— In the southern parts of Hampshire Odd Fellows have 11,000 adult and 33,000 juvenile members, 4750.

If any member of their society becomes disreputable, there is power to expel him, but it would not be used except for breach of rules, unless the matter was very notorious, probably not for drunkenness, 4769-75——The scale of payments in the Bill would not pecuniarily affect their society as their benefits do not reach the limit, 4738-40;—but hopes that their scale will be raised with increasing prosperity and habits of thrift of working classes, 4753—— The Bill may injure them, as conveying the idea that the societies are not fit to be allowed to manage their own affairs, 4763-6.

Very desirable to alter the Friendly Societies Act, so as to allow all children under three years to be insured, 4741 ;—that friendly societies might be better able to compete with the collecting societies, 4742 ;—who have a great advantage in sending their agents to collect premiums from door to door, 4744 ;—but friendly societies can yet hold their own, 4746——Opinion that, if any fresh legislation takes place, a distinction should be made between the friendly and the collecting societies, 4754-7 ;— but friendly societies do not desire to see present Act altered, except in minor particulars, 4758, 4765.

Waugh, Rev. Benjamin. Moved, that the Rev. Benjamin Waugh be examined on oath ; on question, resolved in the negative, after division. *See* Proceedings of Committee, page vii.

Waugh, Rev. Benjamin. (Analysis of his Evidence.)—Has been Director of the Society for the Prevention of Cruelty to Children since its formation in 1884 ; 2027-8——His services are gratuitous, 2029, 2228——Decides, on all reports of society's officers, if proceedings shall be taken, 2030-4—-—The metropolitan police have been directed to report to society every case against a child, 2105——Several coroners give notice to society of bad child cases, 2151-2——Since 1884 5314 cases of cruelty in London and provinces have been reported to society, 2035-6 ;—in 752 of which they prosecuted, with a result of 670 convictions, 2037-8——Out of the 752 cases, 335 were either fathers or mothers, 2040——Some of the worst cases of cruelty were by parents ; instances given, 2041-4.

Attention first called to connection of cruelty and insurance by number of starved children being insured, 2045-9 ;—and number of children overlaid ; coroners' returns showing that 50 per cent. of children overlaid were known to be insured, 2050-1.

Had five cases of prosecution during last week ; in one case four children insured for together, 28 *l.* 12 *s.* ; in another, two children for 5 *l.* 13 *s.* 9 *d.,* 2054 ——Another case of boy whose insurance at a certain age rose from 10 *l.* to 20 *l.* ; till he had come into benefit for 20 *l.* he was well treated, then starvation began ; other cases mentioned ; society took proceedings last week on behalf of twelve children who were insured altogether for 87 *l.* ; all offenders but one sent to gaol, 2055-6——Case of acquittal need not mean no guilt, but only no proof of guilt, 2057——Society does not always prosecute in bad cases, 2058——Considers the temptation and low characters of persons tempted ; Cardiff list shows seven cases of warning given for every one of prosecution, 2059—— Considers that failures to convict are harmful to the cause of the society, 2235—— Prosecutes less frequently in cases where cruelty results in death, because of removal of principal witness, the child, 2061-2.

Cases of murder and manslaughter are only indictable at common law, 2067-73 — — At common law to convict parent of starvation "means" to support it must be proved, 2063-5——In prosecutions under the Guardians Act of 32 & 33 Vict., and the Prevention of Cruelty to Children Act of last year, power to resort to the parish is accounted "means," 2066—— Case mentioned where Mr. Justice Wills dismissed case for want of "means," 2079 ;—though judge said parents were poor voluntarily, and it was proved that child was starved as soon as it came into benefit, 2080-2——In case (Ernest Bastan) where child was starved on his insurance increasing from 10 *l.* to 20 *l.,* father pleaded he was 50 *l.* in arrears of rent from being out of work, 2083-5—— Has had other similar cases, 2088.

In the "Sidney Bolton" case at Greenwich (Deptford) a boy and girl were insured on twenty-two policies in the Liverpool Victoria Legal Friendly Society, and thirteen in the

(225—Ind).   P P 3

Waugh, Rev. Benjamin. (Analysis of his Evidence)—*continued.*

the Prudential, 2097——Their policies were increased at the time poison was administered, 2098-9——Woman committed for trial died before it, 2100——Suspicion was only excited by neighbours hearing father and woman quarrelling over insurance money, 2120——Cases of poisoning rarely discovered except by some accident afterwards, 2118-20——In the Birkdale baby-poisoning case the baby farmer got drunk out of the insurance money, and police had to be fetched, and suspicion was aroused, and two other children were exhumed, and all three were found to have been poisoned, 2106 ——In all these cases medical certificates of natural deaths had been given, 2101-2, 2106, 2115——In the case of a child beggar found in the street it was discovered he was insured in the Liverpool Legal Friendly Society for 20 *l.* 12 *s* , 2269.

Baby farmers are often paid a sum down, but if paid so much a week their interest is to keep the child as cheap as possible, so it may possibly die, 2111——In the Swindon baby-farming case, out of seven children, no more payments were due on four, and they were insured and dying; and on the other four payments were still due, and they were well and uninsured, 2179-83——Had seven baby-farming cases, in all of which children insured, 2112——Another baby-farming case at Upper Broughton, 2187—— The words in the Friendly Societies Act, that no money may be paid on a child's death to anyone but parent or his personal representative, have no effect, 2229——Insurance companies and agents consider that a person adopting a child for a lump sum stands in the parent's place, 2240-1——Crimes by parents quite as common as by baby farmers, 2189 ——Easy to convict baby farmers, as neighbours dislike them, and are willing to give evidence, 2192.

Under the Cruelty to Children Act the fact of insurance may be put in after the verdict of the jury has been given; in summary proceedings it cannot be put in at all, 2090-2.

Treatment of illegitimate children varies, as of other children, natural love often existing for them, 2247.

Very difficult to find out if children are insured, 2131——Return of insured cases dealt with by various branches of society, 2124-5——Table of number of children on whom inquests were held by Dr. Macdonald, showing that, of forty-six who died under three months, five were insured; under six months, thirty-six died, twenty-two insured; under twelve months, thirty-six died, twenty-six insured; under two years, twenty died, twelve insured; under three years, eighteen died, eleven insured, &c., 2141;— showing that insurance increased with the age, especially after three months old, when a child first comes into benefit, 2142 ——Children die much faster in the earlier months, so that proportion of deaths of insured children appears least where in ordinary cases it should be highest, 2147-9.

Statistics of Prudential and other offices, showing that a smaller proportion of insured children die than uninsured, are fallacious; because (1) children not often insured under three months, as they do not come into benefit till then, and that is time of greatest mortality; (2) they do not insure illegitimate children; and (3) many policies lapse, and so never appear as deaths on society's returns, 2123-5——House of Commons Committee reported those statistics were, for above reasons, not reliable, 2196-201;—but also that there were considerations making comparison of their mortality with that of general death-rate unfair to them, 2302-3.

Case of difficulty of conviction (Dorin case) from child having been in charge of two persons, impossible to say which guilty, 2153-62 ——Another similar case, 2164—— Another child had been passed from one baby farmer to another, 2117——Committee of House of Commons reported that crimes committed in privacy of bedroom cannot be traced, 2166——In case mentioned above coroner said, " I hope you will get conviction, but I think you will not," 2169——Law not favourable for convictions ; for example, father and mother cannot give evidence against each other, 2236-7.

Has never had assistance from an agent or insurance company, though it would be to their interest, in detecting cases of criminal neglect, 2266-9.

First remedy for evils of child-life insurance is to take away the temptation of handling the money, by paying money direct to undertaker; funeral insurance is substituted for life insurance, 2204, 2254;—or funeral might be conducted by an agent, as the grave is provided by a public body, at the expense of insurance company, 2248-9—— No life ought to be insured by another in which the insurer has not an insurable interest, which is the law as far as the upper and middle classes are concerned, 2210 ——Working classes carry this principle out in their sick clubs, where they give no sick pay till child is of an age to earn money, 2211-2.

The sums insured for should be diminished, 2204——A child under five years can now be insured for 6 *l.*, and of five years six months for 10 *l.*, 2205-9——Undertakers have agreed to bury children dying at refuge of Protection of Children Society for 15 *s.*, 17 *s.*, and 18 *s.*, 2252——If sum were diminished to lowest cost of funeral, there would be nothing to prevent a respectable artizan from adding money of his own to outlay, 2213, 2250——The scale in present Bill was framed by Mr. Ludlow, Chief Registrar of Friendly Societies, and adopted by Committee of House of Commons, 2216-7.

If

Waugh, Rev. Benjamin. (Analysis of his Evidence)—*continued*.

If sum payable on death were reduced there would be a great saving to the insurance companies, and an endowment fund could be formed, to be paid to child on attaining age of fourteen or sixteen, 2219-20.

Admits superiority of mutual burial societies over collecting societies, 2259-62 ;—though evidence of Dr. Ritchie, of Leeds, points to their being not much better, 2258.

Wills, Mr. Justice. (Analysis of his Evidence.)—Has been for six years one of the Judges of the High Court, 1849-50——His conviction that there is connection between infant insurance and death of children has been gradually formed from cases he has tried and conversations with other judges ; there would be no insurance if a large proportion of children were done to death for it, and much cruelty exists without insurance, 1926 ;—but still a considerable residuum where they coincide; temptation of comparatively large sum, where there is already a tendency to neglect, very great, 1851-2——Immediate possession of 5 *l.* a greater temptation than the wish to avoid burden of supporting child, 1887-90 ;—and the one strengthens the other, 1888, 1933——There are many parents who would starve their children to death for 5 *s.*, 1876, 1887 ;—would happen oftener, but is often stopped by interposition of charity, or sometimes by visit of doctor required to see patient alive to enable him to give certificate, 1884.

There ought to be no chance of making profit out of a death, 1878, 1897-8, 1911——A child can be buried for about 20 *s.*, and insurances go up to 6 *l.* for child under five, 1885, 1917——Better to limit amount than to complicate matters by allowing only actual expenses to be paid, 1886——As long as there is this chance mischiefs will ensue, 1912 ;—or balance be spent on unsuitable merrymaking, 1900——Believes that the majority insure for perfectly good motives, 1902——Sees no objection to insurance for absolute expenses of funeral, 1906, 1919—— Applies to the poor no other principles than he would apply to all other classes, 1871, 1911-2 ;—human nature being the same, 1871, 1936 ;—and such as the law now applies to all classes in other matters, 1939——Limitations exist on fire and marine insurance, that no one shall recover more than he loses, 1939 ;—and no one is allowed, except in the case of insurable interest, to insure the lives of others, except in the case of insurances under the Friendly Societies Act, which are a special exception, as a boon to the working classes, to the principle of the Statute of George III., that there should be no wagering or gambling on human life, 1861-74, 1940.

Insurance of children should be limited to the amount of funeral expenses, 1899——There is now a tendency on the part of the poor to extravagant expenditure on funerals, which should in the interest of thrift be discouraged, 1897, 1900.

The premiums on child-life insurance are very high, 1892——This is not noticed, on account of the small sums in which they are collected, 1895 ;—and lapsed policies, which are a source of profit to all insurance companies, are especially so in the case of the poor, who are improvident, or from misfortune are often unable to keep them up, 1860-1, 1893-4, 1922.

Agents tout very keenly for custom, 1852, 1921 ;—and put a good deal of pressure on the poor to insure, 1853——Has tried many cases of fraud by insurance agents on their companies, 1854-5 ;—which are much in their agents' hands, 1847 ;—and they, for the sake of the commission, take insurances recklessly, regardless of the health or condition of the child, 1859-9——Evil effect of having people going about explaining the advantages to be gained if death occurs, 1852.

There is difficulty in getting convictions, 1881, 1932——Judges and juries are, and ought to be, very cautious, 1932——Has tried many cases that have (and properly) ended in acquittal, when he had no moral doubt of guilt, 1932——Difficulty, too, from husband or wife not being able to give evidence against each other, 1879-81——Believes that in many cases, on account of these difficulties, parents are convicted on a minor charge, instead of for murder or manslaughter ; but attaches little importance to this, as certainty of conviction more important than amount of sentence, 1882-4——Opinion that proposed change in criminal law, that prisoners should be examined, would be beneficial, 1917.

Believes the other judges generally share his opinions ; has had leave from Baron Pollock to say that he does, 1924.

Wood, Mr. E. N. Letter of Mr. E. N. Wood, Deputy Coroner for Greenwich Division, to the Home Secretary, read by the Chairman ; conveys rider of a jury to the effect that the present loose system of life insurance by some companies is an incentive to wilful murder. *See* page 52.

Y.

Yarmouth. Presentment of grand jury at quarter sessions at Great Yarmouth, recommending that lunatics and imbeciles should be included in the Children's Life Insurance Bill [H.L.] ; put in by Chairman. *See* page 191, and *App.* B., page 228.

Lightning Source UK Ltd.
Milton Keynes UK
UKHW021518050119
334855UK00008B/1336/P